ALSO BY THE EDITORS AT AMERICA'S TEST KITCHEN

100 Recipes: The Absolute Best Ways to Make the True Essentials

The New Family Cookbook

The Complete Cooking for Two Cookbook

The America's Test Kitchen Cooking School Cookbook

The Cook's Illustrated Meat Book

The Cook's Illustrated Baking Book

The Cook's Illustrated Cookbook

The Science of Good Cooking

The America's Test Kitchen Menu Cookbook

The America's Test Kitchen Quick Family Cookbook

The America's Test Kitchen Healthy Family Cookbook

The America's Test Kitchen Family Baking Book

Kitchen Hacks: How Clever Cooks Get Things Done

THE AMERICA'S TEST KITCHEN LIBRARY SERIES

Foolproof Preserving

Paleo Perfected

The Best Mexican Recipes

The Make-Ahead Cook

The How Can It Be Gluten-Free Cookbook Volume 2

The How Can It Be Gluten-Free Cookbook

Healthy Slow Cooker Revolution

Slow Cooker Revolution Volume 2: The Easy-Prep Edition

Slow Cooker Revolution

The Six-Ingredient Solution

Pressure Cooker Perfection

Comfort Food Makeovers

The America's Test Kitchen D.I.Y. Cookbook

Pasta Revolution

Simple Weeknight Favorites

The Best Simple Recipes

THE TV COMPANION SERIES

The Complete Cook's Country TV Show Cookbook

The Complete America's Test Kitchen TV Show Cookbook 2001–2016

America's Test Kitchen: The TV Companion Cookbook
(2009 and 2011–2015 Editions)

AMERICA'S TEST KITCHEN ANNUALS

The Best of America's Test Kitchen (2007–2016 Editions)

Cooking for Two (2010–2013 Editions)

Light & Healthy (2010–2012 Editions)

THE COOK'S COUNTRY SERIES

Cook It in Cast Iron

Cook's Country Eats Local

From Our Grandmothers' Kitchens

Cook's Country Blue Ribbon Desserts

Cook's Country Best Potluck Recipes

Cook's Country Best Lost Suppers

Cook's Country Best Grilling Recipes

The Cook's Country Cookbook

America's Best Lost Recipes

THE BEST RECIPE SERIES

The New Best Recipe

More Best Recipes

The Best One-Dish Suppers

Soups, Stews & Chilis

The Best Skillet Recipes

The Best Slow & Easy Recipes

The Best Chicken Recipes

The Best International Recipe

The Best Make-Ahead Recipe

The Best 30-Minute Recipe

The Best Light Recipe

The Cook's Illustrated Guide to Grilling and Barbecue

Best American Side Dishes

Cover & Bake

Steaks, Chops, Roasts & Ribs

Italian Classics

American Classics

FOR A FULL LISTING OF ALL OUR BOOKS

CooksIllustrated.com

AmericasTestKitchen.com

PRAISE FOR AMERICA'S TEST KITCHEN TITLES

"A terrifically accessible and useful guide to grilling in all its forms that sets a new bar for its competitors on the bookshelf. . . . The book is packed with practical advice, simple tips, and approachable recipes."

PUBLISHERS WEEKLY (STARRED REVIEW) ON *MASTER OF THE GRILL*

"This encyclopedia of meat cookery would feel completely overwhelming if it weren't so meticulously organized and artfully designed. This is *Cook's Illustrated* at its finest."

THE KITCHN ON *THE COOK'S ILLUSTRATED MEAT BOOK*

"Carnivores with an obsession for perfection will likely have found their new bible in this comprehensive collection."

PUBLISHERS WEEKLY (STARRED REVIEW) ON *THE COOK'S ILLUSTRATED MEAT BOOK*

"The sum total of exhaustive experimentation . . . anyone interested in gluten-free cookery simply shouldn't be without it."

NIGELLA LAWSON ON *THE HOW CAN IT BE GLUTEN-FREE COOKBOOK*

"The 21st-century *Fannie Farmer Cookbook* or *The Joy of Cooking*. If you had to have one cookbook and that's all you could have, this one would do it."

CBS SAN FRANCISCO ON *THE NEW FAMILY COOKBOOK*

"This book upgrades slow cooking for discriminating, 21st-century palates—that is indeed revolutionary."

THE DALLAS MORNING NEWS ON *SLOW COOKER REVOLUTION*

"One bag, 3 meals? Get the biggest bang for your buck."

FOX NEWS ON *THE MAKE-AHEAD COOK*

"The go-to gift book for newlyweds, small families, or empty nesters."

ORLANDO SENTINEL ON *THE COMPLETE COOKING FOR TWO COOKBOOK*

"Some 2,500 photos walk readers through 600 painstakingly tested recipes, leaving little room for error."

ASSOCIATED PRESS ON *THE AMERICA'S TEST KITCHEN COOKING SCHOOL COOKBOOK*

"A one-volume kitchen seminar, addressing in one smart chapter after another the sometimes surprising whys behind a cook's best practices. . . . You get the myth, the theory, the science and the proof, all rigorously interrogated as only America's Test Kitchen can do."

NPR ON *THE SCIENCE OF GOOD COOKING*

"This book is a comprehensive, no-nonsense guide . . . a well-thought-out, clearly explained primer for every aspect of home baking."

THE WALL STREET JOURNAL ON *THE COOK'S ILLUSTRATED BAKING BOOK*

"Buy this gem for the foodie in your family, and spend the extra money to get yourself a copy too."

THE MISSOURIAN ON *THE BEST OF AMERICA'S TEST KITCHEN 2015*

"The perfect kitchen home companion . . . The practical side of things is very much on display . . . cook-friendly and kitchen-oriented, illuminating the process of preparing food instead of mystifying it."

THE WALL STREET JOURNAL ON *THE COOK'S ILLUSTRATED COOKBOOK*

"If this were the only cookbook you owned, you would cook well, be everyone's favorite host, have a well-run kitchen, and eat happily every day."

THECITYCOOK.COM ON *THE AMERICA'S TEST KITCHEN MENU COOKBOOK*

"This comprehensive collection of 800-plus family and global favorites helps put healthy eating in an everyday context, from meatloaf to Indian curry with chicken."

COOKING LIGHT ON *THE AMERICA'S TEST KITCHEN HEALTHY FAMILY COOKBOOK*

"There are pasta books . . . and then there's this pasta book. Flip your carbohydrate dreams upside down and strain them through this sieve of revolutionary, creative, and also traditional recipes."

SAN FRANCISCO BOOK REVIEW ON *PASTA REVOLUTION*

"These dishes taste as luxurious as their full-fat siblings. Even desserts are terrific."

PUBLISHERS WEEKLY ON *THE BEST LIGHT RECIPE*

"Further proof that practice makes perfect, if not transcendent. . . . If an intermediate cook follows the directions exactly, the results will be better than takeout or Mom's."

THE NEW YORK TIMES ON *THE NEW BEST RECIPE*

"The entire book is stuffed with recipes that will blow your dinner-table audience away like leaves from a sidewalk in November."

SAN FRANCISCO BOOK REVIEW ON *THE COMPLETE COOK'S COUNTRY TV SHOW COOKBOOK*

MASTER OF THE GRILL

**FOOLPROOF RECIPES, TOP-RATED
GADGETS, GEAR, AND INGREDIENTS
PLUS CLEVER TEST KITCHEN TIPS
AND FASCINATING FOOD SCIENCE**

BY THE EDITORS AT
AMERICA'S TEST KITCHEN

AMERICA'S TEST KITCHEN

17 Station Street, Brookline, MA 02445

Library of Congress Cataloging-in-Publication Data

Names: America's Test Kitchen (Firm)
Title: Master of the grill : foolproof recipes, top-rated gadgets, gear, and
    ingredients plus clever test kitchen tips and fascinating food science / by
    the editors at America's Test Kitchen.
Description: Brookline, MA : America's Test Kitchen, [2016] | Includes index.
Identifiers: LCCN 2015040405 | ISBN 9781940352541 (paperback)
Subjects: LCSH: Barbecuing. | Outdoor cooking. | LCGFT: Cookbooks.
Classification: LCC TX840.B3 M387 2016 | DDC 641.5/78--dc23
LC record available at http://lccn.loc.gov/2015040405

Paperback: US $29.95 / $35.00 CAN

Manufactured in the United States of America

10 9 8 7 6 5 4 3 2 1

DISTRIBUTED BY
Penguin Random House Publisher Services
Tel: 800-733-3000

Pictured: Grilled Caesar Salad (page 286), Grilled Blackened Red Snapper (page 278)

CHIEF CREATIVE OFFICER: Jack Bishop
EDITORIAL DIRECTOR, BOOKS: Elizabeth Carduff
EXECUTIVE EDITOR: Lori Galvin
ASSOCIATE EDITOR: Rachel Greenhaus
EDITORIAL ASSISTANTS: Samantha Ronan and Alyssa Langer
BOOK DESIGN: Amy Klee
DESIGN DIRECTOR: Greg Galvan
DEPUTY ART DIRECTOR: Taylor Argenzio
ASSOCIATE ART DIRECTORS: Allison Boales and Jen Hoffman
DESIGNER: Aleko Giatrakis
PHOTOGRAPHY DIRECTOR: Julie Cote
ASSOCIATE ART DIRECTOR, PHOTOGRAPHY: Steve Klise
SENIOR STAFF PHOTOGRAPHER: Daniel J. van Ackere
PHOTOGRAPHY: Keller + Keller and Carl Tremblay
FOOD STYLING: Catrine Kelty, Marie Piraino, and Sally Staub
PHOTOSHOOT KITCHEN TEAM:
    ASSOCIATE EDITOR: Chris O'Connor
    TEST COOK: Daniel Cellucci
    ASSISTANT TEST COOKS: Allison Berkey and Matthew Fairman
ILLUSTRATION: John Burgoyne and Jay Layman
ASSISTANT PHOTOGRAPHY PRODUCER: Mary Ball
PRODUCTION DIRECTOR: Guy Rochford
SENIOR PRODUCTION MANAGER: Jessica Quirk
PRODUCTION MANAGER: Christine Walsh
IMAGING MANAGER: Lauren Robbins
PRODUCTION AND IMAGING SPECIALISTS: Heather Dube, Sean MacDonald, Dennis Noble, and Jessica Voas
PROJECT MANAGER: Britt Dresser
COPY EDITOR: Cheryl Redmond
PROOFREADER: Elizabeth Wray Emery
INDEXER: Elizabeth Parson

CONTENTS

VIII **Welcome to America's Test Kitchen**

1 CHAPTER 1 **The Basics**

125 CHAPTER 2 **The Easy Upgrades**

307 CHAPTER 3 **The Serious Projects**

426 **Conversions and Equivalents**

428 **Index**

Welcome to America's Test Kitchen

This book has been tested, written, and edited by the folks at America's Test Kitchen, a very real 2,500-square-foot kitchen located just outside of Boston. It is the home of *Cook's Illustrated* magazine and *Cook's Country* magazine and is the home to more than 60 test cooks, editors, and cookware specialists. Our mission is to test recipes over and over again until we understand how and why they work and until we arrive at the "best" version.

We start the process of testing a recipe with a complete lack of preconceptions, which means that we accept no claim, no theory, no technique, and no recipe at face value. We simply assemble as many variations as possible, test a half-dozen of the most promising, and taste the results blind. We then construct our own hybrid recipe and continue to test it, varying ingredients, techniques, and cooking times until we reach a consensus. The result, we hope, is the best version of a particular recipe, but we realize that only you can be the final judge of our success (or failure). As we like to say in the test kitchen, "We make the mistakes, so you don't have to."

All of this would not be possible without a belief that good cooking, much like good music, is indeed based on a foundation of objective technique. Some people like spicy foods and others don't, but there is a right way to sauté, there is a best way to cook a pot roast, and there are measurable scientific principles involved in producing perfectly beaten, stable egg whites. This is our ultimate goal: to investigate the fundamental principles of cooking so that you become a better cook. It is as simple as that.

If you're curious to see what goes on behind the scenes at America's Test Kitchen, check out our daily blog, The Feed, at AmericasTestKitchenFeed.com, which features kitchen snapshots, exclusive recipes, video tips, and much more. You can watch us work (in our actual test kitchen) by tuning in to *America's Test Kitchen* (AmericasTestKitchen.com) or *Cook's Country from America's Test Kitchen* (CooksCountryTV.com) on public television. Tune in to *America's Test Kitchen Radio* (ATKradio.com) on public radio to listen to insights, tips, and techniques that illuminate the truth about real home cooking. Want to hone your cooking skills or finally learn how to bake—from an America's Test Kitchen test cook? Enroll in a cooking class at our online cooking school at OnlineCookingSchool.com. And find information about subscribing to *Cook's Illustrated* magazine at CooksIllustrated.com or *Cook's Country* magazine at CooksCountry.com. Both magazines are published every other month. However you choose to visit us, we welcome you into our kitchen, where you can stand by our side as we test our way to the best recipes in America.

facebook.com/AmericasTestKitchen

twitter.com/TestKitchen

youtube.com/AmericasTestKitchen

instagram.com/TestKitchen

pinterest.com/TestKitchen

americastestkitchen.tumblr.com

google.com/+AmericasTestKitchen

1
THE
BASICS

BEEF

4 Perfect Grilled Hamburgers
  Perfect Grilled Cheeseburgers
  with Garlic, Chipotle, and Scallion
  with Cognac, Mustard, and Chives
6 Grilled Well-Done Hamburgers
  Grilled Well-Done Bacon Cheeseburgers
14 Grilled Beef Kebabs with Lemon-Rosemary Marinade
  with North African Marinade
  with Red Curry Marinade
24 Grilled Boneless Steaks
29 Grilled Porterhouse or T-Bone Steaks
  Grilled Tuscan Steaks with Garlic Essence
30 Grilled Filets Mignons
  Blue Cheese Butter
  Roasted Red Pepper and Smoked Paprika Butter
  Lemon, Garlic, and Parsley Butter
32 Grilled Chuck Steaks
36 Grilled Steak Tips
  Garlic and Herb Marinade
  Southwestern Marinade
  Garlic, Ginger, and Soy Marinade
38 Grilled Flank Steak with Garlic-Herb Sauce
40 Grilled Beef Teriyaki
42 Grilled Marinated Skirt Steak
  Grilled Hoisin-Scallion Marinated Skirt Steak
  Grilled Black Pepper–Honey Marinated Skirt Steak

PORK

17 Grilled Pork Skewers with Grilled Tomato Relish
44 Grilled Boneless Pork Chops
  Onion, Olive, and Caper Relish
  Tomato, Fennel, and Almond Relish
  Orange, Jícama, and Pepita Relish
46 Grilled Thin-Cut Pork Chops
  Grilled Caribbean Thin-Cut Pork Chops
  Grilled Mediterranean Thin-Cut Pork Chops
  Grilled Spicy Thai Thin-Cut Pork Chops
48 Grilled Thick-Cut Bone-In Pork Chops
50 Grilled Honey-Glazed Pork Chops
54 Chinese-Style Glazed Pork Tenderloin

LAMB

18 Grilled Lamb Kebabs
  Warm Spice Parsley Marinade with Ginger
  Garlic and Cilantro Marinade with Garam Masala
  Sweet Curry Marinade with Buttermilk
57 Grilled Lamb Shoulder Chops
  with Near East Red Pepper Paste
  with Garlic-Rosemary Marinade
59 Grilled Lamb Loin or Rib Chops
  with Mediterranean Herb and Garlic Paste
  with Zucchini and Mint Sauce

POULTRY

10 Easy Turkey Burgers
  Chicken Burgers
20 Grilled Chicken Kebabs with Garlic and Herb Marinade
  with Curry Marinade
  with Caribbean Marinade
  with Middle Eastern Marinade
  with Southwestern Marinade
  with Mediterranean Marinade
60 Grilled Lemon-Parsley Chicken Breasts
  Grilled Chipotle-Lime Chicken Breasts
  Grilled Orange-Tarragon Chicken Breasts
62 Grilled Glazed Boneless Chicken Breasts
  Spicy Hoisin Glaze
  Honey-Mustard Glaze
  Coconut-Curry Glaze
  Miso-Sesame Glaze
  Molasses-Coffee Glaze
66 Grilled Bone-In Chicken
  Cajun Spice Rub
  Jamaican Spice Rub
  Tex-Mex Spice Rub
  Basic Barbecue Sauce
68 Grilled Glazed Bone-In Chicken Breasts
  Orange-Chipotle Glaze
  Soy-Ginger Glaze
  Curry-Yogurt Glaze
70 Classic Barbecued Chicken
  Kansas City Barbecue Sauce

73 Grilled Chicken Diavolo
74 Grilled Chicken Leg Quarters with Lime Dressing
76 Grilled Chicken Wings
     Grilled BBQ Chicken Wings
     Grilled Creole Chicken Wings
     Grilled Tandoori Chicken Wings

FISH & SEAFOOD

23 Grilled Swordfish Skewers with Basil Oil
81 Sweet and Saucy Lime-Jalapeño Glazed Salmon
     Orange-Sesame Glazed Salmon
     Spicy Apple Glazed Salmon
82 Wood-Grilled Salmon
     Chinese-Style Wood-Grilled Salmon
     Barbecued Wood-Grilled Salmon
     Lemon-Thyme Wood-Grilled Salmon
84 Grilled Red Curry Mahi-Mahi with Pineapple Salsa
86 Grilled Halibut Steaks with Chipotle-Lime Butter
89 Grilled Swordfish Steaks with Salsa Verde
90 Grilled Shrimp with Spicy Lemon-Garlic Sauce
     with Fresh Tomatoes, Feta, and Olives
92 Grilled Scallops
     Chile-Lime Vinaigrette
     Basil Vinaigrette
     Barbecue Sauce Vinaigrette

VEGETABLES, TOFU & FRUIT

12 Grilled Portobello Burgers
78 Grilled Soy-Ginger Glazed Tofu
     Grilled Asian Barbecue Glazed Tofu
101 Grilled Asparagus
     with Chili-Lime Butter
     with Cumin Butter
     with Garlic Butter
     with Orange-Thyme Butter
103 Grilled Butternut Squash
     Spicy Grilled Butternut Squash with
         Garlic and Rosemary

104 Grilled Cabbage
105 Easy Grilled Coleslaw
106 Grilled Corn with Flavored Butter
     Basil and Lemon Butter
     Honey Butter
     Latin-Spiced Butter
     New Orleans "Barbecue" Butter
     Spicy Old Bay Butter
108 Grilled Eggplant with Yogurt Sauce
110 Grilled Marinated Portobello Mushrooms
     with Tarragon
111 Grilled Onions
112 Grill-Roasted Peppers
     with Rosemary
113 Grilled Plantains
114 Grilled Potatoes with Garlic and Rosemary
     with Oregano and Lemon
116 Grilled Potato Hobo Packs
     Grilled Spanish-Style Potato Hobo Packs
     Grilled Spicy Home Fry Potato Hobo Packs
     Grilled Vinegar and Onion Potato Hobo Packs
118 Grilled Vegetable Salad
120 Grilled Ratatouille
122 Grilled Fruit
     Simplified Caramel Sauce
     Sour Orange Glaze
     Rum-Molasses Glaze

BREAD

94 Bruschetta with Tomatoes and Basil
     with Fresh Herbs
     with Red Onions, Herbs, and Parmesan
     with Sautéed Sweet Peppers
     with Grilled Eggplant, Rosemary, and Feta
     with Arugula, Red Onion, and Rosemary–White
         Bean Spread

1 Great Backyard Burgers

RECIPE FOR SUCCESS

✓ WHY THIS RECIPE WORKS

Burgers often come off the grill tough, dry, and bulging in the middle. We wanted a moist and juicy burger with a texture that was tender and cohesive. Just as important, we wanted a flavorful, deeply caramelized crust and a nice level surface capable of holding as many condiments as we could pile on. For juicy, robustly flavored meat, we chose 80 percent lean ground chuck. We formed the meat into fairly thick 6-ounce patties. Our first few batches came off the grill puffed up like tennis balls, but we quickly figured out that slightly indenting, or dimpling, the center of each burger helped them cook to a perfectly even thickness. Grilling the burgers over a superhot, concentrated fire ensured that they developed a good crust without overcooking. For our cheeseburger variation, we took an unconventional approach and mixed the cheese in with the meat for an even distribution of flavor. We also made two other flavor variations with savory add-ins that complemented the grilled burgers' smokiness.

Perfect Grilled Hamburgers

SERVES 4

Weighing the meat on a kitchen scale is the most accurate way to portion it. If you don't own a scale, do your best to divide the meat evenly into quarters. Eighty percent lean ground chuck is our favorite for flavor, but 85 percent lean works, too. If you like, toast the hamburger buns on the grill while the burgers rest.

- 1½   pounds 80 percent lean ground chuck
- 1   teaspoon salt
- ½   teaspoon pepper
- 4   hamburger buns

1 Break meat into small pieces in bowl, sprinkle with salt and pepper, and toss lightly to mix. Divide meat into 4 portions. Working with 1 portion at a time, lightly toss from hand to hand to form ball, then gently flatten into ¾-inch-thick patty. Press center of patties down with your fingertips to create ¼-inch-deep depression.

2A FOR A CHARCOAL GRILL Open bottom vent completely. Light large chimney starter filled with charcoal briquettes (6 quarts). When top coals are partially covered with ash, pour evenly over half of grill. Set cooking grate in place, cover, and open lid vent completely. Heat grill until hot, about 5 minutes.

2B FOR A GAS GRILL Turn all burners to high, cover, and heat grill until hot, about 15 minutes. Leave all burners on high.

3 Clean and oil cooking grate. Place burgers on grill (on hotter side if using charcoal) and cook, without pressing on them, until well browned on first side, 2 to 3 minutes. Flip burgers and continue to grill until burgers register 120 to 125 degrees (for medium-rare) or 130 to 135 degrees (for medium), 2½ to 4 minutes.

4 Transfer burgers to platter, tent with aluminum foil, and let rest for 5 minutes. Serve on buns.

VARIATIONS

2 Perfect Grilled Cheeseburgers

Mix ¾ cup shredded cheddar, Swiss, or Monterey Jack cheese or ¾ cup crumbled blue cheese into meat with salt and pepper.

3 Perfect Grilled Hamburgers with Garlic, Chipotle, and Scallion

Toast 3 unpeeled garlic cloves in 8-inch skillet over medium heat until fragrant, about 8 minutes. When cool enough to handle, peel and mince. Mix garlic, 2 tablespoons minced scallion, and 1 tablespoon minced canned chipotle chile in adobo sauce into meat with salt and pepper.

4 Perfect Grilled Hamburgers with Cognac, Mustard, and Chives

Mix 1½ tablespoons cognac, 1 tablespoon minced fresh chives, and 2 teaspoons Dijon mustard into meat with salt and pepper.

6

FOOD SCIENCE
Dimples Aren't Just Cute

To prevent hamburgers from puffing up during cooking, many sources recommend making a slight depression in the center of the raw patty before placing it on the heat.

But we find that the need for a dimple depends entirely on how the burger is cooked. Meat inflates upon cooking when its connective tissue, or collagen, shrinks at temperatures higher than 140 degrees. If burgers are cooked on a grill or under a broiler, a dimple is in order. Cooked with these methods, the meat is exposed to direct heat not only from below or above but also on its sides; as a result, the edges of the patty shrink, cinching the hamburger like a belt, compressing its interior up and out.

But when the patty is cooked in a skillet, only the part of the patty in direct contact with the pan gets hot enough to shrink the collagen. Because the edges of the burger never directly touch the heat, the collagen it contains doesn't shrink much at all, and the burger doesn't puff.

THE BOTTOM LINE When grilling (or broiling) burgers a dimple is in order to prevent burger bulge. On the stovetop, no dimple is necessary.

5

GRILL HACK
Tagging with Toothpicks

When grilling for a crowd, you need a way to tell well-done burgers from medium-rare at a glance. Try assigning each level of doneness a particular number of toothpicks (e.g., one for medium-rare, two for medium, three for well-done) and pegging the proper marker into the patties as they come off the fire.

7 American Cheese, Please

American cheese is polarizing. A good American cheese is mild, but not bland, and melts like a dream in grilled cheese sandwiches and atop burgers. But in this age of slow food, plastic-wrapped cheese slices have become a symbol of hyperprocessing. We sampled seven nationally available American cheeses plain and in grilled cheese sandwiches and noticed a pattern: The shorter the ingredient list, the better-tasting the cheese. Food experts explained that some manufacturers cut costs by using less actual cheese in their products and more comparatively cheap dairy ingredients. Since cheese is higher in fat and protein than other dairy products, products with more natural cheese will also usually have significantly more fat and protein than products that use whey or milk concentrates, meaning more richness and better flavor. Our top product listed just five ingredients—cheese, water, cream, sodium phosphates, and salt—and was praised by tasters for its cheddar-like sharpness, while the bland bottom-ranked cheeses contained up to 20 ingredients, many of them processed dairy derivatives like whey or milk protein. Unfortunately, quality also added to the price. Since real cheese is a more expensive ingredient than fillers, our top products cost two to three times as much as lower-rated entries.

THE BOTTOM LINE Our winner, **Boar's Head American Cheese**, boasts great flavor and meltability.

WINNER

BOAR'S HEAD American Cheese
Tasting Comments Our winning cheese, which is made from a blend of cheddar cheeses, had "nutty," "sharp" tanginess and a "slightly soft," "tender" texture. These "superthin" slices melted perfectly.

RUNNERS-UP

KRAFT Deli Deluxe American Cheese
Tasting Comments These "crumbly" slices made "molten" and "melty" grilled cheese that was "rich," "sharp," and "cheddary," with "balanced" notes of "cream" and "butter."

LAND O'LAKES Deli American Cheese Product
Tasting Comments Though this "cheese product" contains added whey and milk protein concentrates, a lower moisture level made these "thicker" slices "crumbly" like "aged" cheese, with "cheddar-like sharpness" to match. This product's "tangy" acidity made for "rich" and "assertive" grilled cheese.

8 Burgers for Everyone

✔ WHY THIS RECIPE WORKS

These days, many backyard cooks prefer grilling burgers to medium-well and beyond. The problem is that the meat comes off the grill not just cooked through, but completely dry and tough. We wanted a well-done burger that was still as tender and as moist as it could be. Taste tests proved that well-done burgers made with 80 percent lean chuck were noticeably moister than burgers made from leaner beef, but they still weren't juicy enough. Because we couldn't force the meat to retain moisture, we opted to pack the patties with a panade, a paste made from bread and milk that's often used to keep meatloaf and meatballs moist. Mixing the panade into the beef created burgers that were juicy and tender even when cooked to well-done. To punch up the flavor, we also added minced garlic and tangy steak sauce. We cooked the burgers over high heat to create a flavorful sear; the panade helped to stem moisture loss even over a hot fire. For a variation, we went beyond simply using bacon as a condiment and mixed in some cooled bacon fat with the ground beef for unmistakable bacon flavor in every bite.

Grilled Well-Done Hamburgers
SERVES 4

Stick with 80 percent lean ground beef; a leaner ground beef will result in a drier burger. If you like, toast the hamburger buns on the grill while the burgers rest.

- 1 slice hearty white sandwich bread, crust removed, chopped
- 2 tablespoons whole milk
- 2 teaspoons steak sauce
- 1 garlic clove, minced
- ¾ teaspoon salt
- ¾ teaspoon pepper
- 1½ pounds 80 percent lean ground chuck
- 4 hamburger buns

1 Mash bread and milk in large bowl into paste with fork. Stir in steak sauce, garlic, salt, and pepper. Break meat into small pieces, add to bowl, and toss lightly to mix. Divide meat into 4 portions. Working with 1 portion at a time, lightly toss from hand to hand to form ball, then gently flatten into ¾-inch-thick patty. Press center of patties down with your fingertips to create ¼-inch-deep depression.

2A FOR A CHARCOAL GRILL Open bottom vent completely. Light large chimney starter filled with charcoal briquettes (6 quarts). When top coals are partially covered with ash, pour evenly over half of grill. Set cooking grate in place, cover, and open lid vent completely. Heat grill until hot, about 5 minutes.

2B FOR A GAS GRILL Turn all burners to high, cover, and heat grill until hot, about 15 minutes. Leave all burners on high.

3 Clean and oil cooking grate. Place burgers on grill (on hotter side if using charcoal) and cook, without pressing on them, until well browned on first side, 2 to 4 minutes. Flip burgers and continue to grill until burgers register 140 to 145 degrees (for medium-well) or 150 to 155 degrees (for well-done), 3 to 5 minutes.

4 Transfer burgers to platter, tent with aluminum foil, and let rest for 5 minutes. Serve on buns.

VARIATION

9 Grilled Well-Done Bacon Cheeseburgers
Cook 8 slices bacon in 12-inch nonstick skillet over medium heat until crisp, 7 to 9 minutes; transfer to paper towel–lined plate. Refrigerate 2 tablespoons rendered bacon fat until just warm, then mix into meat with salt and pepper. Top burgers with sliced cheese of choice during final 2 minutes of grilling. Top burgers with bacon before serving.

10 FOOD SCIENCE
Panade to the Rescue

Our quest for a juicy well-done burger ended when we hit upon a surprisingly effective addition—a panade. A panade is a mixture of a starch and liquid. It can be simple (bread and milk) or it can be complex (panko or saltines, buttermilk or yogurt, or even gelatin). But it always has the same goal: to keep ground meat moist and tender. Panades aren't just limited to burgers—they're used in meatloaf and meatballs too. How does a panade work? Starches from the bread absorb liquid from the milk to form a gel that coats and lubricates the protein molecules in the meat, much in the same way as fat, keeping them moist and preventing them from linking together and shrinking into a tough matrix.

A panade prevented the burger on the left from becoming dense and dried out, like the one on the right.

TEST KITCHEN TIP

11 Safety First! Best Practices for Grilling

Some people enjoy grilling just for the primal thrill of playing with fire. Here are four tips to keep that thrill accident-free.

LOCATION IS EVERYTHING Always set up your grill at least 10 feet from your home on a flame-safe surface—a driveway or patio rather than grass or a wooden deck—and away from where children and pets might wander. Pay special attention when cooking with charcoal in windy weather, as sparks can fly out of the grill.

CLEANLINESS COUNTS It is important that the interior basin of your grill, whether gas or charcoal, be cleaned a few times each season to wash away built-up food matter that can ignite or lend off-flavors to whatever you're cooking. Empty drip pans and ash-catchers frequently to reduce mess.

FOOD SAFETY MATTERS Always use separate platters for raw and cooked foods to avoid cross-contamination, and always dispose of excess marinade. Wait to apply sauces to meat until the end of cooking to prevent them from burning and to keep your basting brush from becoming con-taminated by uncooked meat.

AVOID SLOPPY FOOD PREP Flare-ups are often caused by fat or by excess oily marinade dripping off the meat and catching fire. Be sure to trim meat carefully and pat dry any foods marinated with oil with paper towels before grilling.

AND IN CASE OF FLARE-UPS Despite your best efforts, flare-ups may still occur. Keep long tongs and grill gloves handy so that you can quickly and safely move the food to an area of the grill not directly over the fire. The flare-up will die down fast, and you'll have the grill back under your control. Briefly covering the grill can also help squelch flare-ups. We do not recommend using a spray bottle filled with water to douse flare-ups unless you want your food covered in ashes.

12 TEST KITCHEN TIP
Outdoor Cooking Basics

The words "grilling" and "barbecuing" are often used interchangeably, but they are actually different cooking techniques. Whereas grilling works best with quick-cooking foods that are smallish in size (such as shrimp and skewered meats) or foods that are individually portioned (such as steaks and chops), barbecuing and grill roasting work best with larger, slower-cooking foods. It may help to think of grilling, grill roasting, and barbecuing along a cooking-time continuum.

GRILLING is the speediest and simplest cooking method performed on the grill, and typically uses high or moderately high heat. Most of the cooking takes place directly over the fire, and the lid is often not used, especially on a charcoal grill. Grilled foods derive their "grilled" flavor from the dripping juices and fat that hit the heat source and create smoke that subtly seasons the exterior of the food.

GRILL ROASTING involves longer cooking times than grilling simply because the foods are larger, and this method calls for heat that is more moderate. The grill is set up for indirect cooking—that is, part of the grill is left free of coals, or some of the gas burners are turned off. The lid is employed to create an oven-like cooking environment. As a result, foods can be cooked through without danger of scorching the exterior.

BARBECUING takes even longer than grill roasting—it's not unusual for cooking times to exceed 3 hours—because the beef, pork, or poultry is cooked until proteins break down to a meltingly tender texture. This type of cooking requires low, gentle heat. As with grill roasting, food is not cooked directly over the coals or the lit burner. Barbecued foods derive their "barbecued" flavor from wood chips or chunks. The wood generates a deep, intense smoke that permeates the food.

To make indoor cooking method analogies, grilling is like sautéing on the stovetop in a hot skillet, and grill roasting is like roasting in the oven—both cook foods until just done and no further. Barbecuing is like braising—food is cooked past the point of what's considered well-done, until the collagen breaks down and the meat is fork-tender. The table below summarizes the differences between the three cooking methods.

	GRILLING	GRILL ROASTING	BARBECUING
Best For	Small foods that are naturally tender and cook quickly	Large foods that are naturally tender but require more time to cook through	Foods that are naturally tough and sinewy and require prolonged cooking
Prime Examples	Steaks, chops, vegetables, seafood	Beef tenderloin, pork loin, whole birds	Ribs, brisket, pork shoulder
Grill Setup	Cooked directly over fire, often uncovered	Cooked by indirect heat with cover on; sometimes seared first	Cooked by indirect heat with cover on
Cooking Time	5 to 20 minutes	20 minutes to 2 hours	At least 2 hours
Temperature	400 to 600 degrees	300 to 400 degrees	250 to 300 degrees
Use of Wood Chips or Chunks	Rarely	Optional	Required

13 A Turkey Burger Worth Eating

✓ WHY THIS RECIPE WORKS

The average turkey burger—lean, dry, and seasoned with simple salt and pepper—is a poor stand-in for an all-beef burger. We wanted a turkey burger that grilled up juicy and full of flavor to help even the playing field. We took a close look at the ground turkey sold in supermarkets and found several kinds: ground white meat, ground dark meat, and generically labeled 93 percent lean ground turkey. We went with the 93 percent lean turkey, which our tasters liked and which is widely available. For extra richness, we added mild ricotta cheese, which kept the burgers moist without adding any off-putting flavors to the meat. We found that a little bit of Worcestershire sauce and Dijon mustard gave the burgers a pleasant tang and avoided the dreaded blandness usually associated with this healthful option. A two-level fire allowed us to sear the burgers over high heat and then cook them through at a lower, gentler temperature, for a final product that could hold its own against any all-beef burger. Our variation also provides instructions for making these with ground chicken, if you prefer. For the ultimate turkey burger with home-ground meat, see page 140.

Easy Turkey Burgers

SERVES 4

Be sure to use ground turkey, not ground turkey breast (also labeled 99 percent fat-free). We prefer the richer flavor and softer texture of whole-milk ricotta here, but part-skim or fat-free will also work. Because these burgers are made of ground poultry, be sure to cook them through completely in step 4. If you like, toast the hamburger buns on the grill while the burgers rest.

1¼	**pounds 93 percent lean ground turkey**
½	**cup whole-milk ricotta cheese**
2	**teaspoons Worcestershire sauce**
2	**teaspoons Dijon mustard**
½	**teaspoon salt**
¼	**teaspoon pepper**
4	**hamburger buns**

1 Break turkey into small pieces in bowl and add ricotta, Worcestershire, mustard, salt, and pepper. Using your hands, lightly knead mixture until thoroughly combined. Divide meat into 4 portions. Working with 1 portion at a time, lightly toss from hand to hand to form ball, then gently flatten into 1-inch-thick patty. Press center of patties down with your fingertips to create ¼-inch-deep depression.

2A FOR A CHARCOAL GRILL Open bottom vent completely. Light large chimney starter three-quarters filled with charcoal briquettes (4½ quarts). When top coals are partially covered with ash, pour two-thirds evenly over half of grill, then pour remaining coals over other half of grill. Set cooking grate in place, cover, and open lid vent completely. Heat grill until hot, about 5 minutes.

2B FOR A GAS GRILL Turn all burners to high, cover, and heat grill until hot, about 15 minutes. Leave all burners on high.

3 Clean and oil cooking grate. Place burgers on grill (on hotter side if using charcoal) and cook, without pressing on them, until well seared on both sides, 5 to 7 minutes, turning as needed.

4 Slide burgers to cooler part of grill if using charcoal, or turn all burners to medium if using gas. Cover and continue to cook until burgers register 160 degrees, 5 to 7 minutes, flipping them halfway through cooking. Transfer burgers to platter, tent with aluminum foil, and let rest for 5 minutes. Serve on buns.

VARIATION

14 Chicken Burgers

Ground chicken tends to be much moister than ground turkey and therefore requires less ricotta.

Substitute ground chicken for ground turkey and reduce amount of ricotta to ¼ cup.

15 STEP BY STEP
Testing Burgers for Doneness

It's difficult to get an accurate temperature reading even in the thickest burgers. While we like to hold steaks and chops with tongs and slide an instant-read thermometer through the side, we find that this technique can cause delicate burgers to break apart. Instead, we like to slide the tip of the thermometer into the burger at the top edge and push it toward the center. Note that beef burgers may be cooked to medium-rare (125 degrees), but turkey or chicken burgers should be cooked to well-done (160 degrees).

16 SHOPPING IQ
Ketchup Counts

Since the 1980s, most ketchup has been made with high-fructose corn syrup; manufacturers like this ingredient because it's cheap and easy to mix with other ingredients. But in the past few years, many manufacturers have started offering alternatives, such as ketchup made with white sugar. For our recent taste test of eight national brands, we focused on classic tomato ketchups. Tasters tried each plain and with fries. It was clear they wanted ketchup that tasted the way they remembered it: boldly seasoned, with all the flavor elements—salty, sweet, tangy, and tomatoey. Our top three ketchups were all sweetened with sugar.

THE BOTTOM LINE Old-fashioned trumps modern versions. **Heinz Organic Tomato Ketchup** earned our top spot.

17 SHOPPING IQ
Goat Cheese

It's not hard to see why fresh goat cheese is so popular: With its unmistakable tang, it can be eaten straight on crackers, enliven the simplest salad or pasta dish, enhance pizza toppings, or add creamy richness to a burger. Once exclusively made in France, goat cheese's popularity has driven the United States to produce this cheese domestically. With so many domestic choices now available, which one comes out on top? We gathered nine widely available samples (seven of them stateside products) and set to work finding out. We first tasted the cheese straight out of the package on plain crackers. Then, to see if heat changed its character, we rolled it in bread crumbs and baked it. The good news: Sampled straight from the fridge, the majority of our nine selections were smooth and creamy, with a tangy, grassy taste—just what we want in goat cheese. Only a few had issues, including a chalky, Spackle-like texture; a too-neutral flavor; or an overly gamy taste. Products that were chalky straight out of the package didn't improve with baking—and several that were creamy sampled plain surprised us by baking into crumbly, grainy blobs. When we investigated further, we found that much of this difference was due to the cheeses' salt content. The ions in salt help the proteins in cheese bind and retain water, which means that more moisture is retained during cooking and that the cheese melts more smoothly; the products with more salt stayed smooth and cohesive when baked.

THE BOTTOM LINE Our favorite product, **Laura Chenel's Chèvre** is "mildly goaty" and "rich-tasting," with a "grassy" and "tangy" finish straight out of the package. Either baked or tossed with hot pasta, it stayed "lemony" and "bright," with a "creamy, buttery texture."

WINNER

LAURA CHENEL'S CHÈVRE Fresh Chèvre Log

Tasting Comments "Rich-tasting," "grassy," and "tangy," our favorite goat cheese was "smooth" and "creamy" both unheated and baked, and it kept its "lemony, bright flavor" in both iterations.

RUNNER-UP

VERMONT CREAMERY Fresh Goat Cheese, Classic Chèvre

Tasting Comments This was one of our favorite goat cheeses for sampling straight from the package. Its moderate salt content allowed it to turn slightly "mealy" when baked, but its "grassy," "citrus-like" flavors earned raves from tasters.

18 RECIPE FOR SUCCESS
A Meaty-Tasting Mushroom Burger

✓ WHY THIS RECIPE WORKS

Portobello mushrooms sound like the perfect vegetarian replacement for traditional meat burgers, but mushrooms present some natural pitfalls that have to be taken into account. First off, to avoid muddy flavors, we scraped out the dark brown gills on the underside of the mushrooms. Then, to prevent soggy buns, we knew we had to find a way to rid the mushrooms of a lot of their excess moisture. We used a technique that had worked for us in the past when oven-roasted mushrooms—scoring. Before cooking, we lightly scored the mushrooms on the smooth, non-gill side in a crosshatch pattern. This helped expedite the release of moisture, which then dripped out and evaporated on the grill, ensuring intense mushroom flavor and dry, toasty buns. The scored mushrooms also soaked up more of the flavors of our simple marinade. We added some red onions to the grill so we could cook our topping alongside the mushrooms. Finally, we sprinkled the hot grilled mushrooms with tangy goat cheese and topped the finished product with grilled red onion, peppery arugula with balsamic vinegar, and thinly sliced tomato for a delicious, meatless burger that won't make you ask "Where's the beef?"

Grilled Portobello Burgers
SERVES 4

If your mushrooms are larger or smaller than 4 to 5 inches, you may need to adjust the cooking time accordingly.

- 4 (4- to 5-inch) portobello mushroom caps, stems and gills removed
- 1 large red onion, sliced into ½-inch-thick rounds (do not separate rings)
- 3 tablespoons plus 1 teaspoon olive oil

Salt and pepper

2 garlic cloves, minced

2 teaspoons minced fresh thyme

2 ounces goat cheese, crumbled (½ cup)

4 hamburger buns

1 cup baby arugula

¼ teaspoon balsamic vinegar

1 tomato, cored and sliced thin

1 Using tip of sharp knife, lightly score top of each mushroom cap in crosshatch pattern. Brush onion rounds with 1 tablespoon oil and season with salt and pepper. Combine 2 tablespoons oil, garlic, thyme, ¼ teaspoon salt, and ¼ teaspoon pepper in bowl.

2A FOR A CHARCOAL GRILL Open bottom vent completely. Light large chimney starter three-quarters filled with charcoal briquettes (4½ quarts). When top coals are partially covered with ash, pour evenly over grill. Set cooking grate in place, cover, and open lid vent completely. Heat grill until hot, about 5 minutes.

2B FOR A GAS GRILL Turn all burners to high, cover, and heat grill until hot, about 15 minutes. Turn all burners to medium-high.

3 Clean and oil cooking grate. Place mushrooms, gill side down, and onion rounds on grill. Cook mushrooms until lightly charred and beginning to soften on gill side, 4 to 6 minutes. Flip mushrooms, brush with garlic-oil mixture, and cook until tender and browned on second side, 4 to 6 minutes. Sprinkle with goat cheese and let melt, about 2 minutes.

4 Meanwhile, cook onions, turning as needed, until spottily charred on both sides, 8 to 12 minutes. As they finish cooking, transfer mushrooms and onions to platter and tent with aluminum foil. Split hamburger buns open and grill until warm and lightly charred, about 30 seconds. Transfer to platter.

5 Toss arugula with balsamic vinegar and remaining 1 teaspoon oil in bowl and season with salt and pepper to taste. Separate onion rings. Assemble mushroom caps, arugula, tomato, and onion on buns and serve.

STEP BY STEP

Preparing Portobellos for the Grill

1 REMOVE GILLS Use spoon to scrape gills off underside of portobello. (Gills can muddy the flavor and appearance of a dish.)

2 SCORE CAPS Using tip of sharp knife, lightly score top of each mushroom cap in crosshatch pattern.

20 GRILL HACK Dressed to Grill

Grilling requires a lot of equipment. To keep everything at the ready and easy to find, and keep your hands free at the same time, you can wear a carpenter's tool belt. Slip everything from grill brushes to timer and thermometer into it.

21

FOOD SCIENCE
Marinade Magic

Contrary to popular opinion, almost none of the flavors in a marinade penetrate to the center of the meat. But studies published in the *Journal of Food Science* indicate that salts—ordinary table salt as well as sodium glutamates, the naturally occurring flavor enhancers found in many foods—actually travel far into meat and beef up taste as they go. With this in mind, we created a turbocharged marinade with three key ingredients for our kebabs.

Salt

Not only does salt penetrate meat to thoroughly season it, but it also swells and dissolves some of the proteins, allowing them to retain juices.

Tomato Paste

This condiment is a potent source of naturally occurring glutamates.

Beef Broth

Many commercial beef broths contain yeast extract, a rich source of two flavor-enhancing molecules: glutamates and nucleotides. The latter amplify flavor twentyfold, so that even ⅓ cup of broth in the marinade has a big impact.

22

RECIPE FOR SUCCESS
Beef Kebabs That Have It All

✓ WHY THIS RECIPE WORKS

Most beef kebabs are disappointing, with bland, over-cooked meat and raw or mushy vegetables. We wanted foolproof kebabs: chunks of beef with a thick char and a juicy interior, all thoroughly seasoned and paired with browned, tender-firm vegetables. For the meat, we avoided precut chunks from the supermarket and instead made our own. We chose well-marbled steak tips for their beefy flavor and tender texture and cut the meat into generous 2-inch cubes. For the marinade, we combined salt for moisture, oil for flavor, and sugar for browning. For depth of flavor, we added tomato paste, seasonings and herbs, and beef broth. Just an hour of marinating gave the meat all the seasoning it needed. We chose three grill favorites for the vegetables: pepper, onion, and zucchini. Grilling the beef and vegetables on separate skewers over our tweaked version of a two-level fire allowed the vegetables to cook at a lower temperature while the beef seared over the hotter center area so both parts came out perfectly cooked within a few minutes of each other. The flavors of the marinade are easy to change up for a wealth of variations; try our spicy red curry or savory North African–inspired mixes.

Grilled Beef Kebabs with Lemon-Rosemary Marinade

SERVES 4 TO 6

Sirloin steak tips are sometimes sold as whole steaks labeled "flap meat." To ensure even-size chunks, we prefer to purchase whole steaks and cut them ourselves. If you can't find sirloin steak tips, sometimes labeled flap meat, substitute 2½ pounds blade steak (if using, cut each steak in half to remove the gristle). If you have long, thin pieces of meat, roll or fold them into approximate 2-inch cubes. You will need four 12-inch metal skewers for this recipe. For more information on how to cut up onions for kebabs, see page 19.

MARINADE

- 1 onion, chopped
- ⅓ cup beef broth
- ⅓ cup vegetable oil
- 3 tablespoons tomato paste
- 6 garlic cloves, chopped
- 2 tablespoons chopped fresh rosemary
- 2 teaspoons grated lemon zest
- 2 teaspoons salt
- 1½ teaspoons sugar
- ¾ teaspoon pepper

BEEF AND VEGETABLES

- 2 pounds sirloin steak tips, trimmed and cut into 2-inch chunks
- 1 large zucchini, halved lengthwise and sliced 1 inch thick
- 1 large red bell pepper, stemmed, seeded, and cut into 1½-inch pieces
- 1 large red onion, cut into 1-inch pieces, 3 layers thick

1 FOR THE MARINADE Process all ingredients in blender until smooth, about 45 seconds. Measure out ¾ cup marinade and set aside for vegetables.

2 FOR THE BEEF AND VEGETABLES Combine remaining marinade and beef in 1-gallon zipper-lock bag and toss to coat; press out as much air as possible and seal bag. Refrigerate for 1 to 2 hours, flipping bag every 30 minutes. Gently combine zucchini, bell pepper, and onion with reserved marinade in bowl. Cover and let sit at room temperature for 30 minutes.

3 Remove beef from bag, pat dry with paper towels, and thread tightly onto two 12-inch metal skewers. Thread vegetables onto two 12-inch metal skewers, in alternating pattern of zucchini, bell pepper, and onion.

4A FOR A CHARCOAL GRILL Open bottom vent completely. Light large chimney starter mounded with charcoal briquettes (7 quarts). When top coals are partially covered with ash, pour evenly over center of grill, leaving 2-inch gap between grill wall and charcoal. Set cooking grate in place, cover, and open lid vent completely. Heat grill until hot, about 5 minutes.

4B FOR A GAS GRILL Turn all burners to high, cover, and heat grill until hot, about 15 minutes. Leave primary burner on high and turn other burner(s) to medium-low.

5 Clean and oil cooking grate. Place beef skewers on grill (directly over coals if using charcoal or over hotter side if using gas). Place vegetable skewers on cooler part(s) of grill (near edge of coals if using charcoal). Cook (covered if using gas), turning skewers every 3 to 4 minutes, until beef is well browned and registers 120 to 125 degrees (for medium-rare) or 130 to 135 degrees (for medium), 12 to 16 minutes.

6 Transfer beef skewers to platter and tent with aluminum foil. Continue cooking vegetable skewers until tender and lightly charred, about 5 minutes longer. Serve.

VARIATIONS

23 Grilled Beef Kebabs with North African Marinade
Substitute 20 cilantro sprigs, 2 teaspoons paprika, 1½ teaspoons ground cumin, and ½ teaspoon cayenne pepper for lemon zest and rosemary in marinade.

24 Grilled Beef Kebabs with Red Curry Marinade
Substitute 3 tablespoons red curry paste, 2 teaspoons grated lime zest, ½ cup packed fresh basil leaves, and 2 teaspoons grated fresh ginger for lemon zest and rosemary in marinade.

25 Making Beef Kebabs from Start to Finish

1 MARINATE STEAK TIPS
Combine meat chunks with some of marinade in zipper-lock bag and toss to coat; press out air and seal bag. Refrigerate for 1 to 2 hours, flipping bag every 30 minutes.

2 MARINATE VEGETABLES
Gently combine zucchini, bell pepper, and onion with reserved marinade in bowl, cover, and let sit at room temperature for 30 minutes.

3 SKEWER 'EM Remove beef from bag, pat dry, and thread tightly onto metal skewers. Thread vegetables, in alternating pattern of zucchini, bell pepper, and onion, on separate skewers.

4 USE TWO-LEVEL FIRE Place beef kebabs on hotter part of grill and vegetable skewers on cooler part(s) of grill. Cook (covered if using gas), turning skewers occasionally, for 12 to 16 minutes.

26 SHOPPING IQ
Country-Style Pork Ribs

These meaty, tender, boneless ribs are cut from the upper side of the rib cage from the fatty blade end of the loin. Butchers usually cut them into individual ribs and package several ribs together. They're great for grilling as well as pan-searing (pound them flat) or braising.

27

Pork Skewers Loaded with Flavor

✓ WHY THIS RECIPE WORKS

Compared with beef, chicken, and even shrimp, pork skewers get little love from grillers. Without the right ingredients and techniques, the texture of the meat and the overall flavor both tend to be very unsatisfactory. For grilled pork skewers that were moist and flavorful, we turned to boneless country-style ribs, which are quick cooking and tender, yet have enough fat to keep them from drying out. A flavorful spice rub—garlic, coriander, cumin, nutmeg, cinnamon, and lemon—did triple duty, first in a marinade, later in a basting sauce (mixed with butter and honey to promote browning), and again as part of a relish for the finished pork. As a base for that relish, we grilled cherry tomatoes, lemons, and scallions alongside the pork for a bright, potent sauce to complement the skewers. With this quick relish and a marinade that gets to work in just 30 minutes, these skewers offer an easy, flavorful new addition to your grilling options.

Grilled Pork Skewers with Grilled Tomato Relish

SERVES 4 TO 6

You will need seven 12-inch metal skewers for this recipe.

2	lemons
¼	cup vegetable oil
5	garlic cloves, minced
1	tablespoon ground coriander
2	teaspoons ground cumin
	Salt and pepper
½	teaspoon ground nutmeg
½	teaspoon ground cinnamon
2	pounds boneless country-style pork ribs, trimmed and cut into 1-inch pieces
12	ounces cherry tomatoes
2	tablespoons unsalted butter
2	tablespoons honey
6	scallions

1 Grate 1 tablespoon zest from 1 lemon over large bowl. Halve both lemons and set aside. Add oil, garlic, coriander, cumin, 1½ teaspoons salt, ½ teaspoon pepper, nutmeg, and cinnamon to bowl with lemon zest and whisk together. Set aside 2 tablespoons marinade. Add pork to remaining marinade in bowl and refrigerate for at least 30 minutes or up to 24 hours.

2 Remove pork from marinade and thread onto four 12-inch metal skewers so pieces are touching; discard any remaining used marinade. Thread tomatoes onto three 12-inch metal skewers.

3 Combine butter, honey, and reserved marinade in small saucepan and cook over medium heat, whisking constantly, until butter is melted and mixture is fragrant, about 1 minute. Divide honey mixture evenly between 2 bowls. (Use 1 bowl for grilling pork in step 5 and second bowl for sauce in step 6.)

4A FOR A CHARCOAL GRILL Open bottom vent completely. Light large chimney starter filled with charcoal briquettes (6 quarts). When top coals are partially covered with ash, pour evenly over grill. Set cooking grate in place, cover, and open lid vent completely. Heat grill until hot, about 5 minutes.

4B FOR A GAS GRILL Turn all burners to high, cover, and heat grill until hot, about 15 minutes. Turn all burners to medium.

5 Clean and oil cooking grate. Place pork skewers, tomato skewers, scallions, and reserved lemon halves, cut side down, on grill. Cook pork (covered if using gas), turning every 2 minutes and basting with honey mixture reserved for grilling, until meat registers 145 degrees, 12 to 15 minutes. Cook tomatoes, scallions, and lemon halves until charred, turning scallions and tomatoes as needed to brown evenly, 5 to 10 minutes. Transfer items to platter as they finish grilling.

6 Tent pork with aluminum foil and let rest while preparing tomato relish. Slide tomatoes from skewers into large bowl. Chop scallions and add to tomatoes along with honey mixture reserved for sauce; squeeze lemon halves into tomato mixture. Using potato masher, coarsely mash tomato mixture. Add any accumulated pork juices. Season with salt and pepper to taste. Serve tomato relish with pork.

28

Sharpen Your Own Skewers

While we prefer metal skewers, you can pinch hit by turning to the collection of wooden takeout chopsticks lingering in your kitchen drawer: Transform them into sturdy skewers for meat or veggies by honing one end with a pencil sharpener.

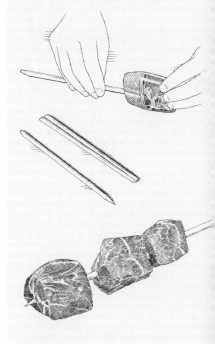

30 RECIPE FOR SUCCESS
Real Shish Kebab

✓ WHY THIS RECIPE WORKS

Shish kebab—skewers of lamb and vegetables—is perhaps the greatest "barbecue" dish from Turkey and the Middle East. When done right, the lamb is well browned and the vegetables are crisp and tender. But shish kebab has its challenges: The components cook at different rates, and the grill temperature has to be just right. We wanted a foolproof method that would give us perfectly cooked vegetables and meat every time. We opted to use the shank end of a boneless leg of lamb: It's inexpensive, requires little trimming, and yields the perfect amount of meat for six people. After extensive testing, we found two vegetables that worked well with the timing and heat required to cook the lamb: red onions and bell peppers. These two options have similar textures and cook through at about the same rate; cut fairly small they added flavor and color to the kebabs without demanding any special attention. Marinating added moisture and allowed us to tweak the flavors of the dish for a wide selection of variations. As little as 2 hours was long enough to give the kebabs good flavor and marinating for 12 hours, or overnight, was even better.

Grilled Lamb Kebabs
SERVES 6

You will need twelve 12-inch metal skewers for this recipe.

- 1 recipe marinade (recipes follow)
- 2¼ pounds boneless leg of lamb (shank end), trimmed and cut into 1-inch pieces
- 3 bell peppers (1 red, 1 yellow, and 1 orange), stemmed, seeded, and each cut into twenty-four 1-inch pieces
- 1 large red onion, cut into thirty-six ¾-inch pieces
  Lemon or lime wedges (optional)

29 TEST KITCHEN TIP
When Recycling Is NOT OK

Used marinade is contaminated with raw meat juice and is therefore unsafe to consume. Even boiling might not make it safe. If you want a sauce to serve with cooked meat, make a little extra marinade and set it aside before adding the rest to the raw meat.

1 Toss marinade and lamb in 1-gallon zipper-lock plastic bag or large bowl; seal bag, pressing out as much air as possible, or cover bowl and refrigerate for at least 2 hours or up to 24 hours.

2 Starting and ending with meat, thread 4 pieces meat, 3 pieces onion (three 3-layer stacks), and 6 pieces bell pepper in mixed order on each of 12 metal skewers.

3A FOR A CHARCOAL GRILL Open bottom vent completely. Light large chimney starter filled with charcoal briquettes (6 quarts). When top coals are partially covered with ash, pour evenly over grill, then spread additional 6 quarts unlit briquettes over lit coals. Set cooking grate in place, cover, and open lid vent completely. Heat grill until hot, about 5 minutes.

3B FOR A GAS GRILL Turn all burners to high, cover, and heat grill until hot, about 15 minutes. Leave all burners on high.

4 Clean and oil cooking grate. Place kebabs on grill. Cook (covered if using gas), turning each kebab one-quarter turn every 1½ to 2 minutes, until meat is well browned all over, grill-marked, and registers 120 to 125 degrees (for medium-rare), about 7 minutes, or 130 to 135 degrees (for medium), about 8 minutes. Transfer kebabs to serving platter; squeeze lemon wedges over kebabs, if using; and serve.

31 Warm Spice Parsley Marinade with Ginger
MAKES ABOUT 1 CUP

½	cup olive oil
½	cup fresh parsley leaves
1	jalapeño chile, stemmed, seeded, and chopped coarse
2	tablespoons grated fresh ginger
3	garlic cloves, peeled
1	teaspoon ground cumin
1	teaspoon ground cardamom
1	teaspoon ground cinnamon
1	teaspoon salt
⅛	teaspoon pepper

Process all ingredients in food processor until smooth, about 1 minute.

32 Garlic and Cilantro Marinade with Garam Masala
MAKES ABOUT ¾ CUP

Garam masala is a warm spice blend that typically contains black pepper, dried chiles, cinnamon, cardamom, and coriander.

½	cup olive oil
½	cup fresh cilantro leaves
¼	cup raisins
1½	tablespoons lemon juice
3	garlic cloves, peeled
1	teaspoon salt
½	teaspoon garam masala
⅛	teaspoon pepper

Process all ingredients in food processor until smooth, about 1 minute.

33 Sweet Curry Marinade with Buttermilk
MAKES ABOUT ¾ CUP

¾	cup buttermilk
1	tablespoon lemon juice
3	garlic cloves, minced
1	tablespoon packed brown sugar
1	tablespoon curry powder
1	teaspoon red pepper flakes
1	teaspoon ground coriander
1	teaspoon chili powder
1	teaspoon salt
⅛	teaspoon pepper

Combine all ingredients in 1-gallon zipper-lock plastic bag or large bowl.

34
STEP BY STEP
Preparing Onions for Kebabs

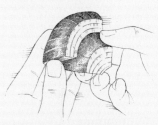

1 TRIM AND QUARTER Trim off stem and root ends and cut onion into quarters. Peel 3 outer layers of onion away from core.

2 QUARTER LENGTHWISE Working with outer layers only, cut each quarter lengthwise into equal strips.

3 CUT CROSSWISE Cut each of 12 strips crosswise into 3 pieces. You should have thirty-six 3-layer stacks of separate pieces of onion.

36 Easy Chicken Kebabs with Global Flavors

✓ WHY THIS RECIPE WORKS

Chicken kebabs are a great way to take boneless, skinless chicken breasts up a notch, but the lean meat requires some help to keep from getting dried out and tasteless over the hot flames. To solve this problem, we started with a simple olive oil marinade, but that wasn't enough for truly juicy chicken. Another great way to help meat retain moisture when cooked is to brine it first, but we worried that a true brine would make the small pieces of chicken used for the kebabs too salty; there was tons of surface area to soak up the brine, which was good for moisture but potentially bad for flavor. Instead, we just added a teaspoon of salt to the marinade along with the oil, plus a simple mix of herbs and garlic—you can tweak the herbs based on what you like best, or try one of our spiced-up variations. Because there is no acid in the marinade and thus no danger of breaking down the texture of the meat, the chicken can be soaked for up to 24 hours before cooking. Cooking the chicken and vegetables together on the same skewers enhances the flavor of both.

Grilled Chicken Kebabs with Garlic and Herb Marinade
SERVES 4

You will need four 12-inch metal skewers for this recipe. For more information on how to cut onions for kebabs, see page 19.

- ½ cup olive oil
- 6 small garlic cloves, minced (about 2 tablespoons)
- ¼ cup chopped fresh chives, minced fresh basil, parsley, tarragon, oregano, cilantro, or mint; or 2 tablespoons minced fresh thyme or rosemary
- 1 teaspoon salt
  Pepper
- 1½ pounds boneless, skinless chicken breasts, trimmed and cut into 1-inch cubes
- 2 red bell peppers, stemmed, seeded, and cut into 1-inch pieces
- 1 large red onion, cut into 1-inch pieces, 3 layers thick

1 Whisk olive oil, garlic, herbs, and salt in small bowl and season with pepper.

2 Mix marinade and chicken in 1-gallon zipper-lock plastic bag; seal bag and refrigerate, turning once or twice, at least 3 hours or up to 24 hours.

3 Remove chicken from marinade. Thread each of four 12-inch skewers with 2 pieces bell pepper, 1 section onion, 2 pieces chicken, and 1 section onion. Repeat twice more, ending with 2 additional pieces bell pepper.

4A FOR A CHARCOAL GRILL Open bottom vent completely. Light large chimney starter filled with charcoal briquettes (6 quarts). When top coals are partially covered with ash, pour evenly over grill. Set cooking grate in place, cover, and open lid vent completely. Heat grill until hot, about 5 minutes.

35 Seeking Superior Skewers

We've been burned by skewers before. Superthin double prongs are flimsy; smooth, rounded prongs let food spin in place when you're trying to flip it. Still, manufacturer innovations promise improvement, so we gathered six sets, including our previous no-frills favorite, the Norpro 12-Inch Stainless Steel Skewers, and threaded them with chicken-vegetable kebabs; scallops; and kofte, a kebab of ground meat and herbs. Metal was best, but solid tab handles on one set retained heat, so serving was a burn risk; loop handles on our two favorite models dispersed heat quickly. One model's "heat-resistant" plastic slider melted. Double-pronged skewers splayed out awkwardly, so threading them through food was a struggle. Their thickness also tore tender scallops. Curved rods occupied too much grill real estate, tangled easily, and only let us turn food 180 degrees.

THE BOTTOM LINE We'll stick with our former champ, **Norpro 12-Inch Stainless Steel Skewers**. Not only do they have the smartest design, but they are also the cheapest at $6.85 for six skewers.

4B FOR A GAS GRILL Turn all burners to high, cover, and heat grill until hot, about 15 minutes. Leave all burners on high.

5 Clean and oil cooking grate. Place kebabs on grill. Cook (covered if using gas), turning as needed, until vegetables and chicken are charred around edges and chicken is cooked through, about 12 minutes. Transfer kebabs to platter and serve.

VARIATIONS

37 **Grilled Chicken Kebabs with Curry Marinade**
Substitute ¼ cup minced fresh cilantro or mint for herbs and add 1 teaspoon curry powder to marinade.

38 **Grilled Chicken Kebabs with Caribbean Marinade**
Substitute ¼ cup minced fresh parsley for herbs and add 1 teaspoon ground cumin, 1 teaspoon chili powder, ½ teaspoon ground allspice, ½ teaspoon pepper, and ¼ teaspoon ground cinnamon to marinade.

39 **Grilled Chicken Kebabs with Middle Eastern Marinade**
Substitute ¼ cup minced fresh mint or parsley (alone or in combination) for herbs and add ½ teaspoon ground cinnamon, ½ teaspoon ground allspice, and ¼ teaspoon cayenne pepper to marinade.

40 **Grilled Chicken Kebabs with Southwestern Marinade**
Substitute ¼ cup minced fresh cilantro for herbs. Decrease salt to ½ teaspoon and add 1 teaspoon ground cumin, 1 teaspoon chili powder, 1 teaspoon turmeric, and 1 medium chile, such as jalapeño, seeded and minced.

41 **Grilled Chicken Kebabs with Mediterranean Marinade**
Substitute following mixture for herb marinade: Combine ½ cup plain whole-milk yogurt, ¼ cup extra-virgin olive oil, 3 minced garlic cloves, 2 teaspoons dried thyme, 2 teaspoons dried oregano, 1 teaspoon salt, 1 teaspoon pepper, and ¼ teaspoon cayenne pepper. In step 2, marinate chicken for 3 to 6 hours. Whisk ¼ cup extra-virgin olive oil, 1 minced garlic clove, 2 tablespoons chopped fresh basil, and 3 tablespoons lemon juice together in bowl; set aside. Skewer chicken and grill as directed. Brush cooked kebabs with lemon dressing before serving.

42 STEP BY STEP
Stemming, Seeding, and Slicing Bell Peppers

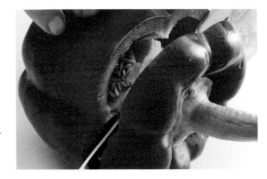

1 SLICE AND STEM Slice ¼ inch from top and bottom of pepper, then gently remove stem from top lobe.

2 CORE Pull core out of pepper.

3 REMOVE RIBS AND SEEDS Slit down 1 side of pepper, then lay it flat, skin side down, in long strip. Use sharp knife to slide along inside of pepper, removing all ribs and seeds. Slice into pieces as directed in recipe.

43 Perfecting the Flavors of Swordfish Skewers

RECIPE FOR SUCCESS

✔ WHY THIS RECIPE WORKS

Swordfish has a taste all its own and needs co-starring ingredients that are strong and robust to complement the flavor of the fish. For these skewers, we paired swordfish with pieces of red onion and lemon. Once grilled, the onion pieces softened slightly yet retained some texture, and the lemon went from tart and acidic to sweet and rich. A simple basil oil, brushed over our skewers once they came off the grill, complemented the bright lemon flavor. Rubbing the swordfish with a bit of ground coriander added complexity and provided flavor that popped with the lemon and basil.

Grilled Swordfish Skewers with Basil Oil

SERVES 4

We like the flavor of swordfish here but you can substitute other firm-fleshed fish such as mahi-mahi or halibut. You will need four 12-inch metal skewers for this recipe.

- 1½   **pounds skinless swordfish steak, cut into 1¼-inch pieces**
- 4   **teaspoons ground coriander**
  -   **Salt and pepper**
- 3   **lemons, quartered lengthwise and halved crosswise**
- 1   **large red onion, cut into 1-inch pieces, 3 layers thick**
- ¼   **cup extra-virgin olive oil**
- 2   **tablespoons chopped fresh basil**

1 Pat swordfish dry with paper towels, rub with coriander, and season with salt and pepper. Thread fish, lemons, and onion evenly in alternating pattern onto four 12-inch metal skewers. Brush skewers with 1 tablespoon oil. Combine remaining 3 tablespoons oil and basil in bowl and season with salt and pepper to taste.

2A FOR A CHARCOAL GRILL Open bottom vent completely. Light large chimney starter three-quarters filled with charcoal briquettes (4½ quarts). When top coals are partially covered with ash, pour evenly over grill. Set cooking grate in place, cover, and open lid vent completely. Heat grill until hot, about 5 minutes.

2B FOR A GAS GRILL Turn all burners to high, cover, and heat grill until hot, about 15 minutes. Turn all burners to medium-high.

3 Clean cooking grate, then repeatedly brush grate with well-oiled paper towels until black and glossy, 5 to 10 times. Place skewers on grill. Cook (covered if using gas), turning as needed, until fish is opaque and flakes apart when gently prodded with paring knife, 5 to 8 minutes.

4 Transfer skewers to platter, tent with aluminum foil, and let rest for 5 to 10 minutes. Brush skewers with basil oil before serving.

44   GADGETS & GEAR   A Charcoal Grill for the Road

A portable charcoal grill offers the smoky flavors of charcoal grilling in a convenient size. We gathered six portable grills with prices ranging from just over $20 to $140 and tested them with burgers, flank steak, and butterflied whole chickens. We appreciated lightweight grills that don't require assembly every time we want to cook, as well as features like clips to secure the lid for easy transport. We preferred grills that fit at least six burgers and three-quarters of a chimney's worth of briquettes. We also saw the value of a raised lip, which kept the food from falling off.

THE BOTTOM LINE For the best all-around portable grill, we recommend the **Weber Smokey Joe Gold** ($34.70), which offers an ample cooking surface, a cover that can be secured for travel, a convenient raised lip, and a reasonable price. This smaller version of one of our favorite full-size charcoal grills shares many of its attributes. The ample cooking surface fit six to eight burgers at a time or a 1½-pound flank steak. The domed cover allowed us to grill-roast a butterflied chicken perfectly. Adjustable vents on the cover and on opposite sides of the grill's body gave us plenty of control over the fire.

45   TEST KITCHEN TIP   Storing Citrus

Unlike bananas or peaches, which ripen at room temperature, citrus fruits stop ripening the moment they are picked, thus beginning a slow and steady decline in texture and flavor. To improve their shelf life, commercially grown citrus are buffed with a thin layer of food-safe wax that prevents moisture from escaping through the fruits' porous rind. To test how well the wax coating works, we bought lemons, limes, and oranges and stored half in the refrigerator and half at room temperature. The fruit that was refrigerated remained firm and juicy for about three weeks, while citrus that was left at room temperature began to discolor and dehydrate in as little as five days. Ultimately, the only downside to storing citrus in the fridge is that it's more difficult to squeeze juice from a cold citrus fruit. To make life easier, let your citrus sit at room temperature for about 15 minutes before juicing.

47 RECIPE FOR SUCCESS
Easy Grilled Steak with a Great Sear

✔ WHY THIS RECIPE WORKS

Turning out a perfectly grilled steak with a flavorful, charred exterior and a rosy, medium-rare interior required a few tricks. The first trick was to buy decent steak. We preferred strip steaks, rib-eye steaks, filets mignons, sirloin steak, or flank steak. Second, to bring out its flavor, we seasoned the meat with salt and let it sit before cooking. Third, we brushed the steaks with oil (and seasoned them with pepper) in order to get a good sear; the oil was especially helpful for thin or lean steaks like flank and filet mignon. Then, to ensure that these steaks came off the grill with a charred exterior and perfectly tender interior, we built a fire with two heat zones, starting the steaks over the hotter side and moving them to the cooler side to finish cooking through. We found that resting the steaks before serving is key—if sliced into right off the grill, the meat will exude its flavorful juices and be dry.

46 FOOD SCIENCE
Rest Meat for Maximum Juiciness

You've taken the meat off the fire and are ready to dig in. But not so fast! A final but very important step when cooking all red meat and pork is a resting period after the meat comes off the heat. As the proteins in the meat heat up during cooking they coagulate, which basically means they uncoil and then reconnect in a different configuration. When the proteins coagulate, they squeeze out part of the liquid that was trapped in their coiled structures and in the spaces between the individual molecules. The heat from the cooking source drives these freed liquids toward the center of the meat.

This process of coagulation explains why experienced chefs can determine the "doneness" of a piece of meat by pushing on it and judging the amount of resistance: The firmer the meat, the more done it is. But the coagulation process is apparently at least partly reversible, so as you allow the meat to rest and return to a lower temperature after cooking, some of the liquid is reabsorbed by the protein molecules as their capacity to hold moisture increases. As a result, if given a chance to rest, the meat will lose less juice when you cut into it, which in turn makes for much juicier and more tender meat.

Grilled Boneless Steaks
SERVES 4

Try to buy steaks of even thickness so they cook at the same rate. If cooking filet mignon, look for steaks that are a bit thicker, about 2 inches. Depending on the size and thickness of the steaks and the desired doneness, the cooking time can vary dramatically. Use a thermometer to determine the doneness. We prefer these steaks cooked to medium-rare.

2–2½ pounds boneless beef steaks, 1 to 2 inches thick, trimmed
Kosher salt and pepper
Vegetable oil

1 Sprinkle steaks evenly with 1 teaspoon salt and let sit at room temperature for 1 hour. Pat steaks dry with paper towels, brush lightly with oil, and season with pepper.

2A FOR A CHARCOAL GRILL Open bottom vent completely. Light large chimney starter filled with charcoal briquettes (6 quarts). When top coals are partially covered with ash, pour two-thirds evenly over half of grill, then pour remaining coals over other half of grill. Set cooking grate in place, cover, and open lid vent completely. Heat grill until hot, about 5 minutes.

2B FOR A GAS GRILL Turn all burners to high, cover, and heat grill until hot, about 15 minutes. Leave primary burner on high and turn other burner(s) to medium.

3 Clean and oil cooking grate. Place steaks on hotter side of grill. Cook (covered if using gas), turning steaks as needed, until nicely charred on both sides, 4 to 6 minutes. Slide steaks to cooler side of grill and continue to cook until they register 120 to 125 degrees (for medium-rare), 4 to 8 minutes.

4 Transfer steaks to platter, tent with aluminum foil, and let rest for 5 to 10 minutes before serving.

48 SHOPPING IQ Choosing the Best Steaks for Grilling

Even a steakhouse can't make a tough, flavorless steak tender and delicious. Starting with a thick steak is key, but which cut? With all of the options at the market, it's hard to know what to choose. Here are our favorites.

Rib-Eye Steak

Very flavorful with lots of marbling and a smooth, fine texture

Filet Mignon

Mild flavor (too mild for some), meltingly tender, surprisingly lean

T-Bone

Strip and tenderloin in one, fatty (in a good way) flavor and texture

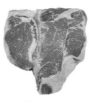

Porterhouse

Strip and tenderloin in one, but tenderloin is larger than in T-bone

Strip Steak

Well marbled, with a big, beefy flavor

49 GADGETS & GEAR
Putting Gas Grills to the Test

Let's be honest. Most people choose a gas grill because it's convenient: Turn a knob and you can start cooking in minutes. But whether that grill performs as it should is another matter. For simple grilling you want uniform, strong heat. What you often get: one instant-burn zone we'll call "The Inferno," and another zone so cool you could set your drink down on it. The rest—an area about the size of a dinner plate—is just about right. You can ruin a lot of expensive food before you find that sweet spot.

We went shopping for gas grills priced $500 or less, focusing on six major brands (four shown in the following chart) to pit against our previous winner, the Weber Spirit E-310 (and its smaller sibling, the Weber Spirit E-210). We fired them up to cook a variety of foods from burger patties to thick strip steaks and 5-pound pork butts. We checked that a 12-pound turkey fit under each lid with room to spare. With slices of white bread, we mapped each grill's heating pattern, and we measured the temperature of the grills' interiors with a calibrated thermocouple to see how they retained heat over time (essential for tender barbecue). Along the way, we observed design elements of each grill that made cooking easier or more complicated. And rolling them in and out of our grill garage over bumpy pavement revealed grills that fought us and rattled to pieces—literally—while others glided steadily and remained sturdily intact.

What made the difference? We started by looking under the grates. All gas grills share similar construction: at the bottom, perforated metal tubes (the burners) produce a row of flames when the gas is ignited. Above them are metal bars shaped like tents, set like roofs over the burners. Since heat wants to rise straight up from the flames, without these bars to deflect it you'd have hotspots directly over each burner, and cooler zones everywhere else. Our top-performing grills provided extra heat deflection, helping them cook more evenly. One had additional bars that didn't cover flames, set beside those that did; another featured a layer of perforated stainless-steel plates that covered the grill beneath the grates.

Gas grills often fall short when it comes to grill roasting and barbecuing, which rely on indirect heat. On a charcoal grill, cooler and hotter heat zones are partially achieved through the arrangement of the coals. And air is what fuels a charcoal fire, so you adjust vents to customize heat level and airflow.

All of this control is out of your hands with gas grills. Air doesn't fuel the fire, gas does. The clamshell-shaped "cookbox" on a gas grill has non-adjustable vents, and all of those vents are in one place: across the back of the box. That means hot air—and smoke—flow in one direction when the lid is closed: straight out the back of the grill. New grill designs make this even worse for smoking: Since we last tested gas grills, all of the manufacturers in our new lineup have positioned their grills' burner tubes to run from front to back, rather than side to side. Why is this important? When tubes of flame run side to side, you can still send the smoke and heat over the meat by turning on only the burner in the front of the grill, positioning wood chips on the lit front burner, and the meat directly behind. Heat and smoke travel front to back, over the meat, on the way to the vents, providing good smoke flavor.

Therefore, the integrity of the cookbox is essential, and success came down to a few factors: the material of the box, and the number and position of the vents. Lower-performing grills had row after row of vents that perforated the back of their cookboxes. The boxes themselves were thin and closed loosely over the grates, so they couldn't hold as much heat. By contrast, our top grill has a cookbox with bottom and sides of thick cast aluminum, and a heavy double-layered steel lid. That lid seals tightly, and the box has just one narrow vent across the back. As a result, meat cooked properly in a timely manner, every time—and even had smoke flavor. In the end, this grill's thoughtful design and sturdy construction, combined with competence and versatility for everything from direct grilling to indirect cooking and smoking, earned it the top spot in our tests.

HIGHLY RECOMMENDED

Good ★★★   Fair ★★   Poor ★

WEBER Spirit E-310 Gas Grill
Model 461510001
Price $499.99
Burners 3
Grates Enameled Cast Iron
Features Fuel gauge, six tool hooks, thermometer
Size of Cooking Grate 23.5 in by 17 in
Capacity 19 burgers

Grilling	★★★
Indirect Cooking	★★★
Design	★★★
Durability	★★★
Cleanup	★★★

Solidly competent, our winner put a crisp brown crust on juicy burgers and steak. And it was equally good at barbecue, resulting in tender pulled pork with real smoky flavor. Tasters raved: "Perfect smoke, super moist and tender,"; "almost as smoky as bacon,"; "the texture is spot-on."

CHAR-BROIL Commercial Series 4-Burner Gas Grill
Model 463242715
Price $499.99
Burners 4
Grates Enameled Cast Iron
Features Side burner, heat-spreading radiant steel plates under grates, cast iron griddle, cleaning tool
Size of Cooking Grate 29.5 in by 17 in
Capacity 24 burgers

Grilling	★★★
Indirect Cooking	★★
Design	★★
Durability	★★★
Cleanup	★★

Unique, heat-spreading zigzagged steel plates beneath cast-iron grates made this grill a standout for direct grilling, producing beautifully uniform toast and burgers, and crisp crust on steak. But its unusual interior layout left us struggling to figure out where to put water pans (on the bottom of the grill), and there was nowhere to prop wood chip packets above the flames. Pulled pork roasted to tenderness, but utterly lacked smoke flavor.

NOT RECOMMENDED

DYNA-GLO 5-Burner Propane Gas Grill with Side Burner and Rotisserie Burner
Model DGA550SSP-D
Price $483.65
Burners 5
Grates Stainless steel
Features Side burner, rotisserie burner (rotisserie available separately)
Size of Cooking Grate 29 in by 17 in
Capacity 28 burgers

Grilling	★½
Indirect Cooking	★★
Design	★
Durability	★★★
Cleanup	★½

This handsome, roomy grill had five burners plus a side burner, but ran hot and cold in different zones, grilling unevenly. Burgers got wedged under a protruding rotisserie burner in back, and a low warming rack blocked our spatula. A big 2-inch gap at the back lid, open holes in the sides, and an open back panel let too much hot air and smoke escape, so it took fiddling to maintain heat for barbecue. While the pulled pork texture was "nice," it lacked smoky flavor.

NEXGRILL 4 Burner Liquid Propane Gas Grill
Model 720-0830H
Price $269.00
Burners 4
Grates Stainless steel
Features Side burner
Size of Cooking Grate 25.5 in by 17 in
Capacity 15 burgers

Grilling	★
Indirect Cooking	★★
Design	★
Durability	★★
Cleanup	★★

This may be the most economical grill we tested, but we're dubious about its value. Toast was white with black stripes. The back of the grill surface was hotter than the front. We got visible grill marks on some burgers, but steak was pale and soft. The open lid's shape sent smoke straight into our faces, and the low warming rack blocked our spatula. Nine large vents and a 2-inch gap across the back of the cookbox let smoke and heat escape.

50

Slicing T-Bone and Porterhouse Steaks

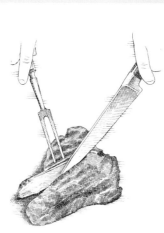

1 REMOVE LARGE SECTION
Cut along bone to remove large strip section.

2 REMOVE SMALLER SECTION Turn steak around and cut tenderloin section off bone.

3 SLICE Cut each piece cross-wise into ¼-inch-thick slices.

RECIPE FOR SUCCESS

51. Boning Up on Great Grilled Steak

✓ WHY THIS RECIPE WORKS

Porterhouse and T-bone steaks are really two steaks in one—a tender New York strip steak on one side of the bone and a buttery, quicker-cooking tenderloin on the other. The trick is to cook both parts to the perfect doneness at the same time. As with boneless steaks, we made a two-level fire and seared the steaks over the hotter side first, then slid them to the cooler side to cook through. The key is to position the tenderloin so it always faces the cooler side of the grill—this prevents it from overcooking. Also, when moving the steak to the cooler side, position it so that the big bone along the bottom of the steak faces the hotter side of the grill. This protects the narrow top of the steak from drying out. Salting the meat for 1 hour before grilling boosted flavor from crust to bone.

Grilled Porterhouse or T-Bone Steaks

SERVES 4 TO 6

Be sure to buy steaks that are at least 1 inch thick.

- 2 (1¾-pound) porterhouse or T-bone steaks, 1 to 1½ inches thick, trimmed
  Salt and pepper

1 Sprinkle each steak evenly with 1 teaspoon salt and let sit at room temperature for 1 hour. Pat steaks dry with paper towels and season with pepper.

2A FOR A CHARCOAL GRILL Open bottom vent completely. Light large chimney starter three-quarters filled with charcoal briquettes (4½ quarts). When top coals are partially covered with ash, pour evenly over half of grill. Set cooking grate in place, cover, and open lid vent completely. Heat grill until hot, about 5 minutes.

2B FOR A GAS GRILL Turn all burners to high, cover, and heat grill until hot, about 15 minutes. Leave primary burner on high and turn other burner(s) to low.

3 Clean and oil cooking grate. Place steaks on hotter side of grill with tenderloin sides facing cooler side of grill. Cook (covered if using gas) until dark crust forms, 6 to 8 minutes. Flip and turn steaks so that tenderloin sides are still facing cooler side of grill. Continue to cook until dark brown crust forms on second side, 6 to 8 minutes.

4 Slide steaks to cooler side of grill and turn so that bone side is facing hotter side of grill. Cover grill and cook, turning as needed, until meat registers 120 to 125 degrees (for medium-rare) or 130 to 135 degrees (medium), 2 to 4 minutes.

5 Transfer steaks to carving board, tent with aluminum foil, and let rest for 5 to 10 minutes. Cut strip and tenderloin pieces off bones, then slice each piece ¼ inch thick. Serve.

VARIATION

52 Grilled Tuscan Steaks with Garlic Essence

Rub halved garlic cloves over bone and meat on each side of steaks before seasoning with salt and pepper.

53

SHOPPING IQ

Two Types of T-Bones

Both T-bone and porterhouse steaks contain a strip steak (left) and a tenderloin steak (right) connected by a T-shaped bone. Technically, a T-bone must have a tenderloin portion at least ½ inch across, and a porterhouse's tenderloin must measure at least 1¼ inches across.

T-Bone

Porterhouse

54 Classy, Classic Filet Mignon

RECIPE FOR SUCCESS

✓ WHY THIS RECIPE WORKS

Filet mignon is the Superman of tenderness, yet its flavor is as mild as Clark Kent, which is why filets are so great when they're grilled. The fire sears the exterior of the steaks, concentrating the flavor by forming a deep brown, crisp, aromatic crust. To get grilled filets mignons with a great crust and juicy interior, we knew a very hot fire was essential, but the thick steaks cooked over consistently high heat burned. Instead, we turned to a two-level fire. We seared the steaks first over high heat and then finished cooking them through on the cooler side. Rubbing the steaks with olive oil before grilling improved browning and added flavor. Judging the doneness of the meat is key, and we found that an instant-read thermometer is the best tool for the job. For an accurate reading, insert it from the side and make sure that the tip of the probe does not go past the center of the steak. To add a little richness to the steaks, we made a variety of savory compound butters—perfect for melting down the sides of the still-warm steaks.

Grilled Filets Mignons

SERVES 4

We suggest serving the steaks with one of our flavored butters (recipes follow).

- 4 (7- to 8-ounce) center-cut filets mignons, 1½ to 2 inches thick, trimmed
- 4 teaspoons olive oil
  Salt and pepper

1A FOR A CHARCOAL GRILL Open bottom vent completely. Light large chimney starter filled with charcoal briquettes (6 quarts). When top coals are partially covered with ash, pour two-thirds evenly over half of grill, then pour remaining coals over other half of grill. Set cooking grate in place, cover, and open lid vent completely. Heat grill until hot, about 5 minutes.

1B FOR A GAS GRILL Turn all burners to high, cover, and heat grill until hot, about 15 minutes. Leave all burners on high.

2 Meanwhile, pat steaks dry with paper towels and lightly rub with oil. Season steaks with salt and pepper.

3 Clean and oil cooking grate. Place steaks on grill (on hotter side if using charcoal) and cook (covered if using gas) until well browned on both sides, 4 to 6 minutes, flipping halfway through cooking. Move steaks to cooler side of grill (if using charcoal) or turn all burners to medium (if using gas) and continue to cook (covered if using gas), until meat registers 115 to 120 degrees (for rare) or 120 to 125 degrees (for medium-rare), 5 to 9 minutes longer.

4 Transfer steaks to serving platter, tent with aluminum foil, and let rest for 10 minutes before serving.

55 Blue Cheese Butter

MAKES ¼ CUP

4	tablespoons unsalted butter, softened
3	tablespoons crumbled blue cheese
1	small shallot, minced
1	teaspoon chopped fresh parsley
1	small garlic clove, minced
¼	teaspoon salt
⅛	teaspoon pepper

Combine all ingredients in bowl and mix until smooth. While steaks are resting, spoon 1 tablespoon butter on each one.

56 Roasted Red Pepper and Smoked Paprika Butter

MAKES ¼ CUP

4	tablespoons unsalted butter, softened
2	tablespoons finely chopped jarred roasted red peppers
1	tablespoon minced fresh thyme
¾	teaspoon smoked paprika
½	teaspoon salt
	Pinch pepper

Combine all ingredients in bowl and mix until smooth. While steaks are resting, spoon 1 tablespoon butter on each one.

57 Lemon, Garlic, and Parsley Butter

MAKES ¼ CUP

4	tablespoons unsalted butter, softened
1	tablespoon minced fresh parsley
1	garlic clove, minced
½	teaspoon grated lemon zest
½	teaspoon salt
	Pinch pepper

Combine all ingredients in bowl and mix until smooth. While steaks are resting, spoon 1 tablespoon butter on each one.

58 STEP BY STEP Checking Your Steak for Doneness

Put down that knife you're about to stab your steak with to see if the meat is done to your liking. Instead, get yourself an instant-read thermometer (see page 60 for our ratings). Do you know how your thermometer works? You should. Understanding how it works will help you take an accurate reading of the meat's temperature. Location is key. You might assume that the sensor on your thermometer is right at the tip, but on some models it is in fact an inch or two up.

To find out where the sensor is on your thermometer, bring a pot of water to a boil and slowly lower your thermometer into the pot until it registers 212 degrees (adjusting, of course, for high altitudes). Knowing the location of the sensor is only half the battle, however. Now you have to insert the thermometer into the steak so that the sensor is right in the middle.

Make sure the thermometer is not touching any bone, which will throw off the reading. And make sure to check each steak, if cooking more than one—some will cook faster than others depending on their thickness and their location on the grill.

59 STEP BY STEP Dealing with Misshapen Filets

To correct for unevenly or oddly cut filets, tie a 12-inch piece of kitchen twine around each steak. Snip off the excess twine at the knot to make sure it does not ignite on the grill. Adjust the shape of the tied filet by gently rolling or patting it with your hand until it is more uniform in appearance and thickness.

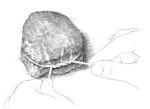

60

STEP BY STEP

Turning Chuck-Eye Roasts into Steaks

1 SEPARATE AND HALVE
After separating roast at its natural seam, turn each piece on its side and cut it in half lengthwise, against grain.

2 TRIM FAT Remove and discard chewy silverskin and any excess fat.

61

RECIPE FOR SUCCESS

Great Grilled Steak on the Cheap

✔ WHY THIS RECIPE WORKS

Treated like pricier cuts, inexpensive chuck steaks can turn tough and chewy on the grill. We wanted to develop a recipe that would produce tender steaks, while capitalizing on chuck's beefy flavor and moderate price. The chuck (also called the shoulder) contains several different cuts, but we found that not all chuck steaks are created equal. Chuck-eye steaks have the best texture and good flavor, but despite their wide availability, the chuck-eye steaks we were getting from the store were inconsistent in size and shape, so they cooked at very different rates. We decided to avoid this problem by buying a boneless chuck-eye roast and cutting the steaks ourselves. This bit of extra (and easy) work resulted in four thick steaks that were a snap to cook evenly. Chipotle chile powder and salt made an assertive base for our spice rub, while granulated garlic and ground coriander provided complementary flavors, but we found that a surprising ingredient—cocoa powder—added great depth. Brown sugar helped smooth out the bitter edges. Letting the spice-rubbed steaks sit in the refrigerator for at least 6 hours allowed the flavors to really sink into the meat before they hit the grill.

Grilled Chuck Steaks

SERVES 4

We prefer to buy a whole chuck-eye roast and cut the steaks ourselves to ensure even thickness and even cooking. Choose a roast without too much fat at the natural seam.

1	tablespoon kosher salt
1	tablespoon chipotle chile powder
1	teaspoon unsweetened cocoa powder
1	teaspoon packed brown sugar
½	teaspoon ground coriander
½	teaspoon granulated garlic
1	(2½- to 3-pound) boneless beef chuck-eye roast
2	tablespoons vegetable oil

1 Combine salt, chile powder, cocoa, sugar, coriander, and garlic in bowl. Separate roast into 2 pieces along natural seam. Turn each piece on its side and cut in half lengthwise against grain. Remove silverskin and trim fat to ¼-inch thickness. Pat steaks dry with paper towels and rub with spice mixture. Transfer steaks to 1-gallon zipper-lock bag and refrigerate for at least 6 hours or up to 24 hours.

2A FOR A CHARCOAL GRILL Open bottom vent halfway. Light large chimney starter filled with charcoal briquettes (6 quarts). When top coals are partially covered with ash, pour evenly over half of grill. Set cooking grate in place, cover, and open lid vent halfway. Heat grill until hot, about 5 minutes.

2B FOR A GAS GRILL Turn all burners to high, cover, and heat grill until hot, about 15 minutes. Turn primary burner to medium-high and other burner(s) to medium-low.

3 Clean and oil cooking grate. Brush steaks all over with oil. Place steaks on hotter side of grill and cook (covered if using gas) until well charred on both sides, about 5 minutes per side. Move steaks to cooler side of grill and continue to cook (covered if using gas) until steaks register 120 to 125 degrees (for medium-rare) or 130 to 135 degrees (for medium), 5 to 8 minutes.

4 Transfer steaks to carving board, tent loosely with aluminum foil, and let rest for 10 minutes. Slice steaks thin against grain and serve.

62

TEST KITCHEN TIP

How to Give Steaks a Garlic Boost

Mixing minced garlic into a steak rub might seem like a logical way to incorporate that flavor but over the high heat of the grill, the garlic can burn. We came up with an alternative approach: treating the steak like bruschetta. Rubbing a smashed garlic clove over the grilled meat's surface imparts a burst of flavor and aroma. Use the technique with any plain grilled or pan-seared steak.

63 TEST KITCHEN TIP
Preventing and Eliminating Flare-Ups

Beyond being scary and dangerous, flare-ups also can make the difference between pleasant charred grill flavor and burnt food. Flare-ups are usually caused by fat or by excess oily marinade dripping off the meat and catching fire. To avoid them, trim meat carefully and pat dry any foods marinated with oil with paper towels before grilling.

Additionally, many gas grills have grease traps on their undersides; when your grill is completely cool, remove the shallow pan from under your grill and give it a good cleaning to prevent it from catching fire. Sometimes, despite our best preventive measures, we still get flare-ups. Keep long tongs and grill gloves handy so that you can quickly and safely move the food to an area of the grill not directly over the fire. The flare-up will die down fast, and you'll have the grill back under your control. Briefly covering the grill can also help squelch flare-ups.

THE BOTTOM LINE Minimize flare-ups by removing excess fat and marinade from food before grilling. Keep long tongs and grill gloves handy so you can safely move food while managing a flare-up.

64 In Search of a Charcoal Grill That Has It All

GADGETS & GEAR

There's a lot to be said for the basic kettle. But it's not a perfect package. The tripod base can be wobbly and when we're adding food to or removing it from the fire, we wish there was a place to set down a platter. If you're willing to spend more money, can you buy a better charcoal grill? To answer this question, we set an upper price limit of $400 (spending more on a charcoal grill seems a bit crazy) and tested seven promising grills.

Our battery of cooking tests included both grilling and low, slow tasks: big batches of burgers, skewers of sticky glazed beef satay, and thick salmon fillets, as well as barbecued ribs. We ran a height check by shutting—or, in some cases, cramming—each grill's lid over a whole turkey; we threaded thermocouple wires under the lids to monitor temperature retention; and we kept track of how easy the grills were to set up when new and to clean up after cooking.

The good news was that most of the grills did a decent job grilling, and several models also fared well with barbecued ribs. The problem was that even when a grill was capable of both grilling and slow-cooking food, some models had design flaws that limited how easy they were to use. In the end, we found three models that we liked well enough to recommend, and all are an upgrade from your basic kettle grill.

HIGHLY RECOMMENDED   Good ★★★   Fair ★★   Poor ★

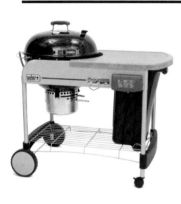

WEBER Performer Deluxe Charcoal Grill
Model 15501001   **Price** $399
Grate Steel, 363 sq in
Favorite Features Push-button gas ignition, rolling cart, charcoal storage bin, Tuck-Away lid holder, ash catcher, thermometer

Grilling	★★★
BBQ/heat retention	★★★
Design	★★★
Assembly	★★★
Cleanup	★★★
Capacity	★★★
Construction quality	★★★

The convenience of gas plus the flavor of charcoal makes this grill a worthwhile (albeit pricey) upgrade from the basic model. Built around our favorite 22.5-inch Weber kettle is a roomy, easy-to-roll cart (much sturdier than the kettle's legs) with a pullout charcoal storage bin; a lid holder; and, most significant, a gas ignition system that lights coals with the push of a button—no chimney starter needed.

WEBER Original Kettle Premium 22-Inch Charcoal Grill
Model 14401001   **Price** $149
Grate Steel, 363 sq in
Favorite Features Ash catcher, thermometer (on newest model), hinged grate

Grilling	★★★
BBQ/heat retention	★★★
Design	★★½
Assembly	★★★
Cleanup	★★★
Capacity	★★★
Construction quality	★★½

Weber's versatile, well-designed classic kettle is an expert griller and maintains heat well, and its well-positioned vents allow for excellent air control. The sturdy ash catcher makes cleanup a breeze, and it is the fastest and easiest model to assemble and move. We wish its tripod legs were sturdier and that the hinged portions of its grate were slightly larger.

RÖSLE 24-Inch Charcoal Grill
Model 25004   **Price** $400
Grate Steel, 416 sq in
Favorite Features Ash catcher, lever that marks vent position, hinged lid, thermometer

Grilling	★★★
BBQ/heat retention	★★
Design	★★½
Assembly	★★★
Cleanup	★★★
Capacity	★★★
Construction quality	★★★

This pricey kettle offers ample cooking space, plus a few perks: a lever that marks vent positions and a hinged lid. But while it grilled well, its roomy interior lost heat relatively quickly. Its top vent sits in the center of the lid—a disadvantage for indirect cooking.

65 Restaurant Steak Tips at Home

RECIPE FOR SUCCESS

✓ WHY THIS RECIPE WORKS

Steak tips are a restaurant-chain staple, but are often tough, dry, or mushy. In addition, steak tips can come from multiple parts of the cow and are packaged in a variety of shapes and sizes. We wanted to clear up the confusion and come up with a recipe that would be worth making at home. After testing more than 50 pounds of tips, we determined that the only ones worth grilling were made from what butchers refer to as "flap meat," also known as sirloin steak tips. Flap meat has good flavor, and although it was a bit chewy when we grilled it on its own, we knew it had potential. To improve the texture, we developed several marinades with plenty of salt (in the form of soy sauce), which acted like a brine, giving the meat a tender texture.

Grilled Steak Tips

SERVES 4 TO 6

Sirloin steak tips, also known as flap meat, are sold as whole steaks, strips, and cubes (see page 37 for more information). We prefer to buy whole steaks for this dish. A two-level fire allows you to brown the steak over the hot side of the grill, then move it to the cooler side if it is not yet cooked through. If your steak is thin, however, you may not need to use the cooler side of the grill. If you use the garlic, ginger, and soy marinade, serve the steak tips with orange wedges instead of lime wedges.

 1 **recipe marinade (recipes follow)**
 2 **pounds sirloin steak tips, trimmed**
    Lime wedges

1 Combine marinade and beef in 1-gallon zipper-lock bag and toss to coat; press out as much air as possible and seal bag. Refrigerate for 1 hour, flipping bag halfway through marinating.

2A FOR A CHARCOAL GRILL Open bottom vent completely. Light large chimney starter filled with charcoal briquettes (6 quarts). When top coals are partially covered with ash, pour two-thirds evenly over half of grill, then pour remaining coals over other half of grill. Set cooking grate in place, cover, and open lid vent completely. Heat grill until hot, about 5 minutes.

2B FOR A GAS GRILL Turn all burners to high, cover, and heat grill until hot, about 15 minutes. Leave all burners on high.

3 Clean and oil cooking grate. Remove beef from bag and pat dry with paper towels. Place steak tips on grill (on hotter side if using charcoal) and cook (covered if using gas) until well browned on first side, about 4 minutes. Flip steak tips and continue to cook (covered if using gas) until meat registers 120 to 125 degrees (for medium-rare) or 130 to 135 degrees (for medium), 6 to 10 minutes longer. If exterior of meat is browned but steak is not yet cooked through, move to cooler side of grill (if using charcoal) or turn down burners to medium (if using gas) and continue to cook to desired doneness.

4 Transfer steak tips to carving board, tent with aluminum foil, and let rest for 5 to 10 minutes. Slice steak tips very thin against grain on bias and serve with lime wedges.

66 Garlic and Herb Marinade
MAKES ABOUT ¾ CUP

⅓ cup soy sauce
⅓ cup olive oil
3 garlic cloves, minced
1 tablespoon minced fresh rosemary
1 tablespoon minced fresh thyme
1 tablespoon packed dark brown sugar
1 tablespoon tomato paste
1 teaspoon pepper

Combine all ingredients in bowl.

67 Southwestern Marinade
MAKES ABOUT ¾ CUP

⅓ cup soy sauce
⅓ cup vegetable oil
3 garlic cloves, minced
1 tablespoon packed dark brown sugar
1 tablespoon tomato paste
1 tablespoon chili powder
2 teaspoons ground cumin
¼ teaspoon cayenne pepper

Combine all ingredients in bowl.

68 Garlic, Ginger, and Soy Marinade
MAKES ABOUT ⅔ CUP

⅓ cup soy sauce
3 tablespoons vegetable oil
3 tablespoons toasted sesame oil
2 tablespoons packed dark brown sugar
1 tablespoon grated fresh ginger
2 teaspoons grated orange zest
1 scallion, sliced thin
3 garlic cloves, minced
½ teaspoon red pepper flakes

Combine all ingredients in bowl.

69 SHOPPING IQ
Will the Real Steak Tip Please . . .

Steak tips can be cut from a half-dozen muscles and are sold in three basic forms: cubes, strips, and steaks. To make sure that you are buying the most flavorful cut (called flap meat sirloin tips by butchers and pictured at right), buy whole steaks.

Cubes   **Strips**   **Steaks**

70 RECIPE FOR SUCCESS
Easy Grilled Flank Steak

✓ WHY THIS RECIPE WORKS

For a simple, economical steak for a backyard barbecue, we turned to flank steak. Like other cuts from the chest and side of the cow, such as skirt steak and hanger steak, flank steak has rich, full, beefy flavor. Also, because it is very thin, it cooks quite fast, making it an ideal candidate for grilling. We found that there's no need to marinate this cut before cooking; with just a little salt, pepper, and sugar (to aid in browning), it is ready to hit the grill. For this quick-cooking steak, we used a half-fire grill setup: We spread the coals over half of the grill to concentrate the heat for optimal char on the steak, and left the other side of the grill much cooler so we could move the steak over if it started to burn. In about 10 minutes, the steak was perfectly done. For a bright counterpoint, we made a quick herb sauce. Fresh parsley contributed a grassy, herbal element, pungent garlic stood up to the meaty flavor of the steak, and lemon juice added a touch of acidity. A bit of sugar contributed sweetness and helped to mellow the potent sauce.

Grilled Flank Steak with Garlic-Herb Sauce
SERVES 4 TO 6
We prefer flat-leaf parsley as opposed to curly parsley.

- 1 (2-pound) flank steak, trimmed
- 1 teaspoon sugar
  Salt and pepper
- 1 cup minced fresh parsley
- ⅓ cup extra-virgin olive oil
- 2 tablespoons lemon juice
- 3 garlic cloves, minced

1 Pat steak dry with paper towels, sprinkle with ¾ teaspoon sugar, and season with salt and pepper. Combine parsley, oil, lemon juice, garlic, remaining ¼ teaspoon sugar, ¼ teaspoon salt, and ¼ teaspoon pepper in small bowl and set aside for serving.

2A FOR A CHARCOAL GRILL Open bottom vent completely. Light large chimney starter filled with charcoal briquettes (6 quarts). When top coals are partially covered with ash, pour evenly over half of grill. Set cooking grate in place, cover, and open lid vent completely. Heat grill until hot, about 5 minutes.

2B FOR A GAS GRILL Turn all burners to high, cover, and heat grill until hot, about 15 minutes. Leave primary burner on high and turn other burner(s) to medium.

3 Clean and oil cooking grate. Place steak on hotter side of grill. Cook (covered if using gas), turning as needed, until lightly charred and meat registers 120 to 125 degrees (for medium-rare), 8 to 12 minutes.

4 Transfer steak to carving board, tent with aluminum foil, and let rest for 5 to 10 minutes. Slice steak very thin on the bias and serve with garlic-herb sauce.

71 STEP BY STEP
Slicing Flank Steak

With its pronounced longitudinal grain, flank steak can be tough and chewy if sliced the wrong way. Make sure to cut the meat into thin slices on the bias, against the grain. This cuts through the connective tissue in the meat and makes it more tender.

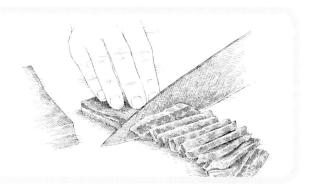

72 SHOPPING IQ
Pass the Steak Sauce

A.1. Steak Sauce reigns supreme in the United States, accounting for the majority of steak sauce sold, but it's not the only brand on the market. We gathered seven brands to see if A.1. deserved its de facto popularity. Steak sauce ingredients tend toward the eclectic and the pungent: raisin paste, turmeric, tamarind, grapefruit puree, malt vinegar, and salty anchovies all appeared on various ingredient lists. We like a steak sauce that can cut through rich, meaty beef with a jolt of flavor that's at once sweet, sour, and salty. Tasters preferred a sauce with a mellow, balanced flavor, a smooth texture, and enough body to cling to the steak without being stiff and gluey.

THE BOTTOM LINE Step aside, A.1. When we're in the mood for a steak sauce to give a boost of flavor to our steak, we'll be reaching for **Heinz 57 Sauce**.

WINNER

HEINZ 57 Sauce
Tasting Comments Our top-rated brand provided "a nice counterpoint that let the meat shine through without overwhelming it." The "smooth" texture was spot-on: "Coats the steak but isn't gloppy."

RUNNER-UP

LEA & PERRINS Traditional Steak Sauce
Tasting Comments This flavorful sauce had hints of "prune," "tamarind," and "molasses." It was bolder than our winner, a quality that some tasters liked. A "kick of vinegar" added a zippy "tartness" that wasn't "metallic, like others."

73

RECIPE FOR SUCCESS
Better-Than-Takeout Teriyaki

✓ WHY THIS RECIPE WORKS

This Japanese-American standard is sadly synonymous with chewy, flavorless meat shellacked in saccharine-sweet sauce. We wanted great teriyaki: juicy, charred steak embellished by a well-balanced glaze robust enough to stand up to the beef. For the meat, we used inexpensive steak tips, which became very tender and flavorful when marinated in a soy sauce–based marinade flavored with scallions, ginger, garlic, and a bit of orange zest. We also found that adding a couple tablespoons of oil to the marinade prevented the meat from sticking to the grill. Slicing the meat into "cutlets" across the grain shortened the muscle fibers so the texture was more tender. The ½-inch-thick cutlets also provided plenty of surface area for charring on the grill. We cooked the marinated meat on a modified two-level fire that concentrated the heat of the grill and let our steak cook up charred and juicy. For a well-balanced sweet and savory sauce that came together quickly, we added cornstarch to sake, mirin, soy sauce, fresh ginger, and sugar. It took only 15 minutes of cooking to give the sauce a nice syrupy texture that was perfect for glazing the meet on the grill and also passing at the table.

Grilled Beef Teriyaki
SERVES 4

If you can't find sirloin steak tips, sometimes labeled "flap meat," flank steak is a good alternative. Mirin, a sweet Japanese rice wine, is a key component of teriyaki; it can be found in Asian markets and the international section of most supermarkets. Alternatively, substitute ¼ cup vermouth or sake and 2 teaspoons sugar for every ¼ cup mirin. Serve with rice.

STEAK

- 2 pounds sirloin steak tips, trimmed
- ⅓ cup soy sauce
- ¼ cup mirin
- 2 tablespoons vegetable oil
- 3 garlic cloves, minced
- 1 tablespoon grated fresh ginger
- 1 tablespoon sugar
- 1 teaspoon grated orange zest
- 2 scallions, white parts minced, green parts sliced thin on bias

SAUCE

- ½ cup sugar
- ½ cup sake or vermouth
- ½ cup mirin
- ⅓ cup soy sauce
- 1 teaspoon grated fresh ginger
- 1 teaspoon cornstarch

1 FOR THE STEAK Cut each steak with grain into 2 or 3 even pieces. Holding knife at 45-degree angle to meat, slice each piece against grain into 4 or 5 slices about ½ inch thick.

2 Combine soy sauce, mirin, oil, garlic, ginger, sugar, orange zest, and scallion whites in bowl. Place marinade and beef in 1-gallon zipper-lock bag and toss to coat; press out as much air as possible and seal bag. Refrigerate for 30 minutes to 1 hour, flipping bag every 15 minutes.

3A FOR A CHARCOAL GRILL Open bottom vent completely. Light large chimney starter filled with charcoal briquettes (6 quarts). When top coals are partially covered with ash, pour evenly over half of grill. Set cooking grate in place, cover, and open lid vent completely. Heat grill until hot, about 5 minutes.

3B FOR A GAS GRILL Turn all burners to high, cover, and heat grill until hot, about 15 minutes. Leave all burners on high.

4 FOR THE SAUCE Meanwhile, whisk all ingredients together in small saucepan, bring to simmer, and cook over medium-low heat until syrupy and reduced to 1 cup, 12 to 15 minutes. Measure out ¾ cup sauce and set aside for serving.

5 Clean and oil cooking grate. Remove beef from bag and pat dry with paper towels. Place beef on grill (on hotter side if using charcoal) and cook (covered if using gas) until dark brown on both sides, 6 to 8 minutes, flipping halfway through cooking. Brush with 2 tablespoons sauce, flip, and cook for 30 seconds. Brush with remaining 2 tablespoons sauce, flip, and continue to cook for 30 seconds longer.

6 Transfer meat to serving platter, tent with aluminum foil, and let rest for 5 to 10 minutes. Sprinkle with scallion greens and serve, passing reserved sauce separately.

74 STEP BY STEP Cutting Sirloin Steak Tips

1 CUT PIECES Cut steak with grain into 2 or 3 even pieces.

2 CUT SLICES Hold knife at 45-degree angle to meat and cut against grain into ½-inch-thick slices.

3 READY STEAK TIPS Each piece of steak should yield 4 to 5 slices.

75 RECIPE FOR SUCCESS
Steak with a Double-Duty Marinade

✓ WHY THIS RECIPE WORKS

Intensely beefy skirt steak is a popular cut because its loose, open grain makes it an ideal candidate for soaking up a flavorful marinade. But while a marinade might add flavor, it can also cause problems. The thin, wet marinated meat can end up simply steaming on the grill instead of browning and forming a crust. To avoid this and ensure a perfectly charred crust, we reversed the usual order of things: First we seared our steaks after seasoning them with salt, pepper, and sugar, and only then, once they were already well charred, did we add a sweet and savory marinade into the mix. We poured our marinade over the top of the just-grilled steaks and let them soak it in. Poking the grilled steaks with a fork let the bold, savory flavors penetrate into the meat even more effectively and, since the marinade never touched raw meat, we could also serve it on the side as a sauce. We developed a trio of marinades to suit different tastes.

Grilled Marinated Skirt Steak
SERVES 4 TO 6

Keep the marinade at room temperature or it will cool down the steaks.

MARINADE
- ½ **cup soy sauce**
- ¼ **cup Worcestershire sauce**
- 2 **scallions, sliced thin**
- 4 **garlic cloves, minced**
- 1 **tablespoon Dijon mustard**
- 2 **teaspoons balsamic vinegar**
- 2 **tablespoons sugar**
- 1½ **teaspoons pepper**
- ¼ **cup vegetable oil**

STEAK
- 2 **(12-ounce) skirt steaks, trimmed and cut crosswise into 4-inch pieces**
- 2 **teaspoons sugar**
- ½ **teaspoon salt**
- ½ **teaspoon pepper**

1 FOR THE MARINADE Combine soy sauce, Worcestershire, scallions, garlic, mustard, vinegar, sugar, and pepper in bowl. Slowly whisk in oil until incorporated and sugar has dissolved; set aside.

2 FOR THE STEAK Pat meat dry with paper towels and sprinkle evenly with sugar, salt, and pepper.

3A FOR A CHARCOAL GRILL Open bottom vent completely. Light large chimney starter mounded with charcoal briquettes (7 quarts). When top coals are partially covered with ash, pour evenly over half of grill. Set cooking grate in place, cover, and open lid vent completely. Heat grill until hot, about 5 minutes.

3B FOR A GAS GRILL Turn all burners to high, cover, and heat grill until hot, about 15 minutes. Leave all burners on high.

4 Clean and oil cooking grate. Place steaks on hotter side of grill. Cook (covered if using gas), turning as needed, until well browned on both sides and meat registers 120 to 125 degrees (for medium-rare), 4 to 8 minutes.

5 Transfer steaks to 13 by 9-inch pan and poke all over with fork. Pour marinade over top, tent with aluminum foil, and let rest for 5 to 10 minutes. Transfer meat to carving board and slice thin against grain. Pour marinade into serving bowl. Serve.

VARIATIONS

76 Grilled Hoisin-Scallion Marinated Skirt Steak

Substitute following mixture for marinade: Combine ½ cup soy sauce, ¼ cup hoisin sauce, 2 thinly sliced scallions, 2 tablespoons sugar, 1 to 2 teaspoons Asian chili-garlic sauce, and 1 teaspoon grated fresh ginger in bowl. Slowly whisk in ¼ cup vegetable oil and 1 teaspoon toasted sesame oil until incorporated and sugar has dissolved.

77 Grilled Black Pepper–Honey Marinated Skirt Steak

Substitute following mixture for marinade: Combine ½ cup soy sauce, 3 tablespoons honey, 2 tablespoons Dijon mustard, 2 teaspoons pepper, and ½ teaspoon minced fresh thyme in bowl. Slowly whisk in ¼ cup vegetable oil until incorporated

78 FOOD SCIENCE
Why Poking Meat During Cooking Does Not Cause Moisture Loss

A widespread belief holds that piercing meat with a fork during cooking should be avoided since it allegedly allows precious juices to escape. To put this theory to the test, we cooked two sets of five steaks to medium-rare. We gently turned one set with a pair of tongs, the other by jabbing the steaks with a sharp fork. We then compared the raw and cooked weights of each steak. Both sets of steaks lost exactly the same amount of moisture during cooking—an average of 19.6 percent of their weight. The reason: Virtually all moisture that is lost when meat is cooked is a result of muscle fibers contracting in the heat and squeezing out their juices. Piercing does not damage the fibers enough to cause additional juices to leak out (any more than poking a wet sponge with a fork would expel its moisture).

THE BOTTOM LINE When it comes to the moisture level and tenderness of meat, cooking time and temperature are the most important factors.

80 RECIPE FOR SUCCESS
The Juiciest Boneless Pork Chops

✓ WHY THIS RECIPE WORKS

Pork chops are a prime candidate for the grill, since it can imbue the lean meat with smoky, savory flavor, but too often the results are disappointing—either the chops end up juicy but have no color or they get plenty of char and become totally dried out in the process. To produce moist, well-charred boneless pork chops on the grill, we used a two-pronged approach. First, we brined the chops to improve their ability to stay juicy during cooking and increase their tenderness. Next, to ensure we'd get a substantial browned crust before the interior overcooked, we developed a unique coating of anchovy paste and honey for the chops. The anchovies' amino acids worked with the fructose from the honey to jumpstart the flavorful Maillard browning reaction. We also chose to cook the chops over the concentrated heat of a modified two-level fire to give them a fighting chance at browning before they were cooked through. Finally, we developed some flavorful relishes using combinations of sweet and savory ingredients to complement the grilled chops.

79 SHOPPING IQ
Fish from a Tube?

When just a single anchovy fillet is all you need for most recipes, we wondered whether a tube of anchovy paste might be a more convenient option than whole anchovies.

Made from pulverized anchovies, vinegar, salt, and water, anchovy paste promises all the flavor of oil-packed anchovies without the mess of rinsing, drying, and chopping the whole fillets.

A head-to-head tasting of our Grilled Caesar Salad (page 286) recipe prepared with equal amounts of anchovy paste and anchovy fillets revealed little difference, although a few astute tasters felt that the paste had a "saltier" and "slightly more fishy" flavor. In such small quantities, however, it was deemed an acceptable substitute. For dishes that use just a touch of anchovy, such as our Grilled Boneless Pork Chops, the squeeze-and-go convenience of the tube is hard to beat.

Grilled Boneless Pork Chops
SERVES 4 TO 6

If your pork is enhanced (injected with a salt solution), do not brine it in step 1. Very finely mashed anchovy fillets (rinsed and dried before mashing) can be used instead of anchovy paste. If desired, serve with one of the following relishes. Prepare the relish while the chops are brining.

6	(6- to 8-ounce) boneless pork chops, ¾ to 1 inch thick
3	tablespoons salt
1	tablespoon vegetable oil
1½	teaspoons honey
1	teaspoon anchovy paste
½	teaspoon pepper

1 Cut 2 slits about 1 inch apart through outer layer of fat and connective tissue on each chop to prevent buckling. Dissolve salt in 1½ quarts cold water in large container. Submerge chops in brine, cover, and let stand at room temperature for 30 minutes.

2 Whisk together oil, honey, anchovy paste, and pepper to form smooth paste. Remove pork from brine and pat dry with paper towels. Using spoon, spread half of oil mixture evenly over 1 side of each chop (about ¼ teaspoon per side).

3A FOR A CHARCOAL GRILL Open bottom vent completely. Light chimney starter filled with charcoal briquettes (6 quarts). When top coals are partially covered with ash, pour evenly over half of grill. Set cooking grate in place, cover, and open lid vent completely. Heat grill until hot, about 5 minutes.

3B FOR A GAS GRILL Turn all burners to high, cover, and heat grill until hot, about 15 minutes. Leave primary burner on high and turn off other burner(s).

4 Clean and oil cooking grate. Place chops, oiled side down, on hotter side of grill and cook, uncovered, until well browned on first side, 4 to 6 minutes. While chops are grilling, spread remaining oil mixture evenly over second side of chops. Flip chops and continue to cook until chops register 145 degrees, 4 to 6 minutes longer (if chops are well browned but register less than 140 degrees, move to cooler part of grill to finish cooking). Transfer chops to plate and let rest for 5 minutes. Serve.

81 Onion, Olive, and Caper Relish
MAKES ABOUT 2 CUPS

- ¼ cup olive oil
- 2 onions, cut into ¼-inch pieces
- 6 garlic cloves, sliced thin
- ½ cup pitted kalamata olives, chopped coarse
- ¼ cup capers, rinsed
- 3 tablespoons balsamic vinegar
- 2 tablespoons minced fresh parsley
- 1 teaspoon minced fresh marjoram
- 1 teaspoon sugar
- ½ teaspoon anchovy paste
- ½ teaspoon pepper
- ¼ teaspoon salt

Heat 2 tablespoons oil in 10-inch nonstick skillet over medium heat until shimmering. Add onions and cook until softened, about 5 minutes. Stir in garlic and cook until fragrant, about 30 seconds. Transfer onion mixture to medium bowl; stir in remaining 2 tablespoons oil, olives, capers, vinegar, parsley, marjoram, sugar, anchovy paste, pepper, and salt. Serve warm or at room temperature.

82 Tomato, Fennel, and Almond Relish
MAKES ABOUT 2 CUPS

- ¼ cup olive oil
- 1 fennel bulb, stalks discarded, bulb halved, cored, and cut into ¼-inch pieces
- 6 garlic cloves, sliced thin
- 2 tomatoes, cored and cut into ½-inch pieces
- ¼ cup green olives, pitted and chopped
- 3 tablespoons sherry vinegar
- ¼ cup slivered almonds, toasted
- 3 tablespoons minced fresh parsley
- 1 teaspoon sugar
- Salt and pepper

Heat 2 tablespoons oil in 10-inch skillet over medium heat until shimmering. Add fennel and cook until slightly softened, about 5 minutes. Stir in garlic and cook until fragrant, about 30 seconds. Stir in tomatoes and continue to cook until tomatoes break down slightly, about 5 minutes. Transfer fennel mixture to medium bowl; stir in remaining 2 tablespoons oil, olives, vinegar, almonds, parsley, sugar, ¾ teaspoon salt, and ½ teaspoon pepper. Serve warm or at room temperature.

83 Orange, Jícama, and Pepita Relish
MAKES ABOUT 3 CUPS

- 1 orange, peel and pith removed
- ¼ cup olive oil
- 2 jalapeños, stemmed, seeded, and sliced into thin rings
- 3 shallots, sliced thin
- 6 garlic cloves, sliced thin
- 14 ounces jícama, peeled and cut into ¼-inch pieces (2 cups)
- ¼ cup pepitas, toasted
- 3 tablespoons chopped fresh cilantro
- 3 tablespoons lime juice (2 limes)
- 1 teaspoon sugar
- Salt and pepper

Quarter orange, then slice crosswise into ¼-inch-thick pieces. Heat 2 tablespoons oil in 10-inch skillet over medium heat until shimmering. Add jalapeños and shallots and cook until slightly softened, about 5 minutes. Stir in garlic and cook until fragrant, about 30 seconds. Transfer jalapeño-shallot mixture to medium bowl; stir in orange, jícama, pepitas, cilantro, lime juice, sugar, ¾ teaspoon salt, and ½ teaspoon pepper. Serve warm or at room temperature.

STEP BY STEP
Preparing Fennel

1 TRIM Cut off stalks and feathery fronds. (Fronds can be minced and used for garnish.) Trim very thin slice from base and remove any tough or blemished outer layers from bulb.

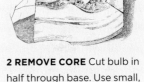

2 REMOVE CORE Cut bulb in half through base. Use small, sharp knife to remove pyramid-shaped core.

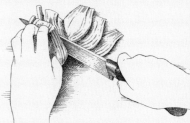

3 SLICE Cut fennel halves into pieces as directed in recipe.

85 RECIPE FOR SUCCESS
Tender, Not Tough, Thin-Cut Pork Chops

✔ WHY THIS RECIPE WORKS

Thick pork chops are relatively easy to grill, but thin chops are a challenge. If you leave them on the grill long enough to get a good char, they become overcooked and dry inside. However, thin-cut chops are widely available and make a quick and easy dinner, so we wanted to come up with a way to make this cut work on the grill. To ensure that our thin-cut pork chops would brown quickly, we partially froze them before grilling to eliminate excess moisture from the exterior. Salting them before freezing prevented them from drying out and allowed us to skip the step of soaking them in a more traditional brine. We created a flavorful golden-brown crust by spreading a combination of softened butter and brown sugar over the chops. Topping the chops with a chive-and-mustard-spiked butter when they came off the grill added even more flavor by creating an instant sauce. Mixing up the flavorings and spices in the butter was an easy way to create simple and effective variations.

Grilled Thin-Cut Pork Chops
SERVES 4 TO 6

6	bone-in pork rib or center-cut chops, about ½ inch thick, trimmed
¾	teaspoon salt
4	tablespoons unsalted butter, softened
1	teaspoon packed brown sugar
½	teaspoon pepper
1	teaspoon minced fresh chives
½	teaspoon Dijon mustard
½	teaspoon grated lemon zest

1 Set wire rack in rimmed baking sheet. Pat chops dry with paper towels. Cut 2 slits, about 2 inches apart, through outer layer of fat and silverskin on each chop. Rub chops with salt. Arrange on prepared rack and freeze until chops are firm, at least 30 minutes but no more than 1 hour. Combine 2 tablespoons

butter, sugar, and pepper in small bowl; set aside. Mix remaining 2 tablespoons butter, chives, mustard, and lemon zest in second small bowl and refrigerate until firm, about 15 minutes. (Butter-chive mixture can be refrigerated, covered, for 24 hours.)

2A FOR A CHARCOAL GRILL Open bottom vent completely. Light large chimney starter filled with charcoal briquettes (6 quarts). When top coals are partially covered with ash, pour evenly over grill. Set cooking grate in place, cover, and open lid vent completely. Heat grill until hot, about 5 minutes.

2B FOR A GAS GRILL Turn all burners to high, cover, and heat grill until hot, about 15 minutes. Leave all burners on high.

3 Pat chops dry with paper towels. Spread softened butter-sugar mixture evenly over both sides of each chop. Grill, covered, over hot fire until well browned and meat registers 145 degrees, 6 to 8 minutes, flipping chops halfway through grilling. Transfer chops to platter and top with chilled butter-chive mixture. Tent with aluminum foil and let rest for 5 minutes. Serve.

VARIATIONS
86 Grilled Caribbean Thin-Cut Pork Chops
Substitute 1 teaspoon grated fresh ginger, ½ teaspoon minced fresh thyme, and ½ teaspoon grated orange zest for chives, mustard, and lemon zest.

87 Grilled Mediterranean Thin-Cut Pork Chops
Substitute 1½ teaspoons black olive tapenade and ½ teaspoon minced fresh oregano for chives and mustard.

88 Grilled Spicy Thai Thin-Cut Pork Chops
Substitute 1½ teaspoons Asian chili-garlic sauce, 1 teaspoon minced fresh cilantro, and ½ teaspoon grated lime zest for chives, mustard, and lemon zest.

89 FOOD SCIENCE
Help! I Forgot to Thaw My Meat!

Don't panic. To prevent the growth of harmful bacteria when thawing frozen meat, we typically use one of two methods: We defrost thicker (1 inch or greater) cuts in the refrigerator and place thinner cuts on a heavy cast-iron or steel pan at room temperature, where the metal's rapid heat transfer safely thaws the meat in about an hour. But what if you just walk in the door from work and don't have an hour? A recent article by food scientist Harold McGee in *The New York Times* alerted us to a faster way to thaw small cuts—a method that's been studied by and won approval from the USDA: Soak cuts such as chops, steaks, cutlets, and fish fillets in hot water. Intrigued, we had to test his method.

Following this approach, we sealed chicken breasts, steaks, and chops in zipper-lock bags and submerged the packages in very hot (140-degree) water. The chicken thawed in less than 8 minutes, the other cuts in roughly 12 minutes—both fast enough that the rate of bacterial growth fell into the "safe" category, and the meat didn't start to cook. (Large roasts or whole birds are not suitable for hot thawing because they would need to be in the bath so long that bacteria would proliferate.) Note: The chicken breasts turned slightly opaque after thawing. Once cooked, however, the hot-thawed breasts and other cuts were indistinguishable from cold-thawed meat.

90 SHOPPING IQ
Chop Shop(ping)

Many recipes calling for pork chops simply specify "loin" chops—a vague and unhelpful term, since all pork chops are cut from the loin of the pig. Butchers further break down the loin into four different types of chop—blade, rib, center cut, and sirloin—each of which cooks differently, depending on the muscles they contain.

Here's what you need to know to buy the right chop for the job whether you're cooking outdoors or in.

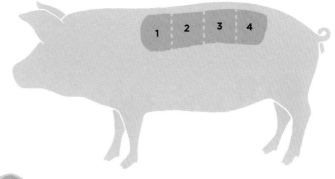

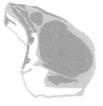

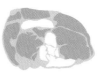

1 BLADE Cut near the fatty shoulder end, this chop's high proportion of marbled dark meat and connective tissue makes it ideal for braising, but not for the grill.

2 RIB Featuring one large eye of loin muscle, this chop is very tender as well as flavorful and a good choice for both grilling and pan-searing.

3 CENTER CUT This chop is good for grilling but because the loin and tenderloin muscles in this chop are bisected by bulky bone or cartilage, it doesn't lie flat and thus makes a poor choice for pan-searing.

4 SIRLOIN This muscle mosaic contains the loin, the tenderloin, and part of the hip section. Because it's generally tough and dry, we don't recommend this cut.

92 RECIPE FOR SUCCESS
Secrets of Thick-Cut Pork Chops on the Grill

✓ WHY THIS RECIPE WORKS

Thick-cut pork chops are generally easier to cook on the grill than thin-cut chops are, but they still have their potential pitfalls. These hulking chops may look as if they are the perfect fit for the grill but, like any lean pork, they aren't immune to drying out. Brining the chops kept the meat juicy. (We don't brine thin chops because the extra moisture would slow down the browning.) A two-step cooking method over our two-level grill fire ensured a charred exterior and slightly pink interior. We seared the chops over high heat and finished them over moderate heat so they could slowly come up to the ideal 145 degrees. For a simple way to flavor the meat in the few minutes between grilling and serving, we topped the grilled chops with a zesty chive, mustard, and lemon butter.

91 FOOD SCIENCE
Why Charcoal Browns Best

We love the convenience of gas grills, but only the most powerful models can produce the same dark, crusty exterior on food as charcoal. Here's why: Grilled foods brown quickly through intense radiant heat produced by the frenetic motion of charged particles in the air around the food. Charcoal, once it has burned down to glowing coals and ash, emits almost all radiant heat. Gas, on the other hand, though it burns about 75 percent hotter than charcoal, gives off very little radiant heat. To compensate, manufacturers insert ceramic rods, metal bars, or lava rocks above the flames of gas grills to capture the energy from the burning fuel and convert it into radiant heat. But as the hot gases travel from the flames to these radiant surfaces, some are simply carried away by air currents. This makes it difficult to raise the temperature of the radiant emitters as high as that of glowing coals, putting most gas grills at a disadvantage. See page 26–27 for our rating of gas grills.

THE BOTTOM LINE We love the convenience of gas grills, but only the most powerful models can produce the same dark, crusty exterior on food as charcoal.

Grilled Thick-Cut Bone-In Pork Chops
SERVES 4

If the pork you're using is enhanced (injected with a salt solution), skip the brining and season the chops with salt along with the pepper in step 1.

Salt and pepper
4 (12-ounce) bone-in pork rib or center-cut chops, 1½ inches thick, trimmed
2 tablespoons unsalted butter, softened
1 teaspoon minced fresh chives
½ teaspoon Dijon mustard
½ teaspoon grated lemon zest

1 Dissolve 3 tablespoons salt in 1½ quarts cold water in large container. Submerge pork in brine, cover, and refrigerate for 1 hour. Remove pork from brine, pat dry with paper towels, and cut slits about 2 inches apart through fat around each chop. Season with pepper. Mix butter, chives, mustard, and lemon zest in bowl and refrigerate until firm, about 15 minutes. (Chive butter can be refrigerated, covered, for up to 24 hours.)

2A FOR A CHARCOAL GRILL Open bottom vent completely. Light large chimney starter filled with charcoal briquettes (6 quarts). When top coals are partially covered with ash, pour two-thirds evenly over half of grill, then pour remaining coals over other half of grill. Set cooking grate in place, cover, and open lid vent completely. Heat grill until hot, about 5 minutes.

2B FOR A GAS GRILL Turn all burners to high, cover, and heat grill until hot, about 15 minutes. Leave primary burner on high and turn other burner(s) to medium-low.

3 Clean and oil cooking grate. Place chops on hotter side of grill. Cook (covered if using gas), until browned, about 3 minutes per side. Slide chops to cooler side of grill and cook until meat registers 145 degrees, 7 to 9 minutes, flipping halfway through grilling. Transfer chops to platter and top with chilled chive butter. Tent with aluminum foil and let rest for 5 to 10 minutes. Serve.

RECIPE FOR SUCCESS
Chops with a Sweet and Tangy Glaze

✔ WHY THIS RECIPE WORKS

Pork chops and honey are a natural pairing, and grilling should enhance the combination, with the sweet honey glaze complementing the smoky char of the meat. Unfortunately, when we tried to bring this combination to life, we battled glazes that slid right off the chops, while to get a chop that appeared even slightly lacquered we had to resort to such lengthy grilling and basting times that the meat ended up as dry as a bone under the glaze. Painting the chops with glaze partway through cooking showed the most promise. To get a glaze with strong honey flavor and sticky staying power, we cooked down the honey to remove the extra water. Next, we rubbed our chops with a sugar mixture that caramelized on the grill, creating a rough surface for our super-reduced glaze to stick to. We cooked the chops over indirect heat until almost done, brushed them with the glaze, and finished with a fast sear. The glaze never even had time to melt off. (And the meat was perfectly cooked, too!)

Grilled Honey-Glazed Pork Chops
SERVES 4

Cutting slits through the fat of the pork chops prevents them from buckling during cooking.

- 4 **(10-ounce) bone-in pork rib or center-cut chops, 1 inch thick, trimmed**
- ¼ **cup sugar**
- 1 **teaspoon salt**

- 1 **teaspoon pepper**
- 2 **tablespoons cider vinegar**
- ½ **teaspoon cornstarch**
- ¼ **cup honey**
- 1½ **tablespoons Dijon mustard**
- ½ **teaspoon minced fresh thyme**
- ⅛ **teaspoon cayenne pepper**

1 Pat chops dry with paper towels and cut 2 slits about 2 inches apart through fat on edges of each chop. Combine sugar, salt, and pepper in bowl, then rub thoroughly over chops.

2 Whisk vinegar and cornstarch together in small saucepan until smooth, then stir in honey, mustard, thyme, and cayenne. Bring mixture to boil, then reduce heat to medium-low and simmer until thickened and measures ¼ cup, 5 to 7 minutes.

3A FOR A CHARCOAL GRILL Open bottom vent completely. Light large chimney starter filled with charcoal briquettes (6 quarts). When top coals are partially covered with ash, pour two-thirds evenly over half of grill, then pour remaining coals over other half of grill. Set cooking grate in place, cover, and open lid vent completely. Heat grill until hot, about 5 minutes.

3B FOR A GAS GRILL Turn all burners to high, cover, and heat grill until hot, about 15 minutes. Leave primary burner on high and turn other burner(s) to medium-low.

4 Clean and oil cooking grate. Place chops on cooler side of grill. Cook (covered if using gas), turning as needed, until meat registers 145 degrees, 6 to 10 minutes.

5 Brush tops of chops with glaze, flip glazed side down, and grill over hotter part of grill until caramelized, about 1 minute. Repeat with second side of chops. Transfer chops to platter, tent with aluminum foil, and let rest for 5 to 10 minutes. Brush chops with remaining glaze before serving.

94 Getting the Glaze to Cling

1 REDUCE Thin glaze runs off the chop in the heat of the grill. Simmering the glaze until it's thick and sticky helps it cling.

2 RUB Smooth chops offer nothing for a glaze to grab. A sugar rub melts into a bumpy, caramelized crust as the chops grill, which gives the glaze a hold.

3 BRUSH The chops cook over indirect heat until almost done. Then they're brushed with glaze and get a fast, hot sear; the glaze never has time to melt off.

TEST KITCHEN TIP

95 Nonstick Measures

Honey, molasses, corn syrup and other sticky fluid ingredients can stubbornly cling to the inside of a measuring cup. To vanquish sticking woes, spray the inside of the measuring up with vegetable oil spray. The nonstick coating helps sticky ingredients release quickly and cleanly.

96 How to Set Up a Gas Grill

STEP BY STEP

First and foremost, read all instructions in your owner's manual thoroughly, and follow the directions regarding the order in which the burners must be lit. On most gas grills, an electric igniter lights the burners, though we have found that electric igniters can fail occasionally, especially in windy conditions. For these situations, most models have a hole for lighting the burners with a match. Be sure to wait several minutes (or as directed) between attempts at lighting the grill. This waiting time allows excess gas to dissipate and is an important safety measure. (For our ratings of our gas grills, see pages 26–27.)

1 CHECK PROPANE LEVEL If grill is equipped with gas gauge or tank scale, check to make sure you have enough fuel. If grill doesn't have gauge, bring about 1 cup water to boil in teakettle or saucepan, then pour boiling water over side of tank. Place your hand on tank. Where water succeeds in warming tank, tank is empty; where tank remains cool to touch, there is fuel inside.

2 LIGHT WITH LID UP With grill cover open, turn all burners to high and ignite. (Note that lighting the grill with the lid down can trap gas and cause a dangerous explosion of fire.)

3 COVER GRILL AND GET GRATE HOT Cover grill and let it heat for about 15 minutes. (Most grills will reach their maximum heat level within 15 minutes, although you might need to heat the grill a few extra minutes on a cold or windy day.)

4 SCRAPE GRATE CLEAN, THEN SLICK DOWN GRATE Once grill is hot, scrape cooking grate clean with grill brush to remove any burnt-on residue. Using tongs, dip wad of paper towels in vegetable oil and wipe grate several times. Adjust burners as directed in recipe to create fire as directed in recipe.

97 STEP BY STEP
How to Set Up a Charcoal Grill

A charcoal grill offers some advantages over gas, including more options for creating custom fires and a better ability to impart smoke flavor. Here's how to get going. (For our ratings of charcoal grills, see pages 34–35.)

1 GET COALS HOT Remove cooking grate from grill and open bottom grill vent halfway or completely, according to recipe. Fill bottom section of chimney starter with crumpled newspaper, set starter on charcoal rack, and fill top of starter with charcoal briquettes according to recipe. Ignite newspaper and allow charcoal to burn until briquettes on top are partly covered with thin layer of gray ash.

2 GET GRATE HOT Empty briquettes onto grill and distribute as indicated in recipe. Set cooking grate in place, cover, and heat grate for about 5 minutes, but no longer, or fire will start to die.

3 SCRUB GRATE CLEAN Use grill brush to scrape cooking grate clean. (You wouldn't cook in a dirty pan, would you?)

4 SLICK DOWN GRATE Using tongs, dip wad of paper towels in vegetable oil and wipe cooking grate several times. (The oil offers another layer of protection against sticking. For really delicate foods such as fish, we recommend slicking down the grate as many as five or 10 times, almost like seasoning a cast-iron skillet. Read more on oiling the grill grate on page 145.)

98 RECIPE FOR SUCCESS
Chinese Pork that Tops Takeout

✓ WHY THIS RECIPE WORKS

Boneless barbecue spareribs are a restaurant favorite that most cooks probably wouldn't attempt at home, but we wanted to try. For an easy dish that could simulate grilled Chinese-style glazed and charred pork, we opted for pork tenderloin, which cooks quickly over a hot fire and stays very tender. Butterflying and pounding the meat gave us maximum surface area for faster, more even cooking and approximated the consistency of boneless spareribs. A combination of thick, sweet apricot preserves and ketchup flavored with molasses, hoisin, fresh ginger, sesame oil, sherry, garlic, and five-spice powder gave us a salty-sweet sauce that acted as both marinade and glaze. Although the test kitchen typically recommends glazing meats during the last minute or two of cooking to avoid burning or sticking, this method didn't give the pork the sticky, lacquered exterior we were looking for. Instead, we found that by flipping and glazing the meat throughout grilling, we could produce a charred, caramelized layer on the meat. Leftover pork from this dish makes an excellent addition to fried rice or noodle soup.

Chinese-Style Glazed Pork Tenderloin

SERVES 4 TO 6

Chinese five-spice powder is a combination of cinnamon, clove, fennel, star anise, and Sichuan peppercorns. For information on grilling baby bok choy, see page 120.

- 2 (12- to 16-ounce) pork tenderloins, trimmed
- ½ cup soy sauce
- ½ cup apricot preserves
- ¼ cup hoisin sauce
- ¼ cup dry sherry
- 2 tablespoons grated fresh ginger
- 1 tablespoon toasted sesame oil
- 2 garlic cloves, minced
- 1 teaspoon five-spice powder
- 1 teaspoon pepper
- ¼ cup ketchup
- 1 tablespoon molasses
- 2 teaspoons vegetable oil

1 Lay tenderloins on cutting board with long side running almost perpendicular to counter edge. Cut horizontally down length of each tenderloin, stopping ½ inch from edge so tenderloin remains intact. Working with one at a time, open up tenderloins, place between 2 sheets of plastic wrap, and pound to ¾-inch thickness.

2 Combine soy sauce, preserves, hoisin, sherry, ginger, sesame oil, garlic, five-spice powder, and pepper in bowl. Measure out ¾ cup of marinade and set aside. Place pork in large zipper-lock bag and pour remaining marinade into bag with pork. Seal bag, turn to coat, and refrigerate for at least 30 minutes or up to 4 hours.

3 Combine reserved marinade, ketchup, and molasses in small saucepan. Cook over medium heat until syrupy and reduced to ¾ cup, 3 to 5 minutes. Reserve ¼ cup glaze for glazing cooked pork.

4A FOR A CHARCOAL GRILL Open bottom vent completely. Light large chimney starter filled with charcoal briquettes (6 quarts). When top coals are partially covered with ash, pour evenly over grill. Set cooking grate in place, cover, and open lid vent completely. Heat grill until hot, about 5 minutes.

4B FOR A GAS GRILL Turn all burners to high, cover, and heat grill until hot, about 15 minutes. Turn all burners to medium-high.

5 Clean and oil cooking grate. Pat pork dry with paper towels, then rub with vegetable oil. Place pork on grill and cook (covered if using gas) until lightly charred on first side, about 2 minutes. Flip and brush grilled side of pork evenly with 2 tablespoons glaze. Continue grilling until lightly charred on second side, about 2 minutes. Flip and brush evenly with 2 tablespoons glaze. Repeat flipping and glazing twice more, until pork registers 145 degrees and is thickly glazed, about 4 minutes longer. Transfer pork to cutting board and brush with reserved glaze. Tent with aluminum foil and let rest for 5 minutes. Slice and serve.

99 Prepping the Tenderloins

1 BUTTERFLY Place the tenderloins on a cutting board and slice each down the side, leaving ½ inch of meat uncut. Now open each like a book. This will give you extra surface for glazing.

2 POUND Place each butterflied tenderloin between two sheets of plastic wrap. Using a meat pounder, pound each to a ¾-inch thickness. These pounded tenderloins will cook quickly and evenly.

100

Chops on the Lamb

As indicated by their names, shoulder, rib, and loin lamb chops all come from different primal cuts of the animal. Shoulder chops come from the shoulder cut, which is the area from the neck through the fourth rib. Meat from this area is flavorful, although it contains a fair amount of connective tissue and can be tough, so shoulder chops tend to be less expensive. Rib chops come from the rib cut, which is the area directly behind the shoulder, extending from the fifth to the 12th rib. All eight ribs taken together are called the rack—when they're cut into individual chops, you get rib chops. Meat from this area has a fine, tender grain and a mild flavor. Loin chops come from the loin cut, which extends from the last rib down to the hip area. Like the rib chop, the loin chop is tender and has a mild, sweet flavor. The other two primal cuts of lamb are the leg, which runs from the hip to the hoof, and the foreshank/breast, from the underside of the animal.

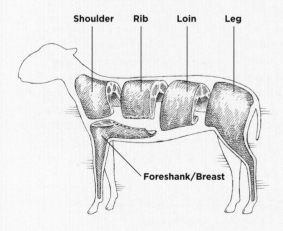

Shoulder   Rib   Loin   Leg

Foreshank/Breast

101 RECIPE FOR SUCCESS
Affordable Lamb Chops on the Grill

✓ WHY THIS RECIPE WORKS

When done right, grilled lamb chops are juicy and tender, with just a touch of gamy richness. But preparing them well is easier said than done. The high heat of a hot fire can scorch the meat or generate flare-ups as rendered fat splatters on the coals. The first step to grilling great-tasting lamb chops is choosing the right cut. Inexpensive shoulder chops, with a gutsier flavor than loin or rib chops (they actually taste like lamb) and a satisfyingly chewy texture, were our top choice. We also found them to be the most versatile of the bunch, holding up in both taste and texture when cooked to varying degrees of doneness. Because shoulder chops contain a fair amount of fat, they are particularly prone to flare-ups, so we built a two-level fire to cook our chops: a pile of coals on one side of the grill and a single layer on the other. Starting the chops on the hotter side gave them a well-browned crust, and sliding them to the cooler side to finish cooking through reduced the risk of flare-ups.

Grilled Lamb Shoulder Chops
SERVES 4

Try to purchase lamb shoulder chops that are at least ¾ inch thick, since they are less likely to overcook. If you can only find chops that are ½ inch thick, reduce the cooking time on the cooler side of the grill by about 30 seconds on each side. If you prefer your lamb medium-well (140 to 145 degrees), it will take about 9 minutes total to finish cooking on the cooler side of the grill.

4   (8- to 12-ounce) lamb shoulder chops
    (blade or round bone), ¾ to 1 inch thick,
    trimmed
2   tablespoons extra-virgin olive oil
    Salt and pepper

1A FOR A CHARCOAL GRILL Open bottom vent completely. Light large chimney starter filled with charcoal briquettes (6 quarts). When top coals are partially covered with ash, pour two-thirds evenly over half of grill, then pour remaining coals over other half of grill. Set cooking grate in place, cover, and open lid vent completely. Heat grill until hot, about 5 minutes.

1B FOR A GAS GRILL Turn all burners to high, cover, and heat grill until hot, about 15 minutes. Leave primary burner on high and turn other burner(s) to medium.

2 Clean and oil cooking grate. Rub chops with oil and season with salt and pepper. Place chops on hotter side of grill and cook (covered if using gas) until well browned, about 2 minutes per side. Slide chops to cooler side of grill and continue to cook until meat registers 120 to 125 degrees (for medium-rare) or 130 to 135 degrees (for medium), 2 to 4 minutes per side. Transfer chops to large platter, tent with aluminum foil, and let rest for 5 minutes before serving.

VARIATIONS

102 Grilled Lamb Shoulder Chops with Near East Red Pepper Paste

Heat 1 tablespoon extra-virgin olive oil in 8-inch skillet over medium-high heat until shimmering. Add ½ red bell pepper, chopped coarse, and ½ serrano or jalapeño chile, chopped coarse, and cook, stirring frequently, until just beginning to soften, about 2 minutes. Reduce heat to medium-low and continue to cook until softened, about 5 minutes. Transfer bell pepper mixture to food processor. Add 2 tablespoons extra-virgin olive oil, 2 teaspoons lemon juice, 1½ teaspoons chopped fresh mint, 1 garlic clove, minced, ½ teaspoon ground cumin, ½ teaspoon dried summer savory, and ¼ teaspoon ground cinnamon and process until almost smooth (some chunky pieces of bell pepper will remain), about 20 seconds. Rub chops with pepper paste. Transfer chops to 13 by 9-inch baking dish, cover with plastic wrap, and refrigerate for at least 20 minutes or up to 24 hours. Grill as directed.

103 Grilled Lamb Shoulder Chops with Garlic-Rosemary Marinade

Combine 2 tablespoons extra-virgin olive oil, 1 tablespoon minced fresh rosemary, 2 minced large garlic cloves, and pinch cayenne pepper in small bowl. Rub chops with mixture. Transfer chops to 13 by 9-inch baking dish, cover with plastic wrap, and refrigerate for at least 20 minutes or up to 24 hours. Grill as directed.

104 Treating Pricey Lamb Right on the Grill

✓ WHY THIS RECIPE WORKS

Lamb and the grill have great chemistry. The intense heat of the coals produces a great crust and helps melt the meat's abundant fat, distributing flavor. While we love the bold flavor and pleasantly chewy texture of lamb shoulder chops, sometimes we want something a bit more refined. Chops from the rib and loin have a milder, sweeter flavor and a more tender texture—but at $12 or more a pound, they aren't cheap. If we were going to splurge on these pricey, elegant chops, we wanted to make sure we had a foolproof technique for grilling them. Chops 1¼ to 1½ inches thick were ideal; they could spend enough time on the grill to develop plenty of smoky flavor. A two-level fire was essential; it allowed us to sear the chops over the hotter portion and then move them to the cooler side to gently finish cooking through. This dual-heat fire also helped with flare-ups; we could simply move the chops to the cooler part of the grill to allow the flames to die down. We also developed two fresh flavor variations that enhanced the delicate flavor of loin or rib chops without overwhelming them.

Grilled Lamb Loin or Rib Chops

SERVES 4

While loin and rib chops are especially tender cuts of lamb, they tend to dry out if cooked past medium since they have less intramuscular fat than shoulder chops. To make these chops worth their high price tag, keep an eye on the grill to make sure the meat does not overcook. These chops are smaller than shoulder chops, so you will need two for each serving. Their flavor is more delicate and refined, so season lightly with just salt and pepper, or perhaps herbs (as in the variations that follow). Aggressive spices don't make sense with these rarefied chops.

- 8 (4-ounce) lamb rib or loin chops, 1¼ to 1½ inches thick, trimmed
- 2 tablespoons extra-virgin olive oil
  Salt and pepper

1A FOR A CHARCOAL GRILL Open bottom vent completely. Light large chimney starter filled with charcoal briquettes (6 quarts). When top coals are partially covered with ash, pour two-thirds evenly over half of grill, then pour remaining coals over other half of grill. Set cooking grate in place, cover, and open lid vent completely. Heat grill until hot, about 5 minutes.

1B FOR A GAS GRILL Turn all burners to high, cover, and heat grill until hot, about 15 minutes. Leave primary burner on high and turn other burner(s) to medium.

2 Clean and oil cooking grate. Rub chops with oil and season with salt and pepper. Place chops on hotter side of grill and cook (covered if using gas) until well browned, about 2 minutes per side. Slide chops to cooler side of grill and continue to cook until meat registers 120 to 125 degrees (for medium-rare) or 130 to 135 degrees (for medium), 2 to 4 minutes per side. Transfer chops to large platter, tent with aluminum foil, and let rest for 5 minutes before serving.

VARIATIONS

105 Grilled Lamb Loin or Rib Chops with Mediterranean Herb and Garlic Paste
Combine ¼ cup extra-virgin olive oil, 3 minced garlic cloves, 1 tablespoon chopped fresh parsley and 2 teaspoons each chopped fresh sage, thyme, rosemary, and oregano in small bowl. Rub chops with herb paste and refrigerate for at least 20 minutes or up to 24 hours. Omit oil, season chops with salt and pepper, and grill as directed.

106 Grilled Lamb Loin or Rib Chops with Zucchini and Mint Sauce
Combine ½ cup extra-virgin olive oil, ½ cup minced fresh mint, 2 tablespoons minced fresh chives, 1 small minced shallot, 2 tablespoons lemon juice, and salt and pepper to taste in medium bowl. Lay 3 medium zucchini, trimmed and sliced thin lengthwise, on a baking sheet and brush both sides of each slice with 2 tablespoons extra-virgin olive oil and season with salt and pepper to taste. Once chops are removed from grill, place zucchini over hotter side of grill. Grill, turning once, until streaked with dark grill marks, 8 to 10 minutes. Transfer zucchini to platter with lamb. Spoon mint sauce over lamb and zucchini and serve after resting.

107 SHOPPING IQ
Domestic Versus Imported Lamb

While almost all the beef and pork sold in American markets is raised domestically, you can purchase imported as well as domestic lamb. Domestic lamb is distinguished by its larger size and milder flavor, while lamb imported from Australia or New Zealand features a far gamier taste. The reason for this difference in taste boils down to diet and the chemistry of lamb fat. Imported lamb is pasture-fed on mixed grasses, while lamb raised in the United States begins on a diet of grass but finishes with grain. The switch to grain has a direct impact on the composition of the animal's fat, reducing the concentration of the medium-length branched fatty-acid chains that give lamb its characteristic "lamby" flavor—and ultimately leading to sweeter-tasting meat.

108 RECIPE FOR SUCCESS
Boneless Chicken Breasts Don't Have to Be Boring

✓ WHY THIS RECIPE WORKS

Because they have no skin and little fat, plain boneless chicken breasts frequently turn out dry and leathery when grilled. A common solution, marinating them in bottled salad dressing—which is usually laden with artificial ingredients—can impart unpleasant off-flavors. We wanted grilled chicken breasts that would come off the grill juicy and flavorful, and we wanted to look beyond bottled salad dressing to get there. A simple combination of olive oil, lemon juice, garlic, parsley, salt, pepper, and a bit of sugar tasted worlds better than any store-bought option. We kept the marinade's acidity low by reducing the lemon juice to avoid mushy chicken but added the bright lemon flavor back in by drizzling the cooked chicken with a complementary vinaigrette before serving. Cooked over a hot, single-level fire, the outer layers of the chicken breasts burned before the inside was cooked through, so we ended up using a two-level fire. We cooked the chicken, covered, over the cooler side of the grill until it was almost done and then finished it with a quick sear for perfectly cooked breasts. The flavors of the citrus-herb marinade are easy to switch up—we provide two other flavor options.

Grilled Lemon-Parsley Chicken Breasts
SERVES 4

The chicken should be marinated for no less than 30 minutes and no more than 1 hour. Serve with a simply prepared vegetable or use in sandwiches or salad.

- 6 tablespoons olive oil
- 2 tablespoons lemon juice
- 1 tablespoon minced fresh parsley
- 1¼ teaspoons sugar
- 1 teaspoon Dijon mustard
  Salt and pepper
- 2 tablespoons water
- 3 garlic cloves, minced
- 4 (6- to 8-ounce) boneless, skinless chicken breasts, trimmed

1 Whisk 3 tablespoons oil, 1 tablespoon lemon juice, parsley, ¼ teaspoon sugar, mustard, ¼ teaspoon salt, and ¼ teaspoon pepper together in bowl and set aside for serving.

2 Whisk water, garlic, remaining 3 tablespoons oil, remaining 1 tablespoon lemon juice, remaining 1 teaspoon sugar, 1½ teaspoons salt, and ½ teaspoon pepper together in bowl. Place marinade and chicken in 1-gallon zipper-lock bag and toss to coat; press out as

109 GADGETS & GEAR
Instant-Read Thermometers

A fast, accurate thermometer is one of the simplest ways to improve the safety and quality of your food. Look for one with a wide temperature range (at least -10 to 425 degrees). We prefer digital models because they are faster and easier to read. A long stem (at least 4 inches) is necessary to reach the center of whole birds and large roasts. Water-resistant models are easier to clean.

THE BOTTOM LINE We use our favorite thermometer, the **ThermoWorks Thermapen Mk4**, every day.

WINNER

THERMOWORKS Thermapen Mk4
Price $99.00
Testing Comments Our winner is pricey, but worth it. It has an incredibly fast digital display with a wide temperature range and automatic shut-off. It's also more water-resistant than the Classic, able to survive a half-hour bath.

RUNNER-UP

THERMOWORKS Classic Super-Fast Thermapen
Price $79.00
Testing Comments Reads out accurate temperatures in 2 to 3 seconds. While it lacks the bells and whistles of the Mk4, it works just as well—and is cheaper to boot.

much air as possible and seal bag. Refrigerate for at least 30 minutes or up to 1 hour, flipping bag every 15 minutes.

3A FOR A CHARCOAL GRILL Open bottom vent completely. Light large chimney starter filled with charcoal briquettes (6 quarts). When top coals are partially covered with ash, pour evenly over half of grill. Set cooking grate in place, cover, and open lid vent completely. Heat grill until hot, about 5 minutes.

3B FOR A GAS GRILL Turn all burners to high, cover, and heat grill until hot, about 15 minutes. Leave primary burner on high and turn off other burner(s).

4 Clean and oil cooking grate. Remove chicken from bag, allowing excess marinade to drip off. Place chicken on cooler side of grill, smooth side down, with thicker sides facing coals and flames. Cover and cook until bottom of chicken just begins to develop light grill marks and is no longer translucent, 6 to 9 minutes.

5 Flip chicken and rotate so that thinner sides face coals and flames. Cover and continue to cook until chicken is opaque and firm to touch and registers 140 degrees, 6 to 9 minutes longer.

6 Move chicken to hotter side of grill and cook until dark grill marks appear on both sides and chicken registers 160 degrees, 2 to 6 minutes longer.

7 Transfer chicken to carving board, tent with aluminum foil, and let rest for 5 to 10 minutes. Slice each breast on bias into ¼-inch-thick slices and transfer to individual plates. Drizzle with reserved sauce and serve.

VARIATIONS

110 **Grilled Chipotle-Lime Chicken Breasts**
Substitute lime juice for lemon juice and use 1 extra teaspoon juice in reserved sauce. Substitute 1 teaspoon minced canned chipotle chile in adobo sauce for mustard and cilantro for parsley.

111 **Grilled Orange-Tarragon Chicken Breasts**
Substitute orange juice for lemon juice and tarragon for parsley. Add ¼ teaspoon grated orange zest to reserved sauce.

immediately after the chicken was flipped meant less glaze stuck to the grill; it also meant the glaze applied to the top of the chicken had time to dry out and cling.

Grilled Glazed Boneless Chicken Breasts

SERVES 4

If using kosher chicken, do not brine.

- ¼ **cup salt**
- ¼ **cup sugar**
- 4 **(6- to 8-ounce) boneless, skinless chicken breasts, trimmed**
- 2 **teaspoons nonfat dry milk powder**
- ¼ **teaspoon pepper**
    Vegetable oil spray
- 1 **recipe glaze (recipes follow)**

1 Dissolve salt and sugar in 1½ quarts cold water in large container. Submerge chicken in brine, cover, and refrigerate for at least 30 minutes or up to 1 hour. Remove chicken from brine and pat dry with paper towels. Combine milk powder and pepper in bowl.

2A FOR A CHARCOAL GRILL Open bottom vent completely. Light large chimney starter mounded with charcoal briquettes (7 quarts). When top coals are partially covered with ash, pour two-thirds evenly over half of grill, then pour remaining coals over other half of grill. Set cooking grate in place, cover, and open lid vent completely. Heat grill until hot, about 5 minutes.

2B FOR A GAS GRILL Turn all burners to high, cover, and heat grill until hot, about 15 minutes. Leave primary burner on high and turn other burner(s) to medium-high.

3 Clean and oil cooking grate. Sprinkle half of milk powder mixture over 1 side of chicken breasts. Lightly spray coated side of breasts with oil spray until milk powder is moistened. Flip chicken and sprinkle remaining milk powder mixture over second side. Lightly spray with oil spray.

4 Place chicken, skinned side down, on hotter part of grill and cook until browned on first side, 2 to 2½ minutes. Flip chicken, brush with 2 tablespoons glaze, and cook until browned on second side, 2 to 2½ minutes. Flip chicken, move to cooler side of grill, brush with 2 tablespoons glaze, and cook for 2 minutes.

112 Smoky, Saucy Boneless, Skinless Chicken Breasts

RECIPE FOR SUCCESS

✔ WHY THIS RECIPE WORKS

Throwing some boneless, skinless chicken breasts on the grill and painting them with a glaze sounds like a great simple dinner idea, in theory. But if you apply the glaze after the meat is browned, the chicken ends up dry and leathery. If you apply the glaze too soon, however, the chicken won't brown, and the sugary glaze burns before the meat cooks through. Our solution was to brown the chicken faster with the help of an unusual ingredient: dry milk powder. Just ½ teaspoon per breast browned the chicken twice as fast; it also created a tacky surface that was perfect for holding on to the glaze. We created a variety of glazes featuring ingredients such as coconut milk, mustard, and hoisin. For balance and complexity, we introduced acidity from citrus juice or vinegar, as well as flavor from spices and aromatics. Corn syrup provided stickiness and a small amount of cornstarch thickened the glazes to just the right consistency. Applying the glaze

Repeat flipping and brushing 2 more times, cooking for 2 minutes on each side. Flip chicken, brush with remaining glaze, and cook until chicken registers 160 degrees, 1 to 3 minutes. Transfer chicken to plate and let rest for 5 minutes before serving.

113 Spicy Hoisin Glaze
MAKES ABOUT ⅔ CUP

For a spicier glaze, use the larger amount of Sriracha sauce.

- 2 tablespoons rice vinegar
- 1 teaspoon cornstarch
- ⅓ cup hoisin sauce
- 2 tablespoons corn syrup
- 1-2 tablespoons Sriracha sauce
- 1 teaspoon grated fresh ginger
- ¼ teaspoon five-spice powder

Whisk vinegar and cornstarch in small saucepan until cornstarch has dissolved. Whisk in hoisin, corn syrup, Sriracha, ginger, and five-spice powder. Bring mixture to boil over high heat. Cook, stirring constantly, until thickened, about 1 minute. Transfer glaze to bowl.

114 Honey-Mustard Glaze
MAKES ABOUT ⅔ CUP

- 2 tablespoons cider vinegar
- 1 teaspoon cornstarch
- 3 tablespoons Dijon mustard
- 3 tablespoons honey
- 2 tablespoons corn syrup
- 1 garlic clove, minced
- ¼ teaspoon ground fennel seeds

Whisk vinegar and cornstarch in small saucepan until cornstarch has dissolved. Whisk in mustard, honey, corn syrup, garlic, and fennel seeds. Bring mixture to boil over high heat. Cook, stirring constantly, until thickened, about 1 minute. Transfer glaze to bowl.

115 Coconut-Curry Glaze
MAKES ABOUT ⅔ CUP

- 2 tablespoons lime juice
- 1½ teaspoons cornstarch
- ⅓ cup canned coconut milk
- 3 tablespoons corn syrup
- 1 tablespoon fish sauce
- 1 tablespoon Thai red curry paste
- 1 teaspoon grated fresh ginger
- ¼ teaspoon ground coriander

Whisk lime juice and cornstarch in small saucepan until cornstarch has dissolved. Whisk in coconut milk, corn syrup, fish sauce, curry paste, ginger, and coriander. Bring mixture to boil over high heat. Cook, stirring constantly, until thickened, about 1 minute. Transfer glaze to bowl.

116 Miso-Sesame Glaze
MAKES ABOUT ⅔ CUP

- 3 tablespoons rice vinegar
- 1 teaspoon cornstarch
- 3 tablespoons white miso
- 2 tablespoons corn syrup
- 1 tablespoon toasted sesame oil
- 2 teaspoons grated fresh ginger
- ¼ teaspoon ground coriander

Whisk vinegar and cornstarch in small saucepan until cornstarch has dissolved. Whisk in miso, corn syrup, oil, ginger, and coriander. Bring mixture to boil over high heat. Cook, stirring constantly, until thickened, about 1 minute. Transfer glaze to bowl.

117 Molasses-Coffee Glaze
MAKES ABOUT ⅔ CUP

- 3 tablespoons balsamic vinegar
- 1½ teaspoons cornstarch
- ¼ cup molasses
- 2 tablespoons corn syrup
- 2 tablespoons brewed coffee
- 1 garlic clove, minced
- ¼ teaspoon ground allspice

Whisk vinegar and cornstarch in small saucepan until cornstarch has dissolved. Whisk in molasses, corn syrup, coffee, garlic, and allspice. Bring mixture to boil over high heat. Cook, stirring constantly, until thickened, about 1 minute. Transfer glaze to bowl.

118
FOOD SCIENCE
The Power of Milk Powder

To make sure that our chicken breasts could be both browned and glazed in the time it took the chicken to cook, we had to accelerate browning. A surprising ingredient—milk powder—was the solution. Milk powder contains both protein and so-called reducing sugar (in this case, lactose), the keys to the Maillard reaction, the chemical process that causes browning. Faster browning gave us more time to layer on the glaze.

119 GADGETS & GEAR
Essential Equipment at a Glance

Outdoor cooking requires some specialized equipment, but less than what you may think. These are what we consider the true essentials.

Charcoal Grill

The test kitchen's charcoal grill standard is the 22-inch kettle grill. But any charcoal grill will cook your food—the difference being that some grills have features that make them easier to use. A generous cooking surface is always best; a deep lid can cover large foods like a whole turkey; a built-in thermometer is a handy tool; and a side table is the ultimate convenience. Charcoal grills also come in small portable versions; while they may be fine for cookouts in the park or camping excursions, they are simply too small to use for most grilling applications.

Charcoal

Many grill aficionados are fans of hardwood charcoal (aka lump charcoal), but we find that it can be inconsistent in its heat output and that it burns too quickly. For consistently great results, we prefer to use regular charcoal briquettes. We avoid using instant-lighting briquettes because we find that they have a slightly off-odor as they burn and because we simply prefer to use a less-processed product.

Chimney Starter

For igniting charcoal briquettes, nothing is safer or more effective than a chimney starter (aka flue starter). You place briquettes in the top chamber, then you crumple a sheet of newspaper, place it in the smaller chamber under the coals, and light it. In about 20 minutes, the coals are covered in a fine, gray ash and are ready to be poured into the grill. We prefer large chimney starters—ones that can hold at least 6 quarts of briquettes.

Gas Grill

A gas grill is convenient and easy to use; all you need to do to start the fire is open the valve and press the igniter. It doesn't deliver the woodsy, smoky flavor that a charcoal grill does, but for some cooks that's a fair swap. Our gas grill testing revealed that it is not necessary to break the bank to get a good performer, and that even heat distribution and good fat drainage are two important factors. We like our gas grills to have a generous cooking surface area and three independently operating burners.

Grill Brush

Nothing works better than a good grill brush for getting burnt-on gunk off a cooking grate. Most feature stiff metal bristles, but sticky goo can quickly get stuck in the bristles. We prefer grill brushes with replaceable scouring pads as the scrubbers. Whichever type you opt for, make sure that it has a long handle to keep your hands a safe distance from fire; wood is preferable over plastic.

Tongs

Tongs are the most useful tool for turning foods, from slender asparagus spears to racks of ribs, when grilling. But forget tongs made especially for grilling—many are cumbersome to use and are ill suited for picking up smaller or more delicate items. A pair of 16-inch standard kitchen tongs keeps your hands a safe distance from the fire and affords you ample dexterity. For more details on what to look for, see page 107.

Barbecue Mitt

A good mitt is invaluable; if you can't pick up a hot cooking grate or reach over the coals to tend to the food, you might as well stay indoors. It should meet two core requirements: enough heat resistance to keep hands from burning and enough pliability to keep cooks from inadvertently dropping grates or smashing food.

Instant-Read Thermometer

For a variety of foods, using an instant-read thermometer is the only way to reliably test the doneness. A good digital instant-read thermometer will quickly register the food's temperature and is much easier to read than a dial-face thermometer. For more details on what to look for, see page 60.

Basting Brush

When you're trying to brush sauce on chicken or meat that's on a ripping-hot grill, you want to keep your fingers safe. Look for a basting brush with a long handle made from a heat-resistant material that is dishwasher-safe. An angled brush head facilitates basting. We prefer silicone brush bristles, which won't melt or singe, to nylon or boar bristles.

120 How to Engineer Your Fire

STEP BY STEP

Two of the biggest mistakes outdoor grillers make happen before the food even hits the grill: creating too much fire and setting up the fire incorrectly. The first problem is easy to avoid—add the amount of charcoal called for in recipes or, if cooking on a gas grill, adjust the burner temperatures as directed. The second problem is more complicated. Depending on the food being cooked, we use one of the five grill set-ups outlined below. You might have to adapt these setups based on the shape, depth, and/or circumference of your grill.

	TYPE/DESCRIPTION	CHARCOAL	GAS
	**Single-Level Fire** A single-level fire delivers a uniform level of heat across the entire cooking surface and is often used for small, quick-cooking pieces of food, such as sausages, some fish, and some vegetables.	Distribute the lit coals in an even layer across the bottom of the grill.	After preheating the grill, turn all the burners to the heat setting as directed in the recipe.
	**Two-Level Fire** This setup creates two cooking zones: a hotter area for searing and a slightly cooler area to cook food more gently. It is often used for thick chops and bone-in chicken pieces.	Evenly distribute two-thirds of the lit coals over half of the grill, then distribute the remainder of the coals in an even layer over the other half of the grill.	After preheating the grill, leave the primary burner on high and turn the other(s) to medium. The primary burner is the one that must be left on; see your owner's manual if in doubt.
	**Modified Two-Level (Half-Grill) Fire** Like a two-level fire, this fire has two cooking zones. One side is intensely hot, and the other side is comparatively cool. It's great for cooking fatty foods because the cooler zone provides a place to set food while flare-ups die down. For foods that require long cooking times, you can brown the food on the hotter side, then set it on the cooler side to finish with indirect heat. It's also good for cooking chicken breasts over the cooler side gently, then giving them a quick sear on the hotter side.	Distribute the lit coals over half of the grill, piling them in an even layer. Leave the other half of the grill free of coals.	After preheating the grill, adjust the primary burner as directed in the recipe, and turn off the other burner(s).
	**Banked Fire** A banked fire is similar to a modified two-level fire, except the heat is concentrated in an even smaller part of the grill. The large coal- or flame-free area can accommodate a pan of water and large cuts of meat. This setup is often used for large foods that require hours on the grill, such as brisket or pulled pork.	Bank all the lit coals steeply against one side of the grill, leaving the rest of the grill free of coals.	After preheating the grill, adjust the primary burner as directed in the recipe, and turn off the other burner(s).
	**Double-Banked Fire** This fire sets up a cool area in the middle so that the food cooks evenly without having to rotate it. Since the flame-free area is narrow and the heat output is not steady over an extended time, this type of fire is good for relatively small, quick-cooking foods such as a whole chicken. We sometimes place a disposable pan in the empty center area to catch drips and prevent flareups. The pan also keeps the coals banked against the sides. This type of fire can be created in a gas grill only if the grill has at least three burners—and burners that ideally run from front to back on the grill.	Divide the lit coals into two steeply banked piles on opposite sides of the grill, leaving the center free of coals.	After preheating the grill, leave the primary burner and burner at the opposite end of the grill on medium-high, medium, or as directed in the recipe, and turn off the center burner(s).

4 pounds bone-in chicken pieces (split breasts cut in half, drumsticks, and/or thighs), trimmed
Salt and pepper
1 (13 by 9-inch) disposable aluminum roasting pan (if using charcoal)

1 Pat chicken dry with paper towels and season with salt and pepper.

2A FOR A CHARCOAL GRILL Open bottom vent completely and place disposable pan in center of grill. Light large chimney starter filled with charcoal briquettes (6 quarts). When top coals are partially covered with ash, pour into 2 even piles on either side of disposable pan. Set cooking grate in place, cover, and open lid vent completely. Heat grill until hot, about 5 minutes.

2B FOR A GAS GRILL Turn all burners to high, cover, and heat grill until hot, about 15 minutes. Turn all burners to medium-low.

3 Clean and oil cooking grate. Place chicken, skin side down, on grill (over disposable pan if using charcoal). Cover and cook until skin is crisp and golden, about 20 minutes.

4 Slide chicken to hotter sides of grill if using charcoal, or turn all burners to medium-high if using gas. Cook (covered if using gas), turning as needed, until well browned on both sides and breasts register 160 degrees and drumsticks/thighs register 175 degrees, 5 to 15 minutes.

5 Transfer chicken to platter, tent with aluminum foil, and let rest for 5 to 10 minutes before serving.

122 Cajun Spice Rub
MAKES ABOUT 1 CUP
Store leftover spice rub for up to 3 months. Omit the salt from the spice rub if brining the chicken.

½ cup paprika
2 tablespoons kosher salt
2 tablespoons garlic powder
1 tablespoon dried thyme
2 teaspoons ground celery seeds

121 RECIPE FOR SUCCESS
Simple Bone-In Chicken Parts

✔ WHY THIS RECIPE WORKS
Flare-ups can turn chicken into a charred mess if you're not paying attention. The method we developed for bone-in chicken avoids this pitfall by starting the chicken over a relatively cool area of the grill. This allows the fat in the chicken skin to render slowly, thereby avoiding flare-ups and encouraging ultracrisp skin. Finishing it over the hotter side yields browned parts. In addition to the quality of the finished product, we like this approach because it is effectively hands-off: You don't have to constantly move and monitor the chicken pieces. This recipe works with breasts, legs, thighs, or a combination of parts.

Grilled Bone-In Chicken
SERVES 4 TO 6
For extra flavor, rub the chicken with one of the spice rubs before cooking, or brush with barbecue sauce (recipes follow) during the final few minutes of grilling.

2   teaspoons pepper
2   teaspoons cayenne pepper

Combine all ingredients in bowl.

123 Jamaican Spice Rub

MAKES ABOUT 1 CUP

Store leftover spice rub for up to 3 months. Omit the salt from the spice rub if brining the chicken.

¼   cup packed brown sugar
3   tablespoons kosher salt
3   tablespoons ground coriander
2   tablespoons ground ginger
2   tablespoons garlic powder
1   tablespoon ground allspice
1   tablespoon pepper
2   teaspoons cayenne pepper
2   teaspoons ground nutmeg
1½ teaspoons ground cinnamon

Combine all ingredients in bowl.

124 Tex-Mex Spice Rub

MAKES ABOUT 1 CUP

Store leftover spice rub for up to 3 months. Omit the salt from the spice rub if brining the chicken.

¼   cup ground cumin
2   tablespoons chili powder
2   tablespoons ground coriander
2   tablespoons dried oregano
2   tablespoons garlic powder
4   teaspoons kosher salt
2   teaspoons unsweetened cocoa powder
1   teaspoon cayenne pepper

Combine all ingredients in bowl.

125 Basic Barbecue Sauce

MAKES ABOUT 2 CUPS

For a thinner, smoother texture, strain the sauce after it has finished cooking. This recipe can be doubled or tripled.

1   tablespoon vegetable oil
1   onion, chopped fine
    Salt and pepper
1   garlic clove, minced
1   teaspoon chili powder

¼   teaspoon cayenne pepper
1¼ cups ketchup
6   tablespoons molasses
3   tablespoons cider vinegar
2   tablespoons Worcestershire sauce
2   tablespoons Dijon mustard
1   teaspoon hot sauce

1. Heat oil in medium saucepan over medium heat until shimmering. Add onion and pinch salt and cook until softened, 5 to 7 minutes. Stir in garlic, chili powder, and cayenne and cook until fragrant, about 30 seconds.

2. Whisk in ketchup, molasses, vinegar, Worcestershire, mustard, and hot sauce. Bring sauce to simmer and cook, stirring occasionally, until thickened and measures 2 cups, about 25 minutes.

3. Let sauce cool to room temperature. season with salt and pepper to taste and serve.

126 STEP BY STEP
Great Grilled Bone-in Chicken Parts

1 START CHICKEN OVER COOLER CENTER Once coals are heated, bank them on either side of disposable aluminum pan. Place chicken skin side down in center of grill, over pan. Cover and cook for 20 minutes

2 FINISH OVER HOTTER SIDES Slide chicken to hotter sides of grill and cook, turning as needed, until well browned and cooked through, 5 to 15 minutes longer.

127

Salt Isn't Just for Seasoning

Cleaning a basting brush can be risky business, with lots of goo and grease clinging stubbornly to its bristles—and the brush just gets worse with every use. Try this clever technique to ensure a thorough cleaning job. After washing the dirty brushes with liquid dish soap and very hot water, rinsing them well, and shaking them dry, place the brushes, bristles pointing down, in a cup and fill the cup with coarse salt until the bristles are covered. The salt draws moisture out of the bristles and keeps them dry and fresh between uses.

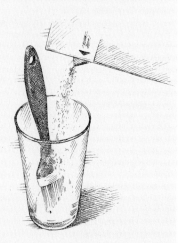

128

RECIPE FOR SUCCESS

Sweet and Tangy Glazed Bone-In Chicken

✓ WHY THIS RECIPE WORKS

There's a lot to admire about a perfectly grilled, glazed chicken breast. Cooked bone-in with the skin on for extra flavor and juiciness, the smoke-infused meat should be tender and succulent and the skin crisp and evenly lacquered. To keep every element of this dish on track, we started with our grill setup. A half-fire arrangement meant we had a super-hot side for an initial sear and a much cooler side to allow the chicken to cook through gently over indirect heat. Arranging the chicken breasts so that thicker sides faced the fire promoted even cooking. To get all the breasts to cook at a similar rate, we placed a sheet of aluminum foil over them before closing the grill lid. Moving the breasts back to the hotter side for the final few minutes of cooking resulted in even crispier skin. For the glazes we balanced sweet ingredients with bold flavors and waited until the last few minutes of cooking to brush them on, which prevented them from burning on the grill. For extra flavor, we reserved half of the glaze for serving as a sauce at the table.

Grilled Glazed Bone-In Chicken Breasts

SERVES 4

If using kosher chicken, do not brine in step 1, but season with salt as well as pepper. Remember to reserve half of the glaze for serving.

    Salt
 4 (10- to 12-ounce) bone-in split chicken
    breasts, trimmed
    Pepper
 1 recipe glaze (recipes follow)

1 Dissolve ½ cup salt in 2 quarts cold water in large container. Submerge chicken breasts in brine, cover, and refrigerate for 30 minutes to 1 hour. Remove chicken from brine and pat dry with paper towels. Season chicken with pepper.

2A FOR A CHARCOAL GRILL Open bottom vent completely. Light large chimney starter filled with charcoal briquettes (6 quarts). When top coals are partially covered with ash, pour evenly over half of grill. Set cooking grate in place, cover, and open lid vent completely. Heat grill until hot, about 5 minutes.

2B FOR A GAS GRILL Turn all burners to high, cover, and heat grill until hot, about 15 minutes. Leave primary burner on high and turn off other burner(s). (Adjust primary burner as needed to maintain grill temperature of 350 degrees.)

3 Clean and oil cooking grate. Place chicken on hotter side of grill, skin side up, and cook (covered if using gas) until lightly browned on both sides, 6 to 8 minutes. Move chicken, skin side down, to cooler side of grill, with thicker end of breasts facing hotter side. Cover loosely with aluminum foil. Cover and continue to cook until chicken registers 150 degrees, 15 to 20 minutes longer.

4 Brush bone side of chicken generously with half of glaze, move to hotter side of grill, and cook until browned, 5 to 10 minutes. Brush skin side of chicken with remaining glaze, flip chicken, and continue to cook until chicken registers 160 degrees, 2 to 3 minutes longer.

5 Transfer chicken to serving platter, tent with aluminum foil, and let rest for 5 to 10 minutes before serving, passing reserved glaze separately.

129 Orange-Chipotle Glaze

MAKES ABOUT ¾ CUP

For a spicier glaze, use the greater amount of chipotle chile.

 1–2 tablespoons minced canned chipotle
      chile in adobo sauce
   1 small shallot, minced
   2 teaspoons minced fresh thyme
   1 teaspoon grated orange zest plus ⅔ cup
      juice (2 oranges)
   1 tablespoon molasses
  ¾ teaspoon cornstarch
      Salt

Combine chipotle, shallot, thyme, and orange zest and juice in small saucepan. Whisk in molasses and cornstarch, bring to simmer, and cook over medium heat until thickened, about 5 minutes. Season with salt to taste. Reserve half of glaze for serving and use remaining glaze to brush on chicken.

130 Soy-Ginger Glaze

MAKES ABOUT ¾ CUP

Reduce the amount of salt in the brine to ¼ cup when using this glaze.

- ⅓ cup water
- ¼ cup soy sauce
- 2 tablespoons mirin
- 1 tablespoon grated fresh ginger
- 2 garlic cloves, minced
- 3 tablespoons sugar
- ¾ teaspoon cornstarch
- 2 scallions, minced

Combine water, soy sauce, mirin, ginger, and garlic in small saucepan, then whisk in sugar and cornstarch. Bring to simmer over medium heat and cook until thickened, about 5 minutes; stir in scallions. Reserve half of glaze for serving and use remaining glaze to brush on chicken.

131 Curry-Yogurt Glaze

MAKES ABOUT ¾ CUP

- ¾ cup plain whole-milk yogurt
- 2 garlic cloves, minced
- 2 teaspoons grated fresh ginger
- 2 teaspoons minced fresh cilantro
- 1½ teaspoons curry powder
- ½ teaspoon grated lemon zest
- ½ teaspoon sugar
   Salt and pepper

Whisk all ingredients together in bowl and season with salt and pepper to taste. Reserve half of glaze for serving and use remaining glaze to brush on chicken.

132 GADGETS & GEAR Cooking Grate Cleaning Block

The GrillStone Value Pack Cleaning Kit by Earthstone International ($9.99) promises to deliver a deeper clean than the typical grill brush. We used this pumice block (two are included in the kit), which is attached to a plastic handle, to clean messy charcoal and gas cooking grates. We routinely clean preheated grates just before we put the food on to cook, and this block's short handle put testers' hands too close to the heat. However, we found that this strong scrubber quickly stripped off all the accumulated gunk even from cold grates. As we scrubbed, the pumice wore into a grooved shape that conformed to that of the grate, allowing it to clean even more thoroughly. Because each block lasted for only three or four cleanings (replacement blocks cost $4.49), and it generated abundant pumice dust that had to be rinsed off before we could use the grate, we find that it's best used as a once-per-season grill grate reconditioning tool. Still, it's one that we'd recommend to get grates shining like new.

THE BOTTOM LINE The tough-scrubbing pumice block on the **GrillStone Value Pack Cleaning Kit by Earthstone International** ($9.99) is ideal for the occasional cooking grate deep cleaning.

133 RECIPE FOR SUCCESS
Great Barbecued Chicken

✔ WHY THIS RECIPE WORKS

Classic barbecued chicken is one of America's favorite summer meals. But despite its popularity, barbecued chicken recipes cause backyard grillers plenty of headaches. We set out to develop a recipe for barbecued chicken with perfect, evenly cooked meat; golden-brown skin; and intense, multidimensional barbecue flavor. Most recipes call for searing chicken quickly over high heat, but we found that starting barbecued chicken over low heat slowly rendered the fat without the danger of flare-ups and gave us evenly cooked meat all the way through. Our homemade sauce has the perfect balance of sweetness and smokiness from brewed coffee, vinegar, and molasses. We created a complex layer of barbecue flavor by applying the sauce in coats and turning the chicken as it cooked over moderate heat. The sauce turned out thick and caramelized, and it perfectly glazed the chicken.

Classic Barbecued Chicken

SERVES 4 TO 6

Using homemade barbecue sauce makes a big difference, but you can substitute 3 cups of store-bought sauce. Don't try to grill more than 10 pieces of chicken at a time; you won't be able to line them up as directed in step 4. You can use a mix of chicken breasts, thighs, and drumsticks, making sure they add up to about 10 pieces.

- 1 teaspoon salt
- 1 teaspoon pepper
- ¼ teaspoon cayenne pepper
- 3 pounds bone-in chicken pieces (split breasts cut in half, drumsticks, and/or thighs), trimmed
- 1 recipe Kansas City Barbecue Sauce (recipe follows)
- 1 (13 by 9-inch) disposable aluminum roasting pan (if using charcoal)

1 Combine salt, pepper, and cayenne in bowl. Pat chicken dry with paper towels and rub with spices. Reserve 2 cups barbecue sauce for cooking; set aside remaining 1 cup sauce for serving.

2A FOR A CHARCOAL GRILL Open bottom vent completely and place disposable pan on 1 side of grill. Light large chimney starter filled with charcoal briquettes (6 quarts). When top coals are partially covered with ash, pour evenly over other side of grill. Set cooking grate in place, cover, and open lid vent completely. Heat grill until hot, about 5 minutes.

2B FOR A GAS GRILL Turn all burners to high, cover, and heat grill until hot, about 15 minutes. Leave primary burner on high and turn off other burner(s). (Adjust primary burner as needed to maintain grill temperature around 350 degrees.)

3 Clean and oil cooking grate. Place chicken, skin side down, on cooler side of grill. Cover and cook until chicken begins to brown, 30 to 35 minutes.

4 Slide chicken into single line between hotter and cooler sides of grill. Cook uncovered, flipping chicken and brushing every 5 minutes with some of sauce reserved for cooking, until sticky, about 20 minutes.

5 Slide chicken to hotter side of grill and cook, uncovered, flipping and brushing with remaining sauce for cooking, until well glazed, breasts register 160 degrees, and drumsticks/thighs register 175 degrees, about 5 minutes. Transfer chicken to platter, tent with aluminum foil, and let rest for 5 to 10 minutes. Serve with remaining sauce.

134 Kansas City Barbecue Sauce

MAKES ABOUT 4 CUPS

For a thinner, smoother texture, strain this thick, sweet, and smoky tomato-based sauce after it has finished cooking.

- 1 tablespoon vegetable oil
- 1 onion, chopped fine
  Salt and pepper
- 4 cups chicken broth
- 1 cup brewed coffee
- 1¼ cups cider vinegar
- ¾ cup molasses
- ½ cup tomato paste
- ½ cup ketchup

2	tablespoons brown mustard
1	tablespoon hot sauce
½	teaspoon garlic powder
¼	teaspoon liquid smoke

1 Heat oil in large saucepan over medium heat until shimmering. Add onion and pinch salt and cook until softened, 5 to 7 minutes. Whisk in broth, coffee, vinegar, molasses, tomato paste, ketchup, mustard, hot sauce, and garlic powder.

2 Bring sauce to simmer and cook, stirring occasionally, until thickened and measures 4 cups, about 1 hour.

3 Off heat, stir in liquid smoke. Let sauce cool to room temperature. Season with salt and pepper to taste and use as directed in recipe.

135 Bottled BBQ Sauce

SHOPPING IQ

We generally recommend making your own barbecue sauce at home—it's not that hard and you'll definitely get superior results. But sometimes supermarket brands are more convenient. We tested eight national brands to find one that would work in recipes and as a dipping sauce. Barbecue styles vary greatly by region, but we'd argue there's an all-American supermarket style. It's on the sweet side and balances tang, smoke, and tomato flavor. The sauces in our test that fit that profile rated better than those closer to authentic regional barbecue styles. The latter failed, in part, because they weren't sweet enough. But not all sugars are created equal. Our top picks were the only two in our lineup that list molasses as their third ingredient; other brands contain it, but in lower relative concentrations.

THE BOTTOM LINE If you're looking for the convenience and affordability of a supermarket barbecue sauce, make sure you choose one with a good amount of sugar, preferably from molasses, like our winner, **Bull's-Eye Original Barbecue Sauce**.

136

RECIPE FOR SUCCESS

Chicken Diavolo Redeemed on the Grill

✓ WHY THIS RECIPE WORKS

Chicken *diavolo* is one of those dishes that has no universally accepted recipe. The one constant (other than the chicken, of course) is heat provided by plenty of black and/or dried red pepper. To make a chicken diavolo that was truly fiery, we used a mixture of herbs, spices, lemon zest, oil, sugar, and two kinds of pepper—black and red. This seasoning did double duty, first as a marinade for bone-in, skin-on chicken parts and then as a sauce for the cooked chicken. We used parts instead of a whole chicken because they were easier to handle and picked up more grill flavor. We found that the chicken could marinate for as little as 1 hour or up to 24 hours, for extra convenience. When it was time to grill, we built a two-level fire, starting the chicken on the cooler side of the grill and then moving it over a hot fire to char the outside and crisp the skin. Using a wood chip packet added smoky depth. Cooking the reserved marinade mixture mellowed the garlic bite, and a splash of lemon juice finished the sauce, which added the perfect extra kick to the grilled chicken.

Grilled Chicken Diavolo

SERVES 4

To use wood chunks on a charcoal grill, substitute one medium wood chunk, soaked in water for 1 hour, for the wood chip packet.

3	pounds bone-in chicken pieces (split breasts cut in half, drumsticks, and/or thighs), trimmed
½	cup extra-virgin olive oil
4	garlic cloves, minced
1	tablespoon chopped fresh rosemary
2	teaspoons grated lemon zest plus 4 teaspoons juice
2	teaspoons red pepper flakes
1	teaspoon sugar
	Salt and pepper
½	teaspoon paprika
1	cup wood chips

1 Pat chicken dry with paper towels. Whisk oil, garlic, rosemary, lemon zest, pepper flakes, sugar, 1 teaspoon pepper, and paprika together in bowl until combined. Measure out ¼ cup oil mixture and set aside for sauce. (Oil mixture can be covered and refrigerated for up to 24 hours.) Whisk 2¼ teaspoons salt into oil mixture remaining in bowl and transfer to 1-gallon zipper-lock bag. Add chicken, turn to coat, and refrigerate for at least 1 hour or up to 24 hours. Just before grilling, soak wood chips in water for 15 minutes, then drain. Using large piece of heavy-duty aluminum foil, wrap soaked chips in 8 by 4½-inch foil packet. (Make sure chips do not poke holes in sides or bottom of packet.) Cut 2 evenly spaced 2-inch slits in top of packet.

2A FOR A CHARCOAL GRILL Open bottom vent halfway. Light large chimney starter filled with charcoal briquettes (6 quarts). When top coals are partially covered with ash, pour two-thirds evenly over half of grill, then pour remaining coals over other half of grill. Place wood chip packet on larger pile of coals. Set cooking grate in place, cover, and open lid vent halfway. Heat grill until hot and wood chips are smoking, about 5 minutes.

2B FOR A GAS GRILL Place wood chip packet over primary burner. Turn all burners to high, cover, and heat grill until hot and wood chips are smoking, about 15 minutes. Turn primary burner to medium and turn other burner(s) to low. (Adjust primary burner as needed to maintain grill temperature of 400 to 425 degrees.)

3 Remove chicken from marinade and pat dry with paper towels. Discard used marinade. Clean and oil cooking grate. Place chicken on cooler side of grill, skin side up. Cover and cook until underside of chicken is lightly browned, 8 to 12 minutes. Flip chicken, cover, and cook until breasts register 155 degrees and drumsticks/thighs register 170 degrees, 7 to 10 minutes.

4 Transfer chicken to hotter side of grill, skin side down, and cook (covered if using gas) until skin is well browned, about 3 minutes. Flip and continue to cook (covered if using gas) until breasts register 160 degrees and drumsticks/thighs register 175 degrees, 1 to 3 minutes. Transfer chicken to platter, tent with foil, and let rest for 5 to 10 minutes.

5 Meanwhile, heat reserved oil mixture in small saucepan over low heat until fragrant and garlic begins to brown, 3 to 5 minutes. Off heat, whisk in lemon juice and ¼ teaspoon salt. Spoon sauce over chicken. Serve.

137 GRILL HACK
No Chimney Starter? No Problem.

Open the bottom vent and place eight sheets of balled newspaper beneath the bottom grate. Pile the charcoal in an even pile in the center of the rack and light the paper. After about 20 minutes, the coals will be covered with gray ash and ready to be rearranged for cooking. (Don't use instant-light charcoal, which can impart unpleasant flavors to food.)

138 SHOPPING IQ
Pass on Packaged Parts

Packaged chicken parts are convenient, but the same chicken parts inside aren't required to be the same weight and their size can vary dramatically. For example, the U.S. Department of Agriculture permits leg quarters sold together to weigh between 8.5 and 24 ounces; in other words, one leg quarter in a package can weigh almost three times as much as another. Breasts can come from chickens that weigh between 3 and 5.5 pounds—a difference that can't help but translate to the breasts themselves. Such a disparity can be a problem when you're trying to get food to cook at the same rate. This lack of standardization showed up in our own shopping. We bought 26 packages of split breasts and leg quarters (representing five brands) from five different Boston-area supermarkets. When we weighed each piece and calculated the maximum weight variation within each package, the differences were startling: The largest pieces were twice the size of the smallest. Worse, some leg quarters came with attached backbone pieces that had to be cut off and discarded (which means throwing away money).

THE BOTTOM LINE Whenever possible, buy chicken parts individually from a butcher, who can select similar-size pieces.

These leg quarters came in the same package, yet the one on the left weighs twice as much as the one on the right—a discrepancy that can lead to uneven cooking.

139

RECIPE FOR SUCCESS
Tackling Whole Chicken Leg Quarters

✔ WHY THIS RECIPE WORKS

Chicken leg quarters seem like a perfect candidate for the grill—the leg and thigh have dark, rich meat and plenty of skin to crisp up. But the thick joint takes longer to cook than the rest of the leg, so grilling to complete doneness often results in overcooking. To remedy this, we took a two-pronged approach. To prepare the chicken, we made slashes down to the bone, a technique often used for large cuts of meat. This helped the chicken cook evenly. It also ensured that the seasonings we used to flavor the chicken would penetrate deep into the meat. We rubbed a seasoning paste with bold, Latin-inspired flavors into the slashes and let the legs sit for an hour before grilling. We then used a two-level grilling technique, starting the chicken over lower heat and allowing some of the fat to render before moving it over a hot fire where it could sear and finish cooking. A quick, easy, citrus-y dressing provided a welcome hit of brightness to the cooked chicken.

Grilled Chicken Leg Quarters with Lime Dressing
SERVES 4

A garlic press makes quick work of mincing the six cloves called for here. You can use 1 teaspoon of dried oregano in place of the fresh called for in the dressing. Do not (ever) use dried cilantro.

- 2 teaspoons plus ¼ cup extra-virgin olive oil
- 6 garlic cloves, minced
- 4 teaspoons kosher salt
- 1 tablespoon sugar
- 2 teaspoons grated lime zest plus 2 tablespoons juice
- 1½ teaspoons ground cumin
- 1 teaspoon pepper
- ½ teaspoon cayenne pepper

4 (10-ounce) chicken leg quarters, trimmed
2 tablespoons chopped fresh cilantro
2 teaspoons chopped fresh oregano

1 Combine 2 teaspoons oil, garlic, salt, sugar, lime zest, cumin, pepper, and cayenne in bowl and mix to form paste. Set aside 2 teaspoons garlic paste for dressing.

2 Position chicken skin side up on cutting board and pat dry with paper towels. Leaving drumsticks and thighs attached, make 4 parallel diagonal slashes in chicken: one across drumsticks, one across leg joints; and two across thighs (each slash should reach bone). Flip chicken over and make 1 more diagonal slash across back of drumsticks. Rub remaining garlic paste all over chicken and into slashes. Refrigerate chicken for at least 1 hour or up to 24 hours.

3A FOR A CHARCOAL GRILL Open bottom vent completely. Light large chimney starter filled with charcoal briquettes (6 quarts). When top coals are partially covered with ash, pour two-thirds evenly over half of grill, then pour remaining coals over other half of grill. Set cooking grate in place, cover, and open lid vent completely. Heat grill until hot, about 5 minutes.

3B FOR A GAS GRILL Turn all burners to high, cover, and heat grill until hot, about 15 minutes. Turn primary burner to medium and turn other burner(s) to low. (Adjust primary burner as needed to maintain grill temperature of 400 to 425 degrees.)

4 Clean and oil cooking grate. Place chicken on cooler side of grill, skin side up. Cover and cook until underside of chicken is lightly browned, 9 to 12 minutes. Flip chicken, cover, and cook until leg joint registers 165 degrees, 7 to 10 minutes.

5 Transfer chicken to hotter side of grill, skin side down, and cook (covered if using gas) until skin is well browned, 3 to 5 minutes. Flip chicken and continue to cook until leg joint registers 175 degrees, about 3 minutes longer. Transfer to platter, tent with aluminum foil, and let rest for 5 to 10 minutes.

6 Meanwhile, whisk remaining ¼ cup oil, lime juice, cilantro, oregano, and reserved garlic paste together in bowl. Spoon half of dressing over chicken and serve, passing remaining dressing separately.

140 STEP BY STEP Making Flavorful Chicken Leg Quarters

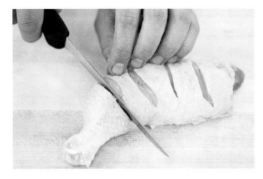

1 SLASH Make bone-deep slashes in each quarter so the seasonings can penetrate and the meat cooks more readily.

2 RUB Massage the garlicky seasoning paste into the slashes and all over the chicken and refrigerate for up to 24 hours.

3 DRESS Transform the remaining seasoning paste into a bright dressing for the cooked chicken.

141

It's in the Bag

Instead of using old newspapers to light a chimney starter, try saving your empty bags of charcoal briquettes to light the next fire.

1 CUT PIECES Cut or tear charcoal bag (separating paper layers) into pieces small enough to crumple and fit in bottom of chimney starter.

2 STUFF CHIMNEY Stuff few pieces of bag in bottom of chimney and light. Charcoal residue on bag will help paper to stay lit.

142

RECIPE FOR SUCCESS

A Happy Hour Favorite with a Grilled Twist

✔ WHY THIS RECIPE WORKS

To take this barroom classic from the fryer to the grill we had to figure out how to handle the fat and connective tissue from the wings, which creates a problem as it drips into the fire. To get crisp, well-rendered chicken wings with lightly charred skin, succulent, smoky meat and minimal flare-ups, we quick-brined the wings and tossed them in cornstarch and pepper. These steps helped the meat retain moisture and kept the wings from sticking to the grill. We then cooked them right over a gentle medium-low fire. The moderate temperature minimized flare-ups and the direct heat accelerated the cooking process. Also, though we normally cook white chicken meat to 160 degrees, wings are chock-full of collagen, which begins to break down upwards of 170 degrees. Cooking the wings to 180 degrees produced meltingly tender wings. These few minor adjustments gave us crispy, juicy chicken that made a great alternative to fried wings. We also developed several easy spice rubs to take the wings up a notch if you're looking for some new flavor options.

Grilled Chicken Wings

MAKES 2 DOZEN WINGS

If you buy whole wings, cut them into two pieces before brining. Don't brine the wings for more than 30 minutes or they'll be too salty.

½	**cup salt**
2	**pounds chicken wings, wingtips discarded, trimmed**
1½	**teaspoons cornstarch**
1	**teaspoon pepper**

1 Dissolve salt in 2 quarts cold water in large container. Prick chicken wings all over with fork. Submerge chicken in brine, cover, and refrigerate for 30 minutes.

2 Combine cornstarch and pepper in bowl. Remove chicken from brine and pat dry with paper towels. Transfer wings to large bowl and sprinkle with cornstarch mixture, tossing until evenly coated.

3A FOR A CHARCOAL GRILL Open bottom vent completely. Light large chimney starter half filled with charcoal briquettes (3 quarts). When top coals are partially covered with ash, pour evenly over grill. Set cooking grate in place, cover, and open lid vent completely. Heat grill until hot, about 5 minutes.

3B FOR A GAS GRILL Turn all burners to high, cover, and heat grill until hot, about 15 minutes. Turn all burners to medium-low.

4 Clean and oil cooking grate. Grill wings (covered if using gas), thicker skin side up, until browned on bottom, 12 to 15 minutes. Flip chicken and grill until skin is crisp and lightly charred and meat registers 180 degrees, about 10 minutes. Transfer chicken to platter, tent with aluminum foil, and let rest for 5 to 10 minutes. Serve.

VARIATIONS

143 Grilled BBQ Chicken Wings

Reduce pepper to ½ teaspoon. Add 1 teaspoon chili powder, 1 teaspoon paprika, ½ teaspoon garlic powder, ½ teaspoon dried oregano, and ½ teaspoon sugar to cornstarch mixture in step 2.

144 Grilled Creole Chicken Wings

Add ¾ teaspoon dried oregano, ½ teaspoon garlic powder, ½ teaspoon onion powder, ½ teaspoon white pepper, and ¼ teaspoon cayenne pepper to cornstarch mixture in step 2.

145 Grilled Tandoori Chicken Wings

Reduce pepper to ½ teaspoon. Add 1 teaspoon garam masala, ½ teaspoon ground cumin, ¼ teaspoon garlic powder, ¼ teaspoon ground ginger, and ⅛ teaspoon cayenne pepper to cornstarch mixture in step 2.

146 STEP BY STEP Getting Wings Ready for Grilling

1 CUT Using chef's knife, cut into skin between 2 larger sections of wings until you hit joint.

2 BREAK JOINT Bend back 2 sections to pop and break joint.

3 SEPARATE Cut through skin and flesh to completely separate 2 meaty portions.

4 REMOVE WINGTIP Hack off wingtip and discard or use for stock.

147 RECIPE FOR SUCCESS
Tofu That's the Tops

✓ WHY THIS RECIPE WORKS

Tofu has a soft, silky texture that contrasts nicely with the crisp, browned crust that results from a quick stint on the grill, and its mild flavor gets a boost from the sweet-and-sour flavors of this Asian-style glaze. First we made the glaze by simmering soy sauce, sugar, mirin, fresh ginger, garlic, and chili-garlic sauce. Some cornstarch helped to thicken the sauce so it would cling to the tofu. We found the key to successfully grilled tofu was cutting it to the right shape and handling it carefully on the grill. We tried grilling tofu that had been cut into planks, strips, and cubes, and found that tofu cut lengthwise into 1-inch-thick planks fared best. This shape maximized surface contact, and the larger pieces were easier to turn. Using two spatulas provided the best leverage for flipping the delicate tofu.

Grilled Soy-Ginger Glazed Tofu

SERVES 4 TO 6

You can use either firm or extra-firm tofu in this recipe. In order for this recipe to be gluten-free, you must use gluten-free soy sauce or tamari. Dry sherry or white wine can be substituted for the mirin in this recipe. Be sure to handle the tofu gently on the grill, or it may break apart.

GLAZE

- ⅓ cup soy sauce
- ⅓ cup water
- ⅓ cup sugar
- ¼ cup mirin
- 1 tablespoon grated fresh ginger
- 2 garlic cloves, minced
- 2 teaspoons cornstarch
- 1 teaspoon Asian chili-garlic sauce

TOFU

- 28 ounces firm tofu, sliced lengthwise into 1-inch-thick planks
- 2 tablespoons vegetable oil
  Salt and pepper
- ¼ cup minced fresh cilantro

1 FOR THE GLAZE Simmer soy sauce, water, sugar, mirin, ginger, garlic, cornstarch, and chili-garlic sauce in small saucepan over medium-high heat until thickened and reduced to ¾ cup, 5 to 7 minutes; transfer to bowl.

2 FOR THE TOFU Spread tofu over paper towel–lined baking sheet, let drain for 20 minutes, then gently press dry with paper towels. Brush tofu with oil and season with salt and pepper.

3A FOR A CHARCOAL GRILL Open bottom vent completely. Light large chimney starter filled with charcoal briquettes (6 quarts). When top coals are partially covered with ash, pour two-thirds evenly over half of grill, then pour remaining coals over other half of grill. Set cooking grate in place, cover, and open lid vent completely. Heat grill until hot, about 5 minutes.

3B FOR A GAS GRILL Turn all burners to high, cover, and heat grill until hot, about 15 minutes. Leave all burners on high.

4 Clean and oil cooking grate. Gently place tofu on grill, perpendicular to grate bars (on hotter part of grill if using charcoal). Cook (covered if using gas) until lightly browned on both sides, 6 to 10 minutes, gently flipping tofu halfway through cooking using 2 spatulas.

5 Slide tofu to cooler side of grill (if using charcoal) or turn all burners to medium (if using gas). Brush tofu with ¼ cup glaze and cook until well browned, 1 to 2 minutes. Flip tofu, brush with ¼ cup glaze, and cook until well browned, 1 to 2 minutes. Transfer tofu to platter, brush with remaining ¼ cup glaze, and sprinkle with cilantro. Serve.

VARIATION

148 Grilled Asian Barbecue Glazed Tofu

In order for this recipe to be gluten-free, you must use gluten-free soy sauce or tamari.

Substitute following mixture for glaze: Simmer ⅓ cup hoisin sauce, ⅓ cup ketchup, 2 tablespoons rice vinegar, 1½ tablespoons soy sauce, 1½ tablespoons toasted sesame oil, 1 tablespoon grated fresh ginger, and 1 minced scallion in small saucepan over medium-high heat until thickened and reduced to ¾ cup, 5 to 7 minutes.

149 Grill Gloves

GADGETS & GEAR

When you're reaching over a red-hot grill to turn burgers or steak, you need serious protection for your arms and hands. We tested grill gloves and mitts in leather, cotton, and combinations of high-tech synthetics alongside our favorite regular oven mitt. Most gloves were oversize, thick, and stiff, barely letting us grab grates or tongs, never mind doing any cooking. Our favorite is protective but thin enough for dexterity, with elbow-length sleeves that kept us safe over the coals.

THE BOTTOM LINE Heat protection isn't the whole equation; gloves with individual fingers like the **Steve Raichlen Ultimate Suede Grilling Gloves** ($29.99 per pair) are better for dexterity than mitts. The pliant leather gave us great control when manipulating tongs and grabbing hot grill grates. Long cuffs protected our forearms. Our only gripe? They're not machine-washable.

150 SHOPPING IQ
Fishing for Fish

It goes without saying that freshness and quality are paramount with seafood. With whole fish, you can check for bright eyes and gills and an overall shine. It's harder to know if fillets are fresh, so investigate your surroundings for clues. It's mostly common sense: The store should be clean, with a clean ocean scent; if it smells fishy or like ammonia, shop elsewhere. Whole fish should rest on lots of ice (not be sitting in puddles), while fillets should not be displayed directly on ice, as it could "burn" them. Rather, the fish should sit on a stainless-steel tray on top of the ice.

Even if they look fresh, the fillets you buy at the store may have been previously frozen. That's not necessarily a bad thing. Fish that's flash-frozen at sea immediately after it's caught and then stored and thawed properly may actually be fresher than a never-frozen fillet that's been sitting around. By federal regulation, the store must label previously frozen seafood. In either case, look for fillets that appear moist and that aren't flaking into segments. And don't be afraid to ask at the fish counter which fish is the freshest.

151 Stick-No-More Glazed Salmon

✔ WHY THIS RECIPE WORKS

Salmon is perfect for glazing and for grilling, but try to do both things at once and the fish inevitably sticks to the grill grate. The promise of sweet, smoky glazed grilled salmon made this recipe very appealing, but we needed a way to guarantee an intact piece of fish at the end of it. For the glaze, we preferred the concentrated sweetness of a jelly-based glaze, which also had just the right consistency to coat and cling to the salmon. We developed three glazes with different flavor profiles that all work great with salmon. But no matter how much we scrubbed the grill grate or how well we oiled it, the sticky, sweet glaze adhered to the grill and wouldn't let go. So we came up with a solution that avoided the issue altogether: placing our salmon on the grill on individual pieces of aluminum foil. We were able to get great grill marks, full smoke flavor, no sticking, and, if we removed the skin (which most people discard anyway), we could glaze both sides of the salmon. We even added extra glaze, enriched with butter, which caramelized in the foil "boat" for deep, full flavor.

Sweet and Saucy Lime-Jalapeño Glazed Salmon

SERVES 4

See page 143 for information on skinning the salmon. Use any brand of heavy-duty aluminum foil to make the grill trays, but be sure to spray the foil with vegetable oil spray.

½	cup jalapeño jelly
½	cup packed fresh cilantro leaves and stems
2	scallions, chopped coarse
2	garlic cloves, minced
1	teaspoon grated lime zest plus
2	tablespoons juice
2	tablespoons unsalted butter
4	(6- to 8-ounce) skinless salmon fillets, 1¼ inches thick
	Salt and pepper

1 Process jelly, cilantro, scallions, garlic, and lime zest and juice in food processor or blender until smooth. Heat glaze in small saucepan over medium heat until just bubbling, 2 to 3 minutes. Remove from heat and transfer ¼ cup glaze to small bowl to cool slightly. Stir butter into glaze remaining in saucepan, cover, and set aside.

2A FOR A CHARCOAL GRILL Open bottom vent completely. Light large chimney starter filled with charcoal briquettes (6 quarts). When top coals are partially covered with ash, pour evenly over three-quarters of grill. Set cooking grate in place, cover, and open lid vent completely. Heat grill until hot, about 5 minutes.

2B FOR A GAS GRILL Turn all burners to high, cover, and heat grill until hot, about 15 minutes. Leave all burners on high.

3 Using 4 large sheets of heavy-duty aluminum foil, crimp edges of each sheet to make 4 trays, each measuring 7 by 5 inches. Brush each side of each fillet with ½ tablespoon reserved glaze (without butter), and place 1 fillet skinned side up on each tray.

4 Place trays with salmon on hotter side of grill and cook (covered if using gas) until glaze forms golden-brown crust, 6 to 8 minutes. (Move fillets to cooler part of grill if they darken too soon.) Using tongs, flip salmon and cook for 1 minute. Spoon half of buttered glaze on salmon and cook until center of each fillet is still translucent, about 1 minute. Transfer salmon to platter and spoon remaining buttered glaze over it. Serve.

VARIATIONS

152 Orange-Sesame Glazed Salmon

Substitute orange marmalade, lemon zest, and lemon juice for the jalapeño jelly, lime zest, and lime juice. Add 2 tablespoons oyster sauce and 1 teaspoon toasted sesame oil to food processor or blender in step 1. Stir in 1 teaspoon toasted sesame seeds with butter in step 1.

153 Spicy Apple Glazed Salmon

Substitute apple jelly for the jalapeño jelly. Omit lime zest and lime juice. Add 2 tablespoons cider vinegar and ½ teaspoon red pepper flakes to food processor or blender in step 1.

154

Wood-Grilled Salmon without a Plank

✔ WHY THIS RECIPE WORKS

The premise of grilled cedar-planked salmon is simple: Fillets are set on a soaked plank of aromatic cedar, and the plank is placed on the grill to cook. We wondered if there was a way to create this distinctive flavor without the planks. We turned instead to wood chips. To replicate the wood-to-fish proximity, we made individual aluminum foil trays to hold the chips and salmon. To prevent the salmon from sticking to the wood chips, we left the skin on (it easily separated from the cooked fish). Poking a few slits in the bottom of the foil allowed more heat to reach the wood chips, which caused them to release more of their woodsy flavor. Coating each fillet with olive oil and a light sprinkling of sugar created a golden, mildly sweet exterior that looked as good as it tasted.

Wood-Grilled Salmon

SERVES 4

Coating each fillet with a thin layer of olive oil and a light sprinkling of granulated sugar produces a golden, mildly sweet exterior. Aromatic woods such as cedar and alder give the most authentic flavor.

- 1½ teaspoons sugar
- ½ teaspoon salt
- ¼ teaspoon pepper
- 4 (6- to 8-ounce) skin-on salmon fillets, 1¼ inches thick
- 1 tablespoon olive oil
- 2 cups wood chips, soaked in water for 15 minutes and drained

1 Combine sugar, salt, and pepper in small bowl. Pat salmon dry with paper towels. Brush flesh side of salmon with oil and sprinkle with sugar mixture. Using 4 large sheets of heavy-duty aluminum foil, crimp edges of each sheet to make 4 trays, each measuring 7 by 5 inches. Using tip of paring knife, make several small slits in bottom of each tray. Divide wood chips evenly among trays and lay 1 fillet skin side down on top of wood chips in each tray.

2A FOR A CHARCOAL GRILL Open bottom vent completely. Light large chimney starter filled with charcoal briquettes (6 quarts). When top coals are partially covered with ash, pour evenly over grill. Set cooking grate in place, cover, and open lid vent completely. Heat grill until hot, about 5 minutes.

2B FOR A GAS GRILL Turn all burners to high, cover, and heat grill until hot, about 15 minutes. Leave all burners on high.

3 Place trays with salmon on grill and cook, covered, until center of each fillet is still translucent when checked with tip of paring knife and registers 125 degrees (for medium-rare), about 10 minutes. Remove trays from grill. Slide metal spatula between skin and flesh of fish and transfer to platter. Serve.

VARIATIONS

155 Chinese-Style Wood-Grilled Salmon
Add ½ teaspoon five-spice powder and ¼ teaspoon cayenne pepper to sugar mixture. Omit oil and brush salmon with 2 tablespoons hoisin sauce before sprinkling with sugar mixture.

156 Barbecued Wood-Grilled Salmon
Add ¾ teaspoon chili powder and ¼ teaspoon cayenne pepper to sugar mixture. Omit oil and brush salmon with mixture of 1 tablespoon Dijon mustard and 1 tablespoon maple syrup before sprinkling with sugar mixture.

157 Lemon-Thyme Wood-Grilled Salmon
Add 2 teaspoons minced fresh thyme and 1½ teaspoons grated lemon zest to sugar mixture. Omit oil and brush salmon with 2 tablespoons Dijon mustard before sprinkling with sugar mixture.

158 STEP BY STEP Preparing Wood-Grilled Salmon

1 PREP FOIL TRAY Cut out 4 rectangles of heavy-duty aluminum foil and crimp edges until each tray measures 7 by 5 inches. Using paring knife, poke small slits in bottom of trays. (These vents will help to heat the chips.)

2 ARRANGE FISH ON CHIPS Place soaked wood chips in foil trays and arrange salmon skin side down directly on top of wood chips.

3 SERVE Once salmon is cooked, slide metal spatula between flesh and skin; fish should release easily.

159 SHOPPING IQ Wild Versus Farmed

In season, we prefer the more pronounced flavor of wild-caught salmon to farmed Atlantic salmon (traditionally the main farm-raised variety in the United States). If you're going to spend the extra money for wild salmon, make sure it looks and smells fresh, and realize that high-quality wild salmon is available only from late spring through the end of summer.

160 RECIPE FOR SUCCESS
Mahi-Mahi Goes Sweet and Spicy

✓ WHY THIS RECIPE WORKS

Mahi-mahi boasts a hearty, meaty texture that makes it a great candidate for the grill and a sweet, delicate taste that's well suited to robust flavors. Charring over high heat contributes rich, smoky notes to this mild-tasting fish. To give ours even more flavor, we added a layer of red curry paste before tossing it on the grill. Store-bought red curry paste gave us nuanced, complex flavors without the intimidating ingredient list of a do-it-yourself curry paste. The fillets cooked through in just a few minutes per side. Now all we needed was a fruit salsa to sweeten things up. Pineapple, cut into small pieces and combined with scallion and cilantro, gave us a sweet but bright and zingy salsa that perfectly complemented the hot, smoky grilled fish.

Grilled Red Curry Mahi-Mahi with Pineapple Salsa
SERVES 4

See page 278 for information on how to prep the pineapple.

12	ounces pineapple, cut into ¼-inch pieces
1	scallion, sliced thin
¼	cup minced fresh cilantro
2	tablespoons vegetable oil
	Salt and pepper
4	(6-ounce) skin-on mahi-mahi fillets, 1 to 1½ inches thick
1	tablespoon red curry paste

1 Combine pineapple, scallion, cilantro, and 1 table-spoon oil in bowl and season with salt and pepper to taste. Pat mahi-mahi dry with paper towels. Combine curry paste with remaining 1 tablespoon oil in bowl and brush over flesh of mahi-mahi.

2A FOR A CHARCOAL GRILL Open bottom vent completely. Light large chimney starter filled with charcoal briquettes (6 quarts). When top coals are partially covered with ash, pour evenly over grill. Set cooking grate in place, cover, and open lid vent completely. Heat grill until hot, about 5 minutes.

2B FOR A GAS GRILL Turn all burners to high, cover, and heat grill until hot, about 15 minutes. Leave all burners on high.

3 Clean cooking grate, then repeatedly brush grate with well-oiled paper towels until black and glossy, 5 to 10 times. Place mahi-mahi skin side up on grill. Cook (covered if using gas) until well browned on first side, about 3 minutes. Gently flip mahi-mahi and continue to cook until flesh flakes apart when gently prodded with paring knife and registers 140 degrees, 3 to 8 minutes. Transfer mahi-mahi to platter and serve with pineapple salsa.

161 SHOPPING IQ
Pineapple

When it comes to pineapple, we prefer Costa Rican-grown pineapples, also labeled "extra-sweet" or "gold." We find this fruit to be consistently "honey-sweet" in comparison to the "acidic" Hawaiian pineapple with greenish, not yellow, skin. Pineapples will not ripen further once picked, so be sure to purchase golden, fragrant fruit that gives slightly when pressed.

162 RECIPE FOR SUCCESS
Halibut: Tender, Moist, and Full of Flavor

✔ WHY THIS RECIPE WORKS

Halibut is a mild-flavored, lean, white fish with firm flesh, making it a perfect choice for those who like other mild-flavored, steak-like fish such as swordfish or tuna. Like those, halibut is also a great choice for the grill, but sticking and tearing were big issues when we were developing our grilled halibut recipe. Because of this, oiling the grill thoroughly is crucial. Cooking the fish over a single-level, moderately hot fire also helped. Halibut is best simply prepared. No marinades are necessary, just a brush of oil. Like swordfish, however (and like beef steaks), halibut takes well to the rich addition of a flavored butter. Here we opted for a spicy, zesty mix of chipotle chile and lime. Chipotles are actually dried, smoked jalapeño chiles. A small amount of chopped chipotle adds gentle heat to the butter in this recipe.

Grilled Halibut Steaks with Chipotle-Lime Butter

SERVES 4

In this recipe, we use boneless, skin-on halibut steaks. If your market carries only half steaks, which consist of two sections of flesh separated by a long, thin bone, you will need two steaks, about 1 pound each and 1 inch thick, for this recipe. If your market carries only whole halibut steaks (they have four sections of flesh divided by a bone and a membrane), you will need only one 2-pound steak, about 1 inch thick.

- 4 tablespoons unsalted butter, softened
- 1 tablespoon chopped fresh cilantro
- 2 teaspoons lime juice
- 1 chipotle chile in adobo sauce, chopped fine
- 1 garlic clove, minced
  Salt and pepper
- 4 (7- to 8-ounce) boneless skin-on halibut steaks, 1 inch thick
- 2 tablespoons extra-virgin olive oil
  Lemon wedges

1 Beat butter with large fork in medium bowl until light and fluffy. Add cilantro, lime juice, chipotle, garlic, and ¼ teaspoon salt and stir to combine. Transfer butter to piece of plastic wrap and roll butter into log about 3 inches long and 1½ inches in diameter. Refrigerate until firm, at least 2 hours or up to 3 days. (Butter can be frozen for up to 2 months. When ready to use, let soften just until butter can be cut, about 15 minutes).

2A FOR A CHARCOAL GRILL Open bottom vent completely. Light large chimney starter filled with charcoal briquettes (6 quarts). When top coals are partially covered with ash, pour evenly over grill. Set cooking grate in place, cover, and open lid vent completely. Heat grill until hot, about 5 minutes.

2B FOR A GAS GRILL Turn all burners to high, cover, and heat grill until hot, about 15 minutes. Leave all burners on high.

3 Clean cooking grate, then repeatedly brush grate with well-oiled paper towels until black and glossy, 5 to 10 times. Brush halibut with oil and season with salt and pepper.

4 Grill halibut, uncovered and turning once (using metal spatula), until barely translucent at very center of the steak and halibut registers 140 degrees, 7 to 9 minutes. Transfer steaks to individual plates and top each with slice of chipotle butter. Serve immediately with lemon wedges.

163 Fish for the Grill

Salmon (Atlantic and Pacific)

Most supermarket Atlantic salmon is farmed and is available year-round whole, in fillets, or as cross-cut steaks, Atlantic salmon has a meaty texture and a mild flavor that pairs well with fragrant herbs like dill or chives. Most Pacific salmon—including sockeye, coho, and Chinook (also called king)—are caught in the wild. Wild salmon is available seasonally between late spring and early fall (although frozen can be found year-round). Wild salmon has deep red flesh and a stronger flavor than Atlantic salmon.

Trout

Common types of this mostly freshwater fish include rainbow, lake, brown, and brook trout. Available wild or farmed, trout has a soft texture and delicate flavor. Trout is often prepared whole (look out for translucent pinbones) but is also available in fillets. The freshest trout has clear, bright eyes.

Tuna

Yellowfin (or ahi) tuna is usually cut into steaks. The uncooked flesh is a bright ruby red with a firm texture. Tuna is best when cooked to rare or medium-rare; well-done tuna turns gray and loses its moisture.

Swordfish

Swordfish caught off the Atlantic coast is available fresh year-round, although its peak season is summer. Most swordfish is sold in steaks. It has a slightly sweet flavor and meaty texture. Look for firm flesh without discolored edges.

Snapper

Snapper varieties abound in the Atlantic, but only one variety (L. campechanus) is recognized by the FDA as "red snapper." With beautiful, deep-red skin, it is often sold whole, but snapper is also available in firm, pink fillets. Be sure to remove the gills (bright red gills are an indicator of freshness) when preparing this fish whole.

Halibut

Halibut yields fillets and steaks that are firm, meaty, and mild. Look for flesh that is almost translucent, without a yellowish cast. Halibut's low fat content makes it prone to overcooking, so keep an eye on it on the grill.

164

How Do I Reheat Fish— and Do I Even Want To?

Fish is notoriously susceptible to overcooking, so reheating previously cooked fillets is something that makes nearly all cooks balk. But since almost everyone has leftover fish from time to time, we decided to figure out the best approach to warming it up.

As we had suspected, we had far more success reheating thick fillets and steaks than thin ones. Both swordfish and halibut steaks reheated nicely, retaining their moisture well and with no detectable change in flavor. Likewise, salmon reheated well, but thanks to the oxidation of its abundant fatty acids into strong-smelling aldehydes, reheating brought out a bit more of the fish's pungent aroma. There was little we could do to prevent trout from drying out and overcooking when heated a second time.

To reheat thicker fish fillets, use this gentle approach: Place the fillets on a wire rack set in a rimmed baking sheet, cover them with foil (to prevent the exteriors of the fish from drying out), and heat them in a 275-degree oven until they register 125 to 130 degrees, about 15 minutes for 1-inch-thick fillets (timing varies according to fillet size). We recommend serving leftover cooked thin fish in cold applications like salads.

165

In Search of a Great Grill Spatula

Grill spatulas are long-handled turners designed to keep your hands away from the flames while grilling. In our lineup of eight models, none worked perfectly in all three of our tests, which included handling pizza, swordfish, and burgers, but one stood out as the best possible compromise. Its midsize head got all the jobs done, and its nimble offset handle and comfortable, rounded plastic grip made it the class leader, hands down. As an added bonus, it was among the least expensive of the grill spatulas in our testing. The winner was the Weber Original Stainless Steel Spatula. Testers of all sizes loved this spatula's slim, rounded, offset handle, remarking on the agility, sense of control, and confidence that it inspired. Its relatively small head was also able to lift and move large swordfish steaks. Particularly when the grill is really packed, this is your spatula.

THE BOTTOM LINE Safety is always a good investment. Thus, we recommend a long-handled spatula, such as the **Weber Original Stainless Steel Spatula** ($14.99) to make grilling more comfortable and safe.

166 RECIPE FOR SUCCESS Simple Grilled Swordfish with Italian Flavors

✓ WHY THIS RECIPE WORKS

Swordfish steaks are a favorite on the grill. Their dense, meaty flesh keeps the steaks from falling apart. When developing our recipe, our first step was to choose thicker steaks, since thinner steaks overcooked easily. Since they can stay on the grill longer, the thicker steaks also pick up more smoky flavor. We found it was important to leave the fish in place long enough that it developed good grill marks before moving it. A two-level fire was necessary so the fish could sear over the hot fire and then cook through on the cooler part of the grill. A piquant Italian salsa verde made from parsley, anchovies, capers, garlic, lemon, and olive oil was perfect with the grilled swordfish. A slice of sandwich bread pureed into the sauce kept the flavors balanced and gave the sauce body. Toasting the bread rid it of excess moisture that would otherwise make for a gummy sauce.

Grilled Swordfish Steaks with Salsa Verde

SERVES 4

Because of the shape and size of swordfish, individual steaks are quite large. This recipe serves four—or more, if you want to cut the steaks into smaller pieces. Salsa verde is best served immediately after it is made, but can be refrigerated for up to 2 days. Bring the sauce to room temperature and stir to recombine it before serving.

SALSA VERDE

- 1 large slice hearty white sandwich bread
- ½ cup extra-virgin olive oil
- 2 tablespoons lemon juice
- 2 cups fresh parsley leaves
- 2 anchovy fillets
- 2 tablespoons capers, rinsed
- 1 small garlic clove, minced
- ⅛ teaspoon salt

FISH

- 2 (1-pound) skin-on swordfish steaks, 1 to 1½ inches thick

- 2 tablespoons extra-virgin olive oil
  Salt and pepper
  Lemon wedges

1 FOR THE SALSA VERDE Toast bread in toaster at lowest setting until surface is dry but not browned, about 15 seconds. Remove crust and cut bread into rough ½-inch pieces (you should have about ½ cup).

2 Process bread pieces, oil, and lemon juice in food processor until smooth, about 10 seconds. Add parsley, anchovies, capers, garlic, and salt. Pulse until mixture is finely chopped (mixture should not be smooth), about 5 pulses, scraping down bowl with rubber spatula after 3 pulses. Transfer mixture to small bowl and set aside.

3A FOR A CHARCOAL GRILL Open bottom vent completely. Light large chimney starter filled with charcoal briquettes (6 quarts). When top coals are partially covered with ash, pour two-thirds evenly over half of grill, then pour remaining coals over other half of grill. Set cooking grate in place, cover, and open lid vent completely. Heat grill until hot, about 5 minutes.

3B FOR A GAS GRILL Turn all burners to high, cover, and heat grill until hot, about 15 minutes. Leave primary burner on high and turn other burner(s) to medium-high.

4 FOR THE FISH Cut swordfish steaks in half to make 4 equal pieces. Brush fish with oil and season with salt and pepper.

5 Clean cooking grate, then repeatedly brush grate with well-oiled paper towels until black and glossy, 5 to 10 times. Place swordfish on hotter part of grill and cook uncovered, turning once (using metal spatula) until steaks are streaked with dark grill marks, 6 to 9 minutes. Move swordfish to cooler part of grill and cook, uncovered, turning once, until center is no longer translucent and swordfish registers 140 degrees, 3 to 6 minutes. Top each portion of grilled swordfish with generous tablespoon of salsa and serve immediately with lemon wedges.

168 RECIPE FOR SUCCESS
Perfect, Saucy Grilled Shrimp

✔ WHY THIS RECIPE WORKS

Shrimp can turn from moist and juicy to rubbery and dry in the blink of an eye over the heat of a grill. While grilling shrimp in their shells can shield them from the coals' scorching heat, any seasonings you add are stripped off along with the shells when it's time to eat. For juicy, boldly seasoned shrimp we decided to go with peeled shrimp and find a way to prevent them from drying out. We seasoned the shrimp with salt, pepper, and sugar (to encourage browning) and set them over the hot side of a half-grill fire. This worked well with jumbo shrimp, but smaller shrimp overcooked before charring. However, since jumbo shrimp cost as much as $25 per pound, we wanted a less expensive solution, so we created faux jumbo shrimp by cramming a skewer with several normal-size shrimp pressed tightly together. The final step was to take the shrimp off the fire before they were completely cooked and finish cooking them in a heated sauce waiting on the cooler side of the grill; this final simmer infused them with bold flavor. The flavors of the sauce can easily be changed to taste; one variation is included here.

Grilled Shrimp with Spicy Lemon-Garlic Sauce
SERVES 4

To fit all of the shrimp on the cooking grate at once, you will need three 14-inch metal skewers. Serve with grilled bread.

LEMON-GARLIC SAUCE
- 4 tablespoons unsalted butter, cut into 4 pieces
- ¼ cup lemon juice (2 lemons)
- 3 garlic cloves, minced
- ½ teaspoon red pepper flakes
- ⅛ teaspoon salt
- 1 (10-inch) disposable aluminum pie pan
- ⅓ cup minced fresh parsley

SHRIMP
- 1½ pounds extra-large shrimp (21 to 25 per pound), peeled and deveined
- 2–3 tablespoons vegetable oil
  Salt and pepper
- ¼ teaspoon sugar
  Lemon wedges

1 FOR THE LEMON-GARLIC SAUCE Combine butter, lemon juice, garlic, pepper flakes, and salt in disposable pan.

2 FOR THE SHRIMP Pat shrimp dry with paper towels. Thread shrimp tightly onto three 14-inch metal skewers, alternating direction of heads and tails. Brush shrimp with oil and season with salt and pepper. Sprinkle 1 side of each skewer evenly with sugar.

167 FOOD SCIENCE
Why Shrimp Turns Pink

Most cooks know that when you throw a batch of shrimp into a pot of boiling water or a hot skillet, they change color almost immediately. The gray-white shells and flesh are transformed into a bright red/orange/pink.

The color comes from a carotene-like pigment called astaxanthin, found not only in shrimp but also in salmon, lobster, crabs, crawfish, red seabream, and some fish eggs.

Usually astaxanthin is the reddish color we associate with salmon and most crustaceans. But in shrimp, astaxanthin is bound to a protein that masks the color, making the shrimp appear gray, not pink, when raw. When heat is applied, a chemical reaction occurs, and the bond between the protein and the pigment is broken, allowing the reddish color to show through.

THE BOTTOM LINE Once shrimp turn pink, they are cooked.

3A FOR A CHARCOAL GRILL Open bottom vent completely. Light large chimney starter filled with charcoal briquettes (6 quarts). When top coals are partially covered with ash, pour evenly over half of grill. Set cooking grate in place, cover, and open lid vent completely. Heat grill until hot, about 5 minutes.

3B FOR A GAS GRILL Turn all burners to high, cover, and heat grill until hot, about 15 minutes. Leave primary burner on high and turn other burner(s) to medium-low.

4 Clean cooking grate, then repeatedly brush grate with well-oiled paper towels until black and glossy, 5 to 10 times. Place disposable pan with sauce ingredients on hotter side of grill and cook until hot, 1 to 3 minutes; slide pan to cooler side of grill.

5 Place shrimp skewers, sugared side down, on hotter side of grill; use tongs to push shrimp together on skewers if they have separated. Cook shrimp until lightly charred on first side, 4 to 5 minutes. Flip skewers and cook until second side is pink and slightly translucent, 1 to 2 minutes.

6 Using potholder, carefully lift each skewer from grill and use tongs to slide shrimp off skewers and into pan with sauce. Toss shrimp and sauce to combine. Slide pan to hotter side of grill and cook, stirring, until shrimp are opaque throughout, about 30 seconds.

7 Stir in parsley. Transfer shrimp to platter and serve with lemon wedges.

VARIATION

169 **Grilled Shrimp with Fresh Tomatoes, Feta, and Olives**

Substitute following mixture for lemon-garlic sauce: Combine ¼ cup extra-virgin olive oil, 1 finely chopped large tomato, 1 tablespoon minced fresh oregano, and ⅛ teaspoon salt in disposable pan; cook as directed. Stir 1 cup crumbled feta cheese, ⅓ cup chopped kalamata olives, 3 thinly sliced scallions, and 2 tablespoons lemon juice into shrimp before serving.

170 Making Saucy Grilled Shrimp

1 PREP SAUCE IN PAN Combine butter, lemon juice, garlic, red pepper flakes, and salt in disposable pan that can go onto the grill.

2 PACK ONTO SKEWERS Pat shrimp dry with paper towels. Thread shrimp onto 3 skewers, alternating direction of heads and tails.

3 SPRINKLE WITH SUGAR Sprinkle 1 side of each skewer evenly with sugar.

4 GRILL THEN SAUCE Grill sugared side of shrimp for 4 to 5 minutes, then grill second side for 1 to 2 minutes. Slide shrimp into pan with sauce and finish cooking on hotter side of grill.

172 Perfecting Grilled Scallops

✔ WHY THIS RECIPE WORKS

In theory, scallops are tailor-made for the grill. The blazing-hot fire should deeply brown the bivalves' exteriors while leaving their centers plump and moist, with a hint of smoke. Unfortunately, in reality, by the time the scallops develop a good sear, they're usually overcooked and rubbery. And then there's the problem of trying to flip them when they inevitably stick to the cooking grate. To avoid overcooking the scallops but still develop a brown crust, we needed a quick blast of blazing heat, so we built the hottest fire possible by corralling the coals in a disposable aluminum pan set in the bottom of the grill. We found that using large "dry" scallops kept them from falling through the grate and avoided the soapy flavor that afflicts "wet" scallops. To make flipping easier, we incorporated a couple of techniques into our recipe: We lightly coated the scallops with a slurry of vegetable oil, flour, cornstarch, and sugar and we threaded them onto doubled metal skewers. The slurry kept the scallops from sticking to the grill grate, the sugar promoted browning, and the two skewers prevented the scallops from spinning when turned. Thoroughly oiling the grate also helped get our scallops off the grill in one piece. We whipped up a trio of boldly flavored vinaigrettes to complement these juicy, smoky scallops.

Grilled Scallops
SERVES 4

Double-skewering the scallops makes flipping easier. To skewer, thread four to six scallops onto one skewer and then place a second skewer through the scallops parallel to and about ¼ inch from the first. You will need eight to twelve 12-inch metal skewers for this recipe. If you use a charcoal grill, make sure the roasting pan you use is at least 2¾ inches deep.

171 Trial by Fire

Creating a good sear on scallops without overcooking them requires a quick blast of the hottest heat possible. We use a disposable aluminum pan filled with 7 quarts of coals to create a tall, super-hot, even fire in the center of the grill.

1½ pounds large sea scallops, tendons removed
1 (13 by 9-inch) disposable roasting pan (if using charcoal)
2 tablespoons vegetable oil
1 tablespoon all-purpose flour
1 teaspoon cornstarch
1 teaspoon sugar
  Kosher salt and pepper
  Lemon wedges
1 recipe vinaigrette (optional) (recipes follow)

1 Place scallops on rimmed baking sheet lined with clean dish towel. Place second clean dish towel on top of scallops and press gently on towel to blot liquid. Let scallops sit at room temperature, covered with towel, for 10 minutes. With scallops on counter, thread onto doubled 12-inch metal skewers so that flat sides will directly touch grill grate, 4 to 6 scallops per pair of skewers. Return skewered scallops to towel-lined sheet; refrigerate, covered with second towel, while preparing grill.

2A FOR A CHARCOAL GRILL Light large chimney starter mounded with charcoal briquettes (7 quarts). Poke twelve ½-inch holes in bottom of disposable pan and place in center of grill. When top coals are partially covered with ash, pour into disposable pan.

2B FOR A GAS GRILL Turn all burners to high, cover, and heat grill until very hot, about 15 minutes. Leave all burners on high.

3 Clean cooking grate, then repeatedly brush grate with well-oiled paper towels until grate is black and glossy, 5 to 10 times.

4 Whisk oil, flour, cornstarch, and sugar together in small bowl. Brush both sides of skewered scallops with oil mixture and season with salt and pepper. Place skewered scallops directly over hot grate. Cook (covered if using gas) without moving scallops until lightly browned, 2½ to 4 minutes. Carefully flip skewers and continue to cook until second side is browned, sides of scallops are firm, and centers are opaque, 2 to 4 minutes. Serve immediately with lemon wedges and vinaigrette, if using.

173 Chile-Lime Vinaigrette
MAKES ABOUT 1 CUP

1 teaspoon finely grated lime zest plus
  3 tablespoons juice (2 limes)
1 tablespoon Sriracha sauce
2 tablespoons honey
2 teaspoons fish sauce
½ cup vegetable oil

Whisk lime zest and juice, Sriracha, honey, and fish sauce until combined. Whisking constantly, slowly drizzle in oil until emulsified.

174 Basil Vinaigrette
MAKES ABOUT 1 CUP

1 cup packed fresh basil leaves
3 tablespoons minced fresh chives
2 tablespoons champagne vinegar
2 garlic cloves, minced
2 teaspoons sugar
1 teaspoon salt
½ teaspoon pepper
⅔ cup vegetable oil

Pulse basil, chives, vinegar, garlic, sugar, salt, and pepper in blender until roughly chopped. With blender running, slowly drizzle in oil until emulsified, scraping down sides as necessary.

175 Barbecue Sauce Vinaigrette
MAKES ABOUT 1 CUP

Bulls-Eye Original Barbecue Sauce and Pork Barrel Original Barbecue Sauce are our top-rated brands supermarket brands. For more information, see pages 71 and 358.

3 tablespoons barbecue sauce
2 tablespoons cider vinegar
1 tablespoon ketchup
2 teaspoons sugar
½ teaspoon salt
½ cup vegetable oil

Whisk barbecue sauce, vinegar, ketchup, sugar, and salt together in medium bowl until combined. Whisking constantly, slowly drizzle in oil until emulsified.

176 RECIPE FOR SUCCESS
Classic Italian Appetizers off the Grill

✓ WHY THIS RECIPE WORKS

Authentic Italian garlic bread, called bruschetta, consists of crisp, toasted slices of country bread brushed with extra-virgin olive oil (never butter), rubbed with raw garlic, and then slathered with various toppings. The toppings can be as simple as salt and pepper and fresh herbs or they can incorporate a variety of fresh vegetables, cheeses, and other more substantial ingredients. We used crusty rustic oblong or round loaves that yielded large slices. Cutting the bread about an inch thick provided enough heft to support weighty toppings and give a good chew. After grilling the bread, we brushed the oil over the surface for even coverage. Grilling gave the bread little jagged edges that pulled off tiny bits of garlic when we rubbed the raw clove over the slices. Grill the bread as close as possible to the time at which you plan to assemble the bruschetta.

Bruschetta with Tomatoes and Basil
SERVES 8 TO 10

This is the classic bruschetta, although you can substitute other herbs. Decrease the quantity if using stronger herbs, such as thyme or oregano.

- 4 medium ripe tomatoes, cored and cut into ½-inch pieces
- ⅓ cup shredded fresh basil leaves
  Salt and pepper
- 1 (12 by 5-inch loaf) rustic bread, sliced 1 inch thick, ends discarded (8 to 10 slices)
- 3 tablespoons extra-virgin olive oil
- 1 large garlic clove, peeled

1A FOR A CHARCOAL GRILL Open bottom vent completely. Light large chimney starter filled with charcoal briquettes (6 quarts). When top coals are partially covered with ash, pour evenly over grill. Set cooking grate in place, cover, and open lid vent completely. Heat grill until hot, about 5 minutes.

1B FOR A GAS GRILL Turn all burners to high, cover, and heat grill until hot, about 15 minutes. Leave all burners on high.

2 Meanwhile, mix tomatoes and basil in medium bowl; season with salt and pepper to taste.

3 Clean and oil cooking grate. Grill bread, turning once, until golden brown on both sides, 1 to 1½ minutes. Remove bread from grill, brush both sides of each slice with oil, and rub with garlic clove. Use slotted spoon to divide tomato mixture among grilled bread slices. Serve immediately.

177 Bruschetta with Fresh Herbs
SERVES 8 TO 10

- ½ cup extra-virgin olive oil
- 1½ tablespoons minced fresh parsley
- 1 tablespoon minced fresh oregano or thyme
- 1 tablespoon minced fresh sage
  Salt and pepper
- 1 (12 by 5-inch loaf) rustic bread, sliced 1 inch thick, ends discarded (8 to 10 slices)
- 1 large garlic clove, peeled

1A FOR A CHARCOAL GRILL Open bottom vent completely. Light large chimney starter filled with charcoal briquettes (6 quarts). When top coals are partially covered with ash, pour evenly over grill. Set cooking grate in place, cover, and open lid vent completely. Heat grill until hot, about 5 minutes.

1B FOR A GAS GRILL Turn all burners to high, cover, and heat grill until hot, about 15 minutes. Leave all burners on high.

2 Meanwhile, mix 5 tablespoons oil, parsley, oregano, and sage in small bowl; season with salt and pepper.

3 Clean and oil cooking grate. Grill bread, turning once, until golden brown on both sides, 1 to 1½ minutes. Remove bread from grill, brush both sides of each slice with remaining 3 tablespoons oil, and rub with garlic clove. Brush grilled bread with herb oil and serve immediately.

178 Bruschetta with Red Onions, Herbs, and Parmesan

SERVES 8 TO 10

The sautéed onions may be prepared in advance; be sure to bring them to room temperature before serving.

- 6 tablespoons extra-virgin olive oil
- 4 red onions, halved lengthwise and sliced thin
- 4 teaspoons sugar
- 2 tablespoons balsamic vinegar
- 1½ tablespoons minced fresh herbs such as parsley, basil, or chives
   Salt and pepper
- 1 (12 by 5-inch loaf) rustic bread, sliced 1 inch thick, ends discarded (8 to 10 slices)
- 1 large garlic clove, peeled
- 3 tablespoons grated Parmesan cheese

1 Heat 3 tablespoons oil in 12-inch skillet over medium-high heat. Add onions and sugar and cook, stirring often, until onions are softened, 7 to 8 minutes. Reduce heat to medium-low and continue to cook, stirring often, until onions are sweet and tender, 7 to 8 minutes longer. Stir in vinegar and herbs and season with salt and pepper to taste.

2A FOR A CHARCOAL GRILL Open bottom vent completely. Light large chimney starter filled with charcoal briquettes (6 quarts). When top coals are partially covered with ash, pour evenly over grill. Set cooking grate in place, cover, and open lid vent completely. Heat grill until hot, about 5 minutes.

2B FOR A GAS GRILL Turn all burners to high, cover, and heat grill until hot, about 15 minutes. Leave all burners on high.

3 Clean and oil cooking grate. Grill bread, turning once, until golden brown on both sides, 1 to 1½ minutes. Remove bread from grill, brush both sides of each slice with remaining 3 tablespoons oil, and rub with garlic clove. Divide onion mixture evenly among grilled bread slices, then sprinkle with Parmesan. Serve immediately.

continued

179

STEP BY STEP
Coring and Dicing Tomatoes

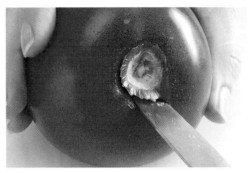

1 CORE Remove core of tomato using paring knife.

2 SLICE Slice tomato crosswise.

3 CUT INTO PIECES Stack several slices of tomato, then slice both crosswise and widthwise into pieces as desired.

180 Bruschetta with Sautéed Sweet Peppers

SERVES 8 TO 10

  6 tablespoons plus 1 teaspoon extra-virgin olive oil
  4 large red bell peppers, stemmed, seeded, and cut into 3 by ¼-inch strips
  2 onions, halved and sliced thin
     Salt
  4 garlic cloves (3 minced, 1 large peeled)
  ¼ teaspoon red pepper flakes
  1 (14.5-ounce) can diced tomatoes, drained, ¼ cup juice reserved
  1½ teaspoons chopped fresh thyme
  4 teaspoons sherry vinegar
  1 (12 by 5-inch loaf) rustic bread, sliced 1 inch thick, ends discarded (8 to 10 slices)
  2 ounces Parmesan cheese, shaved with vegetable peeler (½ to 1 cup shavings)

1 Heat 3 tablespoons oil, bell peppers, onions, and ½ teaspoon salt in 12-inch skillet over medium-high heat; cook, stirring occasionally, until vegetables are softened and browned around edges, 10 to 12 minutes. Reduce heat to medium, push vegetables to side of skillet, and add 1 teaspoon oil, minced garlic, and pepper flakes to clearing. Cook garlic, mashing it with wooden spoon, until fragrant, about 30 seconds, then stir into vegetables. Reduce heat to low and stir in tomatoes, reserved juice, and thyme. Cover and cook, stirring occasionally, until moisture has evaporated, 15 to 18 minutes. Off heat, stir in vinegar and ¼ teaspoon salt.

2A FOR A CHARCOAL GRILL Open bottom vent completely. Light large chimney starter filled with charcoal briquettes (6 quarts). When top coals are partially covered with ash, pour evenly over grill. Set cooking grate in place, cover, and open lid vent completely. Heat grill until hot, about 5 minutes.

2B FOR A GAS GRILL Turn all burners to high, cover, and heat grill until hot, about 15 minutes. Leave all burners on high.

3 Clean and oil cooking grate. Grill bread, turning once, until golden brown on both sides, 1 to 1½ minutes.
continued

181 Making Parmesan Shavings

Thin shavings of Parmesan can be used to garnish a variety of dishes. Simply run a sharp vegetable peeler along the length of a piece of cheese to remove paper-thin curls.

Remove bread from grill, brush both sides of each slice with remaining 3 tablespoons oil, and rub with large garlic clove. Divide pepper mixture evenly among bread slices, top with Parmesan, and serve immediately.

182 Bruschetta with Grilled Eggplant, Rosemary, and Feta

SERVES 8 TO 10

If desired, the eggplant can be grilled ahead of time, refrigerated, and brought back to room temperature before serving on the bruschetta. You can substitute an equal amount of ricotta salata (a firm, salted cheese) or goat cheese for the feta cheese if you choose.

- 7 tablespoons extra-virgin olive oil
- 1½ tablespoons balsamic vinegar
- 2 garlic cloves (1 minced, 1 large peeled)
- 1 teaspoon chopped fresh rosemary
- 1½ pounds eggplant, sliced into ¾-inch-thick rounds
  Salt and pepper
- 1 (12 by 5-inch loaf) rustic bread, sliced 1 inch thick, ends discarded (8 to 10 slices)
- 3 ounces feta cheese, crumbled (¾ cup)

1A FOR A CHARCOAL GRILL Open bottom vent completely. Light large chimney starter filled with charcoal briquettes (6 quarts). When top coals are partially covered with ash, pour evenly over grill. Set cooking grate in place, cover, and open lid vent completely. Heat grill until hot, about 5 minutes.

1B FOR A GAS GRILL Turn all burners to high, cover, and heat grill until hot, about 15 minutes. Leave all burners on high.

2 Meanwhile, mix ¼ cup oil, vinegar, minced garlic, and rosemary together in small bowl. Lay eggplant slices on baking sheet and brush both sides of each slice with vinegar-oil mixture. Season with salt and pepper.

3 Clean and oil cooking grate. Place eggplant on grill and cook, turning once, until streaked with dark grill marks, about 8 to 10 minutes. Transfer eggplant to cutting board, cut each slice crosswise into 1-inch strips, and cover to keep warm.

4 Grill bread, turning once, until golden brown on both sides, 1 to 1½ minutes. Remove bread from grill, brush both sides of each slice with remaining 3 tablespoons oil, and rub with large garlic clove. Divide eggplant strips evenly among bread slices, top with feta, and serve immediately.

183 Bruschetta with Arugula, Red Onion, and Rosemary–White Bean Spread

SERVES 8 TO 10

1	(15-ounce) can cannellini beans, rinsed
6	tablespoons extra-virgin olive oil
2	tablespoons water
1	tablespoon lemon juice
2	garlic cloves (1 small crushed, 1 large peeled)
	Salt and pepper
¼	teaspoon chopped fresh rosemary
1	tablespoon balsamic vinegar
¼	cup thinly sliced red onion
2	ounces (2 cups) arugula, cut into ½-inch strips
1	(12 by 5-inch loaf) rustic bread, sliced 1 inch thick, ends discarded (8 to 10 slices)

1 Process two-thirds of beans, 2 tablespoons oil, water, lemon juice, crushed garlic, ½ teaspoon salt, and ⅛ teaspoon pepper in food processor until smooth, about 10 seconds. Add rosemary and remaining beans; pulse until incorporated but not smooth, about 5 pulses.

2 Whisk vinegar, 1 tablespoon oil, ¼ teaspoon salt, and ⅛ teaspoon pepper in medium bowl; add onion and toss.

3A FOR A CHARCOAL GRILL Open bottom vent completely. Light large chimney starter filled with charcoal briquettes (6 quarts). When top coals are partially covered with ash, pour evenly over grill. Set cooking grate in place, cover, and open lid vent completely. Heat grill until hot, about 5 minutes.

3B FOR A GAS GRILL Turn all burners to high, cover, and heat grill until hot, about 15 minutes. Leave all burners on high.

4 Clean and oil cooking grate. Grill bread, turning once, until golden brown on both sides, 1 to 1½ minutes. Remove bread from grill, brush both sides of each slice with remaining 3 tablespoons oil, and rub with large garlic clove. Divide bean spread evenly among bread slices. Toss arugula with onion until coated, then top bread slices with onion and arugula; serve immediately.

184 SHOPPING IQ White Beans

The creamy texture and mildly nutty flavor of cannellini beans round out soups, casseroles, pasta dishes, and salads, and they make appealing dips. We've always appreciated the convenience of canned beans for use in quick recipes, but we've also always been a little prejudiced in favor of dried beans, considering their flavor and texture superior. We included five brands each of canned and dried beans, including two dried "heirloom" varieties. We held six blind tastings, serving two rounds each of the beans plain, in dip, and in soup. We didn't tell participants whether the beans they were evaluating were canned or dried. Surprisingly, top scores for canned beans actually edged out top scores for dried beans. In both canned and dried varieties, tasters liked beans that were firm and intact, with meltingly tender skins, creamy texture, and clean bean flavor. It turns out that beans destined for canning are processed quickly and efficiently, often suffering less degradation than dried beans.

THE BOTTOM LINE The choice is up to you, but today's best canned white beans, **Goya**, can match—and even greatly surpass—the quality of dried beans.

WINNER (CANNED)

GOYA Cannellini
Tasting Comments Tasters' favorite canned beans were "well seasoned" (they had the highest sodium level of the lineup), as well as "big and meaty," with both "earthy sweetness" and "savory flavor." Their texture was consistently "ultra-creamy and smooth," with a "nice firm bite"—all evidence of carefully calibrated processing.

WINNER (DRIED)

RANCHO GORDO Classic Cassoulet Bean
Tasting Comments This heirloom bean purveyor has stopped carrying cannellini beans, and instead sells a variety grown in California from French Tarbais beans. Our tasters found them "creamy and smooth, nutty and sweet," with a "fresh, clean" taste and a "lovely texture and appearance."

185 RECIPE FOR SUCCESS
Great Asparagus off the Grill

✔ WHY THIS RECIPE WORKS

The main challenge with throwing delicate asparagus on the grill is protecting it from overcooking while still developing a good char. For great grilled asparagus, we opted for thicker spears, which combined maximum browning with a meaty, crisp-tender texture. A simple medium-hot fire worked best—the spears were on and off the grill in less than 10 minutes. Brushing the spears with butter rather than oil before grilling gave us crispy, nutty asparagus. We tried adding flavor with zesty marinades but because asparagus has a naturally tough outer skin, most of the seasonings were left in the bowl or on the basting brush. Instead, we decided to add flavorings directly to the butter we were brushing on the asparagus, which worked perfectly.

Grilled Asparagus

SERVES 4 TO 6

Use asparagus that is at least ½ inch thick near the base. Do not use pencil-thin asparagus; it cannot withstand the heat and will overcook. Age affects the flavor of asparagus enormously. For the sweetest taste, look for spears that are bright green and firm, with tightly closed tips.

- 1½ **pounds thick asparagus spears, trimmed**
- 3 **tablespoons unsalted butter, melted**
  Salt and pepper

1A FOR A CHARCOAL GRILL Open bottom vent completely. Light large chimney starter three-quarters filled with charcoal briquettes (4½ quarts). When top coals are partially covered with ash, pour evenly over grill. Set cooking grate in place, cover, and open lid vent completely. Heat grill until hot, about 5 minutes.

1B FOR A GAS GRILL Turn all burners to high, cover, and heat grill until hot, about 15 minutes. Turn all burners to medium-high.

2 Brush asparagus with melted butter and season with salt and pepper.

3 Clean and oil cooking grate. Place asparagus in even layer on grill and cook until just tender and browned, 4 to 10 minutes, turning halfway through cooking. Transfer asparagus to platter and serve.

VARIATIONS

186 Grilled Asparagus with Chili-Lime Butter

Add 1 teaspoon grated lime zest, ½ teaspoon chili powder, ¼ teaspoon cayenne pepper, and ⅛ teaspoon red pepper flakes to butter.

187 Grilled Asparagus with Cumin Butter

Add 2 minced small garlic cloves, 1 teaspoon grated lemon zest, ½ teaspoon ground cumin, and ½ teaspoon ground coriander to butter.

188 Grilled Asparagus with Garlic Butter

Add 3 minced small garlic cloves to butter.

189 Grilled Asparagus with Orange-Thyme Butter

Add 1 teaspoon grated orange zest and 1 teaspoon minced fresh thyme to butter.

190 STEP BY STEP
Trimming Asparagus

1 BEND Remove 1 stalk of asparagus from bunch and bend it at thicker end until it snaps.

2 TRIM With broken asparagus as guide, trim tough ends from remaining asparagus bunch, using chef's knife.

191 Yes, You Can Grill Butternut Squash

✔ WHY THIS RECIPE WORKS

Like roasting, grilling brings out the best in this vegetable, leaving it tender and caramelized with a smoky finish. In early fall, while grilling is still possible and squash fills markets, this dish is a no-brainer. We chose to peel the squash to remove not only the tough outer skin but also the rugged fibrous layer of white flesh just beneath for supremely tender squash. However, our first few attempts at grilling the peeled, sliced squash resulted in raw-on-the-inside, burnt-on-the-outside orange lumps. The squash was just too dense to cook through evenly on the grill. Next we tried parboiling the squash before grilling to make sure it would cook through on the grill before it got dry and overcooked. This extra step helped jump-start the cooking process so the squash could finish cooking relatively quickly over a medium-hot fire that had enough heat to caramelize its surface.

Grilled Butternut Squash

SERVES 4 TO 6

This recipe calls for a lot of squash slices. Depending on the space between the bars on your cooking grate, you might want to cook them on a grill grid to prevent any slices from dropping down into the fire.

1   **small butternut squash (about 2 pounds), peeled, seeded, and cut into ½-inch-thick slices**
     Salt and pepper
3   **tablespoons extra-virgin olive oil**

1 Place squash slices in large pot. Cover with 2 quarts cold water. Add 1 teaspoon salt and bring to boil over high heat. Reduce heat to medium and simmer until squash is barely tender, about 3 minutes. Drain squash in colander, being careful not to break up squash slices. Transfer squash to large bowl; drizzle oil over top. Season with salt and pepper to taste, and gently turn squash to coat both sides of each slice with oil.

2A FOR A CHARCOAL GRILL Open bottom vent completely. Light large chimney starter three-quarters filled with charcoal briquettes (4½ quarts). When top coals are partially covered with ash, pour evenly over grill. Set cooking grate in place, cover, and open lid vent completely. Heat grill until hot, about 5 minutes.

2B FOR A GAS GRILL Turn all burners to high, cover, and heat grill until hot, about 15 minutes. Turn all burners to medium-high.

3 Clean and oil cooking grate. Place squash slices on grill and cook, turning once, until dark brown caramelization occurs and flesh becomes very tender, 8 to 10 minutes. Serve hot, warm, or at room temperature.

VARIATION

192 Spicy Grilled Butternut Squash with Garlic and Rosemary

Add 1 tablespoon extra-virgin olive oil to squash in step 1. After oiling, sprinkle squash with 2 tablespoons brown sugar, 1 teaspoon chopped fresh rosemary, 1 minced garlic clove, and ½ teaspoon red pepper flakes in place of salt and pepper. Turn squash to coat in oil-spice mixture. Grill as directed.

193 STEP BY STEP Cutting Up Squash for Grilling

1 PEEL Using sharp vegetable peeler or chef's knife, remove skin and fibrous threads just below skin from squash.

2 TRIM Trim off top and bottom and cut squash in half where narrow neck and wide curved bottom meet.

3 HALVE Cut squash base in half lengthwise, then scoop out and discard seeds and fibers. Slice both sections into ½-inch-thick pieces.

194 RECIPE FOR SUCCESS
Cabbage Everyone Will Like

✓ WHY THIS RECIPE WORKS

Cabbage is an underappreciated vegetable—except for coleslaw, few people give it much thought. We were looking for a new way to use this underdog when we discovered that putting cabbage over fire can transform it into a soft, sweet, deliciously smoky dish. To prevent the cabbage from falling apart on the grill, we sliced it into thick wedges, keeping the core intact. High heat helped develop browning, which meant that the cabbage tasted sweeter, but the timing was tricky. We needed to get the inside to cook before the exterior got overcooked. In the test kitchen we prevent soggy coleslaw by salting chopped cabbage. The salt draws out moisture, which we drain off before we dress the coleslaw. Following that same principle, we salted our cabbage wedges so the moisture would turn to steam on the grill. The steam then helped the interior of the wedges cook through. Brushing a simple lemon-herb vinaigrette on the cabbage instead of plain oil both before and after grilling added bright flavor.

Grilled Cabbage
SERVES 4

Leave the core intact so the cabbage wedges don't fall apart on the grill.

Salt and pepper
1   head green cabbage (2 pounds), cut into 8 wedges through core
1   tablespoon minced fresh thyme
2   teaspoons minced shallot
2   teaspoons honey
1   teaspoon Dijon mustard
½   teaspoon grated lemon zest plus 2 tablespoons juice
6   tablespoons extra-virgin olive oil

1 Sprinkle 1 teaspoon salt evenly over cabbage wedges and let sit for 45 minutes. Combine thyme, shallot, honey, mustard, lemon zest and juice, and ¼ teaspoon pepper in bowl. Slowly whisk in oil until incorporated. Measure out ¼ cup vinaigrette and set aside.

2A FOR A CHARCOAL GRILL Open bottom vent completely. Light large chimney starter half-filled with charcoal briquettes (3 quarts). When top coals are partially covered with ash, pour evenly over grill. Set cooking grate in place, cover, and open lid vent completely. Heat grill until hot, about 5 minutes.

2B FOR A GAS GRILL Turn all burners to high, cover, and heat grill until hot, about 15 minutes. Turn all burners to medium.

3 Clean and oil cooking grate. Brush 1 cut side of cabbage wedges with half of vinaigrette. Place cabbage on grill, vinaigrette side down, and cook (covered if using gas) until well browned, 7 to 10 minutes. Brush tops of wedges with remaining vinaigrette; flip and cook (covered if using gas) until second side is well browned and fork-tender, 7 to 10 minutes. Transfer cabbage to platter and drizzle with reserved vinaigrette. Season with salt and pepper to taste. Serve.

195 STEP BY STEP
Cutting Cabbage

To keep cabbage wedges together, quarter the cabbage, taking care to cut directly through the core. Cut each quarter in half for eight 2-inch wedges.

196 Coleslaw with Character

✓ WHY THIS RECIPE WORKS

We love the fresh crunch of cold and creamy cole-slaw, but sometimes a change of course is in order. In this recipe, we use the grill to tame the raw bite of cabbage. A modest amount of mayo seasoned with puckery cider vinegar binds the cabbage together. Carrot adds earthy sweetness and fresh cilantro takes this slaw further from the workaday picnic classic to something a bit more spirited.

Easy Grilled Coleslaw

SERVES 4

Do not remove the core from the cabbage; it will keep the leaves intact on the grill.

½	**head green cabbage (1 pound), cut into 2 wedges**
2	**tablespoons olive oil**
	Salt and pepper
¼	**cup mayonnaise**
1	**shallot, minced**
4	**teaspoons cider vinegar**
1	**carrot, peeled and shredded**
2	**tablespoons minced fresh cilantro**

1A FOR A CHARCOAL GRILL Open bottom vent completely. Light large chimney starter filled with charcoal briquettes (6 quarts). When top coals are partially covered with ash, pour evenly over grill. Set cooking grate in place, cover, and open lid vent completely. Heat grill until hot, about 5 minutes.

1B FOR A GAS GRILL Turn all burners on high, cover, and heat grill until hot, about 15 minutes. Leave all burners on high.

2 Brush cabbage wedges with oil and season with salt and pepper.

3 Clean and oil cooking grate. Place cabbage on grill. Cook (covered if using gas), turning as needed, until cabbage is lightly charred on all sides, 8 to 12 minutes. Transfer cabbage to platter; tent with aluminum foil and let rest.

4 Whisk mayonnaise, shallot, and vinegar together in large bowl. Slice cabbage into thin strips, discarding core. Stir cabbage, carrot, and cilantro into mayonnaise mixture. Season with salt and pepper to taste. Serve.

197 Great Grilled Corn

✓ WHY THIS RECIPE WORKS

Fresh corn and the hot lick of the grill flame are a perfect matchup. Fire does something magical to the kernels, toasting them and deepening their natural sweetness. We wanted to take this pairing to the next level by introducing flavored butter into the mix. However, while whipping up a flavored butter is easy, getting it to penetrate the corn is another story. Simply slathering grilled corn with compound butter failed to infuse the kernels with flavor, so we knew we'd have to apply the butter before or during cooking. When we buttered the corn before grilling, however, the butter dripped into the fire and caused major flare-ups. Eventually, we ended up with a foolproof method where we first charred the husked corn ears over a hot fire and then sizzled them in a disposable pan along with the flavored butter right on the grill. For the flavors of our compound butters, we combined sweet and spicy elements to create options for every palate.

Grilled Corn with Flavored Butter
SERVES 4 TO 6

Use a disposable aluminum roasting pan that is at least 2¾ inches deep.

- 1 recipe flavored butter (recipes follow)
- 1 (13 by 9-inch) disposable aluminum roasting pan
- 8 ears corn, husks and silk removed
- 2 tablespoons vegetable oil
  Salt and pepper

1 Place flavored butter in disposable pan. Brush corn evenly with oil and season with salt and pepper.

2A FOR A CHARCOAL GRILL Open bottom vent completely. Light large chimney starter three-quarters filled with charcoal briquettes (4½ quarts). When top coals are partially covered with ash, pour evenly over grill. Set cooking grate in place, cover, and open lid vent completely. Heat grill until hot, about 5 minutes.

2B FOR A GAS GRILL Turn all burners to high, cover, and heat grill until hot, about 15 minutes. Turn all burners to medium-high.

3 Clean and oil cooking grate. Place corn on grill and cook, turning occasionally, until lightly charred on all sides, 5 to 9 minutes. Transfer corn to disposable pan and cover tightly with aluminum foil.

4 Place disposable pan on grill and cook, shaking pan frequently, until butter is sizzling, about 3 minutes. Remove pan from grill and carefully remove foil, allowing steam to escape away from you. Serve corn, spooning any butter in pan over individual ears.

198 Basil and Lemon Butter

Serve with lemon wedges, if desired.

- 6 tablespoons unsalted butter, softened
- 2 tablespoons chopped fresh basil
- 1 tablespoon minced fresh parsley
- 1 teaspoon finely grated lemon zest
- ½ teaspoon salt
- ¼ teaspoon pepper

Combine all ingredients in small bowl.

199 Honey Butter

- 6 tablespoons unsalted butter, softened
- 2 tablespoons honey
- ½ teaspoon salt
- ¼ teaspoon red pepper flakes

Combine all ingredients in small bowl.

200 Latin-Spiced Butter

Serve with orange wedges, if desired.

- 6 tablespoons unsalted butter, softened
- 2 tablespoons minced fresh cilantro
- 1 tablespoon minced fresh parsley
- 1 teaspoon minced canned chipotle chile in adobo sauce
- ½ teaspoon finely grated orange zest
- ½ teaspoon salt

Combine all ingredients in small bowl.

201 New Orleans "Barbecue" Butter

- 6 tablespoons unsalted butter, softened
- 1 garlic clove, minced
- 1 tablespoon Worcestershire sauce
- 1 teaspoon tomato paste
- ½ teaspoon minced fresh rosemary
- ½ teaspoon minced fresh thyme
- ½ teaspoon cayenne pepper

Combine all ingredients in small bowl.

202 Spicy Old Bay Butter

Serve with lemon wedges, if desired.

- 6 tablespoons unsalted butter, softened
- 1 tablespoon hot sauce
- 1 tablespoon minced fresh parsley
- 1½ teaspoons Old Bay seasoning
- 1 teaspoon finely grated lemon zest

Combine all ingredients in small bowl.

203 GADGETS & GEAR
Top Tongs

To the uninitiated, all grill tongs look the same. But small design nuances have a huge impact on how well tongs handle asparagus or corn, flip a whole chicken, or turn an awkward, floppy rack of ribs on the grill. We bought eight pairs and headed to the backyard to assess how different styles of tongs could handle foods of varying shapes and weights. Tongs are extensions of our arms and hands, and a great pair should work nearly as naturally.

The main difference between kitchen and grill tongs is length: Grill tongs must keep us a comfortable distance from the fire. The usable length of these tongs ranged from 13 to 22 inches, but we found that about 16 inches is best. Any longer, and we had to work to lever heavy foods or contort our arms to stand close enough to work over the grill; shorter, and we risked getting scorched.

THE BOTTOM LINE Comfortable, lightweight, and sturdy, **OXO Good Grips 16-inch Locking Tongs** took top honors in our tests.

WINNER

OXO GOOD GRIPS 16-inch Locking Tongs
Price $14.99
Testing Comments These tongs passed every test with top marks. The pincers picked up multiple spears of asparagus in one swoop, cupped corn firmly, and did not damage tender rib meat. One tester said, "I could perform heart surgery with these."

RUNNER-UP

WEBER STYLE Tongs
Price $10.99
Testing Comments Almost identical to our top tongs, these felt comfortable in our hands. Shorter than advertised—a usable length of 16 inches instead of 19, with a 3-inch lock—they gripped ribs, hot coals, and multiple asparagus spears. But the pincers angled inward sharply, cutting into rib meat.

204 RECIPE FOR SUCCESS
Eggplant on the Grill— a Match Made in Heaven

✓ WHY THIS RECIPE WORKS

The biggest challenge that confronts the cook when preparing eggplant in any form is excess moisture; often it has to be salted before being cooked to draw out its juices. That's why grilling is such an ideal method for cooking eggplant. On the grill there's no need to draw out moisture before cooking. The moisture will vaporize or fall harmlessly through the cooking grate. The eggplant browns and crisps beautifully on the grill. To get grilled eggplant that isn't leathery or spongy, the size of the slice is crucial; we cut ¼-inch-thick slices to produce a charred exterior and tender flesh. For flavor, we quickly infused olive oil with garlic and red pepper flakes in the microwave and brushed it on the eggplant slices before grilling. We saved a tablespoon of the oil and mixed it with yogurt, lemon, and fresh herbs for a Mediterranean-inspired sauce to drizzle on at the end.

Grilled Eggplant with Yogurt Sauce
SERVES 6 TO 8

For spicier eggplant, increase the amount of red pepper flakes to ¼ teaspoon.

- 6 tablespoons extra-virgin olive oil
- 5 garlic cloves, minced
- ⅛ teaspoon red pepper flakes
- ½ cup plain whole-milk yogurt
- 3 tablespoons minced fresh mint
- 1 teaspoon grated lemon zest plus 2 teaspoons juice
- 1 teaspoon ground cumin
- Salt and pepper
- 2 pounds eggplant, sliced into ¼-inch-thick rounds

1 Microwave oil, garlic, and pepper flakes in bowl until garlic is golden and crisp, about 2 minutes. Strain oil through fine-mesh strainer into clean bowl; reserve oil and crispy garlic mixture separately.

2 Combine 1 tablespoon strained garlic oil, yogurt, mint, lemon zest and juice, cumin, and ¼ teaspoon salt in bowl; set aside. Brush eggplant thoroughly with remaining garlic oil and season with salt and pepper.

3A FOR A CHARCOAL GRILL Open bottom vent completely. Light large chimney starter three-quarters filled with charcoal briquettes (4½ quarts). When top coals are partially covered with ash, pour evenly over grill. Set cooking grate in place, cover, and open lid vent completely. Heat grill until hot, about 5 minutes.

3B FOR A GAS GRILL Turn all burners to high, cover, and heat grill until hot, about 15 minutes. Turn all burners to medium-high.

4 Clean and oil cooking grate. Place half of eggplant on grill. Cook (covered if using gas), turning as needed, until browned and tender, 8 to 10 minutes. Transfer to platter and repeat with remaining eggplant. Before serving, drizzle with yogurt sauce and sprinkle with crispy garlic mixture.

205 TEST KITCHEN TIP
Slice It Right

If the eggplant slices are too thick, the exterior will char nicely but the inside will be spongy and underdone. We found that ¼-inch-thick slices are the optimal size for eggplant rounds destined for the grill.

206 RECIPE FOR SUCCESS
Big Mushrooms Are Built for the Grill

✓ WHY THIS RECIPE WORKS

When grilled, portobello mushrooms often turn limp and flaccid, burning on the outside before the interior fully cooks. We wanted perfect grilled portobello mushrooms: plump, juicy, and slightly charred, with all the smoky flavor of the grill. Cooking over direct heat charred the outside before the mushrooms had a chance to cook through. We tried cooking over indirect heat, away from the fire, but while this solved the charring problem it didn't address the cooking problem. We solved this by digging out an old tool of the campfire trade: aluminum foil. By wrapping each mushroom in a packet of foil, we were able to cook them through in about 10 minutes. We then unwrapped each mushroom and let it grill uncovered for 30 to 60 seconds to sear in the grilled flavor. We cooked them gill side up the whole time to trap the juices and flavor in the meaty mushrooms without sacrificing any of the grill's smoky attributes. For a different take on these mushrooms, try our tarragon-flavored variation.

Grilled Marinated Portobello Mushrooms
SERVES 4 TO 6

We prefer large 5- to 6-inch portobellos for grilling because they are sold loose—not prepackaged—and are typically fresher. However, if you cannot find large ones, use six 4- to 5-inch portobellos, which are usually sold three to a package; decrease their grilling time wrapped in foil to about 8 minutes.

- ½ cup olive oil
- 3 tablespoons lemon juice
- 6 garlic cloves, minced
- ¼ teaspoon salt
- 4 portobello mushrooms (5 to 6 inches in diameter), stemmed

1 Combine oil, lemon juice, garlic, and salt in 1-gallon zipper-lock bag. Add mushrooms and toss to coat; press out as much air as possible and seal bag. Let sit at room temperature for 1 hour.

2 Meanwhile, cut four 12-inch square pieces of aluminum foil (or six 9-inch square pieces if using smaller mushrooms).

3A FOR A CHARCOAL GRILL Open bottom vent completely. Light large chimney starter three-quarters filled with charcoal briquettes (4½ quarts). When top coals are partially covered with ash, pour evenly over grill. Set cooking grate in place, cover, and open lid vent completely. Heat grill until hot, about 5 minutes.

3B FOR A GAS GRILL Turn all burners to high, cover, and heat grill until hot, about 15 minutes. Turn all burners to medium-high.

4 Clean and oil cooking grate. Remove mushrooms from marinade and place each on foil square, gill side up. Fold foil around each mushroom and seal edges. Place foil packets on grill, sealed side up, and cook (covered if using gas) until juicy and tender, 9 to 12 minutes.

5 Using tongs, unwrap mushrooms, place gill side up on grill, and cook until grill-marked, 30 to 60 seconds. Transfer to platter and serve.

VARIATION
207 Grilled Marinated Portobello Mushrooms with Tarragon

Substitute 2 teaspoons rice vinegar for lemon juice, reduce garlic to 1 clove, and add 1 tablespoon chopped fresh tarragon to marinade.

208
Sweet on Grilled Onions

✔ WHY THIS RECIPE WORKS

Grilling onions sounds like a great idea. Ideally the onions will caramelize and crisp up into the perfect side dish. However, it turns out that onions are actually pretty hard to manage on the grill. They slip through the grate, burn, or cook to a leathery texture on the outside while remaining raw on the inside. We wanted to find a way to make our dreams of perfect grilled onions come true. Because slicing onions into rounds exposes the greatest surface area, that was the logical shape for grilling, and we found that slices cut ½ half inch thick were best. Onions were simply too susceptible to burning over high heat; moderate heat, with the onions covered, was just right. We prevented the rounds from falling through the grate by skewering them. After developing our grilling technique, we conducted a taste test to choose the best variety. Spanish onions won; tasters loved their meaty texture and complex flavor profile.

Grilled Onions

SERVES 4

You will need four 12-inch metal skewers for this recipe.

- **2 large Spanish onions, each cut crosswise into four ½-inch-thick rounds**
- **3 tablespoons olive oil**
  Salt and pepper

1 Thread onion rounds, from side to side, onto four 12-inch metal skewers. Brush onions with oil and season with salt and pepper.

2A FOR A CHARCOAL GRILL Open bottom vent completely. Light large chimney starter three-quarters filled with charcoal briquettes (4½ quarts). When top coals are partially covered with ash, pour evenly over grill. Set cooking grate in place, cover, and open lid vent completely. Heat grill until hot, about 5 minutes.

2B FOR A GAS GRILL Turn all burners to high, cover, and heat grill until hot, about 15 minutes. Turn all burners to medium-high.

3 Clean and oil cooking grate. Place onions on grill, cover, and cook until deep golden brown and just tender, 15 to 20 minutes, flipping and rotating skewers as needed. Transfer onions to platter and remove skewers; discard any charred outer rings. Serve hot, warm, or at room temperature.

209
STEP BY STEP
Skewering Onions

For easy grilling, skewer onion rounds from side to side.

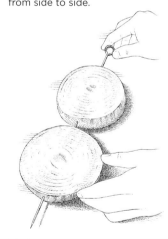

210

The Best Roasted Peppers

✓ WHY THIS RECIPE WORKS

Grill roasting is an easy way to add smoky flavor to sweet bell peppers. To infuse the peppers with even more flavor and ensure that they were perfectly softened but not mushy, we started by steaming them in a disposable pan with a mixture of olive oil, garlic, salt, and pepper. We then transferred the softened peppers to the cooking grate to blacken. After the peppers were done grilling, we used the remaining oil mixture from the disposable pan—now boosted with pepper juices and a hit of sherry vinegar—as a tangy vinaigrette for the tender, peeled peppers. Take care not to overroast the peppers—when the skin of a pepper puffs up and turns black, it has reached the point at which the flavor is maximized and the texture of the flesh is soft but not mushy.

Grill-Roasted Peppers

SERVES 4

These peppers can be refrigerated for up to five days.

¼	cup extra-virgin olive oil
3	garlic cloves, peeled and smashed
	Salt and pepper
1	(13 by 9-inch) disposable aluminum pan
6	red bell peppers
1	tablespoon sherry vinegar

1 Combine oil, garlic, ½ teaspoon salt, and ¼ teaspoon pepper in disposable pan. Using paring knife, cut around stems of peppers and remove cores and seeds. Place peppers in pan and turn to coat with oil. Cover pan tightly with aluminum foil.

2A FOR A CHARCOAL GRILL Open bottom vent completely. Light large chimney starter filled with charcoal briquettes (6 quarts). When top coals are partially covered with ash, pour evenly over half of grill. Set cooking grate in place, cover, and open lid vent completely. Heat grill until hot, about 5 minutes.

2B FOR A GAS GRILL Turn all burners to high, cover, and heat grill until hot, about 15 minutes. Turn all burners to medium-high.

3 Clean and oil cooking grate. Place pan on grill (hotter side if using charcoal) and cook, covered, until peppers are just tender and skins begin to blister, 10 to 15 minutes, rotating and shaking pan halfway through cooking.

4 Remove pan from heat and carefully remove foil (reserve foil to use later). Using tongs, remove peppers from pan, allowing juices to drip back into pan, and place on grill (hotter side if using charcoal). Grill peppers, covered, turning every few minutes until skins are blackened, 10 to 15 minutes.

5 Transfer juices and garlic in pan to medium bowl and whisk in vinegar. Remove peppers from grill, return to now-empty pan, and cover tightly with foil. Let peppers steam for 5 minutes. Using spoon, scrape blackened skin off each pepper. Quarter peppers lengthwise, add to vinaigrette in bowl, and toss to combine. Season with salt and pepper to taste, and serve.

VARIATION

211 Grill-Roasted Peppers with Rosemary

Add 1 sprig rosemary to oil in step 1. Discard rosemary sprig after grilling. Replace sherry vinegar with red wine vinegar in step 5.

212
Plantains—Not the Same Old Side

✓ WHY THIS RECIPE WORKS

Plantains are a staple in Latin American cuisine. They are widely available in many supermarkets and are always sold in Latino markets. You may also see them in some Asian food stores. Although plantains are technically a fruit rather than a vegetable (they closely resemble bananas in appearance), they are usually served as a side dish instead of dessert. They are starchier and less sweet than bananas. We prefer ripe, black-skinned plantains for grilling. (Green plantains are most often fried to make a side dish called tostones.) Ripe plantains are also easier to peel than green ones, which is key since plantains must be peeled and oiled for grilling or they will stick to the cooking grate. By the time the plantains are streaked with grill marks, they will be cooked through, tender, and ready to serve.

Grilled Plantains

SERVES 4

Plantains absorb the flavor of the grill well and can be served with almost anything. Try these plantains with grilled chicken, fish, beef, or pork. For this recipe, the plantains are quartered, peeled, and then cut in half lengthwise.

- 2 **large ripe plantains**
- 2 **tablespoons vegetable oil**
- **Salt**

1 Trim ends from plantains, then cut crosswise into 4 pieces. With paring knife, make slit in peel of each piece, from 1 end to other end, and then peel away skin with your fingers. Cut each piece of plantain in half lengthwise. Place plantains in large bowl, add oil, season with salt, and gently toss to coat.

2A FOR A CHARCOAL GRILL Open bottom vent completely. Light large chimney starter three-quarters filled with charcoal briquettes (4½ quarts). When top coals are partially covered with ash, pour evenly over grill. Set cooking grate in place, cover, and open lid vent completely. Heat grill until hot, about 5 minutes.

2B FOR A GAS GRILL Turn all burners to high, cover, and heat grill until hot, about 15 minutes. Turn all burners to medium-high.

3 Clean and oil cooking grate. Place plantains on grill and cook, turning once, until grill marks appear, 7 to 8 minutes.

213

Plantains

This large, starchy variety of banana is popular in Latin American, African, and Asian cuisines. Plantains mature from green to yellow to black. Though fully ripe plantains can be eaten out of hand, most plantains are cooked when they are still underripe. Their flavor is reminiscent of "squash and potato," and they have a "dense, spongy texture."

214 RECIPE FOR SUCCESS
Grilled Potatoes with Flair

✓ WHY THIS RECIPE WORKS

Grilled potatoes are a summer classic. We wanted to put a new spin on this dish by adding rosemary and garlic. Unfortunately, we found it was difficult to add enough flavor to plain grilled potatoes. Coating the potatoes with oil, garlic, and rosemary produced burnt, bitter garlic and charred rosemary. It turned out that we needed to introduce the potatoes to the garlic-oil mixture not once, but three times. Before cooking, we pierced the potatoes, skewered them, seasoned them with salt, brushed on the garlic-rosemary oil, and precooked them in the microwave. Then, before grilling, we brushed them again with the infused oil. After grilling, we tossed them with the oil yet again. We finally had it—tender grilled potatoes infused with the smoky flavor of the grill and enlivened with the bold flavors of garlic and rosemary.

Grilled Potatoes with Garlic and Rosemary
SERVES 4

This recipe allows you to grill an entrée while the hot coals burn down in step 4. Once that item is done, start grilling the potatoes. This recipe works best with small potatoes that are about 1½ inches in diameter. If using medium potatoes, 2 to 3 inches in diameter, cut them into quarters. If the potatoes are larger than 3 inches in diameter, cut each potato into eighths. Since the potatoes are first cooked in the microwave, use wooden skewers.

- ¼ cup olive oil
- 9 garlic cloves, minced
- 1 teaspoon chopped fresh rosemary
  Salt and pepper
- 2 pounds small red potatoes, unpeeled, halved, and threaded onto wooden skewers
- 2 tablespoons chopped fresh chives

1 Heat oil, garlic, rosemary, and ½ teaspoon salt in 8-inch skillet over medium heat until sizzling, about 3 minutes. Reduce heat to medium-low and continue to cook until garlic is light blond, about 3 minutes. Pour mixture through fine-mesh strainer into small bowl; press on solids. Measure 1 tablespoon solids and 1 tablespoon oil into large bowl and set aside. Discard remaining solids but reserve remaining oil.

2 Place skewered potatoes in single layer on large plate and poke each potato several times with skewer. Brush with 1 tablespoon strained oil and season with salt. Microwave until potatoes offer slight resistance when pierced with paring knife, about 8 minutes, turning halfway through microwaving. Transfer potatoes to baking sheet coated with 1 tablespoon strained oil. Brush with remaining 1 tablespoon strained oil and season with salt and pepper to taste.

3A FOR A CHARCOAL GRILL Open bottom vent completely. Light large chimney starter filled with charcoal briquettes (6 quarts). When top coals are partially covered with ash, pour two-thirds evenly over half of grill, then pour remaining coals over other half of grill. Set cooking grate in place, cover, and open lid vent completely. Heat grill until hot, about 5 minutes.

3B FOR A GAS GRILL Turn all burners to high, cover, and heat grill until hot, about 15 minutes. Turn all burners to medium-high.

4 Clean and oil cooking grate. Place potatoes on grill (on hotter side if using charcoal) and cook (covered if using gas) until grill marks appear, 3 to 5 minutes, flipping halfway through cooking. Move potatoes to cooler side of grill (if using charcoal) or turn all burners to medium-low (if using gas). Cover and continue to cook until paring knife slips in and out of potatoes easily, 5 to 8 minutes longer.

5 Remove potatoes from skewers and transfer to bowl with reserved garlic-oil mixture. Add chives, season with salt and pepper to taste, and toss until thoroughly coated. Serve.

VARIATION

215 Grilled Potatoes with Oregano and Lemon

Reduce garlic to 3 cloves, substitute 2 tablespoons chopped fresh oregano for rosemary, and add 2 teaspoons grated lemon zest to oil in skillet. Substitute 2 teaspoons chopped fresh oregano for chives and add additional 1 teaspoon grated lemon zest to potatoes when they come off grill.

216

RECIPE FOR SUCCESS

Easy Grilled Potato Packs

✓ WHY THIS RECIPE WORKS

The appeal of this campfire classic is partly convenience: All you need is fire, food, and tin foil, no pots or pans required. But the method has other virtues: Because the food is cooked in a contained environment over the fire, the technique combines freshness and clear flavors with the deep caramelized taste of grilling. Unfortunately, it also frequently results in food that is both burnt and undercooked. We set out to create a foolproof recipe that would avoid both extremes. After multiple tests, we found that Yukon Golds were preferable to starchy, mealy russets and "slippery" red potatoes. To ensure evenly grilled potatoes, we cut them into evenly sized wedges and microwaved them for a few minutes before grilling them. Tossing the potatoes with a little oil prevented them from sticking to the foil. A quick flip halfway through cooking on the grill ensured perfectly cooked, spotty brown potatoes. The contained cooking environment of the foil pack created the perfect opportunity to add all kinds of flavors in our variations, from simple herbs to more creative ingredients like chorizo sausage or wine vinegar.

Grilled Potato Hobo Packs

SERVES 4

To keep the packs from tearing, use heavy-duty aluminum foil or two layers of regular foil.

- 2 pounds Yukon Gold potatoes, unpeeled
- 1 tablespoon olive oil
- 2 garlic cloves, peeled and chopped
- 1 teaspoon minced fresh thyme
- 1 teaspoon salt
- ½ teaspoon pepper

1 Cut each potato in half crosswise, then cut each half into 8 wedges. Place potatoes in large bowl, cover, and microwave until edges of potatoes are translucent,

4 to 7 minutes, shaking bowl to redistribute potatoes halfway through microwaving. Drain well. Gently toss potatoes with oil, garlic, thyme, salt, and pepper.

2 Cut four 14 by 10-inch sheets of heavy-duty aluminum foil. Working with one at a time, spread one-quarter of potato mixture over half of foil, fold foil over potatoes, and crimp edges tightly to seal.

3A FOR A CHARCOAL GRILL Open bottom vent completely. Light large chimney starter filled with charcoal briquettes (6 quarts). When top coals are partially covered with ash, pour evenly over grill. Set cooking grate in place, cover, and open lid vent completely. Heat grill until hot, about 5 minutes.

3B FOR A GAS GRILL Turn all burners to high, cover, and heat grill until hot, about 15 minutes. Turn all burners to medium-high.

4 Clean cooking grate. Place hobo packs on grill and cook, covered, until potatoes are completely tender, about 10 minutes, flipping packs halfway through cooking. Cut open foil and serve.

VARIATIONS

217 Grilled Spanish-Style Potato Hobo Packs
Add 6 ounces thinly sliced cured chorizo sausage, 1 seeded and chopped red bell pepper, and 1 teaspoon paprika to cooked potatoes as they are tossed in step 1.

218 Grilled Spicy Home Fry Potato Hobo Packs
Omit chopped garlic. Add 1 teaspoon paprika, ½ teaspoon garlic powder, ½ teaspoon onion powder, and ¼ teaspoon cayenne pepper to cooked potatoes as they are tossed in step 1.

219 Grilled Vinegar and Onion Potato Hobo Packs
Microwave 1 halved and thinly sliced small onion with potatoes in step 1. Add 2 tablespoons white wine or red wine vinegar to cooked potatoes as they are tossed in step 1.

220 STEP BY STEP Making Potato Hobo Packs

1 JUMP-START POTATOES Microwave potatoes first to help them cook quickly on grill.

2 FORM FOIL PACKETS Arrange microwaved potatoes on foil, fold over, and crimp.

3 GRILL Flip packs halfway through grilling for evenly charred potatoes.

221 RECIPE FOR SUCCESS
Vegetable Salad off the Grill

✔ WHY THIS RECIPE WORKS

Charred veggies infused with a tangy vinaigrette may not seem technically difficult, but we found that the devil is in the details. Hearty veggies that can be cut into large plank shapes are easiest for grilling, but not all veggies benefit from the same marinating method. A combination of eggplant, bell pepper, zucchini, and red onion made for a good variety of flavors, and when sliced all the vegetables took the same amount of time to cook—about 5 minutes per side. Next we tried marinating the vegetables before grilling for stronger flavors. Unfortunately, it turned out that while the zucchini, bell peppers, and onions could stand up to the pregrill marinade, the marinated eggplant turned unpleasantly squishy on the grill. Shortening the marinating time or cutting the eggplant into thicker slices didn't help. We decided to leave the eggplant unmarinated but saved a few tablespoons of the marinade mixture to use as a dressing for the salad, which would help flavor the grilled eggplant. The eggplant, since it was not marinated, also needed a few extra minutes on the grill, so it went on first and came off last.

Grilled Vegetable Salad
SERVES 4 TO 6

Keep the onion rounds together when you add them to the marinade or they'll be difficult to grill.

- **3   tablespoons white wine vinegar**
- **3   garlic cloves, minced**
- **1½   teaspoons Dijon mustard**
- **Salt and pepper**
- **6   tablespoons olive oil**
- **3   zucchini (8 ounces each), halved lengthwise**
- **1   red onion, sliced into ½-inch-thick rounds**
- **1   red bell pepper, stemmed, seeded, and halved lengthwise**
- **1   pound eggplant, sliced into ½-inch-thick rounds**
- **3   tablespoons chopped fresh basil**
- **1   tablespoon minced fresh parsley**

1 Whisk vinegar, garlic, mustard, ½ teaspoon salt, and ½ teaspoon pepper together in large bowl. Slowly whisk in oil until thoroughly incorporated. Measure out 2 tablespoons dressing and set aside. Add zucchini, onion, and bell pepper to remaining dressing and turn to coat. Marinate vegetables for 15 minutes, tossing occasionally.

2A FOR A CHARCOAL GRILL Open bottom vent completely. Light large chimney starter three-quarters filled with charcoal briquettes (4½ quarts). When top coals are partially covered with ash, pour evenly over grill. Set cooking grate in place, cover, and open lid vent completely. Heat grill until hot, about 5 minutes.

2B FOR A GAS GRILL Turn all burners to high, cover, and heat grill until hot, about 15 minutes. Turn all burners to medium-high.

3 Clean and oil cooking grate. Place eggplant and marinated vegetables on grill, beginning with eggplant. Grill (covered if using gas) until charred and tender, 4 to 6 minutes per side, removing eggplant last. Chop vegetables into 1-inch pieces and toss with reserved dressing, basil, and parsley. Let cool for 10 minutes. Season with salt and pepper to taste. Serve.

222 GADGETS & GEAR
Grill Pan

You can certainly grill vegetables right on the grill, but a grill pan does make transferring vegetables quick and easy. We like the **Weber Professional-Grade Grill Pan** (Model 6435; $19.99). Narrow slits, rather than holes, prevent even thin-cut vegetables from slipping into the coals. The pan's raised sides keep food from sliding off and are easy to grip, even with heavy mitts.

223 Hot Tips for Grilling Vegetables

TEST KITCHEN TIP

1 BUILD A MEDIUM-HOT FIRE Most vegetables respond better to moderate heat than to a blazing fire. If you're setting up the grill for just vegetables, pour a chimney three-quarters full of lit coals evenly over the grill.

2 MAKE THE (RIGHT) CUT Preparing vegetables for the grill is all about maximizing their surface area to increase flavorful browning and cutting shapes that discourage them from falling apart or slipping through the grill grate.

3 BRUSH WITH OIL Applying a thin layer of extra-virgin olive oil to vegetables before grilling encourages even browning and helps prevent them from sticking to the grill grate. To contain the mess, lay the vegetables on a baking sheet and use a basting brush. Season with salt and pepper before cooking.

4 GO EASY ON THE CHAR Browning vegetables is one thing; incinerating them is another. For the best results, keep the pieces moving to avoid hot spots and grill until they're just tender and streaked with grill marks.

5 GRILL MEAT FIRST ON A CHARCOAL GRILL When grilling vegetables to accompany steak, chicken, or pork, we cook the meat first, while the fire is at its hottest. By the time the meat is done, the heat has subsided a bit and the vegetables can cook at more moderate temperatures while the meat rests. (Note: This plan works equally well on a gas grill, where waiting for the fire to die down is not an issue.)

225 Ratatouille with an American Accent

✔ WHY THIS RECIPE WORKS

A well-made ratatouille embodies the essence of flavors from the south of France, including firm eggplant, zucchini, caramelized onions, heady garlic, and garden-fresh herbs. Bringing the mixture together are the ripest of tomatoes. Yet too often the ingredients in this stew end up indistinguishable from each other in terms of taste, color, and texture. Each of the vegetables has its own set of cooking problems and if they are not handled properly, the resulting dish is a mess. We wanted to address these issues and also translate this classic dish to the grill, since it's prime grilling time when all of these vegetables are in season and a smoky char makes the flavors of the ratatouille even better. The heat of the grill fire also helps all the moisture evaporate from the vegetables faster than it would in an oven. Carefully monitoring the grill time for each separate vegetable was the only major requirement for perfect grilled ratatouille.

Grilled Ratatouille
SERVES 6 TO 8

Depending on the size of your grill, you may have to cook the vegetables in multiple batches. When grilling

224 TEST KITCHEN TIP
Not the Same Old Vegetables for the Grill

These vegetables might seem like unusual grill fare, but they're delicious and easy to prep. Simply coat with olive oil, sprinkle with salt and pepper, and they're good to go on the grill.

VEGETABLE	PREPARATION	COOK
Baby Bok Choy	Halve head through stem; rinse but don't dry. (The water left clinging to the leaves will turn to steam on the grill, helping the bok choy cook evenly.)	6 to 7 minutes, turning once
Endive	Halve lengthwise through core. (Keeping the core intact helps the leaves stay together for easy turning.)	5 to 7 minutes, turning once
Radicchio	Cut head into 4 equal wedges.	4 to 5 minutes, turning every 1½ minutes (Turn each wedge twice so that each side, including the rounded one, spends some time facing the fire.)
Scallions	Trim off root end and discard any loose or wilted outer leaves. (Use scallions that are at least ¼ inch in diameter for a well-charred exterior and a tender interior.)	4 to 5 minutes, turning once
Fennel	Trim fronds from bulbs and discard or save for another use. Cut thin slice from base of bulb, then cut bulb vertically through base into ¼-inch-thick slices, leaving core intact.	7 to 9 minutes, turning once

more than one vegetable at a time, be prepared to take each off the grill as it is done cooking. A rasp-style grater makes quick work of turning the garlic into a paste.

- 1 red onion, cut into ½-inch-thick slices and skewered
- 2 pounds eggplant, sliced into ¾-inch-thick rounds
- 1½ pounds zucchini or summer squash, sliced lengthwise into ½-inch-thick planks
- 2 bell peppers, stemmed, seeded, and halved, each half cut into thirds
- 1 pound tomatoes, cored and halved
- ¼ cup extra-virgin olive oil, plus extra for brushing
  Salt and pepper
- 3 tablespoons sherry vinegar
- ¼ cup chopped fresh basil
- 1 tablespoon minced fresh thyme
- 1 garlic clove, minced to paste

1 Place onion, eggplant, zucchini, bell peppers and tomatoes on baking sheet, brush with oil, and season with salt and pepper. Whisk ¼ cup oil, vinegar, basil, thyme, and garlic together in large bowl.

2A FOR A CHARCOAL GRILL Open bottom vent completely. Light large chimney starter three-quarters filled with charcoal briquettes (4½ quarts). When top coals are partially covered with ash, pour evenly over grill. Set cooking grate in place, cover, and open lid vent completely. Heat grill until hot, about 5 minutes.

2B FOR A GAS GRILL Turn all burners to high, cover, and heat grill until hot, about 15 minutes. Turn all burners to medium-high.

3 Clean and oil cooking grate. Place vegetables on grill and cook, turning once, until tender and streaked with grill marks, 10 to 12 minutes for onion, 8 to 10 minutes for eggplant and squash, 7 to 9 minutes for peppers, and 4 to 5 minutes for tomatoes. Remove vegetables from grill as they are done and let cool slightly.

4 When cool enough to handle, chop vegetables into ½-inch pieces and add to oil mixture; toss to coat. Season with salt and pepper to taste, and serve warm or at room temperature.

226 Getting Fruity on the Grill

✓ WHY THIS RECIPE WORKS

Grilled fruit makes a simple summertime dessert, or it can be used as an accompaniment to grilled pork, chicken, or fish. Grilling intensifies the sweetness of the fruit through caramelization. In the chart on page 123, we have included those fruits that we believe do best on the grill. Use smaller plums, peaches, apples, and pears when grilling, since larger fruits may burn on the outside before heating through to the center. All fruit to be grilled should be ripe, but still firm. Grill delicate fruits with their skins intact, as the skins keep the fruit from falling apart on the grill.

Grilled Fruit

Be sure to clean your cooking grate thoroughly before adding the fruit.

> **Prepared fruit (see chart)**
> **Vegetable oil**

1A FOR A CHARCOAL GRILL Open bottom vent completely. Light large chimney starter three-quarters filled with charcoal briquettes (4½ quarts). When top coals are partially covered with ash, pour evenly over grill. Set cooking grate in place, cover, and open lid vent completely. Heat grill until hot, about 5 minutes.

1B FOR A GAS GRILL turn all burners to high, cover, and heat grill until hot, about 15 minutes. Turn all burners to medium-high.

2 Clean and oil cooking grate. Lightly brush prepared fruit with vegetable oil. Grill fruit as directed in chart. Fruit is done when it is marked on exterior and just barely softened and heated through at center.

227 Simplified Caramel Sauce

MAKES ABOUT ½ CUP

Use this sauce over ice cream and grilled fruit. This recipe makes enough for four servings. Caramel sauce is especially good with grilled bananas, pears, apples, and peaches.

½	cup (3½ ounces) sugar
2½	tablespoons water
⅓	cup heavy cream
1	tablespoon rum or brandy

1 Combine sugar and water in medium saucepan over medium-low heat. Stir until sugar dissolves. Increase heat to high and cook, swirling pan occasionally but not stirring, until caramel is uniformly golden amber in color, about 4 minutes.

2 Wearing oven mitts to protect your hands, remove pan from heat and slowly whisk in cream, about 1 tablespoon at a time, making sure to keep bubbling caramel away from your arms; stir until smooth. Stir in rum. Set caramel sauce aside to thicken and cool.

228 Sour Orange Glaze

MAKES ABOUT ½ CUP

This glaze can be brushed onto fruit during the last minutes of cooking. This recipe glazes four servings of fruit, with extra sauce to drizzle over the fruit before serving. This glaze goes well with any type of fruit.

- ½ cup orange juice
- ¼ cup packed (1¾ ounces) brown sugar
- 3 tablespoons lime juice (2 limes)
- 3 tablespoons unsalted butter, cut into ¼-inch pieces and chilled

1 Combine orange juice, sugar, and 2½ tablespoons lime juice in small saucepan and bring to boil over high heat. Reduce heat to medium-high and cook until reduced to ⅓ cup, about 7 minutes.

2 Remove pan from heat and whisk in butter until melted and incorporated. Stir in remaining 1½ teaspoons lime juice. Use warm or at room temperature.

229 Rum-Molasses Glaze

MAKES ABOUT ½ CUP

This recipe glazes four servings of fruit, with extra sauce to drizzle over the top of each serving. Use half of the mixture to brush onto the fruit during the last minute or two of cooking and the other half to drizzle over the fruit before serving. This glaze goes very well with bananas, pineapple, mangos, pears, peaches, and apples.

- 6 tablespoons molasses
- ¼ cup plus ½ teaspoon dark rum
- 4 teaspoons lime juice
- 3 tablespoons unsalted butter, cut into ¼-inch pieces and chilled

1 Combine molasses, ¼ cup rum, and 1 tablespoon lime juice in small saucepan and bring to boil over high heat. Reduce heat to medium-high and cook until reduced to ⅓ cup, about 5 minutes.

2 Remove pan from heat and whisk in butter until melted and incorporated. Stir in remaining ½ teaspoon rum and remaining 1 teaspoon lime juice. Use warm or at room temperature.

230 TEST KITCHEN TIP Easy-Prep Fruit off the Grill

FRUIT	PREPARATION	GRILLING DIRECTIONS
Apple	Cut in half through core. Remove core with melon baller or sturdy teaspoon measure. Use paring knife to cut out the stem.	Grill skin side up for 5 to 6 minutes; turn and grill skin side down for 5 to 6 minutes.
Banana	Leave skin on; cut in half lengthwise using sharp paring knife.	Grill skin side up for 2 minutes; turn and grill skin side down for 2 minutes.
Mango	Peel, pit, and cut into 4 pieces.	Grill larger pieces for 5 minutes, smaller pieces for 4 minutes, turning all pieces once halfway through cooking time.
Peach	Cut in half and remove pit.	Grill skin side up for 4 minutes; turn and grill skin side down for 3 to 4 minutes.
Pear	Cut in half lengthwise. Remove core with melon baller or sturdy teaspoon measure. Use paring knife to cut out stem.	Grill skin side up for 5 minutes; turn and grill skin side down for 5 minutes.
Pineapple	Cut into half-circles.	Grill for 6 minutes, turning once halfway through cooking time.
Plum	Cut in half and remove pit.	Grill skin side up for 4 minutes; turn and grill skin side down for 2 minutes.

2
THE EASY UPGRADES

BEEF

128 Tender, Juicy Grilled Burgers
 Grilled Scallion Topping
 Grilled Shiitake Mushroom Topping
 Grilled Napa Cabbage and Radicchio Topping
130 All-in-One Grilled Burgers
 Ranch All-in-One Grilled Burgers
 Tex-Mex All-in-One Grilled Burgers
 Italian All-in-One Grilled Burgers
132 Meatloaf Burgers
135 Grilled Steak Burgers
136 Jucy Lucy Burgers
139 Green Chile Cheeseburgers
158 Grilled Steak with New Mexican Chile Rub
160 Grilled Cowboy-Cut Rib Eyes
162 Grilled Beef and Chorizo Skewers
164 Grilled Argentine Steaks with Chimichurri Sauce
166 Drunken Steak
 Margarita Drunken Steak
169 Grilled Free-Form Beef Wellington with Balsamic Reduction
170 Grilled Thai Beef Salad
173 Spinach Salad with Grilled Beef, Mushrooms, and Miso-Ginger Dressing
174 Skirt Steak Fajitas
176 Grilled Skirt Steak and Poblano Tacos
178 Grilled London Broil
 Sweet and Smoky Grilled Tomato Salsa
180 Inexpensive Grill-Roasted Beef with Garlic and Rosemary
 with Shallot and Tarragon
184 Grill-Roasted Beef Tenderloin
 Smoked Grill-Roasted Beef Tenderloin
186 Baltimore Pit Beef
188 California Barbecued Tri-Tip
 Santa Maria Salsa
190 Grilled Beef Satay
 Peanut Sauce

PORK

152 Wisconsin Brats and Beer
154 Grilled Sausages with Onions
 with Peppers and Onions
 with Fennel
157 Texas Smoked Sausages
192 Grilled Pork Kebabs with Hoisin and Five-Spice
 with Sweet Sriracha Glaze
 with Barbecue Glaze
194 Ancho-Rubbed Grilled Pork Chops
196 Grilled Stuffed Pork Chops
 Grilled Sausage-Stuffed Pork Chops
 Grilled Southwestern Stuffed Pork Chops
198 Grill-Smoked Pork Chops
200 Smoked Double-Thick Pork Chops
202 Smoked Pork Loin
 Basic Pantry Barbecue Sauce
 Five-Alarm Barbecue Sauce
 Chinese-Style Barbecue Sauce
 Honey-Scallion Barbecue Sauce
204 Grilled Rosemary Pork Loin
206 Grilled Garlic-Lime Pork Tenderloin Steaks
 Grilled Lemon-Thyme Pork Tenderloin Steaks
 Grilled Spicy Orange-Ginger Pork Tenderloin Steaks
208 Spice-Crusted Grilled Pork Tenderloin
 Everything Bagel–Crusted Grilled Pork Tenderloin
 Coffee-and-Fennel-Crusted Grilled Pork Tenderloin
210 Grilled Glazed Pork Tenderloin Roast
 Miso Glaze
 Sweet and Spicy Hoisin Glaze
 Satay Glaze

LAMB

212 Grilled Lamb Kofte
 Grilled Beef Kofte
214 Grilled Rack of Lamb
 with Sweet Mustard Glaze
216 Grilled Butterflied Leg of Lamb
 with Tandoori Marinade
 with Greek-Style Marinade
 with Soy-Honey Marinade
 with Garlic-Rosemary Marinade

POULTRY

140 Juicy Grilled Turkey Burgers
 Malt Vinegar–Molasses Burger Sauce
 Apricot-Mustard Burger Sauce
 Chile-Lime Burger Sauce
219 Grilled Tequila Chicken with Orange, Avocado, and Pepita Salad
220 Grilled Chicken Tacos with Salsa Verde

222 Monterey Chicken
    Pico de Gallo
224 Easy Stuffed Chicken Breasts
    Greek-Style Grilled Stuffed Chicken Breasts
226 Chicken Souvlaki
229 Barbecued Chicken Kebabs
230 Peach-Glazed Grilled Chicken
233 Kentucky Bourbon Brined Grilled Chicken
234 Sweet and Tangy Barbecued Chicken
236 Citrus-and-Spice Grilled Chicken
238 Cornell Chicken
240 Peri Peri Grilled Chicken
242 Alabama Barbecued Chicken
245 Grilled Indian-Spiced Chicken with Raita
246 Thai-Style Grilled Chicken with Spicy Sweet and
    Sour Dipping Sauce
248 Jerk Chicken
251 Huli Huli Chicken
252 Smoked Chicken
254 Grill-Roasted Chicken
    with Tangy Barbecue Sauce
256 Grilled Butterflied Chicken Diavola
258 Grilled Butterflied Lemon Chicken
260 Grilled Wine-and-Herb Marinated Chicken
262 Glazed Grill-Roasted Chicken
    Honey-Mustard Glaze
    Brown Sugar–Balsamic Glaze
    Spicy Molasses Glaze

FISH & SEAFOOD
142 Salmon Burgers
    Creamy Lemon-Herb Sauce
    Creamy Chipotle-Lime Sauce
144 Tuna Burgers
    Wasabi Mayonnaise
146 Grilled Southern Shrimp Burgers
264 Grilled Fish Tacos
267 Grilled Shrimp Tacos with Jícama Slaw
    Overnight Mexican Crema
    Quick Mexican Crema
268 Grilled Jalapeño and Lime Shrimp Skewers
    Grilled Red Chile and Ginger Shrimp Skewers

270 Grilled Bacon-Wrapped Scallops
272 Grilled Tuna Steaks with Vinaigrette
    with Chermoula Vinaigrette
    with Soy-Ginger Vinaigrette
274 Grilled Salmon Steaks with Lemon-Caper Sauce
    with Orange-Ginger Sauce
    with Lime-Cilantro Sauce
    with Olive Vinaigrette
276 Grill-Smoked Salmon
    "Smoked Salmon Platter" Sauce
278 Grilled Blackened Red Snapper
    Pineapple and Cucumber Salsa with
      Mint Rémoulade
281 Maryland-Style Grilled Shrimp and Corn
282 Grilled Clams, Mussels, or Oysters
    Grilled Mussels
    Grilled Oysters
    with Spicy Lemon Butter
    with Tangy Soy-Citrus Sauce
    with Mignonette Sauce

VEGETABLES
148 Ultimate Veggie Burgers
150 Mediterranean-Style Portobello Burgers
286 Grilled Caesar Salad
288 Grilled Chicken Caesar Salad
290 Grilled Vegetable Kebabs
291 Charred Carrot Salad
293 Charred Fingerling Potato Salad
294 Smoky Grilled Potato Salad
297 Grilled Sweet Potatoes with Chimichurri Sauce
299 Mexican-Style Grilled Corn
300 Grilled Eggplant and Bell Peppers with
    Mint-Cumin Dressing
301 Grilled Zucchini and Red Onion with
    Lemon-Basil Vinaigrette

BREAD
284 Grilled Tomato and Cheese Pizzas
    Spicy Garlic Oil
302 Grilled Vegetable and Bread Salad
304 Tunisian-Style Grilled Vegetables (Mechouia)

231 RECIPE FOR SUCCESS Pull-Out-All-the-Stops Backyard Burgers

✓ WHY THIS RECIPE WORKS

Patties made of preground chuck are easy, but we were after a charred crust, rich beefy taste, and juicy interior that are hard to get from supermarket ground beef. This is because the way ground beef is handled during processing draws out sticky proteins that create a dense texture in the burger. To avoid this, we ground our own meat and switched from chuck to sirloin steak tips, which contain less connective tissue and just the right amount of fat. We froze the meat to make grinding easier and added butter for flavor and richness. We also froze the patties after forming them to ensure that by the time they'd thawed at their centers, they had developed a perfect outer crust. We cooked the burgers over a superhot fire for great char and flavor.

Tender, Juicy Grilled Burgers

SERVES 4

This recipe requires freezing the meat twice, for a total of 1 hour 5 minutes to 1 hour 20 minutes, before grilling. When stirring the salt and pepper into the ground meat and shaping the patties, take care not to overwork the meat or the burgers will become dense. Sirloin steak tips are also sold as flap meat. Serve the burgers with your favorite toppings or one of our grilled-vegetable toppings (recipes follow). If making a grilled-vegetable topping, start preparing the topping while the patties are in the freezer and grill the vegetables before you grill the burgers. Finish the topping while the burgers rest. You can also toast the buns on the grill while the burgers rest.

1½	pounds sirloin steak tips, trimmed and cut into ½-inch chunks
4	tablespoons unsalted butter, cut into ¼-inch pieces
	Kosher salt and pepper
1	(13 by 9-inch) disposable aluminum pan (if using charcoal)
4	hamburger buns

1 Place beef chunks and butter on large plate in single layer. Freeze until meat is very firm and starting to harden around edges but still pliable, about 35 minutes.

2 Place one-quarter of meat and one-quarter of butter cubes in food processor and pulse until finely ground into pieces size of rice grains (about ⅟32 inch), 15 to 20 pulses, stopping and redistributing meat around bowl as necessary to ensure beef is evenly ground. Transfer meat to rimmed baking sheet. Repeat grinding in 3 batches with remaining meat and butter. Spread mixture over sheet and inspect carefully, discarding any long strands of gristle or large chunks of hard meat, fat, or butter.

3 Sprinkle ¾ teaspoon salt and 1 teaspoon pepper and over meat and gently toss with fork to combine. Divide meat into 4 portions. Working with 1 portion at a time, lightly toss from hand to hand to form ball, then gently flatten into ¾-inch-thick patty. Press center of patties down with your fingertips to create ¼-inch-deep depression. Transfer patties to platter and freeze for 30 to 45 minutes.

4A FOR A CHARCOAL GRILL Using skewer, poke 12 holes in bottom of disposable pan. Open bottom vent completely and place disposable pan in center of grill. Light large chimney starter two-thirds filled with charcoal briquettes (4 quarts). When top coals are partially covered with ash, pour into disposable pan. Set cooking grate in place, cover, and open lid vent completely. Heat grill until hot, about 5 minutes.

4B FOR A GAS GRILL Turn all burners to high, cover, and heat grill until hot, about 15 minutes. Leave all burners on high.

5 Clean and oil cooking grate. Season 1 side of patties liberally with salt and pepper. Using spatula, flip patties and season other side. Place burgers on grill (directly over coals if using charcoal) and cook, without pressing on them, until browned and meat easily releases from grill, 4 to 7 minutes. Flip burgers and continue to grill until browned on second side and meat registers 125 degrees (for medium-rare) or 130 degrees (for medium), 4 to 7 minutes longer.

6 Transfer burgers to plate and let rest for 5 minutes. Serve on buns.

232 Grilled Scallion Topping
MAKES ABOUT ¾ CUP

- 2 tablespoons sour cream
- 2 tablespoons mayonnaise
- 2 tablespoons buttermilk
- 1 tablespoon cider vinegar
- 1 tablespoon minced fresh chives
- 2 teaspoons Dijon mustard
- ¼ teaspoon sugar
  Salt and pepper
- 20 scallions
- 2 tablespoons vegetable oil

1 Combine sour cream, mayonnaise, buttermilk, vinegar, chives, mustard, sugar, ½ teaspoon salt, and ⅛ teaspoon pepper in medium bowl. Set aside.

2 Toss scallions with oil in large bowl (do not clean bowl). Grill scallions over hot fire until lightly charred and softened, 2 to 4 minutes per side. Return to bowl and let cool, 5 minutes. Slice scallions thin, then transfer to bowl with reserved sour cream mixture. Toss to combine and season with salt and pepper to taste.

233 Grilled Shiitake Mushroom Topping
MAKES ABOUT ¾ CUP

- 2 tablespoons sour cream
- 2 tablespoons mayonnaise
- 2 tablespoons buttermilk
- 1 tablespoon cider vinegar
- 1 tablespoon minced fresh chives
- 2 teaspoons Dijon mustard
- ¼ teaspoon sugar
  Salt and pepper
- 8 ounces shiitake mushrooms, stemmed
- 2 tablespoons vegetable oil

1 Combine sour cream, mayonnaise, buttermilk, vinegar, chives, mustard, sugar, ½ teaspoon salt, and ⅛ teaspoon pepper in medium bowl. Set aside.

2 Toss mushrooms with oil in large bowl (do not clean bowl). Grill mushrooms over hot fire until lightly charred and softened, 2 to 4 minutes per side. Return to bowl and let cool, 5 minutes. Slice mushrooms thin, then transfer to bowl with reserved sour cream mixture. Toss to combine and season with salt and pepper to taste.

234 Grilled Napa Cabbage and Radicchio Topping
MAKES ABOUT ¾ CUP

- 2 tablespoons sour cream
- 2 tablespoons mayonnaise
- 2 tablespoons buttermilk
- 1 tablespoon cider vinegar
- 1 tablespoon minced fresh parsley
- 2 teaspoons Dijon mustard
- ¼ teaspoon sugar
  Salt and pepper
- ¼ small head napa cabbage
- ½ small head radicchio, cut into 2 wedges
- 2 tablespoons vegetable oil

1 Combine sour cream, mayonnaise, buttermilk, vinegar, parsley, mustard, sugar, ½ teaspoon salt, and ⅛ teaspoon pepper in medium bowl. Set aside.

2 Place cabbage and radicchio on rimmed baking sheet and brush with oil (do not clean sheet). Grill over hot fire until lightly charred and beginning to wilt, 2 to 4 minutes on each cut side. Return to sheet and let cool, 5 minutes. Slice cabbage and radicchio thin, then transfer to bowl with reserved sour cream mixture. Toss to combine and season with salt and pepper to taste.

235 SHOPPING IQ
A Better Bun

A great burger deserves a great bun. In a tasting of supermarket hamburger buns, we were surprised by the differences in flavor and texture. Sunbeam and Wonder were so airy that they all but deflated if grasped too firmly, while heartier brands stood up well to wet condiments. But the dealbreaker was size: Of eight products, six measured less than 3½ inches across—a tight fit for most patties.

THE BOTTOM LINE Size matters (along with taste). **Pepperidge Farm Premium Bakery Rolls** (not the smaller "Classic" variety) boast a generous 4½-inch diameter, hearty texture and "wheaty" taste, and the least amount of sugar in the lineup.

236 RECIPE FOR SUCCESS
Bigger-on-the-Inside Burgers

✔ WHY THIS RECIPE WORKS

We love a burger that's stacked high with add-ons, but we couldn't help but wonder whether there was a way to take some of the "top" out of the toppings. We wanted to put the same bold flavors inside the burger, instead. We started with some classic burger toppings: cheese, bacon, and mustard. Because the cheese and bacon added a good amount of fat to the meat, we switched from 80 percent lean ground beef, which is our usual favorite, to 90 percent lean for this recipe. We also found that we liked these burgers cooked until they were completely well-done. The additions to the meat kept it from getting dried out. We then went on to more adventurous flavor combinations using firm cheese and potent ingredients with minimal moisture (such as garlic, herbs, chiles, and powdered seasoning mixes). These burgers may not be piled high with colorful toppings, but one bite will prove that looks aren't everything—it's what's inside that really counts.

All-in-One Grilled Burgers
SERVES 4

We suggest cooking these burgers completely (to well-done); the extra ingredients tend to make them taste mushy if not cooked all the way through. If you like, toast the hamburger buns on the grill while the burgers rest.

- 8 slices bacon, chopped fine
- 1½ pounds 90 percent lean ground beef
- 4 ounces sharp cheddar cheese, shredded (1 cup)
- 4 teaspoons yellow mustard
- 2 teaspoons Worcestershire sauce
- ½ teaspoon salt
- ½ teaspoon pepper
- 4 hamburger buns

1 Cook bacon in 12-inch skillet over medium heat, stirring occasionally, until brown and crisp, 10 to 12 minutes. Using slotted spoon, transfer bacon to paper towel–lined plate.

2 Break ground beef into small pieces in bowl, then add cheddar, mustard, Worcestershire, salt, pepper, and bacon. Using your hands, lightly knead mixture until combined. Divide meat into 4 equal portions. Working with 1 portion at a time, lightly toss from hand to hand to form loose ball, then gently flatten into 1-inch-thick patty. Press center of patties down with your fingertips to create ¼-inch-deep depression.

3A FOR A CHARCOAL GRILL Open bottom vent completely. Light large chimney starter filled with charcoal briquettes (6 quarts). When top coals are partially covered with ash pour evenly over grill. Set cooking grate in place, cover, and open lid vent completely. Heat grill until hot, about 5 minutes.

3B FOR A GAS GRILL Turn all burners to high, cover, and heat grill until hot, about 15 minutes. Leave all burners on high.

4 Clean and oil cooking grate. Place burgers on grill and cook, without pressing on them, until browned and meat easily releases from grill, 4 to 6 minutes. Flip burgers and continue to grill until browned on second side and meat registers 150 to 155 degrees (for well-done), 4 to 6 minutes longer. Transfer burgers to platter, tent with aluminum foil, and let rest for 5 minutes. Serve on buns.

VARIATIONS

237 **Ranch All-in-One Grilled Burgers**
Omit bacon, cheddar, mustard, and Worcestershire. Add ⅔ cup crumbled blue cheese, 4 teaspoons powdered ranch dressing mix (from packet), and 2 minced garlic cloves to burger mixture in step 2.

238 **Tex-Mex All-in-One Grilled Burgers**
Omit bacon, cheddar, mustard, Worcestershire, salt, and pepper. Add 1 cup shredded Monterey Jack cheese, ¼ cup chopped fresh cilantro, 4 teaspoons minced canned chipotle chile in adobo sauce, and 4 teaspoons taco seasoning (from packet) to burger mixture in step 2.

239 **Italian All-in-One Grilled Burgers**
Omit bacon, cheddar, mustard, and Worcestershire. Add ½ cup grated Parmesan cheese, ¼ cup chopped fresh basil, 4 teaspoons Dijon mustard, and 2 minced garlic cloves to burger mixture in step 2.

240 SHOPPING IQ
Boffo Bacon

Good bacon is meaty, smoky without tasting like an ashtray, salty without imitating a salt lick, and sweet without being cloying—it has what industry experts call "balanced bacon flavor." We rounded up thick-cut and traditional slices of nationally available supermarket bacons. Tasters took off points for strips that were too fatty, and panned the brand that used vaporized smoke instead of traditional smoking techniques. Thick strips with high ratios of protein to fat, which contributed to more complex flavor, consistently topped tasters' rankings. Their "substantial," "crisp" texture also won us over.

THE BOTTOM LINE The best supermarket bacon combines salty, sweet, and smoky elements in a thick-cut strip for optimal flavor. **Farmland Thick-Sliced Bacon** and **Plumrose Premium Thick Sliced Bacon** take top honors in the test kitchen.

WINNERS

FARMLAND Thick-Sliced Bacon
Tasting Comments This thick strip was also one of the meatiest, with saltiness offset by sweetness, all combining to deliver bacon balance. Tasters described it as "a good meaty slice" that was "sweet," "smoky, porky, and salty."

PLUMROSE Premium Thick Sliced Bacon
Tasting Comments With one of the highest amounts of protein, this "substantially meaty" bacon was "pleasantly smoky," "with very little fat." Plumrose is the only brand cured with brown sugar, which contributed to its "deeply browned, Maillard flavor."

241
GRILL HACK
Squeaky-Clean Squeeze Tops

Squeeze bottle tops can get caked with ketchup, mayonnaise, and mustard. Save the cleaned tops from empty bottles and store. When the top of a new bottle gets dirty, unscrew it, throw it in the dishwasher, and replace with a clean one.

242 RECIPE FOR SUCCESS Meatloaf Meets Burger

✓ WHY THIS RECIPE WORKS

We wanted to find a way to take the familiar, homey taste of meatloaf and turn it into a fast and accessible dinner option, in the form of individual meatloaf burgers. We started by switching from the usual ground beef to meatloaf mix, which contains beef, pork, and veal, for distinctive flavor and texture. We then added a few high-impact ingredients to create the taste of meatloaf in our burgers: an egg, Worcestershire sauce, fresh thyme, ketchup, brown sugar, and cider vinegar. While this ingredient list is much shorter than our traditional meatloaf recipe, these additions gave us the essence of meatloaf while keeping this recipe safely within the average home pantry. Cooked to well-done, these easy burgers were a quick fix for a meatloaf craving without ever having to turn on the oven.

243 FOOD SCIENCE How to Prevent Burger Sog Out

Who hasn't eaten a burger on a bun so saturated with meat juices that it was practically falling apart? There's an easy way to mitigate that problem: Let your burgers rest briefly before placing them on buns. In raw meat, most of the juices are stored in individual structures called myofibrils. Cooking causes the proteins to contract and expel some of the liquid. If the meat is given a chance to rest off heat, the proteins relax, allowing some of the juices to be reabsorbed. We advocate a rest for most meat, but it's particularly important for burgers. Burgers are always cooked directly over high heat, which raises their temperature at the surface. This in turn causes the proteins to be squeezed harder, so more moisture is lost. Letting ground beef rest is also important because a significant amount of fat will drain away instead of collecting in the bun.

THE BOTTOM LINE For perfect burgers (and buns), let the burgers rest for 5 minutes, tented with foil and preferably on a rack so moisture doesn't collect underneath, before transferring them to buns.

Meatloaf Burgers

SERVES 4

You can substitute equal parts ground beef and ground pork for the meatloaf mix. If you like, toast the hamburger buns on the grill while the burgers rest.

- 1½ **pounds meatloaf mix**
- 1 **large egg**
- 2 **teaspoons Worcestershire sauce**
- 1 **teaspoon minced fresh thyme**
- ½ **teaspoon salt**
- ½ **teaspoon pepper**
- ½ **cup ketchup**
- 2 **tablespoons packed brown sugar**
- 2 **teaspoons cider vinegar**
- 4 **hamburger buns**

1 Combine meatloaf mix, egg, Worcestershire, thyme, salt, and pepper in bowl. Divide mixture into 4 portions. Working with 1 portion at a time, lightly toss from hand to hand to form ball, then gently flatten into ¾-inch-thick patty. Press center of patties down with your fingertips to create ¼-inch-deep depression. Whisk ketchup, sugar, and vinegar in bowl until combined. Set aside 5 tablespoons glaze for serving.

2A FOR A CHARCOAL GRILL Open bottom vent completely. Light large chimney starter filled with charcoal briquettes (6 quarts). When top coals are partially covered with ash pour evenly over grill. Set cooking grate in place, cover, and open lid vent completely. Heat grill until hot, about 5 minutes.

2B FOR A GAS GRILL Turn all burners to high, cover, and heat grill until hot, about 15 minutes. Leave all burners on high.

3 Clean and oil cooking grate. Place burgers on grill and cook, without pressing on them, until well browned on first side, 5 to 7 minutes. Flip burgers and brush with remaining glaze. Cook until meat registers 150 to 155 degrees (for well-done), about 7 minutes. Transfer burgers to wire rack on plate and tent with aluminum foil; let rest on wire rack for 5 minutes. Serve on buns with reserved glaze.

244

GRILL HACK

Condiment Cups

When serving condiments at your next backyard barbecue, use a jumbo muffin tin to contain condiments like ketchup, mustard, relish, chopped onion, and pickles. The toppings stay together and you have only one container to clean at the end of the party.

245 Have Grill, Can Travel

Not even our favorite no-frills charcoal grill, the Weber Performer Deluxe (see page 34), is compact enough to travel farther than the backyard. Fortunately, there's another option for picnics and beach barbecues: the EZ Grill Disposable Instant Grill. Inside the box is an all-in-one grill—essentially an aluminum pan (perforated for airflow) fitted with a metal grate on top and wire legs on the bottom— plus two packages of "easy to light" charcoal. We had our doubts—the whole kit looked pretty flimsy—but once we struck a match, we were cooking. The spacious cooking surface accommodated three steaks at a time with room to spare, and the heat held steady enough for us to follow up with three chicken breasts—a total of more than 45 minutes of cooking time. Once cool, the grill can be thrown away or recycled.

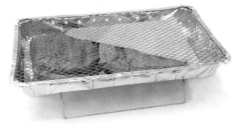

THE BOTTOM LINE We wouldn't use the **EZ Grill** ($10.99) for a big backyard barbecue, but it's ideal for a movable feast.

246 RECIPE FOR SUCCESS
Steak on a Bun

✓ WHY THIS RECIPE WORKS
Most so-called steak burgers are plain beef patties drowning in A.1. Steak Sauce. We wanted something the best steakhouses would be proud to serve: a robust burger with the big beefy flavor and crusty char of a grilled steak. Ground sirloin, the most flavorful ground beef, was a natural choice, but unfortunately it's also quite lean. A seasoned butter mixed in with the meat added richness to the sirloin, but something was missing—steak sauce! Rather than turn to a store-bought sauce, we simmered up our own intensely favored sauce in about 5 minutes. It was perfect for serving with the burger, smearing on the bun, and even mixing into the beef before cooking for intense flavor.

Grilled Steak Burgers
SERVES 4

Use kaiser rolls or other hearty buns for these substantial burgers.

BURGERS

- 8   tablespoons unsalted butter
- 2   garlic cloves, minced
- 2   teaspoons onion powder
- 1   teaspoon pepper
- ½   teaspoon salt
- 2   teaspoons soy sauce
- 1½ pounds 90 percent lean ground sirloin
- 4   hamburger buns

STEAK SAUCE

- 2   tablespoons tomato paste
- ⅔   cup beef broth
- ⅓   cup raisins
- 2   tablespoons soy sauce
- 2   tablespoons Dijon mustard
- 2   tablespoons balsamic vinegar
- 1   tablespoon Worcestershire sauce

1 FOR THE BURGERS Melt butter in 8-inch skillet over medium-low heat. Add garlic, onion powder, pepper, and salt and cook until fragrant, about 1 minute. Pour all but 1 tablespoon butter mixture into bowl and let cool for about 5 minutes.

2 FOR THE STEAK SAUCE While butter mixture cools, add tomato paste to skillet and cook over medium heat until paste begins to darken, 1 to 2 minutes. Stir in broth, raisins, soy sauce, mustard, vinegar, and Worcestershire and simmer until raisins plump, about 5 minutes. Process sauce in blender until smooth, about 30 seconds; transfer to bowl.

3 Add soy sauce and 5 tablespoons cooled butter mixture to ground beef and gently knead until well combined. Divide into 4 portions. Working with 1 portion at a time, lightly toss from hand to hand to form ball, then gently flatten into ¾-inch-thick patty. Press center of patties down with your fingertips to create ¼-inch-deep depression. Brush each patty all over with 1 tablespoon steak sauce. Combine remaining 2 tablespoons cooled butter mixture with 2 tablespoons steak sauce; set aside.

4A FOR A CHARCOAL GRILL Open bottom vent completely. Light large chimney starter filled with charcoal briquettes (6 quarts). When top coals are partially covered with ash, pour evenly over grill. Set cooking grate in place, cover, and open lid vent completely. Heat grill until hot, about 5 minutes.

4B FOR A GAS GRILL Turn all burners to high, cover, and heat grill until hot, about 15 minutes. Leave all burners on high.

5 Clean and oil cooking grate. Place burgers on grill and cook (covered if using gas), without pressing on them, until browned and meat easily releases from grill, 3 to 4 minutes. Flip burgers and continue to grill until browned on second side and meat registers 120 to 125 degrees (for medium-rare) or 130 to 135 degrees (for medium), 4 to 5 minutes longer. Transfer burgers to plate, tent with aluminum foil, and let rest for 5 to 10 minutes. Brush cut side of buns with butter–steak sauce mixture. Grill buns, cut side down, until golden, 2 to 3 minutes. Serve on buns with remaining steak sauce.

247
TEST KITCHEN TIP
Storing Tomato Paste

Recipes often call for only a tablespoon or two of tomato paste. Unfortunately, the rest of the can usually ends up turning brown in the refrigerator and then being discarded. Eliminate this waste by using the following tip.

1 Open both ends of tomato paste can. Remove lid from 1 end and use lid at other end to push paste out onto sheet of plastic wrap. (This method also works as a neat way of getting other solid ingredients, such as frozen juice and almond paste, out of cans.)

2 Wrap tomato paste in plastic wrap and place it in freezer.

3 When paste has frozen, cut off amount needed for recipe and then return frozen log to freezer.

248 Burgers with a Surprise

✓ WHY THIS RECIPE WORKS

Minneapolis taverns are famous for the Jucy Lucy, a moist beef burger stuffed with American cheese. Replicating the Jucy Lucy seemed like it would be easy enough, but our burgers, cooked well-done to melt the cheese inside, were dry and tough. Even worse, the cheese melted right through the meat, leaving an empty cavern in the middle of the burger where the cheese had been. To keep the cheese in place, we created a double-sealed pocket by wrapping the cheese inside a small beef patty and then molding a second, larger patty around it. Adding a panade (a mixture of bread and milk, mashed into a paste) to the ground beef kept the burgers moist and juicy.

Jucy Lucy Burgers

SERVES 4

Buy the American cheese from the deli counter, and ask them to slice it into a ½-inch slab from which you can cut four big cubes to fill the centers of the burgers. You can substitute 1 percent or 2 percent low-fat milk for the whole milk. The cheesy center of these burgers is molten hot when first removed from the grill, so be sure to let the burgers rest for at least 5 minutes before serving. If you like, toast the hamburger buns on the grill while the burgers rest.

2 slices hearty white sandwich bread, torn into 1-inch pieces

¼ cup whole milk

1 teaspoon garlic powder

¾ teaspoon salt

½ teaspoon pepper

1½ pounds 85 percent lean ground beef

1 (½-inch-thick) piece deli American cheese, quartered

4 hamburger buns

1 In large bowl and using potato masher, mash bread, milk, garlic powder, salt, and pepper into smooth paste. Add beef and lightly knead mixture until well combined.

2 Divide meat into 4 equal portions. Using half of 1 portion of meat, encase 1 cube cheese to form mini burger patty. Mold remaining half-portion of meat around mini patty and seal edges to form ball. Flatten ball with palm of your hand, forming ¾-inch-thick patty. Repeat with remaining meat and cheese. Cover and refrigerate patties for at least 30 minutes or up to 24 hours.

3A FOR A CHARCOAL GRILL Open bottom vent completely. Light large chimney starter half filled with charcoal briquettes (3 quarts). When top coals are partially covered with ash, pour evenly over grill. Set cooking grate in place, cover, and open lid vent completely. Heat grill until hot, about 5 minutes.

3B FOR A GAS GRILL Turn all burners to high, cover, and heat grill until hot, about 15 minutes. Turn all burners to medium.

4 Clean and oil cooking grate. Place burgers on grill and cook, without pressing on them, until well browned on first side, 6 to 8 minutes. Flip burgers and cook until well browned and cooked through, 6 to 8 minutes. Transfer burgers to platter, tent with aluminum foil, and let rest for 5 minutes. Serve on buns.

249 STEP BY STEP Form a Jucy Lucy

To avoid a burger blowout, it's essential to completely seal in the cheese. Don't worry about overworking the meat; adding milk and bread to the ground beef ensures tender, juicy burgers every time.

1 ENCASE Using half of each portion of meat, surround cheese to form mini burger patty.

2 SEAL Mold remaining half-portion of meat around mini patty and seal edges to form ball.

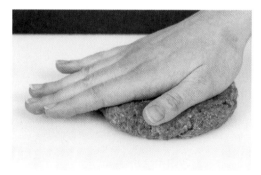

3 FLATTEN Press ball with palm of your hand to flatten, forming ¾-inch-thick patty.

250 RECIPE FOR SUCCESS Turning Up the Heat on Cheeseburgers

☑ WHY THIS RECIPE WORKS

For our version of New Mexico's green chile cheeseburgers—ground beef patties grilled to a crusty brown and topped with chopped fire-roasted chiles and a slice of cheese—we preferred the flavor and fat of 85 percent lean ground beef. For the topping, we used mild Anaheim chiles and spicy jalapeños for a complex chile flavor. We grilled the chiles with onions and then quickly chopped them with fresh garlic in the food processor. For even more chile flavor, we pureed some of the chile topping into a smooth paste and mixed it into the raw ground beef. This gave us burgers with satisfying (but not overwhelming) heat through and through.

Green Chile Cheeseburgers

SERVES 4

For more heat, include the jalapeño ribs and seeds. In step 3, you may need to add a teaspoon or two of water to the food processor to help the chile mixture puree. If you like, toast the hamburger buns on the grill while the burgers rest. Serve the burgers with your favorite toppings.

- 3 Anaheim chiles, stemmed, halved, and seeded
- 3 jalapeño chiles, stemmed, halved, and seeded
- 1 onion, sliced into ½-inch-thick rounds
- 1 garlic clove, minced
  Salt and pepper
- 1½ pounds 85 percent lean ground beef
- 4 slices deli American cheese (4 ounces)
- 4 hamburger buns

1A FOR A CHARCOAL GRILL Open bottom vent completely. Light large chimney starter filled with charcoal briquettes (6 quarts). When top coals are partially covered with ash, pour evenly over grill. Set cooking grate in place, cover, and open lid vent completely. Heat grill until hot, about 5 minutes.

1B FOR A GAS GRILL Turn all burners to high, cover, and heat grill until hot, about 15 minutes. Leave all burners on high.

2 Clean and oil cooking grate. Lay chiles and onion on grill and cook until vegetables are lightly charred and tender, 2 to 4 minutes per side. Transfer vegetables to bowl, cover, and let sit for 5 minutes. Remove skins from chiles and discard; separate onion rounds into rings.

3 Transfer chiles, onion, and garlic to food processor and pulse until coarsely chopped, about 10 pulses. Transfer all but ¼ cup chopped chile mixture to empty bowl and season with salt and pepper to taste; set aside. Process remaining chile mixture until smooth.

4 Combine beef, pureed chile mixture, ½ teaspoon salt, and ¼ teaspoon pepper in large bowl and gently knead until well incorporated. Divide into 4 portions. Working with 1 portion at a time, lightly toss from hand to hand to form ball, then gently flatten into ¾-inch-thick patty. Press center of patties down with your fingertips to create ¼-inch-deep depression.

5 Place burgers on grill and cook, covered, until browned on first side, 3 to 5 minutes. Flip burgers, top each with chopped chile mixture and 1 slice cheese, and continue to grill, covered, until cheese is melted and meat registers 120 to 125 degrees (for medium-rare) or 130 to 135 degrees (for medium), 3 to 5 minutes longer. Serve on buns.

251 GADGETS & GEAR
Don't Run Out of Gas

It happens to all of us: We're right in the middle of grilling dinner and the fire quits because the grill runs out of propane gas. We wondered: Are there products to help us avoid that annoyance, and if so, how do they stack up? We tested three propane level indicators, which are designed to show how much fuel you have in your tank. One model sounds an alarm when you've got two hours of cooking time left. Unfortunately, it works only when the grill is ignited. Another indicator works much like a mood ring, with sporadically illuminating color bars that we found nearly indecipherable. We much preferred the Original Grill Gauge, which looks like a car's gas gauge. You hook the indicator to the collar of the tank; when you lift the tank three inches off the ground, it registers the gas level by weight.

THE BOTTOM LINE The **Original Grill Gauge** ($13.99) is our top pick for propane indicators.

1 (2-pound) bone-in turkey thigh, skinned, boned, trimmed, and cut into ½-inch pieces
1 tablespoon unflavored gelatin
3 tablespoons chicken broth
6 ounces white mushrooms, trimmed
1 tablespoon soy sauce
   Pinch baking soda
2 tablespoons vegetable oil, plus extra for brushing
   Kosher salt and pepper
6 hamburger buns

RECIPE FOR SUCCESS

252 Turkey Burgers with a Meaty Punch

✔ WHY THIS RECIPE WORKS

Most turkey burgers are dry, bland, or loaded up with flavor-blunting fillers. To create juicy, well-textured turkey burgers, we ditched store-bought ground turkey in favor of a home-ground turkey thigh, which boasts more fat and flavor. To ensure that our turkey burger recipe delivered maximum juiciness, we incorporated a paste made from a portion of the ground turkey, gelatin, soy sauce, and baking soda. The gelatin trapped moisture within the burgers while the baking soda helped tenderize the meat by raising its pH, and the soy sauce added savory umami flavor. Finally, we added coarsely chopped raw white mushrooms to keep the meat from binding together too firmly. To top the burgers, we created a variety of sweet and savory sauces that complemented the rich dark meat of the turkey.

Juicy Grilled Turkey Burgers

SERVES 6

To ensure the best texture, don't let the burgers stand for more than an hour before cooking. If you like, toast the hamburger buns on the grill while the burgers rest. Serve with one of our burger sauces (recipes follow) or your favorite toppings.

1 Place turkey pieces on large plate in single layer. Freeze meat until very firm and hardened around edges, 35 to 45 minutes. Meanwhile, sprinkle gelatin over broth in small bowl and let sit until gelatin softens, about 5 minutes. Pulse mushrooms in food processor until coarsely chopped, about 7 pulses, stopping and redistributing mushrooms around bowl as needed to ensure even grinding. Set mushrooms aside.

2 Pulse one-third of turkey in now-empty food processor until coarsely chopped into ⅛-inch pieces, 18 to 22 pulses, stopping and redistributing turkey around bowl as needed to ensure even grinding. Transfer meat to large bowl and repeat 2 more times with remaining turkey.

3 Return ½ cup (about 3 ounces) ground turkey to bowl of again-empty food processor and add soy sauce, baking soda, and softened gelatin. Process until smooth, about 2 minutes, scraping down bowl as needed. With processor running, slowly drizzle in oil, about 10 seconds; leave paste in food processor. Return mushrooms to food processor and pulse to combine with paste, 3 to 5 pulses, stopping and redistributing mixture as needed to ensure even mixing. Transfer mushroom mixture to bowl with ground turkey and use your hands to evenly combine.

4 With lightly greased hands, divide meat mixture into 6 balls. Gently flatten each ball into ¾-inch-thick patty. Press center of patties down with your fingertips to create ¼-inch-deep depression.

5A FOR A CHARCOAL GRILL Open bottom vent completely. Light large chimney starter filled with charcoal briquettes (6 quarts). When top coals are partially covered with ash, pour evenly over half of grill. Set cooking grate in place, cover, and open lid vent completely. Heat grill until hot, about 5 minutes.

5B FOR A GAS GRILL Turn all burners to high, cover, and heat grill until hot, about 15 minutes. Leave primary burner on high and turn off other burner(s).

6 Clean and oil cooking grate. Brush 1 side of patties with oil and season with salt and pepper. Using spatula, flip patties, brush with oil, and season second side. Place burgers on hotter side of grill and cook until well browned on first side, 4 to 7 minutes. Flip burgers and cook until well browned on second side and meat registers 160 degrees, 4 to 7 minutes more. (If cooking frozen burgers: After burgers are browned on both sides, transfer to cooler side of grill, cover, and continue to cook until burgers register 160 degrees.)

7 Transfer burgers to plate and let rest for 5 minutes. Serve on buns.

253 Malt Vinegar–Molasses Burger Sauce
MAKES ABOUT 1 CUP

- ¾ cup mayonnaise
- 4 teaspoons malt vinegar
- ½ teaspoon molasses
- ¼ teaspoon Worcestershire sauce
- ¼ teaspoon salt
- ¼ teaspoon pepper

Whisk all ingredients together in bowl.

254 Apricot-Mustard Burger Sauce
MAKES ABOUT 1 CUP

- ¾ cup mayonnaise
- 5 teaspoons apricot preserves
- 1 tablespoon lemon juice
- 1 tablespoon Dijon mustard
- 1 tablespoon whole-grain mustard
- ¼ teaspoon sugar

Whisk all ingredients together in bowl.

255 Chile-Lime Burger Sauce
MAKES ABOUT 1 CUP

- ¾ cup mayonnaise
- 2 teaspoons chile-garlic paste
- 2 teaspoons lime juice
- 1 scallion, sliced thin
- ¼ teaspoon fish sauce
- ⅛ teaspoon sugar

Whisk all ingredients together in bowl.

256 STEP BY STEP How We Built a Better Burger

Swapping out lean, bland commercial ground turkey for a freshly ground turkey thigh (we use a food processor) was only our first step toward a juicier, more meaty-tasting burger.

1 GRIND DARK MEAT Turkey thighs contain more fat and flavor than lean white meat.

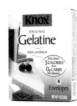

2 MIX IN MUSHROOMS They add moisture and flavor, and lighten the texture of the meat.

3 ADD BAKING SODA Just a pinch tenderizes the meat by raising its pH.

4 ADD GELATIN Gelatin acts like a sponge, holding up to 10 times its own weight in water.

257 RECIPE FOR SUCCESS Nothing Fishy About These Burgers

✓ WHY THIS RECIPE WORKS

The main problem to overcome when making salmon burgers is their relatively low fat content—they tend to get overcooked very fast over the high heat of the grill. Slightly undercooking the burgers helped, but we went looking for other ways to ensure moistness without compromising the unique flavor of the fish. We tried adding melted butter and vegetable oil, but that made the burgers greasy. Egg yolks worked, but they obscured the flavor of the fish. We hit on the right solution when we added mayonnaise—just 2 tablespoons for four burgers gave us plenty of creaminess and moisture. We chopped the fish by hand instead of using a food processor to make sure we ended up

with a texture closer to ground meat than to salmon mousse. Generously coating the cooking grate multiple times with well-oiled paper towels prevented sticking. For flavor, we kept things very simple, with just fresh parsley, onion, lemon juice, and salt and pepper. You can add additional flavor with one of our easy, zesty sauces.

Salmon Burgers
SERVES 4

Be sure that your salmon burgers are refrigerated for at least 15 minutes before being grilled. Chilled burgers are more likely to hold their shape when grilled. Coat a metal spatula with vegetable oil spray so that

the burgers slide easily onto the grill. Serve these burgers on salad greens or toasted hamburger buns with Creamy Lemon-Herb Sauce or Creamy Chipotle-Lime Sauce (recipes follow) or your favorite toppings.

- 1¼ **pounds skinless salmon**
- ¼ **cup chopped fresh parsley**
- 2 **tablespoons mayonnaise**
- 2 **tablespoons finely grated onion**
- 1 **tablespoon lemon juice**
  Salt and pepper

1 Chop salmon into ¼-inch pieces. Using rocking motion, continue to chop salmon until it is coarsely chopped into pieces roughly ⅛ inch each.

2 Place salmon in bowl; add parsley, mayonnaise, onion, lemon juice, ½ teaspoon salt, and pepper to taste; and mix. Divide mixture into 4 portions and use your hands to press each into compact patty about 1 inch thick. Place patties on parchment paper–lined baking sheet and refrigerate for at least 15 minutes.

3A FOR A CHARCOAL GRILL Open bottom vent completely. Light large chimney starter filled with charcoal briquettes (6 quarts). When top coals are partially covered with ash, pour evenly over grill. Set cooking grate in place, set grill grid on cooking grate, cover, and open lid vent completely. Heat grill until hot, about 5 minutes.

3B FOR A GAS GRILL Turn all burners to high, cover, and heat grill until hot, about 15 minutes. Leave all burners on high.

4 Clean cooking grate, then repeatedly brush grate with well-oiled paper towels until black and glossy, 5 to 10 times. Place burgers on grill and cook (covered if using gas) until well browned on first side, 3 to 5 minutes. Flip burgers with greased metal spatula. Continue grilling (covered if using gas) until other side is well browned and burgers are barely translucent at center and register 125 to 130 degrees, 3 to 4 minutes. Serve immediately.

258 Creamy Lemon-Herb Sauce
MAKES ABOUT ⅓ CUP

Other fresh herbs, such as dill, basil, cilantro, mint, or tarragon, can be used in place of the parsley and thyme.

- ¼ **cup mayonnaise**
- 1 **small scallion, minced**
- 1 **tablespoon lemon juice**
- 1½ **teaspoons minced fresh parsley**
- 1½ **teaspoons minced fresh thyme**
- ½ **teaspoon salt**
  Pepper

Mix all ingredients, including pepper to taste, together in small bowl. Refrigerate until flavors blend, at least 30 minutes.

259 Creamy Chipotle-Lime Sauce
MAKES ABOUT ⅓ CUP

This sauce lends a Southwestern flair to burgers. Serve with sliced avocados and tomatoes.

- 2 **small garlic cloves, unpeeled**
- ¼ **cup mayonnaise**
- 1½ **teaspoons lime juice**
- 1 **teaspoon minced chipotle chile in adobo sauce, plus ½ teaspoon adobo sauce**

1 Place garlic cloves in 8-inch skillet over medium heat. Toast, turning cloves occasionally, until fragrant and skins have browned, 10 to 12 minutes. Let cool, peel, and mince. (You should have about 1 teaspoon.)

2 Mix garlic, mayonnaise, lime juice, chipotle, and adobo sauce together in small bowl. Refrigerate for at least 30 minutes.

260
STEP BY STEP
Boning and Skinning Salmon

If your salmon has pinbones and skin, here's how to remove them yourself.

1 TWEEZE OUT BONES Rub your fingers over surface of fillet to feel for pinbones. Remove them using tweezers or needlenose pliers.

2 SEPARATE SKIN Place fillet skin side down on cutting board. Holding sharp knife parallel to board, slice just above skin to separate it from flesh.

261

Burgers from the Sea

✔ WHY THIS RECIPE WORKS

Like salmon burgers, tuna burgers tend to be dry and disappointing. For burgers with good texture and flavor, we hand-chopped the meat and then combined it with a little garlic and ginger. These flavors paired well with the tuna's distinctive taste without overpowering it. The delicate texture of the fish created a lot of problems with sticking so we wiped the cooking grate with well-oiled paper towels multiple times to build up a stick-resistant coating. Coating the spatula with vegetable oil spray also helped loosen the burgers from the cooking grate. Tuna is a very lean fish and the lack of fat makes it hard to keep tuna burgers moist. To avoid burgers with the texture of canned tuna, we undercooked the burgers, taking them off the grill when they reached medium-rare (pink in the center). Our wasabi mayonnaise pairs wonderfully with these burgers.

Tuna Burgers

SERVES 4

Do not let these burgers overcook; tuna tends to get very dry when cooked for too long. The garlic and ginger are subtle additions that we strongly recommend, although they can be omitted if you prefer. Serve these burgers on salad greens or on toasted hamburger buns.

- 1¼ pounds tuna steaks
- 1 garlic clove, minced
- 1 teaspoon minced fresh ginger
  Salt and pepper

1 Chop tuna into ¼- to ⅓-inch pieces. Using rocking motion, continue to chop tuna until it is coarsely chopped into pieces roughly ⅛ inch each. Mix with garlic, ginger, ½ teaspoon salt, and pepper to taste.

Divide mixture into 4 equal portions and use your hands to press each into compact patty about 1 inch thick. Place patties on parchment-lined baking sheet and refrigerate for at least 15 minutes or up to 30 minutes.

2A FOR A CHARCOAL GRILL Open bottom vent completely. Light large chimney starter filled with charcoal briquettes (6 quarts). When top coals are partially covered with ash, pour evenly over grill. Set cooking grate in place, set grill grid on grate, cover, and open lid vent completely. Heat grill until hot, about 5 minutes.

2B FOR A GAS GRILL Turn all burners to high, set grill grid on cooking grate, cover, and heat grill until hot, about 15 minutes. Leave all burners on high.

3 Clean cooking grate, then repeatedly brush grate with well-oiled paper towels until black and glossy, 5 to 10 times. Grill tuna burgers (covered if using gas), until browned on first side, about 3 minutes. Flip burgers with greased metal spatula. Continue grilling (covered if using gas) until burgers register 125 degrees (for medium-rare) 2 to 3 minutes. Serve immediately.

262 Wasabi Mayonnaise
MAKES ABOUT ¼ CUP
This spicy mayonnaise is particularly good with tuna burgers.

- ¼ cup mayonnaise
- 1 teaspoon soy sauce
- 1 teaspoon wasabi powder

Mix all ingredients together in small bowl. Cover with plastic wrap and chill until flavors blend, at least 10 minutes.

263 STEP BY STEP
Prepping Your Cooking Grate for Delicate Foods

Be sure your grill is both hot and clean before you set delicate foods like fish or burgers down. Otherwise the crust will stick and rip.

1 SCRAPE CLEAN Heat grill and scrub with sturdy grill brush to remove any residual debris.

2 SLICK DOWN Dip wad of paper towels in vegetable oil. Using long-handled tongs, run over cleaned cooking grate.

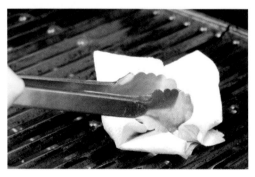

3 BUILD UP SEASONING Oil will burn off at first. Continue to dip towels into oil and slick down grate; it will become "nonstick." When grate turns black and glossy, grill ready.

264 RECIPE FOR SUCCESS
Go Shrimping for a Burger

✓ WHY THIS RECIPE WORKS

A good shrimp burger should be first and foremost about the shrimp. Unfortunately, many shrimp burgers are more reminiscent of fish-flavored rubber patties or overseasoned bread balls than shrimp. We set out to develop a recipe for our ideal shrimp burger: moist, chunky yet still cohesive, and with seasoning that complements the sweet shrimp flavor but doesn't overpower it. After early testing we decided we needed a combination of finely chopped shrimp to help bind the burgers, as well as some larger, bite-size chunks. We achieved this texture with help from the food processor. We wanted to use as little binder as possible, to avoid the soggy, mushy results we'd seen in other shrimp burgers that frequently used a combination of mayonnaise, egg, and bread crumbs. We kept the mayonnaise for the much-needed moisture and fat it added but left out the egg and decreased the bread crumbs. Some minced scallion and parsley, lemon zest, and a touch of cayenne pepper rounded out the flavor of our burgers.

Grilled Southern Shrimp Burgers

SERVES 4

Be sure to use raw, not cooked, shrimp here. Dry the shrimp thoroughly before processing, or the burgers will be mushy. Handle the burgers gently when shaping and grilling; if overhandled while being shaped, the burgers will be dense and rubbery, and if handled roughly during cooking, they will break apart. Serve with salad greens or toasted hamburger buns with Tartar Sauce (page 419).

1	slice hearty white sandwich bread, torn into large pieces
¼	cup mayonnaise
2	scallions, minced
2	tablespoons minced fresh parsley
2	teaspoons grated lemon zest
¼	teaspoon salt
⅛	teaspoon pepper
	Pinch cayenne pepper
1½	pounds extra-large shrimp (21 to 25 per pound), peeled, deveined, and patted dry
	Vegetable oil

1 Pulse bread in food processor to coarse crumbs, about 10 pulses. Transfer to small bowl. Do not clean food processor. Combine mayonnaise, scallions, parsley, lemon zest, salt, pepper, and cayenne in large bowl until uniform.

2 Pulse shrimp in now-empty food processor until some pieces are finely minced and others are coarsely chopped, about 7 pulses. Add shrimp to mayonnaise mixture and gently fold until just combined. Sprinkle bread crumbs over mixture and gently fold until incorporated.

3 Scrape shrimp mixture onto small baking sheet, divide into 4 equal portions, and loosely pack each into 1-inch-thick patty. Cover and refrigerate patties for at least 30 minutes or up to 3 hours.

4A FOR A CHARCOAL GRILL Open bottom vent completely. Light large chimney starter three-quarters filled with charcoal briquettes (4½ quarts). When top coals are partially covered with ash, pour evenly over grill. Set cooking grate in place, cover, and open lid vent completely. Heat grill until hot, about 5 minutes.

4B FOR A GAS GRILL Turn all burners to high, cover, and heat grill until hot, about 15 minutes. Turn all burners to medium-high.

5 Clean and oil cooking grate. Lightly brush tops of burgers with oil, lay them on grill, oiled side down, and lightly brush other side with oil. Cook burgers, without pressing on them, until lightly browned and cooked through, 10 to 14 minutes, flipping them halfway through grilling. Transfer burgers to platter, tent with aluminum foil, and let rest for 5 minutes before serving.

265 GRILL HACK
A Welder's Brush Goes Grilling

Cleaning your grill's hot grate is recommended to keep foods from sticking. A welder's brush, which can be purchased for just a few dollars at a hardware store, has a long wooden handle attached to a wire brush, just like a grill brush and can be used in a pinch. Its long wires and narrow design allow for deep scrubbing between the bars on the cooking grate.

266 Meatless Doesn't Mean Mediocre

✓ WHY THIS RECIPE WORKS

Store-bought veggie burgers often border on inedible, but most homemade renditions are a lot of work. We wanted a recipe that would act like hamburgers, with a modicum of chew, a harmonious blend of savory ingredients, and the ability to go from grill to bun without falling apart. We found veggie burgers made with soy-based products bland and gummy, so we turned to lentils and bulgur, which gave us just the texture we were after. For savory flavor, we turned to foods rich in umami—specifically, cremini mushrooms and cashews. Panko bread crumbs were the perfect binder.

Ultimate Veggie Burgers
SERVES 12

Canned lentils can be used, though some flavor will be sacrificed. Use a 15-ounce can, drain the lentils in a fine-mesh strainer, and thoroughly rinse under cold running water before spreading them on paper towels and drying them as directed in step 1. If you cannot find panko, use 1 cup of plain bread crumbs. If you plan to freeze the patties, note that you will need to increase the amount of bread crumbs since the patties increase in moisture content with freezing and thawing (see make-ahead directions). If you like, toast the hamburger buns on the grill after cooking the burgers.

¾ cup dried brown lentils, picked over and rinsed

Salt and pepper

¾ cup bulgur

2 tablespoons vegetable oil

2 onions, chopped fine

1 celery rib, chopped fine

1 small leek, white and light green parts only, halved lengthwise, chopped fine, and washed thoroughly

2 garlic cloves, minced

1 pound cremini or white mushrooms, trimmed and sliced ¼ inch thick

1 cup raw cashews

⅓ cup mayonnaise

2 cups panko bread crumbs

12 hamburger buns

1 Bring 3 cups water, lentils, and 1 teaspoon salt to boil in medium saucepan over high heat. Reduce heat to medium-low and simmer, uncovered, stirring occasionally, until lentils are just beginning to fall apart, about 25 minutes. Drain in fine-mesh strainer. Line rimmed baking sheet with triple layer of paper towels and spread drained lentils over paper towels. Gently pat lentils dry with additional paper towels. Let lentils cool to room temperature.

2 While lentils simmer, bring 2 cups water and ½ teaspoon salt to boil in small saucepan. Stir bulgur into boiling water and cover immediately; let sit off heat until water is absorbed, 15 to 20 minutes. Drain in fine-mesh strainer, then use rubber spatula to press out excess moisture. Transfer bulgur to medium bowl and set aside.

3 Heat 1 tablespoon oil in 12-inch nonstick skillet over medium-high heat until shimmering. Add onions, celery, leek, and garlic and cook, stirring occasionally, until vegetables begin to brown, about 10 minutes. Spread vegetable mixture onto second rimmed baking sheet to cool; set aside. Heat remaining 1 tablespoon oil in now-empty skillet over high heat until shimmering. Add mushrooms and cook, stirring occasionally, until golden brown, about 12 minutes. Spread mushrooms on baking sheet with vegetable mixture; let cool to room temperature, about 20 minutes.

4 Pulse cashews in food processor until finely chopped, about 15 pulses (do not wash workbowl). Stir cashews into bowl with bulgur, then stir in mayonnaise, cooled lentils, and vegetable-mushroom mixture. Transfer half of mixture to now-empty food processor and pulse until coarsely chopped, 15 to 20 pulses (mixture should be cohesive but roughly textured). Transfer processed mixture to large bowl and repeat with remaining unprocessed mixture; combine with first batch.

5 Stir in panko and 1 teaspoon salt and season with pepper to taste. Line baking sheet with paper towels. Divide mixture into 12 portions, about ½ cup each, shaping each into tightly packed patty about 4 inches in diameter and ½ inch thick. Place patties on prepared sheet (paper towels will absorb excess moisture).

6A FOR A CHARCOAL GRILL Open bottom vent completely. Light large chimney starter filled with charcoal briquettes (6 quarts). When top coals are partially covered with ash, pour evenly over grill. Set cooking grate in place, cover, and open lid vent completely. Heat grill until hot, about 5 minutes.

6B FOR A GAS GRILL Turn all burners to high, cover, and heat grill until hot, about 15 minutes. Leave all burners on high.

7 Clean and oil cooking grate. Place burgers on grill and cook, without moving them, until well browned, about 5 minutes; flip burgers and continue cooking until well browned on second side, about 5 minutes. Serve on buns.

TO MAKE AHEAD Patties can be prepared through step 5 and refrigerated for up to 3 days. Alternatively, you can freeze patties. For each burger to be frozen, add 1 teaspoon panko bread crumbs or ½ teaspoon plain bread crumbs to mixture before shaping. Thaw frozen patties overnight in refrigerator on triple layer of paper towels, covered loosely. Before cooking, pat patties dry with paper towels and reshape to make sure they are tightly packed and cohesive.

267

FOOD SCIENCE

Freeze Your Buns

Bread stales when starches crystallize and incorporate water into the crystalline structure, causing bread to harden. But storage temperature dramatically affects how quickly this happens. We found that refrigerated bread staled in just a day and bread stored at room temperature staled in just two days—but frozen bread held up well for a month. Why? Staling, or retrogradation, occurs about six times faster at refrigerator temperatures (36 to 40 degrees) than at room temperature, but at below-freezing temps, it slows down significantly.

THE BOTTOM LINE Store bread at room temperature for no more than two days; otherwise, freeze it.

269 RECIPE FOR SUCCESS
Ultimate Mushroom Burger

✓ WHY THIS RECIPE WORKS

For a vegetarian burger with unbeatable meaty taste, we turned to grilled portobello mushrooms. Scraping out the gills avoided any muddy off-flavors and marinating the mushrooms in a simple vinaigrette boosted their complexity. Cutting a shallow crosshatch into the caps not only allowed the portobellos to soak up more marinade, but it also prevented the skin from turning chewy while cooking. Before grilling, we mixed together some toppings that complemented the mushrooms' Mediterranean flavor profile. A combination of chopped roasted red peppers, chopped sun-dried tomatoes, and feta cheese made for a bright, briny accompaniment, and a quick basil-boosted mayonnaise promised a creamy component for our finished burgers. Keeping these two toppings close by, we grilled the mushrooms alongside ½–inch-thick sliced red onions. Skewering the slices with toothpicks kept the onion rounds in place for tidy grilling and brushing them with the remaining marinade unified the flavors. Once the mushrooms had taken on plenty of rich char on both sides, we placed them on a platter and filled the gilled sides with the feta mixture. Returning to the grill, we gave the filled mushrooms a final blast of heat to warm them through and then toasted up sturdy kaiser rolls. We assembled our flavor-packed finished product, stacking our stuffed mushrooms, sweet grilled onions, and some peppery baby arugula on top of our basil mayo–smeared buns. These burgers were perfectly rich, and juicy—no meat necessary.

Mediterranean-Style Portobello Burgers
SERVES 4

Our favorite feta cheese is Mt. Vikos Traditional Feta from Greece. If the mushrooms absorb all the marinade, simply brush the onions with olive oil before grilling them in step 4.

- 4 portobello mushroom caps (4 to 5 inches in diameter), gills removed
- ½ cup extra-virgin olive oil
- 3 tablespoons red wine vinegar
- 1 garlic clove, minced
  Salt and pepper
- 4 ounces feta cheese, crumbled (1 cup)
- ½ cup jarred roasted red peppers, patted dry and chopped
- ½ cup oil-packed sun-dried tomatoes, patted dry and chopped
- ½ cup mayonnaise
- ½ cup chopped fresh basil
- 4 (½-inch-thick) slices red onion
- 4 kaiser rolls, split
- 1 ounce (1 cup) baby arugula

---

268 TEST KITCHEN TIP
Preparing Portobellos and Onions for the Grill

A few easy tricks have a lot of impact.

Skewer Onion Slices
Use a toothpick to help hold the onion rounds together.

Score the Cap
Cut a shallow crosshatch into the top of each cap to minimize the rubbery texture.

Remove the Gills
Scrape out the muddy-tasting gills with a spoon.

1 Using tip of paring knife, cut ½-inch crosshatch pattern on tops of mushroom caps, 1⁄16 inch deep. Combine oil, vinegar, garlic, 1 teaspoon salt, and ½ teaspoon pepper in 1-gallon zipper-lock bag. Add mushrooms, seal bag, turn to coat, and let sit for at least 30 minutes or up to 1 hour.

2 Combine feta, red peppers, and sun-dried tomatoes in bowl. Whisk mayonnaise and basil together in separate bowl. Push 1 toothpick horizontally through each onion slice to keep rings intact while grilling.

3A FOR A CHARCOAL GRILL Open bottom vent completely. Light large chimney starter filled with charcoal briquettes (6 quarts). When top coals are partially covered with ash, pour evenly over grill. Set cooking grate in place, cover, and open lid vent completely. Heat grill until hot, about 5 minutes.

3B FOR A GAS GRILL Turn all burners to high, cover, and heat grill until hot, about 15 minutes. Turn all burners to medium-high.

4 Clean and oil cooking grate. Remove mushrooms from marinade, reserving excess. Brush onions all over with reserved mushroom marinade. Place onions and mushrooms, gill side up, on grill. Cook (covered if using gas) until mushrooms have released their liquid and are charred on first side, 4 to 6 minutes. Flip mushrooms and onions and continue to cook (covered if using gas) until mushrooms are charred on second side, 3 to 5 minutes.

5 Transfer onions to platter; remove toothpicks. Transfer mushrooms to platter, gill side up, and divide feta mixture evenly among caps, packing down with your hand. Return mushrooms to grill, feta side up, and cook, covered, until heated through, about 3 minutes.

6 Return mushrooms to platter and tent with aluminum foil. Grill rolls cut sides down until lightly charred, about 1 minute. Spread basil-mayonnaise on roll bottoms and top each with 1 mushroom and 1 onion slice. Divide arugula evenly among burgers, then cap with bun tops. Serve.

270

Makeshift Bottle Opener

During backyard barbecues, it's all too easy to misplace one of the most important tools: the bottle opener. Don't despair if this happens to you and you still want to quench your thirst grillside. Simply use grill tongs, which have an opening inside the handles just large enough to catch the edge of a bottle cap. Sandwich the top of the bottle inside the handle and gently pop off the cap.

271

RECIPE FOR SUCCESS

Bringing a Tailgating Favorite Home

✔ **WHY THIS RECIPE WORKS**
Our first attempts at this Midwest favorite resulted in gray, soggy sausages and bland onions floating in hot beer. To perfect our recipe, we started by letting the sausages marinate in the beer and seasonings to start flavoring them while we prepared the grill (we found that grilling the sausages before marinating them made them turn out soggy). Then we grilled the onions and added them in with the sausages to braise in a disposable aluminum pan on the grill. Grilling the onions before stirring them into the beer gave the mixture serious flavor, and the addition of Dijon mustard lent brightness and body to the sauce. After the braise we threw the sausages directly onto the grill for a final crisping to give them good color and a great sear.

Wisconsin Brats and Beer
SERVES 8 TO 12
For the beer, use a pale lager such as Budweiser.

- 2 **pounds onions, sliced into ½-inch-thick rounds (do not separate rings)**
- 3 **tablespoons vegetable oil**
  Pepper
- 3 **cups beer**
- ⅔ **cup Dijon mustard**
- 1 **teaspoon sugar**
- 1 **teaspoon caraway seeds**
- 1 **(13 by 9-inch) disposable aluminum roasting pan**
- 2 **pounds bratwurst (8 to 12 sausages)**
- 8–12 **(6-inch) sub rolls**

1 Brush onion rounds with oil and season with pepper; set aside. Combine beer, mustard, sugar, caraway seeds, and 1 teaspoon pepper in disposable pan, then add sausages in single layer.

2A FOR A CHARCOAL GRILL Open bottom vent completely. Light large chimney starter filled with charcoal briquettes (6 quarts). When top coals are partially covered with ash, pour evenly over grill. Set cooking grate in place, cover, and open lid vent completely. Heat grill until hot, about 5 minutes.

2B FOR A GAS GRILL Turn all burners to high, cover, and heat grill until hot, about 15 minutes. Leave all burners on high.

3 Clean and oil cooking grate. Place onions on grill and cook, turning as needed, until lightly charred on both sides, 6 to 10 minutes. Transfer onions to disposable pan. Place pan in center of grill, cover grill, and cook for 15 minutes.

4 Move pan to 1 side of grill. Transfer sausages directly to grill and cook until browned on all sides, about 5 minutes. Transfer sausages to platter and tent with aluminum foil. Continue to cook onion mixture in pan until sauce is slightly thickened, about 5 minutes. Serve sausages and onions with rolls.

272

STEP BY STEP

Making a Better Bratwurst

Once the sausages have simmered in the beer-mustard-onion mixture and picked up plenty of flavor, place them on the grill to crisp up while the beer mixture finishes reducing.

273 Beer for Brats

We tested eight lagers in our recipe for Wisconsin Brats and Beer, and tasters overwhelmingly preferred the mellow sweetness of **Budweiser**. Miller Genuine Draft was our second choice; tasters praised its mild, malty flavor. Expensive imported beers, such as Heineken and Spaten, were bitter when reduced in the sauce, so keep those beers for drinking.

274 RECIPE FOR SUCCESS
Improving on a Classic Grill Pairing

✓ WHY THIS RECIPE WORKS

Sausage and onions are a classic pairing that sounds tailor-made for the grill. But the reality is usually onions that are both crunchy and charred and sausages that either dried out or—even worse—catch fire. We wanted a foolproof method for grilling sausages and onions simultaneously that would produce nicely browned links with juicy interiors and tender, caramelized onions. Microwaving the onions—with a little thyme, salt, and pepper—for just 4 minutes jump-started the cooking process and allowed them to finish cooking evenly and thoroughly on the grill. We adapted a ballpark technique, first cooking the meat with the onions away from direct heat in a disposable pan and then finishing the sausages directly over the flames. Keeping the onions cooking on their own in the pan for an extra 5 to 10 minutes allowed the liquid to evaporate and the onions to caramelize to a deep golden brown while the sausages finished up brown and crisp on the grill. Our variations add ingredients that complement the grilled sausages with sweet and aromatic flavors.

Grilled Sausages with Onions
SERVES 4

This recipe will work with any raw, uncooked sausage. Serve the sausages as is or in toasted rolls.

- 2   large onions, sliced thin
- 1   teaspoon minced fresh thyme leaves
- ½   teaspoon salt
- ¼   teaspoon pepper
- 1   (13 by 9-inch) disposable aluminum roasting pan
- 2   pounds sweet or hot Italian sausage (8 to 12 links)

1A FOR A CHARCOAL GRILL Open bottom vent completely. Light large chimney starter filled with charcoal briquettes (6 quarts). When top coals are partially covered with ash, pour evenly over grill. Set cooking grate in place, cover, and open lid vent completely. Heat grill until hot, about 5 minutes.

1B FOR A GAS GRILL: Turn all burners to high, cover, and heat grill until hot, about 15 minutes. Turn all burners to medium-high.

2 Meanwhile, microwave onions, thyme, salt, and pepper in medium bowl, covered, until onions begin to soften and tips turn slightly translucent, 4 to 6 minutes, stirring once halfway through microwaving (be careful of steam). Transfer onions to disposable pan. Place sausages in single layer over onions and wrap pan tightly with aluminum foil.

3 Clean and oil cooking grate. Place disposable pan in center of grill, cover grill, and cook for 15 minutes. Move pan to 1 side of grill and carefully remove foil. Transfer sausages directly to grill and cook (covered if using gas) until golden brown on all sides, 5 to 7 minutes.

4 Transfer sausages to serving platter and tent with foil. Cover grill and continue to cook onions, stirring occasionally, until liquid evaporates and onions begin to brown, 5 to 10 minutes longer. Serve sausages, passing onions separately.

VARIATIONS

275 Grilled Sausages with Peppers and Onions

Omit thyme and add 3 seeded and quartered red bell peppers to roasting pan with sausages. Transfer pepper pieces to cooking grate with sausages and cook until charred patches form, 5 to 7 minutes, flipping halfway through cooking.

276 Grilled Sausages with Fennel

Omit thyme and replace 1 onion with 2 cored and sliced fennel bulbs and 2 tablespoons minced fennel fronds.

277 SHOPPING IQ Fresh Sausage

For grilling, links are better than long coils, which cook unevenly on the grill. We also avoid precooked sausages (these often come in shrink-wrapped packages), as grilling tends to dry them out and turn their texture mealy. Here are some of the most common types of links you'll find at the supermarket.

SWEET OR HOT ITALIAN SAUSAGE Sweet versions of this pork sausage are flavored with fennel seeds, while the hot kind is spiked with chiles. Both types have a meaty flavor that makes them great for grilling, but they're also very fatty and should be carefully monitored when grilled directly over the coals (even after precooking) to avoid flare-ups.

FRESH BRATWURST Authentic versions of these pale, mild German sausages made from pork and veal have a smooth, almost emulsified texture, with all the fat blended thoroughly with the meat, helping to reduce flare-ups.

FRESH CHICKEN SAUSAGE Because chicken sausages tend to be lean, we prefer varieties that contain cheese. The extra fat helps keep the sausage from drying out on the grill and doesn't add to the risk of flare-ups.

FRESH POLISH SAUSAGE The thicker casings of these mild pork sausages mean they may need a little more time over the coals to ensure fully cooked interiors. The smoked, dried version, called kielbasa, usually comes precooked and should be avoided when grilling.

278 STEP BY STEP Grilling Sausages and Onions

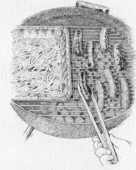

1 MICROWAVE ONIONS
Microwaving onions jump-starts cooking and ensures uniformly tender texture.

2 TOP ONIONS WITH SAUSAGES
Placing sausages on hot onions in an aluminum pan allows the sausages' rendered fat to flavor onions.

3 PLACE FOIL-COVERED PAN ON HOT GRILL Cooking onions in foil-covered pan makes them tender, not crunchy.

4 BROWN SAUSAGE OVER COALS Finish cooking sausages over coals. With most of their fat rendered, there is little risk of flare-ups.

279 Spicy Sausages from the South

RECIPE FOR SUCCESS

✓ WHY THIS RECIPE WORKS

Smoked sausages are a staple of Texas barbecue, a legacy of German butchers who settled in the area. These pork sausages are seasoned with cayenne pepper and garlic and smoked until the casing is wrinkled. At home, most people don't want to make their own sausages, nor do they have a smoker. Could we get the same deep smoky Texas flavor on a grill with store-bought sausages? After we examined the sausage options at the grocery store, hot Italian sausage stood out as the best choice. We set up soaked wood chips on the hotter side of a half-grill fire and then cooked the sausages on the cooler side. To get great smoke flavor, we left them on for 45 minutes; despite the long cooking time, they were still extremely moist and juicy. Best of all, their skins deepened to a dark, slightly wrinkled red, like the sausages from a real Texas barbecue joint.

Texas Smoked Sausages

SERVES 4

If you'd like to use wood chunks instead of wood chips when using a charcoal grill, substitute three medium wood chunks, soaked in water for 1 hour, for the wood chip packet.

> 3 cups wood chips, soaked in water for 15 minutes and drained
>
> 2 pounds hot Italian sausage (8 to 12 links)
>
> 8–12 (6-inch) sub rolls

1 Using large piece of heavy-duty aluminum foil, wrap soaked chips in 8 by 4½-inch foil packet. (Make sure chips do not poke holes in sides or bottom of packet.) Cut 2 evenly spaced 2-inch slits in top of packet.

2A FOR A CHARCOAL GRILL Open bottom vent halfway. Light large chimney starter filled with charcoal briquettes (6 quarts). When top coals are partially covered with ash, pour evenly over half of grill. Place wood chip packet on coals. Set cooking grate in place, cover, and open lid vent halfway. Heat grill until hot and wood chips are smoking, about 5 minutes.

2B FOR A GAS GRILL Remove cooking grate and place wood chip packet directly on primary burner. Set cooking grate in place, turn all burners to high, cover, and heat grill until hot and wood chips are smoking, about 15 minutes. Leave primary burner on high and turn off other burner(s).

3 Clean and oil cooking grate. Lay sausages on cooler side of grill, away from coals and flames. Cover (position lid vent over sausages if using charcoal) and cook until sausages are well browned and cooked through, about 45 minutes, turning every 15 minutes. Serve with rolls.

280 Coarse-Grain Mustard

SHOPPING IQ

Mustard aficionados argue that the coarse-grained condiment improves any ham sandwich or grilled sausage—unless you pick the wrong jar. After sampling 11 brands, tasters appreciated spiciness, tanginess, and the pleasant pop of seeds. They disliked mustards with superfluous ingredients such as xanthan gum, artificial flavors, and garlic and onion powders. But the more noteworthy factor turned out to be salt. Mustards with a meager quantity ranked low, whereas the winners contained roughly twice as much of this flavor amplifier.

THE BOTTOM LINE Tying for first place, both the familiar **Grey Poupon Country Dijon** and the newer **Grey Poupon Harvest Coarse Ground** make good pantry staples.

WINNERS

GREY POUPON Country Dijon Mustard
Tasting Comments Tasters noted this "classic," "moderately coarse" mustard with "wasabi-like heat" went particularly well with grilled sausage.

GREY POUPON Harvest Coarse Ground Mustard
Tasting Comments This mustard boasts "a real burst of mustard flavor" with "big, round, crunchy seeds," "good heat," and just enough vinegar.

281 Keeping Grill Platters Warm

GRILL HACK

If using a gas grill, rest your serving platter on the flat lid to warm it up. The heated platter can be used for serving foods right away or for keeping meat warm as it rests before carving. Make sure to handle the platter with potholders.

282

Using a Mortar and Pestle

The key to using a mortar and pestle effectively is circular grinding, not up-and-down pounding. (Pounding is less efficient and scatters ingredients.) Here's how to effectively grind spices to a fine powder.

Place spices in mortar. Steady mortar with your hand and firmly press pestle's rounded base against inside of mortar with your other hand. Rotate pestle, without lifting head and maintaining downward pressure at all times, until spices are ground to desired consistency.

283

RECIPE FOR SUCCESS
Inexpensive Steak with Fiery Spice Rubs

✔ WHY THIS RECIPE WORKS

Spice rubs can sometimes counteract flavor and texture deficiencies in less-expensive steaks, but only when done right. We wanted a rub that would not only impart good flavor, but would also aid in the creation of a crispy, crunchy crust. Tomato paste and fish sauce are two of the most potent carriers of glutamates, which amp up savory, meaty flavors, and they did their job well here as a wet rub for the steak: The flavor of the meat was noticeably deeper, without tasting like fish or tomatoes. We then built on that base by adding garlic powder and onion powder to completely infuse the steak with flavor even before we added the dry rub. For the dry rub, we turned to paprika, chiles, and peppers, which don't lose flavor over the intense heat of the grill.

Grilled Steak with New Mexican Chile Rub

SERVES 6 TO 8

Spraying the rubbed steaks with oil helps the spices bloom, preventing a raw flavor.

STEAK
- 2 teaspoons tomato paste
- 2 teaspoons fish sauce
- 1½ teaspoons kosher salt
- ½ teaspoon onion powder
- ½ teaspoon garlic powder
- 2 (1½- to 1¾-pound) whole boneless shell sirloin steaks, 1 to 1¼ inches thick, trimmed

SPICE RUB
- 2 dried New Mexican chiles, stemmed, seeded, and torn into ½-inch pieces
- 4 teaspoons cumin seeds
- 4 teaspoons coriander seeds
- ½ teaspoon red pepper flakes
- ½ teaspoon black peppercorns
- 1 tablespoon sugar
- 1 tablespoon paprika
- ¼ teaspoon ground cloves
  Vegetable oil spray

284

TEST KITCHEN TIP
Keeping Chiles Fresher Longer

Fresh chiles like jalapeños and serranos have a relatively brief shelf life in the refrigerator. We tried four different refrigerator storage methods to see if any would help these chiles keep their crisp texture and fresh flavor longer. We sealed whole chiles in a plastic bag; left them loose in the crisper drawer; sliced them in half (to allow liquid to penetrate) and stored them in distilled white vinegar; and sliced them in half and submerged them in a brine solution (1 tablespoon salt per cup of water). In both the bag and the crisper, the chiles began to soften and turn brown within a week. Storing in vinegar was also not ideal; after about a week, the chiles began tasting more pickled than fresh. The brine-covered chiles, however, retained their crispness, color, and bright heat for several weeks and, after a quick rinse to remove excess brine, were indistinguishable from fresh chiles when we sampled them raw and in salsa. After a month they began to soften, but they remained perfectly usable in cooked applications for several weeks.

1 FOR THE STEAK Combine tomato paste, fish sauce, salt, onion powder, and garlic powder in bowl. Pat steaks dry with paper towels. With sharp knife, cut 1/16-inch-deep slits on both sides of steaks, spaced 1/2 inch apart, in crosshatch pattern. Rub salt mixture evenly on both sides of steaks. Place steaks on wire rack set in rimmed baking sheet; let stand at room temperature for at least 1 hour. (After 30 minutes, prepare grill.)

2 FOR THE SPICE RUB Toast New Mexican chiles, cumin, coriander, pepper flakes, and peppercorns in 10-inch skillet over medium-low heat, stirring frequently, until just beginning to smoke, 3 to 4 minutes. Transfer to plate to cool, about 5 minutes. Grind spices in spice grinder or in mortar with pestle until coarsely ground. Transfer spices to bowl and stir in sugar, paprika, and cloves.

3A FOR A CHARCOAL GRILL Open bottom vent completely. Light large chimney starter mounded with charcoal briquettes (7 quarts). When top coals are partially covered with ash, pour two-thirds evenly over half of grill, then pour remaining coals over other half of grill. Set cooking grate in place, cover, and open lid vent completely. Heat grill until hot, about 5 minutes.

3B FOR A GAS GRILL Turn all burners to high, cover, and heat grill until hot, about 15 minutes. Leave primary burner on high and turn other burner(s) to medium.

4 Clean and oil cooking grate. Sprinkle half of spice rub evenly over 1 side of steaks and press to adhere until spice rub is fully moistened. Lightly spray rubbed side of steak with oil spray, about 3 seconds. Flip steaks and repeat process of sprinkling with spice rub and coating with oil spray on second side.

5 Place steaks on hotter side of grill and cook until browned and charred on both sides and center registers 120 to 125 degrees (for medium-rare) or 130 to 135 degrees (for medium), 3 to 4 minutes per side. If steaks have not reached desired temperature, move to cooler side of grill and continue to cook. Transfer steaks to clean wire rack set in rimmed baking sheet, tent with aluminum foil, and let rest for 10 minutes. Slice meat thin against grain and serve.

285 STEP BY STEP Turning Cheaper Steaks into "Choice"

1 SCORE MEAT Shallow slits cut into the steak help the salt paste and spice rub adhere to the meat and penetrate more deeply.

2 APPLY PASTE A paste of onion and garlic powders, salt, tomato paste, and fish sauce boosts beefy flavor and tenderizes the meat.

3 APPLY SPICE RUB Toasting and then grinding dried chiles and spices leads to a more substantial crust with complex flavor.

4 SPRAY WITH OIL A light misting of oil blooms the spices on the grill and helps the rub cling to the meat.

286

RECIPE FOR SUCCESS

The Ultimate Steak

✓ WHY THIS RECIPE WORKS

Cowboy-cut rib eyes are 2-inch-thick, 1½ pound, bone-in behemoths that can cost upwards of $25 each so you want to make sure you know what you're doing when you throw them on the grill. But there are also serious advantages to these steaks, including the fact that they stay on the grill longer than smaller steaks, which means they soak up more smoke and grill flavor. The challenge is to cook the inside to just the right temperature while getting a dark, flavorful sear on the outside. To achieve these goals, we started with room-temperature steaks and cooked them gently over the cooler side of a half-grill fire. We then seared them on the hotter side of the grill (for the charcoal setup we used the Minion method of layering lit briquettes on top of unlit briquettes to help the fire stay hot long enough to finish the job).

287

SHOPPING IQ

Cowboy Steaks

Rib-eye steaks are deeply marbled, tender, and beefy—they're from the same part of the steer that's used for prime rib. Bone-in steaks (like these) have more flavor than boneless, and the bone protects against overcooking. Of special interest is the exterior band of fat and meat on a rib eye called the deckle; connoisseurs say it is the most flavorful part of the cow.

THE BOTTOM LINE Cowboy-cut rib eyes are double-thick bone-in steaks. They take longer to cook than single-serving rib eyes, so they have more time to soak up smoky grill flavor.

Grilled Cowboy-Cut Rib Eyes
SERVES 4 TO 6

Don't start grilling until the steaks' internal temperature has reached 55 degrees. Otherwise, the times and temperatures in this recipe will be inaccurate.

- 2 (1¼- to 1½-pound) double-cut bone-in rib-eye steaks, 1¾ to 2 inches thick, trimmed
- 4 teaspoons kosher salt
- 2 teaspoons vegetable oil
- 2 teaspoons pepper

1 Set wire rack in rimmed baking sheet. Pat steaks dry with paper towels and sprinkle all over with salt. Place steaks on prepared rack and let stand at room temperature until meat registers 55 degrees, about 1 hour. Rub steaks with oil and sprinkle with pepper.

2A FOR A CHARCOAL GRILL Open bottom vent halfway. Arrange 4 quarts unlit charcoal briquettes in even layer over half of grill. Light large chimney starter one-third filled with charcoal briquettes (2 quarts). When top coals are partially covered with ash, pour evenly over unlit coals. Set cooking grate in place, cover, and open lid vent halfway. Heat grill until hot, about 5 minutes.

2B FOR A GAS GRILL Turn all burners to high, cover, and heat grill until hot, about 15 minutes. Turn primary burner to medium-low and turn off other burner(s). (Adjust primary burner as needed to maintain grill temperature around 300 degrees.)

3 Clean and oil cooking grate. Place steaks on cooler side of grill with bones facing fire. Cover and cook until steaks register 75 degrees, 10 to 20 minutes. Flip steaks, keeping bones facing fire. Cover and continue to cook until steaks register 95 degrees, 10 to 20 minutes.

4 If using charcoal, slide steaks to hotter side of grill. If using gas, remove steaks from grill, turn primary burner to high, and heat until hot, about 5 minutes; place steaks over primary burner. Cover and cook until well browned and steaks register 120 to 125 degrees (for medium-rare), about 4 minutes per side. Transfer steaks to clean wire rack set in rimmed baking sheet, tent with aluminum foil, and let rest for 15 minutes. Transfer steaks to carving board, cut meat from bone, and slice into ½-inch-thick slices. Serve.

SHOPPING IQ

Grass-Fed vs. Grain-Fed Beef

Picking out a steak is no longer as simple as choosing the cut, the grade, and whether or not the beef has been aged. There's another aspect to consider: the cow's diet. While most American beef is grain-fed, many supermarkets carry grass-fed options as well.

Grain-fed beef has long been promoted as richer and fattier, while grass-fed beef has gotten a bad rap as lean and chewy, with an overly gamy taste. To judge for ourselves, we went to the supermarket and bought 16 grass-fed and 16 grain-fed rib-eye and strip steaks. Because the grass-fed steaks were dry-aged 21 days, we bought similarly aged grain-fed meat. When we seared the steaks to medium-rare and tasted them side by side, the results surprised us: With strip steaks, our tasters could not distinguish between grass-fed and grain-fed meat. Tasters did, however, notice a difference in the fattier rib eyes, but their preferences were split: Some preferred the "mild" flavor of grain-fed beef; others favored the stronger, more complex, "nutty" undertones of grass-fed steaks. None of the tasters noticed problems with texture in either cut.

What accounts for the apparent turnaround in meat that's often maligned? The answer may lie in new measures introduced in recent years that have made grass-fed beef taste more appealing, including "finishing" the beef on forage like clover that imparts a sweeter profile. Perhaps even more significant is that an increasing number of producers have decided to dry-age. This process concentrates beefy flavor and dramatically increases tenderness.

THE BOTTOM LINE For non-dry-aged grass-fed beef, the jury is still out on whether it tastes any better (or worse) than grain-fed. But if your grass-fed beef is dry-aged—and if you're OK with fattier cuts like rib eye that taste a little gamy—you'll likely find the meat as buttery and richly flavored as regular grain-fed dry-aged beef.

289 Spicy, Meaty Mexican Skewers

✓ WHY THIS RECIPE WORKS

Alambre Mexicano, a dish of skewered meat, chiles, and vegetables grilled over an open flame, is popular in northern Mexico. For the meat, we chose richly marbled steak tips for their beefy flavor and tender texture, as well as chorizo for its spice and assertive flavor profile. We tossed the beef in a mixture of olive oil and spices; we chose oregano for a peppery bite, garlic powder to add savoriness, and cumin for depth. We rounded out our kebabs with spicy jalapeños and sweet red onion. We briefly parcooked the vegetables in the microwave to ensure that they would finish cooking at the same time as the meat. Seeding the jalapeños allowed us to enjoy their flavor without making the dish overly spicy.

Grilled Beef and Chorizo Skewers
SERVES 4 TO 6

If you can't find steak tips, sometimes labeled flap meat, substitute 1¼ pounds blade steaks (if using, cut the steak in half and remove the gristle that runs through it). If you have long, thin pieces of meat, roll or fold them into approximate 2-inch cubes. You will need four 12-inch metal skewers for this recipe. Serve with warm tortillas or rice.

- 1 large red onion, cut into 1-inch pieces, 3 layers thick
- 4 jalapeño chiles, stemmed, halved, seeded, and cut into 1-inch pieces
- 3 tablespoons extra-virgin olive oil
- 1 tablespoon minced fresh oregano or 1 teaspoon dried
- ½ teaspoon garlic powder
  Salt and pepper
- ¼ teaspoon ground cumin
- 1 pound sirloin steak tips, trimmed and cut into 2-inch pieces
- 1 pound Mexican-style chorizo sausage, cut into 2-inch lengths
- 2 tablespoons chopped fresh cilantro
  Lime wedges

1 Gently toss onion and jalapeños with 1 tablespoon oil in bowl. Cover vegetables and microwave until just tender, 3 to 5 minutes. In large bowl, combine oregano, garlic powder, ½ teaspoon salt, ¼ teaspoon pepper, cumin, and remaining 2 tablespoons oil. Add steak and toss to coat. Thread steak, chorizo, onion, and jalapeños tightly onto four 12-inch metal skewers in alternating pattern.

2A FOR A CHARCOAL GRILL Open bottom vent completely. Light large chimney starter filled with charcoal briquettes (6 quarts). When top coals are partially covered with ash, pour evenly over grill. Set cooking grate in place, cover, and open lid vent completely. Heat grill until hot, about 5 minutes.

2B FOR A GAS GRILL Turn all burners to high, cover, and heat grill until hot, about 15 minutes. Leave all burners on high.

3 Clean and oil cooking grate. Place skewers on grill and cook (covered if using gas), turning as needed, until well browned and meat registers 130 to 135 (for medium), 10 to 15 minutes. Transfer skewers to serving platter, tent with aluminum foil, and let rest for 5 to 10 minutes. Sprinkle with cilantro and serve with lime wedges.

290 SHOPPING IQ
Chorizo

Chorizo is a name shared by several styles of sausage. While all versions derive from the Iberian original, each has its own characteristics.

ORIGIN	MEAT TYPE	FLAVOR/APPEARANCE	USES
Spain	Dry-cured pork	Coarsely ground; bright red, with a smoky flavor derived from smoked paprika; depending on the paprika, chorizo can be sweet (*dulce*) or hot (*picante*)	Can be sliced thin and eaten as an hors d'oeuvre; often cooked in dishes like paella or Spanish tortilla
Colombia, Argentina	Fresh or cooked pork	Very coarsely ground; lightly seasoned with garlic, sometimes contains herbs	Usually served grilled or fried
Mexico	Fresh pork (or beef)	Finely ground; pronounced spicy tanginess from chili powder and vinegar	Usually removed from casings before being fried and mashed to a dry, crumbled texture for incorporation into dishes like tinga

SAUCE

- ¼ cup hot tap water
- 2 teaspoons dried oregano
- 1 teaspoon salt
- 1⅓ cups fresh parsley leaves
- ⅔ cup fresh cilantro leaves
- 6 garlic cloves, minced
- ½ teaspoon red pepper flakes
- ¼ cup red wine vinegar
- ½ cup extra-virgin olive oil

STEAKS

- 1 tablespoon cornstarch
- 1½ teaspoons salt
- 4 (1-pound) boneless strip steaks, 1½ inches thick, trimmed
- 4 2-inch unsoaked wood chunks
- 1 (9-inch) disposable aluminum pie plate (if using gas)
  Pepper

1 FOR THE SAUCE Combine water, oregano, and salt in small bowl and let sit until oregano is softened, about 15 minutes. Pulse parsley, cilantro, garlic, and pepper flakes in food processor until coarsely chopped, about 10 pulses. Add water mixture and vinegar and pulse to combine. Transfer mixture to bowl and slowly whisk in oil until emulsified. Cover and let sit at room temperature for 1 hour.

2 FOR THE STEAKS Meanwhile, combine cornstarch and salt in bowl. Pat steaks dry with paper towels and place on wire rack set in rimmed baking sheet. Rub entire surface of steaks with cornstarch mixture and place steaks, uncovered, in freezer until very firm, about 30 minutes.

3A FOR A CHARCOAL GRILL Open bottom vent halfway. Light large chimney starter filled with charcoal briquettes (6 quarts). When top coals are partially covered with ash, pour evenly over grill. Using tongs, place wood chunks directly on top of coals, spacing them evenly around perimeter of grill. Set cooking grate in place, cover, and open lid vent halfway. Heat grill until hot and wood chunks are smoking, about 5 minutes.

3B FOR A GAS GRILL Turn all burners to high, cover, and heat grill until hot, about 15 minutes. Leave all burners on high. Place wood chunks in disposable

291 Grilled Steak the South American Way

RECIPE FOR SUCCESS

✓ WHY THIS RECIPE WORKS

In Argentina, 2-pound steaks are grilled over a hardwood fire so they pick up a lot of smoke flavor. Because these steaks are so big, they spend plenty of time on the grill and emerge with a thick, flavorful browned crust. When translated to smaller American steaks, the method falters. Our goal was to devise a technique that would prolong the grill time (so the steaks could pick up more wood flavor) and maximize browning. We rubbed the steaks with salt and used the freezer as a dehydrator to evaporate all the surface moisture; this helped develop a crisp crust on the grill, and rubbing the dried steaks with cornstarch enhanced browning even more. And covering the grill for the first few minutes of cooking time helped jump-start the flavoring process.

Grilled Argentine Steaks with Chimichurri Sauce

SERVES 6 TO 8

The chimichurri sauce can be made up to three days in advance.

aluminum pie plate and set on cooking grate. Close lid and heat until wood chunks begin to smoke, about 5 minutes.

4 Clean and oil cooking grate. Season steaks with pepper. Place steaks on grill, cover, and cook until beginning to brown on both sides, 4 to 6 minutes, flipping halfway through cooking.

5 Flip steaks and cook, uncovered, until well browned on first side, 2 to 4 minutes. Flip steaks and continue to cook until meat registers 115 to 120 degrees (for rare) or 120 to 125 degrees (for medium-rare), 2 to 6 minutes longer.

6 Transfer steaks to carving board, tent with aluminum foil, and let rest for 10 minutes. Slice each steak ¼ inch thick. Serve, passing sauce separately.

292

TEST KITCHEN TIP
Preserving Salt's Crunch

Since the crunchy texture of a finishing salt is just as important as the seasoning it provides, we were disappointed when the flaky sea salt we sprinkled on fish fillets, steaks, and chicken breasts dissolved almost instantly in the food's juices.

In search of a way to maintain the crunch, we tried tossing Maldon Sea Salt Flakes (our favorite finishing salt) in a spoonful of oil to create a moisture barrier. While the oil-coated crystals indeed stayed intact on food (after 10 minutes they were unchanged), the oil caused the salt to clump, making even sprinkling virtually impossible.

Next, we turned to vegetable oil spray, which produced a gossamer coating that precluded clumping—and dissolving. Simply discharge a ⅓-second spray into a small bowl (say "one," and you're done), add 1½ teaspoons of flaky sea salt, and stir to coat. (Be sure to spritz first and then add the salt, lest the flakes fly everywhere.)

293
STEP BY STEP
Keys to Smoky, Crisp-Crusted Grilled Steak

Here's how we produced our own brand of smoky charred churrasco—even without the aid of a wood-burning Argentine grill.

1 USE THE RIGHT RUB Rubbing the steaks with cornstarch and salt seasons the meat and expedites crust formation by drying the meat's exterior; cornstarch also enhances browning.

2 FREEZE BRIEFLY The freezer's cold, dry air drives off exterior moisture and chills the steaks' interiors, so they can stay on the grill longer, soaking up more smoke flavor.

3 ADD WOOD CHUNKS TO THE FIRE Four large chunks of unsoaked wood added to a single-level fire infuse the meat with wood-grilled flavor. (If using a gas grill, place the chunks in a perforated disposable aluminum pie plate before placing on cooking grate.)

294

Soy Sauce

At its most basic, soy sauce is a fermented liquid made from soybeans and wheat. The soybeans contribute a strong, pungent taste, while the wheat lends sweetness. Soy sauce should add flavor and contribute complexity to your food—not just make it salty. In most supermarkets today, you will find a shelf full of options. How do you choose? We tasted a lineup of 12 soy sauces, first plain, then with rice, and finally cooked in a teriyaki sauce and brushed over broiled chicken thighs. In the test kitchen, we use soy sauce not only in numerous Asian-flavored dishes, but also to enhance meaty flavor in sauces, stews, soups, and braises. Our winner for cooked applications has a robust flavor that holds up during boiling and reducing and a higher sugar content that reacts to heat, causing browning and bringing about a richer, more savory flavor. Our dipping favorite is double-fermented over an unusually long period, which produces a complex bouquet of aroma and flavor and mellows the salt impact, making it preferable for dipping and noncooking applications.

THE BOTTOM LINE Sweeter, saltier sauces like **Lee Kum Kee Table Top Premium** are best for cooking with, while lower-sodium options such as **Ohsawa Nama Shoyu** win out for dipping.

WINNER

(BEST FOR COOKING)

LEE KUM KEE Table Top Premium Soy Sauce

Tasting Comments This Chinese brand won the rice and teriyaki tastings. With rice, its flavor was described as "salty, sweet, roasted, pleasant," and "fruity," with a "great aroma." Cooked in teriyaki, it was "salty, malty, and delicious," with "good depth" and "balance." Contains more sodium than other brands tested.

WINNER

(BEST FOR DIPPING)

OHSAWA NAMA SHOYU Organic Unpasteurized Soy Sauce

Tasting Comments This Japanese brand won the plain tasting, with its flavor described as "clean," "caramel," and "rich and nuanced." A few tasters called it "sweet and dimensional," even "floral," with one adding that it was "lighter in style and flavor than others." Contains less sodium than other brands tested.

295

RECIPE FOR SUCCESS

Steak and Booze—Hold the Hangover

✓ WHY THIS RECIPE WORKS

We tried several drunken steak recipes, but the flavor was all over the place—some steaks were barely tipsy while others had us picking a designated driver. We wanted our recipe to fall somewhere in the middle of these two extremes. Loose-grained steaks, like the flank steak in this recipe, absorbed more marinade, and thus more flavor, than tight-grained steaks. Scoring the surface of the meat allowed the marinade to penetrate into the steak without compromising the interior color or texture. The soy sauce in the marinade not only added intense flavor but also kept the meat moist during cooking due to its salt. The marinade's sugar content (from the alcohol and the brown sugar) encouraged a crust to form on the steak. Since the marinade dulled a little during grilling, we refreshed it by drizzling a bit of reserved marinade over the rested and sliced cooked steak just before serving. For an easy variation, we switched from light rum to tequila for a margarita-flavored take on drunken steak.

Drunken Steak

SERVES 4

Other thin steaks with a loose grain, such as skirt or steak tips, can be substituted for the flank steak. If using a gas grill, grill the steak covered for maximum heat output. Don't marinate the steak for longer than 4 hours or it will turn gray and mushy.

- 1 cup light rum
- ½ cup soy sauce
- 1 tablespoon packed brown sugar
- 1 tablespoon grated fresh ginger
- 1 garlic clove, minced
- 1 scallion, minced
- 1 (1½-pound) flank steak, trimmed

1 Whisk rum, soy sauce, sugar, ginger, and garlic together in bowl to dissolve sugar. Transfer ¼ cup of marinade to separate bowl, stir in scallion, and set aside for serving.

2 Using sharp knife, lightly score both sides of steak at 1½-inch intervals in crosshatch pattern. Combine remaining marinade and steak in 1-gallon zipper-lock bag and toss to coat; press out as much air as possible and seal bag. Refrigerate for 1 to 4 hours, flipping bag every 30 minutes. Before grilling, remove steak from bag and pat dry with paper towels.

3A FOR A CHARCOAL GRILL Open bottom vent completely. Light large chimney starter filled with charcoal briquettes (6 quarts). When top coals are partially covered with ash, pour evenly over half of grill. Set cooking grate in place, cover, and open lid vent completely. Heat grill until hot, about 5 minutes.

3B FOR A GAS GRILL Turn all burners to high, cover, and heat grill until hot, about 15 minutes. Leave primary burner on high and turn other burner(s) to medium.

4 Clean and oil cooking grate. Place steak on hotter side of grill. Cook (covered if using gas), turning as needed, until lightly charred on both sides and meat registers 120 to 125 degrees (for medium-rare), 8 to 12 minutes.

5 Transfer steak to carving board, tent with aluminum foil, and let rest for 5 to 10 minutes. Slice steak thin against grain, drizzle with reserved marinade, and serve.

VARIATION

296 Margarita Drunken Steak

Substitute following mixture for marinade: Whisk ¾ cup tequila, ¼ cup triple sec, 1 tablespoon granulated sugar, ½ teaspoon ground cumin, and ¼ teaspoon cayenne pepper together in bowl. Transfer ¼ cup marinade to small bowl, stir in 1 tablespoon minced fresh cilantro, and set aside for serving.

STEP BY STEP
Secrets to Perfect Drunken Steak

1 SCORE LIGHTLY Scoring both sides of steak at 1½-inch intervals allows marinade to flavor meat more deeply. (Be sure to use sharp knife.)

2 MARINADE The marinade's sugar content (from alcohol and the brown sugar) encourages a crust to form on steak when it's grilled.

3 DRY Pat steak dry before grilling to further facilitate formation of crust.

298

RECIPE FOR SUCCESS

A Fresh Take on an Old Standard

✅ WHY THIS RECIPE WORKS

For a streamlined, modern-day twist on beef Wellington, that classic combination of tender meat, sautéed mushrooms, and rich pâté wrapped in flaky puff pastry, we decided to not only pare back the ingredient list, but also move the cooking outside. We wanted to take this decadent dish from a buffet standard with hours of required preparation to a quick, easy, and accessible meal. First, we grilled our filets mignons and mushrooms and then sliced them thin. Before layering them on thick pieces of grilled country bread—our answer to puff pastry—we applied a thin coating of duck liver pâté. Reduced balsamic vinegar, drizzled over each beef Wellington, was the perfect finishing touch. Our modern take on beef Wellington still had top-shelf taste, but without the fuss and in a fraction of the time.

Grilled Free-Form Beef Wellington with Balsamic Reduction

SERVES 4

½ cup balsamic vinegar

3 (8-ounce) filets mignons, about 2 inches thick, trimmed

4 large portobello mushroom caps, about 4 inches in diameter

2 tablespoons olive oil

Salt and pepper

4 thick slices rustic or country bread

4 ounces smooth duck liver pâté

1 Simmer vinegar in small saucepan over medium heat until reduced to 3 tablespoons, about 5 minutes; transfer to bowl. Pat steaks and mushrooms dry with paper towels, brush with oil, and season with salt and pepper.

2A FOR A CHARCOAL GRILL Open bottom vent completely. Light large chimney starter filled with charcoal briquettes (6 quarts). When top coals are partially covered with ash, pour two-thirds evenly over half of grill, then pour remaining one-third over other half of grill. Set cooking grate in place, cover, and open lid vent completely. Heat grill until hot, about 5 minutes.

2B FOR A GAS GRILL Turn all burners to high, cover, and heat grill until hot, about 15 minutes. Leave primary burner on high and turn other burner(s) to medium.

3 Clean and oil cooking grate. Place steaks on hotter side of grill and cook (covered if using gas) until well browned on first side, 2 to 3 minutes. Slide steaks to cooler side of grill and cook, turning as needed, until meat registers 120 to 125 degrees (for medium-rare), 5 to 9 minutes. Transfer steaks to carving board, tent with aluminum foil, and let rest while grilling mushrooms and bread.

4 Place mushrooms on hotter side of grill. Cook, turning once, until tender and lightly browned, 8 to 10 minutes; transfer to platter. Place bread slices on cooler side of grill until golden brown on both sides, 1 to 1½ minutes; transfer to platter.

5 Spread pâté over grilled bread. Slice mushrooms; lay on top of pâté. Slice steaks ¼ inch thick and lay on top of portobellos. Drizzle with reduced balsamic vinegar and serve.

299

SHOPPING IQ
Balsamic Vinegar

The traditional process for producing balsamic vinegar takes a minimum of 12 years and a vinegar can only be called "tradizionale" if it is created in one of two specific Italian provinces. These rules are thrown out the window when it comes to commercial balsamic vinegar, however. We tasted both top-selling, nationally available supermarket balsamic vinegars and several traditional balsamics both plain and in vinaigrettes and glazes. While even the best of the commercial bunch couldn't compete with the complex, rich flavor of true balsamic vinegar when tasted plain, several of the supermarket options held up just fine in the vinaigrette and cooked applications. In dressing, the traditional stuff did not justify its price tag, and in a pan sauce most of that fine aroma and depth of flavor was cooked away. A good supermarket balsamic vinegar must be sweet and thick (like the real deal), but it should also offer acidity. Our winner worked well both plain and in cooked dishes.

THE BOTTOM LINE Don't waste your money on pricey traditional balsamic vinegar if you're going to toss it on salad or cook with it. The good stuff works best uncooked, as a drizzle to finish a dish. Our favorite is **Cavalli Gold Seal Extra Vecchio Aceto Balsamico Tradizionale**. In vinaigrette or cooked sauce, the sharpness of a supermarket balsamic like **Bertolli Balsamic Vinegar** adds a pleasingly bright contrast to the vinegar's natural sweetness.

**WINNER
(BEST TRADITIONAL)**

CAVALLI GOLD SEAL Extra Vecchio Aceto Balsamico Tradizionale di Reggio Emilia
Price $199.99 for 3.38 oz ($60 per oz)
Tasting Comments Not so surprisingly, the 25-year aging period of this balsamic vinegar paid off. Although you won't find it in supermarkets, tasters waxed poetic about its "pomegranate," "caramel," "smoky" flavor that "coats the tongue" and tastes "amazing."

**WINNER
(BEST SUPERMARKET BRAND)**

BERTOLLI Balsamic Vinegar of Modena
Price $3.49 for 8.5 oz ($0.41 per oz)
Tasting Comments Served plain, this balsamic vinegar tasted of dried fruit like figs, raisins, and prunes. Some of these nuances disappeared once it was reduced or whisked into vinaigrette, but it still tasted pleasantly sweet. While its texture was fairly thin, its flavor earned high marks in the dressing and the glaze.

301 Bright and Balanced Steak Salad

✓ WHY THIS RECIPE WORKS

In the best versions of Thai grilled beef salad, known as *nam tok*, the cuisine's five signature flavor elements—hot, sour, salty, sweet, and bitter—come into balance, making for a light but satisfying dish. We tested a wide variety of cuts and chose our winner, flank steak, for its uniform shape, moderate price, and decent tenderness. We used the test kitchen's standard half-grill fire for grilling the meat, starting the meat over high heat to sear the exterior and then moving it to the cooler side to finish cooking for a perfect medium-rare steak with a nicely charred crust. The dressing for this dish should have a good balance between hot, sour, salty, and sweet to provide a counterpoint to the subtle bitter char of the meat. Fish sauce, lime juice, sugar, and a mix of hot spices provided these elements and the final addition—toasted rice powder made in a food processor—added extra body to the dressing.

Grilled Thai Beef Salad
SERVES 4 TO 6

Serve with rice, if desired. If fresh Thai chiles are unavailable, substitute ½ serrano chile. Don't skip the toasted rice; it's integral to the texture and flavor of the dish. Any variety of white rice can be used. Toasted rice powder (*kao kua*) can also be found in many Asian markets; substitute 1 tablespoon rice powder for the white rice.

- 1 teaspoon paprika
- 1 teaspoon cayenne pepper
- 1 tablespoon white rice
- 3 tablespoons lime juice (2 limes)
- 2 tablespoons fish sauce
- 2 tablespoons water
- ½ teaspoon sugar
- 1 (1½-pound) flank steak, trimmed
  Salt and coarsely ground white pepper

300 Knowing When To Flip Your Steak— Thai Style

This salad's Thai name, *nam tok* (literally "water falling"), refers to the beads of moisture that form on the surface of the steak as it cooks—an age-old Thai cookery clue that the meat is ready to be flipped. While this method sounded imprecise, during testing we found it to be a surprisingly accurate gauge of when the flank steak is halfway done. Here's why: As this steak's interior gets hotter, its tightly packed fibers contract and release some of their interior moisture, which the fire's heat then pushes to the meat's surface. When turned at this point and cooked for an equal amount of time on the second side, the steak emerged deeply charred on the outside and medium-rare within. (Note: We do not recommend this technique across the board for steaks; since the thickness and density of the meat fibers vary from cut to cut, the time it takes for heat to penetrate and for beads of moisture to be pushed to the meat's surface differs.)

Time to Flip
For perfectly cooked meat, flip the steak when beads of moisture appear on its surface.

1 seedless English cucumber, sliced ¼ inch thick on bias

4 shallots, sliced thin

1½ cups fresh mint leaves, torn

1½ cups fresh cilantro leaves

1 Thai chile, stemmed, seeded, and sliced thin into rounds

1 Heat paprika and cayenne in 8-inch skillet over medium heat; cook, shaking pan, until fragrant, about 1 minute. Transfer to small bowl. Return skillet to medium-high heat, add rice and toast, stirring constantly, until deep golden brown, about 5 minutes. Transfer to small bowl and let cool for 5 minutes. Grind rice with spice grinder, mini food processor, or mortar and pestle until it resembles fine meal, 10 to 30 seconds (you should have about 1 tablespoon rice powder).

2 Whisk lime juice, fish sauce, water, sugar, and ¼ teaspoon toasted paprika mixture in large bowl and set aside.

3A FOR A CHARCOAL GRILL Open bottom vent completely. Light large chimney starter filled with charcoal briquettes (6 quarts). When top coals are partially covered with ash, pour in even layer over half of grill. Set cooking grate in place, cover, and open lid vent completely. Heat grill until hot, about 5 minutes.

3B FOR A GAS GRILL Turn all burners to high, cover, and heat grill until hot, about 15 minutes. Leave primary burner on high and turn off other burner(s).

4 Clean and oil cooking grate. Pat steak dry and season with salt and white pepper. Place steak on hotter part of grill and cook until beginning to char and beads of moisture appear on outer edges of meat, 5 to 6 minutes. Flip steak, continue to cook on second side until meat registers 120 to 125 degrees (for medium-rare), about 5 minutes longer. Transfer to carving board, tent with aluminum foil, and let rest for 10 minutes (or let cool to room temperature, about 1 hour).

5 Line large platter with cucumber slices. Slice steak ¼ inch thick against grain on bias. Transfer sliced steak to bowl with fish sauce mixture. Add shallots, mint, cilantro, Thai chile, and half of rice powder, and toss to combine. Arrange steak over cucumber-lined platter. Serve, passing remaining rice powder and remaining toasted paprika mixture separately.

302 RECIPE FOR SUCCESS
Steak Salad with an Asian Twist

✓ WHY THIS RECIPE WORKS

To put a new spin on the classic steakhouse combo of beef and mushrooms, we grilled both ingredients and then served the smoky pair atop a spinach salad with an Asian-inspired dressing. We built our bold dressing from rice vinegar, fresh ginger, soy sauce, and brown sugar; toasted sesame oil and miso paste deepened its flavor. It also doubled as a quick and easy marinade for the mushrooms. If you have time, you can marinate the mushrooms in the dressing for up to 1 hour before grilling for even more flavor.

Spinach Salad with Grilled Beef, Mushrooms, and Miso-Ginger Dressing

SERVES 4

Look for portobello mushrooms that measure 5 to 6 inches in diameter. If using smaller mushrooms, reduce the cooking time by a few minutes. You can substitute rib-eye steaks of a similar thickness for the strip steaks, if desired.

- 3 tablespoons rice vinegar
- 1 tablespoon soy sauce
- 1 tablespoon packed brown sugar
- 1 tablespoon white miso
- 1 teaspoon grated fresh ginger
- ⅓ cup vegetable oil
- 1 tablespoon toasted sesame oil
- 2 large portobello mushroom caps, gills removed
  Salt and pepper
- 2 (10- to 12-ounce) strip steaks, 1 inch thick, trimmed
- 5 ounces (5 cups) baby spinach

1 Whisk vinegar, soy sauce, sugar, miso, and ginger in bowl until sugar dissolves. Slowly whisk in vegetable oil and sesame oil. Toss mushrooms and ¼ cup dressing in second bowl and season with salt and pepper. Pat steaks dry and season with salt and pepper.

2A FOR A CHARCOAL GRILL Open bottom vent completely. Light large chimney starter filled with charcoal briquettes (6 quarts). When top coals are partially covered with ash pour evenly over grill. Set cooking grate in place, cover, and open lid vent completely. Heat grill until hot, about 5 minutes.

2B FOR A GAS GRILL Turn all burners to high, cover, and heat grill until hot, about 15 minutes. Leave all burners on high.

3 Clean and oil cooking grate. Grill steaks and mushrooms until well browned and steaks are cooked and register 115 to 120 degrees (for rare) or 120 to 125 degrees (for medium-rare), 3 to 5 minutes per side, and 4 to 5 minutes per side for mushrooms. Transfer steaks to cutting board, tent with aluminum foil, and let rest for 10 minutes. Transfer mushrooms to plate.

4 Slice steaks thin against grain and slice mushrooms thin. Toss spinach with 2 tablespoons dressing in bowl and season with salt and pepper to taste. Transfer spinach to platter or divide evenly among individual plates and top with steak and mushrooms. Spoon remaining dressing over salad and serve.

303 SHOPPING IQ
Miso

"Miso" is the Japanese word for bean paste. An ingredient commonly found in Asian (most notably Japanese) cuisines, miso is a fermented paste of soy beans and rice, barley, or rye. It is salty and ranges in strength and color from mild, pale yellow (referred to as white) miso to stronger-flavored red or brownish-black miso. The color of miso depends on its fermentation method and ingredients.

Miso paste is an incredibly versatile ingredient; it is suitable for use in soups, braises, dressings, and sauces and as a topping for grilled foods. The lighter misos are typically used in more delicate dishes like soups and salads; the darker misos are best used in heavier recipes. Miso can be found in most supermarkets as well as Japanese and Asian markets. It will keep for up to a year in the refrigerator.

304 Foolproof Steak Fajitas on the Grill

✓ WHY THIS RECIPE WORKS

Skirt steak makes great fajitas, but it can cook up tough if not handled properly. For skirt steak fajitas that packed meaty flavor and wouldn't overcook, we started with a marinade that included soy sauce. This helped brine the steak, keeping the meat moist. Pricking the steak with a fork helped the marinade penetrate the meat and cut the marinating time to only 30 minutes. We cooked the steak along with onions and bell peppers over a half-grill fire, which allowed us to get a good char on everything on the hot side of the grill. Then we moved the vegetables to the cooler side so they could cook through without getting burned. After the steak was cooked, we drizzled it with a second marinade and sliced the meat against the grain to make it more tender.

Skirt Steak Fajitas

SERVES 4

We prefer the beefier flavor of skirt steak, but you can use flank steak, which is wider. Don't marinate the steak for longer than 2 hours or it will begin to turn mushy. To make this dish spicier, add the chile, ribs, and seeds to the marinade in step 1. Toast the cumin in a dry skillet over medium heat until fragrant (about 1 minute) and then remove the pan from the heat so the cumin won't scorch. Serve the fajitas plain or with salsa, shredded cheese, and/or sour cream.

½	cup lime juice (4 limes)
¼	cup vegetable oil
2	tablespoons soy sauce
3	garlic cloves, minced
2	teaspoons ground cumin, toasted
2	teaspoons packed light brown sugar
1	jalapeño chile, stemmed, seeded, and chopped fine
1	tablespoon minced fresh cilantro
2	(12-ounce) skirt steaks, trimmed
2	pounds onions, sliced into ½-inch-thick rounds
3	large bell peppers (1 red and 2 green), stemmed, seeded, and halved, each half cut into thirds
12	(6-inch) flour tortillas

1 Whisk lime juice, 2 tablespoons oil, soy sauce, garlic, cumin, sugar, and jalapeño in bowl. Transfer ¼ cup marinade to second bowl, add cilantro, and set aside. Prick steaks with fork all over on each side, then cut each steak in half crosswise. Place steaks in 1-gallon zipper-lock bag, pour in marinade (without cilantro), seal bag, and refrigerate for at least 30 minutes or up to 2 hours. Remove steaks from bag, pat dry with paper towels, and discard marinade in bag.

2A FOR A CHARCOAL GRILL Open bottom vent completely. Light large chimney starter filled with charcoal briquettes (6 quarts). When top coals are partially covered with ash, pour evenly over half of grill. Set cooking grate in place, cover, and open lid vent completely. Heat grill until hot, about 5 minutes.

2B FOR A GAS GRILL Turn all burners to high, cover, and heat grill until hot, about 15 minutes. Leave primary burner on high and turn off other burner(s).

3 Clean and oil cooking grate. Brush onions and bell peppers with remaining 2 tablespoons oil. Grill onions and bell peppers on hotter side of grill, turning occasionally, until charred and softened, 8 to 12 minutes. (Bell peppers will cook more quickly.) Move vegetables to cooler side of grill. Grill steaks on hotter side of grill until seared on both sides but still pink in center, 4 to 6 minutes per side. Transfer steak and vegetables to serving platter, pour reserved marinade over top, cover with aluminum foil, and let rest for 5 minutes.

4 Meanwhile, warm tortillas on hotter side of grill, about 10 seconds per side. Wrap in dish towel or foil to keep warm. Separate onions into rings, slice bell peppers thin, and slice steak thin against grain. Serve immediately with bell peppers, onions, and warm tortillas.

305 SHOPPING IQ
Steak for Fajitas

We love the beefy flavor of skirt steak, but it's not as widely available as flank steak, which will also work in our Skirt Steak Fajitas. Both steaks share similar characteristics (long and thin and very flavorful), so how do you tell them apart? Skirt steak is narrower, and the grain runs crosswise. Flank steak is wider, and the grain runs lengthwise. When shopping for skirt steak, choose fattier cuts, which will add a lot of flavor to the fajitas. If using flank steak, cut the meat into thirds lengthwise rather than in half crosswise.

Skirt Steak

Flank Steak

306 SHOPPING IQ Corn Tortillas

While we love homemade corn tortillas, we usually rely on the convenience of store-bought. Good corn tortillas should be soft and pliable, with a fresh, light corn flavor. We compared tortillas in two blind taste tests, first assessing them warmed in an oven and served plain, and then pitting the top four products against one another in enchiladas. Tasters faulted many of the tortillas for being either too sweet or bland. Our winner had a hint of sweetness from its light, fresh corn flavor but no added sugar. It also had the most sodium by far, but no one found them too salty. Actually, they were quite flavorful, which makes sense because salt is a flavor booster. Texture is where supermarket corn tortillas can really go wrong; they're often crumbly and dry, and they break as you try to bend them around a filling. Our winner maintained pliability by adding wheat gluten, which binds with water to make the dough more cohesive and elastic, which in turn creates a softer, stronger tortilla. This also means that unlike most corn tortillas, our winner is not gluten-free. For those who need gluten-free tortillas, our second-place finisher, while lacking our winner's firm structure, is still a good option.

THE BOTTOM LINE Low sugar and high salt make the best combination for great flavor. If you're not worried about gluten, a corn tortilla with added protein from wheat, like our winner, **Maria and Ricardo's Handmade Style Soft Corn Tortillas**, is the most strong, supple option.

WINNER

MARIA AND RICARDO'S Handmade Style Soft Corn Tortillas, Yellow
Tasting Comments These "tender yet substantial" tortillas wrapped enchilada fillings securely with the help of wheat gluten that kept them soft and pliable. "Clean" and "mellow," the tortillas had a light, corn-like sweetness with a hint of nuttiness, perhaps from the griddle marks that speckled each tortilla.

RUNNER-UP

MISSION White Corn Tortillas, Restaurant Style
Tasting Comments These "mildly sweet" runner-up tortillas were "earthy," with good corn flavor and a drier yet more traditional texture (there is no added wheat gluten). Their "faint, stone-ground grit" was "pleasant," though some tasters complained that the tortillas were crumbly and disintegrated in the enchiladas.

307
RECIPE FOR SUCCESS
Smoky-Sweet Mexican Tacos

✅ **WHY THIS RECIPE WORKS**
In this popular north Mexican taco filling, rich, smoky beef is perfectly complemented by sweet-hot poblano chiles and piquant onions. The combination is deliciously to the point, unencumbered by competing flavors, and also very simple to put together. We wanted an authentic version of these tacos that could be made on a home grill. First, we tackled the chiles. We grilled the poblanos over a very hot fire; this left the skins charred and blistered while the flesh remained relatively unscathed. Putting the peppers in a covered bowl when they came off the grill made the bitter skins easier to peel off later. The onions needed only a quick stint over the fire to develop good grill marks. We found that marinating the skirt steak was unnecessary; instead, we covered the cooked steak with a flavorful puree of onion, lime juice, garlic, cumin, and salt while it rested. Finally, we sliced our skirt steak thin for a tender texture.

Grilled Skirt Steak and Poblano Tacos
SERVES 6
If you can't find skirt steak, you can substitute flank steak, although the meat will be a bit more chewy. Serve with chopped cilantro and Mexican *crema* or sour cream.

- 4 onions (3 sliced crosswise into ½-inch-thick rounds, 1 chopped coarse)
- 6 tablespoons lime juice (3 limes)
- 3 garlic cloves, minced
- ½ teaspoon ground cumin
- Salt and pepper
- 1½ pounds poblano chiles
- 1 tablespoon vegetable oil
- 2 pounds skirt steak, trimmed
- 18 (6-inch) corn tortillas
- Lime wedges

1 Process chopped onion, lime juice, garlic, cumin, and 1 teaspoon salt in food processor until smooth, about 20 seconds. Set aside. Brush onion rounds and poblanos with oil and season with salt and pepper. Pat steak dry and season with salt and pepper.

2A FOR A CHARCOAL GRILL Open bottom vent completely. Light large chimney starter filled with charcoal briquettes (6 quarts). When top coals are partially covered with ash, pour evenly over half of grill. Set cooking grate in place, cover, and open lid vent completely. Heat grill until hot, about 5 minutes.

2B FOR A GAS GRILL Turn all burners to high, cover, and heat grill until hot, about 15 minutes. Leave primary burner on high and turn off other burner(s).

3 Clean and oil cooking grate. Place poblanos on hotter side of grill and onion rounds on cooler side of grill. Grill (covered if using gas), turning as needed, until poblanos are blistered and blackened and onions are softened and golden, 6 to 12 minutes. Transfer onions to platter and cover to keep warm. Transfer poblanos to bowl, cover, and let steam while cooking steak and tortillas.

4 Place steak on hotter side of grill. Grill (covered if using gas), turning as needed, until well browned on both sides and meat registers 120 to 125 degrees (for medium-rare), 4 to 8 minutes. Transfer steak to 13 by 9-inch pan and poke all over with fork. Pour pureed onion mixture over top, cover, and let rest for 5 to 10 minutes.

5 Working in batches, grill tortillas, turning as needed, until warm and soft, about 30 seconds; wrap tightly in aluminum foil to keep soft.

6 Peel poblanos, then slice thin. Separate onions into rings and chop coarse, then toss with poblanos. Remove steak from marinade, slice into 4- to 6-inch lengths, then slice thin against grain. Serve with warm tortillas, poblano-onion mixture, and lime wedges.

308 SHOPPING IQ
Fresh Chiles

Fresh chiles often have vegetal or grassy flavors, with clean, punchy heat. Chiles get their heat from a compound called capsaicin, which is concentrated mostly in the inner whitish pith (called ribs), with progressively smaller amounts in the seeds and flesh. If you like a lot of heat, you can use the entire chile when cooking. If you prefer a milder dish, remove the ribs and seeds. The same chile can go by different names in different parts of the country and can range from green to red, depending on when it was harvested. To ensure that you're buying the chile called for in a recipe, it's a good idea to look at a photo before shopping. Whatever the variety, you should choose chiles with tight, unblemished skin and flesh that's firm to the touch.

	CHILE	APPEARANCE AND FLAVOR	HEAT	SUBSTITUTIONS
	Poblano	Large, triangular, green to red-brown; crisp, vegetal	🌶	Bell pepper, Anaheim
	Anaheim	Large, long, skinny, yellow-green to red; mildly tangy, vegetal	🌶🌶	Poblano
	Jalapeño	Small, smooth, shiny, green or red; bright, grassy	🌶🌶 ½	Serrano
	Serrano	Small, dark green; bright, citrusy	🌶🌶🌶	Jalapeño
	Habanero	Bulbous, bright orange to red; deeply floral, fruity	🌶🌶🌶🌶	Thai

309 RECIPE FOR SUCCESS
Making the Most of an Inexpensive Cut

✔ WHY THIS RECIPE WORKS

We wanted to perfect the grilling method for London broil, which is a name for inexpensive but robustly flavored top round steak. Using soy sauce as the base for our marinade encouraged moisture retention. By adding Italian-style flavorings, we came up with a potent marinade that provided deep flavor and good texture. We grilled the steak over the hotter side of a half-grill fire and flipped it every minute to help eliminate the gray, overcooked band of meat that often develops under the surface of the steak. Since the cooking time was less than 10 minutes over the hot fire, this level of attention didn't feel like too much work. However, since we were flipping the steak so often, the meat did not have time to develop a nicely charred crust. To remedy this without sacrificing our perfectly pink interior, we crosshatched both sides of the steak to expose additional surface area and create thin ridges that would crisp up quickly. We also patted the steak dry when we removed it from the marinade and added a simple spice rub. Not only did the spices crust nicely on the grill, they also provided a peppery kick to counter the meat's richness.

310 TEST KITCHEN TIP
Gray Bands Aren't Cool

Because London broil is typically 1½ inches thick, by the time the center of the grilled steak is a beautiful rosy pink, the meat near the exterior is overcooked and gray. To avoid the gray bands, we let the steak sit on the counter to take the chill off before grilling it, and we flip it every minute during grilling.

Overcooked Edges
Our technique works to minimize the overcooked bands of gray meat.

Grilled London Broil
SERVES 4

Because it's so lean, this steak is best served medium-rare to medium and sliced very thin (it will be tough and dry if cooked to well or beyond). You can use thyme in place of the rosemary and either sweet or hot paprika. Serve with Sweet and Smoky Grilled Tomato Salsa (recipe follows), if desired, but note that it will need to be prepared ahead.

- 1 (1½- to 2-pound) top round steak, 1½ inches thick, trimmed
- ½ cup soy sauce
- 2 tablespoons balsamic vinegar
- 2 tablespoons ketchup
- 2 tablespoons chopped fresh sage
- 5 garlic cloves, minced
- 1½ tablespoons vegetable oil
- 1 teaspoon chopped fresh rosemary
- 1½ teaspoons coarsely ground pepper
- 1 teaspoon paprika

1 Cut ½-inch crosshatch pattern, ¼ inch deep, on both sides of steak. Place steak in 1-gallon zipper-lock bag. Combine soy sauce, vinegar, ketchup, sage, garlic, oil, and rosemary in blender and process until garlic and herbs are finely chopped, about 30 seconds. Add marinade to bag with steak, seal, and turn to coat. Let sit at room temperature for 2 hours or refrigerate for up to 8 hours. (If refrigerated, bring steak to room temperature before grilling.)

2A FOR A CHARCOAL GRILL Open bottom vent completely. Light large chimney starter filled with charcoal briquettes (6 quarts). When top coals are partially covered with ash, pour evenly over half of grill. Set cooking grate in place, cover, and open lid vent completely. Heat grill until hot, about 5 minutes.

2B FOR A GAS GRILL Turn all burners to high, cover, and heat grill until hot, about 15 minutes. Leave all burners on high.

3 Combine pepper and paprika in bowl. Remove steak from marinade, pat dry with paper towels, and season with pepper mixture.

4 Clean and oil cooking grate. Place steak on grill (on hotter side if using charcoal) and cook for 1 minute. Flip and grill on second side for 1 minute. Repeat, flipping every minute, until steak registers 120 to 125 degrees (for medium-rare) or 130 to 135 degrees (for medium), 5 to 9 minutes. Transfer to carving board, tent with aluminum foil, and let rest for 10 minutes. Slice steak thin against grain and serve.

311 Sweet and Smoky Grilled Tomato Salsa

MAKES ABOUT 3 CUPS

Sugar and lime juice should be added at the end to taste, depending on the ripeness of the tomatoes. To make this salsa spicier, add the jalapeño ribs and seeds. The salsa can be refrigerated for up to two days; bring back to room temperature before serving. Wood chunks are not recommended for this recipe.

- 1 cup wood chips, soaked in water for 15 minutes and drained
- 2 pounds plum tomatoes, cored and halved lengthwise
- 2 large jalapeño chiles
- 2 teaspoons vegetable oil
- 3 tablespoons finely chopped red onion
- 2 tablespoons chopped fresh cilantro
- 2 tablespoons extra-virgin olive oil
- 1 (13 by 9-inch) disposable aluminum pan
  Salt and pepper
- 1–2 tablespoons lime juice
- ½–1 teaspoon sugar

1 Using large piece of heavy-duty aluminum foil, wrap soaked chips in 8 by 4 ½-inch foil packet. (Make sure chips do not poke holes in sides or bottom of packet.) Cut 2 evenly-spaced 2-inch slits in top of packet.

2A FOR A CHARCOAL GRILL Open bottom vent halfway. Light large chimney starter filled with charcoal briquettes (6 quarts). When top coals are partially covered with ash, pour evenly over half of grill. Set cooking grate in place, cover, and open lid vent halfway. Heat grill until hot, about 5 minutes.

2B FOR A GAS GRILL Turn all burners to high, cover, and heat grill until hot, about 15 minutes. Leave all burners on high.

3 Toss tomatoes, jalapeños, and vegetable oil together in bowl. Place tomatoes cut side down on hotter side of grill, cover, and cook until evenly charred on both sides and juices bubble, 8 to 12 minutes, flipping halfway through cooking.

4 Meanwhile, cook jalapeños on hotter side of grill until skins are blackened on all sides, 8 to 10 minutes, turning as needed.

5 Transfer tomatoes and jalapeños to disposable pan. If using charcoal, remove cooking grate and place wood chip packet on coals; set cooking grate in place. If using gas, remove cooking grate and place wood chip packet over primary burner; leave primary burner on high and turn other burner(s) to medium-low.

6 Place tomatoes and jalapeños on cooler side of grill, cover (position lid vent over tomatoes if using charcoal), and cook for 2 minutes. Transfer tomatoes and jalapeños to cutting board and let sit until cool enough to handle.

7 Stem, peel, seed, and finely chop jalapeños. Pulse tomatoes in food processor until broken down but still chunky, about 6 pulses. Transfer tomatoes to clean bowl and stir in jalapeños, onion, cilantro, olive oil, 1 teaspoon salt, and ¼ teaspoon pepper. Season with lime juice, sugar, salt, and pepper to taste. Let sit for 10 minutes before serving.

312

STEP BY STEP
Cut a Grid

To cook the London broil evenly throughout, we continually flipped it on the grill. But we had trouble getting a good crust with this method. For even cooking plus crust, we crosshatched the steak on both sides. As the steak grilled, the crosshatching split apart, exposing more surface area. We also sprinkled the raw steak with spices, which fell between the ridges. The thin ridges crisped and the spices crusted nicely.

Cut ½-inch crosshatch pattern, ¼ inch deep, on both sides of steak.

RECIPE FOR SUCCESS

Grill-Roasting without Breaking the Bank

✔ WHY THIS RECIPE WORKS

We set out to develop a method that would produce tender grill-roasted meat with an affordable price tag. We started with top sirloin, which has good beefy flavor and holds up well on the grill. We rubbed the roast all over with garlic, rosemary, and salt, wrapped it in plastic wrap, and refrigerated it for at least 18 hours to season the meat. Then we turned to our grill setup. Traditional recipes for grill roasting sear the meat over the hot side of the grill, then move it to the cooler side, where it cooks at a gentler pace. To ensure an evenly cooked, pink, tender interior for the top sirloin, we minimized the heat output by using only half a chimney's worth of coals. (To replicate this effect on a gas grill, we turned one burner to medium and the other burners off.) We also shielded the seared roast from excess heat by placing it in a disposable aluminum pan when we moved it to the grill's cooler side. We punched holes in the pan to make sure the meat's juices didn't ruin the seared crust. These changes helped to tenderize the roast by keeping its temperature low.

Inexpensive Grill-Roasted Beef with Garlic and Rosemary
SERVES 6 TO 8

A pair of kitchen shears works well for poking the holes in the aluminum pan. Start this recipe the day before you plan to grill so the salt rub has time to flavor and tenderize the meat.

- 6   garlic cloves, minced
- 2   tablespoons minced fresh rosemary
- 4   teaspoons kosher salt
- 1   tablespoon pepper
- 1   (3- to 4-pound) top sirloin roast, trimmed
- 1   (13 by 9-inch) disposable aluminum roasting pan

1 Combine garlic, rosemary, salt, and pepper in bowl. Sprinkle all sides of roast evenly with garlic mixture, wrap tightly in plastic wrap, and refrigerate for 18 to 24 hours.

2A FOR A CHARCOAL GRILL Open bottom vent halfway. Light large chimney starter half filled with charcoal briquettes (3 quarts). When top coals are partially covered with ash, pour evenly over one-third of grill. Set cooking grate in place, cover, and open lid vent halfway. Heat grill until hot, about 5 minutes.

2B FOR A GAS GRILL Turn all burners to high, cover, and heat grill until hot, about 15 minutes. Leave all burners on high.

3 Clean and oil cooking grate. Place roast on grill (on hotter side if using charcoal) and cook (covered if using gas) until well browned on all sides, 10 to 12 minutes, turning as needed. (If flare-ups occur, move roast to cooler side of grill until flames die down.)

4 Meanwhile, poke fifteen ¼-inch holes in center of disposable pan in area roughly same size as roast. Once browned, place beef in pan over holes and set pan over cooler side of grill (if using charcoal) or turn primary burner to medium and turn off other burner(s) (if using gas). (Adjust primary burner as needed to maintain grill temperature between 250 and 300 degrees.) Cover and cook until meat registers 120 to 125 degrees (for medium-rare) or 130 to 135 degrees (for medium), 40 minutes to 1 hour, rotating pan halfway through cooking.

5 Transfer roast to wire rack set in rimmed baking sheet, tent with aluminum foil, and let rest for 20 minutes. Transfer roast to carving board, slice very thin against grain, and serve.

VARIATION

314 Inexpensive Grill-Roasted Beef with Shallot and Tarragon
Substitute 1 minced shallot for garlic and 2 tablespoons minced fresh tarragon for rosemary.

315 TEST KITCHEN TIP
Keeping the Heat Down

Traditional recipes for grill-roasting call for searing the meat over the hotter side of the grill and then moving it to the cooler side, where it cooks at a slower, gentler pace. To ensure an evenly cooked, rosy-pink, tender interior, we adjusted that approach in two ways: First, we minimized the overall heat output by using only half a chimney's worth of coals—just enough to give the meat a good sear. (To replicate this effect on a gas grill, we turned one burner to medium and the other burners off.) Second, we shielded the seared roast from excess heat by placing it in a disposable aluminum pan when we moved it to the grill's cooler side. Both measures help keep the roast below 122 degrees for as long as possible; past this temperature, the enzymes that tenderize meat are inactivated. And the more time meat has to break down, the more tender the results.

316 STEP BY STEP
How to Grill-Roast

Grill roasting is best for relatively large foods that are already tender and don't require prolonged cooking. Grill-roasting temperatures typically range from 300 to 400 degrees, and cooking times are relatively short, usually less than 1 or 2 hours. (Whole turkeys can take up to 3 hours.) The smokiness from the grill can be the primary flavoring for grill-roasted food, but meat and poultry can also be dusted with a spice rub or seasoned with herbs before roasting. Alternatively the food can be basted with a glaze during the final minutes of cooking.

Another flavoring option for grill roasting is to add wood chips or chunks during cooking to bump up the smoke factor. Steps 1 and 2 and 4 below explain how to use wood. Wood chips will work on either a charcoal or a gas grill, but chunks are suited only to charcoal fires since they must rest in a pile of lit coals to smoke. Both must be soaked and drained before using to add enough moisture to prevent them from igniting as soon as they're set on fire. One medium wood chunk is equivalent to 1 cup of chips. Soaked wood chunks can be added directly to lit charcoal, but wood chips typically require a little more prep before putting them on the fire (although occasionally we put chips directly on lit coals). Wood chips and chunks are made from hardwoods because they burn more slowly than softer woods. Hickory and mesquite are most common, though some stores may also carry apple, cherry, or oak. Resinous woods like pine are not used for grilling because they give foods an off-flavor.

1 SOAK WOOD THOROUGHLY Place amount of chips or chunks specified in recipe in bowl and cover with water. Soak chips for 15 minutes; soak chunks for 1 hour. Drain.

2 WRAP CHIPS IN FOIL Using large piece of heavy-duty aluminum foil, wrap chips in 8 by 4½-inch foil packet. Make sure chips do not poke holes in sides or bottom of packet. Cut 2 evenly spaced 2-inch slits in top of packet.

3 SET UP AN INDIRECT FIRE Set up half-grill fire or double-banked fire so that part of grill has no fire. For double-banked fire on gas grill, after preheating grill, leave primary burner and burner at opposite end of grill on medium-high, medium, or as directed in recipe, and turn off center burner(s).

4 ADD WOOD, IF DESIRED Place aluminum foil packet of chips on lit coals of charcoal grill or over primary burner on gas grill.

5 START BY SEARING Clean and oil cooking grate. Place food on hotter side of grill and cook, turning as infrequently as possible, until well browned.

6 MOVE TO COOLER SIDE After searing, slide food to cooler side of grill and cover. Cook, rotating food once if necessary (particularly if using half-grill fire), until it reaches desired internal temperature. Replenish charcoal if required. Let meat rest, then slice and serve.

317 TEST KITCHEN TIP
Favorite Cuts and How to Handle Them

For the most well-seasoned, juicy results, we recommend salting or brining these grill-roasting go-tos. Salting is best for cuts that are already relatively moist and well marbled; because brining introduces moisture to the meat, it provides added insurance against drying out for leaner cuts. When salting, use 1 teaspoon of kosher salt per pound of meat; for brining, use ¼ cup of table salt per 2 quarts of water (for a chicken, use ½ cup table salt). See page 65 for illustrations of banked and split fire set-ups.

CUT	BRINE/SALT TIME	TYPICAL FIRE	COMMENTS
Top Sirloin Roast (3 to 4 pounds)	Salt 6 to 24 hours	Banked	A lengthy exposure to salt helps tenderize this inexpensive, exceptionally beefy roast.
Beef Tenderloin (6 pounds)	Salt 6 to 24 hours	Banked	Adding a little smoke to the fire will give this mild-tasting roast a flavor boost.
Prime Rib (7 pounds)	Salt 6 to 24 hours	Banked	When trimming, leave a layer of fat about ¼ inch thick to baste the meat and prevent it from drying out.
Whole Chicken (3½ to 4 pounds)	Salt 6 to 24 hours or brine 1 hour	Split	Start the bird breast side down to allow the grill marks to fade and the skin to brown more evenly.
Whole Turkey (12 to 14 pounds)	Salt 24 to 48 hours or brine 6 to 12 hours	Split	Birds larger than 14 pounds risk burning before the interior is cooked through. Propping up the bird on a V-rack helps prevent scorching.
Turkey Breast (5 to 7 pounds)	Salt 6 to 24 hours or brine 3 to 6 hours	Banked	Look for breasts smaller than 7 pounds, which will cook through by the time the fire burns out—no coal replenishing necessary.
Boneless Pork Loin (2½ to 3 pounds)	Salt 6 to 24 hours or brine 1½ to 2 hours	Split	To prevent drying out, look for roasts with at least a ⅛-inch-thick layer of fat on one side.
Bone-In Pork Roast (4 to 5 pounds)	Salt 6 to 24 hours	Banked	Ask your butcher to remove the tip of the chine bone and cut the remainder of the bone between the ribs for easy carving.

318 TEST KITCHEN TIPS
Three Keys to the Best Results

USE A THERMOMETER Since the type of grill and even the weather can affect cooking times, the only way to ensure proper doneness is to take the meat's temperature. We highly recommend the instant-read **Thermoworks Splash-Proof Super-Fast Thermapen** and the **IDevices Kitchen Thermometer**.

RACK IT UP To protect the bottom crust from turning soggy as the meat rests, set the roast on a wire rack as it cools.

DON'T RUSH THE REST Resting meat for at least 20 minutes (or as long as 40 minutes for very large roasts) after cooking helps it hold on to precious juices. Want proof? Four-pound pork roasts cooked at 400 degrees that we sliced immediately after cooking shed an average of 10 tablespoons of liquid, while meat rested for 40 minutes lost an average of just 2 teaspoons.

319 RECIPE FOR SUCCESS Protecting a Major Meat Investment on the Grill

✓ WHY THIS RECIPE WORKS

Grilled tenderloin sounds appealing, but with a whole tenderloin going for as much as $100, uneven cooking, bland flavor, and a tough outer crust just don't cut it. To flavor the meat, we salted it, covered it loosely in plastic, and let it rest on the counter before hitting the hot grill. Tucking the narrow tip end of the tenderloin under and tying it securely gave the tenderloin a more consistent thickness that allowed it to cook through more evenly on the grill. Direct heat was too hot for the roast to endure throughout the entire cooking time, so after briefly searing the meat over the coals and flames, we moved it away from the heat for grill roasting via indirect heat. As a variation, we liked adding wood chips to the grill to gently boost the meat's smoky flavor. To prevent the meat from tasting too smoky, we held off on adding the wood chips to the grill until after we'd seared the meat.

Grill-Roasted Beef Tenderloin

SERVES 10 TO 12

Beef tenderloins purchased from wholesale clubs are significantly less expensive but require a good amount of trimming before cooking; for information on how to trim a beef tenderloin roast, see page 351.

- 1 (6-pound) whole unpeeled beef tenderloin, trimmed
- 1½ tablespoons kosher salt
- 2 tablespoons vegetable oil
- 1 tablespoon pepper

1 Tuck tail end of tenderloin and tie roast at 2-inch intervals with kitchen twine. Pat roast dry with paper towels and rub with salt. Cover loosely with plastic wrap and let sit at room temperature for 1 hour. Pat tenderloin dry with paper towels, rub with oil, and sprinkle with pepper.

2A FOR A CHARCOAL GRILL Open bottom vent halfway. Light large chimney starter filled with charcoal briquettes (6 quarts). When top coals are partially covered with ash, pour evenly over half of grill. Set cooking grate in place, cover, and open lid vent halfway. Heat grill until hot, about 5 minutes.

2B FOR A GAS GRILL Turn all burners to high, cover, and heat grill until hot, about 15 minutes. Leave all burners on high.

3 Clean and oil cooking grate. Place roast on hotter side of grill. Cook (covered if using gas), turning as needed, until well browned on all sides, 8 to 10 minutes. If using gas, leave primary burner on high and turn off other burner(s).

4 Slide beef to cooler side of grill. Cover (position lid vent over meat if using charcoal) and cook until center of meat registers 120 to 125 degrees (for medium-rare), 15 to 30 minutes. (Center of roast will remain a degree more rare than ends.)

5 Transfer roast to carving board, tent with aluminum foil, and let rest for 15 to 20 minutes. Remove twine, cut into ½-inch-thick slices, and serve.

VARIATION

320 Smoked Grill-Roasted Beef Tenderloin

If you'd like to use wood chunks instead of wood chips when using a charcoal grill, substitute two medium wood chunks, soaked in water for 1 hour, for the wood chip packet.

Before grilling, soak 2 cups wood chips in water for 15 minutes, then drain. Using large piece of heavy-duty aluminum foil, wrap soaked chips in 8 by 4½-inch foil packet. (Make sure chips do not poke holes in sides or bottom of packet.) Cut 2 evenly spaced 2-inch slits in top of each foil packet. After browning meat in step 3, transfer to large platter. Remove cooking grate, place wood chip packet directly on coals or primary burner, set grate in place, and cover. Let chips begin to smoke, about 5 minutes, before returning meat to grill and cooking as directed in step 4.

321 Faster Fire Starter

We wouldn't dream of starting a charcoal fire without a chimney starter. These cylindrical canisters, shaped like giant metal coffee mugs, quickly ignite quarts of briquettes without lighter fluid (which can leave residual flavor on food). As an added benefit, these handy tools are hardly a splurge—we didn't test a single model above $26. Here's how they work: You put briquettes in the large top chamber, place a crumpled sheet of newspaper in the smaller chamber under the coals, and light it. In about 20 minutes, the coals are red-hot; covered with fine, gray ash; and ready to pour into your grill.

THE BOTTOM LINE Weber Rapidfire Chimney Starter is about half the price of other models, at $14.99. We loved its sturdy construction, generous capacity, heat-resistant handle, and second handle for pouring control. With the most ventilation holes, this canister ignited coals quickly.

322 GADGETS & GEAR
Carving Knives

A carving knife is indispensable year-round for cutting everything from brisket on the Fourth of July to roasts during the holidays. It's specially designed to cut neatly through meat's muscle fibers and connective tissues—no other knife can cut with such precision in a single stroke. We set out to find the best, and based on previous knife-testing experience we were already aware of key attributes to look for: an extra-long, sturdy, tapered blade with a round tip, which allows for easy, trouble-free strokes; a Granton edge (oval scallops carved into both sides of the blade, making a thinner edge on the blade possible without sacrificing the heft or rigidity carried by the top of the blade), which produces thinner slices with little effort; and, finally, a comfortable handle.

THE BOTTOM LINE After our test of nine knives that fit our criteria, the **Victorinox 12″ Fibrox Granton Edge Slicing/Carving Knife** (Model 47645) came out in front, scoring top points in slicing, sharpness, and comfort.

323
RECIPE FOR SUCCESS
Bringing a Beloved Sandwich Home

✔ WHY THIS RECIPE WORKS

Baltimore's "barbecue" tradition involves superthin slices of grill-roasted beef piled on a soft bun with "tiger sauce," a simple sauce of mayonnaise and horseradish. To figure out which cut of beef to use in this recipe, we went right to the source, and found out that many of Baltimore's pit beef joints use whole top or bottom rounds. Although flavorful, these cuts are huge and require a meat slicer to cut them thin enough to be tender. Instead, we turned to top sirloin roast: Its affordability, tenderness, and flavor make it a perfect candidate for this recipe. In terms of flavor, what sets pit beef apart is the salty, spicy, nearly blackened crust. We used a version of the traditional paprika-based spice rub and cut the roast in half before adding the rub to maximize surface area and speed up the flavoring process. To protect our roasts from developing an overcooked, gray ring around the edges, we wrapped them in aluminum foil and started them over an indirect flame. Later, we removed the foil and cranked up the grill to achieve the signature dark crust with a perfectly rosy interior.

Baltimore Pit Beef
SERVES 10

Top sirloin roast is also known as top butt or center-cut roast. Buy refrigerated prepared horseradish, not the shelf-stable kind, which contains preservatives and additives.

TIGER SAUCE
- ½ cup mayonnaise
- ½ cup hot prepared horseradish
- 1 teaspoon lemon juice
- 1 garlic clove, minced
- Salt and pepper

PIT BEEF

- 4 teaspoons kosher salt
- 1 tablespoon paprika
- 1 tablespoon pepper
- 1 teaspoon garlic powder
- 1 teaspoon dried oregano
- ¼ teaspoon cayenne pepper
- 1 (4- to 5-pound) top sirloin roast, trimmed and halved crosswise
- 10 kaiser rolls, split
- 1 onion, sliced thin

1 FOR THE TIGER SAUCE Whisk mayonnaise, horseradish, lemon juice, and garlic together in bowl. Season with salt and pepper to taste. (Sauce can be refrigerated for up to 2 days.)

2 FOR THE PIT BEEF Combine salt, paprika, pepper, garlic powder, oregano, and cayenne in bowl. Pat roasts dry with paper towels and rub with 2 tablespoons seasoning mixture. Wrap meat tightly with plastic wrap and refrigerate for 6 to 24 hours.

3A FOR A CHARCOAL GRILL Open bottom vent halfway. Light large chimney starter filled with charcoal briquettes (6 quarts). When top coals are partially covered with ash, pour evenly over half of grill. Set cooking grate in place, cover, and open lid vent halfway. Heat grill until hot, about 5 minutes.

3B FOR A GAS GRILL Turn all burners to high, cover, and heat grill until hot, about 15 minutes. Leave primary burner on high and turn off other burner(s).

4 Clean and oil cooking grate. Unwrap roasts and place end to end on long side of 18 by 12-inch sheet of aluminum foil. Loosely fold opposite long side of foil around top of roasts. Place meat on cooler part of grill with foil-covered side closest to heat source. Cover (positioning lid vent over meat if using charcoal) and cook until meat registers 100 degrees, 45 minutes to 1 hour.

5 Transfer roasts to plate and discard foil. Turn all burners to high if using gas. If using charcoal, carefully remove cooking grate and light large chimney starter three-quarters filled with charcoal briquettes (4½ quarts). When top coals are partially covered with ash, pour evenly over spent coals. Set cooking grate in place and cover. Heat grill until hot, about 5 minutes.

6 Pat roasts dry with paper towels and rub with remaining spice mixture. Place meat on hotter part of grill. Cook (covered if using gas), turning occasionally, until charred on all sides and meat registers 120 to 125 degrees (for medium-rare), 10 to 20 minutes. Transfer meat to carving board, tent with foil, and let rest for 15 minutes. Slice meat thin against grain. Transfer sliced beef to rolls, top with onion slices, and drizzle with sauce. Serve.

324 STEP BY STEP Cooking Baltimore Pit Beef

1 SHIELD Even with indirect heat, the sides of the roasts closest to the fire can overcook. A simple foil shield protects them.

2 RESEASON After about 1 hour of grill roasting, we remove the roasts, rub them with more seasoning, and turn up the heat.

3 BLAST With a hot fire and a fresh coating of spices, it's easy to create a flavorful seared crust on the roasts.

325 RECIPE FOR SUCCESS A Butcher's Favorite, Hot off the Grill

✓ WHY THIS RECIPE WORKS

Unlike other barbecue recipes, California barbecued tri-tip recipes call for cooking the meat (bottom sirloin roast) over high heat and seasoning it with only salt, pepper, garlic, and the sweet smoke of the grill. This consistently produces a charred exterior and very rare center—but we wanted the outside cooked less and the inside cooked more. To achieve this, we pushed all the coals in our grill to one side, which created a hot zone for searing and a cooler one for finishing the meat slowly. To prevent the meat from tasting like ashes, we held off on adding the wood chips until after we'd seared the meat.

California Barbecued Tri-Tip

SERVES 4 TO 6

If you'd like to use wood chunks instead of wood chips when using a charcoal grill, substitute two medium wood chunks, soaked in water for 1 hour, for the wood chip packet. Serve with Santa Maria Salsa (recipe follows), if desired.

2	tablespoons vegetable oil
6	garlic cloves, minced
¾	teaspoon salt
1	(2-pound) beef tri-tip roast, trimmed
1	teaspoon pepper
¾	teaspoon garlic salt
2	cups wood chips

1 Combine oil, garlic, and salt in bowl. Pat meat dry with paper towels, poke each side about 20 times with fork, then rub evenly with oil-garlic mixture. Wrap meat in plastic wrap and let sit at room temperature for 1 hour, or refrigerate for up to 24 hours.

2 Unwrap meat, wipe off garlic paste using paper towels, and season with pepper and garlic salt. Soak wood chips in water for 15 minutes, then drain. Using large piece of heavy-duty aluminum foil, wrap soaked chips in 8 by 4½-inch foil packet. (Make sure chips do not poke holes in sides or bottom of packet.) Cut 2 evenly spaced 2-inch slits in top of packet.

3A FOR A CHARCOAL GRILL Open bottom vent halfway. Light large chimney starter filled with charcoal briquettes (6 quarts). When top coals are partially covered with ash, pour evenly over half of grill. Set cooking grate in place, cover, and open lid vent halfway. Heat grill until hot, about 5 minutes.

3B FOR A GAS GRILL Turn all burners to high, cover, and heat grill until hot, about 15 minutes. Leave all burners on high.

4 Clean and oil cooking grate. Place roast on hotter side of grill. Cook (covered if using gas), turning as needed, until well browned on all sides, 8 to 10 minutes. Transfer meat to plate.

5 Remove cooking grate and place wood chip packet directly on coals or primary burner. Set grate in place, cover grill and let chips begin to smoke, about 5 minutes. If using gas, leave primary burner on high and turn off other burner(s).

6 Place meat on cooler side of grill. Cover (position lid vent over meat if using charcoal) and cook until meat registers 120 to 125 degrees (for medium-rare), about 20 minutes. (Center of roast will remain a degree more rare than ends.)

7 Transfer meat to carving board, tent with foil, and let rest for 15 to 20 minutes. Slice meat thin and serve.

326 SHOPPING IQ What Is a Tri-Tip?

Also known as a "bottom sirloin roast," "bottom sirloin butt," or "triangle roast," tri-tip is cut from the bottom sirloin primal, an area near the rear leg of the cow, adjacent to the round and flank. Before being "discovered" as a steak, this cut was thought to be tough and was typically ground into hamburger or cut into stew meat.

327 Santa Maria Salsa

MAKES 4 CUPS

The distinct texture of each ingredient is part of this salsa's appeal, so we don't recommend using a food processor.

- 2 pounds tomatoes, cored and chopped fine
- 2 teaspoons salt
- 2 jalapeño chiles, stemmed, seeded, and chopped fine
- 1 small red onion, chopped fine
- 1 celery rib, chopped fine
- ¼ cup lime juice (2 limes)
- ¼ cup chopped fresh cilantro
- 1 garlic clove, minced
- ⅛ teaspoon dried oregano
- ⅛ teaspoon Worcestershire sauce

Toss tomatoes with salt in strainer and let drain for 30 minutes. Toss drained tomatoes with jalapeños, onion, celery, lime juice, cilantro, garlic, oregano, and Worcestershire in bowl, cover, and let stand at room temperature until flavors have melded, about 1 hour. (Salsa can be refrigerated for up to 2 days.)

328 STEP BY STEP Slicing a Bottom Round Steak

Bottom round is a workable substitute for tri-tip, but its long muscle fibers can make it extremely tough. We found that thinly slicing it straight down on a 45-degree angle dramatically reduced its chewiness.

329

Prepping Lemon Grass

The tender heart of the lemon grass stalk is used to flavor many Southeast Asian dishes, including our Grilled Beef Satay. When buying lemon grass, look for green (not brown) stalks that are firm and fragrant. To mince lemon grass follow the steps below.

1 TRIM Trim dry leafy top and tough bottom of each stalk.

2 REMOVE OUTER LAYER Peel and discard dry outer layer until moist, tender inner stalk is exposed.

3 SMASH Smash peeled stalk with bottom of saucepan to release maximum flavor.

4 CUT Cut smashed stalk into long, thin strips; cut cross-wise to mince.

330 RECIPE FOR SUCCESS
More Than Meat on a Stick

✔ WHY THIS RECIPE WORKS

Beef satay should consist of tender strips of assertively flavored meat grilled to lightly burnished perfection. We chose flank steak for this recipe because of its good flavor. Its symmetrical shape also made for easy slicing. For maximum flavor, we kept the marinade simple, using only fish sauce (for a savory flavor boost), oil, and sugar (to aid with browning). Instead of setting up individual skewers, which would be difficult to flip over a hot flame, we mimicked the setup of Thai street vendors. The vendors use trough-shaped grills, which suspend the meat inches above the hot coals. For our version, we filled a disposable aluminum roasting pan with charcoal and lined up the skewers over the pan. During grilling, we basted the meat heavily with a sauce made of coconut milk redolent with ginger, lemon grass, and spices for a burst of flavor that wouldn't make the meat mushy. The peanut sauce is a key element of satay. Our recipe uses chunky peanut butter as a base and spices things up with Thai red curry paste and garlic.

Grilled Beef Satay
SERVES 6

You will need ten to twelve 12-inch metal skewers for this recipe, or you can substitute bamboo skewers, soaked in water for 30 minutes. The disposable aluminum roasting pan used for charcoal grilling should be at least 2¾ inches deep; you will not need the pan for a gas grill. Kitchen shears work well for punching the holes in the pan. Unless you have a very high-powered gas grill, these skewers will not be as well seared as they would be with charcoal. Serve with Peanut Sauce (recipe follows). To make it a meal, serve this dish with white rice.

BASTING SAUCE
- ¾ cup canned regular or light coconut milk
- 3 tablespoons packed dark brown sugar
- 3 tablespoons fish sauce
- 2 tablespoons vegetable oil
- 3 shallots, minced
- 2 lemon grass stalks, trimmed to bottom 6 inches and minced
- 2 tablespoons grated fresh ginger
- 1½ teaspoons ground coriander
- ¾ teaspoon red pepper flakes
- ½ teaspoon ground cumin
- ½ teaspoon salt

BEEF
- 2 tablespoons vegetable oil
- 2 tablespoons packed dark brown sugar
- 1 tablespoon fish sauce
- 1 (1½- to 1¾-pound) flank steak, trimmed, halved lengthwise, and sliced on slight bias against grain into ¼-inch-thick slices
- 1 (13 by 9-inch) disposable aluminum roasting pan (if using charcoal)

1 FOR THE BASTING SAUCE Whisk all ingredients together in medium bowl. Transfer one-third of sauce to small bowl (to brush on raw meat) and set both bowls aside.

2 FOR THE BEEF Whisk oil, sugar, and fish sauce together in medium bowl. Toss beef with marinade and let stand at room temperature for 30 minutes. Weave beef onto 12-inch metal skewers, 2 to 4 pieces per skewer, leaving 1½ inches at top and bottom of skewer exposed. You should have 10 to 12 skewers.

3A FOR A CHARCOAL GRILL Poke twelve ½-inch holes in bottom of disposable pan. Open bottom vent completely and place disposable pan in center of grill. Light large chimney starter mounded with charcoal briquettes (7 quarts). When top coals are partially covered with ash, pour into disposable pan. Set cooking grate over coals with bars parallel to long side of disposable pan, cover, and open lid vent completely. Heat grill until hot, about 5 minutes.

3B FOR A GAS GRILL Turn all burners to high, cover, and heat grill until hot, about 15 minutes. Leave all burners on high.

4 Clean and oil cooking grate. Place beef skewers on grill (directly over coals if using charcoal) perpendicular to grate bars. Brush meat with all of the basting sauce in small bowl (reserved for raw meat) and cook (covered if using gas) until browned, about 3 minutes. Flip skewers, brush with half of remaining basting sauce in medium bowl, and cook until browned on second side, about 3 minutes. Brush meat with remaining basting sauce and cook 1 minute longer. Transfer to large platter and serve.

331 Peanut Sauce
MAKES ABOUT 1½ CUPS

- 1 tablespoon vegetable oil
- 1 tablespoon Thai red curry paste
- 1 tablespoon packed dark brown sugar
- 2 garlic cloves, minced
- 1 cup canned regular or light coconut milk
- ⅓ cup chunky peanut butter
- ¼ cup dry-roasted peanuts, chopped
- 1 tablespoon lime juice
- 1 tablespoon fish sauce
- 1 teaspoon soy sauce

Heat oil in small saucepan over medium heat until shimmering. Add curry paste, sugar, and garlic; cook, stirring constantly, until fragrant, about 1 minute. Add coconut milk and bring to simmer. Whisk in peanut butter until smooth. Remove from heat and stir in peanuts, lime juice, fish sauce, and soy sauce. Let cool to room temperature, and serve.

332

RECIPE FOR SUCCESS

The Other White Meat Kebabs

✓ WHY THIS RECIPE WORKS

Pork tenderloin has the same assets and liabilities as the ever-popular boneless, skinless chicken breast. On the plus side, it's economical, lean, and quick to prepare. The downside? It lacks flavor and has a tendency to dry out when cooked. Brushing pork tenderloin with a potent glaze and grilling it can mitigate one of the problems, to a degree: The intense heat creates some flavorful char on the outside of the meat—but only on the outside. So we embraced the reality of the situation and increased the amount of available exterior by cutting the meat into pieces and making kebabs. We salted the meat before cooking, which helped it hold on to moisture, and made a mixture of thick, sweet hoisin sauce and five-spice powder to flavor the skewers. Adding cornstarch to the hoisin mixture helped it cling to the pork and we also reserved a small amount of the glaze to brush on halfway through grilling. Thanks to the cornstarch and the second glaze addition, each piece of moist, juicy pork boasted some crusty char and a sticky coating. To adapt this approach to other flavor profiles, we also devised a spicy-sweet variation and an American barbecue version.

Grilled Pork Kebabs with Hoisin and Five-Spice

SERVES 4

You will need four 12-inch metal skewers for this recipe. Spraying the meat with oil not only minimizes sticking but also helps the five-spice powder bloom, preventing a raw spice flavor.

- 2 (12-ounce) pork tenderloins, trimmed, and cut into 1-inch chunks
- 1 teaspoon kosher salt
- 1½ teaspoons five-spice powder
- ¾ teaspoon garlic powder
- ½ teaspoon cornstarch
- 4½ tablespoons hoisin sauce
  Vegetable oil spray
- 2 scallions, sliced thin

1 Toss pork and salt together in large bowl. Set aside for 20 minutes. Meanwhile, whisk five-spice powder, garlic powder, and cornstarch together in bowl. Add hoisin to five-spice mixture and stir to combine. Measure out 1½ tablespoons hoisin mixture and set aside.

2 Add remaining hoisin mixture to pork and toss to coat. Thread pork onto four 12-inch metal skewers, leaving ¼ inch between pieces. Spray both sides of meat generously with oil spray.

3A FOR A CHARCOAL GRILL Open bottom vent completely. Light large chimney starter filled with charcoal briquettes (6 quarts). When top coals are partially covered with ash, pour evenly over half of grill. Set cooking grate in place, cover, and open lid vent completely. Heat grill until hot, about 5 minutes.

3B FOR A GAS GRILL Turn all burners to high, cover, and heat grill until hot, about 15 minutes. Leave primary burner on high and turn off other burner(s).

4 Clean and oil cooking grate. Place skewers on hotter side of grill and grill until well charred, 3 to 4 minutes. Flip skewers, brush with reserved hoisin mixture, and continue to grill until second side is well charred and meat registers 145 degrees, 3 to 4 minutes longer. Transfer to serving platter, tent with foil, and let rest for 5 minutes. Sprinkle with scallions and serve.

VARIATIONS

333 Grilled Pork Kebabs with Sweet Sriracha Glaze

Substitute 3 tablespoons packed brown sugar and 1½ tablespoons Sriracha sauce for five-spice powder, garlic powder, and hoisin sauce. Increase cornstarch to 1 teaspoon. Substitute ¼ cup minced fresh cilantro for scallions.

334 Grilled Pork Kebabs with Barbecue Glaze

Substitute 3 tablespoons ketchup, 1½ tablespoons packed brown sugar, 1 teaspoon chili powder, ¼ teaspoon liquid smoke, and pinch cayenne pepper for five-spice powder, garlic powder, and hoisin sauce. Increase cornstarch to ¾ teaspoon. Omit scallions.

335 SHOPPING IQ
Hoisin Sauce

Hoisin sauce is a mixture of soybeans, sugar, vinegar, garlic, and chiles used in many classic Chinese dishes. We discovered that different brands of this condiment vary dramatically in flavor, consistency, and even color— from gloppy and sweet, like plum sauce, to grainy and spicy, like Asian chili paste. According to our tasters, the perfect hoisin sauce balances sweet, salty, pungent, and spicy elements so that no one flavor dominates. One brand came closest to this ideal, with tasters praising its initial "burn," which mellowed into a harmonious blend of sweet and aromatic flavors.

THE BOTTOM LINE No two brands of this staple condiment are identical; look for one that's balanced between fruity flavor and spiciness, like **Kikkoman**, our winner.

RECIPE FOR SUCCESS

Spicy, Smoky Mexican Pork Chops

✓ WHY THIS RECIPE WORKS

The reality of many grilled pork chops is burnt exteriors, tough meat, and barely a hint of flavor. We wanted a recipe for pork chops with perfectly seared crusts, juicy and tender meat, and bold Mexican-inspired flavor. Rib chops were our top choice for their intense porky flavor and juiciness. Brining the chops in a solution of water, salt, and sugar seasoned the pork throughout and kept it juicy on the grill. A dry rub was the best way to give the brined pork deep flavor: Two different kinds of dried chiles added layers of flavor and a subtle heat, while brown sugar encouraged browning and rounded out the flavor of the pork. Cooking the pork over a two-level fire allowed us to get a good sear over the hotter side of the grill before moving the chops to the cooler side to finish without overcooking.

Ancho-Rubbed Grilled Pork Chops
SERVES 4

If the pork is enhanced (injected with a salt solution), do not brine in step 1, but increase the salt amount in the spice rub to 2 teaspoons in step 2.

  Salt
- 3 tablespoons granulated sugar
- 4 (12-ounce) bone-in pork rib or center-cut chops, 1½ inches thick, trimmed
- 1 dried chipotle chile, stemmed, seeded, and torn into ½-inch pieces (1½ tablespoons)
- ½ dried ancho chile, stemmed, seeded, and torn into ½-inch pieces (2 tablespoons)
- 1 teaspoon dried oregano
- ¼ teaspoon garlic powder
- 2 teaspoons packed brown sugar

1 Dissolve 3 tablespoons salt and granulated sugar in 1½ quarts cold water in large container. Submerge chops in brine, cover, and refrigerate for 30 minutes to 1 hour.

2 Meanwhile, toast chipotle and ancho chiles in 8-inch skillet over medium heat, stirring frequently, until fragrant, 2 to 6 minutes. Transfer chiles to spice grinder and let cool slightly. Add oregano and garlic powder and process until finely ground, about 10 seconds. Transfer mixture to bowl and stir in brown sugar and ¼ teaspoon salt.

3 Just before grilling, remove chops from brine, pat dry with paper towels, and rub with spice rub.

4A FOR A CHARCOAL GRILL Open bottom vent completely. Light large chimney starter filled with charcoal briquettes (6 quarts). When top coals are partially covered with ash, pour two-thirds evenly over half of grill, then pour remaining coals over half of grill. Set cooking grate in place, cover, and open lid vent completely. Heat grill until hot, about 5 minutes.

4B FOR A GAS GRILL Turn all burners to high, cover, and heat grill until hot, about 15 minutes. Leave primary burner on high and turn off other burner(s).

5 Clean and oil cooking grate. Place chops on hotter side of grill and cook (covered if using gas) until well browned on both sides, 2 to 4 minutes per side. Move chops to cooler side of grill, cover, and continue to cook until pork registers 145 degrees, 7 to 9 minutes, flipping chops halfway through cooking. Transfer chops to serving platter, tent with aluminum foil, and let rest for 5 to 10 minutes. Serve.

337 SHOPPING IQ
Dried Chiles

Dried chiles are about more than just incendiary heat; some are as mild as can be and, depending on variety, pack wildly varying flavors—from earthy and fruit-sweet to bright and acidic. While commercially ground chile powder can do in some instances, like a quick batch of chili, we believe that it is worth toasting and grinding dried chiles at home for many dishes. Here are some varieties of chiles that we frequently use and their flavor profiles; when shopping for dried chiles, look for those that are pliable and smell slightly fruity:

CHILE	APPEARANCE AND FLAVOR	HEAT	SUBSTITUTIONS
Ancho (dried poblano)	Wrinkly, dark red; rich, with raisiny sweetness	🌶	Pasilla, mulato. You can use 1 tablespoon powder in place of 1 chile.
Mulato (dried smoked poblano)	Wrinkly, deep brown; smoky with hints of licorice and dried cherry	🌶	Ancho
Pasilla	Long, wrinkled, purplish or dark brown; rich grapey, herby flavor	🌶🌶	Ancho, mulato
Chipotle (dried smoked jalapeño)	Wrinkly, brownish red; smoky and chocolaty with tobacco-like sweetness	🌶🌶	You can use 1 teaspoon powder or 1 teaspoon minced chipotle in adobo sauce in place of 1 chile.
Cascabel	Small, round, reddish brown; nutty, woodsy	🌶🌶	New Mexican
New Mexican	Smooth, brick red; bright with smoky undertones	🌶🌶	Cascabel
Guajillo	Wrinkly, dark red; mild, fruity, smoky	🌶🌶	New Mexican
Arbol	Smooth, bright red; bright with smoky undertones	🌶🌶🌶	Pequín
Pequín	Small, round, deep red; bright, citrusy	🌶🌶🌶🌶	Arbol

RECIPE FOR SUCCESS
Savory, Flavor-Filled Pork Chops

✓ WHY THIS RECIPE WORKS

Brining is one way to make lean pork moist and flavorful, but it takes time. For a quicker solution, we paired the pork with a stuffing. We wanted a filling that would add moisture as well as a big hit of flavor. Our first thought was to start with barbecue sauce, spooning it inside the chops instead of brushing it on the exterior of the meat. That was a good start, but the filling needed some bulk. We tried everything from sautéed mushrooms (too mild) to chutney (too overpowering) before settling on the sweet flavor of caramelized onions. To thicken the filling, we turned to gooey cheese, which turned the barbecue sauce and onions into a stable, hearty filling and added a lot of flavor.

Grilled Stuffed Pork Chops

SERVES 4

The pork chops can be stuffed, wrapped tightly in plastic wrap or stored in an airtight container, and refrigerated for up to 24 hours before grilling. Although we think a homemade barbecue sauce like the one on page 313 tastes best, feel free to substitute your favorite store-bought bottled sauce.

- 1 tablespoon olive oil
- 1 large onion, halved and sliced thin
- 4 ounces smoked gouda or smoked cheddar cheese, shredded (1 cup)
- ¼ cup barbecue sauce
- 4 (8-ounce) boneless loin pork chops, about 1½ inches thick, trimmed
  Salt and pepper

1 Heat oil in 10-inch skillet over medium heat until shimmering. Add onion and cook until softened and deeply browned, 15 to 20 minutes. Transfer to bowl and stir in gouda and barbecue sauce.

2 Use sharp paring knife to cut 1-inch opening into side of each pork chop, then cut pocket for stuffing.

Place one-quarter of onion mixture in pocket of each pork chop. Seal pockets with toothpicks. Pat pork chops dry with paper towels and season with salt and pepper.

3A FOR A CHARCOAL GRILL Open bottom vent completely. Light large chimney starter filled with charcoal briquettes (6 quarts). When top coals are partially covered with ash, pour evenly over half of grill. Set cooking grate in place, cover, and open lid vent completely. Heat grill until hot, about 5 minutes.

3B FOR A GAS GRILL Turn all burners to high, cover, and heat grill until hot, about 15 minutes. Leave primary burner on high and turn off other burner(s).

4 Clean and oil cooking grate. Place pork chops on hotter side of grill. Cook (covered if using gas) until browned on both sides, about 5 minutes, flipping chops halfway through.

5 Slide pork chops to cooler side of grill. Cover and cook until meat registers 145 degrees, 6 to 8 minutes longer.

6 Transfer pork chops to serving platter, tent with aluminum foil, and let rest for 10 minutes. Serve.

VARIATIONS

339 Grilled Sausage-Stuffed Pork Chops

Skip step 1 and substitute following mixture for onion mixture in step 2: Heat 2 teaspoons olive oil in 10-inch skillet over medium-high heat until shimmering. Add 8 ounces Italian sausage, casings removed, and cook, breaking it into small pieces, until well browned, 5 minutes. Using slotted spoon, transfer sausage to bowl and stir in 1 cup shredded mozzarella cheese, ½ cup jarred pizza sauce, and 1 tablespoon grated Parmesan cheese. Proceed as directed.

340 Grilled Southwestern Stuffed Pork Chops

Skip step 1 and substitute following mixture for the onion mixture in step 2: Heat 2 teaspoons olive oil in 10-inch skillet over medium-high heat until shimmering. Add 1 red bell pepper, sliced thin, and cook until soft, about 2 minutes. Transfer pepper to bowl and stir in ½ cup jarred salsa, 2 teaspoons minced chipotle chile in adobo sauce, and 1 cup shredded Monterey Jack cheese. Proceed as directed.

341 STEP BY STEP Stuffing Pork Chops

The key to tidy stuffing is to create a large pocket with a small opening. Here's how we do it.

1 SLICE Insert small sharp knife through side of chop until tip almost reaches opposite edge. Swing knife through meat, creating large pocket.

2 FILL Use your finger to widen pocket almost to edge of chop. Spoon small amount of filling into chop.

3 CLOSE Thread toothpick through side of chop to seal in filling.

RECIPE FOR SUCCESS

Grilled Pork Chops That Have It All

✔ WHY THIS RECIPE WORKS

Getting both good smoke flavor and a charred crust is an elusive grilling goal. We wanted chops that had it all: charred crust, ultramoist meat, and true smoke flavor. We used thick-cut chops for this recipe because more meat on the bone gave us more time on the grill to really infuse the meat with smoke before it became leathery and dry. For the grill setup, we used a disposable aluminum pan to create a double-banked fire. We then put a packet of wood chips on the coals and started the chops on the cooler center of the grill, allowing the smoke plenty of time to do its job. We found it best to rest each chop on its bone instead of laying it flat. To keep them from toppling over, we speared the chops together with skewers, making sure to leave a good inch between chops to allow air to circulate, then stood them upright on the grill. This allowed us to keep the chops over the fire for a full 30 minutes, after which we removed the skewers, applied sauce, and finished the chops over the hot coals for a crusty char.

Grill-Smoked Pork Chops

SERVES 4

Buy chops of the same thickness so they will cook uniformly. Use the large holes of a box grater to grate the onion for the sauce. If you'd like to use wood chunks instead of wood chips when using a charcoal grill, substitute two medium wood chunks, soaked in water for 1 hour, for the wood chip packet. You will need two 10-inch metal skewers for this recipe.

SAUCE

- ½ cup ketchup
- ¼ cup molasses
- 2 tablespoons grated onion
- 2 tablespoons Worcestershire sauce
- 2 tablespoons Dijon mustard
- 2 tablespoons cider vinegar
- 1 tablespoon packed light brown sugar

CHOPS

- 2 **cups wood chips, soaked in water for 15 minutes and drained**
- 4 **(12-ounce) bone-in pork rib or center-cut chops, 1½ inches thick, trimmed**
- 2 **teaspoons salt**
- 2 **teaspoons pepper**
- 1 **(13 by 9-inch) disposable aluminum roasting pan (if using charcoal)**

1 FOR THE SAUCE Bring all ingredients to simmer in small saucepan over medium heat and cook, stirring occasionally, until reduced to about 1 cup, 5 to 7 minutes. Transfer ½ cup sauce to small bowl and set aside remaining sauce for serving.

2 FOR THE CHOPS Using large piece of heavy-duty aluminum foil, wrap soaked chips in 8 by 4 ½-inch foil packet. (Make sure chips do not poke holes in sides or bottom of packet.) Cut 2 evenly spaced 2-inch slits in top of each packet. Pat pork chops dry with paper towels. Cut 2 slits, about 2 inches apart, through outer layer of fat and silverskin on each chop. Season each chop with ½ teaspoon salt and ½ teaspoon pepper. Place chops side by side, facing in same direction, on cutting board with curved rib bone facing down. Pass 2 metal skewers through loin muscle of each chop, close to bone, about 1 inch from each end, then pull chops apart to create 1-inch space between each.

3A FOR A CHARCOAL GRILL Open bottom vent halfway and place disposable pan in center of grill. Light large chimney starter filled with charcoal briquettes (6 quarts). When top coals are partially covered with ash, pour into 2 even piles on either side of disposable pan. Place wood chip packet on 1 pile of coals. Set cooking grate in place, cover, and open lid vent halfway. Heat grill until hot and wood chips are smoking, about 5 minutes.

3B FOR A GAS GRILL Remove cooking grate and place wood chip packet directly on primary burner. Set grate in place, turn all burners to high, cover, and heat grill until hot and wood chips are smoking, about 15 minutes. Turn all burners to medium-high. (Adjust burners as needed during cooking to maintain grill temperature between 300 and 325 degrees.)

4 Clean and oil cooking grate. Place skewered chops bone side down on grill (over pan if using charcoal). Cover and cook until meat registers 120 degrees, 28 to 32 minutes.

5 Remove skewers from chops, tip chops onto flat side and brush surface of each with 1 tablespoon sauce. Transfer chops, sauce side down, to hotter parts of grill (if using charcoal) or turn all burners to high (if using gas) and cook until browned on first side, 2 to 6 minutes. Brush top of each chop with 1 tablespoon sauce, flip, and continue to cook until browned on second side and meat registers 145 degrees, 2 to 6 minutes longer.

6 Transfer chops to serving platter, tent with foil, and let rest for 5 to 10 minutes. Serve, passing reserved sauce separately.

STEP BY STEP

343 Grill-Smoking Barbecued Pork Chops

1 BUILD SPLIT FIRE Place disposable aluminum pan between 2 mounds of coals to create cooler center flanked by 2 hot areas.

2 SKEWER CHOPS Pass 2 skewers through loin muscle of each chop to provide stability when standing on grill.

3 STAND ON GRILL Stand skewered chops, bone side down on cooking grate, in center of grill so smoke can reach all sides.

4 SAUCE AND SEAR Brush chops with sauce and transfer to hotter sides of grill to sear on both sides (brushing top of each chop again before flipping).

345 RECIPE FOR SUCCESS
Double the Meat, Double the Smoke

✓ WHY THIS RECIPE WORKS

Most grilled double-thick pork chop recipes result in a charred exterior and raw interior, or gray meat that tastes steamed. We wanted ours to have great taste, color, and tenderness. These giant chops are almost like mini-roasts, so we treated them to the low-and-slow approach traditionally used in barbecue. Starting the chops over indirect heat made for juicy and tender meat and wood chips infused the pork with a nice smoky flavor. Coating the pork chops with a rub of brown sugar and potent herbs and spices helped produce a flavorful crust, and a quick stint over hot coals at the end of cooking gave the crust a crisp texture and rich mahogany color.

Smoked Double-Thick Pork Chops
SERVES 6 TO 8

We prefer blade chops, which have more fat to prevent drying out on the grill, but leaner loin chops will also work. If you'd like to use wood chunks instead of wood chips when using a charcoal grill, substitute two medium wood chunks, soaked in water for 1 hour, for the wood chip packet. These chops are huge. You may want to slice the meat off the bone before serving.

344 FOOD SCIENCE
A Bone Worth Picking

To find out if there were any differences in perceived taste between bone-in and boneless pork chops, we removed the bones from several rib chops, grilled them, and compared the two in a blind taste test. The results were clear. Every taster thought the meat cooked on the bone tasted more juicy and had more pork flavor. We contacted several food scientists to find out possible reasons for this.

First, bone is a poor conductor of heat and, as such, it causes the meat touching it to cook more slowly. Although this factor doesn't alter the cooking time significantly, having a section of the pork chop cook at a slightly slower rate contributes to a juicier end product. Second, the bone also insulates the muscle closest to it, protecting it from exposure to the air. More muscle is exposed on a boneless chop, so therefore more of the flavorful juices evaporate or drip into the coals during grilling.

Finally, fat—what little of it is left in modern pork—is a crucial source of flavor, and, as it melts during cooking, it also increases the perceived juiciness. In certain cuts of pork, especially ribs and chops, deposits of fat are located next to the bone, so cutting away that fat source subsequently cuts down on flavor.

¼   cup packed dark brown sugar
1   tablespoon ground fennel
1   tablespoon ground cumin
1   tablespoon ground coriander
1   tablespoon paprika
1   teaspoon salt
1   teaspoon pepper
4   (1¼- to 1½-pound) bone-in blade-cut pork
    chops, about 2 inches thick, trimmed
2   cups wood chips

1 Combine sugar, fennel, cumin, coriander, paprika, salt, and pepper in bowl. Pat pork chops dry with paper towels and rub them evenly with spice mixture. Wrap chops in plastic wrap and refrigerate for at least 1 hour or up to 24 hours. Just before grilling, soak wood chips in water for 15 minutes, then drain. Using large piece of heavy-duty aluminum foil, wrap soaked chips in 8 by 4½-inch foil packet. (Make sure chips do not poke holes in sides or bottom of packet.) Cut 2 evenly spaced 2-inch slits in top of each packet.

2A FOR A CHARCOAL GRILL Open bottom vent halfway. Light large chimney starter filled with charcoal briquettes (6 quarts). When top coals are partially covered with ash, pour into steeply banked pile against side of grill. Place wood chip packet on coals. Set cooking grate in place, cover, and open lid vent halfway. Heat grill until hot and wood chips are smoking, about 5 minutes.

2B FOR A GAS GRILL Remove cooking grate and place wood chip packet directly on primary burner. Set grate in place, turn all burners to high, cover, and heat grill until hot and wood chips are smoking, about 15 minutes. Turn primary burner to medium and turn off other burner(s). (Adjust primary burner as needed to maintain grill temperature around 275 degrees.)

3 Clean and oil cooking grate. Place pork chops on cooler side of grill with bone sides facing hotter side of grill. Cover (positioning lid vent over pork if using charcoal) and cook until meat registers 145 degrees, 50 minutes to 1 hour. Slide chops directly over fire (hotter side on gas grill) and cook, uncovered, until well browned, about 4 minutes, flipping chops halfway through grilling. Transfer to platter and let rest for 20 minutes. Serve.

346 GADGETS & GEAR
Plastic Wrap

Plastic wrap is essential for storing, freezing, and keeping food fresh, but using it can drive you crazy: The plastic rips and clings to itself; the sharp metal teeth slice more than the plastic—or merely shred it; and most important, it doesn't keep food from spoiling quickly. Has any brand overcome these failings? We tested for strength, clingability, and preservation power to find a winner. We were looking for an impermeable wrap that prevented air and moisture from passing through. We also preferred packaging with metal teeth on the top edge, inside the cover, to those with teeth on the exposed bottom of the box, which were more apt to snag testers' clothing and skin. We liked boxes with a sticky pad on the front to hold the sheet, keeping it from rolling back on itself and getting tangled and crumpled.

THE BOTTOM LINE Our winner, **Glad Cling Wrap**, features several design innovations as well as superior performance on our freshness test.

WINNER

GLAD Cling Wrap Clear Plastic
Price $1.20 per 100 square feet
Testing Comments This wrap aced the impermeability test. Its box featured teeth that easily tore the plastic and "Glad Grab" (an adhesive pad to hold the cut end of the wrap). It clung slightly less well than some other wraps, but it got the job done and offered good value.

RUNNER-UP

STRETCH-TITE Plastic Food Wrap
Price $1.72 per 100 square feet
Testing Comments This wrap had the most cling and was by far the toughest we tested. Unfortunately, it allowed moisture to penetrate much more quickly than other wraps. And without any adhesive on the box, the plastic wrap kept rolling back on itself.

347
RECIPE FOR SUCCESS
Pork Loin with Smoke and Spice

✔ WHY THIS RECIPE WORKS

Smoked meats are traditionally cooked over indirect heat, which is a method that we already preferred for grilling pork loin, anyway, so making a smoked pork loin seemed like an easy proposition—just add a packet of wood chips and sit back to let the smoke and low heat work their magic. Unfortunately, the leanness of the pork loin caused some problems. Fatty cuts smoke well because they have enough richness to balance the assertive smoke flavor. Pork loin isn't rich or fatty, so smoke easily overwhelms the subtle flavor of the meat. To make the pork flavorful enough to stand up to the smoke, we used a basic barbecue spice rub with paprika, chili powder, cumin, oregano, cayenne, brown sugar, salt, and pepper. We started the meat on the cooler side of the grill and finished by searing it on the hotter side for a flavorful exterior, but the interior was still very mild. To build flavor on the inside of the meat, we made a marinade with flavors like brown sugar and bourbon that complemented the smoke.

Smoked Pork Loin
SERVES 6 TO 8

Look for a pork roast with about ¼ inch of fat on top. While we prefer bourbon for its smoky sweetness, you can substitute whatever American whiskey you have on hand. If you'd like to use wood chunks instead of wood chips when using a charcoal grill, substitute two medium wood chunks, soaked in water for 1 hour, for the wood chip packet. This pork is flavorful enough to stand alone, but it also goes well with any of our no-cook barbecue sauces (recipes follow) or your favorite store-bought sauce. The test kitchen's favorite bottled barbecue sauce is Bull's-Eye Original Barbecue Sauce.

SPICE RUB
- 1 tablespoon packed brown sugar
- 1 tablespoon paprika
- 2 teaspoons chili powder
- 2 teaspoons ground cumin
- 1 teaspoon dried oregano
- 1 teaspoon salt
- 1 teaspoon pepper
- ¼ teaspoon cayenne pepper

MARINADE
- ¼ cup Dijon mustard
- ¼ cup bourbon
- ¼ cup soy sauce
- ¼ cup packed brown sugar
- 2 tablespoons Worcestershire sauce
- 4 garlic cloves, minced

- 1 (2½- to 3-pound) boneless pork loin roast, fat on top scored lightly, and tied at 1-inch intervals
- 2 cups wood chips

1 FOR THE SPICE RUB Combine all ingredients in small bowl. Set aside.

2 FOR THE MARINADE Whisk mustard, bourbon, soy sauce, sugar, Worcestershire, and garlic in bowl. Place marinade and roast in 1-gallon zipper-lock bag. Press air out of bag, seal, and refrigerate for at least 2 hours or up to 8 hours, flipping bag after 1 hour to ensure that roast marinates evenly.

3 Just before grilling, soak wood chips in water for 15 minutes, then drain. Using large piece of heavy-duty aluminum foil, wrap soaked chips in 8 by 4½-inch foil packet. (Make sure chips do not poke holes in sides or bottom of packet.) Cut 2 evenly spaced 2-inch slits in top of each packet. Remove roast from marinade, pat dry with paper towels, and rub spice rub all over roast.

4A FOR A CHARCOAL GRILL Open bottom vent halfway. Light large chimney starter filled with charcoal briquettes (6 quarts). When top coals are partially covered with ash, pour evenly over half of grill. Place wood chip packet on coals. Set cooking grate in place, cover, and open lid vent halfway. Heat grill until hot and wood chips are smoking, about 5 minutes.

4B FOR A GAS GRILL Remove cooking grate and place wood chip packet over primary burner. Set grate in place, turn all burners to high, cover, and heat grill until hot and wood chips are smoking, about 15 minutes. Leave primary burner on high and turn off other burner(s).

5 Clean and oil cooking grate. Arrange roast fat side up on cooler side of grill. Cook, covered, until center of roast registers 130 to 135 degrees, about 1 hour, flipping and rotating roast once halfway through cooking. Slide roast to hotter side of grill and cook, covered, until roast is well browned on all sides and center of roast registers 140 degrees, 5 to 10 minutes. Transfer to carving board, tent with foil, and let rest for 15 minutes. Remove twine. Slice and serve.

348 Basic Pantry Barbecue Sauce
MAKES ABOUT 1¼ CUPS

- 1 cup ketchup
- 3 tablespoons molasses
- 1 tablespoon cider vinegar
- 1 teaspoon hot sauce
- ⅛ teaspoon liquid smoke (optional)

Whisk all ingredients together in small bowl.

349 Five-Alarm Barbecue Sauce
MAKES ABOUT 1¼ CUPS

- 1 cup ketchup
- 3 tablespoons molasses
- 1 tablespoon cider vinegar

352 GADGETS & GEAR It's About Twine

Tying roasts helps them keep their shape and cook evenly, but it's important to pick the right type of twine. After researching and testing a variety of tying materials, we found that unconventional options like unwaxed dental floss (which singed on the grill and cut into the meat) and nylon twine from the hardware store (which bled yellow colorant into the roast) were not viable. Tested on our Smoked Pork Loin, regular kitchen twine, particularly the linen variety (cotton is also available), held a nice overhand knot and pulled away from the cooked meat easily, taking a minimum of seared crust with it. Cotton twine, especially a midweight, 16-ply string, works nearly as well and is more economical.

- 1 tablespoon minced canned chipotle chile in adobo sauce
- 1 jalapeño chile, stemmed, seeded, and minced
- ¼ teaspoon cayenne pepper

Whisk all ingredients together in small bowl.

350 Chinese-Style Barbecue Sauce
MAKES ABOUT 1¼ CUPS

- 1 cup ketchup
- 3 tablespoons hoisin sauce
- 1 tablespoon rice vinegar
- 1 tablespoon Asian chili-garlic sauce
- 1 tablespoon minced cilantro
- 1 teaspoon grated fresh ginger

Whisk all ingredients together in small bowl.

351 Honey-Scallion Barbecue Sauce
MAKES ABOUT 1¼ CUPS

- 1 cup ketchup
- 3 tablespoons honey
- 1 tablespoon cider vinegar
- 2 teaspoons Dijon mustard
- 2 scallions, chopped fine
- ¾ teaspoon pepper

Whisk all ingredients together in small bowl.

RECIPE FOR SUCCESS
Pork Loin with Classic Italian Flavors

✓ **WHY THIS RECIPE WORKS**

What makes boneless pork loin so appealing—its lean nature and lack of sinew or gristle—also makes it a challenge to cook, especially on the grill: Little fat translates to little flavor and meat that easily dries out. Rosemary and garlic can team up to address the flavor issue, but they have to be combined with proper grilling technique. When we developed our recipe, we found it better to score, rather than trim, the thin layer of fat on the top of the pork loin, as scoring encouraged the fat to melt and baste the meat during cooking. To flavor every bite with our garlic, rosemary, parsley, and oil paste, we butterflied the meat, which allowed us to spread the interior of the loin with the flavorful paste. Mincing the parsley, rosemary, and garlic made for a perfectly homogeneous filling. We then rolled up the roast, tied it with kitchen twine, and brushed it with olive oil to help it brown and to reduce sticking on the grill. On the grill, we browned the roast directly over high heat, then finished cooking it on the cooler side of the grill.

Grilled Rosemary Pork Loin
SERVES 6 TO 8

Freezing the pork for 30 minutes will make butterflying it much easier.

- ⅓ cup minced fresh parsley
- 1½ tablespoons minced fresh rosemary
- 2 garlic cloves, minced
  Salt and pepper
- 3 tablespoons extra-virgin olive oil
- 1 (2½- to 3-pound) boneless pork loin roast

1 Combine parsley, rosemary, garlic, ¾ teaspoon salt, ¾ teaspoon pepper, and 2 tablespoons oil in bowl. Using sharp knife, lightly score fat on top of roast in cross-hatch pattern. With roast fat side up, cut horizontally through meat, one-third above bottom, stopping ½ inch from edge. Open roast and press flat; 1 side will be twice as thick. Continue cutting thicker side of roast in half, stopping ½ inch from edge; open roast and press flat.

2 Spread herb mixture over cut side of pork, leaving ½-inch border on sides. Roll pork up tightly and tie at 1-inch intervals with kitchen twine. (Roast can be refrigerated for up to 24 hours.) Rub roast with remaining 1 tablespoon oil and season with salt and pepper.

3A FOR A CHARCOAL GRILL Open bottom vent completely. Light large chimney starter filled with charcoal briquettes (6 quarts). When top coals are partially covered with ash, pour evenly over half of grill. Set cooking grate in place, cover, and open lid vent completely. Heat grill until hot, about 5 minutes.

3B FOR A GAS GRILL Turn all burners to high, cover, and heat grill until hot, about 15 minutes. Leave primary burner on high and turn off other burner(s).

4 Clean and oil cooking grate. Place roast on hotter side of grill. Cook (covered if using gas), turning as needed until well browned on all sides, about 12 minutes. Slide roast to cooler side of grill and turn fat side up. Cover and cook until meat registers 140 degrees, 35 to 45 minutes.

5 Transfer pork to carving board, tent with aluminum foil, and let rest for 15 to 20 minutes. Remove twine, cut into ½-inch-thick slices, and serve.

354

TEST KITCHEN TIP

To Cover or Not to Cover

In general, slow-cooking food is cooked covered so that the grill turns into an oven of sorts. A gas grill requires lidded cooking more often than charcoal because it tends to run cooler. We generally don't use the lid when grilling quick-cooking items on a charcoal grill.

355 STEP BY STEP Packing Herb Flavor into Every Bite

To flavor the pork roast from the inside out, we butterflied the loin and then spread the interior with a heady herb paste. The technique is easier with a relatively short, wide roast (about 7 to 8 inches long and 4 to 5 inches wide). Here's how we did it.

1 SLICE TO OPEN ROAST Place roast fat side up on cutting board. Starting about 1 inch from cutting board, cut horizontally, stopping about ½ inch before edge.

2 FINISH CUT TO FLATTEN Now cut into thicker half of roast again, starting about 1 inch from cutting board and stopping about ½ inch before edge.

3 SPREAD AND ROLL Spread herb mixture evenly over surface of butterflied roast, leaving ½-inch border on all sides. Roll tightly and tie with kitchen twine.

357 Rough Treatment for Perfect Tenderloin

✓ WHY THIS RECIPE WORKS

One of the most common ways to grill pork tenderloin is to turn it into medallions, but this treatment requires you to pay constant attention to the slices lest they overcook or, worse, slip through the grate. But since pork tenderloin is a mild cut, it makes sense to cut the roast into smaller pieces to expose more surface area and build up as much flavor as possible on the exterior. To get these benefits without dealing with fussy medallions, we turned our tenderloins into smaller, flatter "steaks" with almost 30 percent more surface area than the tenderloins for a greatly improved ratio of browned exterior to tender interior. We also cut thin slashes in the steaks to promote better penetration of our garlic-citrus marinade. Finally, we left excess marinade on the steaks to help keep their exteriors from drying out on the grill and then thickened some reserved marinade with mayonnaise for a bold finishing sauce. The marinade also contains honey for better browning and fish sauce for meatiness and the flavors can be easily mixed up for other variations.

Grilled Garlic-Lime Pork Tenderloin Steaks
SERVES 4 TO 6

Since marinating is a key step in this recipe, we don't recommend using enhanced pork.

- 2 (1-pound) pork tenderloins, trimmed
- 1 tablespoon grated lime zest plus ¼ cup juice (2 limes)
- 4 garlic cloves, minced
- 4 teaspoons honey
- 2 teaspoons fish sauce
- ¾ teaspoon salt
- ½ teaspoon pepper
- ½ cup vegetable oil
- 4 teaspoons mayonnaise
- 1 tablespoon chopped fresh cilantro
  Flake sea salt (optional)

1 Slice each tenderloin in half crosswise to create 4 steaks total. Pound each half to ¾-inch thickness. Using sharp knife, cut ⅛-inch-deep slits spaced ½ inch apart in crosshatch pattern on both sides of steaks.

2 Whisk lime zest and juice, garlic, honey, fish sauce, salt, and pepper together in large bowl. Whisking constantly, slowly drizzle oil into lime mixture until smooth and slightly thickened. Transfer ½ cup lime mixture to small bowl and whisk in mayonnaise; set aside sauce. Add steaks to bowl with remaining marinade and toss thoroughly to coat; transfer steaks and marinade to 1-gallon zipper-lock bag, press out as much air as possible, and seal bag. Let steaks sit at room temperature for 45 minutes.

356 TEST KITCHEN TIP The Geometry of Tenderloin

Cylindrical pork tenderloin doesn't have much surface area for browning. Pounding the roast into a flat steak seemed like an obvious way to increase the amount of meat that comes in contact with the grill—and as a result, the flavor in every bite—but we didn't realize how significant the difference actually was until we did the math. Flattening a cylindrical piece of pork tenderloin into a ¾-inch rectangular steak increased its surface area by almost 30 percent.

Cylindrical Tenderloin
Volume: 250 ml
Surface Area: 172.7 sq cm

Pounded Steak
Volume: 250 ml
Surface Area: 220 sq cm

3A FOR A CHARCOAL GRILL Open bottom vent completely. Light large chimney starter filled with charcoal briquettes (6 quarts). When top coals are partially covered with ash, pour evenly over half of grill. Set cooking grate in place, cover, and open lid vent completely. Heat grill until hot, about 5 minutes.

3B FOR A GAS GRILL Turn all burners to high, cover, and heat grill until hot, about 15 minutes. Leave primary burner on high and turn off other burner(s).

4 Clean and oil cooking grate. Remove steaks from marinade (do not pat dry) and place over hotter part of grill. Cook, uncovered, until well browned on first side, 3 to 4 minutes. Flip steaks and cook until well browned on second side, 3 to 4 minutes. Transfer steaks to cooler part of grill, with wider end of each steak facing hotter part of grill. Cover and cook until meat registers 145 degrees, 3 to 8 minutes longer (remove steaks as they come to temperature). Transfer steaks to carving board and let rest for 5 minutes.

5 While steaks rest, microwave reserved sauce until warm, 15 to 30 seconds; stir in cilantro. Slice steaks against grain into ½-inch-thick slices. Drizzle with half of sauce; sprinkle with sea salt, if using; and serve, passing remaining sauce separately.

VARIATIONS

358 Grilled Lemon-Thyme Pork Tenderloin Steaks

Substitute grated lemon zest and juice (2 lemons) for lime zest and juice. Add 1 tablespoon minced fresh thyme to lemon mixture with garlic. Omit cilantro.

359 Grilled Spicy Orange-Ginger Pork Tenderloin Steaks

Reduce lime zest to 1½ teaspoons and juice to 2 tablespoons. Add 1½ teaspoons grated orange zest plus 2 tablespoons juice, 2 teaspoons grated fresh ginger, and ¼ teaspoon cayenne pepper to lime mixture with garlic.

360 RECIPE FOR SUCCESS
Pork Tenderloin Gets Spicy

✓ WHY THIS RECIPE WORKS

A spice crust is a popular treatment for grilled pork tenderloin because it promises to add texture and flavor to this lean, mild cut. To avoid a sandy exterior in our recipe, we used cracked mustard seeds, coriander seeds, black peppercorns, sugar, salt, and cornmeal. To help the crust stay put, we first rolled the tenderloin in cornstarch and then dipped it in lightly beaten egg whites before adding the spices to the exterior. Gently pressing the spices onto the pork also helped the crust stay in place. A spritz of oil spray before grilling further ensured the crust stuck to the pork instead of the grill. To keep the coating from burning, we finished cooking the pork on the cooler side of a half-grill fire setup. Our variations played with other interesting flavor combinations for the spice crust.

Spice-Crusted Grilled Pork Tenderloin

SERVES 4 TO 6

To crack the spices, place them in two zipper-lock bags, one inside the other, and press or gently pound with a skillet, rolling pin, or meat mallet. We prefer Demerara and turbinado sugar for their crunch, but plain brown sugar works too. If you don't have kosher salt, use ½ teaspoon table salt.

SPICE MIXTURE

- 1½ tablespoons mustard seeds, cracked
- 1 tablespoon coriander seeds, cracked
- 1 tablespoon cornmeal
- 1 teaspoon black peppercorns, cracked
- 1 teaspoon Demerara or turbinado sugar
- 1 teaspoon kosher salt

PORK

- ½ cup cornstarch
- 2 large egg whites
- 2 (12- to 16-ounce) pork tenderloins, trimmed
  Vegetable oil spray

1 FOR THE SPICE MIXTURE Combine all ingredients on rimmed baking sheet.

2 FOR THE PORK Place cornstarch in large bowl. Beat egg whites in second large bowl until foamy.

Pat pork dry with paper towels. Working with 1 tenderloin at a time, coat lightly with cornstarch, dip in egg whites, then coat with spice mixture, pressing gently to adhere. Transfer tenderloins to clean baking sheet and spray all sides with oil spray.

3A FOR A CHARCOAL GRILL Open bottom vent completely. Light large chimney starter filled with charcoal briquettes (6 quarts). When top coals are partially covered with ash, pour evenly over half of grill. Set cooking grate in place, cover, and open lid vent completely. Heat grill until hot, about 5 minutes.

3B FOR A GAS GRILL Turn all burners to high, cover, and heat grill until hot, about 15 minutes. Leave primary burner on high and turn off other burner(s).

4 Clean and oil cooking grate. Place tenderloins on hotter side of grill. Cook (covered if using gas), turning as needed, until browned on all sides, 6 to 8 minutes. Slide pork to cooler side of grill, cover, and cook until meat registers 145 degrees, 6 to 12 minutes.

5 Transfer pork to carving board, tent with aluminum foil, and let rest for 5 to 10 minutes. Slice pork thin and serve.

VARIATIONS

361 Everything Bagel–Crusted Grilled Pork Tenderloin

Substitute following mixture for spice mixture: Combine 1 tablespoon cornmeal, 1 tablespoon sesame seeds, 1 tablespoon minced garlic, 1 teaspoon cracked black peppercorns, 1 teaspoon kosher salt, 1 teaspoon poppy seeds, and ½ teaspoon caraway seeds on rimmed baking sheet.

362 Coffee-and-Fennel-Crusted Grilled Pork Tenderloin

Substitute following mixture for spice mixture: Combine 1 tablespoon cornmeal, 2 teaspoons fennel seeds, 1 teaspoon instant espresso powder, 1 teaspoon cracked black peppercorns, 1 teaspoon kosher salt, 1 teaspoon Demerara or turbinado sugar, and ¼ teaspoon red pepper flakes on rimmed baking sheet.

363

Building a Spice Crust That Stays Put

1 COAT A roll in cornstarch will help the egg whites adhere.

2 DIP A dip in lightly beaten egg whites will help the spices adhere.

3 PRESS Gently pressing the spices onto the pork will help the crust stay put.

the glaze to char, further enhancing the rich, flavorful crust, and adding glutamate-rich ingredients such as mirin, hoisin, or fish sauce to the glaze enhanced the savory, meaty flavor of the pork.

Grilled Glazed Pork Tenderloin Roast
SERVES 6

Since brining is a key step in having the two tenderloins stick together, we don't recommend using enhanced pork in this recipe.

> 2 (1-pound) pork tenderloins, trimmed
>   Salt and pepper
>   Vegetable oil
> 1 recipe glaze (recipes follow)

1 Lay tenderloins on cutting board, flat side (side opposite where silverskin was) up. Holding thick end of 1 tenderloin with paper towels and using dinner fork, scrape flat side lengthwise from end to end 5 times, until surface is completely covered with shallow grooves. Repeat with second tenderloin. Dissolve 3 tablespoons salt in 1½ quarts cold water in large container. Submerge tenderloins in brine, cover, and let stand at room temperature for 1 hour.

2 Remove tenderloins from brine and pat dry with paper towels. Lay 1 tenderloin, scraped side up, on cutting board and lay second tenderloin, scraped side down, on top so that thick end of 1 tenderloin matches up with thin end of other. Spray five 14-inch lengths of kitchen twine thoroughly with vegetable oil spray; evenly space twine underneath tenderloins and tie. Brush roast with oil and season with pepper. Transfer ⅓ cup glaze to bowl for grilling; reserve remaining glaze for serving.

3A FOR A CHARCOAL GRILL Open bottom vent completely. Light large chimney starter filled with charcoal briquettes (6 quarts). When top coals are partially covered with ash, pour into steeply banked pile against side of grill. Set cooking grate in place, cover, and open lid vent completely. Heat grill until hot, about 5 minutes.

3B FOR A GAS GRILL Turn all burners to high, cover, and heat grill until hot, about 15 minutes. Leave primary burner on high and turn off other burner(s).

364

Terrific Tenderloin with Asian Glazes

✓ WHY THIS RECIPE WORKS

The tapered shape of a tenderloin makes it difficult to cook evenly. We wanted to find a way to make grilled pork tenderloin a bit more foolproof—and elevate this cut above its "casual supper" status to something more special. For well-seasoned, juicy meat, brining was essential. Grilling pork tenderloin directly over a hot fire the entire time resulted a thick band of dry, overcooked meat below its surface. A better approach was to start the tenderloin over low heat followed by searing over high heat. Even so, the tapered end of the tenderloin still overcooked by the time the rest of the roast reached the ideal temperature. We solved this problem by tying the roasts together, with the thick end of one nestled against the thin end of the other. Scraping the length of each tenderloin with a fork helped bond the two pieces of meat together to create one larger roast. Glazing the tenderloins over high heat allowed

4 Clean and oil cooking grate. Place roast on cooler side of grill, cover, and cook until meat registers 115 degrees, 22 to 28 minutes, flipping and rotating halfway through cooking.

5 Slide roast to hotter part of grill and cook until lightly browned on all sides, 4 to 6 minutes. Brush top of roast with about 1 tablespoon glaze and grill, glaze side down, until glaze begins to char, 2 to 3 minutes; repeat glazing and grilling with remaining 3 sides of roast, until meat registers 140 degrees.

6 Transfer roast to carving board, tent with aluminum foil, and let rest for 10 minutes. Carefully remove twine and slice roast into ½-inch-thick slices. Serve with remaining glaze.

365 Miso Glaze

MAKES ABOUT ¾ CUP

3	tablespoons sake
3	tablespoons mirin
⅓	cup white miso
¼	cup sugar
2	teaspoons Dijon mustard
1	teaspoon rice vinegar
¼	teaspoon grated fresh ginger
¼	teaspoon toasted sesame oil

Bring sake and mirin to boil in small saucepan over medium heat. Whisk in miso and sugar until smooth, about 30 seconds. Remove pan from heat and continue to whisk until sugar is dissolved, about 1 minute. Whisk in mustard, vinegar, ginger, and sesame oil until smooth.

366 Sweet and Spicy Hoisin Glaze

MAKES ABOUT ¾ CUP

1	teaspoon vegetable oil
3	garlic cloves, minced
1	teaspoon grated fresh ginger
½	teaspoon red pepper flakes
½	cup hoisin sauce
2	tablespoons soy sauce
1	tablespoon rice vinegar

Heat oil in small saucepan over medium heat until shimmering. Add garlic, ginger, and pepper flakes; cook until fragrant, about 30 seconds. Whisk in hoisin and soy sauce until smooth. Remove pan from heat and stir in vinegar.

367 Satay Glaze

MAKES ABOUT ¾ CUP

1	teaspoon vegetable oil
1	tablespoon Thai red curry paste
2	garlic cloves, minced
½	teaspoon grated fresh ginger
½	cup canned coconut milk
¼	cup packed dark brown sugar
2	tablespoons peanut butter
1	tablespoon lime juice
2½	teaspoons fish sauce

Heat oil in small saucepan over medium heat until shimmering. Add curry paste, garlic, and ginger; cook, stirring constantly, until fragrant, about 1 minute. Whisk in coconut milk and sugar and bring to simmer. Whisk in peanut butter until smooth. Remove pan from heat and whisk in lime juice and fish sauce.

368 STEP BY STEP Turning Two Tenderloins into One Roast

To get around the usual problems with grilling pork tenderloin, we "fused" two together and cooked them as a single roast.

1 ROUGH UP Scrape up flat sides of each tenderloin with fork until surface is covered with shallow grooves. This releases sticky proteins that will act as "glue."

2 FUSE Arrange tenderloins with scraped sides touching and thick end of one nestled against thin end of other. Tie tenderloins together.

370 RECIPE FOR SUCCESS
New Wave Middle Eastern Kebabs

✓ WHY THIS RECIPE WORKS

In the Middle East, kebabs called *kofte* feature ground meat, not chunks, mixed with lots of spices and fresh herbs. Our challenge was to get their sausage-like texture just right. Because the patties are small, the meat easily overcooks and becomes dry. Plus, since kofte is kneaded by hand in order to get the meat proteins to cross-link and take on a resilient texture, it's easy to make it too springy—or not springy enough. We skipped the traditional bread panade in favor of a little gelatin to keep our kofte moist after grilling. We also added pine nuts to the mixture for richness and texture.

For the spices, we used a variation on the common Middle Eastern spice blend called *baharat*, which contains black pepper, cumin, coriander, and chile pepper. For a cooling sauce to balance the spices of the kofte we made a yogurt-garlic-tahini-lemon mixture.

Grilled Lamb Kofte

SERVES 4 TO 6

Use the large holes of a box grater to grate the onion for this recipe. You will need eight 12-inch metal skewers for the kofte.

YOGURT-GARLIC SAUCE

1	cup plain whole-milk yogurt
2	tablespoons lemon juice
2	tablespoons tahini
1	garlic clove, minced
½	teaspoon salt

KOFTE

½	cup pine nuts
4	garlic cloves, peeled
1½	teaspoons hot smoked paprika
1	teaspoon salt
1	teaspoon ground cumin
½	teaspoon pepper
¼	teaspoon ground coriander
¼	teaspoon ground cloves
⅛	teaspoon ground nutmeg
⅛	teaspoon ground cinnamon
1½	pounds ground lamb
½	cup grated onion, drained
⅓	cup minced fresh parsley
⅓	cup minced fresh mint
1½	teaspoons unflavored gelatin
1	(13 by 9-inch) disposable aluminum roasting pan (if using charcoal)

369 GRILL HACK
Lack of a Grill Brush Won't Foil Your Fun

One of the test kitchen's favorite ways to clean a grill without a grill brush is to use balled-up aluminum foil.

1 FLATTEN FOIL Lay 18 by 12-inch piece of aluminum foil on counter, then center 2 paper towels on foil. Drizzle paper towels with 2 tablespoons vegetable oil.

2 BALL UP FOIL Crumple foil around paper towels and poke several holes in it with skewer.

3 BRUSH GRILL Using long-handled tongs, brush hot grill surface with foil, letting some oil leak out and season grill.

1 FOR THE YOGURT-GARLIC SAUCE Whisk all ingredients together in bowl.

2 FOR THE KOFTE Process pine nuts, garlic, paprika, salt, cumin, pepper, coriander, cloves, nutmeg, and cinnamon into coarse paste in food processor, 30 to 45 seconds; transfer to large bowl. Add lamb, onion, parsley, mint, and gelatin to bowl and knead with your hands until thoroughly combined and mixture feels slightly sticky, about 2 minutes.

3 Divide mixture into 8 equal portions. Shape each portion into 5-inch-long cylinder about 1 inch in diameter. Using eight 12-inch metal skewers, thread 1 cylinder onto each skewer, pressing gently to adhere. Transfer skewers to lightly greased baking sheet, cover with plastic wrap, and refrigerate for 1 hour or up to 24 hours.

4A FOR A CHARCOAL GRILL Using skewer, poke 12 holes in bottom of disposable pan. Open bottom vent completely and place disposable pan in center of grill. Light large chimney starter two-thirds filled with charcoal briquettes (4 quarts). When top coals are partially covered with ash, pour into disposable pan. Set cooking grate in place, cover, and open lid vent completely. Heat grill until hot, about 5 minutes.

4B FOR A GAS GRILL Turn all burners to high, cover, and heat grill until hot, about 15 minutes. Leave all burners on high.

5 Clean and oil cooking grate. Place skewers on grill (directly over coals if using charcoal) at 45-degree angle to grate bars. Cook (covered if using gas) until browned and meat easily releases from grill, 4 to 7 minutes. Flip skewers and continue to cook until browned on second side and meat registers 160 degrees, about 6 minutes. Transfer skewers to platter and serve, passing yogurt-garlic sauce separately.

VARIATION

371 Grilled Beef Kofte
Substitute 80 percent lean ground beef for lamb. Increase garlic to 5 cloves, paprika to 2 teaspoons, and cumin to 2 teaspoons.

372 SHOPPING IQ
Curly-versus Flat-Leaf Parsley

You've probably noticed that your neighborhood grocer has two different varieties of this recognizable herb (though there are actually more than 30 varieties out there): curly-leaf and flat-leaf (also called Italian). Curly-leaf parsley is more popular, but in the test kitchen flat-leaf is by far the favorite. We find flat-leaf to have a sweet, bright flavor that's much preferable to the bitter, grassy tones of curly-leaf. Flat-leaf parsley is also much more fragrant than its curly cousin. If you're making a dish in which parsley gets star billing, go for flat-leaf. However, if you're sprinkling a little parsley into a stew or onto pasta, don't worry if your local supermarket carries only the curly stuff; it won't make a noticeable difference in the flavor of your dish.

373
Racking Up Lamb

✔ WHY THIS RECIPE WORKS

Rack of lamb and the grill have great chemistry. The intense heat of the coals produces a great crust and melts away the meat's abundance of fat, distributing flavor throughout, while imparting a smokiness that's the perfect complement to lamb's rich, gamy flavor. But the rendering fat can cause flare-ups that scorch the meat and impart sooty flavors, ruining this pricey cut. To solve this problem, we trimmed the excess fat from racks of lamb and stacked the coals on the sides of the grill, creating a cooler center where the fat could safely render before we moved the lamb over direct heat to brown the exterior. A simple wet rub of robust herbs and a little oil enhanced the meat's flavor without overwhelming it. Our method gave us a rack of lamb that was pink and juicy, with a well-browned crust that contrasted nicely with the lush, ultratender interior.

Grilled Rack of Lamb
SERVES 4 TO 6

We prefer the milder taste and bigger size of domestic lamb, but you may substitute lamb from New Zealand or Australia. Since imported racks are generally smaller, follow the shorter cooking times given in the recipe. While most lamb is sold frenched (meaning part of each rib bone is exposed), chances are there will still be some extra fat between the bones. Remove the majority of this fat, leaving an inch at the top of the small eye of meat.

- 4 teaspoons vegetable oil
- 4 teaspoons minced fresh rosemary
- 2 teaspoons minced fresh thyme
- 2 garlic cloves, minced
- 2 (1½- to 1¾-pound) racks of lamb (8 ribs each), trimmed and frenched
  Salt and pepper
- 1 (13 by 9-inch) disposable aluminum roasting pan (if using charcoal)

1 Combine 1 tablespoon oil, rosemary, thyme, and garlic in bowl; set aside. Pat lamb dry with paper towels, rub with remaining 1 teaspoon oil, and season with salt and pepper.

2A FOR A CHARCOAL GRILL Open bottom vent completely and place disposable pan in center of grill. Light large chimney starter filled with charcoal briquettes (6 quarts). When top coals are partially covered with ash, pour into 2 even piles on either side of disposable pan. Set cooking grate in place, cover, and open lid vent completely. Heat grill until hot, about 5 minutes.

2B FOR A GAS GRILL Turn all burners to high, cover, and heat grill until hot, about 15 minutes. Leave primary burner on high and turn off other burner(s).

3 Clean and oil cooking grate. Place lamb, bone side up, on cooler part of grill with meaty side of racks very close to, but not quite over, hot coals or lit burner. Cover and cook until meat is lightly browned, faint grill marks appear, and fat has begun to render, 8 to 10 minutes.

4 Flip racks bone side down and slide to hotter part of grill. Cook until well browned, 3 to 4 minutes. Brush racks with herb mixture, flip bone side up, and cook until well browned, 3 to 4 minutes. Stand racks up, leaning them against each other for support, and cook until bottom is well browned and meat registers 120 to 125 degrees (for medium-rare) or 130 to 135 degrees (for medium), 3 to 8 minutes.

5 Transfer lamb to carving board, tent with aluminum foil, and let rest for 15 to 20 minutes. Cut between ribs to separate chops and serve.

VARIATION

374 Grilled Rack of Lamb with Sweet Mustard Glaze

Omit rosemary and add 3 tablespoons Dijon mustard, 2 tablespoons honey, and ½ teaspoon grated lemon zest to oil, thyme, and garlic. Reserve 2 tablespoons of glaze to brush over lamb before serving.

375 STEP BY STEP Grilling Rack of Lamb

1 START COOL Place lamb, bone side up, on cooler part of grill with meaty side of racks very close to, but not quite over, hot coals or lit burner. Cover and cook until meat is lightly browned.

2 GET HOT Flip racks bone side down and slide to hotter part of grill. Cook until well browned, then brush with herb mixture, flip racks, and brown well on second side.

3 FINISH Stand racks up, leaning them against each other for support, and cook until bottom is well browned.

Grilled Butterflied Leg of Lamb

SERVES 8 TO 10

Butterflied leg of lamb is nothing more than a boneless leg of lamb, pounded to an even thickness so that it cooks evenly on the grill. Often, the butcher will pound and trim it for you.

- 1 (3½- to 4-pound) boneless half leg of lamb, trimmed
- 2 tablespoons vegetable oil
  Salt and pepper

1 Cover lamb with plastic wrap and pound to even thickness as needed. Let stand at room temperature, covered loosely with plastic, for 1 hour.

2A FOR A CHARCOAL GRILL Open bottom vent completely. Light large chimney starter filled with charcoal briquettes (6 quarts). When top coals are partially covered with ash, pour evenly over half of grill. Set cooking grate in place, cover, and open lid vent completely. Heat grill until hot, about 5 minutes.

2B FOR A GAS GRILL Turn all burners to high, close lid, and heat grill until very hot, about 15 minutes. Leave primary burner on high and turn other burner(s) to medium.

3 Meanwhile, pat lamb dry with paper towels, then rub with oil and season with salt and pepper.

4 Clean and oil cooking grate. Place lamb fat side down on cooler side of grill. Cover and cook until well browned, about 10 minutes, rotating meat halfway through grilling so that meat facing hotter side is now facing cooler side.

5 Flip lamb fat side up and continue to cook on cooler side of grill, covered, for 5 minutes. Rotate meat and move to hotter side of grill (if using charcoal); cover and cook until meat registers 120 to 125 degrees (for medium-rare) or 130 to 135 degrees (for medium), 5 to 15 minutes.

6 Transfer lamb to carving board, tent with aluminum foil, and let rest for 20 minutes. Slice thin on bias and serve.

376

RECIPE FOR SUCCESS

Simple, Succulent Leg of Lamb

✓ WHY THIS RECIPE WORKS

For our best grilled leg of lamb, we used a butterflied cut, which was easier to manage on the grill than bone-in leg. The butterflied leg was also easier to cook evenly and thick enough to carve into attractive slices when it was done. For a crust that came out caramelized but not blackened, we turned the meat regularly during grilling. While cutting the meat against the grain is one of the cardinal rules of meat cookery for optimal tenderness, we found that in order to produce the largest slices possible, we could sidestep it. Instead, we cut the meat into thin slices on an angle, disregarding the grain. While this cut tastes great with nothing but oil, salt, and pepper, we also developed a set of simple marinades for variations with flavors that complement the rich, smoky taste of the grilled lamb.

377 Grilled Butterflied Leg of Lamb with Tandoori Marinade

This marinade forms an especially thick, browned crust when the lamb is grilled.

Combine ⅓ cup plain yogurt, 2 tablespoons lemon juice, 5 minced garlic cloves, 1 tablespoon grated fresh ginger, 1 tablespoon curry powder, 1 teaspoon cayenne pepper, ½ teaspoon ground cinnamon, ½ teaspoon salt, and ¼ teaspoon pepper. Rub mixture evenly over lamb and marinate for at least 1 hour or up to 24 hours (refrigerate if marinating for more than 1 hour). Omit step 3 and grill as directed.

378 Grilled Butterflied Leg of Lamb with Greek-Style Marinade

Combine ¼ cup extra-virgin olive oil, 2 tablespoons lemon juice, 2 tablespoons minced fresh oregano (or 1 tablespoon dried), 2 tablespoons minced fresh thyme (or 1 tablespoon dried), 3 minced garlic cloves, 1 teaspoon paprika, ½ teaspoon salt, and ¼ teaspoon pepper. Rub mixture evenly over lamb and marinate for at least 1 hour or up to 24 hours (refrigerate if marinating more than 1 hour). Omit step 3 and grill lamb as directed.

379 Grilled Butterflied Leg of Lamb with Soy-Honey Marinade

Add a minced jalapeño chile or ¼ teaspoon red pepper flakes to spice up this marinade.

Combine ⅓ cup soy sauce, ⅓ cup honey, 1 tablespoon grated fresh ginger, 2 minced garlic cloves, 1 teaspoon minced fresh thyme, and pinch cayenne pepper. Rub mixture evenly over lamb and marinate for at least 1 hour or up to 24 hours (refrigerate if marinating more than 1 hour). Omit step 3 and grill lamb as directed.

380 Grilled Butterflied Leg of Lamb with Garlic-Rosemary Marinade

Combine ¼ cup extra-virgin olive oil, 6 minced garlic cloves, and 1½ tablespoons minced fresh rosemary. Rub mixture evenly over lamb and marinate for at least 1 hour or up to 24 hours (refrigerate if marinating more than 1 hour). Omit step 3 and grill lamb as directed.

381 GADGETS & GEAR
Carving Boards

A carving board may seem like a luxury when you pull it out only a few times a year—but anyone who's tried carving a leg of lamb on a flat cutting board knows what a disaster that can be, with juices dribbling onto the counter from all sides. Carving boards are designed to avoid this mess, traditionally by relying on a trench around their perimeter that traps the liquid. We only considered boards that were at least 18 inches long—enough space for a large turkey, with room to work. But bigger wasn't necessarily better. Models that were nearly 2 feet long felt bulky and hogged counter space. As for height, boards around 1 inch tall had enough heft to sit securely on the counter but were still easy to lift. We liked that thinner boards could be stored easily, but they tended to slip on the counter.

We expect a carving board to trap at least ½ cup of liquid. Traditionally, a trench about 1 inch from the board's perimeter is designed to handle the job. Because the fat released during carving gels as it cools, it will cause the juices to slow down, so boards with narrow, shallow trenches tended to clog and overflow. Small grids and pencil-shaped grooves carved into other boards were designed to not only trap liquid but also hold roasts firmly in place during carving. They worked moderately well, but they also hampered slicing.

THE BOTTOM LINE Of the carving boards we tested, none could best our longtime favorite **J.K. Adams Maple Reversible Carving Board** ($69.95). Its reversible design boasts a flat side suited to slicing roasts and an indented side with a poultry-shaped well to hold chicken and turkey snugly in place. Both sides allow for neat, even slicing without interference, and each sports a spacious trench that holds an ample ½ cup of liquid. It's also durable, handsome, and easy to clean and one of the least expensive boards in our lineup. This is one case where simpler really is better.

382 Grilled Chicken Salad with Bright and Harmonious Flavors

RECIPE FOR SUCCESS

✓ WHY THIS RECIPE WORKS

We set out to create a fresh, bright chicken salad inspired by the flavors of Mexico. A simple tequila-lime mixture boosted the chicken's flavor both in a quick marinade before cooking and, when cooked down with some orange juice, as a reduced sauce drizzled over the chicken after cooking. Grilled avocados gave the salad more smoky depth. We cooked the chicken over the hotter part of the grill to get a good char while cooking the more delicate avocados at the same time on the cooler side. To bring the salad together, we created a bright, tangy vinaigrette by combining lime juice and olive oil with cayenne and honey for well-rounded flavor.

Grilled Tequila Chicken with Orange, Avocado, and Pepita Salad

SERVES 4

Ripe but firm avocados are critical for successful grilling. If your avocados are overripe, skip seasoning and grilling and simply peel and slice the avocados before assembling the salad.

- ½ cup tequila
- ½ cup water
- 6 tablespoons lime juice (3 limes)
- 4 garlic cloves, minced
  Salt and pepper
- 4 (6- to 8-ounce) boneless, skinless chicken breasts, trimmed
- 3 oranges, peeled and cut into ½-inch pieces
- 5 tablespoons extra-virgin olive oil
- 1 tablespoon honey
- ¼ teaspoon cayenne pepper
- 2 ripe but firm avocados, halved and pitted
- 6 ounces (6 cups) watercress, chopped
- ⅓ cup pepitas, toasted
- 1 shallot, sliced thin

1 Whisk tequila, water, 3 tablespoons lime juice, garlic, and 2 teaspoons salt together in bowl until salt is dissolved. Transfer ½ cup marinade to small saucepan. Pour remaining marinade into 1-gallon zipper-lock bag, add chicken, and toss to coat. Press out as much air as possible, seal bag, and refrigerate for 30 minutes to 1 hour, flipping bag occasionally.

2 Let oranges drain in colander set over large bowl, reserving juice. In second large bowl, whisk ¼ cup oil, honey, cayenne, ¼ teaspoon salt, ¼ pepper, and remaining 3 tablespoons lime juice together; set aside for salad.

3 Before grilling, brush avocado halves with remaining 1 tablespoon oil and season with salt and pepper. Remove chicken from marinade, let excess marinade drip off, and transfer to plate.

4A FOR A CHARCOAL GRILL Open bottom vent completely. Light large chimney starter filled with charcoal briquettes (6 quarts). When top coals are partially covered with ash, pour two-thirds evenly over half of grill, then pour remaining coals over other half of grill. Set cooking grate in place, cover, and open lid vent completely. Heat grill until hot, about 5 minutes.

4B FOR A GAS GRILL Turn all burners to high, cover, and heat grill until hot, about 15 minutes. Leave primary burner on high and turn other burner(s) to medium.

5 Clean and oil cooking grate. Place chicken on hotter side of grill. Cook (covered if using gas), turning as needed, until chicken is nicely charred and registers 160 degrees, 8 to 12 minutes. Meanwhile, place avocados cut side down on cooler side of grill and cook until lightly charred, 3 to 5 minutes. Transfer chicken and avocados to cutting board and tent with aluminum foil.

6 Add drained orange juice to reserved marinade in saucepan, bring to simmer over medium-high heat, and cook until reduced to ¼ cup, 3 to 5 minutes. Whisk dressing to recombine, then add watercress, pepitas, shallots, and drained oranges and toss gently to coat; transfer to platter. Peel grilled avocado, slice thin, and lay on top of salad. Slice chicken on bias into ½-inch-thick pieces, lay on top of salad, and drizzle with reduced marinade. Serve.

383 SHOPPING IQ
Chill Out, Chicken

Chicken breasts account for 60 percent of the chicken sold in stores, and the vast majority of those breasts are the boneless, skinless variety. We gathered eight different products and called our tasters to find out which is best.

As it turned out, we could recommended only one brand without reservations. What's more, tasters' comments made clear that while flavor is paramount in whole birds and dark meat, chicken breasts are all about texture. Tasters deemed the flavor of this blandest part of the bird more or less the same across the board.

Our investigation into why the texture of some birds is better than that of others homed in on how the breasts are processed. And it was only when we asked the manufacturer of our winner, Bell & Evans, to walk us through its methods that we uncovered a good, albeit peculiar, lead for our findings: Once a Bell & Evans whole chicken is broken down into parts, the breasts are "aged" on the bone in chilled containers for as long as 12 hours before the bones (and skin) are removed. This aging period, it turns out, actually improves tenderness.

THE BOTTOM LINE Thanks to 12 hours of aging before being boned, our top pick, **Bell & Evans Air Chilled Boneless, Skinless Chicken Breasts** are "mega-juicy" and "tender," not to mention full of "clean, chicken-y" flavor.

384 Smoky and Spicy Tacos

✓ **WHY THIS RECIPE WORKS**

Simple grilled chicken, which cooks up quickly with a nice, smoky char, makes a perfect taco filling, especially when accompanied by a piquant green tomatillo salsa. Since it would be paired with other flavorful elements, we found that our chicken needed only a brief stint in a garlic-lime marinade before being grilled over a hot fire. A bit of salt and sugar in our marinade kept the chicken moist as it cooked and rounded out its flavor nicely. To complement the smoky, charred notes of the chicken, we decided to grill some of the salsa ingredients as well: sliced onion, a jalapeño chile, and half of the tomatillos cooked at the same rate as the chicken. We pulsed our grilled vegetables with additional raw tomatillos, cilantro, lime juice, and garlic for freshness and bite. As a final touch, we grilled our tortillas briefly to warm and lightly char them.

Grilled Chicken Tacos with Salsa Verde

SERVES 4

Serve with diced avocado and sliced radishes.

¼	cup vegetable oil
3	tablespoons lime juice (2 limes)
2	tablespoons water
	Sugar
	Salt and pepper
5	cloves garlic, minced
1½	pounds boneless, skinless chicken breasts, trimmed
1	onion, peeled and cut into ½-inch-thick rounds
1	jalapeño chile, stemmed, halved, and seeded
1	pound tomatillos, husks and stems removed, rinsed well and dried
12	(6-inch) corn tortillas
½	cup chopped fresh cilantro

1 Whisk 3 tablespoons oil, 1 tablespoon lime juice, water, 1 teaspoon sugar, 1½ teaspoons salt, ½ teaspoon pepper, and half of garlic together in medium bowl. Add chicken, cover, and refrigerate, turning occasionally, for 30 minutes. Brush onion, jalapeño, and half of tomatillos with remaining 1 tablespoon oil and season with salt. Halve remaining tomatillos; set aside.

2A FOR A CHARCOAL GRILL Open bottom vent completely. Light large chimney starter filled with charcoal briquettes (6 quarts). When top coals are partially covered with ash, pour evenly over grill. Set cooking grate in place, cover, and open lid vent completely. Heat grill until hot, about 5 minutes.

2B FOR A GAS GRILL Turn all burners to high, cover, and heat grill until hot, about 15 minutes. Leave all burners on high.

3 Clean and oil cooking grate. Place chicken and oiled vegetables on grill. Cook (covered if using gas), turning as needed, until chicken registers 160 degrees and vegetables are lightly charred and soft, 10 to 15 minutes. Transfer chicken and vegetables to cutting board and tent with aluminum foil.

4 Working in batches, grill tortillas, turning as needed, until warm and soft, about 30 seconds; wrap tightly in foil to keep soft.

5 Chop grilled vegetables coarse, then pulse with remaining tomatillos, cilantro, remaining garlic, remaining 2 tablespoons lime juice, ½ teaspoon salt, and pinch sugar in food processor until slightly chunky, 16 to 18 pulses. Slice chicken thin on bias and serve with tortillas and tomatillo salsa.

385 SHOPPING IQ
Tomatillos

Called *tomates verdes* in much of Mexico, small green tomatillos have a tangier, more citrusy flavor than true green tomatoes. When choosing tomatillos, look for pale green orbs with firm flesh that fills and splits open the fruit's papery outer husk, which must be removed before cooking. While we prefer the flavor and texture of fresh tomatillos, we have found that you can substitute one 12-ounce can of tomatillos, drained and rinsed, for every 8 ounces of fresh tomatillos.

RECIPE FOR SUCCESS

A Chain-Restaurant Favorite on the Home Grill

✓ WHY THIS RECIPE WORKS

As invented by the Bonanza Steakhouse chain, Chicken Monterey consisted of a boneless chicken breast in the restaurant's "exclusive Monterey marinade," flame-broiled and then topped with bacon strips and melted Monterey Jack cheese. Our challenge was to create a version that would work for home grillers. Recipes that we tried out tended to be bland and dry. To improve on these disappointing results, we started by butterflying boneless, skinless chicken breasts to provide more surface area for tasty char. For our marinade we developed a simple mixture of honey, Dijon mustard, salt, and pepper that could also double as a basting sauce on the grill. While the chicken cooked on the hotter side of the grill, we let red onion slices—basted with the reserved fat from cooking the bacon—soften on the cooler side of the grill. To finish, we slid the chicken away from the fire and topped it with the smoky onions and a mixture of cooked diced bacon and spicy shredded pepper Jack cheese.

Monterey Chicken
SERVES 4

We skewer the onion slices with a toothpick to keep them from falling apart on the grill. You won't need an entire red onion for this recipe; you can use the remainder to make Pico de Gallo (recipe follows).

- ½ cup Dijon mustard
- ¼ cup honey
  Salt and pepper
- 4 (6- to 8-ounce) boneless, skinless chicken breasts, trimmed
- 4 slices bacon, cut into ½-inch pieces
- 6 ounces pepper Jack cheese, shredded (1½ cups)
- 4 (½-inch-thick) slices red onion
  Lime wedges

1 Whisk mustard, honey, 1 teaspoon salt, and ½ teaspoon pepper together in bowl. Reserve ¼ cup honey-mustard mixture for basting chicken. Transfer remaining honey-mustard mixture to 1-gallon zipper-lock bag.

2 Working with 1 breast at a time, starting on thick side, cut chicken in half horizontally, stopping ½ inch from edge so halves remain attached. Open up breast like book, creating single flat piece. Place chicken in bag with honey-mustard mixture, toss to coat, and refrigerate for 30 minutes to 1 hour.

3 Meanwhile, cook bacon in 10-inch skillet over medium heat until crisp, 5 to 7 minutes. Using slotted spoon, transfer bacon to paper towel–lined plate. Reserve bacon fat. Once cool, toss bacon with pepper Jack.

4A FOR A CHARCOAL GRILL Open bottom vent completely. Light large chimney starter filled with charcoal briquettes (6 quarts). When top coals are partially covered with ash, pour two-thirds evenly over half of grill, then pour remaining coals over other half of grill. Set cooking grate in place, cover, and open lid vent completely. Heat grill until hot, about 5 minutes.

4B FOR A GAS GRILL Turn all burners to high, cover, and heat grill until hot, about 15 minutes. Leave primary burner on high and turn other burner(s) to medium.

5 Clean and oil cooking grate. Push toothpick horizontally through each onion slice to keep rings intact while grilling. Brush onion slices lightly with reserved bacon fat and place on cooler side of grill. Place chicken on hotter side of grill, cover, and cook until lightly charred, about 5 minutes. Flip onion slices and chicken. Brush chicken with reserved honey-mustard mixture, cover, and cook until lightly charred on second side, about 5 minutes.

6 Remove onion slices from grill and move chicken to cooler side of grill. Quickly remove toothpicks and separate onion rings. Divide onion rings evenly among chicken breasts. Divide bacon–pepper Jack mixture evenly over onion rings. Cover and cook until pepper Jack is melted and chicken registers 160 degrees, about 2 minutes. Transfer chicken to platter, tent with aluminum foil, and let rest for 5 to 10 minutes. Serve with lime wedges.

387 Pico de Gallo

MAKES ABOUT 1½ CUPS

To make this sauce spicier, include the jalapeño ribs and seeds.

3	tomatoes, cored and chopped
	Salt and pepper
¼	cup finely chopped red onion
¼	cup chopped fresh cilantro
1	jalapeño chile, stemmed, seeded, and minced
1	tablespoon lime juice
1	garlic clove, minced

Toss tomatoes with ¼ teaspoon salt in bowl. Transfer to colander and let drain for 30 minutes. Combine drained tomatoes, onion, cilantro, jalapeño, lime juice, and garlic in bowl. Season with salt and pepper to taste.

388 SHOPPING IQ Pepper Jack Cheese

Add hot pickled peppers to Monterey Jack, a mild California cow's-milk cheese, and you've got pepper Jack. Here in the test kitchen, we like pepper Jack for its creamy melting properties, and we've used it in enchiladas, biscuits, nachos, seven-layer dip, Tex-Mex meatloaf, and more. To select a favorite, we tasted seven nationally available cheeses. Although every product uses jalapeños (with one adding habanero), the heat levels varied. None was tear-inducingly hot, but some were tear-inducingly tame. We preferred the spicier cheeses. Fat played a role in our rankings, providing a buttery, creamy background to the heat of pepper Jack, as well as helping the cheese melt smoothly. With 9 grams of fat per ounce, our winning product was "creamy" and "buttery." It melted nicely, and its cheddar-like tang easily accommodated the "assertive kick" of peppers.

THE BOTTOM LINE For a good mix of bite and creaminess, choose a pepper Jack with a high fat content like our winner, **Boar's Head Monterey Jack with Jalapeño**.

WINNER

BOAR'S HEAD Monterey Jack Cheese with Jalapeño
Tasting Comments This "buttery" cheese had a "tangy," "cheddar-like" flavor that was "clean" and "nicely balanced," and the jalapeños gave it a "bright," "assertive" kick. The texture was "even and firm" yet "creamy."

RUNNER-UP

TILLAMOOK Pepper Jack Cheese
Tasting Comments This cheese's "very strong, sharp flavor" was "more tangy than milky," "fairly acidic," and "complex." The heat was "moderate" and the texture "soft."

389 RECIPE FOR SUCCESS
Stepped-Up Weeknight Chicken

✓ WHY THIS RECIPE WORKS

Because they're so lean, boneless, skinless chicken breasts can be pretty bland and are prone to drying out when cooked. Two promising ways to add flavor are with smoke and char from grilling and with a savory stuffing. We started with our usual easy stuffing technique, in which we cut a pocket in the chicken breast, pack it with stuffing, and seal it with a toothpick. After a few tries, we ruled out bread-based stuffings—they were inevitably pasty. Vegetable fillings required precooking—more work than we wanted to do for a simple weeknight recipe. Herb purees (made with garlic and olive oil) packed the most flavor and came together quickly, but oozed out of the chicken as it cooked. Creamy fontina cheese and a small amount of bread crumbs helped keep the herbs in place. With the added bulk from the stuffing, these chicken breasts had to spend extra time on the grill, so we cooked them gently over indirect heat and incorporated an olive oil–based marinade both before and after cooking to help protect against drying out and add even more flavor. Our variation plays with the flavors in both the stuffing and the marinade.

Easy Stuffed Chicken Breasts
SERVES 4

You will need four sturdy, uncolored toothpicks for this recipe. We prefer the taste and texture of homemade bread crumbs (simply tear one slice of hearty white sandwich bread into pieces, grind in a food processor, and toast in a dry skillet until golden), but store-bought bread crumbs are acceptable here.

6	tablespoons extra virgin olive oil
½	teaspoon grated lemon zest plus 1 tablespoon juice
3	garlic cloves, minced
1	teaspoon sugar
¾	teaspoon salt
½	teaspoon pepper
1	cup chopped fresh basil
2	ounces fontina cheese, shredded (½ cup)
3	tablespoons toasted bread crumbs
4	(6-ounce) boneless, skinless chicken breasts, trimmed

1 Whisk oil, zest and juice, garlic, sugar, salt, and pepper in small bowl. Pulse 2 tablespoons oil mixture, basil, cheese, and bread crumbs in food processor until coarsely ground, about 10 pulses.

2 Cut pocket in thick part of each chicken breast, spoon in filling, and secure with toothpick. Transfer stuffed chicken to large plate or baking dish and toss with ¼ cup oil mixture. Cover with plastic wrap and refrigerate for 30 minutes to 1 hour.

3A FOR A CHARCOAL GRILL Open bottom vent completely. Light large chimney starter filled with charcoal briquettes (6 quarts). When top coals are partially covered with ash, pour evenly over half of grill. Set cooking grate in place, cover, and open lid vent completely. Heat grill until hot, about 5 minutes.

3B FOR A GAS GRILL Turn all burners to high, close lid, and heat grill until very hot, about 15 minutes. Leave primary burner on high and turn off other burner(s).

4 Clean and oil cooking grate. Arrange chicken, smooth side down, on cooler side of grill with thicker side facing hotter side of grill. Cook (covered if using gas) until chicken is beginning to brown and meat registers 140 degrees, 16 to 20 minutes, flipping and rotating breasts halfway through cooking time. Move chicken to hotter side of grill and cook covered, flipping every few minutes, until meat registers 160 degrees, 4 to 8 minutes. Transfer chicken to platter and brush with remaining oil mixture. Tent with aluminum foil and let rest for 5 minutes. Remove toothpicks. Serve.

VARIATION

390 Greek-Style Grilled Stuffed Chicken Breasts

Substitute ¾ cup chopped fresh parsley and ¼ cup chopped fresh oregano for basil. Substitute ⅓ cup crumbled feta for fontina.

392 RECIPE FOR SUCCESS Wrapping Up Great Grilled Chicken

✓ WHY THIS RECIPE WORKS

For our version of this Greek sandwich, we started by brining the chicken and marinating it with a flavorful mixture of olive oil, lemon juice, herbs, black pepper, and honey before skewering and grilling it, which gave the chicken a flavorful crust. Reserving some of the marinade to mix in with the cooked chicken gave it a boost of brightness. To keep the pieces of chicken on the ends of the skewers from overcooking, we strung chunks of bell pepper and red onion along with the chicken pieces to shield them. We tempered the flavor of our tzatziki sauce by mincing the raw garlic and briefly steeping it in lemon juice. Traditionally, souvlaki is wrapped in soft pocketless pitas, which are hard to find at regular supermarkets. Instead, we moistened regular pocketed pitas and wrapped them in foil before putting them on the cooler side of the grill. The gently steamed pitas were soft, warm, and floppy—perfect for wrapping.

Chicken Souvlaki

SERVES 4

If using kosher chicken, do not brine. This tzatziki is fairly mild; if you like a more assertive flavor, double

the garlic. A rasp-style grater makes quick work of turning the garlic into a paste. We like the chicken as a wrap, but you may skip the pita and serve the chicken, vegetables, and tzatziki with rice. You will need four 12-inch metal skewers for this recipe.

TZATZIKI SAUCE

- 1 tablespoon lemon juice
- 1 small garlic clove, minced to paste
- ¾ cup plain Greek yogurt
- ½ cucumber, peeled, halved lengthwise, seeded, and chopped fine (½ cup)
- 3 tablespoons minced fresh mint
- 1 tablespoon minced fresh parsley
- ⅜ teaspoon salt

CHICKEN

- Salt and pepper
- 1½ pounds boneless, skinless chicken breasts, trimmed, and cut into 1-inch pieces
- ⅓ cup extra-virgin olive oil
- 2 tablespoons minced fresh parsley
- 1 teaspoon grated lemon zest plus ¼ cup juice (2 lemons)
- 1 teaspoon honey
- 1 teaspoon dried oregano
- 1 green bell pepper, stemmed, seeded, and quartered, each quarter cut into 4 pieces
- 1 small red onion, ends trimmed, peeled, halved lengthwise, each half cut into 4 chunks
- 4 (8-inch) pita breads

1 FOR THE TZATZIKI SAUCE Whisk lemon juice and garlic together in small bowl. Let stand for 10 minutes. Stir in yogurt, cucumber, mint, parsley, and salt. Cover and set aside.

2 FOR THE CHICKEN Dissolve 2 tablespoons salt in 1 quart cold water in large container. Submerge

391 TEST KITCHEN TIP Brine, Freeze, Grill

We brine chicken breasts both to season them and to help keep them moist during cooking. Because many people freeze chicken to have on hand we began to ponder which is better: brine first, then freeze, or freeze first, then brine? To see, we brined, froze for two weeks, defrosted, and then cooked several boneless chicken breasts. We compared them with breasts we froze plain for the same two weeks, defrosted, and then brined and cooked. We pitted both of these frozen versions against chicken breasts that we freshly brined and cooked. The result? There were slight textural differences, but all three were moist and juicy, and we'd happily use any in our cooking.

chicken in brine, cover, and refrigerate for 30 minutes. While chicken is brining, combine oil, parsley, lemon zest and juice, honey, oregano, and ½ teaspoon pepper in medium bowl. Transfer ¼ cup oil mixture to large bowl and set aside to toss with cooked chicken.

3 Remove chicken from brine and pat dry with paper towels. Toss chicken with remaining oil mixture.

4 Thread 4 pieces of bell pepper, concave side up, onto one 12-inch metal skewer. Thread one-quarter of chicken onto skewer. Thread 2 chunks of onion onto skewer, and place skewer on plate. Repeat skewering remaining chicken and vegetables on 3 more skewers.

5 Lightly moisten 2 pita breads with water. Sandwich 2 unmoistened pita breads between moistened pita breads and wrap stack tightly in lightly greased heavy-duty aluminum foil.

6A FOR A CHARCOAL GRILL Open bottom vent completely. Light large chimney starter mounded with charcoal briquettes (7 quarts). When top coals are partially covered with ash, pour evenly over half of grill. Set cooking grate in place, cover, and open lid vent completely. Heat grill until hot, about 5 minutes.

6B FOR A GAS GRILL Turn all burners to high, cover, and heat grill until hot, about 15 minutes. Leave primary burner on high and turn off other burner(s).

7 Clean and oil cooking grate. Place skewers on hotter side of grill and cook, turning occasionally, until chicken and vegetables are well browned on all sides and chicken registers 160 degrees, 15 to 20 minutes. Using fork, push chicken and vegetables off skewers into bowl of reserved oil mixture. Stir gently, breaking up onion chunks; cover with foil and let sit for 5 minutes.

8 Meanwhile, place packet of pitas on cooler side of grill. Flip occasionally to heat, about 5 minutes.

9 Lay each warm pita on 12-inch square of foil. Spread each pita with 2 tablespoons tzatziki. Place one-quarter of chicken and vegetables in middle of each pita. Roll into cylindrical shape and serve.

STEP BY STEP

393 Softening Supermarket Pita

To soften up dry, tough supermarket pita, we moisten two of the breads with a little water and then stack them on either side of two unmoistened pieces. Then we steam the breads in a foil-wrapped stack on the cooler side of the grill while the cooked chicken rests.

394 RECIPE FOR SUCCESS
Barbecued Chicken Skewers with a Secret Ingredient

✓ WHY THIS RECIPE WORKS

In theory, barbecued chicken kebabs sound pretty great: char-streaked chunks of juicy meat lacquered with sweet and tangy barbecue sauce. But without an insulating layer of skin, even the fattiest thigh meat can dry out and toughen when exposed to the blazing heat of the grill—and forget about ultralean skinless breast meat. Our goal was simple: juicy, tender chicken with plenty of sticky-sweet, smoke-tinged flavor. Brining is one common way to safeguard against dry meat, but in this case the brine made the meat so slick that the barbecue sauce refused to stick. A salt rub worked much better; the rub crisped up on the chicken's exterior as it cooked, forming a craggy surface that the sauce could really cling to. For incredible depth of flavor as well as juicy meat, we turned to an unusual technique: grinding bacon to a paste and applying it to the salted meat. Combined with both sweet and smoked paprika and a little sugar, our bacony rub created chicken that was juicy, tender, and full-flavored, with a smoky depth that complemented the barbecue sauce.

Barbecued Chicken Kebabs

SERVES 6

Use the large holes of a box grater to grate the onion for the sauce. We prefer flavorful dark thigh meat for these kebabs, but white meat can be used. Whichever you choose, don't mix white and dark meat on the same skewer, since they cook at different rates. If you have thin pieces of chicken, cut them larger than 1 inch and roll or fold them into approximate 1-inch cubes. Turbinado sugar is commonly sold as Sugar in the Raw. Demerara sugar can be substituted. You will need four 12-inch metal skewers for this recipe.

SAUCE
- ½ cup ketchup
- ¼ cup molasses
- 2 tablespoons grated onion
- 2 tablespoons Worcestershire sauce
- 2 tablespoons Dijon mustard
- 2 tablespoons cider vinegar
- 1 tablespoon packed light brown sugar

CHICKEN
- 2 tablespoons paprika
- 4 teaspoons turbinado sugar
- 2 teaspoons kosher salt
- 2 teaspoons smoked paprika
- 2 slices bacon, cut into ½-inch pieces
- 2 pounds boneless, skinless chicken thighs or breasts, trimmed, cut into 1-inch chunks

1 FOR THE SAUCE Bring all ingredients to simmer in small saucepan over medium heat and cook, stirring occasionally, until reduced to about 1 cup, 5 to 7 minutes. Transfer ½ cup sauce to small bowl and set remaining sauce aside for serving.

2 FOR THE CHICKEN Combine paprika, sugar, salt, and smoked paprika in large bowl. Process bacon in food processor until smooth paste forms, 30 to 45 seconds, scraping down sides of bowl as needed. Add bacon paste and chicken to spice mixture and mix with your hands or rubber spatula until ingredients are thoroughly blended and chicken is completely coated. Cover with plastic wrap and refrigerate for 1 hour. Thread chicken tightly onto four 12-inch metal skewers.

3A FOR A CHARCOAL GRILL Open bottom vent completely. Light large chimney starter three-quarters filled with charcoal briquettes (4½ quarts). When top coals are partially covered with ash, pour evenly over half of grill. Set cooking grate in place, cover, and open lid vent completely. Heat grill until hot, about 5 minutes.

3B FOR A GAS GRILL Turn all burners to high, cover, and heat grill until hot, about 15 minutes. Turn all burners to medium-high.

4 Clean and oil cooking grate. Place skewers on hotter part of grill (if using charcoal), and cook (covered if using gas), turning kebabs every 2 to 2½ minutes, until well browned and slightly charred, 8 to 10 minutes. Brush top surface of skewers with ¼ cup sauce, flip, and cook until sauce is sizzling and browning in spots, about 1 minute. Brush second side with remaining ¼ cup sauce, flip, and continue to cook until sizzling and browning in spots, about 1 minute longer.

5 Transfer skewers to serving platter, tent with aluminum foil, and let rest for 5 to 10 minutes. Serve, passing reserved sauce separately.

395 TEST KITCHEN TIP
Better With Bacon

To create a protective coating that keeps the chicken moist on the grill, we chop two slices of bacon, pulse them in a food processor until smooth, and then toss the resulting paste (along with sugar and spices) with the raw chicken chunks.

396 Sweet and Smoky Glazed Chicken

✓ WHY THIS RECIPE WORKS

Too many recipes for glazed grilled chicken give you meat that's scorched or sickeningly sweet—or both. We wanted nicely glazed, unimpeachable peachy grilled chicken. To start, we sprinkled the chicken with salt and pepper and let it sit for at least an hour before cooking to season the chicken and enable it to retain more moisture. Then we faced the main challenge: balancing real peach flavor with the necessity of not incinerating our dinner. Cooking chicken covered in sweet preserves led to intense scorching on the grill, but just applying a glaze at the end of cooking didn't yield much flavor. We created a setup that cooked the chicken most of the way through in the sauce without exposing it to open flame by using a disposable aluminum pan. We started the chicken skin side down to render some fat before flipping the pieces skin side up to dry off and crisp up. We then finished the meat over the coals for perfect browning. A fresh peach and a jalapeño chile cooked alongside the chicken and incorporated into the sauce added heat and flavor to the finished dish.

Peach-Glazed Grilled Chicken
SERVES 4

Leave the jalapeño whole for grilling. Note that the salted chicken needs to rest for 1 to 24 hours before grilling. Since the preserves cause the food to brown quickly in step 5, move the items around as necessary to manage any hot spots. If you'd like to use wood chunks instead of wood chips when using a charcoal grill, substitute one medium wood chunk, soaked in water for 1 hour, for the wood chip packet.

3   pounds bone-in chicken pieces (split breasts cut in half, drumsticks, and/or thighs), trimmed
    Salt and pepper
1   cup wood chips
1   cup peach preserves
⅛   teaspoon cayenne pepper
1   (13 by 9-inch) disposable aluminum pan
1   peach, halved and pitted
1   jalapeño chile
2   tablespoons cider vinegar

1 Pat chicken dry with paper towels and sprinkle with 2¼ teaspoons salt and 1 teaspoon pepper. Place in 1-gallon zipper-lock bag and refrigerate for at least 1 hour or up to 24 hours.

2 Just before grilling, soak wood chips in water for 15 minutes, then drain. Using large piece of heavy-duty aluminum foil, wrap soaked chips in 8 by 4½-inch foil packet. (Make sure chips do not poke holes in sides or bottom of packet.) Cut 2 evenly spaced 2-inch slits in top of packet. Whisk preserves and cayenne together in disposable pan. Place peach halves (cut side up), jalapeño, and chicken (skin side down) in pan.

3A FOR A CHARCOAL GRILL Open bottom vent halfway. Light large chimney starter filled with charcoal briquettes (6 quarts). When top coals are partially covered with ash, pour evenly over grill. Place wood chip packet on coals on 1 side of grill. Set cooking grate in place, cover, and open lid vent halfway. Heat grill until hot and wood chips are smoking, about 5 minutes.

3B FOR A GAS GRILL Remove cooking grate and place wood chip packet directly on primary burner. Set grate in place, turn all burners to high, cover, and heat grill until hot and wood chips are smoking, about 15 minutes. Turn all burners to medium. (Adjust burners as needed to maintain grill temperature between 350 and 375 degrees.)

4 Clean and oil cooking grate. Place disposable pan with chicken over side of grill opposite wood chip packet. Cover grill (position lid vent over chicken if using charcoal) and cook for 10 minutes. Flip chicken, and rotate pan 180 degrees. (Open top and bottom vents fully for charcoal grill.) Continue to cook, covered, until breasts register 155 degrees and drumsticks/thighs register 170 degrees, 10 to 14 minutes.

5 Flip chicken, peach halves, and jalapeño to coat with preserves, then transfer to grill grate (skin side down for chicken). Leave pan on grill to let preserves thicken and caramelize slightly around edges, 3 to 5 minutes, then remove pan from grill.

6 Meanwhile, cook chicken, peach halves, and jalapeño until well browned on first side, 2 to 5 minutes. Flip and continue to cook until chicken breasts register 160 degrees and drumsticks/ thighs register 175 degrees and peach halves and jalapeño are well browned on second side, 2 to 5 minutes. Return chicken, skin side up, to pan with preserves, tent loosely with foil, and let rest for 10 minutes. Transfer peach and jalapeño to plate to cool slightly.

7 Remove any loose skin from peach halves and jalapeño (no need to remove all skin); then chop peach halves, seed and mince jalapeño, and transfer both to bowl. Arrange chicken on serving platter. Pour preserves from pan into bowl with chopped peach halves and jalapeño; stir in vinegar. Season glaze with salt and pepper to taste. Spoon glaze over chicken and serve.

397

From Pan to Grate

1 START IN PAN Cook chicken, peach, and jalapeño in disposable roasting pan with peach preserves and cayenne.

2 SEAR ON GRATE Move chicken, peach, and jalapeño onto grill grate to sear while preserves caramelize in the pan.

3 COAT CHICKEN Move just chicken back to pan, now off grill, to coat with glaze and let rest.

4 MAKE SAUCE Chop peach and jalapeño and combine them with reduced glaze and vinegar to make serving sauce.

398 Smoky Bourbon Chicken

✓ WHY THIS RECIPE WORKS

A bourbon-spiked barbecue sauce slathered on grilled chicken is a perfect combination but infusing smoke and bourbon flavors while keeping the meat from drying out is a challenge. We started by using two split chickens so we could cook each half skin side up for crispier skin. For good bourbon flavor, we made a marinade that paired the bourbon with brown sugar, shallot, garlic, and soy sauce. We also slashed the surface of the chickens to help them absorb the marinade. Our science editor suggested heating the marinade, which would help activate the aroma compounds, so we boiled the mixture before adding it to the chickens. Now the meat had smokiness, bold bourbon flavor, and deep, well-rounded seasoning.

Kentucky Bourbon Brined Grilled Chicken

SERVES 4 TO 6

Use a bourbon you'd be happy drinking. Use all the basting liquid in step 5. If you'd like to use wood chunks instead of wood chips when using a charcoal grill, substitute one medium wood chunk, soaked in water for 1 hour, for the wood chip packet.

- 1¼ cups bourbon
- 1¼ cups soy sauce
- ½ cup packed brown sugar
- 1 shallot, minced
- 4 garlic cloves, minced
- 2 teaspoons pepper
- 2 (3½- to 4-pound) whole chickens, giblets discarded
- 1 cup wood chips
- 4 (12-inch) wooden skewers

1 Bring bourbon, soy sauce, sugar, shallot, garlic, and pepper to boil in medium saucepan over medium-high heat and cook for 1 minute. Remove from heat and let cool completely. Set aside ¾ cup bourbon mixture for basting chicken. (Bourbon mixture can be refrigerated for up to 3 days.)

2 With 1 chicken breast side down, use kitchen shears to cut along both sides of backbone. Discard backbone and trim any excess fat or skin at neck. Flip chicken over and, using chef's knife, cut through breastbone to separate chicken into halves. Cut ½-inch-deep slits across breast, thigh, and leg of each half, about ½ inch apart. Tuck wingtips behind backs. Repeat with second chicken. Divide chicken halves between two 1-gallon zipper-lock bags and divide remaining bourbon mixture between bags. Seal bags, turn to distribute marinade, and refrigerate for at least 1 hour or up to 24 hours, flipping occasionally.

3 Just before grilling, soak wood chips in water for 15 minutes, then drain. Using large piece of heavy-duty aluminum foil, wrap soaked chips in 8 by 4½-inch foil packet. (Make sure chips do not poke holes in sides or bottom of packet.) Cut 2 evenly spaced 2-inch slits in top of packet. Remove chicken halves from marinade and pat dry with paper towels; discard marinade. Insert 1 skewer lengthwise through thickest part of breast down through thigh of each chicken half.

4A FOR A CHARCOAL GRILL Open bottom vent halfway. Light large chimney starter filled with charcoal briquettes (6 quarts). When top coals are partially covered with ash, pour into steeply banked pile against side of grill. Place wood chip packet on coals. Set cooking grate in place, cover, and open lid vent halfway. Heat grill until hot and wood chips are smoking, about 5 minutes.

4B FOR A GAS GRILL Remove cooking grate and place wood chip packet directly on primary burner. Set grate in place, turn all burners to high, cover, and heat grill until hot and wood chips are smoking, about 15 minutes. Leave primary burner on high and turn off other burners. (Adjust primary burner as needed to maintain grill temperature between 350 and 375 degrees.)

5 Clean and oil cooking grate. Place chicken halves skin side up on cooler side of grill with legs pointing toward fire. Cover and cook, basting every 15 minutes with reserved bourbon mixture, until breasts register 160 degrees and thighs register 175 degrees, 75 to 90 minutes, switching placement of chicken halves after 45 minutes. (All of bourbon mixture should be used.) Transfer chicken to carving board, tent with foil, and let rest for 20 minutes. Carve and serve.

399 RECIPE FOR SUCCESS Perfecting a Barbecued Classic

✓ WHY THIS RECIPE WORKS

Barbecued chicken falls victim to numerous pitfalls: The chicken cooks unevenly, frequent flare-ups cause the skin to blacken, and the sauce is usually cloyingly thick and sweet. We set out to foolproof this American classic. For chicken that was well seasoned all the way to the bone, we applied a rub: Salt, onion and garlic powders, paprika, a touch of cayenne, and some brown sugar maintained a bold presence even after grilling. Placing a disposable aluminum pan opposite the coals in our grill setup and filling the pan partially with water lowered the temperature inside the grill, which ensured that all the chicken pieces cooked at a slow, steady rate. We smartened the typical ketchup-based barbecue sauce with molasses, while cider vinegar, Worcestershire sauce, and Dijon mustard kept the sweetness in check. We waited to apply the sauce until after searing the chicken, which prevented the sauce from burning and gave the chicken skin a chance to develop color first. Applying the sauce in stages, rather than all at once, ensured that its bright tanginess wasn't lost.

Sweet and Tangy Barbecued Chicken

SERVES 6 TO 8

When browning the chicken over the hotter side of the grill, move it away from any flare-ups. Use the large holes of a box grater to grate the onion for the sauce.

CHICKEN

2	tablespoons packed dark brown sugar
1½	tablespoons kosher salt
1½	teaspoons onion powder
1½	teaspoons garlic powder
1½	teaspoons paprika
¼	teaspoon cayenne pepper
6	pounds bone-in chicken pieces (split breasts and/or leg quarters), trimmed

SAUCE

1	cup ketchup
5	tablespoons molasses
3	tablespoons cider vinegar
2	tablespoons Worcestershire sauce
2	tablespoons Dijon mustard
¼	teaspoon pepper
2	tablespoons vegetable oil
⅓	cup grated onion
1	garlic clove, minced
1	teaspoon chili powder
¼	teaspoon cayenne pepper
1	(13 by 9-inch) disposable aluminum roasting pan (if using charcoal) or 2 disposable aluminum pie plates (if using gas)

1 FOR THE CHICKEN Combine sugar, salt, onion powder, garlic powder, paprika, and cayenne in bowl. Arrange chicken on rimmed baking sheet and sprinkle both sides evenly with spice rub. Cover with plastic wrap and refrigerate for at least 6 hours or up to 24 hours.

2 FOR THE SAUCE Whisk ketchup, molasses, vinegar, Worcestershire, mustard, and pepper together in bowl. Heat oil in medium saucepan over medium heat until shimmering. Add onion and garlic; cook until onion is softened, 2 to 4 minutes. Add chili powder and cayenne and cook until fragrant, about 30 seconds. Whisk in ketchup mixture and bring to boil. Reduce heat to medium-low and simmer gently for 5 minutes. Measure out ⅔ cup sauce and set aside to baste chicken; set aside remaining sauce for serving. (Sauce can be refrigerated for up to 1 week.)

3A FOR A CHARCOAL GRILL Open bottom vent halfway. Place disposable pan on 1 side of grill and add 3 cups water to pan. Light large chimney starter filled with charcoal briquettes (6 quarts). When top coals are partially covered with ash, pour evenly over other side of grill. Set cooking grate in place, cover, and open lid vent halfway. Heat grill until hot, about 5 minutes.

3B FOR A GAS GRILL Remove cooking grate, place 2 disposable pie plates directly on 1 burner (opposite primary burner), and add 1½ cups water to each. Set grate in place, turn all burners to high, cover, and heat grill until hot, about 15 minutes. Turn primary burner to medium-high and turn off other burner(s). (Adjust primary burner as needed to maintain grill temperature between 325 and 350 degrees.)

4 Clean and oil cooking grate. Place chicken, skin side down, over hotter part of grill and cook until browned and blistered in spots, 2 to 5 minutes. Flip chicken and cook until second side is browned, 4 to 6 minutes. Move chicken to cooler side and brush both sides with ⅓ cup sauce for basting. Arrange chicken, skin side up, with leg quarters closest to fire and breasts farthest away. Cover (positioning lid vent over chicken if using charcoal) and cook for 25 minutes.

5 Brush both sides of chicken with remaining ⅓ cup sauce for basting and continue to cook, covered, until breasts register 160 degrees and leg quarters register 175 degrees, 25 to 35 minutes longer.

6 Transfer chicken to serving platter, tent with aluminum foil, and let rest for 10 minutes. Serve, passing reserved sauce separately.

400 FOOD SCIENCE
Why Use a Water Pan in Your Grill?

Some grill experts put an empty aluminum pan in the grill in order to catch drips and prevent flare-ups. For recipes such as our Sweet and Tangy Barbecued Chicken, we not only put a pan on the grill but also fill it with water—for different reasons: Placing a pan of water opposite the coals lowers the heat inside a grill, allowing you to cook more slowly and gently; it also evens out the heat. But we weren't sure which component—the water or the pan—was more responsible for these benefits.

To find out, we gauged the heat disparities on three different grill setups by running a toast test. We built indirect fires in each grill and then placed a disposable aluminum pan opposite the coals in one, an aluminum pan filled with 3 cups of water in another, and nothing in the third grill. We let the coals burn for 15 minutes and then spread six slices of bread over each grill's cooler side and let them cook for 4 minutes.

What did we find? Bread toasted on the grill without a pan turned dark brown and the pieces closest to the coals burned, while the slices cooked on the two grills with aluminum pans were lightly and evenly tanned. The bread toasted over the water-filled pan was slightly paler but not by much. The grill temperatures correlated with the toast results: The grill without the pan registered 415 to 425 degrees, the grill with the empty pan 385 to 395 degrees, and the grill with the water-filled pan 375 to 385 degrees.

Even putting an empty aluminum pan in the grill will significantly drop its temperature. Aluminum is very efficient at absorbing heat, allowing it to lower the temperature inside the grill by about 30 degrees and to even out hot spots. Water added to the pan captures more heat, helping drop the temperature even further, but it's mainly the metal pan that's responsible for the change. So if you ever put an empty pan in the grill to catch drips, be aware that it will lower the temperature as well.

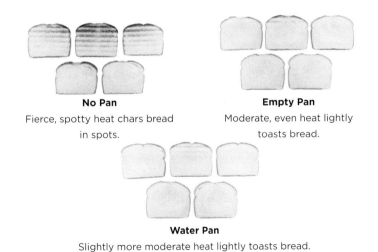

No Pan
Fierce, spotty heat chars bread in spots.

Empty Pan
Moderate, even heat lightly toasts bread.

Water Pan
Slightly more moderate heat lightly toasts bread.

401 Latin Chicken with Tang and Spice

✔ WHY THIS RECIPE WORKS

Grilled citrus- and spice-marinated chicken is a standard menu item at Mexican restaurants, but quality and approach can vary dramatically from recipe to recipe. Sometimes you luck out with chicken that is juicy and full of flavor. More often, though, the chicken is dry, leathery, bland, and lifeless. We wanted to come up with a great version of this dish we could grill up at home. Recipes often call for marinating chicken in a blend of orange and lime juices (to substitute for the more authentic sour oranges, which are hard to come by), along with the aromatics, spices, and herbs, but this combination didn't deliver the bold flavors we were looking for. Instead, we started with just lime juice and gave it a helping hand with orange zest and lime zest; the result was the perfect replacement for sour oranges. Mixed with onion, garlic, and just enough olive oil to make a paste, this gave our chicken great citrus flavor in just 1 hour. Cooking over indirect heat with a brief sear over the fire at the end to crisp the skin and add flavorful char gave us succulent meat, crisp skin, and nicely caramelized seasonings.

Citrus-and-Spice Grilled Chicken
SERVES 4 TO 6

To create a split fire, with a central cooler zone and coals on either side, we place a disposable roasting pan in the center of the grill.

1 onion, chopped coarse

6 garlic cloves, peeled

2 tablespoons olive oil

1 tablespoon grated orange zest

2 teaspoons dried oregano

1½ teaspoons salt

1 teaspoon grated lime zest plus ¼ cup juice (2 limes)

½ teaspoon pepper

½ teaspoon ground cinnamon

½ teaspoon ground cumin

⅛ teaspoon ground cloves

3 pounds bone-in chicken pieces (split breasts cut in half, drumsticks, and/or thighs), trimmed

1 (13 by 9-inch) disposable aluminum roasting pan (if using charcoal)

1 Process onion, garlic, oil, orange zest, oregano, salt, lime zest and juice, pepper, cinnamon, cumin, and cloves in food processor until smooth, about 30 seconds; transfer to 1-gallon zipper-lock bag. Add chicken to bag with marinade and toss to coat; press out as much air as possible and seal bag. Refrigerate for at least 1 hour or up to 24 hours, turning bag occasionally.

2A FOR A CHARCOAL GRILL Open bottom vent completely and place disposable pan in center of grill. Light large chimney starter filled with charcoal briquettes (6 quarts). When top coals are partially covered with ash, pour into 2 even piles on either side of disposable pan. Set cooking grate in place, cover, and open lid vent completely. Heat grill until hot, about 5 minutes.

2B FOR A GAS GRILL Turn all burners to high, cover, and heat grill until hot, about 15 minutes. Turn all burners to medium-low. (Adjust burners as needed to maintain grill temperature around 350 degrees.)

3 Clean and oil cooking grate. Place chicken skin side up on grill (over disposable pan if using charcoal). Cover and cook until bottom is browned and chicken registers 155 degrees, about 25 minutes.

4 Flip chicken skin side down. Slide chicken over coals if using charcoal, or turn all burners to high if using gas. Cook until well browned and breasts register 160 degrees and drumsticks/thighs register 175 degrees, 5 to 10 minutes. Transfer chicken to large platter, tent with aluminum foil, and let rest for 5 to 10 minutes before serving.

402 GADGETS & GEAR Food Processors

Food processors are fixtures in most well-equipped kitchens thanks to their ability to simplify a variety of kitchen tasks at the push of a button. Still, pick the wrong processor and suddenly this great convenience leaves you worse off than when you started. We tested eight models across a variety of price points to find a large-capacity machine that could handle a wide variety of tasks with ease. The elements that made the biggest differences in separating the winners from the losers were the responsiveness of the pulse button, motor strength, blade sharpness, and how easy the machine's parts were to clean. Although there are plenty of machines on the market with extra bells and whistles, our winner was a classic machine that slices and chops as evenly and cleanly as an expertly wielded knife—only much faster—with a simple, sturdy, easy-to-clean design.

THE BOTTOM LINE The **Cuisinart Custom 14-Cup Food Processor** takes the top spot in the test kitchen.

WINNER

CUISINART Custom 14-Cup Food Processor

Price $161.99

Testing Comments This easy-to-use, classic machine consistently outshines its pricier competition. With a powerful, quiet motor, responsive pulsing action, sharp blades, and simple design, this model is both impressive and affordable. It was one of only a few machines that didn't leak at its maximum liquid capacity and it was easy to clean and store. Though only a chopping blade and slicing/coarse shredding disk are included, more blade options are available à la carte.

RUNNER-UP

BREVILLE Sous Chef 12-Cup Food Processor

Price $299.99

Testing Comments This model stood out for its expert chopping, slicing, and shredding, but its motor struggled to mix a double batch of pizza dough and its too-short blades failed to fully emulsify mayonnaise. It boasts a well-designed workbowl that slides smoothly into place and pours neatly, and it was quiet and quick at most tasks. The pulse button is responsive and effective, and its adjustable slicing blade works well, though you have to set the width under the blade before you start to process.

403

Whole Chickens

The ability to pick up a whole chicken at any local market doesn't make shopping easy. On the contrary, there's a multitude of brands and a wide range of prices—not to mention that you need a degree in agribusiness to decode most of the packaging lingo. We wanted to figure out what tasted best when we stripped away the sales pitches so we rounded up eight national and large regional brands of whole fresh supermarket chicken, which we seasoned minimally, roasted, and carved into piles of white and dark meat for tasting. Only a few gave us meat that was rich, clean-tasting, tender, and moist. Others tasted utterly bland or, worse, faintly metallic, bitter, or liver-y. Chalky, dry meat was a common, predictable complaint, but surprisingly, so was too much moisture. The process of water chilling, where the chicken carcasses are chilled in a water bath after processing, helped explain why tasters found the meat in several of the birds to be unnaturally spongy, with washed-out flavor. We preferred birds chilled on a conveyor belt that circulates them along the ceiling of a cold room. Air chilling dilutes flavor less than water chilling, leaving the birds juicy without being soggy.

THE BOTTOM LINE Mary's Free Range Air Chilled Chicken (also sold as Pitman's) was deemed "really perfect" by our tasters.

WINNER

MARY'S Free Range Air Chilled Chicken (also sold as Pitman's)
Tasting Comments Air chilling plus a higher percentage of fat (compared with water-chilled chicken) added up to a bird that tasters raved was "clean," "sweet," "buttery," "savory," "chicken-y," and "juicy," with "richly flavored" dark meat that was "so moist" and "tender." In sum: "Really perfect."

RUNNER-UP

BELL & EVANS Air Chilled Premium Fresh Chicken
Tasting Comments Thanks to almost 3 hours of air chilling, this bird's white meat was "perfectly moist," "rich and nutty," and "concentrated and chicken-y," and its dark meat "silky-tender" yet "firm." Several tasters remarked that it seemed "really fresh" and "clean-tasting." Also helpful to flavor: It had the highest fat percentage of any bird in the tasting.

404

Ivy-League Grilled Chicken

✓ WHY THIS RECIPE WORKS
Invented in the 1940s by Robert Baker, a Cornell University professor, this tangy, crisp-skinned grilled chicken recipe has been a star attraction at the New York State Fair ever since. Grilling two split chickens over gentle heat worked best here. To crisp the skin without burning it, we started the chicken skin side up to render the fat slowly, then flipped the chicken skin side down to brown until crisp. The traditional poultry seasoning worked great as a rub but tasted dusty in the sauce, so we replaced it with fresh rosemary and sage. Dijon mustard contributed even more flavor to the sauce and thickened it perfectly.

Cornell Chicken
SERVES 4 TO 6
If using kosher chicken, do not brine. Do not brine the chicken longer than 2 hours or the vinegar will turn the meat mushy. Poultry seasoning is a mix of herbs and spices that can be found in the supermarket spice aisle.

CHICKEN
- 2 (3½- to 4-pound) whole chickens, giblets discarded
- ¼ cup salt
- 3½ cups cider vinegar

SEASONING AND SAUCE
- 1 tablespoon ground poultry seasoning Salt and pepper
- ½ cup cider vinegar
- 3 tablespoons Dijon mustard
- 1 tablespoon chopped fresh sage leaves
- 1 tablespoon chopped fresh rosemary
- ½ cup olive oil

1 FOR THE CHICKEN With 1 chicken breast side down, use kitchen shears to cut along both sides of backbone. Discard backbone and trim any excess fat or skin at neck. Flip chicken over and, using chef's knife, cut through breastbone to separate chicken into halves. Tuck wingtips behind back. Repeat with second chicken. In large container, dissolve salt in vinegar and 2 quarts cold water. Submerge chickens in brine, cover, and refrigerate for 1 to 2 hours.

2 FOR THE SEASONING AND SAUCE Combine poultry seasoning, 2 teaspoons salt, and 2 teaspoons pepper in small bowl; set aside. Process vinegar, mustard, sage, rosemary, ½ teaspoon salt, and ½ teaspoon pepper in blender until smooth, about 1 minute. With blender running, slowly add oil until incorporated. Measure out ¾ cup vinegar sauce and set aside to baste chicken; set aside remaining sauce for serving.

3 Remove chickens from brine, pat dry with paper towels, and rub evenly with poultry seasoning mixture.

4A FOR A CHARCOAL GRILL Open bottom vent completely. Light large chimney starter three-quarters filled with charcoal briquettes (4½ quarts). When top coals are partially covered with ash, pour evenly over grill. Set cooking grate in place, cover, and open lid vent halfway. Heat grill until hot, about 5 minutes.

4B FOR A GAS GRILL Turn all burners to high, cover, and heat grill until hot, about 15 minutes. Turn all burners to medium-low. (Adjust burners as needed to maintain grill temperature around 350 degrees.)

5 Clean and oil cooking grate. Place chicken skin side up on grill and brush with 6 tablespoons vinegar sauce for basting. Cover and cook chicken until well browned on bottom and thighs register 120 degrees, 25 to 30 minutes, brushing with more sauce for basting halfway through grilling.

6 Flip chicken skin side down and brush with remaining sauce for basting. Cover and continue to cook chicken until skin is golden brown and crisp and breasts register 160 degrees and thighs register 175 degrees, 20 to 25 minutes longer.

7 Transfer chicken to carving board and let rest for 10 minutes. Carve chicken and serve with reserved sauce.

406

RECIPE FOR SUCCESS

Spicy African Barbecued Chicken

✓ WHY THIS RECIPE WORKS

The spicy grilled dish known as peri peri chicken has African roots, but at its most basic, it is chicken marinated in a paste of garlic, herbs, spices, lemon juice, and fiery African peppers called peri peri chiles and then grilled over a hot fire. We wanted to develop a version that kept the spicy yet complex profile while presenting a more accessible alternative to the hard-to-come-by peri peri peppers. We used a half-grill fire along with an aluminum pan filled with water to eliminate hot spots. For the spice paste, we started with a base of olive oil, garlic, shallot, lemon, bay leaves, paprika, and black pepper, plus five-spice powder for complexity. To mimic

the fruity, complex heat of the peri peri peppers we turned to dried arbol chiles and cayenne. Tomato paste and a final savory touch—chopped peanuts—gave the dish a balanced richness and hint of sweetness.

Peri Peri Grilled Chicken

SERVES 6 TO 8

When browning the chicken over the hotter side of the grill, move it away from the direct heat if any flare-ups occur. Serve with white rice.

- ¼ cup salt
- 3   tablespoons extra-virgin olive oil
- 8   garlic cloves, peeled
- 2   tablespoons tomato paste
- 1   shallot, chopped
- 1   tablespoon sugar
- 1   tablespoon paprika
- 1   tablespoon five-spice powder
- 1   teaspoon pepper
- ½   teaspoon cayenne pepper
- 3   bay leaves, crushed
- 2   teaspoons grated lemon zest plus ¼ cup juice (2 lemons), plus lemon wedges for serving
- 4–10 arbol chiles, stems removed
- 6   pounds bone-in chicken pieces (split breasts, thighs, and/or drumsticks), trimmed
- ½   cup dry-roasted peanuts, chopped fine
- 1   (13 by 9-inch) disposable roasting pan (if using charcoal) or 2 (9-inch) disposable pie plates (if using gas)

1 Process salt, oil, garlic, tomato paste, shallot, sugar, paprika, five-spice powder, pepper, cayenne, bay leaves, lemon zest and juice, and 4 arbol chiles in blender until smooth paste forms, 10 to 20 seconds. Taste paste and add up to 6 additional arbol chiles, depending on desired level of heat (spice paste should be slightly hotter than desired heat level of cooked chicken); process until smooth. Using metal skewer, poke skin side of chicken pieces 8 to 10 times. Place chicken parts, peanuts, and spice paste in large bowl or container and toss until chicken is evenly coated with spice paste. Cover and refrigerate for at least 6 hours or up to 24 hours.

2A FOR A CHARCOAL GRILL Open bottom vent halfway. Place disposable pan on 1 side of grill and add 3 cups water to pan. Light large chimney starter filled with charcoal briquettes (6 quarts). When top coals

405

SHOPPING IQ

Picking the Right Stand-In for Peri Peri Peppers

Traditionally, dried African *peri peri* peppers, which are about 10 times hotter than serrano chiles, give this dish its spicy heat, but they are hard to find in the States. Because they have a fruity, complex flavor in addition to heat, we found that no one chile could replace them. Instead, we landed on a combination of cayenne, for a baseline level of heat, and dried arbol chiles, which are spicy but, more important, have the right fruity note that mimics the peri peri chile's flavor.

Peri Peri Peppers

Arbols Plus Cayenne

are partially covered with ash, pour evenly over other side of grill. Set cooking grate in place, cover, and open lid vent halfway. Heat grill until hot, about 5 minutes.

2B FOR A GAS GRILL Remove cooking grate, place 2 disposable pie plates directly on 1 burner (opposite primary burner), and add 1½ cups water to each. Set grate in place, turn all burners to high, cover, and heat grill until hot, about 15 minutes. Turn primary burner to medium-high and turn off other burner(s). (Adjust primary burner as needed to maintain grill temperature between 325 and 350 degrees.)

3 Clean and oil cooking grate. Place chicken, skin side down, on hotter side of grill and cook until browned and blistered in spots, 2 to 5 minutes. Flip chicken and cook until second side is browned, 4 to 6 minutes. Move chicken to cooler side and arrange, skin side up, with drumsticks/thighs closest to fire and breasts farthest away. Cover (positioning lid vent over chicken if using charcoal) and cook for 50 minutes to 1 hour, until breasts register 160 degrees and drumsticks/thighs register 175 degrees, 50 minutes to 1 hour.

4 Transfer chicken to serving platter, tent with aluminum foil, and let rest for 10 minutes before serving with lemon wedges.

407 TEST KITCHEN TIP
Grilling with Water

Whether you're cooking this recipe or barbecued chicken, it's key to cook the meat through gently for tender, juicy results. To do this, in addition to setting up the grill with a cooler side that is left free of coals, we also put an aluminum pan or pie plates filled with water on the grill. Both the pan (or plates) and the water absorb heat, lowering the heat overall and eliminating hot spots. Read more about the science behind grilling with water on page 235.

GAS

1 Place 2 disposable aluminum pie plates on 1 burner, opposite primary burner, and set cooking grate in place.
2 Fill pie plates with 1½ cups water each.
3 Light burners as directed and proceed with recipe.

CHARCOAL

1 Place 13 by 9-inch disposable aluminum pan on 1 side of charcoal grate.
2 Fill pan with 3 cups water.
3 Once coals are lit, pour them next to pan, put cooking grate in place, and proceed with recipe.

a charcoal grill, substitute two medium wood chunks, soaked in water for 1 hour, for the wood chip packet.

SAUCE

- ¾ **cup mayonnaise**
- 2 **tablespoons cider vinegar**
- 2 **teaspoons sugar**
- ½ **teaspoon prepared horseradish**
- ½ **teaspoon salt**
- ½ **teaspoon pepper**
- ¼ **teaspoon cayenne pepper**

CHICKEN

- 1 **teaspoon salt**
- 1 **teaspoon pepper**
- ½ **teaspoon cayenne pepper**
- 2 **(3½- to 4-pound) whole chickens, giblets discarded**
- 2 **cups wood chips, soaked in water for 15 minutes and drained**
- 1 **(13 by 9-inch) disposable aluminum roasting pan (if using charcoal)**

1 FOR THE SAUCE Process ingredients in blender until smooth, about 1 minute. Refrigerate for at least 1 hour or up to 2 days.

2 FOR THE CHICKEN Combine salt, pepper, and cayenne in small bowl. With 1 chicken breast side down, use kitchen shears to cut along both sides of backbone. Discard backbone and trim any excess fat or skin at neck. Flip chicken over and, using chef's knife, cut through breastbone to separate chicken into halves. Tuck wingtips behind back. Repeat with second chicken. Pat chickens dry with paper towels and rub them evenly with spice mixture. Using large piece of heavy-duty aluminum foil, wrap soaked chips in 8 by 4½-inch foil packet. (Make sure chips do not poke holes in sides or bottom of packet.) Cut 2 evenly spaced 2-inch slits in top of each packet.

3A FOR A CHARCOAL GRILL Open bottom vent halfway and place disposable pan in center of grill. Light large chimney starter filled with charcoal briquettes (6 quarts). When top coals are partially covered with ash, pour into 2 even piles on either side of pan. Place wood chip packet on 1 pile of coals. Set cooking grate in place, cover, and open lid vent halfway. Heat grill until hot and wood chips are smoking, about 5 minutes.

408   Introducing White Barbecue Sauce

✔ WHY THIS RECIPE WORKS

For Alabama-inspired barbecued chicken, we ditched the ketchup and slathered a mayonnaise-based sauce on hickory-smoked chicken. Smoking generally takes hours, but we expedited the process by cutting the chickens in half and cooking them in the middle of the grill, sandwiched between piles of smoking coals topped with hickory chips. Splitting the chickens allowed us to get good char and smoke flavor in every bite of meat. We coated our chickens with the traditional mixture of mayonnaise seasoned with vinegar, sugar, horseradish, salt, pepper, and cayenne. The chickens were basted in this sauce two times during cooking so that the hot chicken absorbed the sauce and was flavored throughout.

Alabama Barbecued Chicken

SERVES 4 TO 6

Hickory wood chips are traditional here; however, any type of wood chips will work fine. If you'd like to use wood chunks instead of wood chips when using

3B FOR A GAS GRILL Remove cooking grate and place wood chip packet directly on primary burner. Set grate in place. Turn all burners to high, cover, and heat grill until hot and wood chips are smoking, about 15 minutes. Turn all burners to medium-low. (Adjust burners as needed to maintain grill temperature around 350 degrees.)

4 Clean and oil cooking grate. Place chicken skin side down on grill (in center if using charcoal). Cover (positioning lid vent over chicken if using charcoal) and cook chicken until well browned on bottom and thighs register 120 degrees, 35 to 45 minutes.

5 Flip chicken skin side up. Cover and continue to cook chicken until skin is golden brown and crisp and breasts register 160 degrees and thighs register 175 degrees, 15 to 20 minutes longer.

6 Transfer chicken to carving board and brush with 2 tablespoons sauce. Tent chicken with foil and let rest for 10 minutes. Brush chicken with remaining sauce, carve, and serve.

409

STEP BY STEP

Promoting Smoking Flavor

To get as much smoke flavor into the chicken as possible we recommend this arrangement.

Arrange coals on opposite sides of the grill and chicken halves in middle, away from direct heat. Alternating direction of chicken halves allows all four to fit snugly on standard grill.

410

SHOPPING IQ

Mayonnaise

Whether it's dressing potato salad, moistening a BLT, or holding crumbs in place on baked fish, mayonnaise is a kitchen staple. To find the best one, we gathered 15 top-selling jars, everything from classic mayo to olive oil– or canola-based versions to reduced-fat brands. After a preliminary tasting round, in which we sampled the mayos plain we trimmed the list to seven and tried these brands in macaroni salad. In spite of a lineup of condiments with bells and whistles, we found that the best-tasting brands had the fewest ingredients and the simplest flavors. Tasters downgraded dressed-up variations that used cider vinegar instead of more neutral distilled white vinegar, or honey instead of sugar for sweetness. They also didn't like add-ins such as dried garlic or onion, which turned plain mayonnaise into something closer to salad dressing. Our top-rated brand didn't even include lemon juice or mustard, though we use both in the test kitchen recipe for mayonnaise. Surprisingly, fat levels in the mayonnaises didn't affect the rankings; aside from the "light" version, all contained roughly the same amount. Not surprisingly, salt levels did make a difference, with tasters preferring brands with more salt rather than less.

THE BOTTOM LINE Mayonnaise is best when it's kept simple and straightforward, with a minimal ingredient list as in our winner, **Blue Plate Real Mayonnaise**. Make sure you pick a brand that has plenty of salt but no other add-ins.

WINNER

BLUE PLATE Real Mayonnaise Tasting Comments Tasters praised Blue Plate's "great balance of taste and texture," calling it "solid, straight-up mayo" and "a close second to homemade." But while it's one of the top-selling brands in the country, you'll have to mail-order it unless you live in the South or Southeast.

RUNNER-UP

HELLMANN'S Real Mayonnaise Tasting Comments Our previous favorite, Hellmann's is the top-selling mayonnaise by a wide margin and is available nationwide (it's sold as Best Foods west of the Rockies). Tasters praised it as "creamy and tangy," with a "nice eggy flavor."

411 RECIPE FOR SUCCESS
Adapting an Indian Technique for American Grills

✔ WHY THIS RECIPE WORKS

Inspired by yogurt-marinated chicken cooked in an Indian tandoor oven, this dish packs in surprising flavor in spite of its short ingredient list. As with authentic tandoori recipes, we marinated the chicken in yogurt. For the spice rub, curry powder alone tasted harsh and one-dimensional. Garam masala added complexity, but the raw taste remained. Adding the spices to the yogurt marinade solved the problem—the yogurt kept the chicken moist and tender; plus, it helped to deepen the spices once they hit the grill. To prevent the marinade from burning, we started the chicken on the cooler side of the grill and then finished it on the hotter side so it would brown. More yogurt, plus garlic and cilantro, provided a cool, creamy counterpoint to the grilled meat.

Grilled Indian-Spiced Chicken with Raita

SERVES 4

1½ cups plain whole-milk yogurt
1 tablespoon curry powder
1 tablespoon garam masala
Salt and pepper
4 (10- to 12-ounce) bone-in split chicken breasts, trimmed
2 tablespoons minced fresh cilantro
1 small garlic clove, minced

1 Whisk ¾ cup yogurt, curry powder, garam masala, 1 teaspoon salt, and ¼ teaspoon pepper together in bowl. Combine marinade and chicken in 1-gallon zipper-lock bag and toss to coat; press out as much air as possible and seal bag. Refrigerate for 1 to 6 hours, flipping bag occasionally.

2 Combine remaining ¾ cup yogurt, cilantro, and garlic in bowl and season with salt and pepper to taste. Cover and refrigerate until ready to serve. Remove chicken from bag and let excess marinade drip off but do not pat dry.

3A FOR A CHARCOAL GRILL Open bottom vent completely. Light large chimney starter filled with charcoal briquettes (6 quarts). When top coals are partially covered with ash, pour evenly over half of grill. Set cooking grate in place, cover, and open lid vent completely. Heat grill until hot, about 5 minutes.

3B FOR A GAS GRILL Turn all burners to high, cover, and heat grill until hot, about 15 minutes. Leave primary burner on high and turn other burner(s) to medium-low.

4 Clean and oil cooking grate. Place chicken on cooler side of grill, skin side down with thicker ends facing hotter side of grill. Cover and grill until chicken begins to brown and registers 155 degrees, 25 to 35 minutes.

5 Slide chicken to hotter side of grill, or turn all burners to high if using gas, and cook, turning as needed, until well browned and registers 160 degrees, 3 to 5 minutes. Transfer chicken to platter and let rest for 5 to 10 minutes. Serve with yogurt-cilantro sauce.

---

412 Whole-Milk Yogurt

SHOPPING IQ

Full fat yogurt is less acidic and can have three times as much fat as low-fat yogurt, which gives it far more flavor. Of the four national brands of whole-milk yogurt that we tasted, we found two of them too sour. Tasters preferred the two whole-milk yogurts with the most fat; one had a slightly richer flavor profile that made it the overall winner.

THE BOTTOM LINE The fat makes all the difference for our winner, **Brown Cow Cream Top Plain Yogurt**.

WINNER

BROWN COW Cream Top Plain Yogurt
Tasting Comments The favorite among tasters, this yogurt won praise for its especially "creamy," "smooth" texture and "rich," "well-rounded" flavor.

RUNNER-UP

STONYFIELD FARM Organic Whole Milk Plain Yogurt
Tasting Comments This was a close second for most tasters, and a first choice for others. Mild "lemony" flavors broke through the "rich, buttery" sample for a balanced flavor profile.

---

413 Double Duty Dishes

TEST KITCHEN TIP

Keep your food safe and clean while still saving yourself from having to wash any extra dishes by reusing the same platter to hold meat before and after cooking. Simply cover the dish with plastic wrap or foil before putting the meat on it. Remove the protective layer after all the meat is in the pan or on the grill and *voilà*—you have a clean platter ready for the cooked food.

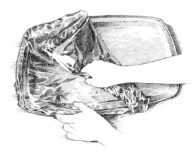

415 RECIPE FOR SUCCESS Chicken with True Thai Flavors

✓ WHY THIS RECIPE WORKS

Thai-style grilled chicken is coated in an herb and spice mixture and served with a sweet and spicy dipping sauce. The flavors are wonderfully aromatic and complex, a refreshing change from typical barbecue. We set out to develop our own version. We chose bone-in chicken breasts for our recipe. After testing numerous rub combinations, we liked the simplest version, made only with cilantro, black pepper, lime juice, and garlic, accented with the earthy flavor of coriander and fresh ginger. To flavor the meat and skin, we placed a thick layer of the rub under the skin as well as on top of it. The true Thai flavors of this dish come through in the sauce, a classic combination of sweet and spicy. Most recipes suffered from extremes, but we found balance in a blend of sugar, lime juice, distilled white vinegar, hot red pepper flakes, fish sauce, and garlic for our dipping sauce. We cooked the chicken over a half-grill fire, searing it over the hotter side first to get good browning before moving it to the cooler side to cook through.

Thai-Style Grilled Chicken with Spicy Sweet and Sour Dipping Sauce
SERVES 4

For even cooking, the chicken breasts should be of comparable size. Some of the rub is inevitably lost to the grill, but the chicken will still be flavorful.

CHICKEN AND BRINE
- ½ cup sugar
- ½ cup salt
- 4 (12-ounce) bone-in split chicken breasts, trimmed

414 STEP BY STEP Splitting Chicken Breasts

We've found store-bought split chicken breasts to be problematic. Some are so sloppily cut that the tenderloins are missing, some retain only tiny shreds of tattered skin, and some packages contain wildly divergent sizes. Consequently, we advise purchasing whole breasts and splitting them yourself.

Whether you buy them split or split your own, you should always trim off the rib section from each split breast prior to cooking. This ensures even cooking.

1 SPLIT With whole breast skin side down on cutting board, center knife on breastbone, then apply pressure to cut through and separate breast into 2 halves.

2 TRIM Using kitchen shears, trim off rib section from each breast, following vertical line of fat from tapered end of breast up to socket where wing was attached. Also trim excess fat and skin from chicken breasts prior to cooking.

DIPPING SAUCE

- ⅓ cup sugar
- ¼ cup distilled white vinegar
- ¼ cup lime juice (2 limes)
- 2 tablespoons fish sauce
- 3 small garlic cloves, minced
- 1 teaspoon red pepper flakes

RUB

- ⅔ cup chopped fresh cilantro
- 12 garlic cloves, minced
- ¼ cup lime juice (2 limes)
- 2 tablespoons grated fresh ginger
- 2 tablespoons pepper
- 2 tablespoons ground coriander
- 2 tablespoons vegetable oil

1 FOR THE CHICKEN AND BRINE Dissolve sugar and salt in 2 quarts cold water in large container. Submerge chicken in brine, cover, and refrigerate for at least 30 minutes or up to 1 hour. Remove chicken from brine and pat dry with paper towels.

2 FOR THE DIPPING SAUCE Whisk all ingredients together in bowl until sugar dissolves. Let stand for 1 hour at room temperature to allow flavors to meld.

3 FOR THE RUB Combine all ingredients in small bowl; work mixture with your fingers to thoroughly combine. Slide your fingers between chicken skin and meat to loosen skin, taking care not to detach skin. Rub about 2 tablespoons rub under skin of each breast. Thoroughly rub even layer of rub onto all exterior surfaces, including bottom and sides. Place chicken in bowl, cover with plastic wrap, and refrigerate while preparing grill.

4A FOR A CHARCOAL GRILL Open bottom vent completely. Light large chimney starter filled with charcoal briquettes (6 quarts). When top coals are partially covered with ash, pour evenly over half of grill. Set cooking grate in place, cover, and open lid vent completely. Heat grill until hot, about 5 minutes.

4B FOR A GAS GRILL Turn all burners to high, cover, and heat grill until hot, about 15 minutes. Leave primary burner on high and turn other burner(s) to low.

5 Clean and oil cooking grate. Place chicken skin side down on hotter side of grill; cook until browned, about 3 minutes (1 to 2 minutes longer for gas grill). Using tongs, flip chicken and cook until browned on second side, about 3 minutes longer. Move chicken skin side up to cooler side of grill and cover. Continue to cook until thickest part of breasts (not touching bone) register 160 degrees, 10 to 15 minutes longer. Transfer chicken to platter; let rest for 10 minutes. Serve, passing dipping sauce separately.

416 SHOPPING IQ
Fish Sauce

Fish sauce is a very potent Asian condiment made of the liquid from salted, fermented fish. It has a very concentrated flavor and, like anchovy paste, when used in appropriately small amounts it lends foods a salty complexity that is nearly impossible to replicate. We gathered six brands of fish sauce and tasted them plain and in a dipping sauce with grilled chicken. With such a limited ingredient list—most of the brands contained some combination of fish extract, water, salt, and sugar—the differences between the sauces were minimal. And because fish sauce is used in such small amounts, minute flavor differences get lost among the other flavors of a dish. Because most supermarkets don't carry a wide selection of fish sauce, we recommend buying whatever is available.

THE BOTTOM LINE Our winner, **Red Boat 40° N Fish Sauce**, is acceptable for most applications, although if you are a fan of fish sauce and use it often, you might want to make a special trip to an Asian market.

WINNER

RED BOAT 40° N Fish Sauce
Tasting Comments Thanks to its abundance of protein, which far outstripped the other products, this fish sauce tasted intensely rich and flavorful. Despite having the most sodium in the lineup, it never tasted overly salty. Our panel detected earthy, slightly "sweet" notes for a flavor that was "complex, not just fishy."

RUNNER-UP

THAI KITCHEN Premium Fish Sauce
Tasting Comments This product earned solid marks in every tasting. It was slightly more mild than our winner, and many tasters thought that it provided a "good base flavor" that allowed other more subtle ingredients in the dipping sauce and chicken to shine.

417

Smoky, Spicy Jamaican Chicken

✔ WHY THIS RECIPE WORKS

Modern-day jerk chicken recipes call for marinating the meat with an intensely flavorful liquid paste of allspice berries, fiery Scotch bonnet chiles, herbs, and spices and then smoking it over pimento wood. But most recipes are rife with pitfalls: Dense, thick spice pastes are tricky to spread evenly and tend to burn, while thinner concoctions run right off the chicken and into the fire. We wanted a marinade that struck the ideal aromatic-sweet-spicy balance, and we needed to find a replacement for the traditional pimento wood. For authentic jerk flavor we settled on a bold and complex list of ingredients: chiles, scallions, plenty of garlic and salt, plus a mixture of dried thyme, basil, and rosemary. Ground nutmeg and ginger, plus a touch of brown sugar, provided warmth and sweetness; grated lime zest and yellow mustard offered brightness; and soy sauce contributed a savory boost. Starting the chicken pieces on the cooler side of the grill gave the marinade a chance to dry out and set on the skin, which prevented the pieces from sticking to the grate. To ensure that the hotter side was still plenty hot for a good sear at the end of cooking, we placed a pile of unlit coals underneath the lit ones; this approach extended the life of the fire significantly. Smoking allspice berries, thyme, and rosemary along with the hickory chips gave our chicken authentic jerk flavor, mimicking pimento wood's fresh, sweet, herbal smoke.

Jerk Chicken

SERVES 4

For a milder dish, use one seeded chile. If you prefer your food very hot, use up to three chiles including their seeds and ribs. Scotch bonnet chiles can be used in place of the habaneros. Wear gloves when working with the chiles. If you'd like to use wood chunks instead of wood chips when using a charcoal grill, substitute one medium wood chunk, soaked in water for 1 hour, for the wood chip packet.

JERK MARINADE

- 1½ tablespoons coriander seeds
- 1 tablespoon allspice berries
- 1 tablespoon black peppercorns
- 1–3 habanero chiles, stemmed, seeded, and quartered
- 8 scallions, chopped
- 6 garlic cloves, peeled
- 3 tablespoons vegetable oil
- 2 tablespoons soy sauce
- 2 tablespoons grated lime zest (3 limes), plus lime wedges for serving
- 2 tablespoons yellow mustard
- 1 tablespoon dried thyme
- 1 tablespoon ground ginger
- 1 tablespoon packed brown sugar
- 2¼ teaspoons salt
- 2 teaspoons dried basil
- ½ teaspoon dried rosemary
- ½ teaspoon ground nutmeg

CHICKEN

- 3 pounds bone-in chicken pieces (split breasts cut in half, drumsticks, and/or thighs), trimmed
- 2 tablespoons allspice berries
- 2 tablespoons dried thyme
- 2 tablespoons dried rosemary
- 2 tablespoons water
- 1 cup wood chips (preferably hickory), soaked in water for 15 minutes and drained

1 FOR THE JERK MARINADE Grind coriander seeds, allspice berries, and peppercorns in spice grinder or mortar and pestle until coarsely ground. Transfer spices to blender jar. Add habanero(s), seeds and ribs (if using), scallions, garlic, oil, soy sauce, lime zest, mustard, thyme, ginger, sugar, salt, basil, rosemary, and nutmeg and process until smooth paste forms, 1 to 3 minutes, scraping down sides of blender jar as necessary. Transfer marinade to 1-gallon zipper-lock bag.

2 FOR THE CHICKEN Place chicken pieces in bag with marinade and toss to coat; press out as much air as possible and seal bag. Let stand at room temperature for 30 minutes while preparing grill, flipping bag after 15 minutes. (Marinated chicken can be refrigerated for up to 24 hours.)

3 Combine allspice berries, thyme, rosemary, and water in bowl and set aside to moisten for 15 minutes. Using large piece of heavy-duty aluminum foil, wrap soaked chips and moistened allspice mixture in 8 by 4½-inch foil packet. (Make sure chips do not poke holes in sides or bottom of packet.) Cut 2 evenly spaced 2-inch slits in top packet.

4A FOR A CHARCOAL GRILL Open bottom vent halfway. Arrange 1 quart unlit charcoal briquettes in single layer over half of grill. Light large chimney starter one-third filled with charcoal briquettes (2 quarts). When top coals are partially covered with ash, pour on top of unlit charcoal, keeping coals arranged over half of grill. Place wood chip packet on top of coals. Set cooking grate in place, cover, and open lid vent halfway. Heat grill until hot and wood chips are smoking, about 5 minutes.

4B FOR A GAS GRILL Remove cooking grate and place wood chip packet directly on primary burner. Set grate in place, turn all burners to high, cover, and heat grill until hot and wood chips are smoking, 15 to 25 minutes. Turn primary burner to medium and turn off other burner(s).

5 Clean and oil cooking grate. Place chicken on cooler side of grill, with marinade clinging and skin side up, as far away from fire as possible, with thighs closest to heat and breasts farthest away. Cover (positioning lid vent over chicken if using charcoal) and cook for 30 minutes.

6 Move chicken skin side down to hotter side of grill; cook until browned and skin renders, 3 to 6 minutes. Using tongs, flip chicken pieces and cook until browned on second side and breasts register 160 degrees and thighs and drumsticks register 175 degrees, 5 to 12 minutes longer.

7 Transfer chicken to serving platter, tent with foil, and let rest for 5 to 10 minutes. Serve warm or at room temperature with lime wedges.

418 Sweet and Tangy Hawaiian Rotisserie Chicken

✔ WHY THIS RECIPE WORKS

Authentic Hawaiian *huli huli* chicken is typically something home cooks buy instead of make. The birds are continually basted with a sticky-sweet glaze and "huli"-ed, which means "turned" in Hawaiian. To adapt this recipe for an achievable homemade option, we had to change both the sauce and the technique. For the teriyaki-like glaze, we developed a version with soy sauce, rice vinegar, ginger, garlic, chili sauce, ketchup, brown sugar, and lots and lots of pineapple juice. We reduced the sauce until it was thick, glossy, and sweet to get the same effect as constantly basting without having to babysit the chicken on the grill. To mimic a Hawaiian rotisserie, we spread the coals in a single layer. The direct heat rendered the fat and crisped the skin, but the chicken was far enough from the coals to avoid burning.

Huli Huli Chicken

SERVES 4 TO 6

When basting the chicken with the glaze in step 4, be careful not to drip too much of it onto the coals or flames or the grill may flare up. If you'd like to use wood chunks instead of wood chips when using a charcoal grill, substitute two medium wood chunks, soaked in water for 1 hour, for the wood chip packet.

CHICKEN

- 2 (3½- to 4-pound) whole chickens, giblets discarded
- 2 cups soy sauce
- 1 tablespoon vegetable oil
- 6 garlic cloves, minced
- 1 tablespoon grated fresh ginger

GLAZE

- 3 (6-ounce) cans pineapple juice
- ¼ cup packed light brown sugar
- ¼ cup soy sauce
- ¼ cup ketchup
- ¼ cup rice vinegar
- 2 tablespoons grated fresh ginger
- 4 garlic cloves, minced
- 2 teaspoons Asian chili-garlic sauce
- 2 cups wood chips

1 FOR THE CHICKEN With 1 chicken breast side down, use kitchen shears to cut along both sides of backbone. Discard backbone and trim any excess fat or skin at neck. Flip chicken over and, using chef's knife, cut through breastbone to separate chicken into halves. Tuck wingtips behind back. Repeat with second chicken. Combine soy sauce and 2 quarts cold water in large container. Heat oil in large saucepan over medium-high heat until shimmering. Add garlic and ginger and cook until fragrant, about 30 seconds. Stir into soy sauce mixture. Add chicken and refrigerate, covered, for at least 1 hour or up to 8 hours.

2 FOR THE GLAZE Combine pineapple juice, sugar, soy sauce, ketchup, vinegar, ginger, garlic, and chili-garlic sauce in empty saucepan and bring to boil. Reduce heat to medium and simmer until thick and syrupy (you should have about 1 cup), 20 to 25 minutes. Soak wood chips in water for 15 minutes, then drain. Using large piece of heavy-duty aluminum foil, wrap soaked chips in 8 by 4½-inch foil packet. (Make sure chips do not poke holes in sides or bottom of packet.) Cut 2 evenly spaced 2-inch slits in top of packet.

3A FOR A CHARCOAL GRILL Open bottom vent halfway. Light large chimney starter three-quarters filled with charcoal briquettes (4½ quarts). When top coals are partially covered with ash, pour evenly over grill. Place foil packet on coals. Set cooking grate in place, cover, and open lid vent open halfway. Heat grill until hot and wood chips are smoking, about 5 minutes.

3B FOR A GAS GRILL Remove cooking grate and place wood chip packet directly on primary burner. Set grate in place, turn all burners to high, cover, and heat grill until hot and wood chips are smoking, about 15 minutes. Turn all burners to medium-low. (Adjust burners as needed to maintain grill temperature around 350 degrees.)

4 Clean and oil cooking grate. Remove chicken from brine and pat dry with paper towels. Place chicken skin side up on grill (do not place chicken directly above foil packet). Cover and cook chicken until well browned on bottom and thighs register 120 degrees, 25 to 30 minutes. Flip chicken skin side down and continue to cook, covered, until skin is well browned and crisp , breasts register 160 degrees, and thighs register 175 degrees, 20 to 25 minutes longer. Transfer chicken to platter, brush with half of glaze, and let rest for 5 minutes. Serve, passing remaining glaze at table.

TO MAKE AHEAD Both brine and glaze can be made ahead and refrigerated for up to 3 days. Do not brine chicken for longer than 8 hours or it will become too salty.

TEST KITCHEN TIP

Key to Bold Flavor

Authentic huli huli chicken is grilled over kiawe wood, from a hardwood tree that is a species of mesquite. The test kitchen finds mesquite wood chips too assertive for long-cooked chicken and pork dishes; after an hour or two, the smoke turns the meat bitter. But we liked them in this comparatively quick recipe. Our Huli Huli Chicken recipe will work with any variety of wood chips, but if you care about authenticity, mesquite is the chip of choice.

420 Simple, Smoke-Infused Chicken Pieces

✓ WHY THIS RECIPE WORKS

Smoking is a gentle process in which a low fire burns slowly to keep pieces of wood smoldering, allowing chicken to cook gradually. But getting the heat just right is a challenge, and the smoke flavor can be fickle. We wanted a fire setup and specific window of smoking time that would produce tender, juicy meat with clean, full-bodied smoke flavor. We started by brining the chicken for additional moisture, which kept it from drying out. We used chicken parts rather than a whole bird so we could arrange the white meat as far from the heat as possible. Covering a small pile of unlit coals with a batch of lit coals in our grill allowed the heat from the lit briquettes to trickle down and light the cold coals—a technique that extended the life of the fire. A pan of water under the chicken on the cooler side of the grill provided humidity, which helped stabilize the temperature of the grill and prevented the delicate breast meat from drying out. Adding wood chunks just once at the beginning of cooking—and not refueling them once they had burned out—gave us fresh, clean-tasting smoke flavor.

Smoked Chicken

SERVES 6 TO 8

If using kosher chicken, do not brine in step 1. If you'd like to use wood chunks instead of wood chips when using a charcoal grill, substitute two medium wood chunks, soaked in water for 1 hour, for the wood chip packets.

      Salt
 1   cup sugar
 6   pounds bone-in chicken pieces (split breasts, drumsticks and/or thighs), trimmed
 3   tablespoons vegetable oil
      Pepper
 3   cups wood chips (1½ cups soaked in water for 15 minutes and drained, 1½ cups unsoaked)
 1   (16 by 12-inch) disposable aluminum roasting pan (if using charcoal) or 2 (9-inch) disposable aluminum pie plates (if using gas)

1 Dissolve 1 cup salt and sugar in 4 quarts cold water in large container. Submerge chicken pieces in brine, cover, and refrigerate for 30 minutes to 1 hour. Remove chicken from brine and pat dry with paper towels. Brush chicken evenly with oil and season with pepper.

2 Using large piece of heavy-duty aluminum foil, wrap soaked chips in 8 by 4½-inch foil packet. (Make sure chips do not poke holes in sides or bottom of packet.) Cut 2 evenly spaced 2-inch slits in top packet. Repeat with another sheet of foil and unsoaked wood chips.

3A FOR A CHARCOAL GRILL Open bottom vent halfway. Place disposable pan on 1 side of grill and add 2 cups water to pan. Arrange 2 quarts unlit charcoal banked against other side of grill. Light large chimney starter half filled with charcoal briquettes (3 quarts). When top coals are partially covered with ash, pour on top of unlit charcoal, to cover one-third of grill with coals steeply banked against side of grill. Place wood chip packets on top of coals. Set cooking grate in place, cover, and open lid vent halfway. Heat grill until hot and wood chips begin to smoke, about 5 minutes.

3B FOR A GAS GRILL Remove cooking grate and place wood chip packets directly on primary burner. Place disposable pie plate on other burner(s) and add 2 cups water to plate. Set cooking grate in place, turn all burners to high, cover, and heat grill until hot and wood chips begin to smoke, about 15 minutes. Turn primary burner to medium-high and turn off other burner(s). (Adjust primary burner as needed to maintain grill temperature around 325 degrees.)

4 Clean and oil cooking grate. Place chicken on cooler side of grill, skin side up, as far away from heat as possible with thighs closest to heat and breasts farthest away. Cover (positioning lid vent over chicken if using charcoal) and cook until breasts register 160 degrees and thighs and drumsticks register 175 degrees, 1¼ to 1½ hours.

5 Transfer chicken to serving platter, tent with foil, and let rest for 5 to 10 minutes. Serve.

421 FOOD SCIENCE Achieving Smoky, Not Sooty, Chicken

To infuse our chicken pieces with full-bodied smoke flavor, we figured it was necessary to keep the wood chunks smoldering for the entire time that the meat was on the grill. But when the finished product tasted not just smoky, but also harsh and ashy, we wondered: Was there a limit to the amount of smoke that the chicken could take?

To find out, we smoked two batches of chicken. For the first, we added two soaked wood chunks to the fire at the beginning of cooking; when those had burned out about 45 minutes later, we added two more soaked chunks to keep the smoldering going for the duration of cooking. For the second batch, we didn't replenish the wood after the initial chunks had burned out.

What were the results? The chicken exposed to smoke the entire time tasted bitter and sooty, while the pieces that were exposed to smoke for only 45 minutes or so (about half of the overall cooking time) had just enough smoky depth.

A consultation with our science editor explains why. Smoke contains both water- and fat-soluble compounds. As the chicken cooks, water evaporates and fat drips away, eventually halting meat's capacity to continue absorbing smoke flavor. Once that happens, any additional smoke flavor that's not absorbed by the meat gets deposited on the exterior of the chicken, where the heat of the grill breaks it down into harsher—flavored compounds.

422 RECIPE FOR SUCCESS Whole Chicken with Serious Smoke Flavor

✓ WHY THIS RECIPE WORKS

Many people avoid grilling whole chickens because the exterior of the bird chars before the interior cooks through. For well-seasoned meat that wouldn't dry out, we brined the chicken and then coated it with an aromatic spice rub. We arranged the coals on either side of the grill with a disposable aluminum roasting pan in the middle and cooked the chicken over the roasting pan where it wouldn't burn, but would receive ample heat from both piles of coals. The chicken only had to be turned once, halfway through cooking, to get perfect, evenly roasted meat. For maximum smoky flavor, we used wood chips. It's easy to add sauce to this recipe as it roasts—see our variation below for more information.

Grill-Roasted Chicken

SERVES 3 TO 4

If using kosher chicken, do not brine in step 1. If you'd like to use wood chunks instead of wood chips when using a charcoal grill, substitute two medium wood chunks, soaked in water for 1 hour, for the wood chip packets.

- ½ **cup salt**
- 1 **(3½- to 4-pound) whole chicken, giblets discarded**
- 3 **tablespoons spice rub (recipes follow)**
- 2 **cups wood chips**
- 1 **(16 by 12-inch) disposable aluminum roasting pan (if using charcoal)**

1 Dissolve salt in 2 quarts cold water in large container. Submerge chicken in brine, cover, and refrigerate for 1 hour. Remove chicken from brine and pat dry with paper towels. Tuck wingtips behind back. Rub chicken evenly, inside and out, with spice rub, lifting up skin over breast and rubbing spice rub directly onto meat.

2 Soak wood chips in water for 15 minutes, then drain. Using large piece of heavy-duty aluminum foil, wrap 1 cup soaked chips in 8 by 4½-inch foil packet. (Make sure chips do not poke holes in sides or bottom of packet.) Repeat with remaining 1 cup chips. Cut 2 evenly spaced 2-inch slits in top of each packet.

3A FOR A CHARCOAL GRILL Open bottom vent halfway and place disposable pan in center of grill. Light large chimney starter filled with charcoal briquettes (6 quarts). When top coals are partially covered with ash, pour into 2 even piles on either side of disposable pan. Place 1 wood chip packet on each pile of coals. Set cooking grate in place, cover, and open lid vent halfway. Heat grill until hot and wood chips are smoking, about 5 minutes.

3B FOR A GAS GRILL Remove cooking grate and place wood chip packets directly on primary burner. Set cooking grate in place, turn all burners to high, cover, and heat grill until hot and wood chips are smoking, about 15 minutes. Turn all burners to medium. (Adjust burners as needed to maintain grill temperature around 325 degrees.)

4 Clean and oil cooking grate. Place chicken on center of grill (over disposable) pan if using charcoal), breast side down, cover (position lid vent over meat if using charcoal), and cook for 30 minutes.

5 Working quickly, remove lid and, using 2 large wads of paper towels, turn chicken breast side up. Cover and continue to cook until breast registers 160 degrees and thighs register 175 degrees, 25 to 35 minutes longer. Transfer chicken to carving board, tent with foil, and let rest for 15 minutes before carving and serving.

423 Fragrant Dry Spice Rub

MAKES ABOUT ½ CUP

Store leftover spice rub at room temperature for up to 3 months.

- 2 **tablespoons ground cumin**
- 2 **tablespoons curry powder**
- 2 **tablespoons chili powder**
- 1 **tablespoon ground allspice**
- 1 **tablespoon pepper**
- 1 **teaspoon ground cinnamon**

Combine all ingredients in bowl.

424 Citrus-Cilantro Wet Spice Rub

MAKES ABOUT 3 TABLESPOONS

For more heat, add up to ½ teaspoon cayenne pepper.

- 1   tablespoon minced fresh cilantro
- 1   tablespoon orange juice
- 1½ teaspoons lime juice
- 1½ teaspoons extra-virgin olive oil
- 1   small garlic clove, minced
- ½   teaspoon ground cumin
- ½   teaspoon chili powder
- ½   teaspoon paprika
- ½   teaspoon ground coriander

Combine all ingredients in bowl. Use immediately.

VARIATION

425 Grill-Roasted Chicken with Tangy Barbecue Sauce

If you like, barbecue sauce can be used along with the spice rub. Wait until the bird is almost done to brush on the barbecue sauce, so that it does not scorch. See our Sweet and Tangy Barbecue Sauce (page 313) or use your favorite.

After rotating chicken breast side up in step 5, cook until thighs register 160 degrees, about 15 minutes. Working quickly, remove lid and brush outside and inside of chicken with ½ cup barbecue sauce. Cover and continue to cook until breast registers 160 degrees and thighs register 175 degrees, 10 to 15 minutes longer. Serve, passing additional barbecue sauce separately.

Turning Up the Heat on Butterflied Chicken

✔ WHY THIS RECIPE WORKS

Butterflying a chicken is a win-win when it comes to grilling. It allows the chicken to cook through more quickly and evenly and also exposes more skin to the grill so it can brown and become ultracrisp. But crisp skin and tender meat are only half the battle—the chicken has to be flavorful, too. To that end, we set out to infuse our bird with bold heat and garlicky flavor. Adding two heads of garlic to a brine was our first move. Next, we created a potent garlic-pepper oil and rubbed some under the skin of the chicken before grilling. For one last punch of flavor, we reserved some of the garlicky oil to serve with the chicken.

Grilled Butterflied Chicken Diavola

SERVES 3 TO 4

If using a kosher chicken, do not brine in step 1. This dish is very spicy; for milder heat, reduce the amount of red pepper flakes.

- 1 (3- to 4-pound) whole chicken, giblets discarded
- 2 garlic heads, plus 4 cloves minced
- 3 bay leaves
  Salt and pepper
- ¼ cup extra-virgin olive oil
- 2 teaspoons red pepper flakes
- 1 (13 by 9-inch) disposable aluminum roasting pan (if using charcoal)
  Lemon wedges

1 Place chicken breast side down on cutting board. Using kitchen shears, cut through bones on either side of backbone. Discard backbone and trim any excess fat or skin at neck. Flip chicken over and use heel of your hand to flatten breastbone. Cover chicken with plastic wrap and pound breasts with meat pounder to even thickness.

2 Combine 2 garlic heads, bay leaves, and ½ cup salt in zipper-lock bag, crush gently with meat pounder, and transfer to large container. Stir in 2 quarts cold water to dissolve salt. Submerge chicken in brine, cover, and refrigerate for 2 hours.

3 Cook oil, minced garlic, pepper flakes, and 2 teaspoons pepper in small saucepan over medium heat until fragrant, about 3 minutes. Let oil cool, then measure out 2 tablespoons and set aside.

4 Remove chicken from brine and pat dry with paper towels. Gently loosen skin covering breast and thighs and rub remaining garlic-pepper oil underneath skin. Tuck wingtips behind back.

5A FOR A CHARCOAL GRILL Open bottom vent completely and place disposable pan in center of grill. Light large chimney starter filled with charcoal briquettes (6 quarts). When top coals are partially covered with ash, pour into 2 even piles on either side of disposable pan. Set cooking grate in place, cover, and open lid vent completely. Heat grill until hot, about 5 minutes.

5B FOR A GAS GRILL Turn all burners to high, cover, and heat grill until hot, about 15 minutes. Turn all burners to medium-low. (Adjust burners as needed to maintain grill temperature around 350 degrees.)

6 Clean and oil cooking grate. Place chicken, skin side down, in center of grill (over disposable pan if using charcoal). Cover and cook until skin is crisp, breast registers 160 degrees, and thighs register 175 degrees, 30 to 45 minutes.

7 Transfer chicken to carving board and let rest for 5 to 10 minutes. Carve chicken and serve with reserved garlic oil and lemon wedges.

427 STEP BY STEP
Butterflying Chicken

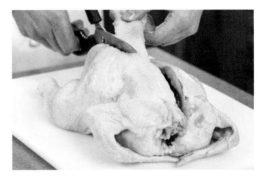

1 REMOVE BACKBONE Cut through bones on either side of backbone and trim any excess fat or skin at neck.

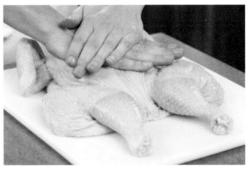

2 FLATTEN Flip chicken over and use heel of your hand to flatten breastbone.

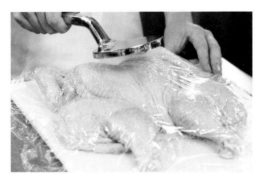

3 POUND BREAST Cover chicken with plastic wrap. Using meat pounder or rubber mallet, pound breast to same thickness as leg and thigh meat.

428 RECIPE FOR SUCCESS
A Bold and Lemony Butterflied Bird

✓ WHY THIS RECIPE WORKS

Butterflying a chicken not only helps the bird cook faster and more evenly on the grill, it also makes it easier to rub seasonings directly under the skin to flavor the meat and it creates especially crisp skin. To infuse a butterflied bird with classic lemon flavor, we tried slipping various combinations of seasonings under the skin and eventually ended up with a simple mixture of lemon zest, salt, and pepper. To infuse even more lemon flavor, we made a vinaigrette with fresh lemon juice and olive oil and poured it over the cooked chicken. To keep the vinaigrette from tasting too sour, we quickly caramelized the lemon halves over the grill. This gave us a bright, smoky juice that infused the vinaigrette and the chicken with lemon flavor. We used a grill-roasting technique to cook the chicken, placing the legs nearest the coals and keeping the white meat further away from the heat. The relatively gentle cooking gave us a moister bird. A final sear directly over the dying coals at the end of cooking crisped and browned the skin nicely—without the risk of flare-ups.

Grilled Butterflied Lemon Chicken
SERVES 6 TO 8

2   (4-pound) whole chickens, giblets
    discarded
5   lemons
    Salt and pepper
1   (13 by 9-inch) disposable aluminum pan
    (if using charcoal)
1   garlic clove, minced
2   tablespoons minced fresh parsley
2   teaspoons Dijon mustard
1   teaspoon sugar
⅔   cup extra-virgin olive oil

1 Set wire rack in rimmed baking sheet. With 1 chicken breast side down, use kitchen shears to cut along both sides of backbone. Discard backbone and trim any excess fat or skin at neck. Flip chicken over and use heel of your hand to flatten breastbone. Cover chicken with plastic wrap and pound breast with meat pounder to even thickness. Repeat with second chicken.

2 Grate 2 teaspoons zest from 1 lemon (halve and reserve lemon) and mix with 2 teaspoons salt and 1 teaspoon pepper in bowl. Pat chickens dry with paper towels and, using your fingers or handle of wooden spoon, gently loosen skin covering breasts and thighs. Rub zest mixture under skin, then season exterior of chicken with salt and pepper. Tuck wingtips behind back and transfer chickens to prepared rack. Refrigerate, uncovered, for at least 1 hour or up to 24 hours.

3A FOR A CHARCOAL GRILL Open bottom vent completely and place disposable pan on 1 side of grill. Light large chimney starter filled with charcoal briquettes (6 quarts). When top coals are partially covered with ash, pour evenly over other side of grill. Scatter 20 unlit coals on top of lit coals. Set cooking grate in place, cover, and open lid vent completely. Heat grill until hot, about 5 minutes.

3B FOR A GAS GRILL Turn all burners to high, cover, and heat grill until hot, about 15 minutes. Leave primary burner on high and turn other burner(s) to low. (Adjust primary burner as needed to maintain grill temperature between 350 and 375 degrees.)

4 Clean and oil cooking grate. Halve remaining 4 lemons and place, along with reserved lemon halves, cut side down on hotter side of grill. Place chickens skin side down on cooler side of grill, with legs pointing toward fire; cover, placing lid vent over chickens on charcoal grill.

5 Grill lemons until deep brown and caramelized, 5 to 8 minutes; transfer to bowl. Continue to grill chickens, covered, until breasts register 160 degrees and thighs register 175 degrees, 40 to 50 minutes longer.

Slide chickens to hotter side of grill and cook, uncovered, until skin is well browned, 2 to 4 minutes. Transfer chickens to carving board skin side up, tent with aluminum foil, and let rest for 15 minutes.

6 Meanwhile, squeeze ⅓ cup juice from grilled lemons into bowl. (Cut any unsqueezed lemons into wedges for serving.) Using flat side of knife, mash garlic and ½ teaspoon salt into paste and add to bowl with lemon juice. Whisk in parsley, mustard, sugar, and ½ teaspoon pepper. Slowly whisk in oil until emulsified.

7 Carve chickens, transfer to serving platter, and pour ⅓ cup vinaigrette over chicken. Serve, passing remaining vinaigrette and grilled lemon wedges separately.

429 TEST KITCHEN TIP
Zesting Citrus

To quickly and easily make finely grated zest, rub fruit against holes of rasp-style grater, grating over same area of fruit only once or twice to avoid grating bitter white pith beneath skin.

430 Summery Grilled Chicken with a Wine Pairing

✔ WHY THIS RECIPE WORKS

Wine is a natural fit with chicken. The bold acidity and fruity, complex flavors of both red and white wines pair beautifully with mild chicken meat. We wanted to develop a recipe for winey, herby grilled chicken that could be enjoyed in warmer months. First off, we used a dry white wine, which imparted a more distinct flavor to the meat. Whizzing our marinade in a blender broke down the herbs for optimal flavor and distribution and poking holes in the chicken with a skewer helped the flavors of the marinade penetrate the bird. Butterflying increased the meat's exposure to heat, allowing it to cook more quickly and evenly. We started the chicken over the cooler part of the grill with the skin side down until the meat was almost done before flipping it and finishing directly above the fire, which ensured evenly cooked meat with a crisp skin. We also included a thin basting sauce, or mop, to add complexity and freshness to the grilled meat by reserving a small amount of marinade to brush on the chicken near the end of cooking.

Grilled Wine-and-Herb Marinated Chicken

SERVES 4

Use a dry white wine, such as Sauvignon Blanc, for this recipe. An inexpensive wine will work just fine, but pick one that's good enough to drink on its own.

- 2 cups dry white wine
- 3 tablespoons lemon juice
- 3 tablespoons extra-virgin olive oil
- 2 tablespoons chopped fresh parsley
- 2 tablespoons chopped fresh thyme
- 2 tablespoons packed light brown sugar
- 4 garlic cloves, minced
- 1 teaspoon pepper
- 2 tablespoons salt
- 1 (4-pound) whole chicken, giblets discarded

1 Process wine, lemon juice, oil, parsley, thyme, sugar, garlic, and pepper in blender until emulsified, about 40 seconds. Measure out ¼ cup marinade and set aside. Add salt to remaining marinade in blender and process to dissolve, about 20 seconds.

2 With chicken breast side down, use kitchen shears to cut along both sides of backbone. Discard backbone and trim any excess fat or skin at neck. Flip chicken over and use heel of your hand to flatten breastbone. Tuck wingtips behind back.

3 Poke holes all over chicken with skewer. Place chicken in 1-gallon zipper-lock bag, pour in salted marinade, seal bag, and turn to coat. Set bag in baking dish, breast side down, and refrigerate for 2 to 3 hours.

4A FOR A CHARCOAL GRILL Open bottom vent completely. Light large chimney starter filled with charcoal briquettes (6 quarts). When top coals are partially covered with ash, pour evenly over half of grill. Set cooking grate in place, cover, and open lid vent completely. Heat grill until hot, about 5 minutes.

4B FOR A GAS GRILL Turn all burners to high, cover, and heat grill until hot, about 15 minutes. Turn primary burner to medium and other burner(s) to low. (Adjust primary burner as needed to maintain grill temperature between 350 and 375 degrees.)

5 Remove chicken from marinade and pat dry with paper towels. Discard used marinade. Clean and oil cooking grate. Place chicken skin side down on cooler side of grill, with legs closest to hotter side of grill. Cover and cook until chicken is well browned and thighs register 160 degrees, 50 minutes to 1 hour 5 minutes. Brush chicken with half of reserved marinade. Flip chicken skin-side up, move it to hotter side of grill, and brush with remaining reserved marinade. Cook, covered, until breasts register 160 degrees and thighs register 175 degrees, 10 to 15 minutes longer.

6 Transfer chicken to carving board, tent with aluminum foil, and let rest for 15 minutes. Carve and serve.

431

SHOPPING IQ

Nothing to Whine About

When a recipe calls for "dry white wine," it's tempting to grab whatever open bottle is in the fridge, regardless of grape varietal. Are we doing our dishes a disservice? Sure, Chardonnay and Pinot Grigio may taste different straight from the glass, but how much do those distinctive flavor profiles really come through once the wines get cooked down with other ingredients?

To find out, we tried four different varietals and a supermarket "cooking wine" in five recipes: braised fennel, risotto, a basic pan sauce, a beurre blanc, and chicken chasseur. In our tests, only Sauvignon Blanc consistently boiled down to a "clean" yet sufficiently acidic flavor—one that played nicely with the rest of the ingredients. Differences between the wines were most dramatic in gently flavored dishes, such as the risotto and beurre blanc. In contrast, all five wines produced similar (and fine) results when used in chicken chasseur, no doubt because of all the other strong flavors in this dish.

But what's a cook without leftover Sauvignon Blanc to do? Is there a more convenient option than opening a fresh bottle? To find out, we ran the same cooking tests with sherry and dry vermouth, wines fortified with alcohol to increase their shelf life. Sherry was too distinct and didn't fare well in these tests, but vermouth was surprisingly good.

THE BOTTOM LINE Sauvignon Blanc is a safe bet when cooking, but if you're out, dry vermouth works too.

432

RECIPE FOR SUCCESS

Sweet, Smoky Glazed Chicken

✓ WHY THIS RECIPE WORKS

We wanted a recipe for smoky grill-roasted chicken finished with a sweet, sticky glaze that avoided common pitfalls: unevenly cooked meat and potential flare-ups. To get direct heat on the chicken without burning it, we used a V-rack to elevate the birds above the flame. We pricked the chicken skin all over with a skewer to allow the fat an escape route. To evenly brown and render the skin before glazing, we grilled the chickens on each side, rotating the V-rack 180 degrees halfway through. To ensure the glaze had a viscous texture that adhered when brushed on the skin, we precooked the glaze, which thickened the mixture and concentrated its flavor. Glazing the chickens too soon slowed their cooking to a crawl. We found it best to wait until the chickens had reached an internal temperature of 155 degrees before beginning to glaze them. For a substantial coating, we brushed the chickens with the glaze and turned the birds at least three times during their final minutes on the grill.

Glazed Grill-Roasted Chicken
SERVES 6 TO 8
To prevent flare-ups, be sure that your grill is clean.

- 2 (3½- to 4-pound) whole chickens, giblets discarded
- 1 tablespoon sugar
- 1 tablespoon salt
- 1 teaspoon pepper
- 1 recipe glaze (recipes follow)

1 Spray V-rack with vegetable oil spray. Pat chickens dry with paper towels and prick skin all over with skewer or paring knife. Combine sugar, salt, and pepper in small bowl, then rub seasoning mixture all over chickens. Tuck wings behind back and tie legs together with kitchen twine. Arrange chickens, breast side up, head to tail on prepared V-rack.

2A FOR A CHARCOAL GRILL Open bottom vent completely. Light large chimney starter filled with charcoal briquettes (6 quarts). When top coals are partially covered with ash, pour evenly over grill. Set cooking grate in place, cover, and open lid vent completely. Heat grill until hot, about 5 minutes.

2B FOR A GAS GRILL Turn all burners to high, cover, and heat grill until hot, about 15 minutes. Turn all burners to low. (Adjust primary burner as needed to maintain grill temperature around 325 degrees.)

3 Arrange V-rack on cooking grate and grill, covered, until back of each chicken is well browned, about 30 minutes, carefully rotating V-rack 180 degrees after 15 minutes. Flip chickens and repeat until breasts are well browned and thighs register 155 degrees, 30 to 40 minutes longer. Brush chickens with glaze and continue grilling with lid on, flipping and glazing chicken every 5 minutes, until lightly charred in spots and breasts register 160 degrees and thighs register 175 degrees, 15 to 25 minutes.

4 Transfer chickens to carving board, tent with aluminum foil, and let rest for 10 minutes. Carve and drizzle chicken with remaining glaze. Serve.

433 Honey-Mustard Glaze

MAKES ABOUT ½ CUP

Simmer ⅓ cup honey, ¼ cup Dijon mustard, and ¼ teaspoon salt in small saucepan over medium heat until thickened, 3 to 5 minutes. (Glaze can be refrigerated for up to 3 days. Gently warm glaze in small saucepan or microwave before using.)

434 Brown Sugar–Balsamic Glaze

MAKES ABOUT ½ CUP

Simmer ⅓ cup packed dark brown sugar, ¼ cup balsamic vinegar, and ¼ teaspoon salt in small saucepan over medium heat until thickened, 3 to 5 minutes. (Glaze can be refrigerated for up to 3 days. Gently warm glaze in small saucepan or microwave before using.)

435 Spicy Molasses Glaze

MAKES ABOUT ½ CUP

Simmer ⅓ cup molasses, ¼ cup cider vinegar, ½ teaspoon red pepper flakes, and ¼ teaspoon salt in small saucepan over medium heat until thickened, 3 to 5 minutes. (Glaze can be refrigerated for up to 3 days. Gently warm glaze in small saucepan or microwave before using.)

436 STEP BY STEP
Perfectly Glazed Grill-Roasted Chicken

1 ARRANGE ON V-RACK Place chickens breast side up and head-to-tail on V-rack. Make sure they are well balanced on rack.

2 GRILL AND ROTATE To evenly brown and render skin before glazing, grill chickens about 30 minutes per side, rotating V-rack 180 degrees after 15 minutes. When flipping chickens, be sure to rotate them as well to promote even browning.

3 GLAZE AND ROTATE Once chickens have reached 155 degrees in thickest part of thigh, begin glazing, flipping, and rotating every 5 minutes until they are cooked through.

438

RECIPE FOR SUCCESS

Fresh Mexican Fish Tacos

✔ WHY THIS RECIPE WORKS

For traditional Mexican grilled fish tacos, a whole fish is split in half lengthwise, bathed in a chile-citrus marinade, and grilled. The flavor-packed fish is eaten with tortillas and some simple sides. We wanted grilled fish tacos featuring a similarly bold flavor profile, but a simpler approach—no dealing with whole, skin-on fish. Although traditional recipes use whole snapper or grouper, swordfish was easier to find and stood up to flipping on the grill. Swordfish steaks that were 1 inch thick spent enough time on the grill to pick up plenty of flavorful char before the interior cooked through. Cutting the fish into 1-inch-wide strips meant that the fish could go from grill to taco with minimal additional prep. We created a flavorful paste from ancho and chipotle chile powders, oregano, and ground coriander, which we

437

TEST KITCHEN TIP

Don't Flake Out

When grilling fish, avoid flaky varieties like grouper, hake, or cod, which will stick to the grill and fall apart when you try to flip them.

Shredded Snapper
For fillets that stay intact, choose a denser variety like swordfish, mahi-mahi, tuna, or halibut.

bloomed in oil to bring out their flavors. Tomato paste provided a savory-sweet punch. To replicate the flavor of traditional sour oranges, we used a combination of lime and orange juices. A fresh pineapple salsa was the perfect accompaniment to our spicy, earthy fish.

Grilled Fish Tacos
SERVES 6

Grouper, mahi mahi, and snapper fillets are all suitable substitutes for the swordfish. To ensure best results, buy 1-inch-thick fillets. The recipe for the pineapple salsa makes more than is needed for the tacos; leftovers can be refrigerated for up to two days.

- 3   tablespoons vegetable oil
- 1   tablespoon ancho chile powder
- 2   teaspoons chipotle chile powder
- 2   garlic cloves, minced
- 1   teaspoon dried oregano
- 1   teaspoon ground coriander
      Salt
- 2   tablespoons tomato paste
- ½   cup orange juice
- 6   tablespoons lime juice (3 limes)
- 2   pounds skinless swordfish steaks, 1 inch thick, cut lengthwise into 1-inch-wide strips
- 1   pineapple, peeled, quartered lengthwise, cored, and each quarter halved lengthwise
- 1   jalapeño chile
- 18   (6-inch) corn tortillas
- 1   red bell pepper, stemmed, seeded, and cut into ¼-inch pieces
- 2   tablespoons minced fresh cilantro, plus extra for serving
- ½   head iceberg lettuce (4½ ounces), cored and sliced thin
- 1   avocado, halved, pitted, and sliced thin
      Lime wedges

1 Heat 2 tablespoons oil, ancho chile powder, and chipotle chile powder in 8-inch skillet over medium heat, stirring constantly, until fragrant and some bubbles form, 2 to 3 minutes. Add garlic, oregano, coriander, and 1 teaspoon salt and continue to cook until fragrant, about 30 seconds longer. Add tomato paste and, using spatula, mash tomato paste with spice mixture until combined, about 20 seconds. Stir in orange juice and 2 tablespoons lime juice. Cook, stirring constantly, until thoroughly mixed and reduced slightly, about 2 minutes. Transfer chile mixture to large bowl and let cool for 15 minutes.

2 Add swordfish to bowl with chile mixture and stir gently with rubber spatula to coat fish. Cover and refrigerate for at least 30 minutes or up to 2 hours.

3A FOR A CHARCOAL GRILL Open bottom vent completely. Light large chimney starter mounded with charcoal briquettes (7 quarts). When top coals are partially covered with ash, pour evenly over grill. Set cooking grate in place, cover, and open lid vent completely. Heat grill until hot, about 5 minutes.

3B FOR A GAS GRILL Turn all burners to high, cover, and heat grill until hot, about 15 minutes. Turn all burners to medium-high.

4 Clean cooking grate, then repeatedly brush grate with well-oiled paper towels until grate is black and glossy, 5 to 10 times. Brush both sides of pineapple with remaining 1 tablespoon oil. Place swordfish on half of grill. Place pineapple and jalapeño on other half. Cover and cook until swordfish, pineapple, and jalapeño have begun to brown, 3 to 5 minutes. Using thin spatula, flip swordfish, pineapple, and jalapeño over. Cover and continue to cook until second sides of pineapple and jalapeño are browned and swordfish registers 140 degrees, 3 to 5 minutes. Transfer swordfish to large platter, flake into pieces, and tent with aluminum foil. Transfer pineapple and jalapeño to cutting board.

5 Clean cooking grate. Working in batches, grill tortillas, turning as needed, until warm and soft, about 1 to 1½ minutes; wrap tightly in aluminum foil to keep soft.

6 When cool enough to handle, chop pineapple and jalapeño fine. Transfer to medium bowl and stir in bell pepper, cilantro, and remaining ¼ cup lime juice. Season with salt to taste. Top tortillas with flaked fish, salsa, lettuce, and avocado. Serve with lime wedges and extra cilantro.

439 STEP BY STEP Grilled Fish Tacos That Taste Light But Not Lean

For grilled fish that's infused with flavor, it wasn't enough to simply create nice char marks. We also boosted flavor with a bold spice paste and a grilled-fruit salsa.

1 MAKE PASTE
A thick spice paste, brightened by lime and orange juices, adds complexity to the fish.

2 CHILL FISH
Refrigerating the paste-covered fish for at least 30 minutes allows the salt in the paste to penetrate and season the fish.

3 GRILL FISH, FRUIT, AND JALAPEÑO
The grill deepens the flavor of the pineapple and chile destined for the salsa.

4 WARM TORTILLAS
Grill the tortillas for about 30 seconds per side and then wrap them in a dish towel or foil to keep them warm.

5 FINISH SALSA
Finely chop the pineapple and jalapeño and then combine them with red bell pepper, cilantro, and lime juice.

440 Spiced and Charred Mexican Shrimp Tacos

✓ WHY THIS RECIPE WORKS

We wanted a fresh-tasting, easy-to-make taco featuring grilled Mexican-spiced shrimp. But delicate shrimp can turn from tender to rubbery in the blink of an eye, especially over the high heat of the grill. Although their shells can shield them from the heat, any seasonings are then stripped off along with the shells when it's time to eat. We decided to go with peeled shrimp, and coated them with an ultraflavorful spice rub. We crammed several extra-large shrimp together on each skewer, which protected them from overcooking. For a lively slaw to accompany our spicy shrimp, we started by thinly slicing delicately flavored, crunchy jícama and tossed it with tangy orange juice, bold red onion, and bright cilantro leaves.

Grilled Shrimp Tacos with Jícama Slaw

SERVES 6

You will need four 12-inch metal skewers for this recipe. To cut the jícama, use the shredding disk of a food processor, a V-slicer, or a sharp chef's knife. Serve with chopped onion, diced avocado, and thinly sliced radishes.

- 1 **pound jícama, peeled and cut into 3-inch-long matchsticks**
- ¼ **cup thinly sliced red onion**
- 3 **tablespoons chopped fresh cilantro**
- 1 **teaspoon grated orange zest plus ⅓ cup juice**
  Salt
- 3 **tablespoons vegetable oil**
- 1 **tablespoon minced fresh oregano or 1 teaspoon dried**
- 2 **teaspoons chipotle chile powder**
- 1 **teaspoon garlic powder**
- 2 **pounds extra-large shrimp (21 to 25 per pound), peeled, deveined, and tails removed**
- 18 **(6-inch) corn tortillas**
- 1 **cup Mexican crema (recipes follow)**
  Lime wedges

1 Combine jícama, onion, cilantro, orange zest and juice, and ½ teaspoon salt in bowl, cover, and refrigerate until ready to serve.

2 Whisk oil, oregano, chile powder, garlic powder, and ½ teaspoon salt together in large bowl. Pat shrimp dry with paper towels, add to spice mixture, and toss to coat. Thread shrimp tightly onto four 12-inch metal skewers, alternating direction of heads and tails.

3A FOR A CHARCOAL GRILL Open bottom vent completely. Light large chimney starter mounded with charcoal briquettes (7 quarts). When top coals are partially covered with ash, pour evenly over grill. Set cooking grate in place, cover, and open lid vent completely. Heat grill until hot, about 5 minutes.

3B FOR A GAS GRILL Turn all burners to high, cover, and heat grill until hot, about 15 minutes. Leave all burners on high.

4 Clean and oil cooking grate. Place shrimp on grill and cook (covered if using gas) until lightly charred on first side, about 4 minutes. Flip shrimp, pushing them together on skewer if they separate, and cook until opaque throughout, about 2 minutes. Transfer to platter and cover with aluminum foil.

5 Working in batches, grill tortillas, turning as needed, until warm and soft, about 1 to 1½ minutes; wrap tightly in aluminum foil to keep soft.

6 Slide shrimp off skewers onto cutting board and cut into ½-inch pieces. Serve with tortillas, jícama slaw, crema, and lime wedges.

441 Overnight Mexican Crema
MAKES ABOUT 1 CUP

Thick, slightly tangy Mexican *crema* is a popular way to impart a touch of richness to many dishes. Drizzled atop creamy soups it adds a bright finishing touch, and dishes like tacos just don't seem complete without it. Avoid ultrapasteurized cream, which has been heated to higher temperatures, killing enzymes and bacteria and even altering the cream's protein structure, making it hard to achieve the right texture.

- 1 **cup cream**
- 2 **tablespoons buttermilk**
- ⅛ **teaspoon salt**
- 2 **teaspoons lime juice**

Stir together cream and buttermilk in container. Cover and place in warm location (75 to 80 degrees is ideal; lower temperatures will lengthen fermentation time) until mixture is thickened but still pourable, 12 to 24 hours. Dissolve salt in lime juice and add to mixture. (Sauce can be refrigerated for up to 2 months.)

442 Quick Mexican Crema
MAKES ABOUT 1¼ CUPS

- ½ **cup mayonnaise**
- ½ **cup sour cream**
- 2 **tablespoons lime juice**
- 2 **tablespoons milk**

Whisk all ingredients together in bowl. (Sauce can be refrigerated for up to 2 days.)

443
STEP BY STEP
Skewering Shrimp for the Grill

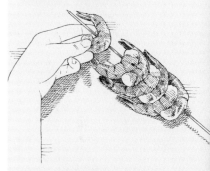

Thread shrimp onto 4 skewers, alternating direction of heads and tails. Packing the shrimp onto the skewers in this manner helps prevent overcooking.

444

RECICE FOR SUCCESS

Spicy Grilled Shrimp Skewers

✓ WHY THIS RECIPE WORKS

Jolts of grill flavor and spicy heat can enhance the delicately sweet and briny flavor of shrimp, but it's easy to overdo it. Most recipes overcook the shrimp and finish them in a bath of mouth-numbing sauce; we wanted juicy shrimp with a smoky crust and chile flavor that was more than just superficial. To achieve this, we sprinkled one side of the shrimp with sugar to promote browning and grilled this side for a few minutes. Then we flipped the skewers to finish gently cooking on the cooler side of the grill. We created a flavorful marinade with pureed jalapeños, garlic, cumin, and cayenne to give our shrimp skewers a spicy, assertive kick, and then set some aside to double as a sauce. Butterflying the shrimp before marinating and grilling them opened up more shrimp flesh for the marinade and finishing sauce to flavor. We also packed the shrimp very tightly onto the skewers so they would cook more slowly.

Grilled Jalapeño and Lime Shrimp Skewers

SERVES 4

You will need four 14-inch metal skewers for this recipe.

MARINADE

- 1–2 jalapeño chiles, stemmed, seeded, and chopped
- 3 tablespoons olive oil
- 6 garlic cloves, minced
- 1 teaspoon grated lime zest plus 5 tablespoons juice (3 limes)
- ½ teaspoon ground cumin
- ¼ teaspoon cayenne pepper
- ½ teaspoon salt

SHRIMP

- 1½ pounds extra-large shrimp (21 to 25 per pound), peeled and deveined
- ½ teaspoon sugar
- 1 tablespoon minced fresh cilantro

1 FOR THE MARINADE Process all ingredients in food processor until smooth, about 15 seconds. Reserve 2 tablespoons marinade; transfer remaining marinade to medium bowl.

2 FOR THE SHRIMP Pat shrimp dry with paper towels. To butterfly shrimp, use paring knife to make shallow cut down outside curve of shrimp. Add shrimp to bowl with marinade and toss to coat. Cover and refrigerate for at least 30 minutes or up to 1 hour.

3A FOR A CHARCOAL GRILL Open bottom vent completely. Light large chimney starter filled with charcoal briquettes (6 quarts). When top coals are partially covered with ash, pour evenly over half of grill. Set cooking grate in place, cover, and open lid vent completely. Heat grill until hot, about 5 minutes.

3B FOR A GAS GRILL Turn all burners to high, cover, and heat grill until hot, about 15 minutes. Leave all burners on high.

4 Clean and oil cooking grate. Thread marinated shrimp onto four 14-inch metal skewers. (Alternate direction of each shrimp as you pack them tightly on skewer to allow about a dozen shrimp to fit snugly on each skewer.) Sprinkle 1 side of skewered shrimp with sugar. Place shrimp skewers sugared side down on hotter side of grill (covered if using gas) and cook until lightly charred, 3 to 4 minutes. Flip skewers and move to cooler side of grill (if using charcoal) or turn all burners off (if using gas) and cook, covered, until other side of shrimp is no longer translucent, 1 to 2 minutes. Using tongs, slide shrimp into clean medium bowl and toss with reserved marinade. Sprinkle with cilantro and serve.

VARIATIONS

445 **Grilled Red Chile and Ginger Shrimp Skewers**

Substitute 1 to 3 seeded and chopped small red chiles (or jalapeños), 1 minced scallion, 3 tablespoons rice vinegar, 2 tablespoons soy sauce, 1 tablespoon toasted sesame oil, 1 tablespoon grated fresh ginger, 2 teaspoons sugar, and 1 minced garlic clove for the marinade. Prepare and grill shrimp as directed. Substitute 1 thinly sliced scallion for cilantro and serve with lime wedges.

446 **Grilled Caribbean Shrimp Skewers**

Substitute with 1 to 2 seeded and chopped habanero or serrano chiles, ¼ cup pineapple juice, 2 tablespoons olive oil, 1 tablespoon white wine vinegar, 3 minced garlic cloves, 1 teaspoon grated fresh ginger, 1 teaspoon packed brown sugar, 1 teaspoon dried thyme, ½ teaspoon salt, and ¼ teaspoon ground allspice for marinade. Prepare and grill shrimp as directed. Substitute 1 tablespoon minced fresh parsley for cilantro.

447 SHOPPING IQ
Shrimp Basics

BUYING SHRIMP

Virtually all of the shrimp sold in supermarkets today have been previously frozen, either in large blocks of ice or by a method called "individually quick-frozen," or IQF for short. Supermarkets simply defrost the shrimp before displaying them on ice at the fish counter. We highly recommend purchasing bags of still-frozen shrimp and defrosting them as needed at home, since there is no telling how long "fresh" shrimp may have been kept on ice at the market. IQF shrimp have a better flavor and texture than shrimp frozen in blocks, and they are more convenient because it's easy to defrost just the amount you need. Shrimp are sold both with and without their shells, but we find shell-on shrimp to be firmer and sweeter. Also, shrimp should be the only ingredient listed on the bag; some packagers add preservatives, but we find treated shrimp to have an unpleasant, rubbery texture.

SORTING OUT SHRIMP SIZES

Shrimp are sold both by size (small, medium, etc.) and by the number needed to make 1 pound, usually given in a range. Choosing shrimp by the numerical rating is more accurate, because the size label varies from store to store. Here's how the two sizing systems generally compare:

Small	51 to 60 per pound
Medium	41 to 50 per pound
Medium-Large	31 to 40 per pound
Large	26 to 30 per pound
Extra-Large	21 to 25 per pound
Jumbo	16 to 20 per pound

DEFROSTING SHRIMP

You can thaw frozen shrimp overnight in the refrigerator in a covered bowl. For a quicker thaw, place them in a colander under cold running water; they will be ready in a few minutes. Thoroughly dry the shrimp before cooking.

448

Prepping Scallops

Use your fingers to peel away the small crescent-shaped muscle that is sometimes attached to scallops, as this tendon becomes incredibly tough when cooked.

449

Upgrading a Classic Appetizer for Dinnertime

✓ WHY THIS RECIPE WORKS

Smoky, salty bacon beautifully accents sweet, succulent scallops, and we thought taking it to the grill would make a great thing even better. We set out to make this classic appetizer into a grilled entrée. We knew we needed to parcook the bacon to prevent the grease from dripping into the fire and incinerating our scallops. Microwaving proved a perfect solution: We layered strips of bacon between paper towels (to absorb grease) and weighed them down with a plate to prevent curling. We wrapped each strip of bacon around two scallops for an ideal scallop-to-bacon ratio. Tossing the scallops in melted butter added richness, and pressing the scallops firmly together on the skewers prevented them from spinning when flipped. A two-level fire cooked both scallops and bacon to perfection. A spritz of juice from grilled lemons and a sprinkling of chopped chives gave the dish a bright finish.

Grilled Bacon-Wrapped Scallops
SERVES 4

Use regular bacon, as thick-cut bacon will take too long to crisp on the grill. When wrapping the scallops, the bacon slice should fit around both scallops, overlapping just enough to be skewered through both ends. We recommend buying "dry" scallops, which don't have chemical additives and taste better than "wet." Dry scallops will look ivory or pinkish; wet scallops are bright white. This recipe was developed with large sea scallops (sold 10 to 20 per pound). You will need four 12-inch metal skewers for this recipe.

12	slices bacon
24	large sea scallops, tendons removed
3	tablespoons unsalted butter, melted
½	teaspoon salt
⅛	teaspoon pepper
2	lemons, halved
¼	cup chopped fresh chives

1 Place 4 layers paper towels on large plate and arrange 6 slices bacon over towels in single layer. Top with 4 more paper towels and remaining 6 slices bacon. Cover with 2 layers of paper towels; place second large plate on top and press gently to flatten. Microwave until fat begins to render but bacon is still pliable, about 4 minutes. Toss scallops, melted butter, salt, and pepper together in bowl until scallops are thoroughly coated with butter.

2 Press 2 scallops together, side to side, and wrap with 1 slice bacon, trimming excess as necessary. Thread onto metal skewer through bacon. Repeat with remaining scallops and bacon, threading 3 bundles onto each of 4 skewers.

3A FOR A CHARCOAL GRILL Open bottom vent completely. Light large chimney starter filled with charcoal briquettes (6 quarts). When top coals are partially covered with ash, pour two-thirds evenly over half of grill, then pour remaining coals over other half of grill. Set cooking grate in place, cover, and open lid vent completely. Heat grill until hot, about 5 minutes.

3B FOR A GAS GRILL Turn all burners to high, cover, and heat grill until hot, about 15 minutes. Leave primary burner on high and turn other burner(s) to medium.

4 Clean and oil cooking grate. Place skewers, bacon side down, and lemon halves, cut side down, on cooler side of grill. Cook (covered, if using gas) until bacon is crispy on first side, about 4 minutes. Flip skewers onto other bacon side and cook until crispy, about 4 minutes longer. Flip skewers scallop side down and move to hotter side of grill. Grill until sides of scallops are firm and centers are opaque, about 4 minutes on 1 side only. Transfer skewers to platter, squeeze lemons over top, and sprinkle with chives. Serve.

450 Color Coding Scallops

The part of the scallop that's sold at the fish counter is the large adductor muscle that opens and closes its shell. This muscle takes its color from the reproductive gland that lies next to it inside the shell. In male scallops, the gland is grayish white and hence the muscle remains white. Female scallops turn pink only when they're spawning; during this period, their glands fill with orange roe and turn bright coral, giving the adductor muscle a rosy hue.

To see if there were any differences besides color, we pan-seared and tasted white male scallops alongside peachy female scallops. They cooked in the same amount of time and had identical textures, although tasters did note that the pink scallops—which retained their tint even after cooking—had a somewhat sweeter, richer flavor. Both colors, however, are absolutely normal and do not indicate anything about the freshness, doneness, or edibility of a scallop.

Female   **Male**

451

Well-Dressed Tuna Steaks

☑ WHY THIS RECIPE WORKS

Perfectly grilled tuna steaks should combine a hot, smoky, charred exterior with a cool, rare center. For a home cook, this ideal can be an elusive goal. For grilled tuna steaks with an intense smoky char and a tender interior, we started with a hot grill. We moistened the tuna steaks' flesh with a vinaigrette to promote browning and allow the oil to penetrate the meat of the tuna steaks. And instead of using sugar in our vinaigrette, we used honey. Both promote browning, but honey does it faster, which was important with the quick cooking times for tuna on the grill. It's easy to add complementary flavors to this dish by mixing up the seasoning in the vinaigrette; see our variations for one with North African flavors and another with an Asian profile.

Grilled Tuna Steaks with Vinaigrette
SERVES 6

We prefer our tuna served rare or medium-rare. If you like your tuna cooked medium, observe the timing for medium-rare, then tent the steaks with foil for 5 minutes before serving.

3	tablespoons plus 1 teaspoon red wine vinegar
2	tablespoons chopped fresh thyme or rosemary
2	tablespoons Dijon mustard
2	teaspoons honey
	Salt and pepper
¾	cup olive oil
6	(8-ounce) tuna steaks, 1 inch thick

1A FOR A CHARCOAL GRILL Open bottom vent completely. Light large chimney starter filled with charcoal briquettes (6 quarts). When top coals are partially covered with ash, pour evenly over half of grill. Set cooking grate in place, cover, and open lid vent completely. Heat grill until hot, about 5 minutes.

1B FOR A GAS GRILL Turn all burners to high, cover, and heat grill until hot, about 15 minutes.

2 Meanwhile, whisk vinegar, thyme, mustard, honey, ½ teaspoon salt, and pinch pepper together in large bowl. Whisking constantly, slowly drizzle oil into vinegar mixture until lightly thickened and emulsified. Measure out ¾ cup vinaigrette and set aside for cooking tuna. Reserve remaining vinaigrette for serving.

3 Clean cooking grate, then repeatedly brush grate with well-oiled paper towels until grate is black and glossy, 5 to 10 times.

4 Pat tuna dry with paper towels. Generously brush both sides of tuna with vinaigrette and season with salt and pepper. Place tuna on grill (on hotter side if using charcoal) and cook (covered if using gas) until grill marks form and bottom surface is opaque, 1 to 3 minutes.

5 Flip tuna and cook until opaque at perimeter and translucent red at center when checked with tip of paring knife and registers 110 degrees (for rare), about 1½ minutes, or until opaque at perimeter and reddish pink at center when checked with tip of paring knife and registers 125 degrees (for medium-rare), about 3 minutes. Serve, passing reserved vinaigrette.

VARIATIONS

452 Grilled Tuna Steaks with Chermoula Vinaigrette

Substitute 2 tablespoons minced fresh parsley for thyme and add ¼ cup minced fresh cilantro, 4 minced garlic cloves, 1 teaspoon paprika, 1 teaspoon ground cumin, and ½ teaspoon ground coriander to vinaigrette.

453 Grilled Tuna Steaks with Soy-Ginger Vinaigrette

Substitute rice vinegar for red wine vinegar and 2 thinly sliced scallions for thyme. Omit salt and add 3 tablespoons soy sauce, 1 tablespoon toasted sesame oil, 2 teaspoons grated fresh ginger, and ½ teaspoon red pepper flakes to vinaigrette.

454 SHOPPING IQ
Red Wine Vinegar

Red wine vinegar has a sharp but clean flavor, making it the most versatile choice in salad dressings. While acidity is the obvious key factor in vinegar, it is actually the inherent sweetness of the grapes used to make the vinegar that makes its flavor appealing to the palate.

After tasters sampled 10 red wine vinegars plain, in vinaigrette, and in pickled onions, it was clear that they found highly acidic vinegars too harsh; brands with moderate amounts of acidity scored higher. Tasters also preferred those brands that were blends—either blends of different grapes or blends of different vinegars—as they offered more complex flavor.

THE BOTTOM LINE Tasters ranked French import **Laurent du Clos Red Wine Vinegar** first. Made from a mix of red and white grapes, this vinegar won the day with its "good red wine flavor."

WINNER

LAURENT DU CLOS Red Wine Vinegar

Tasting Comments "Good red wine flavor" won the day for this French import. Tasters liked the "nicely rich," "well-balanced," and "fruity" flavor that came through in the pickled onions, and they praised the "clean, light, pleasant taste" and "subtle zing" it added to the vinaigrette.

WINNER

POMPEIAN GOURMET Red Wine Vinegar

Tasting Comments Tasters were enthusiastic about this "very mild, sweet, pleasant" red wine vinegar with "tang" that was in "harmonious balance." It was "not harsh at all," but had a "bright, potent taste" with "really pleasing red wine flavor."

Grilled Salmon Steak Woes Solved

✓ WHY THIS RECIPE WORKS

Hearty salmon steaks are a common choice for grilling, but in spite of their thick cut they often end up with a burnt exterior and a dry, flavorless interior. Plus, no matter how much seasoning goes on the outside, it never seems to permeate the whole steak. To make the process foolproof, we first turned the oblong steaks into sturdy medallions. By carefully removing a bit of skin from one tail of the steak, tightly wrapping the skin of the other tail around the skinned portion, and then tying the whole thing with kitchen twine, we made neat steaks that cooked evenly and could be easily moved around the grill. We used a two-level cooking approach, beginning with an initial sear over the hotter part of the grill. While the steaks seared, we made a simple bright lemon and caper sauce directly in a disposable aluminum pan over the cooler side of the grill. When the steaks were browned, we transferred them to the pan, coated them with the sauce, and finished cooking them over the lower heat directly in the sauce, which ensured they remained moist and tender.

Grilled Salmon Steaks with Lemon-Caper Sauce

SERVES 4

Before eating, lift out the small circular bone from the center of each steak.

LEMON-CAPER SAUCE

- 3   tablespoons unsalted butter, cut into 3 pieces
- 1   teaspoon grated lemon zest plus 6 tablespoons juice (2 lemons)
- 1   shallot, minced
- 1   tablespoon capers, rinsed
- ⅛   teaspoon salt
- 1   (13 by 9-inch) disposable aluminum roasting pan

SALMON

- 4 (10-ounce) skin-on salmon steaks, 1 to 1½ inches thick
  Salt and pepper
- 2 tablespoons vegetable oil
- 2 tablespoons minced fresh parsley

1 FOR THE SAUCE Combine butter, lemon zest and juice, shallot, capers, and salt in disposable pan.

2 FOR THE SALMON Pat salmon dry with paper towels. Working with 1 steak at a time, carefully trim 1½ inches of skin from 1 tail. Tightly wrap other tail around skinned portion and tie steak with kitchen twine. Season salmon with salt and pepper and brush both sides with oil.

3A FOR A CHARCOAL GRILL Open bottom vent completely. Light large chimney starter filled with charcoal briquettes (6 quarts). When top coals are partially covered with ash, pour evenly over half of grill. Set cooking grate in place, cover, and open lid vent completely. Heat grill until hot, about 5 minutes.

3B FOR A GAS GRILL Turn all burners to high, cover, and heat grill until hot, about 15 minutes. Leave primary burner on high and turn off other burner(s).

4 Clean cooking grate, then repeatedly brush grate with well-oiled paper towels until black and glossy, 5 to 10 times. Place salmon on hotter side of grill. Cook, turning once, until browned on both sides, 4 to 6 minutes. Meanwhile, set disposable pan with butter mixture on cooler side of grill and cook until butter has melted, about 2 minutes.

5 Transfer salmon to disposable pan and gently turn to coat with butter mixture. Cook (covered if using gas) until center of salmon is still translucent when checked with tip of paring knife and registers 125 degrees (for medium-rare), 6 to 14 minutes, flipping salmon and rotating pan halfway through grilling. Remove twine and transfer salmon to platter. Off heat, whisk parsley into sauce. Drizzle sauce over steaks. Serve.

VARIATIONS

456 **Grilled Salmon Steaks with Orange-Ginger Sauce**

Replace lemon zest and juice with orange zest and orange juice. Omit shallot and capers; add 1 tablespoon grated fresh ginger and 1 tablespoon soy sauce to mixture in step 1. Substitute 1 thinly sliced scallion for parsley in step 3.

457 **Grilled Salmon Steaks with Lime-Cilantro Sauce**

Replace lemon zest and juice with lime zest and juice. Omit shallot and capers; add 2 minced garlic cloves and ½ teaspoon ground cumin to mixture in step 1. Substitute cilantro for parsley in step 3.

458 STEP BY STEP
Prepping Salmon

1 TRIM For salmon steaks that are sturdy enough to grill easily, remove 1½ inches of skin from 1 tail of each steak.

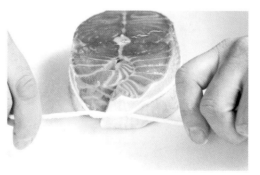

2 WRAP AND TIE Next, tuck skinned portion into center of steak, wrap other tail around it, and tie with kitchen twine.

459 Good for More Than Just Bagels

✓ WHY THIS RECIPE WORKS

We wanted to capture the intense, smoky flavor of smoked fish, but we also wanted to skip the specialized equipment and make this dish less of a project recipe. To prepare the salmon for smoking, we quick-cured the fish with a mixture of salt and sugar, which firmed it up and seasoned it inside and out. We then cooked the fish indirectly over a gentle fire with ample smoke. We also cut our large fillet into individual portions to make serving simple. This small step delivered big results: First, it ensured more thorough smoke exposure (without increasing the time) by creating more surface area. Second, the smaller pieces of delicate salmon were far easier to get off the grill intact than one large fillet.

Grill-Smoked Salmon

SERVES 6

If you'd like to use wood chunks instead of wood chips when using a charcoal grill, substitute two medium wood chunks, soaked in water for 1 hour, for the wood chip packet. Serve the salmon with "Smoked Salmon Platter" Sauce (recipe follows), if desired.

- 2 **tablespoons sugar**
- 1 **tablespoon kosher salt**
- 6 **(6- to 8-ounce) center-cut skin-on salmon fillets**
- 2 **cups wood chips**

1 Combine sugar and salt in bowl. Set salmon, skin side down, on wire rack set in rimmed baking sheet and sprinkle flesh side evenly with sugar mixture. Refrigerate, uncovered, for 1 hour. Just before grilling, soak 1 cup wood chips in water for 15 minutes, then drain. Combine soaked and unsoaked chips. Using large piece of heavy-duty aluminum foil, wrap chips in 8 by 4½-inch foil packet. (Make sure chips do not poke holes in sides or bottom of packet.) Cut 2 evenly spaced 2-inch slits in top of packet.

2 Brush any excess salt and sugar from salmon using paper towels and blot salmon dry. Return fish to wire rack and refrigerate, uncovered, until ready to cook. Fold piece of heavy-duty foil into 18 by 6-inch rectangle.

3A FOR A CHARCOAL GRILL Open bottom vent halfway. Light large chimney starter one-third filled with charcoal briquettes (2 quarts). When top coals are partially covered with ash, pour into steeply banked pile against side of grill. Place wood chip packet on coals. Set cooking grate in place, cover, and open lid vent halfway. Heat grill until hot and wood chips are smoking, about 5 minutes.

3B FOR A GAS GRILL Remove cooking grate and place wood chip packet directly on primary burner. Set cooking grate in place and turn primary burner to high (leave other burner(s) off). Cover and heat grill until hot and wood chips begin to smoke, 15 to 25 minutes. Turn primary burner to medium. (Adjust primary burner as needed to maintain grill temperature between 275 and 300 degrees.)

4 Place foil rectangle on cooler side of grill and place salmon fillets on foil, spaced at least ½ inch apart. Cover (position lid vent over fish if using charcoal) and cook until center of salmon is still translucent when checked with tip of paring knife and registers 125 degrees (for medium-rare), 30 to 40 minutes. Transfer to platter. Serve warm or at room temperature.

460 "Smoked Salmon Platter" Sauce

MAKES 1½ CUPS

- 1 **large egg yolk, plus 1 large hard-cooked egg, chopped fine**
- 2 **teaspoons Dijon mustard**
- 2 **teaspoons sherry vinegar**
- ½ **cup vegetable oil**
- 2 **tablespoons capers, rinsed, plus 1 teaspoon caper brine**
- 2 **tablespoons minced shallot**
- 2 **tablespoons minced fresh dill**

Whisk egg yolk, mustard, and vinegar together in medium bowl. Whisking constantly, slowly drizzle in oil until emulsified, about 1 minute. Gently fold in hard-cooked egg, capers and brine, shallot, and dill.

461

GRILL HACK

Advanced Charcoal Prep

Hoisting a huge bag of charcoal to pour some into a chimney starter can be messy and difficult, especially if you're dressed nicely for a summertime dinner party. To get around this sloppy situation, try this tip.

1 REPACK When you first bring home the sack, divide the briquettes into smaller paper bags. Different recipes call for different amounts of charcoal, so you may want to have some bags with 2 quarts (25 briquettes) and some with 4 quarts (50 briquettes).

2 UNPACK When you need to build a fire, just cut a hole in the bottom of the small bag, and the charcoal flows right into the chimney.

462

STEP BY STEP
Preparing Pineapple for Salsa

1 TRIM AND QUARTER Trim ends of pineapple so that it will sit flat on work surface. Cut pineapple through ends into quarters.

2 REMOVE SKIN Place each quarter, cut side up, on work surface, and slide knife between skin and flesh to remove skin.

3 REMOVE CORE AND SLICE Stand each quarter on end and slice off tough, light-colored core attached to inside of each piece. Discard core. Peeled and cored pineapple can be diced or sliced, as desired.

463

RECIPE FOR SUCCESS
Blackened Fish Without the Burn

✔ WHY THIS RECIPE WORKS

Blackened fish is usually prepared in a cast-iron skillet, but it can lead to one smoky kitchen. We were done with the smoke—and were ready for our fillets to have a dark brown, crusty, sweet-smoky, toasted spice exterior, providing a rich contrast to the moist, mild-flavored fish inside. We thought we'd solve our problems by throwing the fish on the grill. Unfortunately, this move created a host of other issues, including that the fish stuck to the grate, the outside of the fish was way overdone by the time the flesh had cooked through, and the skin-on fillets curled midway through cooking. The curling problem was easy to fix: We simply needed to score the skin. To prevent sticking, we made sure the grill was hot when we put the fish on and oiled the grate multiple times to ensure a clean surface. Finally, to give the fish its flavorful blackened-but-not-burned coating, we bloomed our spice mixture in melted butter, allowed it to cool, and then applied the coating to the fish. Once on the grill, the spice crust acquired the proper depth and richness while the fish cooked through.

Grilled Blackened Red Snapper
SERVES 4

Serve the snapper with Pineapple and Cucumber Salsa with Mint or Rémoulade (recipes follow).

- 2 **tablespoons paprika**
- 2 **teaspoons onion powder**
- 2 **teaspoons garlic powder**
- ¾ **teaspoon ground coriander**
- ¾ **teaspoon salt**
- ¼ **teaspoon pepper**
- ¼ **teaspoon cayenne pepper**
- ¼ **teaspoon white pepper**
- 3 **tablespoons unsalted butter**
- 4 **(6- to 8-ounce) skin-on red snapper fillets, ¾ inch thick**

1 Combine paprika, onion powder, garlic powder, coriander, salt, pepper, cayenne, and white pepper in bowl. Melt butter in 10-inch skillet over medium heat. Stir in spice mixture and cook, stirring often, until fragrant and spices turn dark rust color, 2 to 3 minutes. Transfer mixture to pie plate and let cool to room temperature. Use fork to break up any large clumps.

2 Pat snapper dry with paper towels. Using sharp knife, make shallow diagonal slashes every inch along skin side of fish, being careful not to cut into flesh. Using your fingers, rub spice mixture evenly over top, bottom, and sides of fish (you should use all of spice mixture).

3A FOR A CHARCOAL GRILL Open bottom vent completely. Light large chimney starter two-thirds filled with charcoal briquettes (4 quarts). When top coals are partially covered with ash, pour evenly over half of grill. Set cooking grate in place, cover, and open lid vent completely. Heat grill until hot, about 5 minutes.

3B FOR A GAS GRILL Turn all burners to high, cover, and heat grill until hot, about 15 minutes. Leave all burners on high.

4 Clean cooking grate, then repeatedly brush grate with well-oiled paper towels until black and glossy, 5 to 10 times.

5 Place snapper skin side down on grill (on hotter side if using charcoal) with fillets perpendicular to grate. Cook until skin is very dark brown and crisp, 3 to 5 minutes. Carefully flip snapper and continue to cook until dark brown and beginning to flake when prodded with paring knife and registers 140 degrees, about 5 minutes longer. Serve.

464 Pineapple and Cucumber Salsa with Mint

MAKES ABOUT 3 CUPS

To make this dish spicier, reserve and add the chile seeds.

- ½ large pineapple, peeled, cored, and cut into ¼-inch pieces
- ½ cucumber, peeled, halved lengthwise, seeded, and cut into ¼-inch pieces
- 1 small shallot, minced
- 1 serrano chile, stemmed, seeded, and minced
- 2 tablespoons chopped fresh mint
- 1 tablespoon lime juice, plus extra as needed
- ½ teaspoon grated fresh ginger
  Salt
  Sugar

Combine pineapple, cucumber, shallot, chile, mint, lime juice, ginger, and ½ teaspoon salt in bowl and let sit at room temperature for 15 to 30 minutes. Season with extra lime juice, salt, and sugar to taste before serving.

465 Rémoulade

MAKES ABOUT ½ CUP

- ½ cup mayonnaise
- 1½ teaspoons sweet pickle relish
- 1 teaspoon hot sauce
- 1 teaspoon lemon juice
- 1 teaspoon minced fresh parsley
- ½ teaspoon capers, rinsed
- ½ teaspoon Dijon mustard
- 1 small garlic clove, minced
  Salt and pepper

Pulse all ingredients in food processor until well combined but not smooth, about 10 pulses. Season with salt and pepper to taste and serve. (Sauce can be refrigerated for up to 3 days.)

466 STEP BY STEP Secrets to Grilling Fish

1 CHILL Keep fish fillets refrigerated until you're ready to grill. (At room temperature, they become floppy and are harder to maneuver on the grill.)

2 GRILL SKIN SIDE DOWN Place fish perpendicular to bars of cooking grate, skin side down. (This makes it easier to slide a spatula underneath when it's time to flip.)

3 FLIP To neatly flip fish, slide 1 spatula underneath fillet to lift, and use second spatula to support it.

467 RECIPE FOR SUCCESS Quick-and-Easy Shrimp and Corn

✓ WHY THIS RECIPE WORKS

Shrimp are often grilled in their shells to protect their delicate flesh, but this means you have to remove the shells before eating—a task that can be messy. For easier access to our grilled shrimp, we peeled them first and then crowded the shrimp onto skewers to prevent them from overcooking. A very hot fire ensured that they were cooked to perfection in just minutes. We took advantage of the rest of the space on the grate to grill corn, and since we seemed to be on our way to a seaside supper, we combined butter and Old Bay seasoning for a flavor-packed sauce. To complete our Chesapeake-inspired meal, we microwaved tender red potatoes and then tossed everything in our buttery sauce.

Maryland-Style Grilled Shrimp and Corn

SERVES 4

We prefer to use extra-large shrimp (21 to 25 per pound) for this recipe; if your shrimp are smaller or larger, they will have slightly different cooking times. You will need four 12-inch metal skewers for this recipe.

1	pound small red potatoes, unpeeled
4	ears corn, husks and silk removed and halved crosswise
8	tablespoons unsalted butter
1	tablespoon Old Bay seasoning
1½	pounds extra-large shrimp (21 to 25 per pound), peeled and deveined
2	tablespoons minced fresh parsley

1 Halve potatoes, combine with 1 tablespoon water in bowl, cover, and microwave until potatoes are tender, 5 to 7 minutes; keep warm. Cook butter and Old Bay together in medium saucepan over medium heat until butter melts, about 2 minutes.

2 Pat shrimp dry with paper towels and toss with 1 tablespoon butter mixture. Thread shrimp tightly onto four 12-inch metal skewers, alternating direction of heads and tails.

3A FOR A CHARCOAL GRILL Open bottom vent completely. Light large chimney starter mounded with charcoal briquettes (7 quarts). When top coals are partially covered with ash, pour evenly over grill. Set cooking grate in place, cover, and open lid vent completely. Heat grill until hot, about 5 minutes.

3B FOR A GAS GRILL Turn all burners to high, cover, and heat grill until hot, about 15 minutes. Leave all burners on high.

4 Clean and oil cooking grate. Place shrimp skewers and corn on grill. Cook (covered if using gas), turning as needed, until lightly charred and cooked through, about 6 minutes for shrimp and 8 minutes for corn; transfer to platter and tent with aluminum foil.

5 Toss shrimp, corn, and potatoes with remaining melted butter; arrange on platter. Sprinkle parsley over top and serve.

468 SHOPPING IQ Old Bay Seasoning

Old Bay seasoning is a spice mix that's essential for many shrimp and crab dishes. Created in the 1940s, this spice mix is a regional favorite along the coast of Maryland and Virginia. The predominant flavors in Old Bay are celery, mustard, and paprika. At your local supermarket, you can find it in the spice aisle or near the seafood department; many fish markets carry it as well.

470
RECIPE FOR SUCCESS
Simple Shellfish on the Grill

✔ WHY THIS RECIPE WORKS

Clams, mussels, and oysters belong to the group of shellfish known as bivalves, and they can all be grilled in the same fashion. These two-shelled creatures are easy to cook; when they open, they are done. One of the biggest challenges when cooking bivalves is making sure they are clean. Even perfectly cooked clams and mussels can be made inedible by lingering sand. Over the course of developing our recipe, we learned that careful shopping plays the most important role in minimizing your kitchen work and ensuring that your shellfish are free of grit. While steaming is the easiest way to cook clams and mussels (oysters are often eaten raw on the half shell), grilling these bivalves is an appealing option, especially for summer entertaining. It's also an incredibly simple preparation. The key to great bivalves on the grill is not to move the shellfish around too much, and to handle them carefully once

they open. You want to preserve the natural juices, so when they open, transfer them with tongs to a platter, holding them steady so as not to spill any of the liquid. Add an easy sauce or flavored butter to complement the natural brininess of the shellfish.

Grilled Clams, Mussels, or Oysters
SERVES 4 TO 6 AS AN APPETIZER

Hard-neck clams (that is, littlenecks or cherrystones) are worth the extra money because they remain tightly closed when harvested, keeping the meat inside free of sand. We recommend purchasing rope-cultured mussels for the same reason. In general, we prefer oysters from cold northern waters, because they tend to be briny and have a flavor that's more crisp than that of oysters from warmer southern waters. And always look for tightly closed clams, mussels, and oysters (avoid any that are gaping; they may be dying or dead). The clams may take slightly longer to cook on a gas grill than they do on a charcoal grill. If you like, serve the clams with lemon wedges, hot sauce, and some tomato salsa.

24   hard-shell clams, scrubbed

1A FOR A CHARCOAL GRILL Open bottom vent completely. Light large chimney starter filled with charcoal briquettes (6 quarts). When top coals are partially covered with ash, pour evenly over grill. Set cooking grate in place, cover, and open lid vent completely. Heat grill until hot, about 5 minutes.

1B FOR A GAS GRILL Turn all burners to high, cover, and heat grill until hot, about 15 minutes. Leave all burners on high.

2 Clean and oil cooking grate. Place clams on grill and cook (covered if using gas), without turning, until clams open, 6 to 10 minutes.

3 Using tongs, carefully transfer clams to platter, trying to preserve juices. If desired, discard top shells and loosen meat in bottom shells before serving.

VARIATIONS
471   Grilled Mussels
Substitute 2 pounds scrubbed and debearded mussels for clams. Grill as directed in step 2, decreasing cooking time to 3 to 5 minutes.

469
TEST KITCHEN TIP
Serving Clams, Mussels, And Oysters

The easiest way to serve grilled clams, mussels, or oysters is to divide them among small plates and give each person a small fork. However, if you want guests to eat them while milling about the grill, try the following method.

Holding each clam, mussel, or oyster in a kitchen towel as it comes off the grill, pull off and discard the top shell, then slide a paring knife under the meat to detach it from the bottom shell. By the time you have done this to each clam, mussel, or oyster, the shells should have cooled enough to permit everyone to pick them up and slurp the meat directly from the shells.

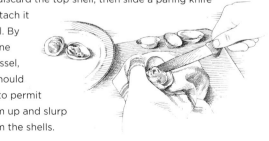

472 Grilled Oysters

Substitute 24 oysters for clams. Grill as directed in step 2, decreasing cooking time to 3 to 5 minutes.

473 Grilled Clams, Mussels, or Oysters with Spicy Lemon Butter

Prepare the butter while the grill heats up. Have your guests remove the meat of the shellfish with small forks and dip it into this tangy, spicy butter.

Melt 4 tablespoons unsalted butter in small saucepan over medium-low heat. Off heat, add 1 tablespoon hot sauce, 1 teaspoon lemon juice, and ¼ teaspoon salt; cover to keep warm. Grill clams, mussels, or oysters as directed. Discard top shells. Pour warm butter mixture into serving bowl; serve shellfish with lemon wedges and warm butter for dipping.

474 Grilled Clams, Mussels, or Oysters with Tangy Soy-Citrus Sauce

Prepare the sauce while the grill heats up.

Combine ½ cup low-sodium soy sauce, 1 tablespoon lemon juice, 1 tablespoon lime juice, 1 thinly sliced scallion, and 1 teaspoon grated fresh ginger in small bowl. Grill clams, mussels, or oysters as directed. Discard top shells. Drizzle sauce over shellfish and serve immediately.

475 Grilled Clams, Mussels, or Oysters with Mignonette Sauce

Prepare the sauce while the grill heats up. Have your guests remove the meat of the shellfish with small forks and dip it into this tangy, potent sauce.

Combine ½ cup red wine vinegar, 2 finely chopped shallots or ¼ cup minced red onion, 2 tablespoons lemon juice, and 1½ tablespoons minced fresh parsley in small bowl. Grill clams, mussels, or oysters as directed. Discard top shells. Pour warm butter mixture into serving bowl; serve shellfish with sauce for dipping.

476 Debearding Mussels

TEST KITCHEN TIP

Mussels often contain a weedy beard protruding from between the two shells. It's fairly small and can be difficult to tug out. The easiest way to remove it is to trap the beard between the side of a small paring knife and your thumb and pull. The flat surface of the knife gives you some leverage to extract the pesky beard.

477

Perfect Pizza From the Grill

✓ WHY THIS RECIPE WORKS

Grilled pizza is not baked pizza—leave all preconceptions behind. When grilling a pizza, the demands placed on both the pizza and the cook are far different, and far more challenging. To begin with, the dough for our grilled pizza recipe was a challenge: It had to be slack enough to be stretched, yet strong enough not to rip. We strengthened the dough by using high-protein bread flour and increased elasticity by adding plenty of water and olive oil to prevent the crust from sticking to the grill. We also discovered that we needed drier and more potent toppings than usual for our grilled pizza recipe. We salted and drained the tomatoes to keep the crust crisp, and we mixed full-bodied, soft fontina cheese with a little Parmesan for a potently flavored cheese blend that didn't ooze. If you prefer, you can also eat just the crust plain as a flatbread, merely slicked with our Spicy Garlic Oil, or dressed with any number of simple toppings. Flatbread can serve as a quick appetizer or a light accompaniment to a meal—once it's been cooked, the coals should still be hot enough to grill meat or fish.

Grilled Tomato and Cheese Pizzas
MAKES FOUR 9-INCH PIZZAS

The pizzas cook very quickly on the grill, so before you begin grilling them, have all the equipment and ingredients you need at hand. Equipment includes a pizza peel (or a rimless baking sheet), a pair of tongs, a paring knife, a large cutting board, and a pastry brush; ingredients include all the toppings and a small bowl of flour for dusting. Timing and coordination are crucial; if you are unsure of your skill level, try cooking the first two pizzas one at a time, then work up to cooking the final two in tandem. The pizzas are best served hot off the grill but can be kept warm for 20 to 30 minutes on a wire rack in a 200-degree oven.

DOUGH

- 1 cup water, room temperature
- 2 tablespoons extra-virgin olive oil
- 2 cups (11 ounces) bread flour plus extra as needed
- 1 tablespoon whole-wheat flour (optional)
- 2 teaspoons sugar
- 1¼ teaspoons salt
- 1 teaspoon instant or rapid-rise yeast

TOPPING

1½ **pounds plum tomatoes, cored, seeded, and cut into ½-inch pieces**

¾ **teaspoon salt**

6 **ounces fontina cheese, shredded (1½ cups)**

1½ **ounces Parmesan cheese, grated fine (¾ cup)**

1 **recipe Spicy Garlic Oil (recipe follows)**

½ **cup chopped fresh basil**
   Kosher salt

1 FOR THE DOUGH Combine water and oil in liquid measuring cup. Process bread flour; whole-wheat flour, if using; sugar; salt; and yeast in food processor until combined, about 5 seconds. With processor running, slowly add water mixture; process until dough forms tacky, elastic ball that clears sides of workbowl, about 1½ minutes. If dough ball does not form, add more bread flour 1 tablespoon at a time and process until dough ball forms. Spray medium bowl lightly with vegetable oil spray. Transfer dough to bowl and press down to flatten surface; cover tightly with plastic wrap and set in draft-free spot until doubled in volume, 1½ to 2 hours.

2 When dough has doubled, press down gently to deflate; turn dough out onto counter and divide into 4 equal pieces. With your cupped palm, form each piece into smooth, tight ball. Set dough balls on well-floured counter. Press dough rounds with your hand to flatten; cover loosely with plastic and let rest about 15 minutes.

3 FOR THE TOPPING Meanwhile, toss tomatoes and salt in medium bowl; transfer to colander and let drain for 30 minutes. (Wipe out and reserve bowl.) Shake colander to drain off excess liquid; transfer tomatoes to now-empty bowl and set aside. Combine cheeses in second medium bowl and set aside.

4 Gently stretch dough rounds into disks about ½ inch thick and 5 to 6 inches in diameter. Working with 1 piece at a time and keeping others covered, roll out each disk to ⅛-inch thickness, 9 to 10 inches in diameter, on well-floured sheet of parchment, dusting with additional bread flour as needed to prevent sticking. (If dough shrinks when rolled out, cover with plastic wrap and let rest until relaxed, 10 to 15 minutes.) Dust surface of rolled dough with flour and set aside. Repeat with remaining dough, stacking sheets of rolled dough on top of each other (with parchment in between) and covering stack with plastic; set aside until grill is ready.

5A FOR A CHARCOAL GRILL Open bottom vent completely. Light large chimney starter filled with charcoal briquettes (6 quarts). When top coals are partially covered with ash, pour evenly over three-quarters of grill. Set cooking grate in place, cover, and open lid vent completely. Heat grill until hot, about 5 minutes.

5B FOR A GAS GRILL Turn all burners to high, cover, and heat grill until hot, about 15 minutes. Leave all burners on high.

6 Clean and oil cooking grate. Lightly flour pizza peel; invert 1 dough round onto peel, gently stretching it as needed to retain shape. (Do not stretch dough too thin; thin spots will burn quickly.) Peel off and discard parchment; carefully slide round onto hotter side of grill. Immediately repeat with another dough round. Cook (covered if using gas) until tops are covered with bubbles (pierce larger bubbles with tip of paring knife) and bottoms are grill-marked and charred in spots, 1 to 2 minutes; while rounds cook, check undersides and slide to cooler side of grill if browning too quickly. Transfer crusts to cutting board, browned sides up. Repeat with 2 remaining dough rounds.

7 Brush 2 crusts generously with garlic oil; top each evenly with one-quarter of cheese mixture and one-quarter of tomatoes. Return pizzas to grill and cover; cook until bottoms are well browned and cheese is melted, 2 to 6 minutes, checking bottoms frequently to prevent burning. Transfer pizzas to cutting board; repeat with remaining 2 crusts. Sprinkle pizzas with basil and kosher salt to taste; cut into wedges and serve immediately.

478 Spicy Garlic Oil
MAKES ABOUT ⅓ CUP

⅓ **cup extra-virgin olive oil**

4 **garlic cloves, minced**

½ **teaspoon red pepper flakes**

Cook all ingredients in small saucepan over medium heat, stirring occasionally, until garlic begins to sizzle, 2 to 3 minutes. Transfer to small bowl and set aside.

479 Surprisingly Successful Smoky Caesar Salad

✓ WHY THIS RECIPE WORKS

Adding smoky char to a Caesar salad sounded like an intriguing idea, as long as we could avoid scorched, limp lettuce. Using just the firm, compact romaine hearts without the delicate outer leaves was a step in the right direction, and grilling them over a hot fire let them pick up char faster to avoid the danger of wilting. We made a simple dressing with mayonnaise instead of raw eggs for bold flavor and brushed some of it on the cut side of the lettuce before cooking to aid browning. Baguette slices brushed with oil and rubbed with raw garlic crisped up in a few minutes and made a sturdy, grill-safe replacement for croutons. We finished the whole thing with more dressing and plenty of Parmesan cheese.

Grilled Caesar Salad

SERVES 6

DRESSING

- 1 tablespoon lemon juice
- 1 garlic clove, minced
- ½ cup mayonnaise
- ¼ cup grated Parmesan cheese
- 1 tablespoon white wine vinegar
- 1 tablespoon Worcestershire sauce
- 1 tablespoon Dijon mustard
- 2 anchovy fillets, rinsed
- ½ teaspoon salt
- ½ teaspoon pepper
- ¼ cup extra-virgin olive oil

SALAD

- 1 (12-inch) baguette, cut on bias into 5-inch-long, ½-inch-thick slices
- 3 tablespoons extra-virgin olive oil
- 1 garlic clove, peeled
- 3 romaine lettuce hearts (18 ounces), halved lengthwise through cores
- ¼ cup grated Parmesan cheese

1 FOR THE DRESSING Combine lemon juice and garlic in bowl and let sit for 10 minutes. Process mayonnaise, Parmesan, vinegar, Worcestershire, mustard, anchovies, salt, pepper, and lemon-garlic mixture in blender for about 30 seconds. With blender running, slowly add oil. Measure out 6 tablespoons dressing and set aside for brushing romaine.

2A FOR A CHARCOAL GRILL Open bottom vent completely. Light large chimney starter filled with charcoal briquettes (6 quarts). When top coals are partially covered with ash, pour evenly over half of grill. Set cooking grate in place, cover, and open lid vent completely. Heat grill until hot, about 5 minutes.

2B FOR A GAS GRILL Turn all burners to high, cover, and heat grill until hot, about 15 minutes. Leave all burners on high.

3 FOR THE SALAD Clean and oil cooking grate. Brush bread with oil and grill (on hotter side if using charcoal), uncovered, until browned, about 1 minute per side. Transfer to platter and rub with garlic clove. Brush cut sides of romaine with reserved dressing; place half of romaine, cut side down, on grill (on hotter side if using charcoal). Cook, uncovered, until lightly charred, 1 to 2 minutes. Move to platter with bread. Repeat. Drizzle romaine with remaining dressing. Sprinkle with Parmesan. Serve.

480 STEP BY STEP
Double Duty Dressing

We get twice the flavor by using the dressing before and after grilling.

1 BRUSH WITH DRESSING Brush our easy homemade Caesar dressing onto halved romaine hearts before grilling.

2 GRILL THE ROMAINE Grill dressed romaine halves on just 1 side to keep lettuce from wilting.

3 FINISH WITH MORE DRESSING When charred lettuce comes off grill, finish it with more Caesar dressing.

481 Next-Level Chicken Caesar Salad

✓ WHY THIS RECIPE WORKS

Grilling chicken Caesar salad may seem odd, but the grill can take its ordinary components—plain romaine lettuce, bread, and chicken—and make them extraordinary with the simple addition of a slightly smoky, charred flavor. We used boneless, skinless chicken breasts, firm romaine hearts (cut in half to maximize surface area for charring), and sliced baguette as the components of our salad. However, not all of these ingredients cooked at the same rate or over the same heat. The chicken needed to be cooked over a hot fire but the romaine hearts and bread slices were best over a medium-hot fire. To solve this, we used a two-level fire and placed the chicken over the hotter side; when the chicken was almost done, we added the bread, which cooked quickly, to the cooler side. We then set aside the chicken and the bread, freeing up the cooler side of the grill for the romaine. For a lighter version of Caesar dressing that would complement this grilled version of the salad, we used some unconventional ingredients—buttermilk, mayonnaise and Dijon mustard—which added lightness and tang.

Grilled Chicken Caesar Salad
SERVES 4

If using kosher chicken, do not brine in step 1 but do season with salt in step 4. Cut the bread on an extreme bias so that it is easy to handle on the grill.

SALAD

- 3 tablespoons salt
- 4 (6-ounce) boneless, skinless chicken breasts, trimmed
  Vegetable oil spray
- ⅛ teaspoon pepper
- 3 romaine lettuce hearts (18 ounces), halved lengthwise through cores
- 1 (5-inch) piece baguette, sliced 1 inch thick on bias

DRESSING

- ⅓ cup buttermilk
- 3 tablespoons mayonnaise
- 2 tablespoons lemon juice
- 3 anchovy fillets, rinsed, patted dry, and minced
- 2 garlic cloves, minced
- 2 teaspoons Dijon mustard
- 1 teaspoon Worcestershire sauce
- 2 tablespoons extra-virgin olive oil
- 1 ounce Parmesan cheese, grated (½ cup)
  Salt and pepper

1 FOR THE SALAD Dissolve salt in 1½ quarts cold water in large container. Submerge breasts in brine, cover, and refrigerate for 30 minutes to 1 hour.

2 FOR THE DRESSING Process buttermilk, mayonnaise, lemon juice, 2 tablespoons water, anchovies, garlic, mustard, and Worcestershire in blender until smooth, about 30 seconds. With blender running, add oil in steady stream until incorporated. Transfer dressing to bowl. Set aside 1 tablespoon Parmesan. Stir remaining 7 tablespoons Parmesan into dressing. Season with salt and pepper to taste, and set aside.

3A FOR A CHARCOAL GRILL Open bottom vent completely. Light large chimney starter filled with charcoal briquettes (6 quarts). When top coals are partially covered with ash, pour two-thirds evenly over half of grill, then pour remaining coals over other half of grill. Set cooking grate in place, cover, and open lid vent completely. Heat grill until hot, about 5 minutes.

3B FOR A GAS GRILL Turn all burners to high, cover, and heat grill until hot, about 15 minutes. Leave primary burner on high and turn other burner(s) to medium. (Adjust burners as needed to maintain hot fire and medium fire on separate sides of grill.)

4 Clean and oil cooking grate. Remove chicken from brine and pat dry with paper towels. Lightly spray chicken with oil spray and season with pepper. Lightly spray romaine hearts and bread with oil spray. Place chicken on hotter side of grill and cook until well browned and chicken registers 160 degrees, 8 to 12 minutes, flipping breasts halfway through cooking. Transfer chicken to cutting board and tent with aluminum foil.

5 While chicken cooks, place bread on cooler side of grill and cook until golden brown, 4 to 6 minutes, flipping slices halfway through cooking. Transfer bread to cutting board with chicken. Place romaine halves on cooler side of grill and cook until lightly charred on all sides, 3 to 5 minutes, turning as needed.

6 Slice chicken crosswise into ½-inch-thick strips. Cut bread into 1-inch cubes and chop romaine hearts into 1-inch pieces. Whisk dressing to recombine. In large bowl, toss chicken and lettuce with dressing to coat. Divide salad evenly among 4 plates. Sprinkle bread cubes and reserved Parmesan evenly over top and serve.

482 SHOPPING IQ
Pass the Parm

Genuine Italian Parmigiano-Reggiano cheese offers a buttery, nutty taste and crystalline crunch. Produced for the past 800 years in northern Italy using traditional methods, this hard cow's-milk cheese has a distinctive flavor, but it comes at a steep price.

THE BOTTOM LINE Our top-rated brand, chosen from a lineup of supermarket cheeses, is **Boar's Head Parmigiano-Reggiano**. Our tasters say it offers a "good crunch" and "nice tangy, nutty" flavor; it costs about $18 per pound.

483

Best Vegetable Kebabs

✓ WHY THIS RECIPE WORKS

Vegetables on their own can be a great option for grilled kebabs, because they cook quickly and, when done right, offer a crisp, charred exterior and a juicy, tender interior. Tossing grilled vegetables with a bold dressing can do wonders to brighten up an otherwise boring dinner, but for our take on vegetable kebabs, we took the idea one step further. We tossed the vegetables with half of our dressing base before skewering and grilling them, giving them great flavor from the start. We also grilled lemon quarters to tone down their bright acidity and give the juice a deeper, more complex flavor when added to the dressing. Bell peppers and zucchini are classic grilling vegetables for good reason: Bell peppers sweeten over the flame, while zucchini hold their shape and meaty texture. Portobello mushroom caps were the perfect addition to the kebabs; as they released their moisture on the grill, they picked up great char flavor and developed a deep, meaty taste.

Grilled Vegetable Kebabs

SERVES 4

You will need eight 12-inch metal skewers for this recipe.

- ¼ cup extra-virgin olive oil
- 1 teaspoon Dijon mustard
- 1 teaspoon minced fresh rosemary
- 1 garlic clove, minced
  Salt and pepper
- 6 portobello mushroom caps (5 inches in diameter), quartered
- 2 zucchini, halved lengthwise and sliced ¾ inch thick
- 2 red bell peppers, stemmed, seeded, and cut into 1½-inch pieces
- 2 lemons, quartered

1 Whisk oil, mustard, rosemary, garlic, ½ teaspoon salt, and ¼ teaspoon pepper together in large bowl. Measure half of mixture into separate bowl and set aside for serving. Toss mushrooms, zucchini, and bell peppers with remaining oil mixture, then thread in alternating order onto eight 12-inch metal skewers.

2A FOR A CHARCOAL GRILL Open bottom vent completely. Light large chimney starter half filled with charcoal briquettes (3 quarts). When top coals are partially covered with ash, pour evenly over grill. Set cooking grate in place, cover, and open lid vent completely. Heat grill until hot, about 5 minutes.

2B FOR A GAS GRILL Turn all burners to high, cover, and heat grill until hot, about 15 minutes. Turn all burners to medium.

3 Clean and oil cooking grate. Place kebabs and lemons on grill. Cook (covered if using gas), turning as needed, until vegetables are tender and well browned and lemons are juicy and slightly charred, 16 to 18 minutes. Transfer kebabs and lemons to platter, removing skewers.

4 Juice 2 lemon quarters and whisk into reserved oil mixture. Drizzle vegetables with dressing and serve.

RECIPE FOR SUCCESS

Sweet and Smoky Carrot Salad

✓ WHY THIS RECIPE WORKS

Grilling carrots draws out their natural sugars and intensifies their flavor. That is, if you can prevent them from burning to a crisp. To make sure our carrots would cook all the way through and get a good char without getting overdone, we jump-started the cooking in the microwave. Then we grilled the softened carrots over a hot fire for just a few minutes on each side for perfect charred flavor. Simply halving the carrots lengthwise made them easier to maneuver on the grill grate; we then cut them into smaller pieces after grilling when we assembled the salad. To complement the smoky-sweet flavor of the grilled carrots, we made a vinaigrette with warm spices and a bit of heat from smoked paprika as well as extra sweetness from sugar and raisins, and freshness from minced parsley.

Charred Carrot Salad

SERVES 4

Try to use carrots of a similar size so that they cook at the same rate; very large carrots can be quartered lengthwise. You can substitute white wine vinegar for the white balsamic vinegar.

1½	**pounds carrots, peeled and halved lengthwise**
¼	**cup vegetable oil**
	Salt and pepper
1	**tablespoon packed brown sugar**
2½	**teaspoons smoked paprika**
⅛	**teaspoon ground cinnamon**
⅛	**teaspoon ground allspice**
2	**tablespoons white balsamic vinegar**
⅓	**cup raisins**
2	**tablespoons minced fresh parsley**

1 Toss carrots with 1 tablespoon oil in bowl and season with salt and pepper. Cover and microwave until softened, 6 to 8 minutes, stirring halfway through microwaving; drain well.

2 Meanwhile, mix sugar, paprika, cinnamon, allspice, 1 teaspoon salt, and 1 teaspoon pepper together in bowl; measure out 2 teaspoons spice mixture and set aside for salad.

3A FOR A CHARCOAL GRILL Open bottom vent completely. Light large chimney starter three-quarters filled with charcoal briquettes (4½ quarts). When top coals are partially covered with ash, pour evenly over grill. Set cooking grate in place, cover, and open lid vent completely. Heat grill until hot, about 5 minutes.

3B FOR A GAS GRILL Turn all burners to high, cover, and heat grill until hot, about 15 minutes. Turn all burners to medium-high.

4 Clean and oil cooking grate. Place carrots on grill and cook until tender and browned on both sides, 2 to 4 minutes per side; transfer to cutting board.

5 Cut carrots into 2-inch pieces. Whisk vinegar and spice mixture together in large bowl, then slowly whisk in remaining 3 tablespoons oil until incorporated. Add carrots, raisins, and parsley and toss to coat; season with salt and pepper to taste. Serve.

TEST KITCHEN TIP

485 The Importance of Peeling Carrots

To test whether peeling carrots has a noticeable effect on their flavor or texture, we compared batches of scrubbed unpeeled carrots with peeled carrots. We tasted the samples raw, cut into coins and glazed, and roasted in a 425-degree oven. Although a few tasters found the unpeeled raw carrots to taste earthier than their stripped siblings, most were distracted by their "dusty exterior" and "bitter finish." The results were even more clear-cut when the carrots were cooked. Tasters unanimously preferred the peel-free carrots in the glazed and roasted samples. In both cases, the skins on the unpeeled carrots became wrinkled, tough, and gritty. Their flavor was "earthier, but not in a good way" and they didn't look particularly appealing. The peeled versions remained bright orange, tender, and sweet.

BOTTOM LINE It takes only an extra minute or two to peel carrots. We think it's time well spent.

486 SHOPPING IQ
Smoked Paprika

Paprika is a generic term for a spice made from ground dried red peppers. Smoked paprika, a Spanish favorite, is made by drying red peppers over an oak fire. It has a distinctive rich and smoky taste. Smoked paprika comes in three varieties: sweet (dulce), bittersweet or medium hot (agridulce), and hot (picante). We prefer sweet smoked paprika in this recipe but the choice is up to you.

487 RECIPE FOR SUCCESS Unconventional Potato Salad from the Grill

✓ WHY THIS RECIPE WORKS

Grilled potato salad is a great summer side dish, but grilling potatoes can be a challenge, requiring a deft hand and a good dose of patience. If the fire is too hot, all you're going to get is raw-on-the-inside, burnt-on-the-outside spuds. But if you're nursing a modest, low-fire grill, your potatoes are not going to be done in time for dinner. We found that the best way to get good grilled flavor while still ensuring that the potatoes would be cooked all the way through was to jump-start cooking in the microwave. We then threaded the softened potatoes onto skewers and grilled them for a few minutes. For a new take on the flavors of potato salad that worked with this grilled version, we added a sweet and smoky vinaigrette with warm spices and a few extra ingredients that paired well with the charred potatoes: We got sweetness from roasted red peppers, savory crunch from toasted pecans, and a fresh bite from sliced scallions.

Charred Fingerling Potato Salad

SERVES 4

Fingerling potatoes with a 1-inch diameter work best in this recipe; if your potatoes are thinner, you may not be able to skewer them with the cut sides facing down. You can substitute small halved red potatoes, if necessary. You can substitute white wine vinegar for the white balsamic vinegar. You will need four 12-inch metal skewers for this recipe.

- 1½ pounds fingerling potatoes, unpeeled, halved lengthwise
- ¼ cup vegetable oil
  Salt and pepper
- 1 tablespoon packed brown sugar
- 2½ teaspoons smoked paprika
- ⅛ teaspoon ground cinnamon
- ⅛ teaspoon ground allspice
- 2 tablespoons white balsamic vinegar
- ¾ cup jarred roasted red peppers, sliced thin
- ½ cup pecans, toasted and chopped
- 2 scallions, sliced thin

1 Toss potatoes with 1 tablespoon oil in bowl and season with salt and pepper. Cover and microwave until softened, 6 to 8 minutes, stirring halfway through microwaving. Drain potatoes well, then thread, cut side down, onto four 12-inch metal skewers.

2 Meanwhile, mix sugar, paprika, cinnamon, allspice, 1 teaspoon salt, and 1 teaspoon pepper together in bowl; measure out and 2 teaspoons spice mixture and set aside for salad.

3A FOR A CHARCOAL GRILL Open bottom vent completely. Light large chimney starter three-quarters filled with charcoal briquettes (4½ quarts). When top coals are partially covered with ash, pour evenly over grill. Set cooking grate in place, cover, and open lid vent completely. Heat grill until hot, about 5 minutes.

3B FOR A GAS GRILL Turn all burners to high, cover, and heat grill until hot, about 15 minutes. Turn all burners to medium-high.

4 Clean and oil cooking grate. Place potatoes on grill and cook until tender and browned on both sides, 2 to 4 minutes per side; transfer to plate.

5 Whisk vinegar and reserved spice mixture together in large bowl, then slowly whisk in remaining 3 tablespoons oil until incorporated. Carefully slide potatoes off skewers into bowl of dressing; add red peppers, pecans, and scallions; and toss to coat. Season with salt and pepper to taste, and serve.

488 Bacon-y and Smoky Potato Salad

✓ WHY THIS RECIPE WORKS

For a super-easy grilled potato salad recipe, we looked for a technique that did not call for precooking the potatoes, but it took some work to find one that worked. Grilling whole unpeeled potatoes took over an hour, and the leathery skins were nearly inedible. Cooking cubed potatoes over a medium fire gave us nicely charred and surprisingly tender potatoes, but standing over the grill turning dozens of tiny potato cubes was too laborious. Looking for a middle ground, we tried halving small red potatoes and grilling them directly. This worked perfectly, producing potatoes with nice smoky flavor that were also crisp outside and tender inside. For even more smokiness, we decided to grill onions along with the potatoes and add a bit of smoky chipotle chile to the vinaigrette. As a final touch, we sautéed some bacon and stirred it into the salad at the last minute. Not wanting to waste the bacon fat, we went back and revised our recipe so the potatoes were tossed with it instead of olive oil for great smoky bacon flavor throughout.

Smoky Grilled Potato Salad
SERVES 8

Use small red potatoes 1½ to 2 inches in diameter. If you don't have 2 tablespoons of fat in the skillet after frying the bacon, add olive oil to make up the difference.

- 6 slices bacon
- 3 tablespoons red wine vinegar
- 2 tablespoons mayonnaise
- 2 teaspoons minced canned chipotle chile in adobo sauce
   Salt and pepper
- 3 tablespoons olive oil, plus extra for brushing
- 3 pounds small red potatoes, unpeeled, halved
- 1 large onion, sliced into ½-inch-thick rounds
- 4 scallions, sliced thin

1 Cook bacon in 12-inch skillet over medium heat until crisp, 7 to 9 minutes; transfer to paper towel–lined plate. Set aside 2 tablespoons bacon fat. When cool enough to handle, crumble bacon and set aside. Whisk vinegar, mayonnaise, chipotle, ½ teaspoon salt, and ½ teaspoon pepper together in large bowl. Slowly whisk in 3 tablespoons oil until combined; set aside dressing.

2A FOR A CHARCOAL GRILL Open bottom vent completely. Light large chimney starter three-quarters filled with charcoal briquettes (4½ quarts). When top coals are partially covered with ash, pour evenly over grill. Set cooking grate in place, cover, and open lid vent completely. Heat grill until hot, about 5 minutes.

2B FOR A GAS GRILL Turn all burners to high, cover, and heat grill until hot, about 15 minutes. Turn all burners to medium.

3 Clean and oil cooking grate. Toss potatoes with reserved bacon fat and ½ teaspoon salt. Push toothpick horizontally through each onion round to keep rings intact while grilling. Brush onion rounds lightly with oil and season with salt and pepper. Place potatoes, cut side down, and onion rounds on grill and cook, covered, until charred on first side, 10 to 14 minutes.

4 Flip potatoes and onion rounds and continue to cook, covered, until well browned all over and potatoes are easily pierced with tip of paring knife, 10 to 16 minutes longer. Transfer potatoes and onion rounds to rimmed baking sheet and let cool slightly.

5 When cool enough to handle, halve potatoes; remove toothpicks and chop onion rounds coarse. Add potatoes, onion, scallions, and bacon to dressing and toss to combine. Season with salt and pepper to taste. Serve warm or at room temperature.

489 FOOD SCIENCE
Keeping Potato Salad Safe

Mayonnaise has gotten a bad reputation, being blamed for spoiled potato salads and upset stomachs after many summer picnics and barbecues. The main ingredients in mayonnaise are raw eggs, vegetable oil, and an acid (usually vinegar or lemon juice). The eggs used in commercially made mayonnaise have been pasteurized to kill salmonella and other bacteria. Its high acidity is another safeguard; because bacteria do not fare well in acidic environments, the lemon juice or vinegar inhibits bacterial growth. Mayonnaise, even when homemade, is rarely the problem unless it contains very little acid. It's the potatoes that are more likely to go bad.

The bacteria usually responsible for spoiled potato salad are *Bacillus cereus* and *Staphylococcus aureus* (commonly known as staph). Both are found in soil and dust, and they thrive on starchy, low-acid foods like rice, pasta, and potatoes. If they find their way into your potato salad via an unwashed cutting board or contaminated hands, they can wreak havoc on your digestive system. Most foodborne bacteria grow well at temperatures between 40 and 140 degrees Fahrenheit. This is known as the temperature danger zone, and if contaminated food remains in this zone for too long, the bacteria can produce enough toxins to make you sick. The U.S. Food and Drug Administration recommends refrigerating food within 2 hours of its preparation, or 1 hour if the temperature is above 90 degrees. Heat from the sun is often what causes the trouble at summer picnics.

490 RECIPE FOR SUCCESS
Sweet Potatoes with Bite

✔ WHY THIS RECIPE WORKS

Grill-roasted sweet potatoes have a great caramelized exterior and earthy sweetness. Precooking the sweet potatoes for this dish in the microwave ensured that they cooked evenly on the grill. We then put the par-cooked potatoes over the cooler side of a two-level fire to cook them gently through without the danger of charring or sticking. The fresh, herbal flavors of chimichurri sauce were the perfect complement to the grilled sweet potatoes. The parsley, cilantro, red wine vinegar, garlic, salt, and red pepper flakes all came together easily in a food processor, emulsified into a smooth sauce with extra-virgin olive oil.

Grilled Sweet Potatoes with Chimichurri Sauce
SERVES 4

CHIMICHURRI SAUCE
- 1 cup fresh parsley leaves
- ½ cup fresh cilantro leaves
- ½ cup extra-virgin olive oil
- ¼ cup red wine vinegar
- 2 tablespoons water
- 4 garlic cloves, minced
- 1 teaspoon salt
- ½ teaspoon red pepper flakes

POTATOES
- 1½ pounds sweet potatoes, unpeeled, sliced ½ inch thick
- 1 tablespoon olive oil
- Salt and pepper

1 FOR THE CHIMICHURRI SAUCE Process all ingredients in food processor until smooth, 30 to 60 seconds, scraping down bowl as needed.

2 FOR THE POTATOES Toss potatoes with olive oil in bowl and season with salt and pepper. Cover and microwave until softened, 6 to 8 minutes, stirring halfway through cooking; drain well.

3A FOR A CHARCOAL GRILL Open bottom vent completely. Light large chimney starter filled with charcoal briquettes (6 quarts). When top coals are partially covered with ash, pour two-thirds evenly over half of grill, then pour remaining coals over other half of grill. Set cooking grate in place, cover, and open lid vent completely. Heat grill until hot, about 5 minutes.

3B FOR A GAS GRILL Turn all burners to high, cover, and heat grill until hot, about 15 minutes. Leave primary burner on high and turn other burner(s) to medium.

4 Clean and oil cooking grate. Place potatoes on cooler side of grill. Cook (covered if using gas), turning potatoes as needed until tender, about 8 to 12 minutes.

5 Transfer potatoes to platter. Serve with sauce.

491
TEST KITCHEN TIP
Parcook the Potatoes

Placing raw sweet potato rounds on the grill quickly produced burnt exteriors and raw interiors. After some testing, we found that the key to properly cooking the potatoes was to first soften them in the microwave before placing them on the grill—we also cooked them on the cooler side of the grill.

492 SHOPPING IQ
Cheese Choices

COTIJA CHEESE Cotija is a tangy, salty, aged cheese that is commonly crumbled and used as a garnish for finished dishes. If you can't find Cotija, feta makes a good substitute.

QUESO FRESCO Queso fresco is a soft, fresh cheese that, like Cotija, is used most often as a garnish since it does not melt well. It has a mildly salty flavor that is comparable to mild feta, which you can use as a substitute if you can't find queso fresco.

493 RECIPE FOR SUCCESS
Street Corn at Home

✔ WHY THIS RECIPE WORKS

In Mexico, street vendors add kick to grilled corn by slathering it with a creamy, spicy, cheesy sauce. The corn takes on an irresistibly sweet, smoky, charred flavor, which is heightened by the lime juice and chili powder in the sauce. For our own rendition of this south-of-the-border street fare, we ditched the husks, coated the ears with oil to prevent sticking, and grilled them directly on the grate over a hot fire so the corn could develop plenty of char. The traditional base for the sauce is *crema*, a thick, soured Mexican cream. But given its limited availability in supermarkets, we replaced the crema with a combination of mayonnaise (for richness) and sour cream (for tanginess).

Mexican-Style Grilled Corn

SERVES 6

If you can find queso fresco or Cotija, use either in place of the Pecorino Romano. If you prefer the corn spicy, add the optional cayenne pepper.

1½	ounces Pecorino Romano cheese, grated (¾ cup)
¼	cup mayonnaise
3	tablespoons sour cream
3	tablespoons minced fresh cilantro
4	teaspoons lime juice
1	garlic clove, minced
¾	teaspoon chili powder
¼	teaspoon pepper
¼	teaspoon cayenne pepper (optional)
4	teaspoons vegetable oil
¼	teaspoon salt
6	ears corn, husks and silk removed

1A FOR A CHARCOAL GRILL Open bottom vent completely. Light large chimney starter filled with charcoal briquettes (6 quarts). When top coals are partially covered with ash, pour evenly over half of grill. Set cooking grate in place, cover, and open lid vent completely. Heat grill until hot, about 5 minutes.

1B FOR A GAS GRILL Turn all burners to high, cover, and heat grill until hot, about 15 minutes. Leave all burners on high.

2 Meanwhile, combine Pecorino, mayonnaise, sour cream, cilantro, lime juice, garlic, ¼ teaspoon chili powder, pepper, and cayenne, if using, in large bowl and set aside. In second large bowl, combine oil, salt, and remaining ½ teaspoon chili powder. Add corn to oil mixture and toss to coat evenly.

3 Clean and oil cooking grate. Place corn on grill (on hotter side if using charcoal) and cook (covered if using gas) until lightly charred on all sides, 7 to 12 minutes, turning as needed. Place corn in bowl with cheese mixture, toss to coat evenly, and serve.

494 TEST KITCHEN TIP
Shake It Off

Removing the husk and silk from an ear of corn is a chore, and a "corn de-silker" gadget that we tested proved to be a bust. But now we've found a better way: A short stint in the microwave and a quick shake are all it takes to cleanly slide off the corn husk and silk. The cob will heat up a bit, but the kernels won't be cooked.

1 REMOVE STALK END AND MICROWAVE With sharp chef's knife, cut off stalk end of cob just above first row of kernels. Place 3 or 4 ears at a time on microwave-safe plate and microwave on full power for 30 to 60 seconds.

2 SHAKE OUT COBS Hold each ear by uncut end in 1 hand. Shake ear up and down until cob slips free, leaving behind husk and silk.

495 RECIPE FOR SUCCESS
Making the Most of Grilled Vegetable Pairings

✓ WHY THIS RECIPE WORKS

Our perfect grilled vegetable recipe would have to produce charred-on-the-outside, tender-on-the-inside veggies with great smoky flavor and a lively dressing. To double up our recipe's flavor, we wanted a combination of two vegetables. Mindful of complementary cooking times, we paired eggplant with sweet red bell peppers. A medium-hot fire allowed us to cook the vegetables quickly without any chance of burning them; in less than 20 minutes they were perfectly tender and full of smoky flavor. We also whisked up a quick mint-cumin dressing that perfectly complemented the grilled vegetables. Drizzled with dressing while still warm, the vegetables had enough flavor to be the star attraction of a meal.

496 SHOPPING IQ
One Eggplant to Rule them All

Four of the most common varieties of eggplant found in the supermarket are globe, Italian, Chinese, and Thai. To find out whether they can all be used interchangeably, we prepared each type in five dishes calling for different cooking methods. Only the generously sized globe eggplant was a true multitasker, suitable for all dishes and responding well to all cooking methods.

Globe: Best all-around
Tender texture, mild flavor

Italian: Spicy but seedy
Moist with lots of seeds, spicy flavor

Chinese: Sweet and dry
Dry, firmer interior, lots of seeds, and intense, slightly sweet flavor

Thai: Odd one out
Crisp and relatively dry with bright, grassy, slightly spicy flavor

Grilled Eggplant and Bell Peppers with Mint-Cumin Dressing
SERVES 4 TO 6

After about 5 minutes, faint grill marks should begin to appear on the undersides of the vegetables; if necessary, adjust their position on the grill or adjust the heat level. Serve hot, warm, or at room temperature.

- 1 pound eggplant, sliced into ½-inch-thick rounds
- 2 red bell peppers, stemmed, seeded, and cut into 2-inch planks
- 5 tablespoons extra-virgin olive oil
    Salt and pepper
- 2 tablespoons plain yogurt
- 1 tablespoon chopped fresh mint
- 1 tablespoon lemon juice
- 1 small garlic clove, minced
- ½ teaspoon ground coriander
- ½ teaspoon ground cumin

1 Brush eggplant and bell peppers with ¼ cup oil, sprinkle with 1 teaspoon salt, and season with pepper. Whisk yogurt, mint, lemon juice, garlic, coriander, cumin, remaining 1 tablespoon oil, and ¼ teaspoon salt together in bowl.

2A FOR A CHARCOAL GRILL Open bottom vent completely. Light large chimney starter half filled with charcoal briquettes (3 quarts). When top coals are partially covered with ash, pour evenly over grill. Set cooking grate in place, cover, and open lid vent completely. Heat grill until hot, about 5 minutes.

2B FOR A GAS GRILL Turn all burners to high, cover, and heat grill until hot, about 15 minutes. Turn all burners to medium.

3 Clean and oil cooking grate. Place eggplant and bell peppers, cut sides down, on grill. Cook (covered if using gas), turning as needed, until tender and caramelized, 16 to 18 minutes; transfer to platter as they finish cooking. Whisk dressing to recombine, drizzle over vegetables, and serve.

Grilled Zucchini and Red Onion with Lemon-Basil Vinaigrette

SERVES 4 TO 6

After about 5 minutes, faint grill marks should begin to appear on the undersides of the vegetables; if necessary, adjust their position on the grill or adjust the heat level. The vegetables can be served hot, warm, or at room temperature. You will need two 12-inch metal skewers for this recipe.

1	large red onion, sliced into ½-inch-thick rounds
1	pound zucchini, trimmed and sliced lengthwise into ¾-inch-thick planks
6	tablespoons extra-virgin olive oil
	Salt and pepper
1	teaspoon grated lemon zest plus 1 tablespoon juice
1	small garlic clove, minced
¼	teaspoon Dijon mustard
1	tablespoon chopped fresh basil

1 Thread onion rounds, from side to side, onto 2 metal skewers. Brush onion and zucchini with ¼ cup oil, sprinkle with 1 teaspoon salt, and season with pepper. Whisk lemon zest and juice, garlic, mustard, remaining 2 tablespoons oil, and ¼ teaspoon salt together in bowl.

2A FOR A CHARCOAL GRILL Open bottom vent completely. Light large chimney starter half filled with charcoal briquettes (3 quarts). When top coals are partially covered with ash, pour evenly over grill. Set cooking grate in place, cover, and open lid vent completely. Heat grill until hot, about 5 minutes.

2B FOR A GAS GRILL Turn all burners to high, cover, and heat grill until hot, about 15 minutes. Turn all burners to medium.

3 Clean and oil cooking grate. Place onion and zucchini on grill. Cook (covered if using gas), turning as needed, until tender and caramelized, 18 to 22 minutes; transfer to platter as they finish cooking. Remove onion from skewers and discard any charred outer rings. Whisk dressing to recombine, and drizzle over vegetables. Sprinkle with basil and serve.

497

RECIPE FOR SUCCESS

Grilled Zucchini Bathed in Flavor

✔ WHY THIS RECIPE WORKS

Grilling vegetables can be tricky and, often, the big issue is flavor—there's just not enough of it. We found that matching our vegetables in pairs allowed us to double up on flavor, which cook in sync. We paired zucchini with sweet red onion. For the grilling itself, we built a moderate, medium-hot fire and cooked the vegetables for about 20 minutes for tender, charred perfection. To boost the flavors further, we whisked up a quick lemon-basil vinaigrette to accompany the vegetables after they came off the grill.

498

GRILL HACK

Reminder to Turn Off the Gas

Make sure you remember to turn off the gas tank after grilling with this simple trick: Jog your memory by slipping a rubber band around the knob of the gas tank. When you turn the tank on, place the rubber band around your wrist, and remove it only when you turn the tank off. As long as you're wearing the rubber band, you know that the tank is on.

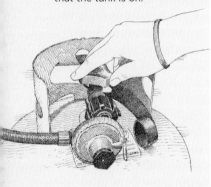

499

RECIPE FOR SUCCESS

Mediterranean-Style Grilled Bread Salad

✓ WHY THIS RECIPE WORKS

Pair grilled vegetable chunks with cubes of rustic bread, fresh herbs, and a bright vinaigrette, and you have a salad that needs little else. We began by choosing the vegetables. We matched zucchini with red onion and red bell pepper since they all cook at a similar rate, and grilled them over a single-level medium-hot fire until they were perfectly browned, tender, and full of smoky flavor. The sturdy texture and strong wheat flavor of a rustic loaf of Italian-style bread paired well with the bolder grilled flavor of the vegetables. Grilling the bread slices (we put them alongside the vegetables) made the pieces sturdier and added an appealing texture. Once the bread and vegetables were grilled, we simply cut them into 1-inch pieces and tossed them with a lemon-based vinaigrette. A few ounces of goat cheese crumbled on top added a creamy finishing touch.

Grilled Vegetable and Bread Salad

SERVES 4

Be sure to use a hearty Italian bread—it is important for both the flavor and the texture of this salad. Thick slices of a French baguette, cut on an extreme bias, also work well here.

- 2 zucchini, halved lengthwise
- 2 red bell peppers, stemmed, seeded, and flattened
- 1 red onion, sliced into ½-inch-thick rounds
- 6 ounces crusty, rustic Italian-style bread, sliced 1 inch thick
- 5 tablespoons extra-virgin olive oil
  Salt and pepper
- 2 tablespoons chopped fresh basil
- 1 teaspoon grated lemon zest plus 4 teaspoons juice
- 1 teaspoon Dijon mustard
- 1 garlic clove, minced
- 2 ounces goat cheese, crumbled (½ cup)

1 Lightly coat zucchini, bell peppers, onion rounds, and bread with 2 tablespoons oil and season with salt and pepper.

2A FOR A CHARCOAL GRILL Open bottom vent completely. Light large chimney starter half filled with charcoal briquettes (3 quarts). When top coals are partially covered with ash, pour evenly over grill. Set cooking grate in place, cover, and open lid vent completely. Heat grill until hot, about 5 minutes.

2B FOR A GAS GRILL Turn all burners to high, cover, and heat grill until hot, about 15 minutes. Turn all burners to medium.

3 Clean and oil cooking grate. Place bread and vegetables on grill. Cook (covered if using gas), turning as needed, until bread is golden, about 4 minutes, and vegetables are spottily charred, 8 to 12 minutes. Transfer bread and vegetables to platter as they finish.

4 Cut vegetables and bread into 1-inch pieces. Whisk remaining 3 tablespoons oil, basil, lemon zest and juice, mustard, and garlic together in large bowl. Add vegetables and bread and toss to coat. Season with salt and pepper to taste, sprinkle with goat cheese, and serve.

500 RECIPE FOR SUCCESS Translating a Tunisian Mechouia Classic for Home Grilling

✓ WHY THIS RECIPE WORKS

For our take on this robustly flavored Tunisian dish of grilled vegetables, we started by prepping the vegetables for the grill. To get good charring, we wanted to expose as much surface area to the heat as possible, so we halved the eggplant, zucchini, and plum tomatoes lengthwise and stemmed and flattened the bell peppers. We also scored the eggplant and zucchini before putting them over the coals so they would release their excess moisture as they cooked. We used a potent combination of coriander, caraway, cumin, paprika, and cayenne to replace the traditional Tunisian spice blend *tabil* and infuse our vegetables with exotic flavor. The heat of the grill worked to bloom the flavor of the spices so they didn't taste raw or harsh, and more of the spices plus garlic, lemon, and a trio of herbs provided a bright, fresh-tasting dressing.

Tunisian-Style Grilled Vegetables (Mechouia)

SERVES 4 TO 6

Serve as a side dish to grilled meats and fish; with grilled pita as a salad course; or with hard-cooked eggs, olives, and premium canned tuna as a light lunch. Equal amounts of ground coriander and cumin can be substituted for the whole spices.

VINAIGRETTE

- 2 teaspoons coriander seeds
- 1½ teaspoons caraway seeds
- 1 teaspoon cumin seeds
- 5 tablespoons olive oil
- ½ teaspoon paprika
- ⅛ teaspoon cayenne pepper
- 3 garlic cloves, minced
- ¼ cup chopped fresh parsley
- ¼ cup chopped fresh cilantro
- 2 tablespoons chopped fresh mint
- 1 teaspoon grated lemon zest plus 2 tablespoons juice
- Salt

VEGETABLES

- 2 bell peppers (1 red and 1 green)
- 1 small eggplant, halved lengthwise
- 1 zucchini (8 to 10 ounces), halved lengthwise
- 4 plum tomatoes, cored and halved lengthwise
- Salt and pepper
- 2 shallots, unpeeled

1 FOR THE VINAIGRETTE Grind coriander seeds, caraway seeds, and cumin seeds in spice grinder until finely ground. Whisk ground spices, oil, paprika, and cayenne together in bowl. Measure out 3 tablespoons oil mixture and set aside. Heat remaining oil mixture and garlic in 8-inch skillet over low heat, stirring occasionally, until fragrant and small bubbles appear, 8 to 10 minutes. Transfer to large bowl and let cool, about 10 minutes. Whisk parsley, cilantro, mint, and lemon zest and juice into oil mixture; season with salt to taste.

2 FOR THE VEGETABLES Slice ¼ inch off tops and bottoms of bell peppers and remove cores. Make slit down 1 side of each bell pepper and then press flat into 1 long strip, removing ribs and remaining seeds with knife as needed. Using sharp knife, cut slits in flesh of eggplant and zucchini, spaced ½ inch apart, in crosshatch pattern, being careful to cut down to but not through skin. Brush cut sides of bell peppers, eggplant, zucchini, and tomatoes with reserved oil mixture and season with salt to taste.

3 Grill vegetables, starting with cut sides down, over medium-hot fire, until tender and well browned and skins of bell peppers, eggplant, tomatoes, and shallots are charred, 8 to 16 minutes, turning and moving vegetables as necessary. Transfer vegetables to baking sheet as they are done. Place bell peppers in bowl, cover with plastic wrap, and let steam to loosen skins.

4 When cool enough to handle, peel bell peppers, eggplant, tomatoes, and shallots. Chop all vegetables into ½-inch pieces and transfer to bowl with vinaigrette; toss to coat. Season with salt and pepper to taste, and serve warm or at room temperature.

501

Prepping Grilled Tunisian-Style Vegetables

1 FLATTEN BELL PEPPERS Trim off top and bottom of bell pepper, then remove stem and seeds. Cut through 1 side of pepper, then press flat and trim away any remaining ribs.

2 SCORE ZUCCHINI AND EGGPLANT Using tip of chef's knife (or paring knife), score cut sides of halved zucchini and eggplant in ½-inch diamond pattern, cutting down to but not through skin.

3

THE SERIOUS PROJECTS

BEEF

329 Chicago-Style Barbecued Ribs

336 Texas Barbecued Beef Ribs

338 Korean Grilled Short Ribs (Kalbi)

340 Grill-Roasted Beef Short Ribs
  Mustard Glaze
  Blackberry Glaze
  Hoisin-Tamarind Glaze

342 Carne Asada
  Red Chile Salsa
  Simple Refried Beans

344 Smoky Chipotle Chili con Carne

346 Grilled Stuffed Flank Steak
  with Spinach and Pine Nuts
  with Sun-Dried Tomatoes and Capers

349 Ultimate Charcoal-Grilled Steaks

350 Smoked Beef Tenderloin

352 Grill-Roasted Prime Rib

354 Kansas City Barbecued Brisket

356 Barbecued Beef Brisket

358 Lone Star Beef Brisket

360 Barbecued Burnt Ends

362 Smoked Roast Beef

PORK

310 Barbecued Baby Back Ribs
  Spice Rub

312 Barbecued Pork Spareribs
  Dry Rub
  Tangy Barbecue Sauce
  Kentucky Smoked Barbecue Sauce
  Louisiana Sweet Barbecue Sauce
  Spicy Rio Grande Barbecue Sauce

314 Sweet and Tangy Grilled Country-Style Pork Ribs

316 Cola-Barbecued Ribs

320 Chinese-Style Barbecued Spareribs

322 Honey-Mustard Barbecued Ribs
  Honey-Mustard Barbecue Sauce

324 Atomic Ribs

326 Kansas City Sticky Ribs

330 Memphis Spareribs

332 Memphis-Style Wet Ribs for a Crowd

334 South Dakota Corncob-Smoked Ribs

364 St. Louis Barbecued Pork Steaks

366 Tacos al Pastor

369 Grilled Citrus-Marinated Pork Cutlets

370 Grilled Stuffed Pork Tenderloin
  Olive and Sun-Dried Tomato Stuffing
  Porcini and Artichoke Stuffing

372 Grilled Pork Loin with Apple-Cranberry Filling
  with Apple-Cherry Filling with Caraway

375 Grill-Roasted Bone-In Pork Rib Roast
  Orange Salsa with Cuban Flavors

376 Cuban-Style Grill-Roasted Pork
  Mojo Sauce

379 Kalua Pork

380 Tennessee Barbecued Pork Shoulder
  Hoecakes

382 Barbecued Pulled Pork
  Dry Rub for Barbecue
  Eastern North Carolina Barbecue Sauce
  Western South Carolina Barbecue Sauce
  Mid–South Carolina Mustard Sauce

384 Lexington Pulled Pork
  South Carolina Pulled Pork
  Lexington Barbecue Sauce

POULTRY

386 Barbecued Pulled Chicken
 Barbecued Pulled Chicken with Peach Sauce
 Barbecued Pulled Chicken for a Crowd
389 Grilled Pesto Chicken
390 Grilled Stuffed Chicken Breasts with Prosciutto
 and Fontina
 with Black Forest Ham and Gruyère
 with Salami and Mozzarella
392 Sinaloa-Style Grill-Roasted Chickens
394 Grill-Roasted Cornish Game Hens
 Barbecue Glaze
 Asian Barbecue Glaze
396 Grill-Roasted Boneless Turkey Breast
 with Herb Butter
 with Olives and Sun-Dried Tomatoes
399 Smoked Turkey Breast
400 Classic Grill-Roasted Turkey
402 Simple Grill-Roasted Turkey
 Gravy for Simple Grill-Roasted Turkey
404 Spice-Rubbed Grill-Roasted Turkey
406 Grilled Duck Breasts
 Peach-Habanero Chutney
 Pickled Ginger Relish
 with Tapenade
408 Grill-Roasted Chinese-Style Duck
410 Grill-Roasted Beer Can Chicken
 Spice Rub

FISH & SEAFOOD

412 Barbecued Side of Salmon
 Horseradish Cream Sauce with Chives
 Mustard-Dill Sauce
415 Grilled Whole Red Snapper or Striped Bass
 Orange, Lime, and Cilantro Vinaigrette
 Fresh Tomato-Basil Relish
 Basic Barbecue Spice Rub
 Cajun Spice Rub
418 Long Island–Style Bluefish
 Tartar Sauce
 Sun-Dried Tomato and Caper Mayonnaise
 Chipotle Chile Mayonnaise
420 Grilled Stuffed Trout
423 New England Clambake
424 Grilled Lobsters
 with Chili Butter
 with Herbed Garlic Butter

503 RECIPE FOR SUCCESS
Sweet 'n' Smoky Barbecued Ribs

✔ WHY THIS RECIPE WORKS

Dry, flavorless ribs are a true culinary disaster. More often than not, baby back ribs cooked at home come out tasting like dry shoe leather. We wanted ribs that were juicy, tender, and fully seasoned, with an intense smokiness. In other words, we wanted ribs that would be well worth the time and effort. Meaty ribs—racks as close to 2 pounds as possible—provided substantial, satisfying portions. Leaving the skin-like membrane on the ribs during cooking helped retain flavor and moistness and helped form a crispy crust. A brief stint in a standard salt-and-sugar brine ensured moist, well-seasoned ribs, while a simple spice rub of chili powder, cayenne, cumin, and brown sugar provided a good balance of sweet and spicy flavors and formed a nice, crisp crust. We barbecued the ribs for a couple of hours on the cooler side of the grill with wood chips and then moved them to a baking sheet and covered them with foil to gently finish cooking in the oven, which made for moist, tender baby back ribs with an intense smoky flavor.

Barbecued Baby Back Ribs
SERVES 4

If you'd like to use wood chunks instead of wood chips when using a charcoal grill, substitute two medium wood chunks, soaked in water for 1 hour, for the wood chip packet.

½   cup sugar
    Salt
2   (1½- to 2-pound) racks baby back ribs, trimmed
1   recipe Spice Rub (recipe follows)
2   cups wood chips

1 Dissolve sugar and ½ cup salt in 4 quarts cold water in large container. Submerge racks in brine, cover, and refrigerate for 1 hour. Remove pork from brine and pat dry with paper towels. Rub 1 tablespoon dry rub on each side of each rack of ribs. Let ribs sit at room temperature for 1 hour.

2 Just before grilling, soak wood chips in water for 15 minutes, then drain. Using large piece of heavy-duty aluminum foil, wrap chips in 8 by 4½-inch

502 SHOPPING IQ
Baby Back Ribs

Baby back ribs (also referred to as loin back ribs) are cut from the section of the rib cage closest to the backbone (shaded red in the drawing). Lean center-cut roasts and chops come from the same part of the pig, which explains why baby back ribs can be expensive.

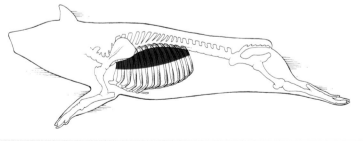

foil packet. (Make sure chips do not poke holes in sides or bottom of packet.) Cut 2 evenly spaced 2-inch slits in top of packet.

3A FOR A CHARCOAL GRILL Open bottom vent halfway. Light large chimney starter three-quarters filled with charcoal briquettes (4½ quarts). When top coals are partially covered with ash, pour evenly over half of grill. Place wood chip packet on coals. Set cooking grate in place, cover, and open lid vent halfway. Heat grill until hot and wood chips are smoking, about 5 minutes.

3B FOR A GAS GRILL Remove cooking grate and place wood chip packet directly on primary burner. Set cooking grate in place, turn all burners to high, cover, and heat grill until hot and wood chips are smoking, about 15 minutes. Turn primary burner to medium-high and turn off other burner(s). (Adjust primary burner as needed to maintain grill temperature of 300 to 325 degrees.)

4 Clean and oil cooking grate. Place ribs meaty side down on cooler side of grill. Cover (position lid vent over meat if using charcoal) and cook until ribs are deep red and smoky, about 2 hours, flipping and rotating racks halfway through grilling. During final 20 minutes of grilling, adjust oven rack to lower-middle position and heat oven to 325 degrees.

5 Transfer ribs to wire rack set in rimmed baking sheet. Cover tightly with foil and cook in oven until tender, 1 to 2 hours.

6 Remove ribs from oven, loosen foil to release steam, and let rest for 30 minutes. Slice ribs between bones and serve.

504 Spice Rub
MAKES ABOUT ¼ CUP

4	teaspoons paprika
1¾	teaspoons ground cumin
1½	teaspoons chili powder
1½	teaspoons packed dark brown sugar
1	teaspoon white pepper
¾	teaspoon dried oregano
¾	teaspoon pepper
½	teaspoon cayenne pepper

Combine all ingredients in bowl.

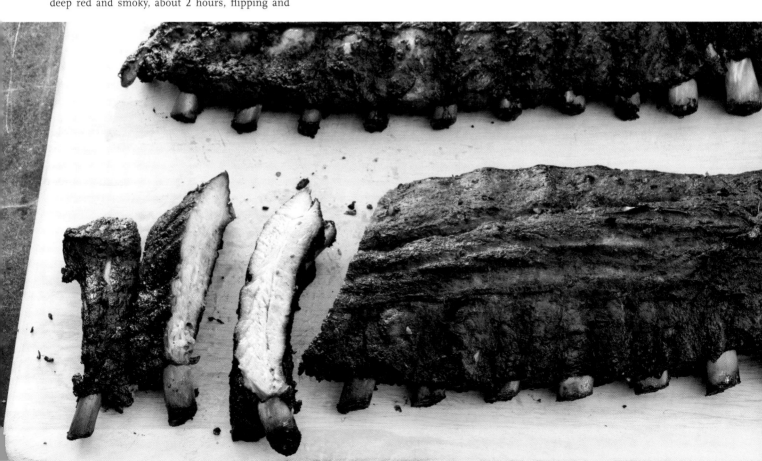

505 RECIPE FOR SUCCESS Classic Barbecued Ribs

✓ WHY THIS RECIPE WORKS

Authentic barbecued ribs are melt-in-your-mouth, fall-off-the-bone tender, with a deeply smoky, meaty flavor. But these irresistibly satisfying ribs come at a cost: They can take a full day in the barbecue pit to develop that deep, smoky flavor. We wanted to find a way to make the magic happen sooner. For bold flavor fast, we applied a spice rub to the ribs; the spices fully infused the meat in just 1 hour. We found that indirect heat came closest to replicating the results of barbecue pit masters. After cooking the ribs on the cooler side of the grill to absorb smoky flavor, we transferred them to the oven to finish. Covering the ribs with foil ensured they remained moist. Of course, barbecued ribs need barbecue sauce, which we applied to the ribs before they went into the oven, reserving a portion to serve alongside the ribs. We also developed some variations on the sauce for sweeter, smokier, or spicier options.

Barbecued Pork Spareribs

SERVES 4 TO 6

St. Louis–style ribs are also simply called spareribs (see page 331 for more information). To remove the membrane from the ribs, use a paring knife to loosen one end, then grasp the membrane with a paper towel and peel it off in one piece. If you'd like to use wood chunks instead of wood chips when using a charcoal grill, substitute two medium wood chunks, soaked in water for 1 hour, for the wood chip packet.

- ¾ cup Dry Rub (recipe follows)
- 2 (2½- to 3-pound) racks St. Louis–style spareribs, trimmed and membrane removed
- 2 cups wood chips
- 1 recipe barbecue sauce (recipes follow)

1 Pat ribs dry. Rub 3 tablespoons dry rub on each side of each rack of ribs. Let ribs sit at room temperature for 1 hour.

2 Just before grilling, soak wood chips in water for 15 minutes, then drain. Using large piece of heavy-duty aluminum foil, wrap chips in 8 by 4½-inch foil packet. (Make sure chips do not poke holes in sides or bottom of packet.) Cut 2 evenly spaced 2-inch slits in top of packet.

3A FOR A CHARCOAL GRILL Open bottom vent halfway. Light large chimney starter two-thirds filled with charcoal briquettes (4 quarts). When top coals are partially covered with ash, pour evenly over half of grill. Place wood chip packet on coals. Set cooking grate in place, cover, and open lid vent halfway. Heat grill until hot and wood chips are smoking, about 5 minutes.

3B FOR A GAS GRILL Remove cooking grate and place wood chip packet directly on primary burner. Set cooking grate in place, turn all burners to high, cover, and heat grill until hot and wood chips are smoking, about 15 minutes. Turn primary burner to medium-high and turn off other burner(s). (Adjust primary burner as needed to maintain grill temperature between 300 and 325 degrees.)

4 Clean and oil cooking grate. Place ribs meaty side down on cooler side of grill; ribs may overlap slightly. Cover (position lid vent over meat if using charcoal) and cook until ribs are deep red and smoky, about 2 hours, flipping and rotating racks halfway through grilling. During final 20 minutes of grilling, adjust oven rack to lower-middle position and heat oven to 325 degrees.

5 Transfer ribs to wire rack set in rimmed baking sheet and brush evenly with ½ cup sauce. Cover tightly with foil and cook in oven until tender, 1 to 2 hours.

6 Remove ribs from oven and let rest, still covered, for 30 minutes. Unwrap ribs, slice between bones, and serve, passing remaining sauce separately.

506 Dry Rub

MAKES ABOUT 1⅓ CUPS

Store leftover spice rub at room temperature for up to three months.

- ¼ cup paprika
- 3 tablespoons celery salt
- 3 tablespoons garlic powder
- 2 tablespoons salt
- 2 tablespoons chili powder
- 2 tablespoons ground cumin
- 2 tablespoons packed dark brown sugar
- 1 tablespoon granulated sugar
- 1 tablespoon dried oregano
- 1 tablespoon white pepper
- 1 tablespoon pepper
- 2 teaspoons cayenne pepper (optional)

Combine all ingredients in bowl.

507 Tangy Barbecue Sauce

MAKES ABOUT 1 CUP

This sauce can be refrigerated for up to four days.

- 4 tablespoons unsalted butter
- 1 small onion, chopped fine
- 2 garlic cloves, minced
- 2 tablespoons lemon juice
- 1 tablespoon pepper
- 1 teaspoon paprika
- 1 teaspoon dry mustard
- ½ teaspoon hot sauce
- ½ teaspoon salt
- 1 (15-ounce) can tomato sauce
- ¼ cup cider vinegar

Melt butter in medium saucepan over medium heat. Add onion and cook, stirring occasionally, until softened, 5 to 7 minutes. Stir in garlic and cook until fragrant, about 30 seconds. Stir in lemon juice, pepper, paprika, mustard, hot sauce, and salt, bring to simmer, and cook for 5 minutes. Add tomato sauce and vinegar and continue to simmer until thickened, about 15 minutes longer.

508 Kentucky Smoked Barbecue Sauce

Increase lemon juice to ¼ cup (2 lemons) and paprika to 2 teaspoons. Add 2 tablespoons packed brown sugar and ½ teaspoon liquid smoke with lemon juice.

509 Louisiana Sweet Barbecue Sauce

Add ¼ cup molasses, 2 tablespoons sweet sherry, and 1 tablespoon packed brown sugar with tomato sauce. Increase vinegar to 6 tablespoons.

510 Spicy Rio Grande Barbecue Sauce

Increase garlic to 4 cloves, lemon juice to ¼ cup (2 lemons), and hot sauce to 1 teaspoon. Add one 7-ounce can diced mild green chiles with lemon juice.

511 STEP BY STEP Removing the Membrane

1 LOOSEN At 1 end of rack, loosen membrane with tip of paring knife.

2 PULL Grab membrane with paper towel and slowly pull off in 1 piece.

512

GRILL HACK

Rib-Rack Stand-In

A barbecue rib rack is a specialized tool that lets you barbecue twice as many ribs at once. However, you probably already own a kitchen tool that could be used as a rib rack. If placed upside down on the grill grate, any fixed V-rack used for roasting easily serves as a rib rack, holding up to six slabs of baby back ribs.

513

RECIPE FOR SUCCESS

Finger Lickin' Pork Ribs

✔ WHY THIS RECIPE WORKS

Country-style ribs are less like baby back ribs or spareribs and more like well-marbled pork chops. They contain both lean loin meat and a section of dark shoulder meat. The trick to cooking these on the grill was getting both parts to cook evenly. We started with a simple dry rub of chili powder, cayenne, salt, and brown sugar, which would encourage browning while adding a complex sweetness. Though cooking the ribs to 175 degrees delivered perfect dark meat, the light meat was woefully dry. On the flip side, pulling the ribs off the grill when they hit 135 to 140 degrees produced juicy light meat but chewy, underdone dark meat. A compromise was in order: 150 degrees. The fat in the ribs moistened the light meat enough that the slight overcooking wasn't noticeable, while the dark meat still had a little tug to it but was nevertheless tender. We started the ribs over the hotter side of the grill for excellent browning, then finished them on the cooler side, where it was easy to baste the ribs with barbecue sauce and allow it to slowly caramelize without burning.

Sweet and Tangy Grilled Country-Style Pork Ribs

SERVES 4 TO 6

When purchasing bone-in country-style ribs, look for those that are approximately 1 inch thick and that contain a large proportion of dark meat. Be sure to carefully trim the pork to reduce the number of flare-ups when the pork is grilled. This recipe requires refrigerating the spice-rubbed ribs for at least 1 hour or up to 24 hours before grilling.

PORK

- 4 teaspoons packed brown sugar
- 1 tablespoon kosher salt
- 1 tablespoon chili powder
- ⅛ teaspoon cayenne pepper
- 4 pounds bone-in country-style pork ribs, trimmed

SAUCE

- 1 cup ketchup
- 5 tablespoons molasses
- 3 tablespoons cider vinegar
- 2 tablespoons Worcestershire sauce
- 2 tablespoons Dijon mustard
- ¼ teaspoon pepper
- 2 tablespoons vegetable oil
- ⅓ cup grated onion
- 1 garlic clove, minced
- 1 teaspoon chili powder
- ¼ teaspoon cayenne pepper

1 FOR THE PORK Combine sugar, salt, chili powder and cayenne in bowl. Pat ribs dry. Rub mixture all over ribs. Wrap ribs in plastic and refrigerate for at least 1 hour or up to 24 hours.

2 FOR THE SAUCE Whisk ketchup, molasses, vinegar, Worcestershire, mustard, and pepper together in bowl. Heat oil in medium saucepan over medium heat until shimmering. Add onion and garlic; cook until onion is softened, 2 to 4 minutes. Add chili powder and cayenne and cook until fragrant, about 30 seconds. Whisk in ketchup mixture and bring to boil. Reduce heat to medium-low and simmer for 5 minutes. Transfer ½ cup of sauce to small bowl for basting and set aside remaining sauce for serving. (Sauce can be refrigerated for up to 1 week.)

3A FOR A CHARCOAL GRILL Open bottom vent halfway. Light large chimney starter filled with charcoal briquettes (6 quarts). When top coals are partially covered with ash, pour over evenly over half of grill. Set cooking grate in place, cover, and open lid vent halfway. Heat grill until hot, about 5 minutes.

3B FOR A GAS GRILL Turn all burners to high, cover and heat grill until hot, about 15 minutes. Leave primary burner on high and turn off other burner(s). (Adjust primary burner as needed to maintain grill temperature around 350 degrees.)

4 Clean and oil cooking grate. Unwrap ribs. Place ribs on hotter side of grill and cook until well browned on both sides, 4 to 7 minutes. Move ribs to cooler side of

514 the Ribs

Racking Up

A standard kettle grill can't hold more than two racks of ribs laid flat. Enter rib racks, which hold at least four slabs upright on the grill grate. The small, angled slots in one otherwise-sturdy product left longer racks drooping and curling over the heat. Another suffered the opposite problem: Its straight (not slanted) walls held the racks upright, and the extra-tall design elevated the ribs within inches of the grill lid. We preferred a rack that stood out for sturdily supporting six racks of ribs. Flipped upside down, it doubles as a roasting rack, big enough to cook a whole chicken or even a small turkey. Its nonstick surface made cleanup a breeze—a plus, since it's not dishwasher-safe.

THE BOTTOM LINE Most models can turn out smoky, moist ribs with good bark, but details like the nonstick coating on the **Charcoal Companion Reversible Rib Rack** can make setup and cleanup much easier.

WINNER

CHARCOAL COMPANION Reversible Rib Rack

Testing Comments This sturdy rack supports six rib racks and cleans up in moments (though not in the dishwasher), thanks to a nonstick coating. It also doubles as a roasting rack, elevating a whole chicken or small turkey above hot grill grates.

RUNNER-UP

WEBER Rib Rack

Testing Comments Though it felt like a lightweight out of the box, this thin, steel-plated, four-slot rack stayed put on the grill and cleaned up nicely in the dishwasher. However, most racks of ribs were too long for the small slots, drooping and curling (though not burning) over the heat.

grill and brush top side with ¼ cup sauce for basting. Cover and cook for 6 minutes. Flip ribs and brush with remaining ¼ cup sauce for basting. Cover and continue to cook until pork registers 150 degrees, 5 to 10 minutes longer. Transfer ribs to serving platter, tent with foil and let rest for 10 minutes. Serve, passing reserved sauce separately.

516 The Real Thing— Cola-Barbecued Ribs

RECIPE FOR SUCCESS

✓ WHY THIS RECIPE WORKS

The premise of cola ribs is simple: Pork ribs are marinated in cola, grilled until tender, and finished with a cola-spiked barbecue sauce. The sweet, spicy flavor of the soda is supposed to lend complexity to the meat and the sauce, but too often the sugary cola burns on the outside of the ribs (even with indirect heat) and the flavor is minimal. For our recipe, we skipped the marinade and added cola flavor in other ways. We started with a spice rub that mimicked and complemented the caramel, vanilla, and warm spices of cola. We covered the ribs with this rub, smoked them over indirect heat on the grill, and then finished them in the oven so they would become tender without overbrowning. For our sauce, we made a super-reduced cola syrup and added it to traditional barbecue sauce ingredients for intense cola flavor. To bring the sauce and ribs together, we brushed plenty of sauce on the ribs before they finished in the oven. Safe from the flame of the grill, the sauce melted into the smoky ribs and carried the distinctive caramel cola flavor right to the bone.

515 Secret to Big Cola Flavor

TEST KITCHEN TIP

The key to adding rich cola flavor to our homemade barbecue sauce was to dramatically reduce the soda before building the sauce.

Before
We start with a full quart of cola.

After
We reduce the quart to a single cup.

Cola-Barbecued Ribs

SERVES 4

For more information on choosing a brand of cola, see "Not All Colas Are Alike." To remove the membrane from the ribs, use a paring knife to loosen one end, then grasp the membrane with a paper towel and peel it off in one piece. If you'd like to use wood chunks instead of wood chips when using a charcoal grill, substitute two medium wood chunks, soaked in water for 1 hour, for the wood chip packet.

SPICE RUB AND RIBS

- 2½ tablespoons packed light brown sugar
- 1½ tablespoons paprika
- 1½ tablespoons pepper
- 2 teaspoons salt
- 1 teaspoon five-spice powder
- 2 (1½-pound) racks baby back ribs, trimmed and membrane removed
- 2 cups wood chips, soaked in water for 15 minutes and drained

COLA BARBECUE SAUCE

- 4 cups cola
- ½ onion, cut into large chunks
- ¼ cup water
- 1¼ cups ketchup
- 1 tablespoon red wine vinegar
- 2 teaspoons yellow mustard
- 1½ teaspoons Worcestershire sauce
- ¼ teaspoon vanilla extract

1 FOR THE SPICE RUB AND RIBS Combine sugar, paprika, pepper, salt, and five-spice powder in small bowl, breaking up any lumps. Set aside 2 tablespoons spice rub for sauce. Pat ribs dry with paper towels and rub each side of each rack with remaining spice rub. (At this point, ribs can be wrapped tightly in plastic wrap and refrigerated for up to 24 hours.)

2 Using large piece of heavy-duty aluminum foil, wrap chips in 8 by 4½-inch foil packet. (Make sure chips do not poke holes in sides or bottom of packet.) Cut 2 evenly spaced 2-inch slits in top of packet.

3A FOR A CHARCOAL GRILL Open bottom vent halfway. Light large chimney starter filled with charcoal briquettes (6 quarts). When top coals are partially covered with ash, pour evenly over half of grill. Place wood chip packet on coals. Set cooking grate in place, cover, and open lid vent halfway. Heat grill until hot and wood chips are smoking, about 5 minutes.

3B FOR A GAS GRILL Remove cooking grate and place wood chip packet directly on primary burner. Set cooking grate in place, turn all burners to high, cover, and heat grill until hot and wood chips are smoking, about 15 minutes. Leave primary burner on high and turn off other burner(s).

4 Clean and oil cooking grate. Place ribs meaty side down on cooler side of grill. Cover (position lid vent over meat if using charcoal) and cook until ribs are deep red and smoky, about 2 hours, flipping and rotating racks halfway through grilling.

5 FOR THE COLA BARBECUE SAUCE While ribs are grilling, heat cola in large saucepan over high heat until boiling. Reduce heat to medium and simmer until cola is reduced to 1 cup, about 40 minutes.

6 While sauce is reducing, process onion and water in food processor until finely ground, about 15 seconds. Transfer mixture to fine-mesh strainer set over bowl and press on solids with rubber spatula to remove as much liquid as possible; discard solids. Whisk ¼ cup strained onion liquid, ketchup, vinegar, mustard, Worcestershire, and reserved spice rub into saucepan with cola syrup. Simmer until slightly thickened, about 10 minutes. Off heat, stir in vanilla.

7 Adjust oven rack to middle position and heat oven to 250 degrees. Brush ribs liberally with sauce and wrap tightly with foil. Arrange foil-wrapped ribs on rimmed baking sheet and cook until ribs are completely tender, about 2 hours. Transfer ribs (still in foil) to cutting board and let rest for 15 minutes. Unwrap ribs and serve, passing remaining sauce at table.

517 TEST KITCHEN TIP
Not All Colas Are Alike

To see if it made a difference what cola we used, we tested cola barbecue sauce made with all the nationally available brands—Coca-Cola, Pepsi, Rally, and RC (as well as diet colas). The winner was clear: Tasters preferred Coca-Cola for its "balanced sweetness" and "warm vanilla" flavor. Rally and RC were passable, but Pepsi tasted "flat" and "one-dimensional." Diet sodas were not acceptable in the sauce.

518 SHOPPING IQ
Five-Spice Powder

Chinese five-spice powder adds a kick that offsets richness in both sweet and savory recipes. In traditional Chinese cooking, the five elements of the cosmos—earth, fire, metal, water, and wood—are represented by five-spice powder. Most blends include cinnamon, cloves, fennel, Sichuan pepper, and star anise, which adds a particular set of piney, licorice notes and tangy heat. We tried six brands in warm sweetened milk (where its flavors would stand out) and in Chinese Braised Beef. The winner and runner-up from our tastings were in the middle range for overall potency and high in star anise. Our favorite won for "lots of licorice" and "anise notes," plus a "piney," "woodsy" taste and a "nice kick" of heat. Our runner-up is a brand whose "five-spice" actually contains seven spices, lending it plenty of "earthy," "complex" flavors.

THE BOTTOM LINE Star anise is a key player in our top pick, **Frontier Natural Products Co-Op Five Spice Powder**.

WINNER

FRONTIER NATURAL PRODUCTS CO-OP Five Spice Powder
Tasting Comments Warmed in milk, this blend had a "rounded," "licorice" flavor that was "woodsy," "sweet," and "aromatic." In braised beef, its "harmonious flavor" had a "nice kick" and was "heaviest on anise, but with cinnamon coming through, too."

RUNNER-UP

DYNASTY Chinese Five Spices
Tasting Comments The "savory" flavor of this blend—which contains seven spices—had an "assertively licorice" aspect in the warmed milk. In braised beef, it was "earthy" and "complex."

519 STEP BY STEP
How to Barbecue

In barbecuing, the goal is to impart a deep, intense smokiness while transforming chewy, tough, fatty cuts into tender, succulent meats. This means a long cooking time (usually several hours) over low heat—hence the barbecue adage: "Low-and-slow is the way to go." Although there is some debate among experts as to the proper heat level for barbecuing, we find a cooking temperature between 250 and 325 degrees to be optimal for most types of meats.

Some barbecue purists would call it heretical to barbecue on a gas grill; we admit that, in comparison with a charcoal grill, a gas grill results in a milder, less-pervasive smoky flavor, but it still yields good results. Either way, you will need to use wood—without smoke you're not barbecuing. See steps 1–2 on page 182 for instruction on setting up wood chips. Remember, you should use wood chunks only with a charcoal grill.

1 USE SPICE RUB Barbecued foods are usually not seared or browned before or after cooking—coating food with a spice rub and using a long cooking time takes care of providing color and crust. Salt and pepper, ground cumin, cinnamon, coriander, or chili powder, and dried herbs such as thyme and bay leaves all work well for a rub. Garlic or onion powder and sugar are also commonly used.

2 BUILD CONCENTRATED FIRE Build half-grill fire or banked fire as directed in recipe so that most of grill has no coals.

3 ADD WOOD CHIPS OR CHUNKS Place foil packet filled with soaked chips on lit coals of charcoal grill or over primary burner on gas grill (or nestle soaked chunks into charcoal).

4 COVER AND COOK ON COOLER SIDE Clean and oil cooking grate. Place food on grill as far from fire as possible. Cover to keep heat, smoke, and moisture trapped inside. Cook, turning as infrequently as possible. Don't open grill more than necessary—otherwise fire might die out before food is cooked.

5 ADD HOT COALS AS NEEDED If necessary, light more coals in chimney and add hot coals to fire to keep it going for entire length of cooking time. For charcoal grill with hinged cooking grate, simply lift part of grate to add hot coals. If not, you will have to don fireproof gloves and remove food and cooking grate to add hot coals. On gas grill, just make sure you have plenty of gas.

6 FINISH IN OVEN Transfer food to rack set in rimmed baking sheet (or other pan as directed); if directed in recipe, wrap in foil to trap steam and speed up cooking process in oven. Finish in oven until meat is fork-tender. Let meat rest, then slice and serve.

520

How Can I Tell When Barbecued Foods Are Done?

Connective tissue makes cuts like brisket or pork shoulder tough. But once the internal temperature of the meat exceeds 140 degrees, the collagen in the connective tissue begins to break down into gelatin, and fat in and around the muscles starts melting and moistening the meat. When held at this temperature, or ideally a bit higher (160 to 180 degrees), for an extended period, tough cuts turn incredibly tender and moist. Low-and-slow barbecuing allows this to happen in a relatively cool grill that won't scorch the exterior. For this process to be successful, barbecued meats must be cooked until they are fork-tender. While it's possible to overcook barbecued meats, undercooking is the bigger risk, so err on the side of cooking too much rather than too little.

521

Hardwood Lump Charcoal versus Briquettes

Irregularly shaped hardwood (or lump) charcoal has gained popularity in recent years, with backyard grillers assuming that it burns hotter than briquettes. To see if that is true, we lit chimneys filled with both types of charcoal and outfitted each grill with seven thermocouple temperature probes. We repeated this test 11 times. The results surprised us: The briquettes burned as hot as, or hotter than, the hardwood every time. The two types of charcoal produced nearly identical heat for about 30 minutes, after which the hardwood charcoal quickly burned out. Meanwhile, the briquettes kept throwing heat for about 2 more hours.

THE BOTTOM LINE Hardwood charcoal is fine for quick grilling tasks but not for long-cooking barbecue. Our recipes call for briquettes, which are cheaper and burn longer.

Hardwood Lump Charcoal   **Briquettes**

522 RECIPE FOR SUCCESS Better-Than-Takeout Barbecued Spareribs

✓ WHY THIS RECIPE WORKS

Chinese sticky ribs are marinated in boldly aromatic seasonings, slow-roasted to tenderness, then glazed and broiled to caramelized perfection. Barbecued ribs, on the other hand, are rubbed with spice and smoked low and slow until they fall off the bone. We wanted to combine the best of both worlds, for tender ribs that were seasoned to the bone, kissed with smoke, and covered with a garlicky, gingery glaze. For ample grill flavor, we determined we'd need to finish our ribs on the grill, so we started with the oven. We skipped marinating and simply cooked the ribs in the oven with the marinade ingredients. After a couple of hours, we moved them to the grill to finish over indirect heat. Instead of using our usual wood chips, we briefly soaked eight black tea bags in water, wrapped them in foil (so they'd burn slower and smoke longer), and set them on the coals. The mellow tea smoke complemented the Asian seasonings perfectly. Adding a cup of red currant jelly to the braising liquid and meat juices made a thick, sticky glaze. We glazed and flipped the ribs every 30 minutes for the last 1 to 1½ hours of cooking, which ensured beautifully shellacked ribs.

Chinese-Style Barbecued Spareribs
SERVES 6

St. Louis–style ribs are also simply called spareribs (see page 331 for more information). To remove the membrane from the ribs, use a paring knife to loosen one end, then grasp the membrane with a paper towel and peel it off in one piece. Cover the edges of the ribs loosely with foil if they begin to burn while grilling.

   2   **(2½- to 3-pound) racks St. Louis–style spareribs, trimmed and membrane removed**
   8   **bags black tea, preferably orange spice or Earl Grey**
1½   **cups ketchup**
   1   **cup soy sauce**
   1   **cup hoisin sauce**
   1   **cup sugar**
   ½   **cup dry sherry**
   6   **garlic cloves, minced**

   2   **tablespoons grated fresh ginger**
   2   **teaspoons toasted sesame oil**
1½   **teaspoons cayenne pepper**
   1   **(13 by 9-inch) disposable aluminum roasting pan**
   1   **cup red currant jelly**

1 Cut rib racks in half. Cover tea bags with water in small bowl and soak for 5 minutes. Squeeze water from tea bags. Using large piece of heavy-duty aluminum foil, wrap soaked tea bags in foil packet and cut several vent holes in top.

2 Adjust oven rack to middle position and heat oven to 300 degrees. Whisk 1 cup ketchup, soy sauce, hoisin, sugar, sherry, garlic, ginger, sesame oil, and cayenne in large bowl; measure out ½ cup and set aside for glaze. Arrange ribs, meaty side down, in disposable pan and pour remaining ketchup mixture over ribs. Cover pan tightly with foil and cook until fat has rendered and meat begins to pull away from bones, 2 to 2½ hours. Transfer ribs to large plate. Pour pan juices into fat separator. Let liquid settle and reserve 1 cup defatted pan juices.

3 Simmer reserved pan juices in medium saucepan over medium-high heat until reduced to ½ cup, about 5 minutes. Stir in jelly, reserved ketchup mixture, and remaining ½ cup ketchup and simmer until reduced to 2 cups, 10 to 12 minutes. Set aside one-third of glaze for serving.

4A FOR A CHARCOAL GRILL Open bottom vent completely. Light large chimney starter filled with charcoal briquettes (6 quarts). When top coals are partially covered with ash, pour evenly over half of grill. Place tea packet on coals. Set cooking grate in place, cover, and open lid vent completely. Heat grill until hot and tea is smoking, about 5 minutes.

4B FOR A GAS GRILL Remove cooking grate and place tea packet directly on primary burner. Set cooking grate in place, turn all burners to high, cover, and heat grill until hot and tea is smoking, about 15 minutes. Leave primary burner on high and turn off other burner(s).

5 Clean and oil cooking grate. Place ribs meaty side down on cooler side of grill; ribs may overlap slightly. Cover and cook until ribs are smoky and edges begin to char, about 30 minutes.

6 Brush ribs with glaze, flip, rotate, and brush again. Cover and cook, brushing with glaze every 30 minutes, until ribs are fully tender and glaze is browned and sticky, 1 to 1½ hours. Transfer ribs to cutting board, tent with foil, and let rest for 10 minutes. Serve with reserved glaze.

TO MAKE AHEAD Ribs and glaze can be prepared through step 3 up to 2 days in advance. Once ribs are cool, wrap tightly in foil and refrigerate. Transfer glaze to bowl, cover with plastic wrap, and refrigerate. Before proceeding with step 4, allow ribs to stand at room temperature for 1 hour. Before proceeding with step 6, microwave glaze until warm, about 1 minute.

523

STEP BY STEP

A Gentler Way to Smoke

Pungent wood smoke overpowered the Asian flavors in this recipe. For a more subtle smoke that enhanced the other seasonings, we turned to tea. To smoke with tea, soak eight black tea bags (we like orange spice or Earl Grey) in water for 5 minutes, then tightly seal them in a foil packet. Cut vent holes in the top of the packet so the smoke can escape and set the packet on the coals.

524 FOOD SCIENCE
Bones Add Flavor, Fat, and Juiciness

Bones have the ability to make juicier, more flavorful roasts, chops, steaks, and ribs. The main structural material of bone is calcium phosphate, an insoluble rigid inorganic compound, but bone also contains a lot of connective tissue. In fact, collagen, the primary protein in connective tissue, comprises about 40 percent of bone. So, given enough cooking time, bones can be made to yield a significant amount of moisture-holding gelatin. When collagen converts to gelatin good things happen. In addition, bone is very porous and thus a relatively poor conductor of heat. This means that the meat located next to the bone doesn't cook as quickly as the rest of the meat—a phenomenon that helps to prevent overcooking and moisture loss and contributes to a noticeably juicier end product. This is why whenever you cut into any bone-in cut of meat, you'll notice that the rarest part is right next to the bone. Bones are also lined with fat, a crucial source of flavor. This is one reason that barbecuing is a popular cooking method for many bone-in cuts. A good number of flavor compounds found in smoke vapor are fat-soluble, and since there is extra fat in the roast or the ribs—courtesy of the bones—the meat is likely to absorb and retain more flavor from the smoke. In addition, as the fat melts during the cooking process, it bastes the meat, increasing the perceived juiciness.

And it doesn't end there. Bones actually add flavor directly to the meat. Here, the credit goes to the marrow, where blood cells are made, which is rich in fat and other flavorful substances. While bone-in cuts cook, the marrow's flavor compounds slowly migrate through the porous bone into the surrounding meat.

525

Sweet on Honey-Mustard Ribs

✓ WHY THIS RECIPE WORKS

Honey-mustard barbecued ribs feature a sticky, sweet sauce with just a touch of heat. We started with lean, tender baby back ribs and cooked them over indirect heat for a couple of hours so they had a chance to pick up smoky flavor and rich brown crust before transferring them to a low oven to finish cooking. We used a deeply flavored sauce that included garlic, honey, Worcestershire, Dijon, and whole-grain mustard. For even more mustard flavor, we used a rub with dry mustard and whole mustard seeds for the ribs. We brushed the ribs with the sauce twice, once before they went into the oven and again just before serving, for a nice sheen.

Honey-Mustard Barbecued Ribs
SERVES 4

If you can't find baby back ribs, St. Louis–style spare-ribs (see page 331) will work fine; just increase the cooking time in the oven in step 5 to 1½ to 2½ hours. To remove the membrane from the ribs, use a paring knife to loosen one end, then grasp the membrane with a paper towel and peel it off in one piece. If you'd like to use wood chunks instead of wood chips when using a charcoal grill, substitute two medium wood chunks, soaked in water for 1 hour, for the wood chip packet.

- ¼ cup mustard seeds
- 2 tablespoons dry mustard
- 2 tablespoons packed brown sugar
- 1 tablespoon salt
- 1 tablespoon garlic powder
- 1 tablespoon pepper
- 2 (1½-pound) racks baby back ribs, trimmed and membrane removed
- 1 recipe Honey-Mustard Barbecue Sauce (recipe follows)
- 2 cups wood chips

1 Combine mustard seeds, dry mustard, sugar, salt, garlic powder, and pepper in bowl. Pat ribs dry with paper towels, and rub evenly with spice mixture. Wrap ribs in plastic wrap and let sit at room temperature for at least 1 hour, or refrigerate for up to 24 hours. (If refrigerated, let sit at room temperature for 1 hour before grilling.) Measure out ½ cup barbecue sauce and set aside for cooking; set aside remaining sauce for serving.

2 Just before grilling, soak wood chips in water for 15 minutes, then drain. Using large piece of heavy-duty aluminum foil, wrap chips in 8 by 4½-inch foil packet. (Make sure chips do not poke holes in sides or bottom of packet.) Cut 2 evenly spaced 2-inch slits in top of packet.

3A FOR A CHARCOAL GRILL Open bottom vent halfway. Light large chimney starter three-quarters filled with charcoal briquettes (4½ quarts). When coals are partially covered with ash, pour them into steeply banked pile against side of grill. Place wood chip packet on top of coals. Set cooking grate in place, cover, and open lid vent halfway. Heat grill until hot and wood chips are smoking, about 5 minutes.

3B FOR A GAS GRILL Remove cooking grate and place wood chip packet directly on primary burner. Set cooking grate in place, turn all burners to high, cover, and heat grill until hot and wood chips are smoking, about 15 minutes. Turn primary burner to medium-high and turn off other burner(s). (Adjust primary burner as needed to maintain grill temperature around 325 degrees.)

4 Clean and oil cooking grate. Unwrap ribs. Place ribs meaty side down on cooler side of grill; ribs may overlap slightly. Cover (position lid vent over meat if using charcoal) and cook until ribs are deep red and smoky, about 2 hours, flipping and rotating racks halfway through grilling. During final 20 minutes of grilling, adjust oven rack to middle position and heat oven to 250 degrees.

5 Remove ribs from grill, brush evenly with ½ cup sauce for cooking, and wrap tightly with foil. Lay foil-wrapped ribs on rimmed baking sheet and cook in oven until tender and fork inserted into ribs meets no resistance, 1 to 2 hours.

6 Remove ribs from oven and let rest, still wrapped, for 30 minutes. Unwrap ribs and brush evenly with some of sauce reserved for serving. Slice ribs between bones and serve with remaining sauce.

526 Honey-Mustard Barbecue Sauce

MAKES ABOUT 2 CUPS

This sauce goes with our Honey-Mustard Barbecued Ribs, but it also pairs well with Classic Barbecued Chicken (page 70).

- 8 tablespoons unsalted butter
- 2 garlic cloves, minced
- ¾ cup honey
- ⅓ cup Dijon mustard
- ⅓ cup whole-grain mustard
- ¼ cup Worcestershire sauce
-    Salt and pepper

Melt butter in small saucepan over low heat. Stir in garlic and cook until fragrant, about 30 seconds. Whisk in honey, mustards, and Worcestershire. Let cool to room temperature, season with salt and pepper to taste, and serve. (Sauce can be refrigerated for up to 4 days.)

527 Barbecue Basting Brushes

GADGETS & GEAR

We wanted a good barbecue basting brush that allowed us to neatly and safely baste our food, even over the highest grilling heat. We tested a sampling of brushes by using them to apply a light oil mixture to bruschetta and a viscous barbecue sauce to chicken pieces. We also simulated normal wear and tear by leaving the brushes next to the grill, exposing them to flare-ups, and putting them through numerous washings.

In the end, we found three features that characterized a comfortable and safe barbecue basting brush: bristle material, handle material, and handle length. Bristles made from silicone were the clear favorite over nylon and boar-bristle, which were damaged both by the high heat of the grill and by the dishwasher. Thin-bristled silicone brushes were best for plain oils and thick sauces alike. As for handles, heat-resistant Bakelite, rubber, and plastic were ideal, and we determined 8 inches to be the minimum length needed to comfortably brush an item at the back of the grill. We were a little surprised, however, to discover that a handle can be too long; brush handles measuring more than 13 inches didn't allow enough precision and control.

THE BOTTOM LINE Choose a brush like **Elizabeth Karmel's Grill Friends Barbecue Brush** made from materials that can handle both the heat of the grill and a trip through the dishwasher, and make sure the handle is between 8 and 13 inches. With its angled brush head and good handle length, this brush let testers baste each food item comfortably and precisely, no matter the shape of the food or its location on the grill. The brush was easy to clean, both in the dishwasher and by hand. (The head can be removed to wash any sticky sauce stuck at the seam of the brush base.) The brush head had enough narrow silicone bristles to do an excellent job of picking up sticky, viscous barbecue sauce and an acceptable job of picking up the thinner oil mixture. This brush was also heat-resistant.

529

RECIPE FOR SUCCESS

Ribs with Fiery Flavor

✔ WHY THIS RECIPE WORKS

Armed with multiple racks of ribs and the entire contents of our spice cabinet and pantry, we set out to develop a recipe for really great (and seriously hot) atomic ribs. We used our basic grill-to-oven method, which allows the meat to develop deep smoky flavor before moving to a low oven to finish. We cranked up the heat in the spice rub with paprika, chili powder, pepper, and cayenne. Salt and brown sugar added flavor and a touch of sweetness for balance. Mustard contributed bright flavor and a thick consistency that helped the sauce cling to the ribs. Heat in the sauce came from habanero chiles and dry mustard. We brushed the ribs with the sauce just before serving so it retained its pungent flavor.

Atomic Ribs

SERVES 4 TO 6

Buy St. Louis–style ribs, which are more manageable than untrimmed pork spareribs. If you can't find them, baby back ribs will work fine; just reduce the cooking time in the oven in step 6 to 1 to 2 hours. To remove the membrane from the ribs, use a paring knife to loosen one end, then grasp the membrane with a paper towel and peel it off in one piece. This sauce is very spicy. For less heat, use only one habanero and remove the ribs and/or seeds before mincing. If you'd like to use wood

chunks instead of wood chips when using a charcoal grill, substitute two medium wood chunks, soaked in water for 1 hour, for the wood chip packet.

SAUCE

¼ cup sliced pickled banana peppers, chopped fine, and 2 tablespoons pickling liquid

¼ cup lemon juice (2 lemons)

¼ cup vegetable oil

¼ cup yellow mustard

4 scallions, sliced thin

3 tablespoons dry mustard

2 tablespoons chili sauce

2 tablespoons packed brown sugar

3 garlic cloves, minced

2 habanero chiles, stemmed and minced
    Salt and pepper

RIBS

3 tablespoons paprika

2 tablespoons chili powder

2 tablespoons packed brown sugar

2 tablespoons pepper

1 tablespoon salt

1 tablespoon cayenne pepper

2 (2½ to 3-pound) full racks pork spareribs, preferably St. Louis–style, trimmed and membrane removed

2 cups wood chips

1 FOR THE SAUCE Whisk all ingredients together in bowl. Season with salt and pepper to taste. (Sauce can be refrigerated for up to 4 days.)

528 FOOD SCIENCE
Don't Get Burned Up Over Chiles

Capsaicin is the chemical in chiles responsible for their heat. It binds to receptors on the tongue or skin, triggering a pain response. Soap and water help lessen the burn on skin a bit, but in our tests oil, vinegar, tomato juice, and baking soda didn't help at all. As for the mouth, water and beer failed, and milk had only a slight impact. What worked on both the skin and the mouth? Hydrogen peroxide. Peroxide changes the structure of capsaicin molecules, rendering them incapable of bonding with our receptors. It works even better in the presence of a base like baking soda: Use a solution of ⅛ teaspoon of baking soda, 1 tablespoon of water, and 1 tablespoon of hydrogen peroxide to wash the affected area or as a mouthwash (swish vigorously for 30 seconds) to tone down a chile's stinging burn. Always keep peroxide and baking soda away from your eyes.

2 FOR THE RIBS Combine paprika, chili powder, sugar, pepper, salt, and cayenne in bowl. Pat ribs dry with paper towels and rub evenly with spice mixture. Wrap ribs in plastic wrap and let sit at room temperature for at least 1 hour, or refrigerate for up to 24 hours. (If refrigerated, let sit at room temperature for 1 hour before grilling.)

3 Just before grilling, soak wood chips in water for 15 minutes, then drain. Using large piece of heavy-duty aluminum foil, wrap chips in 8 by 4½-inch foil packet. (Make sure chips do not poke holes in sides or bottom of packet.) Cut 2 evenly spaced 2-inch slits in top of packet.

4A FOR A CHARCOAL GRILL Open bottom vent halfway. Light large chimney starter three-quarters filled with charcoal briquettes (4½ quarts). When top coals are partially covered with ash, pour into steeply banked pile against side of grill. Place wood chip packet on top of coals. Set cooking grate in place, cover, and open lid vent halfway. Heat grill until hot and wood chips are smoking, about 5 minutes.

4B FOR A GAS GRILL Remove cooking grate and place wood chip packet directly on primary burner. Set cooking grate in place, turn all burners to high, cover, and heat grill until hot and wood chips are smoking, about 15 minutes. Turn primary burner to medium-high and turn off other burner(s). (Adjust primary burner as needed to maintain grill temperature around 325 degrees.)

5 Clean and oil cooking grate. Unwrap ribs. Place ribs, meaty side down, on cooler side of grill; ribs may overlap slightly. Cover (position lid vent over meat if using charcoal) and cook until ribs are deep red and smoky, about 2 hours, flipping and rotating racks halfway through grilling. During final 20 minutes of grilling, adjust oven rack to middle position and heat oven to 250 degrees.

6 Remove ribs from grill and wrap tightly with foil. Arrange foil-wrapped ribs on rimmed baking sheet and cook in oven until tender and fork inserted into ribs meets no resistance, 1½ to 2½ hours.

7 Remove ribs from oven and let rest, still wrapped, for 30 minutes. Unwrap ribs and brush with half of sauce. Slice ribs between bones and serve with remaining sauce.

531 RECIPE FOR SUCCESS Pass-the-Napkins Ribs

✓ WHY THIS RECIPE WORKS

For barbecue fans who like to get their hands dirty, Kansas City sticky ribs are just the ticket. For smoky flavor, tender meat, and signature sticky sauce without hours by the grill, we focused on keeping the ribs moist while speeding up their cooking time. After rubbing the meat with a spicy blend of paprika, brown sugar, salt, pepper, and cayenne, we readied our grill. Wood chips gave the ribs great smoky flavor, and we kept the meat moist by capturing the escaping steam with a sheet of aluminum foil placed directly on top of the ribs. Even on the cooler side of the grill, the ribs still developed a nice crusty exterior. After spreading on a thick coating of our homemade barbecue sauce, we wrapped the ribs tightly in foil to prevent the sauce from charring, added more hot coals and wood chips, and let the ribs cook for a final hour. More sauce brushed on before serving added a final layer of flavor.

Kansas City Sticky Ribs

SERVES 4 TO 6

We like St. Louis–style racks, but if you can't find them, baby back ribs will work fine. To remove the membrane from the ribs, use a paring knife to loosen one end, then grasp the membrane with a paper towel and peel it off in one piece. If you'd like to use wood chunks instead of wood chips when using a charcoal grill, substitute two medium wood chunks, soaked in water for 1 hour, for the wood chip packets.

RIBS
- 3 tablespoons paprika
- 2 tablespoons packed brown sugar
- 1 tablespoon salt
- 1 tablespoon pepper
- ¼ teaspoon cayenne pepper
- 2 (2½- to 3-pound) full racks pork spareribs, preferably St. Louis–style, trimmed and membrane removed
- 2 cups wood chips
- 1 (13 by 9-inch) disposable aluminum roasting pan (if using charcoal)

SAUCE
- 1 tablespoon vegetable oil
- 1 onion, chopped fine
  Salt and pepper
- 4 cups chicken broth
- 1 cup root beer
- 1 cup cider vinegar
- 1 cup dark corn syrup
- ½ cup molasses
- ½ cup tomato paste
- ½ cup ketchup
- 2 tablespoons brown mustard
- 1 tablespoon hot sauce
- ½ teaspoon garlic powder
- ¼ teaspoon liquid smoke

1 FOR THE RIBS Combine paprika, sugar, salt, pepper, and cayenne in bowl. Pat ribs dry with paper towels and rub evenly with spice mixture. Wrap ribs in plastic wrap and let sit at room temperature for at least 1 hour, or refrigerate for up to 24 hours. (If refrigerated, let sit at room temperature for 1 hour before grilling.)

2 FOR THE SAUCE Meanwhile, heat oil in large saucepan over medium heat until shimmering. Add onion and pinch salt and cook until softened, 5 to 7 minutes.

530 FOOD SCIENCE What Exactly Is Liquid Smoke?

Many people assume that the process of making liquid smoke involves distasteful chemical shenanigans, but that's not the case. Liquid smoke is made by collecting smoke from smoldering wood chips in a condenser that quickly cools the vapors, causing them to liquefy. The droplets are captured and filtered twice before being bottled. (Once, we were crazy enough to try making liquid smoke in the test kitchen: The process took an entire day, and all we got was 3 tablespoons! Never again.) Our top-rated brand, **Wright's Liquid Smoke**, contains nothing but smoke and water. Be forewarned, this stuff is extremely concentrated—a few drops go a long way.

Whisk in broth, root beer, vinegar, corn syrup, molasses, tomato paste, ketchup, mustard, hot sauce, and garlic powder. Bring sauce to simmer and cook, stirring occasionally, until reduced to 4 cups, about 1 hour. Off heat, stir in liquid smoke. Let sauce cool to room temperature. Season with salt and pepper to taste. Measure out 1 cup barbecue sauce for cooking; set aside remaining sauce for serving. (Sauce can be refrigerated for up to 4 days.)

3 Just before grilling, soak wood chips in water for 15 minutes, then drain. Using large piece of heavy-duty aluminum foil, wrap 1 cup chips in 8 by 4½-inch foil packet. (Make sure chips do not poke holes in sides or bottom of packet.) Repeat with remaining 1 cup chips. Cut 2 evenly spaced 2-inch slits in top of each packet.

4A FOR A CHARCOAL GRILL Open bottom vent halfway and place disposable pan on 1 side of grill. Light large chimney starter three-quarters filled with charcoal briquettes (4½ quarts). When top coals are partially covered with ash, pour into steeply banked pile against other side of grill. Place 1 wood chip packet on coals. Set cooking grate in place, cover, and open lid vent halfway. Heat grill until hot and wood chips are smoking, about 5 minutes.

4B FOR A GAS GRILL Remove cooking grate and place wood chip packet directly on primary burner. Set grate in place, turn all burners to high, cover, and heat grill until hot and wood chips are smoking, about 15 minutes. Turn primary burner to medium-high and turn off other burner(s). (Adjust primary burner as needed to maintain grill temperature around 325 degrees.)

5 Clean and oil cooking grate. Unwrap ribs and place them meaty side down on cooler side of grill; ribs may overlap slightly. Place sheet of foil directly on top of ribs. Cover (position lid vent over meat if using charcoal) and cook until ribs are deep red and smoky, about 2 hours, flipping and rotating racks halfway through grilling. During final 20 minutes of grilling, if using charcoal, light another large chimney starter three-quarters filled with charcoal briquettes (4½ quarts). When top coals are partially covered with ash, pour hot coals on top of spent coals and top with remaining wood chip packet. Flip and rotate ribs and cook, covered, for 1 hour.

6 Remove ribs from grill, brush evenly with 1 cup sauce for cooking, and wrap tightly with foil. Lay foil-wrapped ribs on grill and cook until tender, about 1 hour longer.

7 Transfer ribs (still in foil) to carving board and let rest for 30 minutes. Unwrap ribs and brush with additional sauce. Slice ribs between bones and serve with remaining sauce.

532 STEP BY STEP
How to Make Tender Ribs

1 REMOVE THE MEMBRANE Ribs have a papery membrane on the underside that can make it hard to pull the meat off the bone. Before cooking, loosen the membrane with the tip of a paring knife and, with the aid of a paper towel, pull it off slowly, all in 1 piece.

2 COVER WITH FOIL Barbecuing the ribs for hours on end won't guarantee super-tender meat. Fortunately, you can trap steam and make the ribs tender by covering them with sheets of aluminum foil.

3 WRAP IT UP During the last hour of barbecuing, wrap the ribs tightly in the foil to keep them from drying out. After removing the ribs from the grill, let them rest for 30 minutes, still wrapped.

533 RECIPE FOR SUCCESS
Windy City Ribs

✓ WHY THIS RECIPE WORKS

Chicago-style barbecued ribs recipes typically call for smoking the ribs at about 200 degrees for at least 8 hours. This slow-and-low cooking method delivers the moist, tender meat that defines Chicago ribs. We wanted to replicate the same method at home. To shorten the cooking time, we started our recipe on the grill—where the ribs picked up good color and smoke flavor—and finished them in the oven. Placing pans of water on the grill and in the oven steamed the ribs, making them extra moist and tender. For Chicago-style barbecue sauce, we used celery salt, allspice, and plenty of cayenne pepper.

Chicago-Style Barbecued Ribs

SERVES 4 TO 6

The dry spices are used to flavor both the rub and the barbecue sauce. To remove the membrane from the ribs, use a paring knife to loosen one end, then grasp the membrane with a paper towel and peel it off in one piece. If you'd like to use wood chunks instead of wood chips when using a charcoal grill, substitute one medium wood chunk, soaked in water for 1 hour, for the wood chip packet. When removing the ribs from the oven, be careful to not spill the hot water in the bottom of the baking sheet.

SPICE RUB AND RIBS

- 1 tablespoon dry mustard
- 1 tablespoon paprika
- 1 tablespoon packed dark brown sugar
- 1½ teaspoons garlic powder
- 1½ teaspoons onion powder
- 1½ teaspoons celery salt
- 1 teaspoon cayenne pepper
- ½ teaspoon ground allspice
- 2 (1½-pound) racks baby back ribs, trimmed and membrane removed
- 1 cup wood chips
- 1 (13 by 9-inch) disposable aluminum roasting pan

SAUCE

- 1¼ cups ketchup
- ¼ cup molasses
- ¼ cup cider vinegar
- ¼ cup water
- ⅛ teaspoon liquid smoke

1 FOR THE SPICE RUB AND RIBS Combine dry mustard, paprika, sugar, garlic powder, onion powder, celery salt, cayenne, and allspice in bowl. Measure out 2 tablespoons spice mixture and set aside for sauce. Pat ribs dry with paper towels and rub evenly with remaining spice mixture. Wrap ribs in plastic wrap and let sit at room temperature for at least 1 hour, or refrigerate for up to 24 hours. (If refrigerated, let sit at room temperature for 1 hour before grilling.)

2 FOR THE SAUCE Whisk all ingredients with reserved 2 tablespoons spice rub in bowl. Just before grilling, soak wood chips in water for 15 minutes, then drain. Using large piece of heavy-duty aluminum foil, wrap chips in 8 by 4½-inch foil packet. (Make sure chips do not poke holes in sides or bottom of packet.) Cut 2 evenly spaced 2-inch slits in top of packet.

3A FOR A CHARCOAL GRILL Open bottom vent completely. Light large chimney starter filled with charcoal briquettes (6 quarts). Place disposable pan on 1 side of grill and add 2 cups water to pan. When top coals are partially covered with ash, pour into steeply banked pile against other side of grill. Place wood chip packet on coals. Set cooking grate in place, cover, and open lid vent completely. Heat grill until hot and wood chips are smoking, about 5 minutes.

3B FOR A GAS GRILL Remove cooking grate and place wood chip packet directly on primary burner. Place disposable pan on secondary burner and add 2 cups water to pan. Set cooking grate in place, turn all burners to high, cover, and heat grill until hot and wood chips are smoking, about 15 minutes. Turn primary burner to medium and turn off other burner(s). (Adjust primary burner as needed to maintain grill temperature around 325 degrees.)

4 Clean and oil cooking grate. Unwrap ribs and place meaty side down on cooler side of grill; ribs may overlap slightly. Cover (position lid vent over meat if using charcoal) and cook until ribs are deep red and smoky, about 1½ hours, flipping and rotating racks halfway through grilling. During final 20 minutes of grilling, adjust oven rack to middle position and heat oven to 250 degrees.

5 Set wire rack in rimmed baking sheet and add just enough water to cover pan bottom. Transfer ribs to rack and cover tightly with foil. Continue to cook ribs in oven until fork slips easily in and out of meat, 1½ to 2 hours.

6 Remove ribs from oven, transfer to platter, tent with foil, and let rest for 30 minutes. Brush ribs evenly with half of sauce. Slice ribs between bones and serve with remaining sauce.

534

GRILL HACK

Easiest Grill Cleaning

No matter how you do it, emptying a kettle grill of cool ashes is a messy procedure. You can neaten things up by fashioning a grill scoop out of a plastic 1-quart or half-gallon milk jug with a handle.

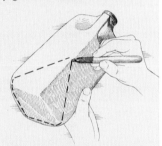

1 CUT Cut off bottom corner of jug to form scoop.

2 SCOOP Plastic conforms to curve of grill bottom, which makes it easier to collect more ashes with single sweep.

535

RECIPE FOR SUCCESS

Ribs with Bark and Bite

✔ WHY THIS RECIPE WORKS

Rather than smothering ribs in sauce, Memphis pit masters rely on a potent spice rub to infuse the meat with unmistakable flavor. To replicate that Memphis-style rub at home, we stared at our spice rack and chose a handful of spices that wouldn't taste too harsh straight from the jar. Beginning with salt and brown sugar for its subtle molasses notes, we combined paprika, chili powder, pepper, garlic powder, onion powder, and cayenne to create a perfectly balanced rub. We worked it over our ribs and then let them sit while the wood chips soaked. After grilling for the first hour, we flipped the ribs and brushed them with a sweet-and-sour mop of apple cider and cider vinegar, repeating this step every half-hour. With the smoky crust in place, wrapping the ribs in foil and moving them to the oven to finish ensured an irresistibly tender texture. We sprinkled them with more of the spice rub and gave them 2 minutes under the broiler for a final browning. While the ribs rested, we reduced the mop into a dipping sauce, adding some reserved spice rub and hot sauce for extra heat.

Memphis Spareribs

SERVES 4 TO 6

These ribs are moderately spicy; adjust the cayenne and hot sauce as you wish. To remove the membrane from the ribs, use a paring knife to loosen one end, then grasp the membrane with a paper towel and peel it off in one piece. If you'd like to use wood chunks instead of wood chips when using a charcoal grill, substitute two medium wood chunks, soaked in water for 1 hour, for the wood chip packet. To reheat leftovers, place the ribs in an ovensafe dish, add a few tablespoons of water, cover with aluminum foil, and place in a 250-degree oven for 20 to 30 minutes.

¼	cup paprika
3	tablespoons packed brown sugar
2	tablespoons chili powder
	Salt and pepper
2	teaspoons garlic powder
2	teaspoons onion powder
1	teaspoon cayenne pepper

2	(2½- to 3-pound) racks St. Louis–style spareribs, trimmed and membrane removed
3	cups apple cider
1	cup cider vinegar
2	cups wood chips
2	teaspoons hot sauce

1 Combine paprika, sugar, chili powder, 2 tablespoons pepper, 1 tablespoon salt, garlic powder, onion powder, and cayenne in bowl. Measure out 7 teaspoons of spice mixture and set aside for finishing ribs and sauce. Pat ribs dry with paper towels and rub evenly with remaining spice mixture. Wrap ribs in plastic wrap and let sit at room temperature for at least 1 hour, or refrigerate for up to 24 hours.

2 Bring cider and vinegar to simmer in small saucepan; remove from heat and cover to keep warm. Just before grilling, soak wood chips in water for 15 minutes, then drain. Using large piece of heavy-duty aluminum foil, wrap chips in 8 by 4½-inch foil packet. (Make sure chips do not poke holes in sides or bottom of packet.) Cut 2 evenly spaced 2-inch slits in top of packet.

3A FOR A CHARCOAL GRILL Open bottom vent halfway. Light large chimney starter three-quarters filled with charcoal briquettes (4½ quarts). When top coals are partially covered with ash, pour into steeply banked pile against side of grill. Place wood chip packet on coals. Set cooking grate in place, cover, and open lid vent halfway. Heat grill until hot and wood chips are smoking, about 5 minutes.

3B FOR A GAS GRILL Remove cooking grate and place wood chip packet directly on primary burner. Set cooking grate in place, turn all burners to high, cover, and heat grill until hot and wood chips are smoking, about 15 minutes. Turn primary burner to medium-high and turn off other burner(s). (Adjust primary burner as needed to maintain grill temperature around 325 degrees.)

4 Clean and oil cooking grate. Unwrap ribs and place meaty side down on cooler side of grill; ribs may overlap slightly. Cover (position lid vent over meat if using charcoal) and cook until ribs are deep red and smoky, about 2 hours, flipping, rotating, and switching ribs and basting with warm cider mop every 30 minutes. During final 20 minutes of grilling, adjust oven rack to middle position and heat oven to 250 degrees.

5 Transfer ribs, meaty side up, to rimmed baking sheet and cover tightly with foil. Cook ribs in oven until tender and fork inserted into ribs meets no resistance, 1½ to 2½ hours, basting with warm mop every 30 minutes.

6 Remove ribs from oven and unwrap. Adjust oven rack 6 inches from broiler element and heat broiler. Sprinkle ribs with 2 tablespoons reserved spice mixture and broil until browned and dry on surface and spices are fragrant, about 2 minutes, flipping ribs halfway through broiling.

7 Remove ribs from oven, tent with foil, and let rest for 30 minutes. While ribs rest, add remaining 1 teaspoon spice mixture to remaining mop and simmer, uncovered, until thickened and saucy, 10 to 15 minutes. Stir in hot sauce and season with salt and pepper to taste. Slice ribs between bones and serve with sauce.

536 SHOPPING IQ Meat Me in St. Louis

Got your map out? "Memphis" and "Kansas City" refer to a style of cooking spareribs. "St. Louis," however, refers to a particular cut of spareribs. A full rack of spareribs contains the brisket bone and surrounding brisket meat and usually weighs around 3½ pounds. The brisket bone and breast meat are often trimmed off to produce a narrower, rectangular rack. These are St. Louis spareribs, and each rack weighs about 2¾ pounds.

We prefer the St. Louis ribs because they fit side by side on the grill, they cook more quickly, and they are easier to slice and eat. That said, regular spareribs work fine. You may need to overlap the racks on the grill, and you can count on a cooking time that's closer to four, rather than three, hours.

537 GADGETS & GEAR Smoker Bags

The SAVU Smoker Bag wowed us with a simple system in which a mixture of ground wood chips, hardwood syrup, and natural sugars are contained within the walls of a large foil bag. This allowed the smoke to pass through small perforations in the foil to get to the food contained within. The ribs emerged juicy, tender, and—after a quick run under the broiler—nicely crusted.

THE BOTTOM LINE While it's possible to get great smoky meat without one, smoker bags like the ones from **SAVU** ($3.50 each) are an easy, inexpensive shortcut to perfect ribs.

539 RECIPE FOR SUCCESS
Ribs for the Whole Gang

✔ WHY THIS RECIPE WORKS

For these saucy Memphis wet ribs, a potent spice rub performs double duty, seasoning the meat and creating the backbone for our barbecue sauce. Tying two racks together allowed us to cook four hefty racks of ribs at once, double our usual yield on the grill. This helped the long cooking time feel more like it was worth it and made this recipe a standout option for summer parties. To keep the ribs moist, we grilled them over indirect heat and basted them with a traditional "mop" of juice and vinegar. After a few hours of smoking them on the grill, we brushed the ribs with our flavorful barbecue sauce and transferred them to the steady, even heat of the oven to finish tenderizing.

Memphis-Style Wet Ribs for a Crowd
SERVES 8 TO 12

To remove the membrane from the ribs, use a paring knife to loosen one end, then grasp the membrane with a paper towel and peel it off in one piece. You'll get the best results from a charcoal grill. If you're cooking with gas, you'll need a large grill with at least three burners. If you'd like to use wood chunks instead of wood chips when using a charcoal grill, substitute two medium wood chunks, soaked in water for 1 hour, for the wood chip packet.

SPICE RUB
- ¼ cup paprika
- 2 tablespoons packed brown sugar
- 2 tablespoons salt
- 2 teaspoons pepper
- 2 teaspoons onion powder
- 2 teaspoons granulated garlic

BARBECUE SAUCE
- 1½ cups ketchup
- ¾ cup apple juice
- ¼ cup molasses
- ¼ cup cider vinegar
- ¼ cup Worcestershire sauce
- 2 tablespoons yellow mustard
- 2 teaspoons pepper

MOP
- ½ cup apple juice
- ¼ cup cider vinegar
- 1 tablespoon yellow mustard

RIBS
- 4 (2½- to 3-pound) racks St. Louis–style spareribs, trimmed and membrane removed
- 2 cups wood chips, soaked in water for 15 minutes and drained
- 1 (13 by 9-inch) disposable aluminum roasting pan (if using charcoal) or 1 (8½ by 4½-inch) disposable aluminum loaf pan (if using gas)

1 FOR THE SPICE RUB Combine all ingredients in bowl.

2 FOR THE BARBECUE SAUCE Combine ketchup, apple juice, molasses, vinegar, Worcestershire, mustard, and 2 tablespoons spice rub in medium saucepan and bring to boil over medium heat. Reduce heat to medium-low and simmer until thickened and reduced to 2 cups, about 20 minutes. Off heat, stir in pepper; set aside.

3 FOR THE MOP Whisk apple juice, vinegar, mustard, and ¼ cup barbecue sauce together in bowl.

538 STEP BY STEP
Making Rib Bundles

Most rib recipes for backyard grills make only one or two racks. Our ribs were so good that we wanted more. We tied racks of ribs together with kitchen twine (with the meaty sides facing out) to create two two-rack bundles that'll feed a small party.

4 FOR THE RIBS Pat ribs dry with paper towels and season all over with remaining spice rub Place 1 rack of ribs, meaty side down, on cutting board. Place second rack of ribs, meaty side up, directly on top of first rack, arranging thick end over tapered end. Tie racks together at 2-inch intervals with kitchen twine. Repeat with remaining 2 racks of ribs. (You should have 2 bundles of ribs.) Using large piece of heavy-duty aluminum foil, wrap chips in 8 by 4 ½-inch foil packet. (Make sure chips do not poke holes in sides or bottom of packet.) Cut 2 evenly spaced, 2-inch slits in top of packet.

5A FOR A CHARCOAL GRILL Open bottom vent halfway. Place disposable roasting pan on 1 side of grill and add 2 quarts water to pan. Arrange 3 quarts unlit charcoal briquettes on other side of grill. Light large chimney starter half filled with charcoal briquettes (3 quarts). When top coals are partially covered with ash, pour evenly over unlit coals. Place wood chip packet on coals. Set cooking grate in place, cover, and open lid vent halfway. Heat grill until hot and wood chips are smoking, about 5 minutes.

5B FOR A GAS GRILL Remove cooking grate, place wood chip packet and disposable loaf pan directly on primary burner and add 2 cups water to pan. Set cooking grate in place, turn primary burner to high (leave other burners off), cover, and heat grill until hot and wood chips are smoking, about 15 minutes. (Adjust primary burner as needed to maintain grill temperature of 275 to 300 degrees.)

6 Clean and oil cooking grate. Place ribs on cooler side of grill (ribs may overlap slightly) and baste with one-third of mop. Cover (position lid vent over meat if using charcoal) and cook for 2 hours, flipping and switching positions of ribs and basting again with half of remaining mop halfway through grilling. During final 20 minutes of grilling, adjust oven racks to upper-middle and lower-middle positions and heat oven to 300 degrees.

7 Line 2 rimmed baking sheets with foil. Cut kitchen twine from racks. Transfer 2 racks, meaty side up, to each sheet. Baste with remaining mop and cook in oven for 2 hours, switching and rotating sheets halfway through cooking.

8 Remove ribs from oven and brush evenly with ½ cup barbecue sauce. Return to oven and continue to cook until tender, basting with ½ cup barbecue sauce and

rotating and switching sheets twice during cooking, about 45 minutes. (Ribs do not need to be flipped and should remain meaty side up during baking.)

9 Transfer ribs to carving board. Brush evenly with remaining ½ cup barbecue sauce, tent with foil, and let rest for 20 minutes. Cut ribs between bones to separate. Serve.

540 GADGETS & GEAR
Basting Pots

Basting food while grilling can be messy; a pot that holds the sauce promises to make it easier. We tried out four, all sold in sets with silicone basting brushes, by holding the pots while slathering barbecue sauce on chicken and olive oil on vegetables. The material proved critical: Cast iron can sit right on the grill grate, whereas stainless-steel models are not heatproof. A pot that can rest on the grate is closer to the food and heats the sauce so that it can be served tableside. Our winner had a comfy handle, a stable shape that won't tip, and handy pouring spouts. While its brush was slightly shorter than we liked, it slathered sauce evenly and cleaned up quickly.

THE BOTTOM LINE Look for a pot made from a material that can withstand the hot temperatures of the grill like the cast iron option from **Lodge**; your basting pot is no better than a normal bowl if you can't set it on the grate.

WINNER

LODGE Sauce Kit
Price $21.95
Testing Comments This cast-iron pot has a comfortable handle and a sturdy design that works both on and off the grill. The brush has silicone bristles that cleaned up easily and held the sauce well. The only drawback was a slightly-too-short brush handle that put our hands too close to the flames. When we substituted our favorite basting brush, the pot worked like a charm.

RUNNER-UP

CHARCOAL COMPANION Sauce Pot and Silicone Basting Brush Set
Price $15.32
Testing Comments This cast-iron pot can rest right on the grill grate and came with a slightly longer-handled brush—helpful for keeping our hands away from the heat. But the pot's awkward, short handle features two tall ridges (designed to cradle the brush) that dug into our hands as we held it while brushing sauce on food.

541 RECIPE FOR SUCCESS

Smoked Ribs with a Secret Ingredient

✓ WHY THIS RECIPE WORKS

Corncob-smoking, a South Dakota specialty, may seem odd, but it gives meat a subtle smokiness hardwoods can't match. For barbecued ribs with mild, nutty sweetness, but without the complicated barbecuing rig, we layered charcoal on our grill with fresh corn-cobs (with the kernels removed) and a foil packet of cornmeal. The cornmeal gave the ribs an initial blast of smoky flavor, and the fresh cobs offered long-lasting smoke and a nutty aroma. We basted the ribs with a simple ketchup-based barbecue sauce with plenty of garlic and some celery seeds for sticky, sweet ribs that we couldn't get enough of.

South Dakota Corncob-Smoked Ribs
SERVES 4 TO 6

To remove the membrane from the ribs, use a paring knife to loosen one end, then grasp the membrane with a paper towel and peel it off in one piece. A gas grill can't do these corncob ribs justice, so please use charcoal. The test kitchen's favorite ketchup is Heinz Organic.

SAUCE
- 1 cup ketchup
- ¼ cup water
- 1 tablespoon pepper
- 1 tablespoon onion powder
- 1 tablespoon Worcestershire sauce
- 1 tablespoon light corn syrup
- 1 tablespoon granulated garlic
- 2 teaspoons celery seeds
- ½ teaspoon liquid smoke

RIBS
- 5 tablespoons packed light brown sugar
- 1 teaspoon salt
- ½ teaspoon pepper
- 2 (2½- to 3-pound) racks baby back ribs, trimmed and membrane removed
- 1 cup cornmeal
- 6 corncobs, kernels removed and reserved for another use
- 1 (13 by 9-inch) disposable aluminum roasting pan

1 FOR THE SAUCE Whisk all ingredients together in medium bowl; set aside.

2 FOR THE RIBS Combine sugar, salt, and pepper in bowl. Pat ribs dry with paper towels and rub with sugar mixture; set aside. Using large piece of heavy-duty aluminum foil, wrap cornmeal in foil packet and cut several vent holes in top.

3 Open bottom vent of charcoal grill halfway. Place disposable pan on 1 side of grill and add 2 quarts water to pan. Arrange 3 quarts unlit charcoal bri-quettes evenly on other side of grill. Place cobs on top of unlit briquettes. Light large chimney starter filled halfway with charcoal briquettes (3 quarts). When top coals are partially covered with ash, pour over cobs and unlit briquettes. Place cornmeal packet on coals. Set cooking grate in place, cover, and open lid vent halfway. Heat grill until hot and cornmeal is smoking, about 5 minutes.

4 Clean and oil cooking grate. Place ribs meaty side up on cooler side of grill; ribs may overlap slightly. Cover, positioning lid vent over meat, and cook until ribs are deep red and tender, 3½ to 4 hours, rotat-ing and switching ribs every hour. (Do not flip ribs.) During last 30 minutes of cooking, baste ribs with sauce every 10 minutes, rotating and switching ribs each time. Transfer ribs to carving board, tent with foil, and let rest for 15 to 20 minutes. Cut ribs between bones. Serve, passing remaining sauce separately.

542

STEP BY STEP

Layering the Fire

In South Dakota, they smoke their ribs on huge custom barbecue rigs using dried corncobs as the sole fuel. It makes sense—corn is what's around, after all. To adapt the method to a backyard kettle grill, we had to figure out how to configure the fire to get 4 hours of steady, corn-tinged smoke. We layered charcoal with fresh corncobs and a foil packet of cornmeal.

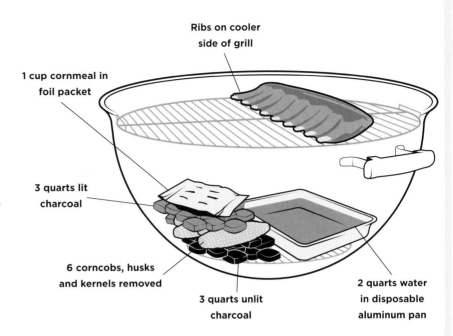

Ribs on cooler side of grill

1 cup cornmeal in foil packet

3 quarts lit charcoal

6 corncobs, husks and kernels removed

3 quarts unlit charcoal

2 quarts water in disposable aluminum pan

543 RECIPE FOR SUCCESS
Fuss-Free Beefy Ribs

✔ WHY THIS RECIPE WORKS

Texas barbecued beef ribs are big, beefy slabs of meat. Unlike their pork-rib cousins, the meat is not fall-off-the-bone tender, but instead retains some chew. The challenge of replicating these ribs at home is twofold: not having a smoke pit to constantly infuse smoky flavor into the ribs, and not wanting to spend 10 hours babysitting the grill. We gave our ribs a head start by steaming them in the oven. This started to break down the connective tissue much sooner than grilling alone. To create a flavorful charred crust—called "bark" by barbecue enthusiasts—we added a basic spice rub. We grilled the ribs over the cooler side of the grill to imitate the low-and-slow heat of professional smoke pits, and we used wood chips to infuse the meat with smoky flavor. Beef ribs don't get a slathering of sauce on the grill; instead they are usually served with a thinner sauce on the side. We came up with a simple one-pot solution for Texas barbecue sauce.

Texas Barbecued Beef Ribs

SERVES 4

Beef ribs are sold in slabs with up to seven bones, but slabs with three to four bones are easier to manage on the grill. If you cannot find ribs with a substantial amount of meat on the bones, don't bother making this recipe. If you'd like to use wood chunks instead of wood chips when using a charcoal grill, substitute one medium wood chunk, soaked in water for 1 hour, for the wood chip packet.

TEXAS BARBECUE SAUCE

- 2 tablespoons unsalted butter
- ½ small onion, chopped fine
- 2 garlic cloves, minced
- 1½ teaspoons chili powder
- 1½ teaspoons pepper
- ½ teaspoon dry mustard
- 2 cups tomato juice
- 6 tablespoons distilled white vinegar
- 2 tablespoons Worcestershire sauce
- 2 tablespoons packed brown sugar
- 2 tablespoons molasses
- Salt

RIBS

- 3 tablespoons packed brown sugar
- 4 teaspoons chili powder
- 1 tablespoon salt
- 2 teaspoons pepper
- ½ teaspoon cayenne pepper
- 3–4 beef rib slabs (3 or 4 ribs per slab, about 5 pounds total), trimmed
- 1 cup wood chips

1 FOR THE TEXAS BARBECUE SAUCE Melt butter in medium saucepan over medium heat. Add onion and cook until softened, about 5 minutes. Stir in garlic, chili powder, pepper, and dry mustard and cook until fragrant, about 30 seconds. Stir in tomato juice, vinegar, Worcestershire, sugar, and molasses and simmer until sauce is reduced to 2 cups, about 20 minutes. Season with salt to taste. (Sauce can be refrigerated for up to 1 week.)

2 FOR THE RIBS Combine sugar, chili powder, salt, pepper, and cayenne in bowl. Pat ribs dry with paper towels and rub them evenly with spice mixture. Wrap ribs in plastic wrap and let sit at room temperature for 1 hour.

3 Adjust oven rack to middle position and heat oven to 300 degrees. Set wire rack in rimmed baking sheet and add just enough water to cover sheet bottom. Arrange ribs on rack meaty side up and cover tightly with aluminum foil. Cook until fat has rendered and meat begins to pull away from bones, about 2 hours. Just before grilling, soak wood chips in water for 15 minutes, then drain. Using large piece of heavy-duty aluminum foil, wrap chips in 8 by 4½-inch foil packet. (Make sure chips do not poke holes in sides or bottom of packet.) Cut 2 evenly spaced 2-inch slits in top of packet.

4A FOR A CHARCOAL GRILL Open bottom vent halfway. Light large chimney starter filled with charcoal briquettes (6 quarts). When top coals are partially covered with ash, pour into steeply banked pile against side of grill. Place wood chip packet on coals. Set cooking grate in place, cover, and open lid vent halfway. Heat grill until hot and wood chips are smoking, about 5 minutes.

4B FOR A GAS GRILL Remove cooking grate and place wood chip packet directly on primary burner. Set cooking grate in place. Turn all burners to high, cover, and heat grill until hot and wood chips are smoking, about 15 minutes. Leave primary burner on high and turn off other burner(s). (Adjust primary burner as needed to maintain grill temperature of 250 to 300 degrees.)

5 Clean and oil cooking grate. Unwrap ribs and place meaty side down on cooler side of grill; ribs may overlap slightly. Cover (position lid vent over meat if using charcoal) and cook until ribs are lightly charred and smoky, about 1½ hours, flipping and rotating racks halfway through grilling. Transfer ribs to carving board, tent with foil, and let rest for 5 to 10 minutes. Serve.

STEP BY STEP
Steam and Smoke

1 STEAM Steam ribs over tray of water in oven to tenderize connective tissue.

2 SMOKE After searing, ribs move to grill with wood chips, where bark will form.

545

SHOPPING IQ
Rib Wrangling

Texas-style barbecued beef ribs are all about the meat. Because beef ribs are located on the cow next to expensive cuts such as rib eye and prime rib, butchers often overtrim the ribs so they can maximize the bulk (and their profits) on the pricier cuts. Be sure to buy slabs with a thick layer of meat that covers the bones. Also, steer clear of the gargantuan seven-rib slabs, which won't fit on a kettle grill. A three- or four-rib slab works best.

Where's the Beef?
These bony ribs are better suited for the stockpot than the smoke pit.

Here's the Beef!
These meaty-but-manageable ribs are worth the time and effort.

Won't Fit
These mammoth ribs are hard to squeeze onto a kettle grill.

546

Prepping the Ribs

If using boneless ribs, skip to step 2

1 DEBONE Remove meat from bone, positioning chef's knife as close as possible to bone.

2 TRIM Trim excess hard fat and silverskin from both sides of meat.

3 SLICE Slice meat at angle into 4 or 5 pieces ranging from ½ to ¾ inch thick.

4 POUND THIN Place plastic wrap over meat and pound into even ¼-inch-thick pieces.

547

RECIPE FOR SUCCESS

Korean Barbecue on an American Grill

✓ WHY THIS RECIPE WORKS

Korean cooks know how to take tough short ribs and transform them into tender barbecued beef, known as *kalbi*, in just minutes. We wanted to learn from their example and modify the recipe to work with readily available equipment and ingredients. Most Korean barbecue recipes use flanken-style short ribs, which are short ribs that are cut across the bones. But we rarely found them in stores, and when we did, they were far too big for a quick-cooking method. We decided to go with English-style short ribs, which consist of a single bone with a thick piece of meat attached. We removed the bones, cut the ribs into four pieces, and pounded the pieces into thin, even slabs. Pureed pear is a common marinade ingredient in kalbi recipes. The acidity in the pear works in concert with the soy sauce and rice vinegar to tenderize the tough meat. Plus, the pear adds a pleasantly sweet, fruity layer of flavor. To re-create the traditional Korean barbecue setup, we used a two-level grill fire and cooked the short ribs over high heat, moving them to the cooler side when flare-ups occurred. The intense heat gave a quick char without making the meat tough.

Korean Grilled Short Ribs (Kalbi)
SERVES 4 TO 6

For more information on short ribs, see page 339. Make sure to buy English-style ribs that have at least 1 inch of meat on top of the bone, avoiding ones that have little meat and large bones. Two pounds of boneless short ribs at least 4 inches long and 1 inch thick can be used instead of bone-in ribs. Alternatively, 2½ pounds of thinly sliced Korean-style ribs can be used (no butchering is required), but if using charcoal, reduce to 3 quarts. Serve with rice, kimchi, and, if available, a spicy bean paste called *gochujang*. Traditionally, all these ingredients are wrapped in a lettuce leaf with the meat and eaten like a taco.

1	ripe pear, peeled, halved, cored, and chopped coarse
½	cup soy sauce
6	tablespoons sugar
2	tablespoons toasted sesame oil
6	garlic cloves, peeled
4	teaspoons grated fresh ginger
1	tablespoon rice vinegar
3	scallions, sliced thin
½	teaspoon red pepper flakes (optional)
5	pounds bone-in English-style short ribs, meat removed from bone, trimmed, sliced widthwise at angle into ½- to ¾-inch-thick pieces, and pounded ¼ inch thick

1 Process pear, soy sauce, sugar, oil, garlic, ginger, and vinegar in food processor until smooth, 20 to 30 seconds. Transfer to medium bowl and stir in scallions and pepper flakes, if using.

2 Spread one-third of marinade in 13 by 9-inch baking dish. Place half of meat in single layer over marinade. Pour half of remaining marinade over meat, followed by remaining meat and remaining marinade. Cover tightly with plastic wrap and refrigerate for at least 4 hours or up to 12 hours, turning meat once or twice.

3A FOR A CHARCOAL GRILL Open bottom vent completely. Light large chimney starter two-thirds filled with charcoal briquettes (4 quarts). When top coals are partially covered with ash, pour into even layer over half of grill. Set cooking grate in place, cover, and open lid vent completely. Heat grill until hot, about 5 minutes.

3B FOR A GAS GRILL Turn all burners to high, cover, and heat grill until hot, about 15 minutes. Leave primary burner on high and turn off other burner(s).

4 Clean and oil cooking grate. Place half of meat on hotter side of grill and cook (covered if using gas), turning every 2 to 3 minutes, until well browned on both sides, 8 to 13 minutes. Move first batch of meat to cooler side of grill and repeat browning with second batch.

5 Transfer second batch of meat to serving platter. Return first batch of meat to hotter side of grill and warm for 30 seconds; transfer to serving platter and serve.

548 SHOPPING IQ
Short Ribs

Depending on butchering technique, short ribs can vary markedly in appearance. Our recipe uses widely available English-style ribs; Korean-style and boneless ribs can also be used. Make sure boneless ribs are at least 4 inches long and 1 inch thick.

English-Style

This common choice contains a single bone, about 4 to 6 inches long. Look for ribs that have at least 1 inch of meat above the bone.

Flanken-Style

The meat has been cut across the ribs and contains 2 to 3 oval-shaped cross-sections of bone. These ribs can be difficult to find in the supermarket.

Korean-Style

The authentic choice (sold only in Asian markets) requires no butchering. The same as flanken-style ribs but cut much thinner, usually about ¼ inch thick.

Boneless

A good option that is available at some markets. Make sure they are at least 4 inches long and 1 inch thick.

549

SHOPPING IQ

Short Ribs for Grill Roasting

Bone-in English-style short ribs (those with long, continuous pieces of meat and a single bone) are a must, but we found that they can vary widely from package to package. Here's what to look for in order for this recipe to work.

- **At least 1 inch of meat on top of the bone**
- **Rib 4 to 6 inches long**

550

RECIPE FOR SUCCESS

Short Ribs Aren't Such a Tall Order

✓ WHY THIS RECIPE WORKS

Flavorful, well-marbled short ribs seem like the perfect candidate for grilling, but getting the texture just right can be a challenge. We wanted meltingly tender meat with the nicely browned exterior that the grill provides—without having to constantly fiddle with the fire. We started with a flavorful spice rub and a sweet-tart glaze. Ground fennel and cumin added more complex layers to the rub. For the glaze, we came up with several options using tangy, bright flavors to help temper the richness of the meat. Short ribs are full of collagen, which converts to gelatin during cooking and produces a tender texture. We went with bone-in ribs to make sure they wouldn't overcook before the collagen had enough time to break down. Even a carefully monitored grill inevitably produces hot and cold spots, and the spotty heat was causing our short ribs to cook unevenly. Starting the ribs in the more even-heat environment of the oven was the optimal solution. When the ribs reached 165 degrees, we moved them to the grill to finish cooking and get a smoky, crunchy crust.

Grill-Roasted Beef Short Ribs

SERVES 4 TO 6

Meaty English-style short ribs are preferred in this recipe to thinner-cut flanken-style ribs (see page 339 for more information). Make sure to choose ribs that are 4 to 6 inches in length and have at least 1 inch of meat on top of the bone.

SPICE RUB

2	tablespoons kosher salt
1	tablespoon packed brown sugar
2	teaspoons pepper
2	teaspoons ground cumin
2	teaspoons garlic powder
1¼	teaspoons paprika
¾	teaspoon ground fennel
⅛	teaspoon cayenne pepper

SHORT RIBS

5	pounds bone-in English-style beef short ribs, trimmed
2	tablespoons red wine vinegar
1	recipe glaze (recipes follow)

1 FOR THE SPICE RUB Combine all ingredients in bowl. Measure out 1 teaspoon rub and set aside for glaze.

2 FOR THE SHORT RIBS Adjust oven rack to middle position and heat oven to 300 degrees. Pat ribs dry. Sprinkle ribs with spice rub, pressing into all sides of ribs. Arrange ribs bone side down in 13 by 9-inch baking dish, placing thicker ribs around perimeter of baking dish and thinner ribs in center. Sprinkle vinegar evenly over ribs. Cover baking dish tightly with aluminum foil. Cook until thickest ribs register 165 to 170 degrees, 1½ to 2 hours.

3A FOR A CHARCOAL GRILL Open bottom vent halfway. Arrange 2 quarts unlit charcoal briquettes into steeply banked pile against side of grill. Light large chimney starter half filled with charcoal briquettes (3 quarts). When top coals are partially covered with ash, pour on top of unlit charcoal to cover one-third of grill with coals steeply banked against side of grill. Set cooking grate in place, cover, and open lid vent halfway. Heat grill until hot, about 5 minutes.

3B FOR A GAS GRILL Turn all burners to high, cover, and heat grill until hot, about 15 minutes. Turn primary burner to medium and turn off other burner(s). (Adjust primary burner as needed to maintain grill temperature of 275 to 300 degrees.)

4 Clean and oil cooking grate. Place short ribs, bone side down, on cooler side of grill about 2 inches from flames. Brush with ¼ cup glaze. Cover and cook until ribs register 195 degrees, 1¾ to 2¼ hours, rotating and brushing ribs with ¼ cup glaze every 30 minutes. Transfer ribs to large platter, tent with foil, and let rest for 5 to 10 minutes before serving.

551 Mustard Glaze
MAKES ABOUT 1 CUP

- ½ cup Dijon mustard
- ½ cup red wine vinegar
- ¼ cup packed brown sugar
- 1 teaspoon reserved spice rub
- ⅛ teaspoon cayenne pepper

Whisk all ingredients together in bowl.

552 Blackberry Glaze
MAKES ABOUT 1 CUP

- 10 ounces (2 cups) fresh or frozen blackberries
- ½ cup ketchup
- ¼ cup bourbon
- 2 tablespoons packed brown sugar
- 1½ tablespoons soy sauce
- 1 teaspoon reserved spice rub
- ⅛ teaspoon cayenne pepper

Bring all ingredients to simmer in small saucepan over medium-high heat. Simmer, stirring frequently to break up blackberries, until reduced to 1¼ cups, about 10 minutes. Strain through fine-mesh strainer, pressing on solids to extract as much liquid as possible. Discard solids.

553 Hoisin-Tamarind Glaze
MAKES ABOUT 1 CUP

Tamarind paste can be found in a well-stocked supermarket or in Asian markets.

- 1 cup water
- ⅓ cup hoisin sauce
- ¼ cup tamarind paste
- 1 (2-inch) piece ginger, peeled and sliced into ½-inch-thick rounds
- 1 teaspoon reserved spice rub
- ⅛ teaspoon cayenne pepper

Bring all ingredients to simmer in small saucepan over medium-high heat. Simmer, stirring frequently, until reduced to 1¼ cups, about 10 minutes. Strain through fine-mesh strainer, pressing on solids to extract as much liquid as possible. Discard solids.

554

RECIPE FOR SUCCESS

Charred Mexican-Style Steak

✓ WHY THIS RECIPE WORKS

Carne asada (literally meaning "grilled meat") is the Mexican answer to steak on the grill. In keeping with tradition, we wanted our steak to have a nicely charred exterior. Skirt steak worked perfectly for our recipe since it is already thin and has good flavor. Instead, of using a traditional marinade, which can impede char, we opted for a dry rub of salt and cumin, and we also let the steak dry out in the refrigerator for 45 minutes. To create the hottest possible grill fire, we corralled the coals using a disposable roasting pan with the bottom cut out. To work in the traditional lime flavor, we squeezed lime juice on the steaks just before serving, and we rubbed them with a clove of garlic for a layer of pungent flavor.

Carne Asada

SERVES 4 TO 6

Two pounds of sirloin steak tips, also sold as flap meat, may be substituted for the skirt steak. Serve with Red Chile Salsa and Simple Refried Beans (recipes follow).

- 2 **teaspoons kosher salt**
- ¾ **teaspoon ground cumin**
- 1 **(2-pound) skirt steak, trimmed, pounded ¼ inch thick and cut with grain into 4 equal steaks**
- 1 **(13 by 9-inch) disposable aluminum roasting pan (if using charcoal)**
- 1 **garlic clove, peeled and smashed Lime wedges**

1 Combine salt and cumin in small bowl. Pat steak dry. Sprinkle salt mixture evenly over both sides of steaks. Transfer steaks to wire rack set in rimmed baking sheet and refrigerate, uncovered, for at least 45 minutes or up to 24 hours. Meanwhile, if using charcoal, use kitchen shears to remove bottom of disposable pan and discard, reserving pan collar.

2A FOR A CHARCOAL GRILL Open bottom vent completely. Light large chimney starter filled with charcoal

briquettes (6 quarts). When top coals are partially covered with ash, place disposable pan collar in center of grill over bottom vent and pour coals into even layer in collar. Set cooking grate in place, cover, and open lid vent completely. Heat grill until hot, about 5 minutes.

2B FOR A GAS GRILL Turn all burners to high, cover, and heat grill until hot, about 15 minutes. Leave all burners on high.

3 Clean and oil cooking grate. Place steaks on grill (if using charcoal, arrange steaks over coals in collar) and cook, uncovered, until well browned on first side, 2 to 4 minutes. Flip steaks and continue to cook until well browned on second side and meat registers 130 to 135 degrees (for medium), 2 to 4 minutes longer. Transfer steaks to carving board, tent with aluminum foil, and let rest for 5 minutes.

4 Rub garlic thoroughly over 1 side of steaks. Slice steaks against grain into ¼-inch-thick slices and serve with lime wedges.

555 Red Chile Salsa
MAKES 2 CUPS

Guajillo chiles are tangy with just a bit of heat. Our favorite brand of fire-roasted tomatoes is DeLallo. Serve the salsa alongside the steak.

- 1¼ ounces dried guajillo chiles, wiped clean
- 1 (14.5-ounce) can fire-roasted diced tomatoes
- ¾ cup water
- ¾ teaspoon salt
- 1 garlic clove, peeled and smashed
- ½ teaspoon distilled white vinegar
- ¼ teaspoon dried oregano
- ⅛ teaspoon pepper
  Pinch ground cloves
  Pinch ground cumin

Toast guajillos in 10-inch nonstick skillet over medium-high heat until softened and fragrant, 1 to 2 minutes per side. Transfer to large plate and, when cool enough to handle, remove stems and seeds. Place guajillos in blender and process until finely ground, 60 to 90 seconds, scraping down sides of blender jar as needed. Add tomatoes and their juice, water, salt, garlic, vinegar, oregano, pepper, cloves, and cumin to blender and process until very smooth, 60 to 90 seconds, scraping

down sides of blender jar as needed. (Salsa can be refrigerated for up to 5 days or frozen for up to 1 month.)

556 Simple Refried Beans
MAKES ABOUT 1½ CUPS

- 2 slices bacon
- 1 small onion, chopped fine
- 2 garlic cloves, minced
- 1 (15-ounce) can pinto beans (do not rinse)
- ¼ cup water
  Kosher salt

Cook bacon in 10-inch nonstick skillet over medium-low heat until crisp, 7 to 10 minutes. Remove bacon and reserve for another use. Increase heat to medium, add onion to fat in skillet, and cook until lightly browned, 5 to 7 minutes. Add garlic and cook until fragrant, about 30 seconds. Add beans and their liquid and water and bring to simmer. Cook, mashing beans with potato masher, until mixture is mostly smooth, 5 to 7 minutes. Season with salt to taste, and serve.

557 FOOD SCIENCE Medium-Rare? Not with This Steak

Cooking most steaks to 125 degrees, or medium-rare, delivers the juiciest, most tender results. But skirt steak is one exception. When a piece of beef is heated, its muscle fibers shrink in width, separating them from one another and making them easier to chew. For cuts like strip steak, which have comparatively thin fibers, the amount of shrinking and tenderizing that occurs at 125 degrees is sufficient. But skirt steak has wider muscle fibers that need to shrink further, and thus must be cooked to 130 degrees for acceptable tenderness. However, this tenderizing effect doesn't continue the more you cook the steak. Once any cut of meat hits 140 degrees, muscle fibers begin to shrink not just in width but also in length, and that causes the meat to toughen again. This lengthwise shrinking also squeezes out juices, so your steak will end up tough and dry.

Before Cooking
Thick, Tough Fibers

After Cooking
Thin, Tender Fibers

558

Toasting and Preparing the Chiles

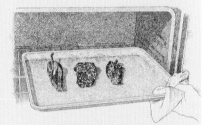

1 TOAST CHILES Toast dried chile pods in 350-degree oven for about 6 minutes until they become fragrant and puffed.

2 PROCESS CHILES When cool enough to handle, remove stems and seeds from pods, rip them into pieces, and process until powdery, 30 to 45 seconds.

559 RECIPE FOR SUCCESS
Chili off the Grill

✓ WHY THIS RECIPE WORKS

True Texas-style chili is all meat—no beans and minimal additional adornment. For big beefy flavor, we started with a chuck roast, seared and cut into sizable, hefty, Texas-size chunks. For the boldest chili flavor, we toasted and ground ancho and New Mexican dried chiles (but store-bought chili powders of the same varieties pack plenty of heat, too). The flavor was also improved by adding bacon, which lent our chili sweetness and smokiness. From among the many recommended liquids to use in chili con carne, we chose water—everything else diluted or competed with the flavor of the chiles. To thicken the sauce to a velvety consistency that would cling to the big chunks of meat, we stirred in masa harina or cornstarch, which made for a smoother, more appealing sauce. Crushed tomatoes provided an underlying tomato flavor and sauciness, and lime juice finished off our chili con carne with a bit of brightness.

Smoky Chipotle Chile con Carne
SERVES 6

For the best flavor, we like to make this chili one day ahead. Make sure you start with a chuck-eye roast that is at least 3 inches thick. The grilling is meant to flavor the meat by searing the surface and smoking it lightly, not to cook it. If you'd like to use wood chunks instead of wood chips when using a charcoal grill, substitute 1 wood chunk, soaked in water for 1 hour, for the wood chip packet. Select dried chiles that are moist and pliant. Toast the cumin seeds in a dry skillet over medium heat until fragrant, about 4 minutes. For hotter chili, boost the heat with a pinch of cayenne or a dash of hot sauce near the end of cooking. Serve the chili with any of the following: warm pinto or kidney beans, cornbread or chips, corn tortillas or tamales, rice, biscuits, or crackers. Top with chopped fresh cilantro, finely chopped onion, diced avocado, shredded cheddar or Monterey Jack cheese, and/or sour cream.

9 garlic cloves, minced
  Salt and pepper
1 (4-pound) boneless beef chuck-eye roast, trimmed
5 tablespoons New Mexican chile powder or 3 medium chiles (about ¾ ounce), toasted and ground
1 cup wood chips, soaked in water for 15 minutes and drained
3 tablespoons ancho chile powder or 3 chiles (about ½ ounce), toasted and ground
2 tablespoons cumin seeds, toasted
2 teaspoons dried oregano, preferably Mexican
7½ cups plus ⅔ cup water
8 slices bacon, cut into ¼-inch pieces
1 onion, chopped fine
2½ tablespoons minced canned chipotle chile in adobo sauce
1 cup canned crushed tomatoes or plain tomato sauce
2 tablespoons lime juice
5 tablespoons masa harina or 3 tablespoons cornstarch

1 Place 4 teaspoons minced garlic on cutting board and sprinkle with 2 teaspoons salt. Using flat side of chef's knife, drag garlic and salt back and forth across cutting board in small circular motions until garlic is ground to paste. Rub beef with garlic paste and sprinkle evenly with 2 tablespoons New Mexican chile powder. Using large piece of heavy-duty aluminum foil, wrap chips in 8 by 4½-inch foil packet. (Make sure chips do not poke holes in sides or bottom of packet.) Cut 2 evenly spaced 2-inch slits in top of packet.

2A FOR A CHARCOAL GRILL Open bottom vent halfway. Light large chimney starter filled with charcoal briquettes (6 quarts). When top coals are partially covered with ash, pour in even layer over half of grill. Place wood chip packet on coals. Set cooking grate in place, cover, and open lid vent halfway. Heat grill until hot and wood chips are smoking, about 5 minutes.

2B FOR A GAS GRILL Remove cooking grate and place wood chip packet directly on primary burner. Set cooking grate in place, turn all burners to high, cover, and heat grill until hot and wood chips are smoking, about 15 minutes. Leave all burners on high.

3 Clean and oil cooking grate. Place meat on hotter side of grill and sear on all sides until well browned, about 12 minutes per side. Transfer roast to carving board, let cool, then cut into 1-inch cubes, discarding excess fat and reserving juices.

4 Combine ancho chile powder, cumin seeds, oregano, and remaining 3 tablespoons New Mexican chile powder in small bowl and stir in ½ cup water to form thick paste; set aside.

5 Cook bacon in Dutch oven over medium-low heat until crisp, about 10 minutes. Using slotted spoon, transfer bacon to paper towel–lined plate. Pour off all but 3 tablespoons fat. Add onion and cook over medium heat until softened, 5 to 7 minutes. Add chipotle and remaining minced garlic and cook until fragrant, about 1 minute. Add chile paste and cook until fragrant, 2 to 3 minutes. Add crushed tomatoes, lime juice, 7 cups water, reserved bacon, and browned beef with any accumulated juices and bring to simmer. Continue to simmer until meat is tender and liquid is dark, rich, and starting to thicken, about 2 hours.

6 Mix masa harina with remaining ⅔ cup water (or cornstarch with 3 tablespoons water) in small bowl to form smooth paste. Increase heat to medium, stir in paste, and simmer until thickened, 5 to 10 minutes. Season with salt and pepper to taste, and serve. (Chili can be refrigerated for up to 2 days.)

560 Draining Wood Chips Outdoors

GRILL HACK

Soaking wood chips or chunks in water prevents them from burning too quickly on the hot coals. Rather than making a trip into the kitchen for a colander to drain the soaked chips, use a clean, perforated flowerpot that you can store outside with your grilling tools. Dump the soaked chips into the flowerpot, allowing the water to drain out the bottom.

562 RECIPE FOR SUCCESS
Savory Steak Pinwheels

WHY THIS RECIPE WORKS

Stuffed steak originated with Italian-American cooking as a way to transform an inexpensive steak into something more exciting and colorful. But the stuffing and the cheese often try to make a run for it, with the cheese oozing out all over the grill, and the stuffing falling out in big clumps. We were sure we could turn this dish into an easy dinner, with tender beef and a juicy, flavorful filling that stayed in place. Thanks to its uniform shape and good beefy taste, flank steak was clearly the best bet. To guarantee that filling would stay in place, we butterflied and pounded the steak flat. As for the filling, the classic Italian-American combo of prosciutto and provolone won raves for its salty savor and the way the dry cheese melted inside the pinwheel yet turned crisp where exposed to the grill. We also came up with variations that featured other salty, savory ingredients. To prevent the meat from shrinking on the grill, we rolled up our flank steak, tied it with twine, and skewered it at 1-inch intervals before slicing and grilling. The twine kept the steak from unraveling, while the skewers prevented the meat from shrinking.

Grilled Stuffed Flank Steak
SERVES 4 TO 6

Depending on the size of the flank steak, you may have between eight and 12 pinwheels of stuffed meat at the end of step 3. Freezing the steak for 30 minutes will make butterflying it easier.

- **2 tablespoons olive oil**
- **2 tablespoons minced fresh parsley**
- **1 small shallot, minced**

561 STEP BY STEP
How to Butterfly and Stuff Flank Steak

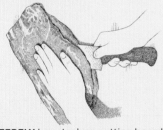

1 BUTTERFLY Lay steak on cutting board with grain running parallel to counter edge. Butterfly meat, leaving ½-inch "hinge" along top edge.

2 OPEN AND POUND Open up steak and pound flat into rough rectangle, trimming any ragged edges.

3 RUB, FILL, AND ROLL Rub with herb mixture; layer with prosciutto and cheese, leaving 2-inch border at top. Roll away from you into tight log.

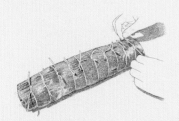

4 TIE Place steak seam side down and tie with string at 1-inch intervals, starting at center.

5 SKEWER Skewer steak directly through each string, allowing skewer to extend ½ inch on opposite side.

6 SLICE Slice steak between strings into 1-inch pinwheels.

2   garlic cloves, minced
1   teaspoon minced fresh sage
8–12 wooden skewers soaked in water for
      30 minutes
1   (2- to 2½-pound) flank steak, trimmed
4   ounces thinly sliced prosciutto
4   ounces thinly sliced provolone cheese
      Kosher salt and pepper

1 Combine oil, parsley, shallot, garlic, and sage in small bowl. Drain and dry skewers, and set aside.

2 Lay steak on cutting board with grain running parallel to counter edge. Cut horizontally through meat, leaving ½-inch "hinge" along top edge. Open up steak, cover with plastic wrap, and pound into rough rectangle, trimming any ragged edges. Rub herb mixture evenly over surface of steak. Lay prosciutto evenly over steak, leaving 2-inch border along top edge. Cover prosciutto with even layer of provolone, leaving 2-inch border along top edge. Starting from bottom edge and rolling away from you, roll beef into tight log and place on cutting board seam side down.

3 Starting ½ inch from end of rolled steak, evenly space eight to twelve 14-inch pieces of kitchen twine at 1-inch intervals underneath steak. Tie middle string first; then, working from outermost strings toward center, tightly tie roll and turn tied steak 90 degrees so seam is facing you. Skewer beef directly through outer flap of steak near seam through each piece of string, allowing skewers to extend ½ inch on opposite side. Using chef's knife, slice roll between pieces of twine into 1-inch-thick pinwheels. Season pinwheels with salt and pepper.

4A FOR A CHARCOAL GRILL Open bottom vent halfway. Light large chimney starter three-quarters filled with charcoal briquettes (4½ quarts). When top coals are partially covered with ash, pour evenly over half of grill. Set cooking grate in place, cover, and open lid vent halfway. Heat grill until hot, about 5 minutes.

4B FOR A GAS GRILL Turn all burners to high, cover, and heat grill until hot, about 15 minutes. Leave primary burner on high and turn off other burner(s).

5 Clean and oil cooking grate. Place pinwheels on hotter side of grill and cook until well browned, 3 to 6 minutes. Using tongs, flip pinwheels; grill until second side is well browned, 3 to 5 minutes longer. Transfer pinwheels to cooler side of grill, cover, and continue to cook until center of pinwheels registers 120 to 125 degrees (for medium-rare), 1 to 4 minutes (slightly thinner pinwheels may not need time on cooler side of grill). Transfer pinwheels to large plate, tent with aluminum foil, and let rest for 5 minutes. Remove and discard skewers and twine and serve immediately.

VARIATIONS

563 Grilled Stuffed Flank Steak with Spinach and Pine Nuts
Microwave 4 ounces chopped spinach, 1 tablespoon water, ½ teaspoon salt, and ½ teaspoon pepper in bowl until spinach is wilted and decreased in volume by half, 3 to 4 minutes. Let cool completely, then squeeze dry. Combine spinach and ¼ cup toasted pine nuts. Replace prosciutto with cooled spinach mixture.

564 Grilled Stuffed Flank Steak with Sun-Dried Tomatoes and Capers
Combine ½ cup drained and chopped sun-dried tomatoes, ½ cup shredded Asiago cheese, and ¼ cup rinsed and chopped capers in bowl. Replace prosciutto with sun-dried tomato mixture.

565 TEST KITCHEN TIP
Knot Surgery

There are plenty of knots to choose from when tying a roast. We like the surgeon's knot. Single pieces of twine are wrapped around the roast at 1½-inch intervals and tied in an initial double loop, which holds the twine in place while a second knot is completed.

Begin by tying a knot as if tying a bow. Pull one end through the loop again. Make a second knot on top of the first knot.

566 Think Outside of the Grill for Great Steak

✔ WHY THIS RECIPE WORKS

For a thick steak that delivered a killer browned crust and even doneness from edge to edge—plus, great charred flavor from the grill—we ditched the actual grill in favor of a superhot charcoal chimney. After trimming the steaks' fat caps in order to eliminate flare-ups, we scored the meat for better browning. We salted the steaks to ensure seasoning throughout and then baked them slowly in a low oven to cook them evenly and dehydrate their surfaces. Skewering them ahead of time made for easy handling and setup. Moving to the grill, we blasted the steaks over the chimney for about 60 seconds per side, and kept the seasoning simple with just a bit of black pepper to finish.

Ultimate Charcoal-Grilled Steaks

SERVES 4

Rib-eye steaks of a similar thickness can be substituted for strip steaks, although they may produce more flare-ups. You will need a charcoal chimney starter with a 7½-inch diameter and four 12-inch metal skewers for this recipe. If your chimney starter has a smaller diameter, skewer each steak individually and cook in four batches. It is important to remove the fat caps on the steaks to limit flare-ups during grilling.

2   (1-pound) boneless strip steaks,
    1¾ inches thick, fat caps removed
    Kosher salt and pepper

1 Adjust oven rack to middle position and heat oven to 200 degrees. Cut each steak in half crosswise to create four 8-ounce steaks. Cut ¹⁄₁₆-inch-deep slits on both sides of steaks, spaced ¼ inch apart, in crosshatch pattern. Sprinkle both sides of each steak with ½ teaspoon salt (2 teaspoons total). Lay steak halves with tapered ends flat on counter and pass two 12-inch metal skewers, spaced 1½ inches apart, horizontally through steaks, making sure to keep ¼-inch space between steak halves. Repeat skewering with remaining steak halves.

2 Place skewered steaks on wire rack set in rimmed baking sheet, transfer to oven, and cook until centers of steaks register 120 degrees, flipping steaks over halfway through cooking and removing them as they come to temperature, 1½ hours to 1 hour 50 minutes. Tent skewered steaks (still on rack) with aluminum foil.

3 Light large chimney starter filled halfway with charcoal briquettes (3 quarts). When top coals are completely covered in ash, uncover steaks (reserving foil) and pat dry with paper towels. Using tongs, place 1 set of steaks directly over chimney so skewers rest on rim of chimney (meat will be suspended over coals). Cook until both sides are well browned and charred, about 1 minute per side. Using tongs, return first set of steaks to wire rack in sheet, season with pepper, and tent with reserved foil. Repeat with second set of skewered steaks. Remove skewers from steaks and serve.

567 FOOD SCIENCE
Grilling Steak Over a Chimney Starter?

Most of us have used a chimney starter only for lighting coals and getting them good and hot before we pour them into the grill. But the coals are actually at their hottest in the chimney—not in the grill, where airflow is far more restricted. So why not leave the coals in the chimney and cook over that? Sure enough, this setup produced a deeply browned sear in just 1 minute per side. Here's how it works.

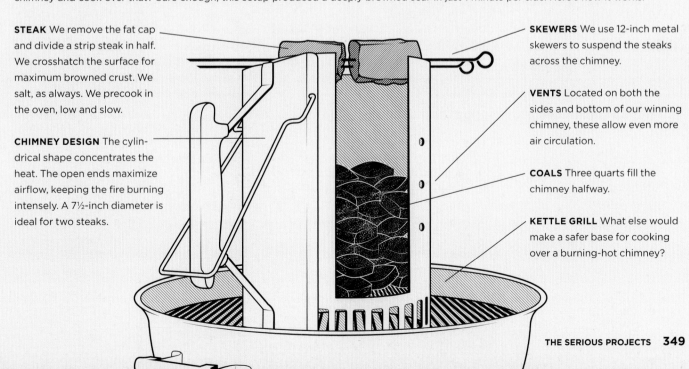

STEAK We remove the fat cap and divide a strip steak in half. We crosshatch the surface for maximum browned crust. We salt, as always. We precook in the oven, low and slow.

CHIMNEY DESIGN The cylindrical shape concentrates the heat. The open ends maximize airflow, keeping the fire burning intensely. A 7½-inch diameter is ideal for two steaks.

SKEWERS We use 12-inch metal skewers to suspend the steaks across the chimney.

VENTS Located on both the sides and bottom of our winning chimney, these allow even more air circulation.

COALS Three quarts fill the chimney halfway.

KETTLE GRILL What else would make a safer base for cooking over a burning-hot chimney?

568

Raked Across the Coals

Arranging lit coals in a grill with a pair of long-handled tongs requires patience: the tongs can only grasp one or two coals at a time. Try using a handheld garden cultivator to arrange the coals as desired.

569

RECIPE FOR SUCCESS

Introducing Tenderloin to the Grill

✓ WHY THIS RECIPE WORKS

Beef tenderloin is a pricey, mild-tasting cut that needs careful attention. We decided to ramp up the flavor by smoking the roast on the grill. We tucked the narrow end under to create a uniform shape and tied the roast with kitchen twine at 1-inch intervals. We seasoned the roast aggressively with an herbed salt mixture and seared it on all sides over a two-level fire with a packet of wood chips underneath the hot coals for subtle, nuanced smoke flavor. Then we moved the beef to the cooler side of the grill so that it could finish cooking evenly in the smoky, gentle heat. We took the roast off the grill when the center reached 125 degrees (for medium-rare) and tented it with foil. For a flavorful sauce to serve alongside, we simmered chopped garlic in olive oil with pepper flakes, rosemary, and thyme; discarded the herbs; and added minced parsley, balsamic vinegar, pepper, and some reserved herb salt. To build layers of flavor, we used some of this potent mixture to baste the meat, and finished it with some chopped grilled scallions for a potent green sauce to complement our deeply flavored grilled tenderloin.

Smoked Beef Tenderloin

SERVES 12 TO 16

For the most economical choice, buy a whole, untrimmed tenderloin from a big-box store and trim it yourself. If you'd like to use wood chunks instead of wood chips when using a charcoal grill, substitute 2 wood chunks, soaked in water for 1 hour, for the wood chip packet.

HERB SALT

- 2   tablespoons kosher salt
- 1   tablespoon minced fresh rosemary
- 2   teaspoons minced fresh thyme

BEEF

- 1   (6-to 7-pound) whole beef tenderloin, trimmed
- 2   bunches scallions, trimmed
- 1   tablespoon pepper
- 1½ cups wood chips

SAUCE

- ¾   cup extra-virgin olive oil
- 6   garlic cloves, chopped
- 1   sprig fresh rosemary
- 1   sprig fresh thyme
- ¼   teaspoon red pepper flakes
- ¼   cup minced fresh parsley
- 1   tablespoon balsamic vinegar
- 1   teaspoon pepper

1 FOR THE HERB SALT Rub salt, rosemary, and thyme together in bowl using your fingers.

2 FOR THE BEEF Tuck tail end of tenderloin under by 2 to 4 inches to create more even shape, then tie with kitchen twine to secure. Tie remainder of tenderloin at 1-inch intervals. Season tenderloin all over with 2 tablespoons herb salt (set remaining herb salt aside, covered, for later use). Wrap tenderloin in plastic wrap and refrigerate for at least 2 hours or up to 2 days. Tie scallions into 2 separate bunches with kitchen twine.

3 FOR THE SAUCE Combine oil, garlic, rosemary sprig, thyme sprig, and pepper flakes in small saucepan. Bring to gentle simmer over low heat, stirring occasionally, and cook until garlic just begins to brown and herbs are fragrant, 8 to 10 minutes. Remove from heat, transfer to bowl, and let cool to room temperature. Discard herb sprigs. Stir in parsley, vinegar, pepper, and 1 teaspoon reserved herb salt.

4 Brush tenderloin all over with 3 tablespoons sauce, then season with pepper. Brush scallion bunches with 1 tablespoon sauce. Set aside remaining ¾ cup sauce for serving.

5 Just before grilling, soak wood chips in water for 15 minutes, then drain. Using large piece of heavy-duty aluminum foil, wrap chips in 8 by 4½-inch foil packet. (Make sure chips do not poke holes in sides or bottom of packet.) Cut 2 evenly spaced 2-inch slits in top of packet.

6A FOR A CHARCOAL GRILL Open bottom vent halfway. Light large chimney starter three-quarters filled with charcoal briquettes (4½ quarts). Place wood chip packet on 1 side of grill. When top coals are partially covered with ash, pour evenly over half of grill on top of wood chip packet. Set cooking grate in place, cover, and open lid vent halfway. Heat grill until hot and wood chips are smoking, about 5 minutes.

6B FOR A GAS GRILL Remove cooking grate and place wood chip packet directly on primary burner. Set cooking grate in place, turn all burners to high, cover, and heat grill until hot and wood chips are smoking, about 15 minutes. Leave primary burner on high and turn off other burners. (Adjust primary burner as needed to maintain grill temperature between 350 and 375 degrees).

7 Clean and oil cooking grate. Place tenderloin and scallions on hotter side of grill. Cook (covered if using gas) until scallions are lightly charred, about 3 minutes, and tenderloin is browned on first side, about 5 minutes. Flip scallions and tenderloin and continue to cook on second sides until scallions are lightly charred, about 3 minutes, and meat is browned, about 5 minutes. Transfer scallions to plate. Move tenderloin to cooler side of grill. Cover and cook for 30 minutes.

8 Move thicker part of tenderloin to hotter side of grill and continue to cook, covered, until tenderloin registers 120 to 125 degrees (for medium-rare), 10 to 20 minutes longer. Transfer tenderloin to carving board, tent with foil, and let rest for 30 minutes.

9 Chop scallions and stir into reserved sauce. Season with salt and pepper to taste. Remove twine and slice meat into ¼-inch-thick slices. Season meat lightly with herb salt and pepper; drizzle with sauce. Serve.

570 STEP BY STEP Preparing an Untrimmed Tenderloin

Save money by buying an untrimmed roast and doing the simple butchering yourself. Here's how:

1 REMOVE CHAIN Use boning or chef's knife to remove fatty strip (or chain) that runs along side of tenderloin.

2 REMOVE SILVERSKIN Insert tip of your knife under sinewy silverskin, then grab it and cut upward against silverskin to remove it. Use paper towel to grasp silverskin if slippery.

3 TUCK NARROW END UNDER Fold narrow end under to make even shape that will cook more consistently.

4 TIE WITH TWINE Tie roast at 1-inch intervals with kitchen twine. Now you're ready to season, let rest, and grill.

571

How to Bone Up on Prime Rib

If your prime rib is without a bone, you can fashion a makeshift "foil bone."

1 ROLL AND COIL Fold 12- to 14-foot sheet of aluminum foil in half lengthwise and then in half lengthwise again; gently roll and scrunch it into narrow tube. Coil foil tube into tight disk about 6 inches across. Flatten to form rectangle.

2 ATTACH TO ROAST Tie foil "bone" to roast (where real bones were removed) and proceed with recipe.

572

RECIPE FOR SUCCESS

Prime Grill Treatment for Prime Rib

✓ WHY THIS RECIPE WORKS

Usually, when we think of grilling, we think of steaks and ribs, but the smoky environment of the grill has plenty to offer for other cuts of meat as well, including prime rib. We wanted a great crust from our prime rib recipe, without the mess and without setting off the smoke detectors, so we moved the proceedings outside. First, we seared the fat-covered side (to minimize flare-ups, we had the butcher trim the fat layer down to a thin ⅛ inch), then we moved the roast to the cooler side of the grill. To get crispiness from our prime rib recipe, we applied a dry salt rub to the roast three hours before grilling. This drew out moisture from just below the surface, allowing for faster evaporation once we began searing.

Grill-Roasted Prime Rib

SERVES 6 TO 8

First-cut beef rib roast is also known as prime rib, loin end, or small end. If all you have is a boneless roast, see our tip at left for making a false bone. If you'd like to use wood chunks instead of wood chips when using a charcoal grill, substitute two medium wood chunks, soaked in water for 1 hour, for the wood chip packet.

- 1 **(7-pound) first-cut beef standing rib roast (3 or 4 bones), meat removed from bones, bones reserved, exterior fat trimmed to ⅛ inch**
- 1 **tablespoon vegetable oil**
  Kosher salt and pepper
- 2 **cups wood chips**
- 1 **(16 by 12-inch) disposable aluminum roasting pan (if using charcoal)**

1 Pat roast dry with paper towels, rub with oil, and season with pepper. Spread ¼ cup salt on rimmed baking sheet and press roast into salt to coat evenly on all sides. Place meat back on ribs so bones fit exactly where they were cut; tie meat to bones with 2 lengths of kitchen twine. Refrigerate roast, uncovered, for 1 hour, then let sit at room temperature for 2 hours.

2 Just before grilling, soak wood chips in water for 15 minutes, then drain. Using large piece of heavy-duty aluminum foil, wrap chips in 8 by 4½-inch foil packet. (Make sure chips do not poke holes in sides or bottom of packet.) Cut 2 evenly spaced 2-inch slits in top of packet.

3A FOR A CHARCOAL GRILL Open bottom vent halfway and place disposable pan on 1 side of grill. Light large chimney starter two-thirds filled with charcoal briquettes (4 quarts). When top coals are partially covered with ash, pour evenly over other side of grill. Set cooking grate in place, cover, and open lid vent halfway. Heat grill until hot, about 5 minutes.

3B FOR A GAS GRILL Turn all burners to high, cover, and heat grill until hot, about 15 minutes. Turn primary burner to medium and turn off other burner(s). (Adjust primary burner as needed to maintain grill temperature of about 325 degrees.)

4 Clean and oil cooking grate. Place roast on hotter side of grill and cook (covered if using gas) until well browned on all sides, 10 to 15 minutes, turning as needed. (If flare-ups occur, move roast to cooler side of grill until flames die down.)

5 Transfer roast to second rimmed baking sheet. If using charcoal, remove cooking grate and place wood chip packet on pile of coals; set cooking grate in place. If using gas, remove cooking grate and place wood chip packet directly on primary burner; set cooking grate in place. Place roast on cooler side of grill, bone side down, with tips of bones pointed away from fire. Cover (position lid vent over meat if using charcoal) and cook until meat registers 115 to 120 degrees (for rare) or 120 to 125 degrees (for medium-rare), 2 to 2½ hours.

6 Transfer roast to carving board, tent with foil, and let rest for 20 minutes. Remove twine and bones, slice meat into ½-inch-thick slices, and serve.

573

Remote Thermometers

Remote thermometers allow you to monitor, from a distance, the temperature of cooking food. One or more temperature probes inserted into the food connect to a battery-powered base that communicates wirelessly with a receiver: either a pager or your smartphone or tablet (via Bluetooth). We tested several pager-style and Bluetooth models on the grill, on the stovetop, and in the oven. Most models were accurate to within 1 degree of the lab thermometer, and all had probes long enough to reach into thick cuts of meat and thin connector cables that didn't obstruct grill lids or oven doors. Distance and functionality were more problematic. No model met its advertised distance range, though each company noted that ranges will vary depending on building materials and interference. When it came to user-friendliness, pager models were categorically fussier to use. They were harder to set up, and we often had to consult the manuals to make adjustments to temperature presets or to reestablish a connection. We preferred the Bluetooth devices, which paired effortlessly with our smartphones and were far easier to operate. Our winner connects quickly and delivers accurate, clear temperature readouts.

THE BOTTOM LINE If you have a smartphone or tablet, remote thermometers with Bluetooth are your best bet for accuracy and functionality.

WINNER

IDEVICES Kitchen Thermometer
Price $78.00
Testing Comments It took seconds to get this sleek Bluetooth device up and running: Download the free app, enter the desired final temperature, stick one of two color-coded probes in the meat, and press start. (For users who need more guidance, the app offers temperature presets for different cuts of meats that mirror our test kitchen recommendations and can display temperature in a helpful graph for estimating remaining cooking time.) It reported accurate readings up to 100 feet from its base, though it sometimes lost connection when we moved behind brick walls or up stairs.

RUNNER-UP

OREGON SCIENTIFIC Grill-Right Bluetooth BBQ Thermometer
Price $48.62
Testing Comments This Bluetooth device worked up to 120 feet from the base. The free app comes with plenty of presets, was easy to customize, and even lets you take and store a photo of your food with a temperature caption for future cooking reference. One gripe: Only the base displays whether or not the Bluetooth is connected, meaning that we could wander off without realizing that the phone had lost communication with the base.

575 RECIPE FOR SUCCESS
Low and Slow Gets an Assist from the Oven

✓ WHY THIS RECIPE WORKS

In researching recipes for barbecued brisket, we found cooks could agree on one thing: cooking low and slow (for up to 12 hours) for the purpose of tenderizing. That seemed like a lot of time. We wanted to figure out a way to make cooking this delicious cut of meat less daunting and less time-consuming, and we wanted to trade in a specialized smoker for a backyard grill. Scoring the fat cap on the brisket helped it render and let the potent spice rub penetrate the meat. (We applied the rub the day before for deep seasoning.) We put the brisket on the cooler side of the grill for gentle cooking, having set it in a disposable aluminum pan to catch the flavorful juices. After a couple of hours of letting it smoke on the grill, we added our homemade barbecue sauce to the pan, covered it, and moved it to the oven, where the steamy environment fully tenderized the meat. Finally, we let the brisket rest in the turned-off oven so that it could reabsorb some of the juices that it had lost, ensuring moist, tender meat.

Kansas City Barbecued Brisket
SERVES 8 TO 10

If you'd like to use wood chunks instead of wood chips when using a charcoal grill, substitute two medium wood chunks, soaked in water for 1 hour, for the wood chip packet.

- 1½ tablespoons paprika
- 1½ tablespoons packed brown sugar
- 1 tablespoon chili powder
- 1 tablespoon pepper
- 2 teaspoons salt
- 1 teaspoon granulated garlic
- 1 teaspoon onion powder
- 1 (5- to 6-pound) beef brisket, flat cut, fat trimmed to ¼ inch
- 2 cups wood chips
- 1 (13 by 9-inch) disposable aluminum roasting pan
- 1 cup ketchup

---

574 SHOPPING IQ
Two Cuts of Brisket

Cut from the cow's breast section, a whole brisket is a boneless, coarse-grained cut comprised of two smaller roasts: the flat (or first) cut and the point (or second) cut. The knobby point cut (A) overlaps the rectangular flat cut (B). The point cut has more marbling and fat, and the flat cut's meat is lean and topped with a thick fat cap. Our recipe calls for the widely available flat cut. Make sure that the fat cap isn't overtrimmed and is ¼ to ½ inch thick.

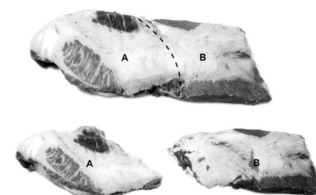

Point Cut   **Flat Cut**

1   cup water
3   tablespoons molasses
1   tablespoon hot sauce

1 Combine paprika, sugar, chili powder, pepper, salt, garlic, and onion powder in bowl. Score brisket fat cap in ½-inch crosshatch pattern, being careful not to cut into meat. Rub brisket with spice mixture. Wrap in plastic wrap and refrigerate for 6 to 24 hours.

2 Just before grilling, soak wood chips in water for 15 minutes, then drain. Using large piece of heavy-duty aluminum foil, wrap chips in 8 by 4½-inch foil packet. (Make sure chips do not poke holes in sides or bottom of packet.) Cut 2 evenly spaced 2-inch slits in top of packet. Unwrap brisket, pat dry with paper towels, and transfer to disposable pan.

3A FOR A CHARCOAL GRILL Open bottom vent halfway. Light large chimney starter filled with charcoal briquettes (6 quarts). When top coals are partially covered with ash, pour evenly over half of grill. Place wood chip packet on coals. Set cooking grate in place, cover, and open lid vent halfway. Heat grill until hot and wood chips are smoking, about 5 minutes.

3B FOR A GAS GRILL Remove cooking grate and place wood chip packet directly on primary burner. Set cooking grate in place, turn all burners to high, cover, and heat grill until hot and wood chips are smoking, about 15 minutes. Leave primary burner on high and turn off other burner(s). (Adjust primary burner as needed to maintain grill temperature around 350 degrees.)

4 Place pan on cooler side of grill. Cover (position lid vent over meat if using charcoal) and cook for 2 hours. During final 20 minutes of grilling, adjust oven rack to lower-middle position and heat oven to 300 degrees.

5 Whisk ketchup, water, molasses, and hot sauce together in bowl, then pour over brisket. Cover pan tightly with foil and transfer to oven. Cook until brisket registers 195 degrees, 2½ to 3 hours. Turn off heat and let brisket rest in oven for 1 hour.

6 Transfer brisket to carving board. Skim fat from sauce. Cut brisket against grain into ¼-inch-thick slices. Serve with sauce.

STEP BY STEP

Smoke, Braise, Rest

To turn this tough cut into juicy, tender barbecue, we used a hybrid method and ended with a rest.

1 USE DISPOSABLE PAN Place brisket in disposable roasting pan to catch juices on grill.

2 MOVE TO OVEN Add sauce, cover pan, and put it in oven to tenderize meat.

3 LET MEAT SIT After braising for 2½ to 3 hours, leave brisket in turned-off oven to fully tenderize.

578

Smokin' Hot Brisket

 WHY THIS RECIPE WORKS

In researching recipes for barbecued brisket, we found that cooks could agree on one thing: slow-cooking (for up to 12 hours) to tenderize the meat. We wanted to figure out a way to make cooking this cut of meat less daunting and less time-consuming, and we wanted to trade in a professional smoker for a backyard grill. We brined the brisket to season it throughout and to make sure the meat remained juicy even after hours on the grill. In our tests, we had trouble figuring out how to maintain a low temperature in the grill without frequently refueling. But then we realized that fire can burn down as well as up. We layered unlit briquettes on the bottom of our grill and added hot coals on top for a fire that burned consistently in the optimal 300-degree range for about 3 hours. We then transferred the brisket to the oven to finish cooking.

Barbecued Beef Brisket

SERVES 8 TO 10

If your brisket is smaller than 5 pounds or the fat cap has been removed, or if you are using a small charcoal grill, it may be necessary to build an aluminum foil shield in order to keep the brisket from becoming too dark. To do this, make two ½ inch folds on the long side of an 18 by 20-inch piece of heavy-duty aluminum foil to form a reinforced edge. Place the foil on the center of the cooking grate, with the reinforced edge over the hotter side of the grill. Position the brisket fat side down over the cooler side of the grill so that it covers about half of the foil. Pull the foil over the brisket to loosely tent it. (For information on making a foil shield, see page 377.) For more information on brisket, see page 354. Some of the traditional accompaniments to barbecued brisket include barbecue sauce (see Texas Barbecue Sauce for Texas Barbecued Beef Ribs page 336), sliced white bread or saltines, pickle chips, and thinly sliced onion.

- 1 **(5- to 6-pound) beef brisket, flat cut, untrimmed**
- ⅔ **cup salt**
- ½ **cup plus 2 tablespoons sugar**
- 3 **wood chunks, preferably hickory, or 2 cups wood chips (if using gas)**

577

Turning Your Grill into a Smoker

The massive smokers used in Texas employ indirect-heat cooking to turn tough cuts like brisket tender. We did the same thing in a kettle grill by pushing the lit coals as far to one side as possible. Placing unlit coals beneath the lit coals keeps the fire going strong for hours. To ensure a slow release of smoke, we placed soaked wood chunks on the coals. We also put a disposable pan filled with water below the brisket to encourage the pink smoke ring under the crust.

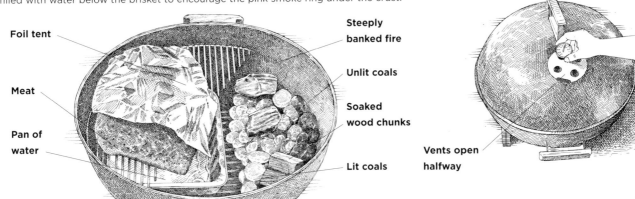

Foil tent
Meat
Pan of water
Steeply banked fire
Unlit coals
Soaked wood chunks
Lit coals
Vents open halfway

3 tablespoons kosher salt

2 tablespoons pepper

1 (13 by 9-inch) disposable aluminum roasting pan (if using charcoal) or 1 (9-inch) disposable aluminum pie plate (if using gas)

1 Lightly score brisket fat cap in 1-inch crosshatch pattern, being careful not to cut into meat. Dissolve salt and ½ cup sugar in 4 quarts cold water in large container. Submerge brisket in brine, cover, and refrigerate for 2 hours.

2 While brisket brines, soak wood chunks in water for at least 1 hour; drain. If using gas, soak wood chips in water for 15 minutes, then drain. Using large piece of heavy-duty aluminum foil, wrap chips in 8 by 4 ½-inch foil packet. (Make sure chips do not poke holes in sides or bottom of packet.) Cut 2 evenly spaced 2-inch slits in top of packet.

3 Combine remaining 2 tablespoons sugar, kosher salt, and pepper in bowl. Remove brisket from brine and pat dry with paper towels. Transfer to rimmed baking sheet and rub salt mixture over entire brisket and into slits.

4A FOR A CHARCOAL GRILL Open bottom vent halfway and place disposable roasting pan on 1 side of grill. Add 2 cups water to pan. Arrange 3 quarts unlit charcoal briquettes banked against other side of grill. Light large chimney starter two-thirds filled with charcoal (4 quarts). When top coals are partially covered with ash, pour on top of unlit charcoal to cover one-third of grill with coals steeply banked against side of grill. Place soaked wood chunks on top of coals. Set cooking grate in place, cover, and open lid vent halfway. Heat grill until hot, about 5 minutes.

4B FOR A GAS GRILL Remove cooking grate and place wood chip packet directly on primary burner. Place disposable pie plate filled with 2 cups water on other burner(s). Set cooking grate in place, turn all burners to high, cover, and heat grill until hot and wood chips are smoking, about 15 minutes. Turn primary burner to medium and turn off other burner(s). (Adjust primary burner as needed to maintain grill temperature of 250 to 300 degrees.)

5 Clean and oil cooking grate. Place brisket on cooler side of grill, fat side down, as far away from coals and flames as possible with thickest side facing coals and flames. Cover (position lid vent over meat if using charcoal) and cook for 3 hours. During final 20 minutes of grilling, adjust oven rack to middle position and heat oven to 325 degrees.

6 Set wire rack in rimmed baking sheet lined with foil and transfer brisket to rack. Roast in oven until tender and meat registers 195 degrees, about 2 hours.

7 Transfer brisket to carving board, tent with foil, and let rest for 30 minutes. Slice brisket against grain into long, thin slices and serve.

580 RECIPE FOR SUCCESS
Deeply Smoky Texas Brisket

✓ WHY THIS RECIPE WORKS

Tender, intensely flavored brisket with a dark crust is the main attraction of Texas-style barbecue. But grill-roasting a large brisket until it's fully cooked can take hours upon hours. Our goal was to make the meat as tender as possible, as quickly as possible. We wanted to rely on the grill for smoky flavor, but we knew that moist-heat cooking methods (such as braising) are ideal for tough cuts. To be successful, we'd need to create a moist-heat environment at some point during the cooking process. We began by coating our brisket with a spice rub and then we put the meat on the grill. Two hours on the grill was enough time for the brisket to absorb plenty of smoke flavor and create a dark brown, crusty exterior. Barbecuing the brisket fat side up ensured that the fat slowly melted into the meat below. Then we wrapped the brisket in foil and moved it to the oven. After a few hours in the oven, our brisket was perfectly cooked and fork-tender.

Lone Star Beef Brisket
SERVES ABOUT 18

If you'd like to use wood chunks instead of wood chips when using a charcoal grill, substitute two medium wood chunks, soaked in water for 1 hour, for the wood chip packet. You can substitute a half brisket (about 5 pounds) if desired. For a half brisket, simply cut the amount of spice mixture in half, grill for just 1½ hours in step 4, and roast for just 2 hours in step 6. Although we think Basic Barbecue Sauce tastes best, feel free to use your favorite store-bought sauce. For extra flavor, consider reserving any accumulated meat juices after the meat has rested and stirring them into the sauce.

- ¼ cup paprika
- 2 tablespoons chili powder
- 2 tablespoons ground cumin
- 2 tablespoons salt
- 2 tablespoons packed brown sugar
- 1 tablespoon granulated sugar
- 1 tablespoon dried oregano
- 1 tablespoon pepper
- 1 tablespoon white pepper
- 2 teaspoons cayenne pepper
- 1 (9- to 11-pound) whole beef brisket, fat trimmed to ¼ inch
- 2 cups wood chips
- 2 cups Basic Barbecue Sauce (page 67)

1 Combine paprika, chili powder, cumin, salt, brown sugar, granulated sugar, oregano, pepper, white pepper, and cayenne in bowl. Pat brisket dry with paper towels and rub it evenly with spice mixture. Wrap brisket in plastic wrap and let sit at room temperature for at least 1 hour or refrigerate for up to 24 hours. (If refrigerated, let sit at room temperature for 1 hour before grilling.)

579 SHOPPING IQ
High-End Barbecue Sauce

Small-batch barbecue sauces promise pit-master magic—but are they worth their higher price tags? To find out, we mail-ordered four products that had some buzz, were award winners, or were marketed by barbecue pros. We sampled the sauces plain and on grilled chicken, focusing on sweetness, complexity, texture, and overall appeal. Our two least favorite sauces were too sweet, containing twice the amount of sugar per serving as the others. A third sauce was watery and mild. But the fourth, our winner, delivered. With generous additions of vinegar, salt, and chili paste along with liquid smoke, it was tart, spicy, and more savory than sweet. It also had enough body to cling to the chicken.

THE BOTTOM LINE If you aren't going to make barbecue sauce yourself, splurge on our high-end winner, **Pork Barrel Original BBQ Sauce**, which is a bold, savory, tangy sauce with a kick.

2 Just before grilling soak wood chips in water, then drain. Using large piece of heavy-duty aluminum foil, wrap chips in 8 by 4½-inch foil packet. (Make sure chips do not poke holes in sides or bottom of packet.) Cut 2 evenly spaced 2-inch slits in top of packet.

3A FOR A CHARCOAL GRILL Open bottom grill vent halfway. Light large chimney starter half filled with charcoal briquettes (3 quarts). When top coals are partially covered with ash, pour them into steeply banked pile against 1 side of grill. Place wood chip packet on top of coals. Set cooking grate in place, cover, and open lid vent halfway. Heat grill until hot and wood chips are smoking, about 5 minutes.

3B FOR A GAS GRILL Remove cooking grate and place wood chip packet directly on primary burner. Set cooking grate in place, turn all burners to high, cover, and heat grill until hot and wood chips are smoking, about 15 minutes. Turn primary burner to medium and turn off other burner(s). (Adjust primary burner as needed to maintain grill temperature between 250 and 300 degrees.)

4 Clean and oil cooking grate. Unwrap brisket and place, fat side up, on cooler side of grill. Cover (position lid vent over meat if using charcoal), and cook for 2 hours.

5 During final 20 minutes of grilling, adjust oven rack to middle position and heat oven to 300 degrees. Make 4 by 3-foot rectangle of heavy-duty foil by overlapping and crimping 2 smaller foil sheets together securely.

6 Place brisket in center of foil and wrap tightly. Transfer wrapped brisket, fat side up, to rimmed baking sheet and roast in oven until fork inserted into center meets no resistance, 3 to 3½ hours.

7 Remove brisket from oven, loosen foil to release steam, and let rest for 30 minutes. Unwrap brisket, transfer it to carving board, and separate meat into 2 sections. Slice meat thin against grain on bias and serve with barbecue sauce.

581

GADGETS & GEAR

Smokers

We tested several "bullet" smoker models: cylindrical-shaped vessels about the size of a kettle grill that feature a large cooking surface atop a charcoal pan. Smoking is all about holding the heat at a low, steady temperature for a long time—a full day, in some cases—to bathe the meat in smoke flavor and tenderize it. We used a 12-hour temperature test, recording the temperature of each model every hour while smoking a variety of foods. In the end, a mid-priced competitor smoked out the competition. It included twin grates, which provided ample room for four pork butts, two whole turkeys, or four rib racks; a water pan; and a multitude of vents for excellent temperature control. Our only complaint? A lack of handles made transport and cleanup difficult.

THE BOTTOM LINE Don't assume that the most expensive choice is necessarily the best one. Look for a model with a large fuel capacity, a water reservoir, and vents (to control the air flow and temperature), like the **Weber Smokey Mountain Cooker**.

WINNER

WEBER Smokey Mountain Cooker–18½-Inch
Price $298.95
Testing Comments Plenty of cooking space, a water pan, and multiple vents for precise temperature control added up to meat that was consistently moist and smoky, with little tending necessary.

RUNNER-UP

BIG GREEN EGG
Price $799.00; stand extra
Testing Comments This ceramic smoker's excellent heat retention and vents that opened all the way still couldn't make up for its cramped cooking surface or the lack of a water pan, which yielded markedly drier meats.

RECIPE FOR SUCCESS

Nothing Bitter About These Ends

✓ WHY THIS RECIPE WORKS

Barbecued burnt ends are usually made from generously marbled point cut brisket, which is smoked for over 12 hours until the exterior is almost black. The meat absorbs plenty of smoky flavor and becomes ultratender from the long cooking time. But for a home barbecue, we wanted to make these flavorful morsels using the more readily available (but much leaner) flat cut brisket. To maximize surface area for crunchy "bark," we cut the meat into 1½-inch-wide strips. Two hours in a brine solution kept the meat moist through cooking. A combined grill- and oven-smoked method provided the burnished exterior and tender meat characteristic of true burnt ends.

Barbecued Burnt Ends

SERVES 8 TO 10

Look for a brisket with a significant fat cap. This recipe takes about 8 hours to prepare. The meat can be brined ahead of time, transferred to a zipper-lock bag, and refrigerated for up to 24 hours. If you don't have ½ cup of juices from the rested brisket, supplement with beef broth. If you'd like to use wood chunks instead of wood chips on a charcoal grill, substitute 3 wood chunks, soaked in water for 1 hour, for the wood chip packet.

BRISKET AND RUB

- 2 cups plus 1 tablespoon kosher salt
- ½ cup granulated sugar
- 1 (5- to 6-pound) beef brisket, flat cut, untrimmed
- ¼ cup packed brown sugar
- 2 tablespoons pepper
- 4 cups wood chips
- 1 (13 by 9-inch) disposable aluminum roasting pan (if using charcoal) or 2 (8½ by 6-inch) disposable aluminum pans (if using gas)

BARBECUE SAUCE
- ¾ **cup ketchup**
- ¼ **cup packed brown sugar**
- 2 **tablespoons cider vinegar**
- 2 **tablespoons Worcestershire sauce**
- 2 **teaspoons granulated garlic**
- ¼ **teaspoon cayenne pepper**

1 FOR THE BRISKET AND RUB Dissolve 2 cups salt and granulated sugar in 4 quarts cold water in large container. Slice brisket with grain into 1½-inch-thick strips. Add brisket strips to brine, cover, and refrigerate for 2 hours. Remove brisket from brine and pat dry with paper towels.

2 Combine brown sugar, pepper, and remaining 1 tablespoon salt in bowl. Rub brisket all over with rub mixture. Just before grilling, soak wood chips in water for 15 minutes, then drain. Using large piece of heavy-duty aluminum foil, wrap 2 cups chips in 8 by 4½-inch foil packet. (Make sure chips do not poke holes in sides or bottom of packet.) Repeat with remaining 2 cups chips. Cut 2 evenly spaced 2-inch slits in top of each packet.

3A FOR A CHARCOAL GRILL Open bottom vent halfway. Place disposable pan on 1 side of grill and add 2 quarts water to pan. Arrange 3 quarts unlit charcoal briquettes evenly on other side of grill and place 1 wood chip packet on coals. Light large chimney starter halfway filled with charcoal briquettes (3 quarts). When top coals are partially covered with ash, pour evenly over unlit coals and wood chip packet. Place remaining wood chip packet on lit coals. Set cooking grate in place, cover, and open lid vent halfway. Heat grill until hot and wood chips are smoking, about 5 minutes.

3B FOR A GAS GRILL Add ½ cup ice cubes to 1 wood chip packet. Remove cooking grate and place both wood chip packets directly on primary burner; place disposable pans directly on secondary burner(s) and add 2 cups water to each. Set cooking grate in place, turn all burners to high, cover, and heat grill until hot and wood chips are smoking, about 15 minutes. Leave primary burner on high and turn off other burner(s). (Adjust primary burner as needed to maintain grill temperature of 275 to 300 degrees.)

4 Clean and oil cooking grate. Arrange brisket on cooler side of grill as far from heat source as possible. Cover (position lid vent over meat if using charcoal) and cook without opening for 3 hours.

5 During final 20 minutes of grilling, adjust oven rack to middle position and heat oven to 275 degrees. Transfer brisket to rimmed baking sheet and cover sheet tightly with foil. Roast until fork slips easily in and out of meat and meat registers about 210 degrees, about 2 hours. Remove from oven, and let rest, covered, for 1 hour. Remove foil, transfer brisket to carving board, and pour accumulated juices into fat separator.

6 FOR THE BARBECUE SAUCE Combine ketchup, sugar, vinegar, Worcestershire, granulated garlic, cayenne, and ½ cup defatted brisket juices in medium saucepan. Bring to simmer over medium heat and cook until slightly thickened, about 5 minutes.

7 Cut brisket strips crosswise into 1- to 2-inch chunks. Combine brisket chunks and barbecue sauce in large bowl and toss to combine. Serve.

583
STEP BY STEP
Cut Brisket into Strips

Slicing a flat-cut brisket into 1½-inch strips creates more surface area to facilitate brining, browning, and smoke absorption. We cube it just before serving.

Go with the Grain
Cut brisket into strips before brining.

584
FOOD SCIENCE
Can You Brine Beef?

We've found that soaking delicate lean white meat, like pork, chicken, turkey, and even shrimp, in a salted water solution, or brine, before cooking results in moist, well-seasoned meat. So why not give beef the same treatment? In general, beef has a higher fat content than lean white meat, so it doesn't need the brine to remain juicy. Secondly, quick-cooking, tender beef cuts such as strip steaks or tenderloin roasts should ideally be cooked only to about 125 degrees (for medium-rare). In comparison, pork and chicken require a higher cooking temperature (145 for pork, 160 for white meat poultry and 175 for dark meat poultry) and are, therefore, in greater danger of drying out. Tougher cuts of beef, however, such as chuck roast or brisket, are cooked to more than 200 degrees. Their extensive marbling of fat and collagen melts and acts as a natural moisturizer, but we found that in a long-cooking, high-temperature grilled brisket recipe, brining can help the beef stay moist even after hours of grill-roasting.

585

Restarting a Grill Fire with Style

When a charcoal fire peters out before it really gets started, you can douse it with lighter fluid and toss on a match, which creates a thrilling ball of flame. Some grillers, however, prefer a tamer, safer approach. Assuming the grill is placed close enough to an outdoor power outlet, simply turn an electric hair dryer to high and aim it toward the base of the pile of coals. The air flow acts as a bellows to get the fire going again in just a few minutes—without a dangerous ball of flames. (If your grill isn't near an outlet, try a bike pump. Three or four blasts provide the intense burst of air that the fire needs for a bit more life.)

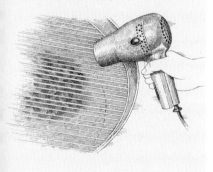

586

RECIPE FOR SUCCESS

Smoky Roast Beef without Spending Big Bucks

✓ WHY THIS RECIPE WORKS

To turn an inexpensive cut into a tender, flavorful roast, we start with an eye-round roast. This cut's cylindrical shape helps it cook evenly on the grill. To tenderize the meat and amp up its beefy flavor, we rubbed the roast with a paste made of herbs, salt, and ketchup. Then we slow-cooked the roast over indirect heat. To moderate the temperature, we put a foil shield around the meat. Finally, we reloaded the grill with fresh coals while the roast rested and then seared the meat over a fresh, hot fire to create a nicely charred crust.

Smoked Roast Beef

SERVES 6 TO 8

If using charcoal, you will need to light two fires: the first to smoke the meat, and the second to sear it after a rest. If using a gas grill, simply turn it off between uses. If you'd like to use wood chunks instead of wood chips when using a charcoal grill, substitute one medium wood chunk, soaked in water for 1 hour, for the wood chip packet. For medium beef, cook to an internal temperature of 130 to 135 degrees. You don't need to rest the meat again after step 5; it may be served immediately.

- 2 tablespoons ketchup
- 4 teaspoons salt
- 2 teaspoons pepper
- ½ teaspoon dried thyme
- ½ teaspoon dried oregano
- ½ teaspoon dried rosemary
- 1 (4-pound) boneless eye-round roast, trimmed
- 1 cup wood chips
- 2 teaspoons vegetable oil

1 Combine ketchup, salt, pepper, thyme, oregano, and rosemary in bowl. Rub ketchup mixture all over roast, then wrap roast in plastic wrap and refrigerate for at least 6 hours or up to 24 hours. Just before grilling, soak wood chips in water for 15 minutes, then drain. Using large piece of heavy-duty aluminum foil, wrap chips in 8 by 4½-inch foil packet. (Make sure chips do not poke holes in sides or bottom of packet.) Cut 2 evenly spaced 2-inch slits in top of packet.

2A FOR A CHARCOAL GRILL Open bottom vent halfway. Light large chimney starter half filled with charcoal briquettes (3 quarts). When top coals are partially covered with ash, pour into steeply banked pile against side of grill. Place wood chip packet on coals. Set cooking grate in place, cover, and open lid vent halfway. Heat grill until hot and wood chips are smoking, about 5 minutes.

2B FOR A GAS GRILL Remove cooking grate and place wood chip packet directly on primary burner. Set cooking grate in place, turn all burners to high, cover, and heat grill until hot and wood chips are smoking, about 15 minutes. Turn primary burner to medium-high and turn off other burner(s). (Adjust primary burner as needed to maintain grill temperature of 325 degrees.)

3 Set wire rack in rimmed baking sheet. Unwrap roast. Make two ½-inch folds on long side of 18-inch length of foil to form reinforced edge. Place foil in center of cooking grate, with reinforced edge over hotter side of grill. Place roast on cooler side of grill so that it covers one-third of foil. Lift and bend edges of foil to shield roast, tucking in edges. Cook, covered, until meat registers 120 to 125 degrees (for medium-rare), 1½ to 1¾ hours. Remove roast from grill, transfer to prepared wire rack, and tent with foil. Let roast rest for 30 minutes or up to 1 hour.

4A FOR A CHARCOAL GRILL Open bottom vent completely. Light large chimney starter filled with charcoal briquettes (6 quarts). When top coals are partially covered with ash, pour into pile over spent coals. Set cooking grate in place, cover, and open lid vent completely. Heat grill until hot, about 5 minutes.

4B FOR A GAS GRILL Turn all burners to high, cover, and heat grill until hot, about 5 minutes. Leave all burners on high.

5 Clean and oil cooking grate. Brush roast all over with oil. Grill (directly over coals if using charcoal; covered if using gas), turning frequently, until charred on all sides, 8 to 12 minutes. Transfer meat to carving board, slice thin, and serve.

The Other Grilled Steak

 WHY THIS RECIPE WORKS

St. Louis barbecued pork steaks are little-known in other parts of America, but in St. Louis, they are so popular that pork steaks are on permanent sale in family packs at the supermarket. When we tried to recreate this regional dish, we found there was no substitute for pork steak, so the only option was to cut our own. We ordered a boneless Boston butt and cut it in half crosswise, then turned each piece on end to slice 1-inch-thick steaks. Inspired by a test kitchen recipe for brats and beer, we used a method of sear, simmer, sear again, cooking the steaks in a disposable pan with barbecue sauce in between stints directly over the coals. This untraditional process gives the steaks a nice char, candy-like edges, and succulent, slightly chewy interiors.

St. Louis Barbecued Pork Steaks

SERVES 4

Pork butt roast is also labeled Boston butt in the supermarket. If pork steaks are available, use them and increase the cooking time in the sauce to 1 to 1½ hours. We use Budweiser in this recipe, since it's made in St. Louis, but any mild-tasting beer will do.

SPICE RUB AND PORK STEAKS
- 1 tablespoon packed brown sugar
- 1 tablespoon paprika
- 2 teaspoons dry mustard
- 2 teaspoons pepper
- 1 teaspoon onion powder
- 1 teaspoon garlic powder
- 1 teaspoon ground cumin
- 1 teaspoon salt
- ¼ teaspoon cayenne pepper
- 1 (5- to 6-pound) boneless pork butt roast, sliced crosswise into 2 pieces, trimmed, and each half cut into three or four 1-inch-thick steaks

BARBECUE SAUCE
- 2 cups beer
- 1½ cups ketchup

- ¼ cup A.1. Steak Sauce
- ¼ cup packed dark brown sugar
- 2 tablespoons cider vinegar
- 2 tablespoons Worcestershire sauce
- 1 teaspoon garlic powder
- 1 teaspoon hot sauce
- 1 teaspoon liquid smoke
- 1 (13 by 9-inch) disposable aluminum roasting pan

1 FOR THE SPICE RUB AND PORK STEAKS Combine sugar, paprika, dry mustard, pepper, onion powder, garlic powder, cumin, salt, and cayenne in bowl. Pat pork steaks dry with paper towels and rub them evenly with spice mixture. Wrap pork in plastic wrap and refrigerate for at least 1 hour or up to 24 hours.

2 FOR THE BARBECUE SAUCE Whisk all ingredients together in bowl and transfer to disposable pan.

3A FOR A CHARCOAL GRILL Open bottom vent halfway. Light large chimney starter filled with charcoal briquettes (6 quarts). When top coals are partially covered with ash, pour evenly over grill. Set cooking grate in place, cover, and open lid vent halfway. Heat grill until hot, about 5 minutes.

3B FOR A GAS GRILL Turn all burners to high, cover, and heat grill until hot, about 15 minutes. Leave primary burner on high and turn off other burner(s). (Adjust primary burner as needed to maintain grill temperature around 350 degrees.)

4 Clean and oil cooking grate. Place pork steaks on grill. Cook (covered if using gas) until well browned on both sides, about 10 minutes, flipping steaks halfway through grilling.

5 Transfer pork steaks to sauce in pan and turn to coat thoroughly. Cover pan with aluminum foil and place on grill. Cover (positioning lid vent over pan if using charcoal) and cook steaks until fork-tender and they register 190 degrees, 45 minutes to 1 hour. Remove steaks from pan and grill until lightly charred around edges, 4 to 8 minutes, flipping steaks halfway through grilling.

6 Transfer steaks to serving platter, tent with foil, and let rest for 10 minutes. Skim excess fat from sauce and serve with steaks.

588 STEP BY STEP
Butchering Boneless Pork Butt

Boneless Boston butt (aka shoulder) steaks can fall apart on the grill if you don't use our easy technique to cut your own steaks from a 5- to 6-pound boneless roast.

1 SLICE Slice pork crosswise in half and remove any large pieces of fat.

2 ROTATE Rotate and stand each half of pork butt on its cut end.

3 CUT INTO STEAKS Cut each half into three or four 1-inch-thick steaks.

589 RECIPE FOR SUCCESS
Braise-and-Grill Pork Tacos

✔ WHY THIS RECIPE WORKS

The traditional pork filling for tacos al pastor, or "shepherd-style" tacos, is made from thin slices of chile-marinated pork that are tightly packed onto a vertical spit and roasted. The pork is often topped with a whole pineapple, the juices of which encourage the pork to caramelize. Of course, most home cooks don't own a vertical rotisserie, so we set out to translate this ultraflavorful taco filling for the American home kitchen. We started off with pork shoulder; its rich marbling created good flavor and helped to keep the pork tender. To infuse the pork with our guajillo chile–tomato marinade, we braised ½-inch-thick slabs (the thinnest we could reasonably create with a chef's knife) in the marinade until they were tender and juicy. To replicate the crisp, browned exterior of authentic versions, we grilled the slabs over a hot fire. Basting the pork with the braising liquid, which was rich with the rendered pork drippings, made the meat ultratender. A few grilled pineapple rounds made a perfect traditional garnish.

Tacos al Pastor

SERVES 6

Pork butt roast is often labeled Boston butt in the supermarket. Serve these tacos with chopped onion, diced avocado, chopped cilantro, and thinly sliced radishes.

12	dried guajillo chiles, stemmed, seeded and torn into ½-inch pieces (1½ cups)
1½	cups water
1¼	pounds plum tomatoes, cored and quartered
8	garlic cloves, peeled
4	bay leaves
	Salt and pepper
¾	teaspoon sugar
½	teaspoon ground cumin
⅛	teaspoon ground cloves
1	(3-pound) boneless pork butt roast, fat cap trimmed to ¼ inch, sliced against grain into ½-inch-thick slabs
1	lime, cut into 8 wedges
½	pineapple, peeled, cored and cut into ½-inch-thick rings
	Vegetable oil
18	(6-inch) corn tortillas
½	cup chopped fresh cilantro

1 Toast guajillos in Dutch oven over medium heat, stirring frequently, until fragrant, 2 to 6 minutes. Stir in water, tomatoes, garlic, bay leaves, 2 teaspoons salt, ½ teaspoon pepper, sugar, cumin, and cloves. Increase heat to medium-high and bring to simmer. Cover, reduce heat to low, and simmer, stirring occasionally, until guajillos are softened and tomatoes mash easily, about 20 minutes.

2 Transfer mixture to blender and process until smooth, about 1 minute. Strain puree through fine-mesh strainer, pressing on solids to extract as much liquid as possible; discard solids and return puree to pot.

3 Add pork to pot, submerge in sauce, and bring to simmer over medium heat. Partially cover, reduce heat, and gently simmer until pork is tender but still holds together, 1½ to 1¾ hours, flipping and rearranging pork halfway through cooking. (Pork and sauce can be refrigerated for up to 2 days.)

4 Transfer pork to large plate, season both sides with salt, and cover tightly with aluminum foil. Whisk sauce to combine. Transfer ½ cup to bowl for grilling. Pour off all but ½ cup sauce left in pot (reserve excess sauce for another use). Squeeze 2 lime wedges into sauce in pot and add spent lime wedges; season with salt to taste. Brush pineapple with oil and season with salt.

5A FOR A CHARCOAL GRILL Open bottom vent completely. Light large chimney starter filled with charcoal briquettes (6 quarts). When top coals are partially covered with ash, pour evenly over grill. Set cooking grate in place, cover, and open lid vent completely. Heat grill until hot, about 5 minutes.

5B FOR A GAS GRILL Turn all burners to high, cover, and heat grill until hot, about 15 minutes. Turn all burners to medium.

6 Clean and oil cooking grate. Place pineapple on grill and cook, turning as needed, until softened and caramelized, 10 to 15 minutes; transfer to cutting board. Meanwhile, brush 1 side of pork with ¼ cup reserved sauce, then place on grill, sauce side down. Cook until well browned and crisp, 5 to 7 minutes. Repeat with second side using remaining ¼ cup reserved sauce; transfer to cutting board and tent with foil.

7 Working in batches, grill tortillas, turning as needed, until warm and soft, about 30 seconds; wrap tightly in foil to keep soft.

8 Chop pineapple and transfer to serving bowl. Using tongs to steady pork, slice each piece crosswise into ⅛-inch pieces. Bring sauce left in pot to simmer over medium heat. Off heat, add sliced pork and toss to coat with sauce. Serve with tortillas, cilantro, pineapple, and remaining 6 lime wedges.

590

SHOPPING IQ

Smoky Spice

This mild, fruity dried chile is easy to find in supermarkets and brings smoky flavor to the pork.

Guajillo Chile

591

Annatto

Annatto, called *achiote* in Mexico, is a very hard brick-red seed from the annatto tree. It is used both for color and for its subtle, earthy flavor in spice rubs and sauces. Look for annatto alongside the other Mexican spices at your market; these spices are often sold in a separate location from the other spices.

592 RECIPE FOR SUCCESS
Tangy Yucatán-Style Pork

✓ WHY THIS RECIPE WORKS

This signature Mexican dish begins with pork cutlets marinated in sour orange juice, annatto powder, and spices and aromatics. The pork is quickly grilled over a hot fire and then served with tortillas and garnishes. We used boneless country-style pork ribs, which stayed moist during cooking (even when pounded into thin cutlets). We marinated our cutlets in a simple lime juice mixture. Placing them over a concentrated fire let the meat quickly brown without overcooking. Per tradition, we scattered fresh toppings over the cutlets before serving. Serve with warm tortillas or rice.

Grilled Citrus-Marinated Pork Cutlets
SERVES 4 TO 6

1½	pounds boneless country-style pork ribs, trimmed
⅓	cup lime juice (3 limes)
⅓	cup extra-virgin olive oil
3	garlic cloves, minced
1	tablespoon annatto powder
¾	teaspoon brown sugar
	Salt and pepper
½	teaspoon ground coriander
1	(13 by 9-inch) disposable aluminum roasting pan (if using charcoal)
1	avocado, halved, pitted, and cut into ½-inch pieces
1	tomato, cored and cut into ½-inch pieces
2	radishes, trimmed and sliced thin
2	tablespoons chopped fresh cilantro

1 Cut each rib lengthwise to create 2 or 3 cutlets about ⅜-inch wide. Place cutlets cut side down between 2 sheets of plastic wrap and gently pound to even ¼-inch thickness.

2 Combine lime juice, oil, garlic, annatto powder, sugar, ¾ teaspoon salt, ½ teaspoon pepper, and coriander in 1-gallon zipper-lock bag. Add pork to bag and toss to coat. Press out as much air as possible, seal bag, and refrigerate for at least 30 minutes or up to 2 hours, flipping bag occasionally.

3 Just before grilling, remove cutlets from bag and pat dry with paper towels; discard marinade. If using charcoal, use kitchen shears to remove and discard bottom of roasting pan; reserve pan collar.

4A FOR A CHARCOAL GRILL Open bottom vent completely. Light large chimney starter filled with charcoal briquettes (6 quarts). When top coals are partially covered with ash, place roasting pan collar in center of grill, oriented over bottom vent, and pour coals into even layer in collar. Set cooking grate in place, cover, and open lid vent completely. Heat grill until hot, about 5 minutes.

4B FOR A GAS GRILL Turn all burners to high, cover, and heat grill until hot, about 15 minutes. Leave all burners on high.

5 Clean and oil cooking grate. Place cutlets on grill (over coals if using charcoal), Cook, uncovered, until lightly browned on first side, about 2 minutes. Flip cutlets and continue to cook until just cooked through, about 30 seconds. Transfer cutlets to serving platter, top with avocado, tomato, radishes, and cilantro, and serve immediately.

593

STEP BY STEP

Making Cutlets

Cut each rib lengthwise into 2 or 3 cutlets about ⅜ inch thick. Place cutlets between 2 sheets of plastic wrap and pound to even ¼-inch thickness.

594

Let There Be Light!

Early- or late-season grillers (and diehards who grill through the winter months) often find themselves grilling the evening meal in the dark. In the absence of a well-placed outdoor light, try a camping headlamp (also know as a spelunker's or miner's light). This contraption not only allows you to point the light directly where you're looking but also keeps your hands free for cooking purposes.

595

Fancy Pork off the Grill

✓ WHY THIS RECIPE WORKS

Pork tenderloin has many advantages that make it an ideal candidate for the grill: It's quick-cooking, is extremely tender, and has a uniform shape that allows for even cooking. But this cut is also mild and lean, making it prone to drying out. Stuffing this roast solves these problems by adding flavor and moisture. For more surface area for the filling and to help prevent leaks, we pounded, filled, and then rolled the tenderloins. And for our flavorful filling, we pulsed bold ingredients—such as olives, sun-dried tomatoes, and porcini mushrooms—in a food processor to produce an intense paste that didn't ooze out. When it came time to fire up the grill, we found that a two-level fire, with the coals spread over half the grill, allowed the pork to cook evenly without drying out. Our last touch was a brown sugar rub on the exterior of each tenderloin, which boosted browning significantly.

Grilled Stuffed Pork Tenderloin
SERVES 4 TO 6

When trimming the tenderloins, be sure to remove the silverskin, the thin swatch of connective tissue underneath the fat. This strip of tissue is very tough and unpleasant to eat.

4	teaspoons packed dark brown sugar
	Kosher salt and pepper
2	(1¼- to 1½-pound) pork tenderloins, trimmed
1	recipe stuffing (recipes follow)
1	cup baby spinach
2	tablespoons olive oil

1 Combine sugar, 2 teaspoons salt, and 1 teaspoon pepper in bowl. Slice each tenderloin in half horizontally, stopping ½ inch from edge so halves remain attached. Open tenderloins like book, cover with plastic wrap, and pound to ¼-inch thickness. Trim any ragged edges to make rough rectangle about 10 inches by 6 inches. Sprinkle interior of each tenderloin with ⅛ teaspoon salt and ⅛ teaspoon pepper.

2 With long side of tenderloin facing you, spread half of stuffing over bottom half of 1 tenderloin and top stuffing with ½ cup spinach. Roll tenderloin away from you into tight cylinder, taking care not to squeeze stuffing out ends. Position tenderloin seam side down. Evenly space 5 pieces of kitchen twine beneath tenderloin and tie to secure, trimming any excess twine. Repeat with remaining tenderloin, stuffing, and spinach.

3A FOR A CHARCOAL GRILL Open bottom vent completely. Light large chimney starter filled with charcoal briquettes (6 quarts). When top coals are partially covered with ash, pour evenly over half of grill. Set cooking grate in place, cover, and open lid vent completely. Heat grill until hot, about 5 minutes.

3B FOR A GAS GRILL Turn all burners to high, cover, and heat grill until hot, about 15 minutes. Leave primary burner on high and turn off other burner(s).

4 Clean and oil cooking grate. Coat tenderloins with oil, then rub entire surface with sugar mixture. Place tenderloins on cooler side of grill, cover, and cook until center of stuffing registers 145 degrees, 25 to 30 minutes, rotating tenderloins halfway through grilling.

5 Transfer tenderloins to carving board, tent with aluminum foil, and let rest for 5 to 10 minutes. Remove twine, slice tenderloins ½ inch thick, and serve.

596 Olive and Sun-Dried Tomato Stuffing
MAKES ABOUT 1 CUP

½	cup pitted kalamata olives
½	cup oil-packed sun-dried tomatoes, rinsed and chopped coarse
4	anchovy fillets, rinsed
2	garlic cloves, minced
1	teaspoon minced fresh thyme
1	teaspoon grated lemon zest
	Salt and pepper

Pulse all ingredients in food processor until coarsely chopped, 5 to 10 pulses; season with salt and pepper to taste.

597 Porcini and Artichoke Stuffing

MAKES ABOUT 1 CUP

Avoid jarred or canned artichokes; frozen artichokes have a much fresher flavor.

- ½ ounce dried porcini mushrooms, rinsed and minced
- 3 ounces frozen artichoke hearts, thawed and patted dry
- 1 ounce Parmesan cheese, grated (½ cup)
- ¼ cup oil-packed sun-dried tomatoes, rinsed and chopped coarse
- ¼ cup fresh parsley leaves
- 2 tablespoons pine nuts, toasted
- 2 garlic cloves, minced
- 1 teaspoon grated lemon zest plus 2 teaspoons juice
  Salt and pepper

Pulse all ingredients in food processor until coarsely chopped, 5 to 10 pulses; season with salt and pepper to taste.

598 The Right (and Wrong) Way to Stuff Pork Tenderloin

TEST KITCHEN TIP

The trick to keeping the stuffing intact depends on how you butcher and bind the roast.

Coming Unhinged
Butterflying the roast and simply folding the hinged flaps of meat around the stuffing can lead to oozing filling.

Pounded and Rolled
Pounding the butterflied roast before stuffing allows the meat to be tightly rolled, not folded, around the filling.

Grilled Pork Loin with Apple-Cranberry Filling

SERVES 6

This recipe is best prepared with a loin that is 7 to 8 inches long and 4 to 5 inches wide and not enhanced (injected with a salt solution). To make cutting the pork easier, freeze it for 30 minutes. If mustard seeds are unavailable, stir an equal amount of whole-grain mustard into the filling after the apples have been processed. For a spicier stuffing, use the larger amount of cayenne. If you'd like to use wood chunks instead of wood chips when using a charcoal grill, substitute two medium wood chunks, soaked in water for 1 hour, for the wood chip packet. The pork loin can be stuffed and tied a day ahead of time, but don't season the exterior until you are ready to grill.

FILLING

1½ cups (4 ounces) dried apples
1 cup apple cider
¾ cup packed light brown sugar
½ cup cider vinegar
½ cup dried cranberries
1 large shallot, halved lengthwise and sliced thin crosswise
1 tablespoon grated fresh ginger
1 tablespoon yellow mustard seeds
½ teaspoon ground allspice
⅛–¼ teaspoon cayenne pepper

PORK

1 (2½-pound) boneless center-cut pork loin roast, trimmed
   Salt and pepper
2 cups wood chips, soaked in water for 15 minutes and drained

1 FOR THE FILLING Bring all ingredients to simmer in medium saucepan over medium-high heat. Cover, reduce heat to low, and cook until apples are very soft, about 20 minutes. Transfer mixture to fine-mesh strainer set over bowl and press with back of spoon to extract as much liquid as possible. Return liquid to saucepan and simmer over medium-high heat until reduced to ⅓ cup, about 5 minutes; set aside for glazing. Pulse apple mixture in food processor until coarsely chopped, about 15 pulses. Transfer filling to bowl and refrigerate until needed.

599

RECIPE FOR SUCCESS

Sweet Stuffed Pork Loin

✔ WHY THIS RECIPE WORKS

Pork loin has a satisfying, meaty texture, but its leanness puts it at a distinct disadvantage in the flavor department. Most grilled pork loin recipes try to compensate with some combination of brining, rubs, sauces, or condiments. We wanted to try something different: using a stuffing to combat the dryness from the inside out. A center-cut loin roast was the ideal cut for this recipe because the solid muscle cut cleanly and stayed together. A chutney-like filling provided deep flavor that was well suited to the pork. The dense, chewy consistency of our stuffing ensured that it stayed put. Making three or four straight, short cuts in the roast allowed us to open it up into one broad, flat piece on which we could easily spread the filling before rolling it back together. Snugly tying up the rolled roast ensured a compact shape that cooked evenly and sliced easily. Reducing the liquid leftover from preparing the filling to a thick, spreadable consistency gave us a sticky-sweet glaze that was the perfect finishing touch.

2 FOR THE PORK Position roast fat side up. Insert knife ½ inch from bottom of roast and cut horizontally, stopping ½ inch before edge. Open up this flap. Cut through thicker half of roast about ½ inch from bottom, stopping about ½ inch before edge. Open up this flap. Repeat until pork is even ½-inch thickness throughout. If uneven, cover with plastic wrap and use meat pounder to even out. Season interior with salt and pepper and spread filling in even layer, leaving ½-inch border. Roll tightly and tie at 1-inch intervals with kitchen twine. Season with salt and pepper.

3 Using large piece of heavy-duty aluminum foil, wrap chips in 8 by 4½-inch foil packet. (Make sure chips do not poke holes in sides or bottom of packet.) Cut 2 evenly spaced 2-inch slits in top of packet.

4A FOR A CHARCOAL GRILL Open bottom vent halfway. Light large chimney starter three-quarters filled with charcoal briquettes (4½ quarts). When top coals are partially covered with ash, pour evenly over half of grill. Place wood chip packet on coals. Set cooking grate in place, cover, and open lid vent halfway. Heat grill until hot and wood chips are smoking, about 5 minutes.

4B FOR A GAS GRILL Remove cooking grate and place wood chip packet directly on primary burner. Set cooking grate in place, turn all burners to high, cover, and heat grill until hot and wood chips are smoking, about 15 minutes. Leave primary burner on medium-high and turn off other burner(s). (Adjust primary burner as needed to maintain grill temperature of 300 to 325 degrees.)

5 Clean and oil cooking grate. Place pork, fat side up, on cooler side of grill, cover (position lid vent over roast if using charcoal), and cook until meat registers 130 to 135 degrees, 55 minutes to 1 hour 10 minutes, flipping roast halfway through grilling.

6 Brush roast evenly with reserved glaze. (Reheat glaze, if necessary, to make it spreadable.) Continue to cook until glaze is glossy and meat registers 140 degrees, 5 to 10 minutes longer. Transfer to carving board, tent with aluminum foil, and let rest for 15 minutes. Remove twine, cut roast into ½-inch-thick slices, and serve.

VARIATION

600 **Grilled Pork Loin with Apple-Cherry Filling with Caraway**
Substitute dried cherries for cranberries and 1 teaspoon caraway seeds for ginger, mustard seeds, and allspice. After processing filling in food processor, transfer to bowl and stir in 2 teaspoons minced fresh thyme.

601 STEP BY STEP How to Stuff a Pork Loin

1 MAKE FIRST CUT Position roast fat side up. Insert knife ½ inch from bottom of roast and cut horizontally, stopping ½ inch before edge. Open this flap up.

2 MAKE SECOND CUT AND OPEN Cut through thicker half of roast about ½ inch from bottom, stopping about ½ inch before edge. Open this flap up.

3 FLATTEN Repeat until pork loin is even ½-inch thickness throughout. If uneven, cover with plastic wrap and use meat pounder to even out.

4 FILL With long side of meat facing you, season meat and spread filling, leaving ½-inch border on all sides.

5 ROLL Starting from short side, roll pork loin tightly.

6 TIE Using twine, tie roast at 1-inch intervals.

602 Smoky Pork off the Grill

RECIPE FOR SUCCESS

✔ WHY THIS RECIPE WORKS

The biggest challenge when grilling a bulky cut of meat like a pork rib roast is getting the interior cooked to the proper temperature without charring the exterior. We wanted a tender, juicy grilled roast with a thick mahogany crust and plenty of deep, rich flavor. After testing three possible cuts from the loin, we determined that we liked the center-cut rib roast for its flavor and simplicity. Because the meat is a single muscle attached along one side to the bones, there is no need to tie the roast for a tidy presentation. We figured that with such a large roast, using a two-level fire would be essential. But we were surprised to discover that we could cook the roast on the cooler side for the duration. After an hour a mahogany crust developed—no high-temperature sear needed. (It's important to position the roast away—but not too far away—from the coals or flames with the bones facing away from the fire.) Letting the roast rest for a full 30 minutes after it finished on the grill allowed the meat to reabsorb some of the juices lost during cooking.

Grill-Roasted Bone-In Pork Rib Roast

SERVES 6 TO 8

For easier carving, ask the butcher to remove the tip of the chine bone and to cut the remainder of the chine bone between each rib. If you'd like to use wood chunks instead of wood chips when using a charcoal grill, substitute one medium wood chunk, soaked in water for 1 hour, for the wood chip packet. Serve this roast with Orange Salsa with Cuban Flavors (recipe follows), if desired.

- 1 **(4- to 5-pound) center-cut bone-in pork rib roast, chine bone removed, fat trimmed to ¼ inch**
- 4 **teaspoons kosher salt**
- 1 **cup wood chips**
- 1½ **teaspoons pepper**

1 Pat roast dry with paper towels. Lightly score fat cap in 1-inch crosshatch pattern, being careful not to cut into meat. Season roast with salt. Wrap roast in plastic wrap and refrigerate for at least 6 hours or up to 24 hours.

2 Just before grilling, soak wood chips in water for 15 minutes, then drain. Using large piece of heavy-duty aluminum foil, wrap chips in 8 by 4½-inch foil packet. (Make sure chips do not poke holes in sides or bottom of packet.) Cut 2 evenly spaced 2-inch slits in top of packet.

3A FOR A CHARCOAL GRILL Open bottom vent halfway. Light large chimney starter filled with charcoal briquettes (6 quarts). When top coals are partially covered with ash, pour into steeply banked pile against side of grill. Place wood chip packet on coals. Set cooking grate in place, cover, and open lid vent halfway. Heat grill until hot and wood chips are smoking, about 5 minutes.

3B FOR A GAS GRILL Remove cooking grate and place wood chip packet directly on primary burner. Set cooking grate in place, turn all burners to high, cover, and heat grill until hot and wood chips are smoking, about 15 minutes. Turn primary burner to medium-high and turn off other burner(s). (Adjust primary burner as needed during cooking to maintain grill temperature of 325 degrees.)

4 Clean and oil cooking grate. Unwrap roast and season with pepper. Place roast on grate with meat near, but not over, coals and flames and bones facing away from coals and flames. Cover (position lid vent over meat if using charcoal) and cook until meat registers 140 degrees, 1¼ to 1½ hours.

5 Transfer roast to carving board, tent with aluminum foil, and let rest for 30 minutes. Carve into thick slices by cutting between ribs. Serve.

603 Orange Salsa with Cuban Flavors

MAKES ABOUT 2½ CUPS

To make this salsa spicier, reserve and add the chile seeds.

- ½ **teaspoon grated orange zest, plus 5 oranges peeled and segmented, each segment quartered crosswise**
- ½ **cup finely chopped red onion**
- 1 **jalapeño chile, stemmed, seeded, and minced**
- 2 **tablespoons lime juice**
- 2 **tablespoons minced fresh parsley**
- 1 **tablespoon extra-virgin olive oil**
- 2 **teaspoons packed brown sugar**
- 1½ **teaspoons distilled white vinegar**
- 1½ **teaspoons minced fresh oregano**
- 1 **garlic clove, minced**
- ½ **teaspoon ground cumin**
- ½ **teaspoon salt**
- ½ **teaspoon pepper**

Combine all ingredients in medium bowl.

604

STEP BY STEP

Carving Pork Rib Roast

Our Grill-Roasted Bone-In Pork Rib Roast can be served on the bone in thick slabs, or the meat can be removed from the bone and sliced into thinner pieces.

For Thick Bone-In Chops

Stand roast on carving board with bones pointing up and cut between bones into separate chops.

For Thin Boneless Slices

1 Holding tip of bones with your hand, use sharp knife to cut along rib to sever meat from bones.

2 Set meat cut side down on carving board and slice against grain into ½-inch-thick slices.

605

Roast Pork with Bold Cuban Flavors

✓ WHY THIS RECIPE WORKS

We wanted a boldly flavored Cuban-style roast pork with crackling-crisp skin and tender meat infused with flavor. To speed up cooking, we abandoned cooking the pork entirely on the grill (which required constant refueling and rotating over several hours) in favor of a combination cooking method: cooking the pork on the grill until our initial supply of coals died down, and then finishing it in the oven. To give the pork added flavor, we again combined methods, first brining the pork in a powerful solution that included two heads of garlic and orange juice, and then rubbing a similarly flavored paste into slits cut all over the pork.

Cuban-Style Grill-Roasted Pork

SERVES 8 TO 10

Let the meat rest for a full hour before serving or it will not be as tender. This roast has a crisp skin that should be served along with the meat. Traditional accompaniments include black beans, rice, and fried plantains. Serve the pork with Mojo Sauce (recipe follows), if desired.

PORK

- 1 (7- to 8-pound) bone-in, skin-on pork picnic shoulder
- 3 cups sugar
- 2 cups salt
- 2 garlic heads, unpeeled cloves separated and crushed
- 4 cups orange juice (8 oranges)

PASTE

- 12 garlic cloves, chopped coarse
- 2 tablespoons ground cumin
- 2 tablespoons dried oregano
- 1 tablespoon salt
- 1½ teaspoons pepper
- 6 tablespoons orange juice
- 2 tablespoons distilled white vinegar
- 2 tablespoons vegetable oil

1 FOR THE PORK Cut 1-inch-deep slits (1 inch long) all over roast, spaced about 2 inches apart. Dissolve sugar and salt in 6 quarts cold water in large container. Stir in garlic and orange juice. Submerge pork in brine, cover, and refrigerate for 18 to 24 hours. Remove pork from brine and pat dry with paper towels.

2 FOR THE PASTE Pulse garlic, cumin, oregano, salt, and pepper in food processor to coarse paste, about 10 pulses. With processor running, add orange juice, vinegar, and oil and process until smooth, about 20 seconds. Rub paste all over pork and into slits. Wrap meat in plastic wrap and let sit at room temperature for 1 hour.

3A FOR A CHARCOAL GRILL Open bottom vent halfway. Light large chimney starter three-quarters filled with charcoal briquettes (4½ quarts). When top coals are partially covered with ash, pour into steeply banked pile against side of grill. Set cooking grate in place, cover, and open lid vent halfway. Heat grill until hot, about 5 minutes.

3B FOR A GAS GRILL Turn all burners to high, cover, and heat grill until hot, about 15 minutes. Turn primary burner to medium-high and turn off other burner(s). (Adjust primary burner as needed to maintain grill temperature around 325 degrees.)

4 Clean and oil cooking grate. Make two ½-inch folds on long side of 18-inch length of aluminum foil to form reinforced edge. Place foil in center of cooking grate, with reinforced edge over hotter side of grill. Place roast, skin side up, on cooler side of grill so that it covers about one-third of foil. Lift and bend edges of foil to shield sides of pork, tucking in edges. Cover (position lid vent over meat if using charcoal) and cook for 2 hours. During final 20 minutes of grilling, adjust oven rack to lower-middle position and heat oven to 325 degrees.

5 Transfer pork to wire rack set in rimmed baking sheet. Roast pork in oven until skin is browned and crisp and meat registers 190 degrees, 3 to 4 hours.

6 Transfer roast to carving board and let rest for 1 hour. Remove skin in 1 large piece. Scrape off and discard fat from top of roast and from underside of skin. Cut meat away from bone in 3 or 4 large pieces, then slice into ¼-inch-thick slices. Cut skin into strips. Serve.

606 Mojo Sauce

MAKES ABOUT 1 CUP

4	garlic cloves, minced
2	teaspoons kosher salt
½	cup extra-virgin olive oil
½	teaspoon ground cumin
¼	cup distilled white vinegar
¼	cup orange juice
¼	teaspoon dried oregano
⅛	teaspoon pepper

1 Place minced garlic on cutting board and sprinkle with salt. Using flat side of chef's knife, drag garlic and salt back and forth across cutting board in small circular motions until garlic is ground into smooth paste.

2 Heat oil in medium saucepan over medium heat until shimmering. Add garlic paste and cumin and cook, stirring, until fragrant, about 30 seconds. Off heat, whisk in vinegar, orange juice, oregano, and pepper. Transfer to bowl and let cool to room temperature. Whisk sauce to recombine before serving. (Sauce can be refrigerated for up to 24 hours; bring to room temperature before serving.)

608 STEP BY STEP
Building a Foil "Shield"

By protecting the pork roast with an aluminum foil shield, we kept it from getting too dark on the side closest to the heat—no rotation required.

1 FOLD Make two ½-inch folds on long side of 18-inch length of foil to form reinforced edge. Place foil on center of cooking grate, with reinforced edge over hot side of grill. Position roast, skin side up, over cool side of grill so that it covers about ⅓ of foil.

2 LIFT Lift and bend edges of foil to shield sides of roast, tucking in edges.

607 SHOPPING IQ
Picking the Perfect Pork Roast

What's the best cut for Cuban-style pork? We tried them all. Widely available Boston butt (the upper portion of the front leg) was an attractive option thanks to its high fat content. But it comes with no skin attached, and the crisp, flavorful skin is one of the highlights of this dish. Fresh ham (from the rear leg) has skin but is usually too lean. We settled on the picnic shoulder (also called pork shoulder), a flavorful cut from the lower portion of the front leg that almost always comes bone-in—and with a fair share of fat and rind to boot.

Boston Butt

Fatty but skinless

Picnic Shoulder

Our choice: great skin, great fat

Fresh Ham

Great skin but too lean

609 RECIPE FOR SUCCESS
Grilled Pork, Luau-Style

✔ WHY THIS RECIPE WORKS

Kalua pork is a traditional Hawaiian dish of shredded smoked suckling pig that's the centerpiece at luaus. There, a whole pig is cooked over a fire of Hawaiian kiawe wood in a pit lined with rocks and banana leaves. Without easy access to most of those flavor builders, we tried to re-create the smoky, tropical notes with common supermarket items. Pork butt's balance of muscle and fat would stay moist and flavorful during low, slow cooking. Kiawe is a species of mesquite, so we created a foil packet of mesquite wood chips for similar smoke. To replicate the earthy, grassy flavor given off by banana leaves, we rubbed the roast with a blend of green tea, brown sugar, salt, and pepper. Using both the grill and the oven gave us all the smoke and tenderness of pit cooking without the wait (or the digging). Placing the pork in an aluminum pan and covering the pan with foil collected the juices and contained the steam.

Kalua Pork

SERVES 8

Pork butt roast is often labeled Boston butt in the supermarket. If your pork butt comes with an elastic netting, remove it before you rub the pork with the tea. If you'd like to use wood chunks instead of wood chips when using a charcoal grill, substitute six medium wood chunks, soaked in water for 1 hour, for the wood chip packets.

- 3   tablespoons green tea leaves (10 to 15 bags)
- 4   teaspoons kosher salt
- 1   tablespoon packed brown sugar
- 2   teaspoons pepper
- 1   (4- to 5-pound) boneless pork butt roast, trimmed
- 6   cups mesquite wood chips
- 1   (13 by 9-inch) disposable aluminum roasting pan

1 Combine tea, salt, sugar, and pepper in bowl. Pat pork dry with paper towels and rub with tea mixture. Wrap roast tightly in plastic wrap and refrigerate for 6 to 24 hours. Place pork in pan and cover pan loosely with aluminum foil. Poke about twenty ¼-inch holes in foil.

2 Just before grilling, soak wood chips in water for 15 minutes, then drain. Using large piece of heavy-duty aluminum foil, wrap 2 cups chips in 8 by 4½-inch foil packet. (Make sure chips do not poke holes in sides or bottom of packet.) Repeat twice with remaining 4 cups chips for total of 3 packets. Cut 2 evenly spaced 2-inch slits in top of each packet.

3A FOR A CHARCOAL GRILL Open bottom vent halfway. Light large chimney starter three-quarters filled with charcoal briquettes (4½ quarts). When top coals are partially covered with ash, pour into steeply banked pile against side of grill. Place wood chip packets on coals. Set cooking grate in place, cover, and open lid vent halfway. Heat grill until hot and wood chips are smoking, about 5 minutes.

3B FOR A GAS GRILL Remove cooking grate and place wood chip packets directly on primary burner. Set cooking grate in place, turn all burners to high, cover, and heat grill until hot and wood chips are smoking, about 15 minutes. Turn primary burner to medium-high and turn off other burner(s). (Adjust primary burner as needed to maintain grill temperature around 300 degrees.)

4 Place disposable pan on cooler side of grill. Cover (position lid vent over meat if using charcoal) and cook for 2 hours. During last 20 minutes of grilling, adjust oven rack to lower-middle position and heat oven to 325 degrees.

5 Remove disposable pan from grill. Cover pan tightly with new sheet of foil, transfer to oven, and cook until pork is tender and fork inserted in meat meets no resistance, 2 to 3 hours. Let pork rest, covered, for 30 minutes. Unwrap and, when meat is cool enough to handle, shred into bite-size pieces, discarding fat. Strain contents of pan through fine-mesh strainer into fat separator. Let liquid settle, then return ¼ cup defatted pan juices to pork. Serve. (Pork can be refrigerated for up to 3 days.)

610 RECIPE FOR SUCCESS Pork and Hoecakes: A Match Made in BBQ Heaven

✔ WHY THIS RECIPE WORKS

This regional recipe features pork shredded so fine that it resembles pâté. In order to get the pork butt tender enough to shred, we used a combination of grill smoking and oven roasting. A stand mixer fitted with a paddle attachment allowed us to achieve the fine texture we were looking for. Returning some of the pork juices to the shredded mixture gave the meat just the right amount of moisture. A simple sauce topped off the pork sandwich, which is traditionally served on two cornmeal hoecakes.

Tennessee Barbecued Pork Shoulder
SERVES 8 WITH LEFTOVERS

Plan ahead: The roast must be seasoned at least 18 hours in advance. Pork butt roast is often labeled Boston butt in the supermarket. After pulling the pork out of the oven in step 7, do not allow it to rest, as the meat shreds more easily while hot. If you'd like to use wood chunks instead of wood chips on a charcoal grill, substitute 2 medium chunks, soaked in water for 1 hour, for the wood chip packet. We prefer to serve the pulled pork on hoecakes (recipe follows), but regular hamburger buns may be substituted. These sandwiches are also great topped with coleslaw. This recipe makes about 1½ cups of barbecue sauce, but can easily be doubled or tripled.

PORK

- 1 (5- to 6-pound) bone-in pork butt roast, trimmed
  Kosher salt
- 2 cups wood chips
- 1 (13 by 9-inch) disposable aluminum roasting pan
- 1 recipe Hoecakes (recipe follows)
  Dill pickle chips

BARBECUE SAUCE

- 1 cup ketchup
- ¼ cup cider vinegar
- ¼ cup water
- 2 tablespoons yellow mustard
- 1 tablespoon Worcestershire sauce
- 1 teaspoon granulated garlic
- 1 teaspoon pepper

1 FOR THE PORK Lightly score fat cap of roast in 1-inch crosshatch pattern, being careful not to cut into meat. Pat roast dry with paper towels. Place roast on large sheet of plastic wrap, and rub 2 tablespoons salt over entire roast and into slits. Wrap roast tightly in plastic and refrigerate for 18 to 24 hours.

2 FOR THE BARBECUE SAUCE Meanwhile, combine ketchup, vinegar, water, mustard, Worcestershire, granulated garlic, and pepper in medium saucepan and bring to boil over medium-high heat. Reduce heat to medium-low and simmer, whisking constantly, until slightly thickened, about 3 minutes. Transfer sauce to bowl and let cool to room temperature.

3 Just before grilling, soak wood chips in water for 15 minutes, then drain. Using large piece of heavy-duty aluminum foil, wrap chips in 8 by 4½-inch foil packet. (Make sure chips do not poke holes in sides or bottom of packet.) Cut 2 evenly spaced 2-inch slits in top of packet.

4A FOR A CHARCOAL GRILL Open bottom vent completely. Light large chimney starter three-quarters filled with charcoal briquettes (4½ quarts). When top coals are partially covered with ash, pour evenly over half of grill. Place wood chip packet on coals. Set cooking grate in place, cover, and open lid vent completely. Heat grill until hot and wood chips are smoking, about 5 minutes.

4B FOR A GAS GRILL Remove cooking grate and place wood chip packet directly on primary burner. Set cooking grate in place, turn all burners to high, cover, and heat grill until hot and wood chips are smoking, about 15 minutes. Turn primary burner to medium-high and turn off other burner(s). (Adjust primary burner as needed to maintain grill temperature of 300 degrees.)

5 Unwrap pork and place fat side down in disposable pan. Place pan on cooler side of grill. Cover grill (position lid vent over meat if using charcoal) and cook until pork registers 120 degrees, about 2 hours. During final 20 minutes of grilling, adjust oven rack to middle position and heat oven to 300 degrees.

6 Transfer pan from grill to rimmed baking sheet. Cover pan tightly with foil and transfer to oven (still on baking sheet). Cook until fork inserted into pork meets little resistance and meat registers 210 degrees, about 3 hours.

7 Carefully remove foil from pan (steam will escape). Remove blade bone from roast using tongs. Immediately transfer hot pork to bowl of stand mixer fitted with paddle attachment. Strain accumulated juices from pan through fine-mesh strainer set over separate bowl; discard solids in strainer.

8 Mix pork on low speed until meat is finely shredded, about 1½ minutes. Whisk pork juices to recombine if separated and add 1½ cups juices to shredded pork. Continue mixing pork on low speed until juices are incorporated, about 15 seconds longer. Season with salt to taste, and add more pork juices if desired. Serve on hoecakes, topped with barbecue sauce and pickles.

611 Hoecakes
MAKES 16 HOECAKES

3	cups (15 ounces) white cornmeal
2	tablespoons sugar
2	teaspoons baking powder
1½	teaspoons salt
2	cups buttermilk
2	large eggs
2	tablespoons bacon fat or vegetable oil

1 Adjust oven rack to middle position and heat oven to 200 degrees. Set wire rack in rimmed baking sheet and place in oven. Whisk cornmeal, sugar, baking powder, and salt together in large bowl. Beat buttermilk and eggs together in separate bowl. Whisk buttermilk mixture into cornmeal mixture until combined.

2A FOR A SKILLET Heat 1 teaspoon fat in 12-inch nonstick skillet over medium heat until shimmering. Using level ¼-cup dry measuring cup, drop 3 evenly spaced scoops of batter into skillet, smoothing tops slightly if necessary.

2B FOR A GRIDDLE Heat 1 tablespoon fat on 400-degree nonstick griddle until shimmering. Using level ¼-cup dry measuring cup, drop 8 evenly spaced scoops of batter onto griddle, smoothing tops slightly if necessary.

3 Cook until small bubbles begin to appear on surface of cakes and edges are set, about 2 minutes. Flip and cook until second side is golden brown, about 2 minutes longer. Transfer hoecakes to prepared sheet in oven. Repeat with remaining fat and batter: 5 additional batches for skillet or 1 additional batch for griddle. Serve.

Barbecued Pulled Pork
SERVES 8

Pork butt roast is often labeled Boston butt in the supermarket. Preparing pulled pork requires little effort, but lots of time. Plan on 10 hours from start to finish. Hickory is the classic choice when it comes to supplying the smoke in this recipe. If you'd like to use wood chunks instead of wood chips when using a charcoal grill, substitute four medium wood chunks, soaked in water for 1 hour, for the wood chip packets. Serve on plain white bread or warmed rolls with dill pickle chips and coleslaw.

- 1 (6- to 8-pound) bone-in pork butt roast, trimmed
- ¾ cup Dry Rub for Barbecue (recipe follows)
- 4 cups wood chips
- 1 (13 by 9-inch) disposable aluminum roasting pan
- 1 brown paper grocery bag
- 2 cups barbecue sauce (recipes follow)

1 Pat pork dry with paper towels, then massage dry rub into meat. Wrap roast in plastic wrap and refrigerate for at least 3 hours or up to 3 days.

2 At least 1 hour prior to cooking, remove roast from refrigerator, unwrap, and let sit at room temperature. Just before grilling, soak wood chips in water for 15 minutes, then drain. Using large piece of heavy-duty aluminum foil, wrap 2 cups chips in 8 by 4½-inch foil packet. (Make sure chips do not poke holes in sides or bottom of packet.) Repeat with remaining 2 cups chips. Cut 2 evenly spaced 2-inch slits in top of each packet.

3A FOR A CHARCOAL GRILL Open bottom vent halfway. Light large chimney starter three-quarters filled with charcoal briquettes (4½ quarts). When top coals are partially covered with ash, pour evenly over half of grill. Place wood chip packets on coals. Set cooking grate in place, cover, and open lid vent halfway. Heat grill until hot and wood chips are smoking, about 5 minutes.

3B FOR A GAS GRILL Remove cooking grate and place wood chip packets directly on primary burner. Set cooking grate in place, turn all burners to high, cover, and heat grill until hot and wood chips are smoking, about 15 minutes. Turn primary burner to medium-high and turn off other burner(s). (Adjust primary burner as needed to maintain grill temperature of 325 degrees.)

612
RECIPE FOR SUCCESS
A BBQ Classic, Simplified

✓ WHY THIS RECIPE WORKS
Most recipes for slow-cooked pulled pork demand the attention of the cook for 8 hours or more. We wanted to find a way to make moist, fork-tender pulled pork without the marathon cooking time and constant attention to the grill. For the seasoning, we found that keeping it simple produced great results. A blend of spices—paprika, chili powder, cumin, and oregano, along with some salt, sugar, and a trio of peppers—provided plenty of complexity and bold flavor. Simply massaging the rub into the meat was straightforward and effective. Placing the roast in a disposable roasting pan on the grill helped protect it from the heat so there was no risk of scorching, while wood chips provided plenty of smoky flavor. We then finished the pork in the oven at a relatively low temperature. This method produced almost the same results as the traditional barbecue, but in considerably less time and with much less effort. Resting the pork for an hour inside a paper grocery sack allowed time for the flavorful juices to be reabsorbed.

4 Set roast in disposable pan, place on cooler side of grill, cover, and cook for 3 hours. During final 20 minutes of cooking, adjust oven rack to lower-middle position and heat oven to 325 degrees.

5 Wrap disposable pan with heavy-duty foil and cook in oven until meat is fork-tender, about 2 hours.

6 Carefully slide foil-wrapped pan with roast into brown paper bag. Crimp end shut and let rest for 1 hour.

7 Transfer roast to carving board and unwrap. Separate roast into muscle sections, removing fat, if desired, and tearing meat into shreds with your fingers. Place shredded meat in large bowl and toss with 1 cup barbecue sauce. Serve, passing remaining sauce separately.

613 Dry Rub for Barbecue

MAKES ABOUT 1 CUP

You can adjust the proportions of spices in this all-purpose rub or add or subtract a spice, as you wish.

- ¼ cup paprika
- 2 tablespoons chili powder
- 2 tablespoons ground cumin
- 2 tablespoons packed dark brown sugar
- 2 tablespoons salt
- 1 tablespoon dried oregano
- 1 tablespoon granulated sugar
- 1 tablespoon pepper
- 1 tablespoon white pepper
- 1-2 teaspoons cayenne pepper

Combine all ingredients in small bowl.

614 Eastern North Carolina Barbecue Sauce

MAKES ABOUT 2 CUPS

This sauce can be refrigerated for up to four days.

- 1 cup distilled white vinegar
- 1 cup cider vinegar
- 1 tablespoon sugar
- 1 tablespoon red pepper flakes
- 1 tablespoon hot sauce
    Salt and pepper

Mix all ingredients together in bowl and season with salt and pepper to taste.

615 Western South Carolina Barbecue Sauce

MAKES ABOUT 2 CUPS

This sauce can be refrigerated for up to four days.

- 1 tablespoon vegetable oil
- ½ cup finely chopped onion
- 2 garlic cloves, minced
- ½ cup cider vinegar
- ½ cup Worcestershire sauce
- 1 tablespoon dry mustard
- 1 tablespoon packed dark brown sugar
- 1 tablespoon paprika
- 1 teaspoon salt
- 1 teaspoon cayenne pepper
- 1 cup ketchup

Heat oil in small saucepan over medium heat. Add onion and cook, stirring occasionally, until softened, 5 to 7 minutes. Stir in garlic and cook until fragrant, about 30 seconds. Stir in vinegar, Worcestershire, mustard, sugar, paprika, salt, and cayenne, bring to simmer, and stir in ketchup. Cook over low heat until thickened, about 15 minutes.

616 Mid-South Carolina Mustard Sauce

MAKES ABOUT 2½ CUPS

This sauce can be refrigerated for up to four days.

- 1 cup cider vinegar
- 1 cup vegetable oil
- 6 tablespoons Dijon mustard
- 2 tablespoons maple syrup or honey
- 4 teaspoons Worcestershire sauce
- 1 teaspoon hot sauce
    Salt and pepper

Mix all ingredients together in bowl and season with salt and pepper to taste.

617

STEP BY STEP

Key Steps to Pulled Pork

1 TRIM If using picnic roast, slide knife under skin and work around to loosen it while pulling it off with your other hand. Boston butt, or shoulder roast, does not need to be trimmed.

2 GRILL Set unwrapped roast in disposable aluminum pan on cooking grate opposite coals and wood.

3 DEBONE When meat has cooled slightly, pull meat from bones and separate major muscle sections; remove fat as desired.

4 SHRED Tear meat into thin shreds.

618 Pulled Pork Made Approachable

✓ WHY THIS RECIPE WORKS

Traditional vinegar-based Lexington-style pulled pork recipes take hours to prepare. We wanted to simplify this recipe without sacrificing flavor. To do so, we used a combination of grilling and oven roasting to reduce the cooking time from all day to just 4 or 5 hours. To infuse the pulled pork with ample smoke flavor despite the abbreviated cooking time, we doubled the amount of wood chips. We opted to use flavorful pork butt, since it has enough fat to stay moist and succulent during long, slow cooking. To bump up the flavor, we coated the pork with a basic barbecue rub and let it sit for at least an hour before placing it on the grill.

Lexington Pulled Pork

SERVES 8

If you'd like to use wood chunks instead of wood chips when using a charcoal grill, substitute four medium wood chunks, soaked in water for 1 hour, for the wood chip packets. Pork butt roast is often labeled Boston butt in the supermarket. The barbecue sauce can be made while the pork is in the oven.

- 2 tablespoons paprika
- 2 tablespoons pepper
- 2 tablespoons packed brown sugar
- 1 tablespoon salt
- 1 (4- to 5-pound) boneless pork butt roast, trimmed
- 4 cups wood chips
- 1 recipe Lexington Barbecue Sauce (page 385), warmed

1 Combine paprika, pepper, sugar, and salt in bowl. Pat pork dry with paper towels and rub evenly with spice mixture. Wrap roast in plastic wrap and let sit at room temperature for at least 1 hour or refrigerate for up to 24 hours. Just before grilling, soak wood chips in water for 15 minutes, then drain. Using large piece of heavy-duty aluminum foil, wrap 2 cups chips in 8 by 4½-inch foil packet. (Make sure chips do not poke holes in sides or bottom of packet.) Repeat with remaining 2 cups chips. Cut 2 evenly spaced 2-inch slits in top of each packet.

2A FOR A CHARCOAL GRILL Open bottom vent halfway. Light large chimney starter half filled with charcoal briquettes (3 quarts). When top coals are partially covered with ash, pour into steeply banked pile against side of grill. Place wood chip packets on coals. Set cooking grate in place, cover, and open lid vent halfway. Heat grill until hot and wood chips are smoking, about 5 minutes.

2B FOR A GAS GRILL Remove cooking grate and place wood chip packets directly on primary burner. Set cooking grate in place, turn all burners to high, cover, and heat grill until hot and wood chips are smoking, about 15 minutes. Turn primary burner to medium and turn off other burner(s). (Adjust primary burner as needed to maintain grill temperature around 275 degrees.)

3 Clean and oil cooking grate. Unwrap roast and place on cooler side of grill. Cover (position lid vent over roast if using charcoal) and cook until pork has dark, rosy crust, about 2 hours. During final 20 minutes of grilling, adjust oven rack to lower-middle position and heat oven to 325 degrees.

4 Transfer pork to large roasting pan, cover pan tightly with foil, and transfer to oven. Roast pork until fork slips easily in and out of meat, 2 to 3 hours. Remove pork from oven and let rest, still covered with foil, for 30 minutes. When cool enough to handle, unwrap pork and pull meat into thin shreds, discarding excess fat and gristle, adding ½ cup barbecue sauce as you shred. Serve with remaining sauce.

VARIATION

619 South Carolina Pulled Pork

This regional recipe, nicknamed "Carolina Gold," has a distinctive mustard-based sauce.

Substitute following mixture for spice mixture in step 1 of Lexington Pulled Pork: 3 tablespoons dry mustard, 2 tablespoons salt, 1½ tablespoons packed light brown sugar, 2 teaspoons pepper, 2 teaspoons paprika, and ¼ teaspoon cayenne pepper.

Substitute following South Carolina mustard barbecue sauce for Lexington sauce: Whisk together ½ cup yellow mustard, ½ cup packed light brown sugar, ¼ cup distilled white vinegar, 2 tablespoons Worcestershire sauce, 1 tablespoon hot sauce, 1 teaspoon salt, and 1 teaspoon pepper. Brush pork with ½ cup sauce before finishing in the oven. (Sauce can be refrigerated for up to 4 days.)

620 Lexington Barbecue Sauce

MAKES ABOUT 2½ CUPS

This vinegary sauce is a standard in North Carolina. It has just enough ketchup and sugar to take the edge off the acidity.

1	**cup water**
1	**cup cider vinegar**
½	**cup ketchup**
1	**tablespoon sugar**
¾	**teaspoon salt**
½	**teaspoon pepper**
½	**teaspoon red pepper flakes**

Whisk all ingredients together in bowl until sugar and salt are dissolved.

621

STEP BY STEP

How to Finish Lexington Pulled Pork

1 FINISH IN OVEN After taking pork off grill, transfer it to roasting pan, cover pan with foil, and finish in 325-degree oven.

2 SHRED AND SAUCE Wearing kitchen gloves to protect your hands from heat, shred (or "pull") pork into thin strands, adding sauce as you go.

622

Tender, Tangy Pulled Chicken

✔ WHY THIS RECIPE WORKS

Barbecuing is the perfect method for cooking fatty cuts of pork or beef, but relatively lean chicken is another story. For an excellent barbecued pulled chicken recipe that wouldn't take all day, we chose whole chicken legs, which combine great flavor, low cost, and resistance to overcooking. The legs cooked gently but thoroughly over indirect heat, absorbing plenty of smoke flavor along the way. Once the chicken finished cooking, we hand-shredded half and machine-processed the other half to produce the perfect texture. The chicken then just had to be combined with a quick barbecue sauce for a truly bun-worthy pulled chicken recipe.

Barbecued Pulled Chicken

SERVES 6 TO 8

Chicken leg quarters consist of drumsticks attached to thighs; often also attached are backbone sections that must be trimmed away. If you'd like to use wood chunks instead of wood chips when using a charcoal grill, substitute two medium wood chunks, soaked in water for 1 hour, for the wood chip packet. Serve the pulled chicken on hamburger rolls or sandwich bread, with pickles and coleslaw.

CHICKEN

- 2 cups wood chips, soaked in water for 15 minutes and drained
- 1 (16 by 12-inch) disposable aluminum roasting pan (if using charcoal)
- 8 (14-ounce) chicken leg quarters, trimmed
  Salt and pepper

SAUCE

- 1 large onion, peeled and quartered
- ¼ cup water
- 1½ cups ketchup
- 1½ cups apple cider
- ¼ cup molasses
- ¼ cup cider vinegar
- 3 tablespoons Worcestershire sauce
- 3 tablespoons Dijon mustard
- ½ teaspoon pepper
- 1 tablespoon vegetable oil
- 1½ tablespoons chili powder
- 2 garlic cloves, minced
- ½ teaspoon cayenne pepper
  Hot sauce

1 FOR THE CHICKEN Using large piece of heavy-duty aluminum foil, wrap chips in 8 by 4 ½-inch foil packet. (Make sure chips do not poke holes in sides or bottom of packet.) Cut 2 evenly spaced 2-inch slits in top of packet.

2A FOR A CHARCOAL GRILL Open bottom vent halfway and place disposable pan in center of grill. Light large chimney starter three-quarters filled with charcoal briquettes (4½ quarts). When top coals are partially covered with ash, pour into 2 even piles on either side of disposable pan. Place wood chip packet on 1 pile of coals. Set cooking grate in place, cover, and open lid vent halfway. Heat grill until hot and wood chips are smoking, about 5 minutes.

2B FOR A GAS GRILL Remove cooking grate and place wood chip packet directly on primary burner. Set cooking grate in place, turn all burners to high, cover, and heat grill until hot and wood chips are smoking, about 15 minutes. Turn all burners to medium. (Adjust burners as needed during cooking to maintain grill temperature between 250 and 300 degrees.)

3 Clean and oil cooking grate. Pat chicken dry with paper towels and season with salt and pepper. Place chicken skin side up on grill (over disposable pan if using charcoal). Cover (position lid vent over meat if using charcoal) and cook until chicken registers 185 degrees, 1 to 1½ hours, rotating chicken pieces halfway through cooking. Transfer chicken to carving board, tent with foil, and let rest until cool enough to handle.

4 FOR THE SAUCE Meanwhile, process onion and water in food processor until mixture resembles slush, about 30 seconds. Strain through fine-mesh strainer set over liquid measuring cup, pressing on solids with rubber spatula (you should have ¾ cup strained onion juice). Discard solids in strainer.

5 Whisk onion juice, ketchup, cider, molasses, 3 tablespoons vinegar, Worcestershire, mustard, and pepper together in bowl. Heat oil in large saucepan over medium heat until shimmering. Stir in chili powder, garlic, and cayenne and cook until fragrant, about 30 seconds. Stir in ketchup mixture, bring to simmer, and cook over medium-low heat until slightly thickened, about 15 minutes (you should have about 4 cups of sauce). Transfer 2 cups sauce to serving bowl; leave remaining sauce in saucepan.

6 Remove and discard skin from chicken legs. Using your fingers, pull meat off bones, separating larger pieces (which should fall off bones easily) from smaller, drier pieces into 2 equal piles.

7 Pulse smaller chicken pieces in food processor until just coarsely chopped, 3 or 4 pulses, stirring chicken with rubber spatula after each pulse. Add chopped chicken to sauce in saucepan. Using your fingers or 2 forks, pull larger chicken pieces into long shreds and add to saucepan. Stir in remaining 1 tablespoon vinegar, cover, and heat chicken over medium-low heat, stirring occasionally, until heated through, about 10 minutes. Add hot sauce to taste, and serve, passing remaining sauce separately.

VARIATIONS

623 **Barbecued Pulled Chicken with Peach Sauce**
In step 5, omit apple cider and molasses. Whisk 1 cup water and ¾ cup peach preserves with onion juice, ketchup, vinegar, Worcestershire, mustard, and pepper. Proceed with sauce as directed.

624 **Barbecued Pulled Chicken for a Crowd**
SERVES 10 TO 12
This technique works well on a charcoal grill but not so well on a gas grill. If your gas grill is large and can accommodate more than eight legs, follow the master recipe, adding as many legs as will comfortably fit in a single layer.

Increase amount of charcoal briquettes to 6 quarts. Use 12 chicken legs and slot them into V-shaped roasting rack set on top of cooking grate over disposable aluminum pan. Increase cooking time in step 3 to 1½ to 1¾ hours. In step 5, remove only 1 cup of sauce from saucepan. In step 7, pulse chicken in food processor in 2 batches.

625 SHOPPING IQ
Wood Smoke Taste Test

Hickory and mesquite are the most readily available types of smoking wood, but some grilling pros swear by more exotic options. To see for ourselves how much difference the wood really makes, we used eight types to smoke chicken, salmon, baby back ribs, and pork chops. Our old standby, hickory, was acceptable but "generic." Mesquite's distinctive flavor was a favorite, while "sweet," "subtle" apple and cherry wood were big hits.

WOOD	CHICKEN	FISH	BEEF/ PORK	COMMENTS
Apple	Great	Great	Great	An all-around hit, with "sweet," "fruity," "subtly complex" flavor.
Cherry	Great	Great	Great	Well liked for "mild," "fruity" sweetness.
Hickory	Good	Good	Good	Overall, "generic but good," with "balanced" flavor.
Oak	Good	Good	Good	"Mild," "nutty," and "herbal," with hints of "vanilla."
Maple	Good	X	Good	Evoked pleasant memories of "bacon" for some but was "resin-y" on salmon.
Alder	X	Good	Good	"Delicate" flavor with notes of "coriander" and "juniper," though some found it "bitter" with chicken.
Pecan	X	X	Good	"Intense" and "spicy" with pork but brought "cigarette-like" off-flavors to chicken and fish.

626

Pesto Isn't Just for Pasta

✓ WHY THIS RECIPE WORKS

Basil pesto isn't just for pasta. We found a way to imbue chicken with basil and garlic that would hold up on the grill. How did we get enough flavor into the chicken? We used homemade pesto, which tastes stronger and fresher than store-bought. We added the pesto base to separate mixtures for marinating, stuffing, and saucing the chicken. We found that bone-in chicken breasts had the most flavor. We cut pockets in them to fill with pesto and then marinated the stuffed breasts in more pesto. We added a third dose of pesto in a sauce to serve with the chicken after it was grilled.

Grilled Pesto Chicken

SERVES 4

- 4 cups fresh basil leaves
- ¾ cup extra-virgin olive oil
- 5 garlic cloves, peeled
- 1½ tablespoons lemon juice
  Salt and pepper
- 2 ounces Parmesan cheese, grated (1 cup)
- 4 (12-ounce) bone-in split chicken breasts, trimmed

1 Process basil, ½ cup oil, garlic, lemon juice, and ¾ teaspoon salt in food processor until smooth, about 1 minute, scraping down bowl as needed. Transfer ¼ cup pesto to large bowl and set aside for marinade. Add Parmesan to pesto left in processor and pulse to incorporate, about 3 pulses; transfer ¼ cup pesto to small bowl and set aside for stuffing. Add remaining ¼ cup oil to pesto left in processor and pulse to incorporate, about 3 pulses; set aside for serving.

2 Starting on thick side of breast, closest to breastbone, cut horizontal pocket in each breast, stopping ½ inch from edge so halves remain attached. Season chicken, inside and out, with salt and pepper. Place 1 tablespoon pesto reserved for stuffing in each pocket. Tie each chicken breast with 2 pieces kitchen twine to secure. In large bowl, rub chicken with pesto reserved for marinade, cover, and refrigerate for 1 hour.

3A FOR A CHARCOAL GRILL Open bottom vent completely. Light large chimney starter filled with charcoal briquettes (6 quarts). When top coals are partially covered with ash, pour evenly over half of grill. Set cooking grate in place, cover, and open lid vent completely. Heat grill until hot, about 5 minutes.

3B FOR A GAS GRILL Turn all burners to high, cover, and heat grill until hot, about 15 minutes. Turn all burners to medium-low. (Adjust burners as needed to maintain grill temperature of 350 degrees.)

4 Clean and oil cooking grate. Place chicken skin side up on grill (cooler side if using charcoal). Cover and cook until chicken registers 155 degrees, 25 to 35 minutes.

5 Slide chicken to hotter side of grill (if using charcoal) or turn all burners to high (if using gas), and flip skin side down. Cover and cook until well browned and chicken registers 160 degrees, 5 to 10 minutes.

6 Transfer chicken to platter, tent with aluminum foil, and let rest for 5 to 10 minutes. Remove twine, carve chicken, and serve with remaining sauce.

STEP BY STEP

Making a Chicken Pocket

To flavor our Grilled Pesto Chicken from the inside out, we cut pockets in the breasts and stuff them with pesto. It's not difficult:

1 SLICE POCKET Starting on thick side closest to breastbone, cut horizontal pocket in each breast, stopping ½ inch from edge.

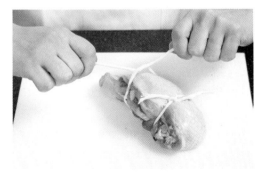

2 TIE After you've stuffed breasts with pesto, tie them with 2 pieces of kitchen twine at even intervals.

628 RECIPE FOR SUCCESS
Chicken Cordon Bleu Takes an Italian Detour

✓ WHY THIS RECIPE WORKS

Chicken cordon bleu solves the problem of dry, mild-flavored chicken breasts with a flavorful stuffing of sharp, nutty melted cheese and salty sliced ham. We wanted to bring this concept to the grill, but leaky cheese can cause flare-ups as it drips from the chicken onto the coals. Off the bat, we knew we needed a strongly flavored stuffing for our chicken to stand up to the grill's smoke. We settled on more flavorful prosciutto and fontina cheese rather than the usual deli ham and Swiss cheese. We butterflied the chicken breasts, placed prosciutto-wrapped fontina inside, and tied each breast up with kitchen twine. Encasing the fontina in prosciutto rather than layering it on top prevented the cheese from leaking. We also added a simple compound butter enlivened by shallot and tarragon for additional moisture and flavor. Cooking the stuffed breasts over a modified two-level fire allowed us to first sear the breasts over the hot coals for color and flavor and finish cooking them over more moderate indirect heat.

Grilled Stuffed Chicken Breasts with Prosciutto and Fontina
SERVES 4

If you're using kosher chicken breasts, do not brine them. For more information on preparing the chicken for the grill, see "Assembling Stuffed Chicken Breasts for Grilling." You can serve the chicken on the bone, but we prefer to carve the breast meat from the bone and slice it before serving.

4   (10- to 12-ounce) bone-in split chicken breasts, trimmed
    Salt and pepper
4   tablespoons unsalted butter, softened
1   shallot, minced
4   teaspoons chopped fresh tarragon
2   ounces fontina cheese, rind removed, cut into four 3 by ½-inch sticks
4   thin slices prosciutto (1½ ounces)

1 Starting on thick side of breast closest to breastbone, cut horizontal pocket in each breast, stopping ½ inch from edge so halves remain attached. Dissolve ¼ cup salt in 2 quarts cold water in large container. Submerge chicken breasts in brine, cover, and refrigerate for 30 minutes to 1 hour. Remove chicken from brine and pat dry with paper towels. Season chicken with pepper.

2A FOR A CHARCOAL GRILL Open bottom vent completely. Light large chimney starter filled with charcoal briquettes (6 quarts). When top coals are partially covered with ash, pour evenly over half of grill. Set cooking grate in place, cover, and open lid vent completely. Heat grill until hot, about 5 minutes.

2B FOR A GAS GRILL Turn all burners to high, cover, and heat grill until hot, about 15 minutes. Leave primary burner on high and turn off other burner(s). (Adjust primary burner as needed to maintain grill temperature of 350 degrees.)

3 Meanwhile, combine butter, shallot, and tarragon in bowl. Roll each piece of fontina in 1 slice prosciutto. Spread equal amount of butter mixture inside each breast. Place 1 prosciutto-wrapped piece of fontina inside each breast and fold breast over to enclose. Evenly space 3 pieces of kitchen twine (each about 12 inches long) beneath each breast and tie, trimming any excess.

4 Clean and oil cooking grate. Place chicken skin side down on hotter side of grill. Cook (covered if using gas) until well browned on first side, 4 to 6 minutes. Flip chicken and cook until second side is just opaque, about 2 minutes. Move chicken to cooler side of grill, skin side up, with thicker side of breasts facing coals and flames. Cover and continue to cook, until chicken registers 160 degrees, 25 to 35 minutes longer.

5 Transfer chicken to carving board, tent with aluminum foil, and let rest for 5 to 10 minutes. Remove twine, cut meat from bone, slice meat ½ inch thick, and serve.

VARIATIONS

629 Grilled Stuffed Chicken Breasts with Black Forest Ham and Gruyère

Substitute 1 teaspoon minced fresh thyme for tarragon and add 1 tablespoon Dijon mustard to butter mixture. Substitute Gruyère cheese for fontina and 4 slices Black Forest ham for prosciutto.

630 Grilled Stuffed Chicken Breasts with Salami and Mozzarella

Substitute 3 minced garlic cloves for shallot, basil for tarragon, low-moisture mozzarella cheese for fontina, and 2 slices Genoa salami for each slice of prosciutto.

631 STEP BY STEP Assembling Stuffed Chicken Breasts for Grilling

1 BUTTERFLY BREAST Starting on thick side closest to breastbone, cut horizontal pocket in each breast, stopping ½ inch from edge.

2 SPREAD BUTTER Spread equal portion of flavorful compound butter inside each breast.

3 ADD FILLING Place 1 prosciutto-wrapped piece of cheese inside each breast and fold breast over to enclose.

4 TIE UP Tie each breast with three 12-inch pieces of kitchen twine at even intervals.

632 RECIPE FOR SUCCESS
South-of-the-Border Grill-Roasted Chicken

✓ WHY THIS RECIPE WORKS

In Mexico's Sinaloa region, chicken is marinated with orange, garlic, and herbs and roasted over embers. To bring this dish to American kitchens, we made our marinade with orange juice concentrate. To help the flavor penetrate, we scored the chicken before marinating it for at least 2 hours. Butterflying, halving, and skewering the chicken made it easier to handle. We also reserved some of the marinade to baste the chicken while grilling. Oregano, thyme, and chipotle chile in adobo rounded out our basting liquid's flavor. Adding a wood chip packet to the grill infused the chicken with savory, smoky flavor.

Sinaloa-Style Grill-Roasted Chickens
SERVES 4 TO 6

You will need four 12-inch metal skewers for this recipe. If you'd like to use wood chunks instead of wood chips when using a charcoal grill, substitute 2 medium wood chunks, soaked in water for 1 hour, for the wood chip packet.

- 2 (3½- to 4-pound) whole chickens, giblets discarded
- 2 onions, chopped
- 1 (12-ounce) can frozen orange juice concentrate, thawed
- ¼ cup extra-virgin olive oil
- 2 garlic heads, cloves separated and peeled (20 cloves)
  Salt and pepper
- 1 tablespoon chopped fresh oregano
- 1 tablespoon minced fresh thyme
- 2 teaspoons minced canned chipotle chile in adobo sauce
- 1½ cups wood chips
  Lime wedges

1 With 1 chicken breast side down, use kitchen shears to cut along both sides of backbone. Discard backbone and trim any excess fat or skin at neck. Flip chicken over and split in half lengthwise through breastbone using chef's knife. Cut ½-inch-deep slits across breast, thighs, and legs, about ½ inch apart. Tuck wingtips behind back. Repeat with second chicken.

2 Process onions, orange juice concentrate, oil, garlic, and 2 tablespoons salt in blender until smooth, about 1 minute. Transfer ¾ cup mixture to bowl and stir in oregano, thyme, and chipotle; set aside for grilling. Divide remaining marinade between two 1-gallon zipper-lock bags. Add chickens to bags and toss to coat. Press out as much air as possible, seal bags, and refrigerate for at least 2 hours or up to 24 hours, flipping occasionally.

3 Before grilling, soak wood chips in water for 15 minutes, then drain. Using large piece of heavy-duty aluminum foil, wrap chips in 8 by 4½-inch foil packet. (Make sure chips do not poke holes in packet.) Cut 2 evenly spaced 2-inch slits in top of packet. Remove chickens from marinade and pat dry with paper towels; discard marinade. Insert 1 skewer lengthwise through thickest part of breast down through thigh of each chicken half.

4A FOR A CHARCOAL GRILL Open bottom vent halfway. Light large chimney starter filled with charcoal briquettes (6 quarts). When top coals are partially covered with ash, pour into steeply banked pile against side of grill. Place wood chip packet on coals. Set cooking grate in place, cover, and open lid vent halfway. Heat grill until hot and wood chips are smoking, about 5 minutes.

4B FOR A GAS GRILL Remove cooking grate and place wood chip packet directly on primary burner. Set cooking grate in place, turn all burners to high, cover, and heat grill until hot and wood chips are smoking, about 15 minutes. Leave primary burner on high and turn off other burner(s). (Adjust primary burner as needed to maintain grill temperature between 350 to 375 degrees.)

5 Clean and oil cooking grate. Place chicken halves skin side up on cooler side of grill with legs pointing toward fire. Cover and cook for 45 minutes, basting every 15 minutes with reserved marinade.

6 Switch placement of chickens, with legs pointing toward fire, and continue to cook, covered, until breasts register 160 degrees and thighs register 175 degrees, 30 to 45 minutes. Transfer to carving board, tent with foil, and let rest for 20 minutes. Carve and serve with lime wedges.

633 STEP BY STEP Sinaloa-Style Grill-Roasted Chickens

1 BUTTERFLY With chickens breast side down, use kitchen shears to cut out backbones; press birds flat.

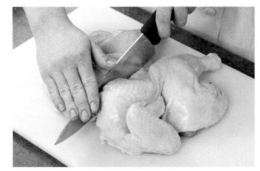

2 HALVE Flip chickens over and split them in half lengthwise through their breastbones using chef's knife to make them easier to grill.

3 SCORE To allow marinade to penetrate meat, cut ½-inch-deep slits across breasts, thighs, and legs, about ½ inch apart.

4 MARINATE Divide chickens and marinade between two 1-gallon zipper-lock bags and refrigerate for 2 to 24 hours.

5 SKEWER To help chickens hold their shape, insert skewer lengthwise through thickest part of each breast and through thigh.

6 GRILL Place chickens skin side up on cooler side of grill with legs pointing toward fire. Cover and cook, basting with reserved marinade.

RECIPE FOR SUCCESS

Game for Grilled Game Hens

✓ WHY THIS RECIPE WORKS

Grilling has the potential to give Cornish game hens great smoky flavor and really crisp skin, but it's not without its problems. Rendered fat from the skin can cause flare-ups, and getting the skin crisp without overcooking the delicate breast meat is tricky. Placing a disposable roasting pan in the middle of the grill allowed us to bank coals on either side and provided a place for the rendered fat to drip without causing flare-ups. Butterflying the hens made each bird a uniform thickness, which promoted even cooking, and also put all of the skin on one side, which could face the coals and crisp more quickly. To keep our Cornish game hens intact once butterflied, we skewered them. Our spice rub emphasized the smoky flavor of the birds and also helped crisp the skin even further.

Grill-Roasted Cornish Game Hens

SERVES 4

To add smoke flavor to the hens, use the optional wood chips. If you'd like to use wood chunks instead of wood chips when using a charcoal grill, substitute four medium wood chunks, soaked in water for 1 hour, for the wood chip packets. You will need four 8- to 10-inch flat metal skewers for this recipe.

- 4 (1¼- to 1½-pound) whole Cornish game hens, giblets discarded
  Salt
- 2 tablespoons packed brown sugar
- 1 tablespoon paprika
- 2 teaspoons garlic powder
- 2 teaspoons chili powder
- 1 teaspoon pepper
- 1 teaspoon ground coriander
- ⅛ teaspoon cayenne pepper
- 4 cups wood chips, soaked in water for 15 minutes and drained (optional)
- 1 (16 by 12-inch) disposable aluminum roasting pan (if using charcoal)
- 1 recipe glaze (recipes follow)

1 With 1 game hen breast side down, use kitchen shears to cut along both sides of backbone; discard backbone. With skin side down, make ¼-inch cut into bone separating breast halves. Lightly press on ribs to flatten hen. Tuck wingtips behind back. Repeat with remaining 3 hens.

2 Dissolve ½ cup salt in 4 quarts cold water in large container. Submerge hens in brine, cover, and refrigerate for 30 minutes to 1 hour.

3 Combine sugar, paprika, garlic powder, chili powder, pepper, coriander, and cayenne in bowl. Remove hens from brine and pat dry with paper towels.

4 Insert flat metal skewer ½ inch from end of drumstick through skin and meat and out other side. Turn leg so that end of drumstick faces wing, then insert tip of skewer into meaty section of thigh under bone. Press skewer completely through breast and second thigh. Fold end of drumstick toward wing and insert skewer ½ inch from end. Press skewer so that blunt end rests against bird and stretches skin tight over legs, thighs, and breast halves. Rub hens evenly with spice mixture and refrigerate while preparing grill.

5 Using large piece of heavy-duty aluminum foil, wrap 2 cups chips, if using, in 8 by 4½-inch foil packet. (Make sure chips do not poke holes in sides or bottom of packet.) Repeat with remaining 2 cups chips. Cut 2 evenly spaced 2-inch slits in top of each packet.

6A FOR A CHARCOAL GRILL Open bottom vent completely and place disposable pan in center of grill. Light large chimney starter filled with charcoal briquettes (6 quarts). When top coals are partially covered with ash, pour into 2 even piles on either side of disposable pan. Place 1 wood chip packet, if using, on each pile of coals. Set cooking grate in place, cover, and open lid vent completely. Heat grill until hot and wood chips are smoking, about 5 minutes.

6B FOR A GAS GRILL Remove cooking grate, if using wood chips, and place wood chip packets directly on primary burner. Set cooking grate in place, turn all burners to high, cover, and heat grill until hot and wood chips are smoking, about 15 minutes. Turn all burners to medium. (Adjust burners as needed during cooking to maintain grill temperature of 325 degrees.)

7 Clean and oil cooking grate. Place hens in center of grill (over disposable pan if using charcoal), skin side down. Cover (position lid vent over birds if using charcoal) and cook until thighs register 160 degrees, 20 to 30 minutes.

8 Using tongs, move hens to hotter sides of grill (2 hens per side if using charcoal), keeping them skin side down, or turn all burners to high (if using gas). Cover and continue to cook until browned, about 5 minutes. Brush hens with half of glaze, flip, and cook for 2 minutes. Brush remaining glaze over hens, flip, and continue to cook until breasts register 160 degrees and thighs register 175 degrees, 1 to 3 minutes longer.

9 Transfer hens to carving board, tent with foil, and let rest for 5 to 10 minutes. Cut hens in half through breastbone and serve.

635 Barbecue Glaze
MAKES ABOUT ½ CUP

- ½ cup ketchup
- 2 tablespoons packed brown sugar
- 1 tablespoon soy sauce
- 1 tablespoon distilled white vinegar
- 1 tablespoon yellow mustard
- 1 garlic clove, minced

Combine all ingredients in small saucepan, bring to simmer, and cook, stirring occasionally, until thickened, about 5 minutes.

636 Asian Barbecue Glaze
MAKES ABOUT ½ CUP

- ¼ cup ketchup
- ¼ cup hoisin sauce
- 2 tablespoons rice vinegar
- 1 tablespoon soy sauce
- 1 tablespoon toasted sesame oil
- 1 tablespoon grated fresh ginger

Combine all ingredients in small saucepan, bring to simmer, and cook, stirring occasionally, until thickened, about 5 minutes.

637 STEP BY STEP Butterflying and Skewering Game Hens

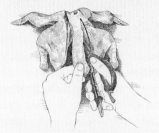

1 REMOVE BACKBONE Use poultry shears to cut through bones on either side of backbone.

2 CUT BREASTBONE With skin side down, make ¼-inch cut into bone separating breast halves.

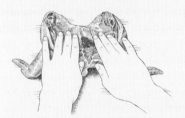

3 FLATTEN BIRD Lightly press on ribs with your fingers to flatten game hen.

4 TUCK WINGS With skin facing up, tuck wingtips behind bird to secure them. Brine birds.

5 INSERT SKEWER Insert flat metal skewer ½ inch from end of drumstick through skin and meat and out other side.

6 SKEWER THIGH Turn leg so that end of drumstick faces wing, then insert tip of skewer into meaty section of thigh under bone.

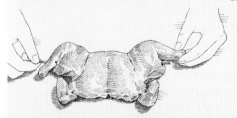

7 SKEWER ACROSS Press skewer completely through breast and second thigh. Fold end of drumstick toward wing and insert skewer ½ inch from end.

8 STRETCH SKIN Press skewer so that blunt end rests against bird and stretches skin tight over legs, thighs, and breast halves.

638 Rich and Juicy Boneless Grilled Turkey

✓ **WHY THIS RECIPE WORKS**

The problem with introducing a mild-mannered turkey breast to the smoky fire of a grill is that the ultralean breast meat easily dries out. We were determined to get around this issue with a recipe that would deliver a grill-roasted breast with crisp, well-rendered skin and rich, juicy meat that was moist all the way through. We started with a bone-in whole breast, removed the skin and bones, then salted the meat to help add flavor and moisture. Next we stacked the breast halves on top of one another, draped them with the turkey skin, and tied the "roast" together. Removing the breast halves from the bone and arranging them so that the thick end of one was pressed against the tapered end of the other created an even thickness throughout. The skin helped protect the meat from the fire and the stacked breasts ensured that the meat cooked more slowly. We started the turkey breast on the cooler side of the grill. A quick sear on the hotter side of the grill at the end of cooking took care of the skin, and after resting, the breast had reached the ideal serving temperature of 165 degrees.

Grill-Roasted Boneless Turkey Breast
SERVES 6 TO 8

We prefer either a natural (unbrined) or kosher turkey breast for this recipe. If using a kosher turkey breast (rubbed with salt and rinsed during processing) or self-basting turkey breast (injected with salt and water), do not salt it in step 1. If the breast has a pop-up timer, remove it before cooking. If you'd like to use wood chunks instead of wood chips when using a charcoal grill, substitute one small wood chunk, soaked in water for 1 hour, for the wood chip packet.

1   **(5- to 7-pound) bone-in whole turkey breast, trimmed**
     Salt and pepper
½   **cup wood chips (optional)**
1   **teaspoon vegetable oil**

1 Remove skin from breast meat and then cut along rib cage to remove breast halves (discard bones or save for stock). Pat turkey breast halves dry with paper towels and season with 2 teaspoons salt. Stack breast halves

639 Turning Bone-In Turkey Breast into Boneless Turkey Roast

1 REMOVE SKIN Starting at 1 side of breast and using your fingers to separate skin from meat, peel skin off breast meat and reserve.

2 REMOVE BONE Using tip of knife, cut along rib cage to remove each breast half completely.

3 ASSEMBLE Arrange 1 breast cut side up; top with second breast, cut side down, thick end over tapered end. Drape skin over breasts and tuck ends under.

4 TIE LENGTHWISE Tie one 36-inch piece of twine lengthwise around roast.

5 TIE CROSSWISE Tie 5 to 7 pieces of twine at 1-inch intervals crosswise along roast, starting at its center, then at either end, and then filling in rest.

on top of one another with cut sides facing each other, and alternating thick and tapered ends. Stretch skin over exposed meat and tuck in ends. Tie kitchen twine lengthwise around roast. Then tie 5 to 7 pieces of twine at 1-inch intervals crosswise along roast. Transfer roast to wire rack set in rimmed baking sheet and refrigerate for 1 hour.

2 Just before grilling, soak wood chips, if using, in water for 15 minutes, then drain. Using large piece of heavy-duty aluminum foil, wrap chips in 8 by 4½-inch foil packet. (Make sure chips do not poke holes in sides or bottom of packet.) Cut 2 evenly spaced 2-inch slits in top of packet.

3A FOR A CHARCOAL GRILL Open bottom vent halfway. Light large chimney starter filled with charcoal briquettes (6 quarts). When top coals are partially covered with ash, pour evenly over half of grill. Place wood chip packet, if using, on coals. Set cooking grate in place, cover, and open lid vent halfway. Heat grill until hot and wood chips are smoking, about 5 minutes.

3B FOR A GAS GRILL Place wood chip packet, if using, directly on primary burner. Turn all burners to high, cover, and heat grill until hot and wood chips are smoking, about 15 minutes. Turn all burners to medium-low. (Adjust burner(s) as needed during cooking to maintain grill temperature of 300 degrees.)

4 Clean and oil cooking grate. Rub surface of roast with oil and season with pepper. Place roast on grill (on cooler side if using charcoal). Cover (position lid vent over meat if using charcoal) and cook until roast registers 150 degrees, 40 minutes to 1 hour, turning roast 180 degrees halfway through grilling.

5 Slide roast to hotter side of grill (if using charcoal) or turn all burners to medium-high (if using gas). Cook until roast is browned and skin is crisp on all sides, 8 to 10 minutes, rotating every 2 minutes.

6 Transfer roast to carving board, tent with foil, and let rest for 15 minutes. Cut into ½-inch-thick slices, removing twine as you cut. Serve.

640 STEP BY STEP
Tying a Butcher's Knot

1 WRAP Wrap piece of butcher's twine around your roast. Hold bottom piece (colored gray) in your right hand and top piece in your left.

2 LOOP With forefinger of your left hand, pull loop from bottom twine to left, underneath top piece.

3 TWIST Twist this loop once toward you to form circle.

4 KNOT Pass end of bottom twine over top piece and through loop. Pull tightly on bottom twine (see arrows) to secure knot.

5 TIGHTEN Pull up and down on top twine to tighten string around roast.

VARIATIONS

641 Grill-Roasted Boneless Turkey Breast with Herb Butter

Mince ¼ cup fresh tarragon leaves, 1 tablespoon fresh thyme leaves, 2 minced garlic cloves, and ¼ teaspoon pepper to fine paste. Combine herb paste and 4 tablespoons softened unsalted butter. Spread butter evenly over cut side of each turkey breast half before assembling roast.

642 Grill-Roasted Boneless Turkey Breast with Olives and Sun-Dried Tomatoes

Combine ¼ cup finely chopped kalamata olives, 3 tablespoons finely chopped sun-dried tomatoes, 1 minced garlic clove, 1 teaspoon minced fresh thyme, ½ teaspoon anchovy paste, and ½ teaspoon red pepper flakes in bowl. Spread olive mixture evenly over cut side of each turkey breast half before assembling roast.

643 RECIPE FOR SUCCESS
Getting Smoky with Mild-Mannered Turkey

✓ WHY THIS RECIPE WORKS

For smoked turkey with plump, juicy meat lightly perfumed with smoke, we chose a turkey breast, which cooked relatively quickly on the grill. Rubbing salt and brown sugar under and over the skin and resting the turkey breast in the refrigerator overnight allowed the seasonings to penetrate the meat. Before grilling, we dried the skin and applied a second round of rub, replacing the salt with pepper for kick. Piercing the skin before grilling allowed some of the fat to drain away, which helped crisp the skin. Two cups of wood chips added enough smokiness without overwhelming the mild meat. After grilling the bird for an hour and a half, we had smoky, well-seasoned, juicy meat with golden, crisp skin.

Smoked Turkey Breast

SERVES 6 TO 8

We prefer either a natural (unbrined) or kosher turkey breast for this recipe. If using a kosher turkey breast (rubbed with salt and rinsed during processing) or self-basting turkey breast (injected with salt and water), do not salt it in step 1, but do sugar. If the breast has a pop-up timer, remove it before cooking. If you'd like to use wood chunks instead of wood chips when using a charcoal grill, substitute two wood chunks, soaked in water for 1 hour, for the wood chip packet.

- 3 **tablespoons packed brown sugar**
- 1 **tablespoon salt**
- 1 **(5-pound) bone-in whole turkey breast, trimmed**
- 2 **teaspoons pepper**
- 2 **cups wood chips**
- 1 **(13 by 9-inch) disposable aluminum roasting pan (if using charcoal)**

1 Combine 2 tablespoons sugar and salt in bowl. Pat turkey dry with paper towels. Using your fingers, gently loosen skin covering each side of breast and rub sugar-salt mixture evenly over and under skin. Tightly wrap turkey with plastic wrap and refrigerate for 8 to 24 hours.

2 Just before grilling, soak wood chips in water for 15 minutes, then drain. Using large piece of heavy-duty aluminum foil, wrap chips in 8 by 4½-inch foil packet. (Make sure chips do not poke holes in sides or bottom of packet.) Cut 2 evenly spaced 2-inch slits in top of packet. Combine remaining 1 tablespoon sugar and pepper in bowl. Unwrap turkey, pat dry with paper towels, and rub sugar-pepper mixture under and over skin. Poke skin all over with skewer.

3A FOR A CHARCOAL GRILL Open bottom vent halfway and place disposable pan in center of grill. Light large chimney starter filled with charcoal briquettes (6 quarts). When top coals are partially covered with ash, pour into 2 even piles on either side of disposable pan. Place wood chip packet on 1 pile of coals. Set cooking grate in place, cover, and open lid vent halfway. Heat grill until hot and wood chips are smoking, about 5 minutes.

3B FOR A GAS GRILL Remove cooking grate and place wood chip packet directly on primary burner. Set cooking grate in place, turn all burners to high, cover, and heat grill until hot and wood chips are smoking, about 15 minutes. Turn all burners to medium-low. (Adjust burners as needed to maintain grill temperature around 350 degrees.)

4 Clean and oil cooking grate. Place turkey breast, skin side up, in center of grill (over disposable pan if using charcoal). Cover (position lid vent over turkey if using charcoal) and cook until skin is well browned and breast registers 160 degrees, about 1½ hours.

5 Transfer turkey to carving board, tent with foil, and let rest for 15 to 20 minutes. Carve turkey and serve.

644 FOOD SCIENCE
Is Pink Turkey Meat Safe to Eat?

We all have experienced the occasional slice of pink turkey meat, even when the bird is fully cooked. (We always rely on an instant-read thermometer to ascertain doneness when roasting poultry. In the case of turkey, look for 160 degrees in the thickest portion of the breast and 175 degrees in the thickest part of the thigh.) Just because a slice of turkey has a pinkish tint doesn't necessarily mean it is underdone. In general, the red or pink color in meat is due to the red protein pigment called myoglobin in the muscle cells that store oxygen. Because the areas that tend to get the most exercise—the legs and thighs—require more oxygen, they contain more myoglobin (and are therefore darker in color) than the breasts. As turkey (or chicken) roasts in the oven, the oxygen attached to the myoglobin is released, and the meat becomes lighter and browner in color. However, if there are trace amounts of other gases formed in a hot oven or grill, they may react to the myoglobin to produce a pink color, even if the turkey is fully cooked.

645

Rethinking Thanksgiving

✔ WHY THIS RECIPE WORKS

Grill-roasting a turkey can be hard to manage, but it can also produce the best-tasting, best-looking turkey ever, with crispy skin and moist meat perfumed with smoke. We wanted to take the guesswork out of preparing the holiday bird on the grill. Because the skin on larger birds will burn before the meat cooks, we chose a small turkey (less than 14 pounds). To season the meat and help prevent it from drying out, we brined the turkey. To protect the skin and promote slow cooking, we placed the turkey on the opposite side of the glowing coals or lit gas burner. Using a V-rack improved air circulation and we turned the turkey three times so all four sides received equal exposure to the hot side of the grill for evenly bronzed skin.

Classic Grill-Roasted Turkey

SERVES 10 TO 12

If using a self-basting turkey (such as a frozen Butterball) or a kosher turkey, do not brine in step 1, but do season with salt after brushing with melted butter in step 2. If you'd like to use wood chunks instead of wood chips when using a charcoal grill, substitute six medium wood chunks, soaked in water for 1 hour, for the wood chip packets.

- 1 cup salt
- 1 (12- to 14-pound) turkey, neck and giblets discarded, wingtips tucked behind back
- 2 tablespoons unsalted butter, melted
- 6 cups wood chips

1 Dissolve salt in 2 gallons cold water in large container. Submerge turkey in brine, cover, and refrigerate or store in very cool spot (40 degrees or less) for 6 to 12 hours.

2 Lightly spray V-rack with vegetable oil spray. Remove turkey from brine and pat dry, inside and out, with paper towels. Brush both sides of turkey with melted butter and place breast side down in prepared V-rack.

3 Just before grilling soak wood chips in water for 15 minutes, then drain. Using large piece of heavy-duty aluminum foil, wrap 2 cups chips in 8 by 4½-inch foil packet. (Make sure chips do not poke holes in sides or bottom of packet.) Repeat twice with remaining 4 cups chips for total of 3 packets. Cut 2 evenly spaced 2-inch slits in top of each packet.

4A FOR A CHARCOAL GRILL Open bottom vent halfway. Light large chimney mounded with charcoal briquettes (7 quarts). When top coals are partially covered with ash, pour into steeply banked pile against side of grill. Place 2 wood chip packets on pile of coals. Set cooking grate in place, cover, and open lid vent halfway. Heat grill until hot and wood chips are smoking, about 5 minutes.

4B FOR A GAS GRILL Remove cooking grate and place 1 wood chip packet directly on primary burner. Set cooking grate in place, turn all burners to high, cover, and heat grill until hot and wood chips are smoking, about 15 minutes. Turn primary burner to medium-high and turn off other burner(s). (Adjust primary burner as needed during cooking to maintain grill temperature around 325 degrees.)

5 Clean and oil cooking grate. Place V-rack with turkey on cooler side of grill with leg and wing facing coals, cover (position lid vent over turkey if using charcoal), and cook for 1 hour.

6 Using potholders, transfer V-rack with turkey to rimmed baking sheet or roasting pan. If using charcoal, remove cooking grate and add 12 new briquettes and third wood chip packet to pile of coals; set cooking grate in place. If using gas, place remaining wood chip packets directly on primary burner. With wad of paper towels in each hand, flip turkey breast side up in rack and return V-rack with turkey to cooler side of grill, with other leg and wing facing coals. Cover (position lid vent over turkey if using charcoal) and cook for 45 minutes.

7 Using potholders, carefully rotate V-rack with turkey (breast remains up) 180 degrees. Cover and continue to cook until breast registers 160 degrees and thighs register 175 degrees, 15 to 45 minutes longer. Transfer turkey to carving board, tent with foil, and let rest for 20 to 30 minutes. Carve and serve.

646 SHOPPING IQ
Heritage Turkeys

Heritage turkeys forage for food and live twice as long as modern birds. They can also cost 10 times as much. Do they taste great enough to command their premium price? To find out, we bought heritage turkeys from farms scattered across the United States. The turkeys we unpacked were a far cry from the usual supermarket turkey, with startlingly long legs and wings, a more angular breast, almost bluish-purple dark meat (a sign of well-exercised birds), and traces of dark pinfeathers in the skin around the tail. We also found their flavor far more rich and flavorful. Tasters found their favorite samples "amazing," "unctuous and silky," with "sweet, succulent flavor," and a texture that was "perfectly tender" and "really moist." A distinct layer of fat under the skin on the breast not only adds flavor but also helps keep the meat moist during cooking. Our top pick is from a large family-owned farm in California that also produces our winning brand of chicken. It has everything we're looking for in turkey, with rich, full flavor and naturally moist meat.

THE BOTTOM LINE A heritage bird is a centerpiece for a special occasion, like beef tenderloin or prime rib (which can cost $75 to $100 at the supermarket), but we'll be happy to splurge on one like **Mary's Free-Range Heritage Turkey** for the holidays—not just to save them from extinction, but for the great taste they bring to our Thanksgiving table.

WINNER

MARY'S Free-Range Heritage Turkey
Price $166.72 for 7- to 14-lb bird, plus shipping
Tasting Comments Our top pick was "richly flavored," with "great texture and moisture." This big turkey was "quite fatty," with "remarkably tender, moist white meat." Dark meat is "dee-lish and also very tender." One taster summed it up: "Amazing."

RUNNER-UP

ELMWOOD STOCK FARM Organic Heritage Turkey
Price $149.00 for 9- to 10.9-lb bird, plus shipping
Tasting Comments This turkey was "supertender and juicy," with white meat "so rich in flavor that it tastes like dark meat." The dark meat was even more tender and flavorful. "Rich without gamy notes," the meat had a "texture like velvet."

647 RECIPE FOR SUCCESS Whole Grilled Turkey Made Even Easier

✓ WHY THIS RECIPE WORKS

Roasting a large turkey monopolizes both your oven and your time. Moving the turkey out to the grill could help and might be even better than the oven since it could eliminate a perennial turkey-roasting problem: unevenly cooked meat. However, we wanted to make sure we could find a way to grill-roast the bird so it emerged tasting pretty much as if it had been roasted in the oven—meaning no smoky or sooty flavors. For the grill, the simplest charcoal cooking setup was a split fire, with heat on both sides of the bird, which eliminates the need for rotating. On the gas grill, we mimicked the split fire by only lighting one burner and rotating the turkey just once during cooking. To roast the bird more gently, eliminating the flare-ups and soot that can give grilled meat a smoky taste, we placed a disposable pan partially filled with water between the heat and the meat. In order to get crisp, golden-brown skin, we cut slits along the backbone to speed up the rendering of excess fat, patted the skin dry with paper towels, and rubbed the skin with salt, pepper, and baking powder, which helped break down its proteins.

Simple Grill-Roasted Turkey

SERVES 10 TO 12

Don't use table salt for this recipe; it is too fine. If using a self-basting turkey (such as a frozen Butterball) or a kosher turkey, don't salt in step 1, but do season with salt in step 2. Check the wings halfway through roasting; if they are getting too dark, slide a small piece of foil between the wing and the cooking grate to shield the wings from the flame. As an accompaniment, try our Gravy for Simple Grill-Roasted Turkey (recipe follows).

- 1 (12- to 14-pound) turkey, neck and giblets removed and reserved for gravy (optional)
  Kosher salt and pepper
- 1 teaspoon baking powder
- 1 tablespoon vegetable oil
- 1 (13 by 9-inch) disposable aluminum roasting pan (if using charcoal) or 2 (9-inch) disposable aluminum pie plates (if using gas)

1 With turkey breast side down, make two 2-inch incisions below each thigh and each side of breast along back of turkey (4 incisions total). Flip turkey over and, using your fingers, gently loosen skin covering breast and thighs. Rub 4 teaspoons salt evenly inside cavity of turkey, 1 tablespoon salt under skin of each side of breast, and 1 teaspoon salt under skin of each leg.

2 Combine 1 teaspoon salt, 1 teaspoon pepper, and baking powder in small bowl. Pat turkey dry with paper towels and evenly sprinkle baking powder mixture all over. Rub in mixture with your hands, coating entire surface evenly. Wrap turkey tightly with plastic wrap; refrigerate for 24 to 48 hours.

3 Remove turkey from refrigerator and discard plastic. Tuck wings behind back. Using hands, rub oil evenly over entire surface.

4A FOR A CHARCOAL GRILL Open bottom vent halfway. Place disposable pan in center of grill and add 3 cups water to pan. Arrange 1½ quarts unlit charcoal briquettes evenly on either side of pan (3 quarts total). Light large chimney starter two-thirds filled with charcoal briquettes (4 quarts). When top coals are partially covered with ash, pour 2 quarts of lit coals on top of each pile of unlit coals. Set cooking grate in place, cover, and open lid vent halfway. Heat grill until hot, about 5 minutes.

4B FOR A GAS GRILL Remove cooking grate. Place 2 disposable pie plates directly on 1 secondary burner and add 2 cups water to each. Set cooking grate in place, turn all burners to high, cover, and heat grill until hot, about 15 minutes. Turn primary burner to medium and turn off other burner(s). (Adjust primary burner as needed to maintain grill temperature of 325 degrees.)

5 Clean and oil cooking grate. Place turkey, breast side up, in center of charcoal grill or on cooler side of gas grill, making sure bird is over disposable pans and not over flame. Cover (position lid vent over turkey if using charcoal) and cook until breast registers 160 degrees and thighs/drumsticks register 175 degrees, 2½ to 3 hours, rotating turkey after 1¼ hours if using gas grill.

6 Transfer turkey to carving board and let rest for 45 minutes. Carve turkey and serve.

648 Gravy for Simple Grill-Roasted Turkey

MAKES 6 CUPS

1	tablespoon vegetable oil
	Reserved turkey neck, cut into 1-inch pieces, and giblets
1	pound onions, chopped coarse
4	cups chicken broth
4	cups beef broth
2	small carrots, peeled and chopped coarse
2	small celery ribs, chopped coarse
6	tablespoons unsalted butter
½	cup all-purpose flour
2	bay leaves
½	teaspoon dried thyme
10	whole black peppercorns
	Salt and pepper

1 Heat oil in Dutch oven over medium-high heat until shimmering. Add turkey neck and giblets; cook, stirring occasionally, until browned, about 5 minutes. Add half of onions and cook, stirring occasionally, until softened, about 3 minutes. Reduce heat to low; cover and cook, stirring occasionally, until turkey parts and onions release their juices, about 20 minutes.

2 Add chicken and beef broths; increase heat to high and bring to boil. Reduce heat to low and simmer, covered, skimming any foam that rises to surface, until broth is rich and flavorful, about 30 minutes. Strain broth into large bowl (you should have about 8 cups), reserving giblets, if desired; discard neck. Reserve broth. If using giblets, when cool enough to handle, remove gristle from giblets, dice, and set aside. (Broth can be refrigerated for up to 2 days.)

3 Pulse carrots in food processor until broken into rough ¼-inch pieces, about 5 pulses. Add celery and remaining onions; pulse until all vegetables are broken into ⅛-inch pieces, about 5 pulses.

4 Melt butter in now-empty Dutch oven over medium-high heat. Add vegetables and cook, stirring frequently, until softened and well browned, about 10 minutes. Reduce heat to medium; stir in flour and cook, stirring constantly, until thoroughly browned and fragrant, 5 to 7 minutes. Whisking constantly, gradually add reserved broth; bring to boil, skimming off any foam that forms on surface. Reduce heat to medium-low and add bay leaves, thyme, and peppercorns; simmer, stirring occasionally, until thickened and reduced to 6 cups, 30 to 35 minutes.

5 Strain gravy through fine-mesh strainer into clean saucepan, pressing on solids to extract as much liquid as possible; discard solids. Stir in diced giblets, if using. Season with salt and pepper to taste, and serve.

649 TEST KITCHEN TIP Cleaning a Grimy Grill Lid

We're fanatics about making sure that we thoroughly clean our cooking grate before grilling, but we often forget to give the same attention to the grill lid. Over time, grease and smoke oxidize and turn into carbon that builds up under the lid and eventually becomes patchy flakes that look like peeling paint. To see if this carbon buildup imparts any ashy off-flavors to food, we took the filthiest lid we could find in the test kitchen and used it to grill-roast turkey and fish, comparing the results after following the same recipes on a new grill with a shiny clean lid. Most of us didn't detect any off-flavors, but we do recommend cleaning the inside of the grill lid on a regular basis to prevent the strips from flaking off and landing on your food. The peeling carbon comes off easily with light scrubbing with steel wool and water. (Don't waste your time trying to clean off any buildup that isn't already flaking. When we attempted to remove every speck of the shiny carbon layer, none of the methods we tried—lemon juice and salt; vinegar and baking soda; S.O.S. pads; or even spraying the surface with Easy-Off, sealing the lid in a plastic garbage bag, and letting it sit in the sun for several hours—made much of a dent.)

650 RECICE FOR SUCCESS Grilled Turkey Gets Spiced Up a Notch

✔ WHY THIS RECIPE WORKS

Mild turkey is a perfect candidate for amping up with smoke and spice on the grill. Moderate, indirect heat and a pan of water placed on the grill helped cook our spice-rubbed turkey gently and kept the meat moist. Setting up the grill with a pile of lit charcoal under unlit briquettes created a long-burning fire that stayed hot long enough to cook the whole bird. A double dose of wood chips imbued the turkey with deeply smoky flavor. We used a flavorful rub both on and under the skin for turkey that was spiced inside and out. More spice mixture was brushed on the turkey with melted butter during cooking for perfectly burnished skin.

Spice-Rubbed Grill-Roasted Turkey
SERVES 10 TO 12

We prefer a Butterball turkey for this recipe. If you prefer natural, unenhanced turkey, we recommend brining: Dissolve 1 cup of salt in 2 gallons of cold water; submerge the turkey in the brine, cover, and refrigerate for 6 to 12 hours. Make sure you have plenty of fuel if you're using a gas grill. If you'd like to use wood chunks instead of wood chips when using a charcoal grill, substitute 2 medium wood chunks, soaked in water for 1 hour, for the wood chip packet.

2	teaspoons five-spice powder
	Salt and pepper
1½	teaspoons ground cumin
1	teaspoon granulated garlic
¼	teaspoon cayenne pepper
¼	teaspoon ground cardamom
2	tablespoons unsalted butter, softened, plus 4 tablespoons unsalted butter
1	tablespoon packed brown sugar
2	tablespoons vegetable oil
1	(12- to 14-pound) turkey, neck and giblets discarded
2	cups wood chips, soaked in water for 15 minutes and drained
1	(13 by 9-inch) disposable aluminum roasting pan (if using charcoal) or 2 (9-inch) disposable aluminum pie plates (if using gas)

1 Combine five-spice powder, 2 teaspoons salt, cumin, 1 teaspoon pepper, granulated garlic, cayenne, and cardamom in bowl. Combine 1 tablespoon spice mixture with softened butter and sugar in second bowl. Combine 1 tablespoon spice mixture with oil in third bowl.

2 Dry turkey thoroughly inside and out with paper towels. With turkey breast side up, use your fingers to gently loosen skin covering each side of breast. Rub spiced butter evenly under skin of breast. Tuck wingtips behind back and tie legs together with kitchen twine. Rub spiced oil evenly over entire surface of turkey. Using large piece of heavy-duty aluminum foil, wrap soaked chips in 8 by 4½-inch foil packet. (Make sure chips do not poke holes in sides or bottom of packet.) Cut 2 evenly spaced 2-inch slits in top of packet.

651 TEST KITCHEN TIP Moderating the Heat

One of the keys to roasting a turkey on the grill for 2 to 3 hours is moderating the heat—the fire needs to be hot enough to cook the turkey, but not so hot that the turkey cooks unevenly or burns. For both gas and charcoal, we place disposable aluminum pans filled with water on the bottom of the grill (next to the briquettes for charcoal, directly on the secondary burners for gas). The water absorbs heat and helps keep the temperature consistently low.

For Charcoal
Use a 13 by 9-inch disposable aluminum roasting pan.

For Gas
Use 9-inch aluminum disposable pie plates.

3A FOR A CHARCOAL GRILL Open bottom vent completely. Place disposable pan on 1 side of grill and add 3 cups water to pan. Arrange 3 quarts unlit charcoal briquettes evenly on other side of grill. Light large chimney starter three-quarters filled with charcoal briquettes (4½ quarts). When top coals are partially covered with ash, pour evenly over unlit coals. Place wood chip packet on coals. Set cooking grate in place, cover, and open lid vent completely. Heat grill until hot and wood chips are smoking, about 5 minutes.

3B FOR A GAS GRILL Remove cooking grate and place wood chip packet directly on primary burner. Place disposable pie plates directly on secondary burner(s) and add 2 cups water to each. Set cooking grate in place, turn all burners to high, cover, and heat grill until hot and wood chips are smoking, about 15 minutes. Leave primary burner on high and turn off other burner(s). (Adjust primary burner as needed to maintain grill temperature of 325 degrees.)

4 Clean and oil cooking grate. Place turkey, breast side up, on cooler side of grill with legs pointing toward hotter side of grill. Cover (position lid vent over turkey if using charcoal) and cook for 1 hour.

5 Meanwhile, melt remaining 4 tablespoons butter in small saucepan over medium heat. Add remaining 2 teaspoons spice mixture and cook until fragrant, about 1 minute. Remove from heat. After turkey has been on grill for 1 hour, brush all over with spiced butter, rotating turkey if using gas grill (if turkey looks too dark, cover breast lightly with foil). Cover and continue to cook until breast registers 160 degrees and thighs/drumsticks register 175 degrees, 1 to 2 hours longer.

6 Transfer turkey to carving board and let rest, uncovered, for 45 minutes. Carve turkey and serve.

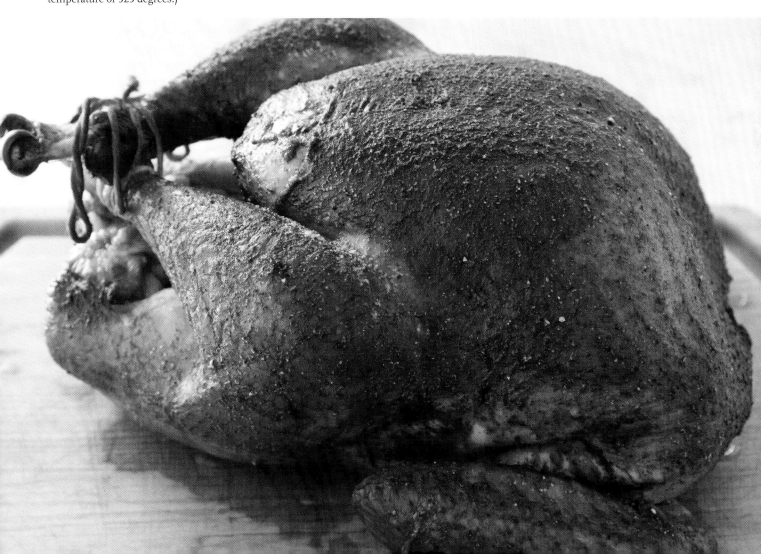

653 RECIPE FOR SUCCESS
Duck off the Grill Is Divine

✓ WHY THIS RECIPE WORKS

Rich and flavorful, duck breasts are perhaps the best part of the bird and they take just minutes to cook. They are also a great pairing with the smoky flavor of the grill. But grilling duck breasts presents a real challenge: How do you render the fat from the skin without overcooking the delicate meat? Trimming all the excess fat minimized flare-ups and charring. Scoring the skin helped it crisp up perfectly. To keep the skin from overwhelming the meat, we trimmed it back. We found that we needed a fairly hot fire to crisp the skin and cook the breasts quickly. Cooking the breasts longer on the skin side kept the meat from drying out. We also developed a set of flavorful accompaniments that suit the duck well.

Grilled Duck Breasts
SERVES 4

Duck breasts tend to cause flare-ups on a gas grill. Be ready to move duck breasts to a cooler spot on the grill if flare-ups occur in the first half of the cooking time. To dress these duck breasts up, serve them with a chutney, relish, or tapenade (recipes follow).

2 (12-ounce) whole boneless duck breasts, split and trimmed of excess skin and fat; remaining skin scored 3 or 4 times diagonally
Salt and pepper

1A FOR A CHARCOAL GRILL Open bottom vent completely. Light large chimney starter filled with charcoal briquettes (6 quarts). When top coals are partially covered with ash, pour evenly over grill. Set cooking grate in place, cover, and open lid vent completely. Heat grill until hot, about 5 minutes.

1B FOR A GAS GRILL Turn all burners to high, cover, and heat grill until hot, about 15 minutes. Turn all burners to medium-high.

2 Clean and oil cooking grate. Sprinkle duck breasts with salt and pepper. Place duck breasts, skin side down, on grill. Cook (covered if using gas) until skin is nicely browned, about 8 minutes. Using tongs, turn duck breasts and continue grilling (covered if using gas) until thickest part of breast registers 140 degrees (for medium-rare), 3 to 4 minutes.

3 Remove breasts from grill, tent with aluminum foil, and let rest for 5 minutes. Slice breasts diagonally into 8 slices, ½ inch thick, and fan 1 sliced breast half on 4 dinner plates. Serve immediately.

654 Peach-Habanero Chutney
MAKES ABOUT 2 CUPS

We recommend using thin plastic gloves when stemming, seeding, and mincing the habanero chile. If you cannot find a habanero, substitute one whole serrano or jalapeño chile. For a spicier chutney, reserve, mince, and add the ribs and seeds from the chile.

1½ tablespoons vegetable oil
1 red onion, chopped fine
2 ripe but firm peaches, halved, pitted, and chopped
½ habanero chile, stemmed, seeded, and minced
¼ teaspoon ground ginger
Pinch ground allspice
Pinch ground cloves

652 SHOPPING IQ
Duck Breasts

The duck breasts and whole ducks sold in supermarkets are usually Pekin, or Long Island, ducks. Once raised on Long Island, these birds are now grown on farms around the country, and the largest producer is in Indiana, a long way from New York. Most duck breasts are sold whole, with the skin on but without the bones. They can be split nicely into two halves, each weighing about 6 ounces.

Other duck species are available if you are willing to order by mail or can shop at a specialty butcher. The Muscovy is a South American bird that is less fatty than the Pekin and has a stronger game flavor. The Moulard is the sterile offspring of a Muscovy and a Pekin duck and is popular in France. Because these birds are so much leaner, the breasts require a different cooking method. Since the Pekin duck is the breed found in supermarkets, we decided to stick with this variety when developing our recipe for grilled duck breasts.

¼ cup packed light brown sugar
¼ cup red wine vinegar
1 tablespoon thinly sliced fresh mint

Heat oil in medium saucepan over medium heat until shimmering. Add onion and cook until soft, about 7 minutes. Add peaches and cook until soft but still intact, about 4 minutes. Add habanero, ginger, allspice, and cloves and cook until fragrant, about 1 minute. Stir in sugar and vinegar and bring to simmer. Reduce heat to low and simmer until liquid is very thick and syrupy, about 9 minutes. Transfer mixture to heatproof bowl and let cool to room temperature. Stir in mint and set chutney aside.

655 Pickled Ginger Relish

MAKES ABOUT ¾ CUP

Simple, fresh-tasting pickled ginger relish offsets the richness of duck breast. You can usually find pickled ginger in the Asian section of the supermarket or at Asian food stores. Serve with steamed rice.

¼ cup vegetable oil
¼ cup rice vinegar
¼ cup finely chopped pickled ginger
2 scallions, sliced thin
2 tablespoons sugar
1 tablespoon minced fresh cilantro
2 teaspoons toasted sesame oil

Mix all ingredients together in medium bowl.

656 Grilled Duck Breasts with Tapenade

Do not be alarmed if some tapenade sticks to the cooking grate; its flavor will still infuse the meat. Grilled bread is a great accompaniment to the duck. (Try Bruschetta with Fresh Herbs on page 94.)

Pulse 1 cup pitted kalamata olives, 4 chopped anchovies, 2 teaspoons drained capers, and 1 chopped garlic clove in food processor until coarsely chopped, about 2 pulses. With motor running, drizzle oil into olive mixture and process until oil is incorporated. (Mixture should still be slightly chunky.) Transfer tapenade to small bowl. In step 2, omit salt and pepper and rub each duck breast with about 1 teaspoon of tapenade before grilling. Serve remaining tapenade with sliced duck.

657 Preparing Duck Breasts

1 SPLIT To prepare whole boneless duck breast for grilling, first split breast into 2 halves.

2 TRIM With sharp chef's knife, trim any overhanging skin and fat from around each half. Slide your fingers under remaining skin along length of breast half to loosen. Turn breast half on its side and slice off some of skin and fat so that skin doesn't overhang breast.

3 SCORE Using paring knife, score skin on each breast half diagonally 3 or 4 times to allow fat to melt during cooking.

659 RECICE FOR SUCCESS
RECIPE FOR SUCCESS
Duck, Duck, Grill

✔ WHY THIS RECIPE WORKS

To re-create the crisp-skinned, salty-sweet, juicy meat of Chinese duck, we turned to grill-roasting. Allowing the fatty duck meat to steam on the stovetop and render fat before moving it to the grill helped minimize flare-ups, encouraged the skin to crisp up, and kept the duck moist. We also made sure to lance the skin to allow for drainage of the fat. When we moved to the grill, we used a double-banked fire and placed the duck in the middle so it would cook evenly without any need for turning or flipping. For a deeply flavored glaze, we turned to an Asian flavor profile built on soy sauce, with five-spice powder and toasted sesame oil. We used this sugar-free glaze during cooking and then added a second, honey-sweetened glaze at the end of cooking (this kept the honey from blackening and burning on the grill). Stuffing the cavity of the duck with more Chinese flavors—scallions and ginger—gave the meat sharp, piquant flavor throughout.

Grill-Roasted Chinese-Style Duck
SERVES 3 TO 4

Buying a duck is usually a simple process: Most stores carry only Pekin ducks. If you'd like to use wood chunks instead of wood chips when using a charcoal grill, substitute two medium wood chunks, soaked in water for 1 hour, for the wood chip packet.

1 (4½-pound) whole Pekin duck, neck and giblets discarded, trimmed
2½ tablespoons soy sauce
2 teaspoons five-spice powder
1 teaspoon toasted sesame oil
3 large scallions, cut into thirds
1 (1½-inch) piece ginger, peeled and sliced into thin coins
2 cups wood chips, soaked in water for 15 minutes and drained
1 (13 by 9-inch) disposable aluminum roasting pan (if using charcoal) or 1 (9-inch) disposable aluminum pie plate (if using gas)
2 tablespoons honey
2 tablespoons rice vinegar

1 Using tip of paring knife, prick skin over entire body of duck. Set V-rack in roasting pan. Place duck, breast side up, on rack. Set roasting pan over 2 stovetop burners and add enough water to come just below bottom of duck. Bring water to boil over high heat, cover pan tightly with aluminum foil, and reduce heat to medium. Steam duck, adding more hot water to maintain level, if necessary, until fat beads on pores of duck and bird is partially cooked, about 30 minutes. Lift duck from rack and, being careful not to break

658 STEP BY STEP
STEP BY STEP
Key Steps to Grill-Roasted Duck

Excess fat is removed by careful trimming and two cooking processes: steaming and grill-roasting.

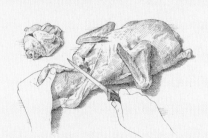

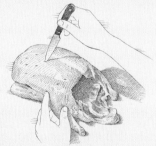

1 TRIM Trim away skin that is not directly above meat or bone. Pull back skin in neck cavity and cut away pieces of fat to expose wing joints.

2 PIERCE To help fat to escape, prick skin all over duck with tip of paring knife, making sure not to cut into meat.

3 STEAM Steam duck on rack set over simmering water to render its fat before grill-roasting.

skin, pat gently with paper towels to remove excess fat and moisture.

2 Mix 1½ tablespoons soy sauce, five-spice powder, and sesame oil together in small bowl. Brush mixture all over duck, being careful not to tear skin. Place scallions and ginger in cavity of duck. Using large piece of heavy-duty aluminum foil, wrap soaked chips in 8 by 4½-inch foil packet. (Make sure chips do not poke holes in sides or bottom of packet.) Cut 2 evenly spaced 2-inch slits in top of packet.

3A FOR A CHARCOAL GRILL Open bottom vent halfway and place disposable pan in center of grill. Light large chimney starter filled with charcoal briquettes (6 quarts). When top coals are partially covered with ash, pour into 2 even piles on either side of disposable pan. Place wood chip packet on 1 pile of coals. Set cooking grate in place, cover, and open lid vent halfway. Heat grill until hot, about 5 minutes. Clean and oil cooking grate. Place duck, breast side up, on grill directly over disposable pan. Cover grill, position lid vent over duck, and cook until skin is crispy, thin, and richly brown, about 1 hour.

3B FOR A GAS GRILL Remove cooking grate and place wood chip packet directly on primary burner. Place disposable pie plate over other burner(s). Set cooking grate in place, turn all burners to high, cover, and heat grill until hot and wood chips are smoking, about 15 minutes. Leave primary burner on high and turn off other burner(s). (Adjust primary burner as needed to maintain grill temperature between 325 and 350 degrees.) Clean and oil cooking grate. Place duck, breast side up, on grill, directly over disposable pie plate. Cover grill and cook until skin just begins to brown, about 30 minutes. Turn secondary burner(s) to low. (Adjust burners as needed to maintain grill temperature between 425 and 450 degrees.) Cook duck until skin is crispy, thin, and richly brown, 40 to 50 minutes.

4 Combine honey, vinegar, and remaining 1 tablespoon soy sauce in small bowl. Brush duck generously with glaze. Cover grill and continue to cook until glaze heats through, 3 to 5 minutes. (Be careful not to let glaze burn.)

5 Transfer duck to carving board and let rest for 10 minutes. Carve and serve.

660 SHOPPING IQ
Duck

The Pekin ducks sold in supermarkets weigh about 4½ pounds, perhaps 5 pounds at the most. Although a chicken in that weight range would serve about 5 people, the same isn't true for duck. Ducks have a larger, heavier bone structure, and they contain a lot more fat, much of which melts away during cooking. A 4½-pound duck feeds three or maybe four people if you serve a lot of side dishes. Ducks are almost always sold frozen.

661 RECIPE FOR SUCCESS
More Than Just a Gimmick

✔ WHY THIS RECIPE WORKS

While it may sound like a gimmick, beer can chicken is the real deal: The bird is rubbed with spices, an open, partially filled beer can is inserted in the chicken's cavity, and the bird is grill-roasted upright. The beer simmers and turns to steam as the chicken roasts, which makes the meat remarkably juicy and rich-textured, similar to braised chicken. And the dry heat crisps the skin and renders the fat away. It's a near-perfect way to cook a chicken—if you can get the details just right. Banking the coals on either side of the grill allowed for a cooler spot in the middle where the chicken could cook through evenly and gently. Filling a chimney starter two-thirds full provided just enough coals to maintain the grill at the proper temperature for the entire time it took to cook the bird. A few wood chips was all it took to contribute a pleasing smoky flavor that didn't overwhelm the chicken.

A simple but flavorful blend of garlic powder, dried thyme, celery seeds, and cayenne provided a rub that was rich and a little bit spicy, the perfect complement to the smokiness imparted by the fire.

Grill-Roasted Beer Can Chicken
SERVES 3 TO 4

If you'd like to use wood chunks instead of wood chips when using a charcoal grill, substitute two medium wood chunks, soaked in water for 1 hour, for the wood chip packet. If you prefer, use lemonade instead of beer; fill an empty 12-ounce soda or beer can with 10 ounces (1¼ cups) of lemonade and proceed as directed.

- 1 (12-ounce) can beer
- 2 bay leaves
- 1 (3½- to 4-pound) whole chicken, giblets discarded

3 **tablespoons spice rub (recipe follows)**
2 **cups wood chips, soaked in water for 15 minutes and drained**
1 **(13 by 9-inch) disposable aluminum roasting pan (if using charcoal)**

1 Open beer can and pour out (or drink) about ¼ cup. With church key can opener, punch 2 more large holes in top of can (for total of 3 holes). Crumble bay leaves into beer.

2 Pat chicken dry with paper towels. Rub chicken evenly, inside and out, with spice rub, gently loosening skin over breast and rubbing spice rub directly onto meat. Using skewer, poke skin all over. Slide chicken over beer can so that drumsticks reach down to bottom of can and chicken stands upright; set aside at room temperature.

3 Using large piece of heavy-duty aluminum foil, wrap chips in 8 by 4½-inch foil packet. (Make sure chips do not poke holes in sides or bottom of packet.) Cut 2 evenly spaced 2-inch slits in top of packet.

4A FOR A CHARCOAL GRILL Open bottom vent halfway and place disposable pan in center of grill. Light large chimney starter two-thirds filled with charcoal briquettes (4 quarts). When top coals are partially covered with ash, pour into 2 even piles on either side of disposable pan. Place wood chip packet on 1 pile of coals. Set cooking grate in place, cover, and open lid vent halfway. Heat grill until hot and wood chips are smoking, about 5 minutes.

4B FOR A GAS GRILL Remove cooking grate and place wood chip packet directly on primary burner. Set cooking grate in place, turn all burners to high, cover, and heat grill until hot and wood chips are smoking, about 15 minutes. Turn all burners to medium. (Adjust burners as needed to maintain grill temperature of 325 degrees.)

5 Clean and oil cooking grate. Place chicken (with can) in center of grill (over roasting pan if using charcoal), using drumsticks to help steady bird. Cover (position lid vent over chicken if using charcoal) and cook until breast registers 160 degrees and thighs register 175 degrees, 1 to 1½ hours.

6 Using large wad of paper towels, carefully transfer chicken (with can) to tray, making sure to keep can upright. Tent with foil and let rest for 15 minutes. Carefully lift chicken off can and onto carving board. Discard remaining beer and can. Carve chicken and serve.

662 Spice Rub

MAKES 1 CUP
Store leftover spice rub at room temperature for up to 3 months.

½ **cup paprika**
2 **tablespoons kosher salt**
2 **tablespoons garlic powder**
1 **tablespoon dried thyme**
2 **teaspoons ground celery seeds**
2 **teaspoons pepper**
2 **teaspoons cayenne pepper**

Combine all ingredients in bowl.

663

STEP BY STEP

Setting Up Beer Can Chicken

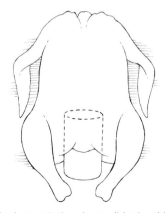

With the legs pointing down, slide the chicken over the open beer can. The two legs and the beer can form a tripod that steadies the chicken on the grill.

FOOD SCIENCE

BPA and Beer Can Chicken

Beer can interiors are coated with an epoxy that contains Bisphenol A (BPA). Is the popular method of cooking a chicken perched on an open beer can really a good idea? Some studies have linked BPA to cancer and other harmful health effects. To evaluate the ramifications of cooking chicken on a beer can, we roasted two whole birds, one set on an open beer can containing 6 ounces of beer and the other on a stainless-steel vertical roaster with the same amount of beer poured into the reservoir. After roasting the chickens, we collected their drippings and stripped each carcass, grinding the meat and skin to create homogeneous samples. We sent the samples to a lab to be evaluated for BPA content. In each chicken, the BPA measured less than 20 micrograms per kilogram, leading us to believe that the beer can cooking method is safe. (The Food and Drug Administration's current standard for exposure is 50 micrograms per kilogram of body weight for adults, or 3,400 micrograms per day for a 150-pound person.) For those who have any remaining concerns, there is always the vertical roaster, which works just as well as a low-tech option.

666 RECIPE FOR SUCCESS
Hot-Smoked Fish on the Grill

✓ WHY THIS RECIPE WORKS

Store-bought smoked salmon is inconsistent in quality and also incredibly expensive. We wanted to create an easy recipe for moist (but not too moist), nicely crusted salmon with a hint of smoked flavor—that could be achieved in just 2 hours. Surprisingly, impatience turned out to be the key to our success. Instead of the traditional cold-smoking technique, which keeps the salmon moist but lacks flavor, we developed a "hot-smoked" method, and kept the salmon moist by brining. We achieved full smoked salmon flavor on the grill using a whole side of salmon. To get a firm but not overly dry texture, complemented by a strong hit of smoke and wood, we slow-cooked the salmon with wood chips or chunks for more than an hour over a half-grill fire, but kept the fish on the cooler part of the grill the whole time. Using two spatulas to transfer the cooked fish from the grill prevented it from falling apart, and cutting through the pink flesh, not the skin, to divide individual portions kept the meat intact while leaving the skin behind.

Barbecued Side of Salmon
SERVES 4 TO 6

The cooking grate must be hot and thoroughly clean before you place the salmon on it; otherwise, the fish might stick. Use the back of a large rimmed baking sheet to get the fish onto the grill. If you'd like to use wood chunks instead of wood chips when using a charcoal grill, substitute 2 medium wood chunks, soaked in water for 1 hour, for the wood chip packet. If desired, serve the salmon with Horseradish Cream Sauce with Chives or Mustard-Dill Sauce (recipes follow).

1	cup sugar
½	cup salt
1	(2½-pound) skin-on salmon fillet
2	tablespoons vegetable oil
2	cups wood chips
1½	teaspoons paprika
1	teaspoon ground white pepper

1 Dissolve sugar and salt in 7 cups cold water in 1-gallon zipper-lock bag. Add salmon, seal bag, and refrigerate for 3 hours. Remove salmon from brine, pat dry with paper towels, and rub thoroughly with oil. Lay salmon skin side down on the back of a rimmed baking sheet and season top and sides with paprika and pepper.

2 Just before grilling, soak wood chips in water for 15 minutes, then drain. Using large piece of heavy-duty aluminum foil, wrap chips in 8 by 4½-inch foil packet. (Make sure chips do not poke holes in sides or bottom of packet.) Cut 2 evenly spaced 2-inch slits in top of packet.

665 STEP BY STEP
How to "Hot-Smoke" and Serve Salmon

1 GRILL Slide salmon off a baking sheet or foil and onto grill. To make it easier to remove salmon from grill, position fillet with long side perpendicular to grate bars.

2 TRANSFER Use 2 spatulas to transfer cooked fish from grill to baking sheet or cutting board.

3 SLICE To serve, cut through pink flesh, but not skin, to divide into individual pieces.

4 REMOVE SKIN Slide spatula between fillet and skin to remove individual pieces, leaving skin behind.

3A FOR A CHARCOAL GRILL Open bottom grill vent halfway. Light large chimney starter half filled with charcoal briquettes (3 quarts). When top coals are partially covered with ash, pour evenly over half of grill. Place wood chip packet on coals. Set cooking grate in place, cover, and open lid vent halfway. Heat grill until hot and wood chips are smoking, about 5 minutes.

3B FOR A GAS GRILL Remove cooking grate and place wood chip packet directly on primary burner. Set cooking grate in place, turn all burners to high, cover, and heat grill until hot and wood chips are smoking, about 15 minutes. Leave primary burner on medium and turn off other burner(s). (Adjust primary burner as needed to maintain grill temperature around 275 degrees.)

4 Clean cooking grate, then repeatedly brush grate with well-oiled paper towels until black and glossy, 5 to 10 times. Gently slide salmon from baking sheet onto cooler side of grill, skin-side down and perpendicular to grate bars. Cover (position lid vent over fish if using charcoal) and cook until heavily flavored with smoke, about 1½ hours.

5 Using 2 spatulas, gently remove salmon from grill. Serve hot or at room temperature.

667 Horseradish Cream Sauce with Chives
MAKES ABOUT 1 CUP

1	cup crème fraîche or sour cream
2	tablespoons prepared horseradish
2	tablespoons minced fresh chives
	Pinch table salt

Combine ingredients in small bowl. (Sauce can be refrigerated for up to 24 hours.)

668 Mustard-Dill Sauce
MAKES ABOUT 1 CUP

Use Dijon, honey, or grainy mustard, as desired. Depending on your choice of mustard, this sauce can be fairly hot.

1	cup mustard
¼	cup minced fresh dill

Combine ingredients in small bowl. (Sauce can be refrigerated for up to 24 hours.)

669 RECIPE FOR SUCCESS
Easy and Elegant Grilled Whole Fish

✔ WHY THIS RECIPE WORKS

Grilling a whole fish presents plenty of problems: The skin sticks fast to the grill and the meat cooks unevenly. We wanted a foolproof way to conquer these challenges. Using semifirm, midsize, mild-flavored fish was the first step to success. Making shallow diagonal slashes on the skin helped ensure even cooking and enabled us to gauge the doneness more easily. To prevent the skin from sticking, we greased the cooking grate and coated the fish with a film of oil. We used two thin metal spatulas to flip the delicate fish once the first side was done. They also made it easier to remove the cooked fish from the grill. The cooked fish needed only a few cuts for us to use one of our spatulas to lift away the meat from the bones on each side in a single piece. A fresh relish or vinaigrette is the perfect complement to the simple grilled fish.

Grilled Whole Red Snapper or Striped Bass

SERVES 4

If your fish are a little larger (between 1½ and 2 pounds), simply grill them a minute or two longer on each side. Fish weighing more than 2 pounds will be hard to maneuver on the grill and should be avoided. Serve the fish with lemon wedges, a vinaigrette, or a relish (recipes follow). Or, for added flavor, season the fish inside and out with a spice rub (recipes follow).

  2 whole red snapper or striped bass
     (about 1½ pounds each), scaled, gutted,
     cleaned, and skin slashed
  3 tablespoons extra-virgin olive oil
     Salt and pepper
     Lemon wedges

1A FOR A CHARCOAL GRILL Open bottom vent completely. Light large chimney starter filled with charcoal briquettes (6 quarts). When top coals are partially covered with ash, pour evenly over grill. Set cooking grate in place, cover, and open lid vent completely. Heat grill until hot, about 5 minutes.

1B FOR A GAS GRILL Turn all burners to high, cover, and heat grill until hot, about 15 minutes. Leave all burners on high.

2 Rub fish with olive oil and season generously with salt and pepper on inside and outside.

3 Clean cooking grate, then repeatedly brush grate with well-oiled paper towels until black and glossy, 5 to 10 times. Place fish on grill. Grill (covered if using gas) until side of fish facing coals is browned and crisp, 6 to 7 minutes. Gently turn fish over using 2 spatulas and cook (covered if using gas) until flesh is no longer translucent at center and skin on both sides of each fish is blistered and crisp, 6 to 8 minutes more. (To check for doneness, peek into slashed flesh or into interior through opened bottom area of each fish.) Use 2 metal spatulas to transfer fish to platter.

4 Fillet fish by making vertical cut just behind head from top of fish to belly. Make another cut along top of fish from head to tail. Use spatula to lift meat from bones, starting at head end and running spatula over bones to lift out fillet. Repeat on other side of fish. Discard head and skeleton. Serve with lemon wedges.

670 Orange, Lime, and Cilantro Vinaigrette

MAKES ABOUT ¾ CUP

If you choose to serve the fish with this vinaigrette, substitute lime wedges for the lemon wedges.

  6 tablespoons vegetable oil
  ¼ cup orange juice
  1 tablespoon lime juice
  2 teaspoons sugar
  1 garlic clove, minced
     Salt and pepper
  1 tablespoon minced fresh cilantro

continued

Whisk oil, orange juice, lime juice, sugar, garlic, ½ teaspoon salt, and pepper to taste together in medium bowl. Whisk in cilantro.

671 Fresh Tomato-Basil Relish

MAKES ABOUT ¾ CUP

If you choose to serve the fish with this relish, omit the lemon wedges.

- 1 pound tomatoes, cored, seeded, and cut into ¼-inch dice
- 2 tablespoons minced shallot
- 2 tablespoons chopped fresh basil
- 2 tablespoons extra-virgin olive oil
- 1 garlic clove, minced
- 1 teaspoon red wine vinegar
  Salt and pepper

Mix all ingredients together in medium bowl. Season with salt and pepper to taste.

674 TEST KITCHEN TIP
Keeping It Spicy

Contrary to what you make think, dried spices and herbs don't last forever. They may not be harmful to you as they age out, but their freshness will diminish. How can you tell when they're less than fresh? Crumble a small amount of the dried herb between your fingers and take a whiff. If it releases a lively aroma, it's still good to go. If the aroma and color of the spice have faded, it's time to restock.

When shopping for spices, try to buy whole, versus ground, and grind them just before using. Grinding releases the volatile compounds that give a spice its flavor and aroma. The longer the spice sits around (or is stored), the more compounds disappear.

As pretty as they might look over or near your stove, remember that heat, light, and moisture shorten their shelf life. Stash your dried herbs and spices in a cool, dark, cabinet away from the stove.

672 Basic Barbecue Spice Rub

MAKES ABOUT ½ CUP

This rub works on any poultry or meat, as well as seafood.

- 3 tablespoons packed brown sugar
- 3 tablespoons paprika
- 2 tablespoons dry mustard
- 2 tablespoons pepper
- 1 tablespoon onion powder
- 1 tablespoon garlic powder
- 1 tablespoon ground cumin
- 2 teaspoons salt
- ¾ teaspoon cayenne pepper

Combine all ingredients in small bowl.

673 Cajun Spice Rub

MAKES ABOUT ¾ CUP

This spicy rub works on any poultry or meat, as well as seafood.

- ½ cup paprika
- 2 tablespoons garlic powder
- 1 tablespoon dried thyme
- 2 teaspoons ground celery seeds
- 2 teaspoons salt
- 2 teaspoons pepper
- 2 teaspoons cayenne pepper

Combine all ingredients in small bowl.

675 STEP BY STEP
Grilling Whole Fish

1 SLASH SKIN Use sharp knife to make shallow diagonal slashes every 2 inches along both sides of fish, beginning just behind dorsal fin to ensure even cooking and to make it easier to check doneness.

2 FLIP FISH When fish is ready to be turned, slide 1 spatula under belly, being careful not to tear skin. Place second spatula under backbone of fish. Lift up spatula under backbone to flip fish, using opposite spatula to ease other side of fish onto grill.

3 REMOVE FROM GRILL When fish is cooked, slide 2 spatulas under belly, lifting gently to make sure skin is not sticking. Quickly move fish to platter.

4 CUT TOP TO BELLY Using sharp knife, make vertical cut just behind head from top of fish to belly.

5 CUT HEAD TO TAIL Make another cut along top of fish from head to tail.

6 REMOVE MEAT CAREFULLY Use spatula to lift meat from bones, starting at head and lifting out fillet. Repeat on other side of fish. Discard head and skeleton.

676

STEP BY STEP
Oiling the Cooking Grate

Dip a wad of paper towels in vegetable oil, grasp the oiled towels with a pair of tongs, and repeatedly rub them over the hot cooking grate. Place the fish fillets on the oiled grate and leave them alone until it is time to flip them.

677

A Fine Grill of Bluefish

✔ WHY THIS RECIPE WORKS

On Long Island, bluefish has long been a favorite choice for the grill. A whole bluefish is typically stuffed with lemon slices and herbs, wrapped in bacon, and grilled. The rich, smoky bacon perfectly balances the strong flavor of the fish. However, working with an entire bluefish, which can weigh 20 pounds, is a bit daunting. We turned to more user-friendly bluefish fillets and added wood chips for extra smoky flavor. We parcooked the bacon for a few minutes in the microwave to render fat and water from the bacon before wrapping it around the fish. Starting the fillets seam side down helped ensure the bacon wrapping stayed sealed. In order to get a good dose of lemon flavor without compromising the crispiness of the bacon, we turned to lemon zest for just the right zing. Adding a healthy shot of fresh thyme along with salt and pepper gave us the most flavorful bluefish yet.

Long Island–Style Bluefish

SERVES 4

Halibut, mahi-mahi, or striped bass can be substituted for the bluefish; if the fish fillets are thicker or thinner, they will have slightly different cooking times. This fish tastes great with any of our flavored mayonnaises (recipes follow). If using one of these sauces, substitute 1 tablespoon of it for the mayonnaise in the recipe. We rely on a wire rack in steps 2 and 4 to keep the bacon crisp. If you'd like to use wood chunks instead of wood chips when using a charcoal grill, substitute 2 medium wood chunks, soaked in water for 1 hour, for the wood chip packet.

12	slices bacon
2	teaspoons minced fresh thyme
1½	teaspoons grated lemon zest, plus lemon wedges for serving
¾	teaspoon salt
¼	teaspoon pepper
4	(6-ounce) skinless bluefish fillets, about 1 inch thick
1	tablespoon mayonnaise
2	cups wood chips, soaked in water for 15 minutes and drained

1 Lay 6 slices bacon evenly on large plate, then lay remaining 6 slices crosswise on top. Weigh bacon down with second plate, and microwave until fat is rendered and bacon is slightly shriveled but still pliable, 1 to 3 minutes. Let cool for 5 minutes.

2 Mix thyme, lemon zest, salt, and pepper in bowl. Pat bluefish fillets dry with paper towels and rub them evenly with thyme mixture. Wrap each fillet with 3 slices cooled bacon, using dollop of mayonnaise to secure ends. Lay fish on wire rack set in rimmed baking sheet and refrigerate until grill is ready. Using large piece of heavy-duty aluminum foil, wrap chips in 8 by 4½-inch foil packet. (Make sure chips do not poke holes in sides or bottom of packet.) Cut 2 evenly spaced 2-inch slits in top of packet.

3A FOR A CHARCOAL GRILL Open bottom vent halfway. Light large chimney starter filled with charcoal briquettes (6 quarts). When top coals are partially covered with ash, pour evenly over grill. Place wood chip packet on coals on 1 side of grill. Set cooking grate in place, cover, and open lid vent halfway. Heat grill until hot and wood chips are smoking, about 5 minutes.

3B FOR A GAS GRILL Remove cooking grate and place wood chip packet directly on primary burner. Set cooking grate in place, turn all burners to high, cover, and heat grill until hot and wood chips are smoking, about 15 minutes. Leave all burners on high.

4 Clean cooking grate, then repeatedly brush grate with well-oiled paper towels until black and glossy, 5 to 10 times. Lay bacon-wrapped fillets, seam side down, on grill, perpendicular to grate bars and opposite wood chip packet. Cover (position lid vent over fish if using charcoal) and cook until bluefish is opaque and flakes apart when gently prodded with paring knife, 10 to 14 minutes, gently flipping fish with 2 spatulas halfway through grilling. Transfer bluefish to clean wire rack, tent with foil, and let rest for 5 minutes. Serve with lemon wedges.

678 Tartar Sauce

MAKES ABOUT 1 CUP

This is a classic sauce for seafood.

- ¾ cup mayonnaise
- 1½ tablespoons minced cornichons (about 3 large) plus 1 teaspoon cornichon juice
- 1 tablespoon minced scallion
- 1 tablespoon minced red onion
- 1 tablespoon capers, minced

Whisk all ingredients together in bowl. Cover and refrigerate until flavors meld, at least 30 minutes. (Sauce can be refrigerated for up to 4 days.)

679 Sun-Dried Tomato and Caper Mayonnaise

MAKES ABOUT 1 CUP

We like this sauce with any grilled fish.

- 1 cup mayonnaise
- 3 tablespoons minced sun-dried tomatoes packed in oil, patted dry
- 1 tablespoon finely chopped capers
- 1 garlic clove, minced
  Salt and pepper

Whisk all ingredients together in bowl; season with salt and pepper to taste. Cover and refrigerate until flavors meld, about 30 minutes. (Mayonnaise can be refrigerated for up to 4 days.)

680 Chipotle Chile Mayonnaise

MAKES ABOUT 1 CUP

This smoky sauce complements fish and chicken well.

- ½ cup mayonnaise
- ½ cup sour cream
- 4 teaspoons minced chipotle chile in adobo sauce
- 1 tablespoon minced fresh cilantro
- 2 teaspoons lime juice
- 1 garlic clove, minced
- ½ teaspoon salt

Whisk all ingredients together in bowl. Cover and refrigerate until flavors meld, about 30 minutes. (Mayonnaise can be refrigerated for up to 4 days.)

681

STEP BY STEP

Wrapping the Bluefish Fillets

1 PREP BACON Microwave bacon between 2 plates to prevent it from curling and to make it easier to wrap around fish fillets.

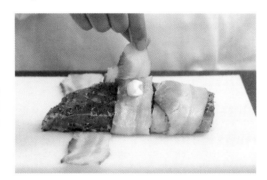

2 WRAP FISH Wrap 3 slices of partially cooked bacon around each fillet, then secure with dollop of mayonnaise.

683 RECIPE FOR SUCCESS Show-Stopping Trout Made Approachable

✓ WHY THIS RECIPE WORKS

One of our favorite ways to prepare trout is stuffed with a simple filling prior to grilling. Oiling the fish as well as the cooking grate helped us avoid any sticking issues. Though making slits in the sides of thicker fish can help with even cooking, it wasn't necessary to make them here since each fish was so thin, and we didn't want to encourage any tearing of the trout's skin or unnecessary release of juices. For the filling, bacon and trout were a classic pairing and spinach, red bell pepper, and onion made ideal additions. Because the fish cooked quickly on the grill and we didn't want the spinach to turn into a soggy mess as it wilted, we precooked our stuffing before it went into the fish. We sautéed the pepper and onion in the fat rendered from the bacon before tossing the spinach into the skillet to wilt. A shot of cider vinegar brightened the flavors. All we had to do was stuff each fish's cavity with some of the stuffing and put them on the grill. In less than 15 minutes, we had perfectly browned trout and a smoky-sweet stuffing.

Grilled Stuffed Trout

SERVES 4

The filling can be made up to a day ahead of time, but the fish should be stuffed just before grilling. To flip the fish in step 5, it's best to use two thin, wide-blade spatulas. If you like, serve the trout with a flavored mayonnaise (see page 419) as well as lemon wedges.

- 4   slices bacon, cut into ¼-inch pieces
- 1   onion, halved and sliced thin
- 1   red bell pepper, stemmed, seeded, and chopped
     Salt and pepper
- 8   ounces (8 cups) baby spinach
- 2   teaspoons cider vinegar
- 4   (7-to 10-ounce) whole rainbow trout, gutted, scaled, and cleaned
- 1   tablespoon vegetable oil
     Lemon wedges

1 Cook bacon in 12-inch skillet over medium heat until browned and crisp, about 8 minutes. Using slotted spoon, transfer bacon to paper towel–lined plate, leaving fat in skillet. Return skillet to medium-high heat, add onion, bell pepper, and ½ teaspoon salt, and cook until vegetables are softened and begin to brown, 5 to 7 minutes.

2 Stir in spinach and vinegar and cook until spinach is wilted and all extra moisture has evaporated, about 5 minutes. Transfer mixture to colander and let drain for 10 minutes. Stir in cooked bacon and season with salt and pepper to taste.

3 Meanwhile, pat trout dry with paper towels, and rub exteriors with oil. Season exteriors and cavities with salt and pepper. Divide spinach mixture evenly among cavities, about generous ¼ cup per fish.

682 STEP BY STEP How to Flip a Whole Fish

1 LIFT EDGE Slide spatula scant 1 inch under backbone edge and lift edge up. Slide second spatula under, then remove first spatula, allowing fish to ease onto second spatula.

2 FLIP FISH OVER Place first spatula on top of fish so it's oriented in same direction as second spatula and flip fish over.

4A FOR A CHARCOAL GRILL Open bottom vent completely. Light large chimney starter filled with charcoal briquettes (6 quarts). When top coals are partially covered with ash, pour evenly over grill. Set cooking grate in place, cover, and open lid vent completely. Heat grill until hot, about 5 minutes.

4B FOR A GAS GRILL Turn all burners to high, cover, and heat grill until hot, about 15 minutes. Leave all burners on high.

5 Clean cooking grate, then repeatedly brush grate with well-oiled paper towels until black and glossy, 5 to 10 times. Lay trout on grill, perpendicular to grate bars. Cook (covered if using gas) until flesh flakes when prodded with paring knife and filling is hot, 10 to 14 minutes, flipping trout halfway through grilling.

6 Transfer trout to wire rack, tent with aluminum foil, and let rest for 5 minutes. Serve with lemon wedges.

684

GADGETS & GEAR

Charcoal Storage Bag

When is a bag that holds a bag a handy thing? When it's holding 20 pounds of charcoal by way of a sturdy Velcro closure that seals out moisture so that the coals are ready for the next grilling session. Late last year we left a bag of coals outdoors in the storage bag for three months, during which time it weathered two major storms, a few snow squalls, and countless rainy days. Our coals stayed dry throughout. On days when we grilled, we used the bag to pour out what we needed—the nylon strap along the length of the bag made it easy to hold it in place as we aimed the coals into the chimney starter. Resealing the bag was a simple matter of pressing together the Velcro strips across the top.

THE BOTTOM LINE For grillers who don't have a shed or a garage, the **Charcoal Companion** bag stashes coals neatly and effectively. This waterproof vinyl bag uses a Velcro closure to protect charcoal from the elements, and it can fit up to one 20-pound bag of coals. A thick nylon strap on the side made it easier to hold the bag when pouring out coals. We left the bag outside for three months during which time we used it intermittently, and our charcoal stayed completely dry.

685 RECIPE FOR SUCCESS

A Rite of Summer Adapted for the Grill

☑ WHY THIS RECIPE WORKS

Clambakes are a rite of summer all along the East Coast. Shellfish and vegetables are layered with seaweed and piled on top of white-hot rocks in a wide sandpit. The food then steams beneath a wet tarp until it's done. This feast usually takes more than a day to prepare and cook. We wanted to make it faster and more approachable by translating it to the grill. The biggest challenge was that our grill was only big enough to handle half the ingredients at a time. Since charcoal dies down as it burns, we had to decide which items would need the hotter temperature of the first round of grilling but could also sit the longest before serving. We chose to lead off with the corn, sausage, and potatoes and follow by the lobsters and clams. We also gave the potatoes a jump-start in the microwave and skewered them to make them more manageable. This grilled clambake captured all the smoky flavor of the traditional version—with no shovel required.

New England Clambake

SERVES 4

Look for potatoes that are 1 to 2 inches in diameter; if your potatoes are larger, quarter them and increase the microwaving time as needed in step 2. Because the skewers go into the microwave, use wooden, not metal, skewers.

> Salt and pepper
> 4 ears corn, husks and silk removed
> 1 pound small red potatoes, unpeeled, scrubbed, and halved
> 4 tablespoons unsalted butter, melted, plus extra for serving
> 2 (1¼- to 1½-pound) live lobsters
> 1 pound kielbasa
> 2 pounds littleneck clams (about 20), scrubbed
> Lemon wedges

1 Dissolve ½ cup salt in 4 quarts cold water in large pot. Add corn and soak for at least 30 minutes or up to 8 hours. Before grilling, remove corn from water, pat dry with paper towels, and season with pepper.

2 Skewer potatoes, then lay them in single layer on large plate. Brush with 1 tablespoon melted butter and season with salt and pepper. Microwave until potatoes begin to soften, about 6 minutes, flipping them halfway through microwaving. Brush with 1 tablespoon melted butter.

3 Split lobsters in half lengthwise, removing internal organs. Using back of chef's knife, whack 1 side of each claw to crack shell. Brush tail meat with 1 tablespoon melted butter, and season with salt and pepper.

4A FOR A CHARCOAL GRILL Open bottom vent completely. Light large chimney starter filled with charcoal briquettes (6 quarts). When top coals are partially covered with ash, pour evenly over grill. Set cooking grate in place, cover, and open lid vent completely. Heat grill until hot, about 5 minutes.

4B FOR A GAS GRILL Turn all burners to high, cover, and heat grill until hot, about 15 minutes. Turn all burners to 325 degrees.

5 Clean and oil cooking grate. Place kielbasa, corn, and skewered potatoes on grill. Cook until kielbasa is seared and hot throughout, corn is lightly charred, and potatoes are brown and tender, 10 to 16 minutes, turning as needed. Transfer vegetables and sausage as they finish cooking to platter, and tent with aluminum foil.

6 Lay lobsters, flesh side down, and clams on grill. Cook until clams have opened and lobsters are cooked through, 8 to 14 minutes, flipping lobsters and brushing lobster tail meat with remaining 1 tablespoon butter halfway through grilling. As lobsters and clams finish cooking, transfer them to platter with vegetables and sausage, preserving any juices that have accumulated inside their shells.

7 Slice kielbasa into 1-inch chunks and remove skewers from potatoes. Serve with lemon wedges and extra melted butter. Use lobster picks to reach meat inside claws and knuckles.

686 SHOPPING IQ How to Buy Lobsters

After some research into the life cycle of the lobster, we discovered that the variations in the texture of lobster meat depended a great deal on what part of the molting cycle a lobster was in. During the late spring, lobsters start to form new shell tissue under their hard shells. By late June and into July or August, depending on the location, lobsters start to molt, meaning that the lobsters available during the later summer weeks and into the early fall are generally soft-shell lobsters, which have less meaty claws and are more perishable than hard-shell lobsters. That said, the meat from soft-shell lobsters is just as flavorful. They should, however, be cooked slightly less than hard-shell lobsters. If serving whole soft-shell lobsters, you may consider buying larger ones or, if the price is good, buying two small ones per person. Markets don't usually advertise which type of lobster they are selling but you can certainly ask. It is also easy to tell which type of lobster you have. Simply squeeze the side of the lobster's body: A soft-shell lobster will yield to pressure while a hard-shell lobster will be hard, brittle, and tightly packed.

687

TEST KITCHEN TIP

Dealing with Claws and Tails

Lobster tastes great when grilled. However, if you've never attempted it before, grilling lobster can be tricky. Not only do the claws take longer to cook than the tails, but the tails have a habit of curling up tightly as they grill, making them difficult to handle. Also, lobster cooks very quickly, which means that there is only a small window of opportunity for it to develop that all-important grilled flavor. These concerns are easily solved by a little butchering beforehand. By cutting the lobster in half lengthwise, you expose the meat to the grill for more flavor. Don't like the idea of butchering a live lobster? Have the fishmonger do it for you at the store. Once lobster is cut up, however, you need to cook and eat it within a few hours. And to help speed the cooking of the claws, crack the shells by whacking them with the back of a chef's knife.

688 RECIPE FOR SUCCESS
A Worthy Indulgence

✔ WHY THIS RECIPE WORKS

The smoky fire of the grill maximizes the sweetness of lobster meat, but you can't simply throw a whole lobster onto the grill. Splitting the lobster lengthwise exposes the meat to the smoky grill fire. We started the lobsters cut side down and then flipped them after 2 minutes to keep them moist. Cracking one side of each claw sped their cooking and covering the claws with a disposable aluminum pan ensured that they cooked through. When you split a lobster for grilling, it's important to remove the tomalley. But don't waste this delicacy: We whipped up a stuffing with the tomalley, bread crumbs, and seasonings and added it to the half-cooked halves after we flipped them. The stuffing lent flavor and texture to the lobster. We also slathered melted garlic butter onto the meat prior to grilling for even richer flavor.

Grilled Lobsters

SERVES 4 AS AN APPETIZER OR 2 AS A MAIN DISH

Lobsters that are 1½ to 2 pounds are large enough to spend enough time on the grill to absorb plenty of smoke flavor, but small enough to fit comfortably on the cooking grate. Don't overcook the lobster; like other shellfish, lobster meat gets tough when cooked for too long. The lobsters are done when the tomalley mixture is bubbling and the tail meat has turned a creamy opaque white. Have all garlic and parsley minced and the bread crumbs ready before you start the grill. For the bread crumbs, use bread that is a few days old, cut it into ½-inch cubes, and pulse the cubes in a food processor until they turn into fine crumbs. Don't halve the lobsters until the charcoal or gas burners have been lit.

6	tablespoons unsalted butter, melted
2	garlic cloves, minced
2	(1½- to 2-pound) live lobsters
¼	cup fresh bread crumbs
2	tablespoons minced fresh parsley
	Salt and pepper
2	(9-inch) disposable aluminum pie plates or small roasting pans
	Lemon wedges

1A FOR A CHARCOAL GRILL Open bottom vent completely. Light large chimney starter filled with charcoal briquettes (6 quarts). When top coals are partially covered with ash, pour evenly over grill. Set cooking grate in place, cover, and open lid vent completely. Heat grill until hot, about 5 minutes.

1B FOR A GAS GRILL Turn all burners to high, cover, and heat grill until hot, about 15 minutes. Leave all burners on high.

2 Meanwhile, mix butter and garlic together in small bowl. Split lobsters in half lengthwise, removing internal organs. Scoop out green tomalley and place in medium bowl. Using back of chef's knife, whack 1 side of each claw to crack shell. Add bread crumbs, parsley, and 2 tablespoons melted garlic butter to bowl with tomalley. Use fork to mix together, breaking up tomalley at same time. Season with salt and pepper.

3 Season tail meat with salt and pepper. Place lobster halves on large tray and brush cut sides with some of remaining garlic butter.

4 Clean cooking grate, then repeatedly brush grate with well-oiled paper towels until black and glossy, 5 to 10 times. Place lobsters on grill flesh side down. Grill (covered if using gas) for 2 minutes. Transfer lobsters to tray, turning them shell side down. Spoon tomalley mixture evenly into open cavities of all 4 lobster halves. Return lobsters to grill, shell side down. Baste lobsters with remaining garlic butter and cover claws with disposable pie plates or roasting pans. Grill (covered if using gas) until tail meat turns opaque creamy white color and tomalley mixture is bubbly, 4 to 7 minutes.

5 Serve immediately with lemon wedges. Use lobster picks to reach meat inside claws and knuckles.

VARIATIONS

689 Grilled Lobsters with Chili Butter

Add 1½ teaspoons chili powder and ¼ to ½ teaspoon cayenne pepper to garlic butter. Serve lobsters with lime wedges instead of lemon wedges.

 **Grilled Lobsters with Herbed Garlic Butter**

Nearly any fresh herbs, including tarragon, chives, parsley, basil, and cilantro (or a combination), can be used to flavor the garlic butter.

Stir 1 tablespoon minced fresh herbs into garlic butter.

691
FOOD SCIENCE
Is the Green Stuff in a Lobster Safe to Eat?

The soft green mass in the body of a lobster is a digestive gland, known to marine biologists as the hepatopancreas and to lobster fans as the tomalley. Many prize the tomalley for its creamy texture and intense flavor. It can be eaten as is, whisked into sauces, or mixed into a compound butter and spread on toast. In recent years there has been concern that eating the tomalley can lead to the contraction of paralytic shellfish poisoning (PSP), the illness caused by red tide, a naturally occurring population explosion of poison-producing plankton that are ingested by filter feeders like clams and scallops. People who eat infected shellfish may experience dizziness and nausea. Lobsters do not filter-feed, but they do consume clams and scallops. If a lobster eats infected bivalves, the PSP could accumulate in its tomalley though not in the meat. So it's fine to eat lobster meat during red tide occurrences, but it's a good idea to forgo the tomalley when there's a shellfish ban in place.

692 STEP BY STEP
Preparing Lobsters for the Grill

1 INSERT KNIFE Plunge chef's knife into body at point where shell forms "T" to kill lobster. Move blade straight down through head. (Freezing lobster for 5 to 10 minutes first will sedate it.)

2 CUT THROUGH TAIL Turn lobster around and, while holding upper body with your hand, cut through body toward tail.

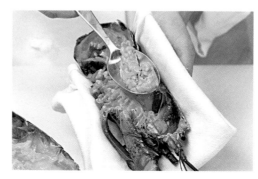

3 REMOVE TOMALLEY AND CRACK CLAWS Remove and discard stomach and intestinal tract. Remove green tomalley and reserve if desired. Remove rubber bands, then crack claw shells slightly by whacking them with back of chef's knife.

Conversions and Equivalents

Some say cooking is a science and an art. We would say that geography has a hand in it, too. Flour milled in the United Kingdom and elsewhere will feel and taste different from flour milled in the United States. So we cannot promise that the loaf of bread you bake in Canada or England will taste the same as a loaf baked in the States, but we can offer guidelines for converting weights and measures. We also recommend that you rely on your instincts when making our recipes. Refer to the visual cues provided. If the bread dough hasn't "come together in a ball," as described, you may need to add more flour—even if the recipe doesn't tell you to. You be the judge.

The recipes in this book were developed using standard U.S. measures following U.S. government guidelines. The charts below offer equivalents for U.S. and metric measures. All conversions are approximate and have been rounded up or down to the nearest whole number.

EXAMPLE:

1 teaspoon	=	4.9292 milliliters, rounded up to 5 milliliters
1 ounce	=	28.3495 grams, rounded down to 28 grams

VOLUME CONVERSIONS

U.S.	METRIC
1 teaspoon	5 milliliters
2 teaspoons	10 milliliters
1 tablespoon	15 milliliters
2 tablespoons	30 milliliters
¼ cup	59 milliliters
⅓ cup	79 milliliters
½ cup	118 milliliters
¾ cup	177 milliliters
1 cup	237 milliliters
1¼ cups	296 milliliters
1½ cups	355 milliliters
2 cups (1 pint)	473 milliliters
2½ cups	591 milliliters
3 cups	710 milliliters
4 cups (1 quart)	0.946 liter
1.06 quarts	1 liter
4 quarts (1 gallon)	3.8 liters

WEIGHT CONVERSIONS

OUNCES	GRAMS
½	14
¾	21
1	28
1½	43
2	57
2½	71
3	85
3½	99
4	113
4½	128
5	142
6	170
7	198
8	227
9	255
10	283
12	340
16 (1 pound)	454

CONVERSIONS FOR COMMON INGREDIENTS

INGREDIENT	OUNCES	GRAMS
1 cup all-purpose flour	5	142
1 cup cake flour	4	113
1 cup whole-wheat flour	5½	156
1 cup granulated (white) sugar	7	198
1 cup packed brown sugar (light or dark)	7	198
1 cup confectioners' sugar	4	113
1 cup cocoa powder	3	85
4 tablespoons butter* (½ stick, or ¼ cup)	2	57
8 tablespoons butter* (1 stick, or ½ cup)	4	113

* In the United States, butter is sold both salted and unsalted. We generally recommend unsalted butter. If you are using salted butter, take this into consideration before adding salt to a recipe.

CONVERTING OVEN TEMPERATURES

FAHRENHEIT	CELSIUS	GAS MARK
225	105	¼
250	120	½
275	135	1
300	150	2
325	165	3
350	180	4
375	190	5
400	200	6
425	220	7
450	230	8
475	245	9

CONVERTING FAHRENHEIT TO CELSIUS

We include doneness temperatures in many of the recipes in this book. We recommend an instant-read thermometer for the job. Refer to the above table to convert Fahrenheit degrees to Celsius. Or, for temperatures not represented in the chart, use this simple formula:

Subtract 32 degrees from the Fahrenheit reading, then divide the result by 1.8 to find the Celsius reading.

EXAMPLE:

"Flip chicken, brush with remaining glaze, and cook until chicken registers 160 degrees, 1 to 3 minutes." To convert:

$160°F - 32 = 128°$
$128° ÷ 1.8 = 71.11°C$, rounded down to 71°C

A

Alabama Barbecued Chicken, *242,* 242–43

All-in-One Grilled Burgers, 130–31

Almond, Tomato, and Fennel Relish, 45

Aluminum foil

    cleaning grill grate with, 212

    making prime rib "foil bone" with, 352

American cheese

    Green Chile Cheeseburgers, *138,* 139

    Jucy Lucy Burgers, *136,* 136–37

    taste tests on, 6

Ancho-Rubbed Grilled Pork Chops, *194,* 194–95

Anchovy(ies)

    Grilled Caesar Salad, 286, *287*

    Grilled Chicken Caesar Salad, 288–89

    Grilled Swordfish Steaks with Salsa Verde, *88,* 89

    Olive and Sun-Dried Tomato Stuffing, 370

    paste, about, 44

Annatto, about, 368

Apple(s)

    -Cherry Filling with Caraway, Grilled Pork Loin with, 373

    -Cranberry Filling, Grilled Pork Loin with, *372,* 372–73

    Glazed Salmon, Spicy, 81

    grilling, 123

Apricot-Mustard Burger Sauce, 141

Argentine Steaks, Grilled, with Chimichurri Sauce, *164,* 164–65

Artichoke and Porcini Stuffing, 371

Arugula, Red Onions, and Rosemary–White Bean Spread, Bruschetta with, 99

Asian Barbecue Glaze, 395

Asian Barbecue Glazed Tofu, Grilled, 78

Asparagus

    Grilled, 101

    Grilled, with Chili-Lime Butter, *100,* 101

    Grilled, with Cumin Butter, 101

    Grilled, with Garlic Butter, 101

    Grilled, with Orange-Thyme Butter, 101

    trimming, 101

INDEX

Note: Page references in *italics* indicate photographs.

Atomic Ribs, *324*, 324–25
Avocado(s)
Grilled Citrus-Marinated Pork Cutlets, *368*, 369
Grilled Fish Tacos, 264–65
Orange, and Pepita Salad, Grilled Tequila
Chicken with, *218*, 219

B

Bacon
All-in-One Grilled Burgers, 130–31
Barbecued Chicken Kebabs, *228*, 229
Cheeseburgers, Grilled Well-Done, *7*, *7*
Grilled Stuffed Trout, 420–21, *421*
Long Island–Style Bluefish, 418
Monterey Chicken, *222*, 222–23
Smoky Grilled Potato Salad, 294, *295*
taste tests on, 131
-Wrapped Scallops, Grilled, 270, *271*

Balsamic
–Brown Sugar Glaze, 263
Reduction, Grilled Free-Form Beef Wellington
with, *168*, 169
vinegar, taste tests on, 169
Baltimore Pit Beef, *186*, 186–87
Bananas, grilling, 123
Barbecued Baby Back Ribs, 310–11, *311*
Barbecued Beef Brisket, 356–57
Barbecued Beef Ribs, Texas, 336–37
Barbecued Brisket, Kansas City, 354–55
Barbecued Burnt Ends, *360*, 360–61
Barbecued Chicken, Alabama, *242*, 242–43
Barbecued Chicken, Classic, 70, *71*
Barbecued Chicken, Sweet and Tangy, *234*, 234–35
Barbecued Chicken Kebabs, *228*, 229
Barbecued foods, testing doneness of, 319
Barbecued Pork Shoulder, Tennessee, *380*, 380–81
Barbecued Pork Spareribs, 312
Barbecued Pork Steaks, St. Louis, *364*, 364–65

Barbecued Pulled Chicken, 386–87

Barbecued Pulled Chicken for a Crowd, 387

Barbecued Pulled Chicken with Peach Sauce, 387

Barbecued Pulled Pork, *382*, 382–83

Barbecued Ribs, Chicago-Style, *328*, 329

Barbecued Ribs, Cola-, 316–17

Barbecued Ribs, Honey-Mustard, 322–23

Barbecued Side of Salmon, 412–13, *413*

Barbecued Spareribs, Chinese-Style, 320–21

Barbecued Tri-Tip, California, 188, *189*

Barbecued Wood-Grilled Salmon, 83

Barbecue Glaze, 395

Barbecue Glaze, Grilled Pork Kebabs with, 192

Barbecue mitt, description of, 64

Barbecue Sauce

    Basic, 67

    Basic Pantry, 203

    bottled, taste tests on, 71

    bottled high-end, taste tests on, 358

    Chinese-Style, 203

    Eastern North Carolina, 383

    Five-Alarm, 203

    Honey-Mustard, 323

    Honey-Scallion, 203

    Kansas City, 70–71

    Kentucky Smoked, 313

    Lexington, 385

    Louisiana Sweet, 313

    Spicy Rio Grande, 313

    Sweet and Tangy, Grill-Roasted Chicken with, 255

    Tangy, 313

    Vinaigrette, 93

    Western South Carolina, 383

Barbecue Spice Rub, Basic, 416

Barbecuing

    cooking temperatures, 9

    cooking times, 9

    defined, 9

    grill setup, 9

    prime examples, 9

    step by step, 318

    use of wood chips, 9

Basic Barbecue Sauce, 67

Basic Barbecue Spice Rub, 416

Basic Pantry Barbecue Sauce, 203

Basil

    Easy Stuffed Chicken Breasts, 224, *225*

    Grilled Pesto Chicken, *388*, 389

    Italian All-in-One Grilled Burgers, 131

    and Lemon Butter, 106

Basil (*cont.*)

    -Lemon Vinaigrette, Grilled Zucchini and Red

        Onion with, 301, *301*

    Mediterranean-Style Portobello Burgers, 150–51, *151*

    Oil, Grilled Swordfish Skewers with, *22*, 23

    and Tomatoes, Bruschetta with, 94, *97*

    -Tomato Relish, Fresh, 416

    Vinaigrette, 93

Basting brushes

    description of, 64

    ratings of, 323

    storing, in salt, 68

Basting pots, ratings of, 333

BBQ Chicken Wings, Grilled, 76

Bean(s)

    Refried, Simple, 343

    White, –Rosemary Spread, Arugula, and Red

        Onions, Bruschetta with, 99

    white, taste tests on, 99

Beef

    All-in-One Grilled Burgers, 130–31

        Italian, 131

        Ranch, 131

        Tex-Mex, 131

    Baltimore Pit, *186*, 186–87

    best cuts, for grill-roasting, 183

    brining, 361

    Brisket

        Barbecued, 356–57

        Barbecued Burnt Ends, *360*, 360–61

        flat cut, about, 354

        Kansas City Barbecued, 354–55

        Lone Star, 358–59

        point cut, about, 354

    and Chorizo Skewers, Grilled, 162, *163*

    chuck-eye roasts, turning into steaks, 32

    grass-fed versus grain-fed, 161

    Green Chile Cheeseburgers, *138*, 139

    Grilled Steak Burgers, *134*, 135

    Grilled Well-Done Bacon Cheeseburgers, 7, *7*

    Grilled Well-Done Hamburgers, 6–7

    Inexpensive Grill-Roasted, with Garlic and Rosemary, 180, *181*

    Inexpensive Grill-Roasted, with Shallot and Tarragon, 180

    Jucy Lucy Burgers, *136*, 136–37

    Kebabs, Grilled, with Lemon-Rosemary Marinade, 14–15, *15*

    Kebabs, Grilled, with North African Marinade, 15

    Kebabs, Grilled, with Red Curry Marinade, 15

    Kofte, Grilled, 213

    Meatloaf Burgers, 132, *133*

    Perfect Grilled Cheeseburgers, 4

Beef *(cont.)*

Perfect Grilled Hamburgers, 4, *5*

Perfect Grilled Hamburgers with Cognac, Mustard, and Chives, 4

Perfect Grilled Hamburgers with Garlic, Chipotles, and Scallions, 4

Prime Rib, Grill-Roasted, 352

ribs, buying, 337

Ribs, Texas Barbecued, 336–37

Roast, Smoked, 362, *363*

Satay, Grilled, 190–91, *191*

Short Ribs

buying, for grill roasting, 340

Grill-Roasted, 340, *341*

Korean Grilled (Kalbi), 338, *339*

styles of, 339

Smoky Chipotle Chile con Carne, 344–45

Tender, Juicy Grilled Burgers, 128

Tenderloin

Grill-Roasted, 184, *185*

Smoked, 350–51

Smoked Grill-Roasted, 184

trimming, 351

Teriyaki, Grilled, *40*, 40–41

tri-tip, about, 188

Tri-Tip, California Barbecued, 188, *189*

see also Steak(s)

Beer

best, for brats, 153

and Brats, Wisconsin, 152, *153*

Beer can chicken, BPA and, 411

Beer Can Chicken, Grill-Roasted, 410–11

Blackberry Glaze, 341

Black Pepper–Honey Marinated Skirt Steak, Grilled, 42

Blue Cheese

Butter, 31

Perfect Grilled Cheeseburgers, 4

Ranch All-in-One Grilled Burgers, 131

Bluefish, Long Island–Style, 418

Bok choy, grilling, 120

Bottle openers, makeshift, 152

Bottle tops, saving, 131

Bourbon, Kentucky, Brined Grilled Chicken, *232*, 233

Bratwurst

about, 155

Wisconsin Brats and Beer, 152, *153*

Bread(s)

Bruschetta

with Arugula, Red Onions, and Rosemary–White Bean Spread, 99

Bread(s), Bruschetta *(cont.)*

with Fresh Herbs, 94–95, *97*

with Grilled Eggplant, Rosemary, and Feta, *97*, 98

with Red Onions, Herbs, and Parmesan, 95

with Sautéed Sweet Peppers, 96–98

with Tomatoes and Basil, 94, *97*

Grilled Caesar Salad, 286, *287*

Grilled Chicken Caesar Salad, 288–89

Grilled Free-Form Beef Wellington with Balsamic Reduction, *168*, 169

pita, softening, 227

and Vegetable, Grilled, Salad, 302, *303*

Brown Sugar–Balsamic Glaze, 263

Bruschetta

with Arugula, Red Onions, and Rosemary–White Bean Spread, 99

with Fresh Herbs, 94–95, *97*

with Grilled Eggplant, Rosemary, and Feta, *97*, 98

with Red Onions, Herbs, and Parmesan, 95

with Sautéed Sweet Peppers, 96–98

with Tomatoes and Basil, 94, *97*

Bulgur

Ultimate Veggie Burger, *148*, 148–49

Burger buns

freezing, 149

soggy, preventing, 132

taste tests on, 129

Burgers

adding panade to, 7

All-in-One Grilled, 130–31

Italian, 131

Ranch, 131

Tex-Mex, 131

Chicken, 11

Green Chile Cheeseburgers, *138*, 139

Grilled Steak, *134*, 135

Grilled Well-Done Bacon Cheeseburgers, 7, *7*

Grilled Well-Done Hamburgers, 6–7

indicating doneness, with toothpicks, 5

Jucy Lucy, *136*, 136–37

Meatloaf, 132, *133*

Perfect Grilled Cheeseburgers, 4

Perfect Grilled Hamburgers, 4, *5*

Perfect Grilled Hamburgers with Cognac, Mustard, and Chives, 4

Perfect Grilled Hamburgers with Garlic, Chipotles, and Scallions, 4

Portobello, Grilled, 12–13

Portobello, Mediterranean-Style, 150–51, *151*

puffy centers, preventing, 5

Burgers *(cont.)*

resting, before serving, 132

Salmon, 142–43

Shrimp, Grilled Southern, 146, *147*

Tender, Juicy Grilled, 128

testing for doneness, 11

Tuna, *144*, 144–45 Turkey, Easy, *10*, 10–11

Turkey, Juicy Grilled, *140* 140–41

Veggie, Ultimate, *148*, 148–49

Burger Sauce

Apricot-Mustard, 141

Chile-Lime, 141

Malt Vinegar–Molasses, 141

Butter

Basil and Lemon, 106

Blue Cheese, 31

Chili, Grilled Lobsters with, 424

Chili-Lime, Grilled Asparagus with, *100,* 101

Chipotle-Lime, Grilled Halibut Steaks with, 86

Cumin, Grilled Asparagus with, 101

Garlic, Grilled Asparagus with, 101

Herb, Grill-Roasted Boneless Turkey Breast with, 398

Herbed Garlic, Grilled Lobsters with, 425

Honey, 107

Latin-Spiced, 107

Lemon, Garlic, and Parsley, *30,* 31

Lemon, Spicy, Grilled Clams, Mussels, or Oysters with, 283

New Orleans "Barbecue," 107

Orange-Thyme, Grilled Asparagus with, 101

Roasted Red Pepper and Smoked Paprika, 31

Spicy Old Bay, 107

Buttermilk, Sweet Curry Marinade with, 19

C

Cabbage

cutting, 104

Easy Grilled Coleslaw, 105

Grilled, 104, *105*

Napa, and Radicchio, Grilled, Topping, 129

Cajun Spice Rub, 66–67, 416

California Barbecued Tri-Tip, 188, *189*

Caper(s)

Grilled Swordfish Steaks with Salsa Verde, *88,* 89

-Lemon Sauce, Grilled Salmon Steaks with, 274–75

Onion, and Olive Relish, 45

"Smoked Salmon Platter" Sauce, 276

and Sun-Dried Tomatoes, Grilled Stuffed Flank Steak with, 347

and Sun-Dried Tomato Mayonnaise, 419

Caramel Sauce, Simplified, 122, *122*

Caribbean Marinade, Grilled Chicken Kebabs with, 21

Caribbean Shrimp Skewers, Grilled, 269

Caribbean Thin-Cut Pork Chops, Grilled, 46

Carne Asada, *342, 342*–43

Carrot(s)

Charred, Salad, 291

peeling, before grilling, 291

Carving boards, ratings of, 217

Carving knives, ratings of, 186

Cashews

Ultimate Veggie Burger, *148*, 148–49

Charcoal

ashes, removing, 330

description of, 64

dividing into smaller bags, 277

hardwood lump versus briquettes, 319

hot, arranging on grill grate, 350

storage bags, ratings of, 421

Charcoal grills

description of, 64

disposable instant grills, ratings of, 134

higher-end, ratings of, 34–35

how to set up, 53

portable, ratings of, 23

turning into a smoker, 356

why foods brown best in, 48

Charred Carrot Salad, 291

Charred Fingerling Potato Salad, 293

Cheddar cheese

Grilled Stuffed Pork Chops, 196, *197*

Perfect Grilled Cheeseburgers, 4

Cheese

All-in-One Grilled Burgers, 130–31

American, taste tests on, 6

Blue, Butter, 31

Bruschetta with Grilled Eggplant, Rosemary, and Feta, *97,* 98

Bruschetta with Red Onions, Herbs, and Parmesan, 95

Bruschetta with Sautéed Sweet Peppers, 96–98

cotija, about, 298

Easy Stuffed Chicken Breasts, 224, *225*

goat, taste tests on, 12

Greek-Style Grilled Stuffed Chicken Breasts, 224

Green Chile Cheeseburgers, *138*, 139

Grilled Caesar Salad, 286, *287*

Grilled Chicken Caesar Salad, 288–89

Grilled Pesto Chicken, *388,* 389

Grilled Portobello Burgers, 12–13

Grilled Shrimp with Fresh Tomatoes, Feta, and Olives, 91

Cheese *(cont.)*

Grilled Stuffed Chicken Breasts with Black Forest
    Ham and Gruyère, 391
Grilled Stuffed Chicken Breasts with Prosciutto
    and Fontina, *390,* 390–91
Grilled Stuffed Chicken Breasts with Salami and
    Mozzarella, 391
Grilled Stuffed Flank Steak, 346–47
Grilled Stuffed Pork Chops, 196, *197*
Grilled Well-Done Bacon Cheeseburgers, 7, *7*
Italian All-in-One Grilled Burgers, 131
Jucy Lucy Burgers, *136,* 136–37
Mediterranean-Style Portobello Burgers, 150–51, *151*
Mexican-Style Grilled Corn, *298,* 299
Monterey Chicken, *222,* 222–23
Parmesan, taste tests on, 287
pepper Jack, taste tests on, 223
Perfect Grilled Cheeseburgers, 4
Porcini and Artichoke Stuffing, 371
queso fresco, about, 298
Ranch All-in-One Grilled Burgers, 131
Sausage-Stuffed Pork Chops, 196
Southwestern Stuffed Pork Chops, 196
Tex-Mex All-in-One Grilled Burgers, 131
and Tomato Pizzas, Grilled, 284–85

**Cherry-Apple Filling with Caraway, Grilled Pork
    Loin with, 373**

Chicago-Style Barbecued Ribs, *328,* 329

Chicken

Alabama Barbecued, *242,* 242–43
Barbecued Pulled, 386–87
Barbecued Pulled, for a Crowd, 387
Barbecued Pulled, with Peach Sauce, 387
Beer Can, Grill-Roasted, 410–11
Bone-In, Grilled, 66
Breasts
    Bone-In, Grilled Glazed, 68, *69*
    bone-in, splitting, 246
    Boneless, Grilled Glazed, *62,* 62–63
    boneless, skinless, taste tests on, 219
    brining, note about, 224
    Easy Stuffed, 224, *225*
    Greek-Style Grilled Stuffed, 224
    Grilled Chipotle-Lime, 61
    Grilled Lemon-Parsley, 60–61, *61*
    Grilled Orange-Tarragon, 61
    Grilled Stuffed, with Black Forest Ham and Gruyère, 391
    Grilled Stuffed, with Prosciutto and Fontina, *390,* 390–91
    Grilled Stuffed, with Salami and Mozzarella, 391

Chicken *(cont.)*

Burgers, 11
butterflying, 257
Citrus-and-Spice Grilled, *236,* 236–37
Classic Barbecued, 70, *71*
Cornell, 238–39
Diavola, Grilled Butterflied, *256,* 256–57
Diavolo, Grilled, *72,* 73
Glazed Grill-Roasted, *262,* 262–63
Grilled, Caesar Salad, 288–89
Grilled, Tacos with Salsa Verde, 220, *221*
Grilled Indian-Spiced, with Raita, *244,* 245
Grilled Tequila, with Orange, Avocado,
    and Pepita Salad, *218,* 219
Grilled Wine-and-Herb Marinated, 260, *261*
Grill-Roasted, 254, *255*
Grill-Roasted, with Sweet and Tangy Barbecue Sauce, 255
Huli Huli, 250–51
Jerk, 248–49, *249*
Kebabs
    Barbecued, *228,* 229
    Grilled, with Caribbean Marinade, 21
    Grilled, with Curry Marinade, 21
    Grilled, with Garlic and Herb Marinade, 20–21
    Grilled, with Mediterranean Marinade, 21
    Grilled, with Middle Eastern Marinade, 21
    Grilled, with Southwestern Marinade, 21
Kentucky Bourbon Brined Grilled, *232,* 233
Leg Quarters, Grilled, with Lime Dressing, 74–75
Lemon, Grilled Butterflied, 258–59, *259*
Monterey, *222,* 222–23
parts, buying, 74
Peach-Glazed Grilled, 230, *231*
Peri Peri Grilled, 240–41, *241*
Pesto, Grilled, *388,* 389
sausages, fresh, for grilling, 155
Sinaloa-Style Grill-Roasted, 392
Smoked, 252, *253*
smoke-infused, achieving, 253
Souvlaki, 226–27, *227*
Sweet and Tangy Barbecued, *234,* 234–35
Thai-Style Grilled, with Spicy Sweet and Sour
    Dipping Sauce, 246–47
whole, grill-roasting, 183
whole, taste tests on, 238
Wings
    Grilled, 76, *77*
    Grilled BBQ, 76
    Grilled Creole, 76

Chicken, Wings *(cont.)*
  Grilled Tandoori, 76
    preparing for grilling, 77
Chile con Carne, Smoky Chipotle, 344–45
Chile(s)
  Anaheim, about, 177
  ancho, about, 195
  Ancho-Rubbed Grilled Pork Chops, *194,* 194–95
  arbol, about, 195
  Atomic Ribs, *324,* 324–25
  cascabel, about, 195
  dried, varieties of, 195
  fresh, storing, 158
  fresh, varieties of, 177
  Green, Cheeseburgers, *138,* 139
  Grilled Beef and Chorizo Skewers, 162, *163*
  Grilled Caribbean Shrimp Skewers, 269
  Grilled Jalapeño and Lime Shrimp Skewers, *268,* 268–69
  Grilled Skirt Steak and Poblano Tacos, 176–77
  Grilled Thai Beef Salad, 170–71
  guajillo, about, 195
  habanero, about, 177
  jalapeño, about, 177
  Jerk Chicken, 248–49, *249*
  -Lime Burger Sauce, 141
  -Lime Vinaigrette, 93
  mouth and skin burn from, remedy for, 324
  mulato, about, 195
  New Mexican, about, 195
  New Mexican, Rub, Grilled Steak with, 158–59
  pasilla, about, 195
  Peach-Habanero Chutney, 406–7
  pequín, about, 195
  Peri Peri Grilled Chicken, 240–41, *241*
  poblano, about, 177
  Red, and Ginger Shrimp Skewers, Grilled, 269
  Red, Salsa, 343
  Santa Maria Salsa, 189
  serrano, about, 177
  Smoky Grilled Potato Salad, 294, *295*
  Spicy Rio Grande Sweet Barbecue Sauce, 313
  Sweet and Saucy Lime-Jalapeño Glazed Salmon, *80,* 81
  Sweet and Smoky Grilled Tomato Salsa, 179
  Tacos al Pastor, 366–67, *367*
  see also Chipotle
Chili Butter, Grilled Lobsters with, 424
Chili-Lime Butter, Grilled Asparagus with, *100,* 101
Chimichurri Sauce
  Grilled Argentine Steaks with, *164,* 164–65
  Grilled Sweet Potatoes and, *296,* 297

Chimney starters
  description of, 64
  grilling steak over, 349
  lighting with empty charcoal bags, 76
  ratings of, 185
  substitute for, 73
Chinese-Style Barbecued Spareribs, 320–21
Chinese-Style Barbecue Sauce, 203
Chinese-Style Glazed Pork Tenderloin, 54, *55*
Chinese-Style Wood-Grilled Salmon, 83
Chipotle
  Chile con Carne, Smoky, 344–45
  Chile Mayonnaise, 419
  chiles, about, 195
  -Lime Butter, Grilled Halibut Steaks with, 86
  -Lime Chicken Breasts, Grilled, 61
  -Lime Sauce, Creamy, 143
  -Orange Glaze, 68–69
  Tex-Mex All-in-One Grilled Burgers, 131
Chopsticks, sharpening, for skewers, 17
Chutney, Peach-Habanero, 406–7
Cilantro
  -Citrus Wet Spice Rub, 255
  and Garlic Marinade with Garam Masala, 19
  Grilled Argentine Steaks with Chimichurri Sauce, *164,* 164–65
  Grilled Chicken Tacos with Salsa Verde, 220, *221*
  Grilled Sweet Potatoes and Chimichurri Sauce, *296,* 297
  Grilled Thai Beef Salad, 170–71
  Grilled Tuna Steaks with Charmoula Vinaigrette, 273
  Latin-Spiced Butter, 107
  -Lime Sauce, Grilled Salmon Steaks with, 275
  Orange, and Lime Vinaigrette, 415–16
Citrus
  -and-Spice Grilled Chicken, *236,* 236–37
  -Cilantro Wet Spice Rub, 255
  storing, 23
  zesting, 259
  see also Lemon(s); Lime(s); Orange(s)
Clams
  grilled, serving, 282
  Mussels, or Oysters, Grilled, 282–83
    with Mignonette Sauce, 283
    with Spicy Lemon Butter, 283
    with Tangy Soy-Citrus Sauce, 283
  New England Clambake, *422,* 423
Classic Barbecued Chicken, 70, *71*
Classic Grill-Roasted Turkey, *400,* 400–401
Cleaning blocks, ratings of, 69
Coconut-Curry Glaze, 63

Coffee
    -and-Fennel-Crusted Grilled Pork Tenderloin, 208
    -Molasses Glaze, 63
Cognac, Mustard, and Chives, Perfect Grilled
        Hamburgers with, 4
Cola-Barbecued Ribs, 316–17
Coleslaw, Easy Grilled, 105
Condiments, serving, in muffin tins, 133
Cooking grates
    cleaning, with aluminum foil, 212
    cleaning, with welder's brush, 147
    cleaning block, ratings of, 69
    oiling, with paper towels, 418
    prepping, for delicate foods, 145
Corn
    Grilled, Mexican-Style, *298*, 299
    Grilled, with Flavored Butter, 106, *106*
    New England Clambake, *422*, 423
    removing husks and silk, 299
    and Shrimp, Maryland-Style Grilled, *280*, 281
Corncob-Smoked Ribs, South Dakota, 334, *335*
Cornell Chicken, 238–39
Cornish Game Hens, Grill-Roasted, 394–95
Cornmeal
    Hoecakes, 381
Corn syrup, measuring, tip for, 51
Cotija cheese
    about, 298
    Mexican-Style Grilled Corn, *298*, 299
Cranberry-Apple Filling, Grilled Pork Loin with, *372*, 372–73
Creamy Chipotle-Lime Sauce, 143
Creamy Lemon-Herb Sauce, 143
Creole Chicken Wings, Grilled, 76
Cuban Flavors, Orange Salsa with, 375
Cuban-Style Grill-Roasted Pork, 376–77
Cucumber(s)
    Grilled Thai Beef Salad, 170–71
    and Pineapple Salsa with Mint, 279
    Tzatziki Sauce, 226
Cumin
    Butter, Grilled Asparagus with, 101
    -Mint Dressing, Grilled Eggplant and Sweet
        Peppers with, 300
    Tex-Mex Spice Rub, 67
Curry
    -Coconut Glaze, 63
    Grilled Indian-Spiced Chicken with Raita, *244*, 245
    Marinade, Grilled Chicken Kebabs with, 21
    Marinade, Sweet, with Buttermilk, 19

Curry *(cont.)*
    Red, Mahi-Mahi, Grilled, with Pineapple Salsa, 84, *85*
    Red, Marinade, Grilled Beef Kebabs with, 15
    -Yogurt Glaze, 69

D
Dill
    -Mustard Sauce, 413
    "Smoked Salmon Platter" Sauce, 276
Disposable instant grills, ratings of, 134
Dressings
    Lime, Grilled Chicken Leg Quarters with, 74–75
    Mint-Cumin, Grilled Eggplant and Sweet Peppers with, 300
    Miso-Ginger, Grilled Beef, and Mushrooms, Spinach Salad
        with, *172*, 173
    see also Vinaigrettes
Drunken Steak, 166–67
Dry Rub, 313
Dry Rub for Barbecue, 383
Duck
    Breasts, Grilled, 406
    Breasts, Grilled, with Tapenade, 407
    breasts, shopping for, 406
    Grill-Roasted Chinese-Style, 408–9, *409*
    Pekin, about, 409

E
Eastern North Carolina Barbecue Sauce, 383
Easy Grilled Coleslaw, 105
Easy Stuffed Chicken Breasts, 224, *225*
Easy Turkey Burgers, *10*, 10–11
Eggplant
    and Bell Peppers, Grilled, with Mint-Cumin Dressing, 300
    Chinese, about, 300
    globe, about, 300
    Grilled, Rosemary, and Feta, Bruschetta with, *97*, 98
    Grilled, with Yogurt Sauce, 108, *109*
    Grilled Ratatouille, 120–21, *121*
    Grilled Vegetable Salad, 118
    Italian, about, 300
    slicing, for grilling, 108
    Thai, about, 300
    Tunisian-Style Grilled Vegetables (Mechouia), 304
Endive, grilling, 120

Equipment, ratings of
  basting brushes, 323
  basting pots, 333
  carving boards, 217
  carving knives, 186
  charcoal storage bags, 421
  chimney starters, 185
  disposable instant grills, 134
  food processors, 237
  gas grills, 26–27
  grill gloves, 79
  grill grate cleaning block, 69
  grill pans, 118
  higher-end charcoal grills, 34–35
  instant-read thermometers, 60
  plastic wrap, 201
  portable charcoal grills, 23
  propane level indicators, 139
  remote thermometers, 353
  rib racks, 315
  skewers, 20
  smoker bags, 331
  smokers, 359
  spatulas, 88
  tongs, 107
Everything Bagel–Crusted Grilled Pork
    Tenderloin, 208

F

Fajitas, Skirt Steak, 174, *175*
Fennel
  Grilled Sausages with, 154
  grilling, 120
  preparing, 45
  Tomato, and Almond Relish, 45
Feta
  Fresh Tomatoes, and Olives, Grilled Shrimp with, 91
  Greek-Style Grilled Stuffed Chicken Breasts, 224
  Grilled Eggplant, and Rosemary, Bruschetta with, *97*, 98
  Mediterranean-Style Portobello Burgers, 150–51, *151*
Fish
  best, for grilling, 87
  buying, 80
  flaky, avoiding, for grilling, 264
  Grilled, Tacos, 264–65
  Grilled Blackened Red Snapper, 278
  Grilled Halibut Steaks with Chipotle-Lime Butter, 86
  Grilled Red Curry Mahi-Mahi with Pineapple Salsa, 84, *85*

Fish *(cont.)*
  Grilled Stuffed Trout, 420–21, *421*
  Grilled Swordfish Skewers with Basil Oil, *22*, 23
  Grilled Swordfish Steaks with Salsa Verde, *88*, 89
  Grilled Tuna Steaks with Charmoula Vinaigrette, 273
  Grilled Tuna Steaks with Soy-Ginger Vinaigrette, 273
  Grilled Tuna Steaks with Vinaigrette, *272*, 272–73
  Grilled Whole Red Snapper or Striped Bass, *414*, 415
  grilling, tips for, 279
  Long Island–Style Bluefish, 418
  reheating, 87
  tuna, about, 87
  Tuna Burgers, *144*, 144–45
  whole, flipping over, 420
  see also Anchovy(ies); Salmon
Fish sauce, taste tests on, 247
Five-Alarm Barbecue Sauce, 203
Five-spice powder, taste tests on, 317
Flare-ups, handling, 8, 33
Fontina
  Easy Stuffed Chicken Breasts, 224, *225*
  Grilled Tomato and Cheese Pizzas, 284–85
  and Prosciutto, Grilled Stuffed Chicken Breasts
      with, *390*, 390–91
Food processors, ratings of, 237
Food science
  adding panade to ground meat, 7
  BPA and beer can chicken, 411
  brining beef, 361
  color coding scallops, 271
  cooking skirt steak, 343
  eating lobster tomalley, 425
  eating pink turkey meat, 399
  faster browning with milk powder, 63
  flavor in bone-in meats, 321
  flavor in bone-in pork chops, 200
  freezing bread, 149
  grilling steak over a chimney starter, 349
  grilling with water, 235
  keeping potato salad safe, 295
  liquid smoke, 326
  marinade ingredients, 14
  poking meat during cooking, 43
  preventing puffy burgers, 5
  preventing soggy burger buns, 132
  resting meat before serving, 24
  smoke-infused chicken, 253
  testing doneness of barbecued foods, 319
  thawing meat quickly, 47
  toning down burn from chiles, 324

Food science *(cont.)*

why charcoal browns best, 48

why shrimp turns pink, 90

Fragrant Dry Spice Rub, 254

Fresh Tomato-Basil Relish, 416

Fruit

Grilled, 122, *122*

see also specific fruits

G

Garam Masala

Garlic and Cilantro Marinade with, 19

Grilled Indian-Spiced Chicken with Raita, *244*, 245

Garlic

Butter, Grilled Asparagus with, 101

Butter, Herbed, Grilled Lobsters with, 425

Chipotles, and Scallions, Perfect Grilled
    Hamburgers with, 4

and Cilantro Marinade with Garam Masala, 19

Cuban-Style Grill-Roasted Pork, 376–77

Essence, Grilled Tuscan Steaks with, 29

Ginger, and Soy Marinade, 37

Grilled Butterflied Chicken Diavola, *256*, 256–57

Grilled Caesar Salad, 286, *287*

Grilled Chicken Caesar Salad, 288–89

Grilled Pesto Chicken, *388*, 389

and Herb Marinade, 37

and Herb Marinade, Grilled Chicken Kebabs with, 20–21

and Herb Paste, Mediterranean, Grilled Lamb Loin
    or Rib Chops with, 59

-Herb Sauce, Grilled Flank Steak with, 38, *39*

Lemon, and Parsley Butter, *30*, 31

-Lemon Sauce, Spicy, Grilled Shrimp with, 90–91

-Lime Pork Tenderloin Steaks, Grilled, 206–7, *207*

Mojo Sauce, 377

Oil, Spicy, 285

and Rosemary, Grilled Potatoes with, 114, *115*

and Rosemary, Inexpensive Grill-Roasted Beef with, 180, *181*

and Rosemary, Spicy Grilled Butternut Squash with, *102*, 103

-Rosemary Marinade, Grilled Butterflied Leg of Lamb with, 217

-Rosemary Marinade, Grilled Lamb Shoulder Chops with, 57

rubbing over grilled steak's surface, 32

Sinaloa-Style Grill-Roasted Chickens, 392

-Yogurt Sauce, 212–13

Gas grills

checking propane levels, 52

description of, 64

how to set up, 52

Gas grills *(cont.)*

propane indicators, ratings of, 139

ratings of, 26–27

remembering to turn off gas, 302

warming serving platter on, 157

Ginger

Garlic, and Soy Marinade, 37

-Miso Dressing, Grilled Beef, and Mushrooms,
    Spinach Salad with, *172*, 173

-Orange Pork Tenderloin Steaks, Grilled Spicy, 207

-Orange Sauce, Grilled Salmon Steaks with, 275

Pickled, Relish, 407

and Red Chile Shrimp Skewers, Grilled, 269

-Soy Glaze, 69

-Soy Glazed Tofu, Grilled, 78, *79*

-Soy Vinaigrette, Grilled Tuna Steaks with, 273

Warm Spice Parsley Marinade with, 19

Glazed Grill-Roasted Chicken, *262*, 262–63

Glazes

Asian Barbecue, 395

Barbecue, 395

Blackberry, 341

Brown Sugar–Balsamic, 263

Coconut-Curry, 63

Curry-Yogurt, 69

Hoisin, Spicy, 63

Hoisin, Sweet and Spicy, 211

Hoisin-Tamarind, 341

Honey-Mustard, 63, 263

Miso, 211

Miso-Sesame, 63

Molasses, Spicy, 263

Molasses-Coffee, 63

Mustard, 341

Orange-Chipotle, 68–69

Rum-Molasses, 123

Satay, 211

Sour Orange, 123

Soy-Ginger, 69

Goat cheese

Grilled Portobello Burgers, 12–13

taste tests on, 12

Gouda cheese

Grilled Stuffed Pork Chops, 196, *197*

Gravy for Simple Grill-Roasted Turkey, 403

Greek-Style Grilled Stuffed Chicken Breasts, 224

Greek-Style Marinade, Grilled Butterflied Leg of
    Lamb with, 217

Green Chile Cheeseburgers, *138*, 139

Grill brushes
   aluminum foil substitute for, 212
   description of, 64
   welder's brush substitute for, 147
Grilled Argentine Steaks with Chimichurri Sauce,
   164, 164–65
Grilled Asian Barbecue Glazed Tofu, 78
Grilled Asparagus, 101
   with Chili-Lime Butter, *100*, 101
   with Cumin Butter, 101
   with Garlic Butter, 101
   with Orange-Thyme Butter, 101
Grilled Bacon-Wrapped Skewers, 270, *271*
Grilled BBQ Chicken Wings, 76
Grilled Beef and Chorizo Skewers, 162, *163*
Grilled Beef Kebabs with Lemon-Rosemary Marinade, 14–15, *15*
Grilled Beef Kebabs with North African Marinade, 15
Grilled Beef Kebabs with Red Curry Marinade, 15
Grilled Beef Kofte, 213
Grilled Beef Satay, 190–91, *191*
Grilled Beef Teriyaki, *40*, 40–41
Grilled Blackened Red Snapper, 278
Grilled Black Pepper–Honey Marinated Skirt Steak, 42
Grilled Bone-In Chicken, 66
Grilled Boneless Pork Chops, 44–45
Grilled Boneless Steaks, 24, *25*
Grilled Butterflied Chicken Diavola, *256*, 256–57
Grilled Butterflied Leg of Lamb, 216
   with Garlic-Rosemary Marinade, 217
   with Greek-Style Marinade, 217
   with Soy-Honey Marinade, 217
   with Tandoori Marinade, 217
Grilled Butterflied Lemon Chicken, 258–59, *259*
Grilled Butternut Squash, *102*, 103
Grilled Caesar Salad, 286, *287*
Grilled Caribbean Shrimp Skewers, 269
Grilled Caribbean Thin-Cut Pork Chops, 46
Grilled Chicken Caesar Salad, 288–89
Grilled Chicken Diavolo, *72*, 73
Grilled Chicken Kebabs
   with Caribbean Marinade, 21
   with Curry Marinade, 21
   with Garlic and Herb Marinade, 20–21
   with Mediterranean Marinade, 21
   with Middle Eastern Marinade, 21
   with Southwestern Marinade, 21
Grilled Chicken Leg Quarters with Lime Dressing, 74–75
Grilled Chicken Tacos with Salsa Verde, 220, *221*
Grilled Chicken Wings, 76, *77*
Grilled Chipotle-Lime Chicken Breasts, 61

Grilled Chuck Steaks, 32, *33*
Grilled Citrus-Marinated Pork Cutlets, *368*, 369
Grilled Clams, Mussels, or Oysters, 282–83
   with Mignonette Sauce, 283
   with Spicy Lemon Butter, 283
   with Tangy Soy-Citrus Sauce, 283
Grilled Cowboy-Cut Rib-Eyes, 160, *161*
Grilled Creole Chicken Wings, 76
Grilled Duck Breasts, 406
Grilled Duck Breasts with Tapenade, 407
Grilled Eggplant and Bell Peppers with Mint-Cumin
   Dressing, 300
Grilled Eggplant with Yogurt Sauce, 108, *109*
Grilled Filets Mignons, 30, *30*
Grilled Fish Tacos, 264–65
Grilled Flank Steak with Garlic-Herb Sauce, 38, *39*
Grilled Free-Form Beef Wellington with Balsamic
   Reduction, *168*, 169
Grilled Fruit, 122, *122*
Grilled Garlic-Lime Pork Tenderloin Steaks, 206–7, *207*
Grilled Glazed Boneless Chicken Breasts, 62, 62–63
Grilled Glazed Pork Tenderloin Roast, *210*, 210–11
Grilled Halibut Steaks with Chipotle-Lime Butter, 86
Grilled Hoisin-Scallion Marinated Skirt Steak, 42, *43*
Grilled Honey-Glazed Pork Chops, *50*, 50–51
Grilled Indian-Spiced Chicken with Raita, *244*, 245
Grilled Jalapeño and Lime Shrimp Skewers, *268*, 268–69
Grilled Lamb Kebabs, *18*, 18–19
Grilled Lamb Kofte, 212–13, *213*
Grilled Lamb Loin or Rib Chops, *58*, 59
Grilled Lamb Loin or Rib Chops with Mediterranean
   Herb and Garlic Paste, 59
Grilled Lamb Loin or Rib Chops with Zucchini
   and Mint Sauce, 59
Grilled Lamb Shoulder Chops, *56*, 57
Grilled Lamb Shoulder Chops with Garlic-Rosemary
   Marinade, 57
Grilled Lamb Shoulder Chops with Near East
   Red Pepper Paste, 57
Grilled Lemon-Parsley Chicken Breasts, 60–61, *61*
Grilled Lemon-Thyme Pork Tenderloin Steaks, 207
Grilled Lobsters, 424
Grilled Lobsters with Chili Butter, 424
Grilled Lobsters with Herbed Garlic Butter, 425
Grilled London Broil, 178–79
Grilled Marinated Portobello Mushrooms, 110
Grilled Marinated Portobello Mushrooms
   with Tarragon, 110
Grilled Marinated Skirt Steak, 42
Grilled Mediterranean Thin-Cut Pork Chops, 46

Grilled Napa Cabbage and Radicchio Topping, 129

Grilled Onions, *110*, 111

Grilled Orange-Tarragon Chicken Breasts, 61

Grilled Pesto Chicken, *388*, 389

Grilled Plantains, 113

Grilled Pork Kebabs with Barbecue Glaze, 192

Grilled Pork Kebabs with Hoisin and Five-Spice, 192

Grilled Pork Kebabs with Sweet Sriracha Glaze, 192, *193*

Grilled Pork Loin with Apple-Cherry Filling
     with Caraway, 373

Grilled Pork Loin with Apple-Cranberry Filling, *372*, 372–73

Grilled Pork Skewers with Grilled Tomato Relish, *16*, 17

Grilled Portobello Burgers, 12–13

Grilled Potatoes with Garlic and Rosemary, 114, *115*

Grilled Potatoes with Oregano and Lemon, 114

Grilled Potato Hobo Packs, *116*, 116–17

    Spanish-Style, 117

    Spicy Home Fry, 117

    Vinegar and Onion, 117

Grilled Rack of Lamb, *214*, 214–15

Grilled Rack of Lamb with Sweet Mustard Glaze, 215

Grilled Ratatouille, 120–21, *121*

Grilled Red Chile and Ginger Shrimp Skewers, 269

Grilled Red Curry Mahi-Mahi with Pineapple Salsa, 84, *85*

Grilled Rosemary Pork Loin, *204*, 204–5

Grilled Salmon Steaks

    with Lemon-Caper Sauce, 274–75

    with Lime-Cilantro Sauce, 275

    with Orange-Ginger Sauce, 275

Grilled Sausages with Fennel, 154

Grilled Sausages with Onions, 154

Grilled Sausages with Peppers and Onions, 154

Grilled Scallion Topping, 129

Grilled Scallops, 92–93

Grilled Shiitake Mushroom Topping, 129

Grilled Shrimp Tacos with Jícama Slaw, *266*, 267

Grilled Shrimp with Fresh Tomatoes, Feta, and Olives, 91

Grilled Shrimp with Spicy Lemon-Garlic Sauce, 90–91

Grilled Skirt Steak and Poblano Tacos, 176–77

Grilled Southern Shrimp Burgers, 146, *147*

Grilled Soy-Ginger Glazed Tofu, 78, *79*

Grilled Spicy Orange-Ginger Pork Tenderloin Steaks, 207

Grilled Spicy Thai Thin-Cut Pork Chops, 46

Grilled Steak Burgers, *134*, 135

Grilled Steak Tips, *36*, 36–37

Grilled Steak with New Mexican Chile Rub, 158–59

Grilled Stuffed Chicken Breasts with Black
     Forest Ham and Gruyère, 391

Grilled Stuffed Chicken Breasts with Prosciutto
     and Fontina, *390*, 390–91

Grilled Stuffed Chicken Breasts with Salami and
     Mozzarella, 391

Grilled Stuffed Flank Steak, 346–47

Grilled Stuffed Flank Steak with Spinach and Pine Nuts, 347

Grilled Stuffed Flank Steak with Sun-Dried Tomatoes
     and Capers, 347

Grilled Stuffed Pork Chops, 196, *197*

Grilled Stuffed Pork Tenderloin, 370–71, *371*

Grilled Stuffed Trout, 420–21, *421*

Grilled Sweet Potatoes and Chimichurri Sauce, *296*, 297

Grilled Swordfish Skewers with Basil Oil, *22*, 23

Grilled Swordfish Steaks with Salsa Verde, *88*, 89

Grilled Tandoori Chicken Wings, 76

Grilled Tequila Chicken with Orange, Avocado,
     and Pepita Salad, *218*, 219

Grilled Thai Beef Salad, 170–71

Grilled Thick-Cut Bone-In Pork Chops, 48, *49*

Grilled Thin-Cut Pork Chops, 46

Grilled Tomato and Cheese Pizzas, 284–85

Grilled Tuna Steaks with Charmoula Vinaigrette, 273

Grilled Tuna Steaks with Soy-Ginger Vinaigrette, 273

Grilled Tuna Steaks with Vinaigrette, *272*, 272–73

Grilled Tuscan Steaks with Garlic Essence, 29

Grilled Vegetable and Bread Salad, 302, *303*

Grilled Vegetable Kebabs, 290, *290*

Grilled Vegetable Salad, 118

Grilled Well-Done Bacon Cheeseburgers, 7, *7*

Grilled Well-Done Hamburgers, 6–7

Grilled Whole Red Snapper or Striped Bass, *414*, 415

Grilled Wine-and-Herb Marinated Chicken, 260, *261*

Grilled Zucchini and Red Onion with Lemon-Basil
     Vinaigrette, 301, *301*

Grill essentials

    barbecuing, about, 9

    charcoal grills, ratings of, 34–35

    essential equipment, 64

    favorite grill-roasting meat cuts, 183

    five grill fire setups, 65

    gas grills, ratings of, 26–27

    grilling, about, 9

    grill roasting, about, 9

    how to barbecue, 318

    how to grill-roast, 182

    safety practices for grilling, 8

    setting up a charcoal grill, 53

    setting up a gas grill, 52

Grill fires

    banked, 65

    double-banked, 65

    five setups, 65

Grill fires *(cont.)*
   modified two-level (half-grill), 65
   restarting, with hair dryer, 362
   single-level, 65
   two-level, 65
Grill gloves, ratings of, 79
Grill hacks
   advanced charcoal prep, 277
   arranging hot charcoal on grill grate, 350
   chimney starter substitute, 73
   cleaning grate with aluminum foil, 212
   cleaning grate with welder's brush, 147
   clean squeeze bottle tops, 131
   draining wood chips outdoors, 345
   grilling in the dark, 370
   keeping serving platters warm, 157
   lighting chimney starter with empty charcoal bags, 76
   makeshift bottle opener, 152
   making a grill scoop, 330
   restarting grill fire, 362
   rib rack substitute, 314
   serving condiments, 133
   sharpening your own skewers, 17
   storing basting brush in salt, 68
   tagging burgers to indicate doneness, 5
   tool belt for grilling equipment, 13
Grilling
   cooking temperatures, 9
   cooking times, 9
   defined, 9
   grill setup, 9
   prime examples, 9
   use of wood chips, 9
Grill lids, cleaning, 403
Grill pans, ratings of, 118
Grill-Roasted Beef Short Ribs, 340, *341*
Grill-Roasted Beef Tenderloin, 184, *185*
Grill-Roasted Beer Can Chicken, 410–11
Grill-Roasted Bone-In Pork Rib Roast, *374,* **375**
Grill-Roasted Boneless Turkey Breast, 396–98
Grill-Roasted Boneless Turkey Breast with Herb Butter, 398
Grill-Roasted Boneless Turkey Breast with Olives
     and Sun-Dried Tomatoes, *397,* **398**
Grill-Roasted Chicken, 254, *255*
Grill-Roasted Chicken with Sweet and Tangy
     Barbecue Sauce, 255
Grill-Roasted Chinese-Style Duck, 408–9, *409*
Grill-Roasted Cornish Game Hens, 394–95
Grill-Roasted Peppers, 112, *112*
Grill-Roasted Peppers with Rosemary, 112

Grill-Roasted Prime Rib, 352
Grill roasting
   cooking temperatures, 9
   cooking times, 9
   defined, 9
   favorite cuts for, 183
   grill setup, 9
   prime examples, 9
   step by step, 182
   tips for, 183
   use of wood chips, 9
Grill-Smoked Pork Chops, *198,* **198–99**
Grill-Smoked Salmon, 276, *277*
Grill spatulas, ratings of, 88
Gruyère and Black Forest Ham, Grilled Stuffed
     Chicken Breasts with, 391

H

Halibut
   about, 87
   Steaks, Grilled, with Chipotle-Lime Butter, 86
Ham
   Black Forest, and Gruyère, Grilled Stuffed
     Chicken Breasts with, 391
   Grilled Stuffed Chicken Breasts with Prosciutto
     and Fontina, *390,* 390–91
   Grilled Stuffed Flank Steak, 346–47
Herbed Garlic Butter, Grilled Lobsters with, 425
Herb(s)
   -and-Wine Marinated Chicken, Grilled, 260, *261*
   Butter, Grill-Roasted Boneless Turkey Breast with, 398
   dried, storing, 416
   dried, testing for freshness, 416
   Fresh, Bruschetta with, 94–95, *97*
   and Garlic Marinade, 37
   and Garlic Marinade, Grilled Chicken Kebabs with, 20–21
   and Garlic Paste, Mediterranean, Grilled Lamb Loin
     or Rib Chops with, 59
   -Lemon Sauce, Creamy, 143
   see also specific herbs
Hobo Packs, Grilled Potato, *116,* **116–17**
   Spanish-Style, 117
   Spicy Home Fry, 117
   Vinegar and Onion, 117
Hoecakes, 381
Hoisin
   and Five-Spice, Grilled Pork Kebabs with, 192
   Glaze, Spicy, 63

Hoisin *(cont.)*

Glaze, Sweet and Spicy, 211

sauce, taste tests on, 193

-Scallion Marinated Skirt Steak, Grilled, 42, *43*

-Tamarind Glaze, 341

Honey

–Black Pepper Marinated Skirt Steak, Grilled, 42

Butter, 107

-Glazed Pork Chops, Grilled, *50,* 50–51

measuring, tip for, 51

-Mustard Barbecued Ribs, 322–23

-Mustard Barbecue Sauce, 323

-Mustard Glaze, 63, 263

-Scallion Barbecue Sauce, 203

-Soy Marinade, Grilled Butterflied Leg of Lamb with, 217

Horseradish

Cream Sauce with Chives, 413

Tiger Sauce, 186–87

Huli Huli Chicken, 250–51

I

Indian-Spiced Chicken, Grilled, with Raita, *244,* 245

Inexpensive Grill-Roasted Beef with Garlic
and Rosemary, 180, *181*

Inexpensive Grill-Roasted Beef with Shallot
and Tarragon, 180

Ingredients, tastings of

bacon, 131

balsamic vinegar, 169

barbecue sauce, commercial, 71

barbecue sauce, high-end, 358

beer for brats, 153

burger buns, 129

cheese, American, 6

cheese, goat, 12

cheese, Parmesan, 287

cheese, pepper Jack, 223

chicken, whole, 238

chicken breasts, boneless, skinless, 219

corn tortillas, 176

fish sauce, 247

five-spice powder, 317

heritage turkeys, 401

hoisin sauce, 193

ketchup, 11

mayonnaise, 243

mustard, coarse-grain, 157

red wine vinegar, 273

Ingredients, tastings of *(cont.)*

soy sauce, 166

steak sauce, 39

white beans, 99

whole-milk yogurt, 245

Instant-read thermometers

description of, 64

how to use, 183

ratings of, 60, 183

Italian All-in-One Grilled Burgers, 131

Italian sausages, about, 155

J

Jamaican Spice Rub, 67

Jerk Chicken, 248–49, *249*

Jícama

Orange, and Pepita Relish, 45

Slaw, Grilled Shrimp Tacos with, *266, 267*

Jucy Lucy Burgers, *136,* 136–37

Juicy Grilled Turkey Burgers, *140* 140–41

K

Kalbi (Korean Grilled Short Ribs), 338, *339*

Kalua Pork, *378, 379*

Kansas City Barbecued Brisket, 354–55

Kansas City Barbecue Sauce, 70–71

Kansas City Sticky Ribs, 326–27

Kebabs

Barbecued Chicken, *228,* 229

Grilled Beef, with Lemon-Rosemary Marinade, 14–15, *15*

Grilled Beef, with North African Marinade, 15

Grilled Beef, with Red Curry Marinade, 15

Grilled Chicken

with Caribbean Marinade, 21

with Curry Marinade, 21

with Garlic and Herb Marinade, 20–21

with Mediterranean Marinade, 21

with Middle Eastern Marinade, 21

with Southwestern Marinade, 21

Grilled Lamb, *18,* 18–19

Grilled Pork, with Barbecue Glaze, 192

Grilled Pork, with Hoisin and Five-Spice, 192

Grilled Pork, with Sweet Sriracha Glaze, 192, *193*

Grilled Vegetable, 290, *290*

preparing onions for, 19

Kentucky Bourbon Brined Grilled Chicken, *232,* 233

Kentucky Smoked Barbecue Sauce, 313
Ketchup
  serving, in muffin tin cups, 133
  taste tests on, 11
Knives, carving, ratings of, 186
Kofte, Grilled Beef, 213
Kofte, Grilled Lamb, 212–13, *213*
Korean Grilled Short Ribs (Kalbi), 338, *339*

L

Lamb
  domestic versus imported, 59
  Kebabs, Grilled, *18*, 18–19
  Kofte, Grilled, 212–13, *213*
  Leg of, Grilled Butterflied, 216
    with Garlic-Rosemary Marinade, 217
    with Greek-Style Marinade, 217
    with Soy-Honey Marinade, 217
    with Tandoori Marinade, 217
  Loin or Rib Chops, Grilled, *58*, 59
  Loin or Rib Chops, Grilled, with Mediterranean
      Herb and Garlic Paste, 59
  Loin or Rib Chops, Grilled, with Zucchini and Mint Sauce, 59
  primal cuts, 56
  Rack of, Grilled, *214*, 214–15
  Rack of, Grilled, with Sweet Mustard Glaze, 215
  Shoulder Chops, Grilled, *56*, 57
  Shoulder Chops, Grilled, with Garlic-Rosemary Marinade, 57
  Shoulder Chops, Grilled, with Near East Red Pepper Paste, 57
Latin-Spiced Butter, 107
Lemon grass, preparing, 190
Lemon(s)
  and Basil Butter, 106
  -Basil Vinaigrette, Grilled Zucchini and Red
      Onion with, 301, *301*
  Butter, Spicy, Grilled Clams, Mussels, or Oysters with, 283
  -Caper Sauce, Grilled Salmon Steaks with, 274–75
  Chicken, Grilled Butterflied, 258–59, *259*
  Garlic, and Parsley Butter, *30*, 31
  -Garlic Sauce, Spicy, Grilled Shrimp with, 90–91
  -Herb Sauce, Creamy, 143
  and Oregano, Grilled Potatoes with, 114
  -Parsley Chicken Breasts, Grilled, 60–61, *61*
  -Rosemary Marinade, Grilled Beef Kebabs with, 14–15, *15*
  storing, 23
  -Thyme Pork Tenderloin Steaks, Grilled, 207
  -Thyme Wood-Grilled Salmon, 83
  zesting, 259

Lentils
  Ultimate Veggie Burger, *148*, 148–49
Lettuce
  Grilled Caesar Salad, 286, *287*
  Grilled Chicken Caesar Salad, 288–89
  Grilled Fish Tacos, 264–65
Lexington Barbecue Sauce, 385
Lexington Pulled Pork, *384*, 384–85
Lime(s)
  -Chile Burger Sauce, 141
  -Chile Vinaigrette, 93
  -Chili Butter, Grilled Asparagus with, *100*, 101
  -Chipotle Butter, Grilled Halibut Steaks with, 86
  -Chipotle Chicken Breasts, Grilled, 61
  -Chipotle Sauce, Creamy, 143
  -Cilantro Sauce, Grilled Salmon Steaks with, 275
  Citrus-and-Spice Grilled Chicken, *236*, 236–37
  Dressing, Grilled Chicken Leg Quarters with, 74–75
  -Garlic Pork Tenderloin Steaks, Grilled, 206–7, *207*
  Grilled Citrus-Marinated Pork Cutlets, *368*, 369
  -Jalapeño Glazed Salmon, Sweet and Saucy, *80*, 81
  and Jalapeño Shrimp Skewers, Grilled, *268*, 268–69
  Orange, and Cilantro Vinaigrette, 415–16
  storing, 23
  zesting, 259
Liquid smoke, about, 326
Lobsters
  claws and tails, note about, 424
  Grilled, 424
  Grilled, with Chili Butter, 424
  Grilled, with Herbed Garlic Butter, 425
  New England Clambake, *422*, 423 preparing for grilling, 425
  soft-shell versus hard-shell, 423
  tomalley in, note about, 425
Lone Star Beef Brisket, 358–59
Long Island–Style Bluefish, 418
Louisiana Sweet Barbecue Sauce, 313

M

Mahi-Mahi, Grilled Red Curry, with Pineapple Salsa, 84, *85*
Malt Vinegar–Molasses Burger Sauce, 141
Mango, grilling, 123
Margarita Drunken Steak, 167
Marinades
  Caribbean, Grilled Chicken Kebabs with, 21
  Curry, Grilled Chicken Kebabs with, 21
  Garlic, Ginger, and Soy, 37
  Garlic and Cilantro, with Garam Masala, 19

Marinades *(cont.)*

Garlic and Herb, 37

Garlic and Herb, Grilled Chicken Kebabs with, 20–21

Garlic-Rosemary, Grilled Butterflied Leg of Lamb with, 217

Garlic-Rosemary, Grilled Lamb Shoulder Chops with, 57

Greek-Style, Grilled Butterflied Leg of Lamb with, 217

key ingredients, 14

Lemon-Rosemary, Grilled Beef Kebabs with, 14–15, *15*

Mediterranean, Grilled Chicken Kebabs with, 21

Middle Eastern, Grilled Chicken Kebabs with, 21

North African, Grilled Beef Kebabs with, 15

Red Curry, Grilled Beef Kebabs with, 15

Southwestern, 37

Southwestern, Grilled Chicken Kebabs with, 21

Soy-Honey, Grilled Butterflied Leg of Lamb with, 217

Sweet Curry, with Buttermilk, 19

Tandoori, Grilled Butterflied Leg of Lamb with, 217

used, disposing of, 8, 18

Warm Spice Parsley, with Ginger, 19

Maryland-Style Grilled Shrimp and Corn, *280, 281*

Mayonnaise

Chipotle Chile, 419

Sun-Dried Tomato and Caper, 419

taste tests on, 243

Wasabi, 145

Meat

ground, adding panade to, 7

poking, during cooking, 43

resting, for maximum juiciness, 24

thawing quickly, 47

see also Beef; Pork; Lamb

Meatloaf Burgers, 132, *133*

Mechouia (Tunisian-Style Grilled Vegetables), 304

Mediterranean Herb and Garlic Paste, Grilled Lamb Loin or Rib Chops with, 59

Mediterranean Marinade, Grilled Chicken Kebabs with, 21

Mediterranean-Style Portobello Burgers, 150–51, *151*

Mediterranean Thin-Cut Pork Chops, Grilled, 46

Memphis Spareribs, 330–31, *331*

Memphis-Style Wet Ribs for a Crowd, 332–33

Mexican Crema

Overnight, 267

Quick, 267

Mexican-Style Grilled Corn, *298*, 299

Middle Eastern Marinade, Grilled Chicken Kebabs with, 21

Mid-South Carolina Mustard Sauce, 383

Mignonette Sauce, Grilled Clams, Mussels, or Oysters with, 283

Milk powder, faster browning with, 63

Mint

-Cumin Dressing, Grilled Eggplant and Sweet Peppers with, 300

Grilled Thai Beef Salad, 170–71

Sauce and Zucchini, Grilled Lamb Loin or Rib Chops with, 59

Miso

about, 173

-Ginger Dressing, Grilled Beef, and Mushrooms, Spinach Salad with, *172, 173*

Glaze, 211

-Sesame Glaze, 63

Mojo Sauce, 377

Molasses

-Coffee Glaze, 63

Glaze, Spicy, 263

–Malt Vinegar Burger Sauce, 141

measuring, tip for, 51

-Rum Glaze, 123

Monterey Chicken, *222, 222–23*

Monterey Jack cheese

Perfect Grilled Cheeseburgers, 4

Southwestern Stuffed Pork Chops, 196

Tex-Mex All-in-One Grilled Burgers, 131

Mortar and pestle, working with, 158

Mozzarella

and Salami, Grilled Stuffed Chicken Breasts with, 391

Sausage-Stuffed Pork Chops, 196

Mushroom(s)

Grilled Beef, and Miso-Ginger Dressing, Spinach Salad with, *172, 173*

Grilled Free-Form Beef Wellington with Balsamic Reduction, *168, 169*

Grilled Vegetable Kebabs, 290, *290*

Juicy Grilled Turkey Burgers, *140* 140–41

Porcini and Artichoke Stuffing, 371

Portobello

Burgers, Grilled, 12–13

Burgers, Mediterranean-Style, 150–51, *151*

Grilled Marinated, 110

Grilled Marinated, with Tarragon, 110

preparing for the grill, 13, 150

Shiitake, Grilled, Topping, 129

Ultimate Veggie Burger, *148*, 148–49

Mussels

Clams, or Oysters, Grilled, 282–83

with Mignonette Sauce, 283

with Spicy Lemon Butter, 283

with Tangy Soy-Citrus Sauce, 283

debearding, 283

grilled, serving, 282

Mustard

-Apricot Burger Sauce, 141

coarse-grain, taste tests on, 157

-Dill Sauce, 413

Glaze, 341

Glaze, Sweet, Grilled Rack of Lamb with, 215

-Honey Barbecued Ribs, 322–23

-Honey Barbecue Sauce, 323

-Honey Glaze, 63, 263

Sauce, Mid-South Carolina, 383

serving, in muffin tin cups, 133

N

Near East Red Pepper Paste, Lamb Shoulder Chops with, 57

New England Clambake, *422, 423*

New Orleans "Barbecue" Butter, 107

North African Marinade, Grilled Beef Kebabs with, 15

North Carolina, Eastern, Barbecue Sauce, 383

Nuts. *See* **Cashews; Peanut(s); Pecans; Pine Nuts**

O

Oils

Basil, Grilled Swordfish Skewers with, *22,* 23

Garlic, Spicy, 285

Old Bay Butter, Spicy, 107

Old Bay seasoning, about, 281

Olive(s)

Fresh Tomatoes, and Feta, Grilled Shrimp with, 91

Grilled Duck Breasts with Tapenade, 407

Onion, and Caper Relish, 45

and Sun-Dried Tomatoes, Grill-Roasted Boneless Turkey Breast with, *397,* 398

and Sun-Dried Tomato Stuffing, 370

Onion(s)

for burgers, serving, in muffin tin cups, 133

Grilled, *110,* 111

Grilled Sausages with, 154

Grilled Skirt Steak and Poblano Tacos, 176–77

Grilled Stuffed Pork Chops, 196, *197*

Grilled Vegetable and Bread Salad, 302, *303*

Olive, and Caper Relish, 45

and Peppers, Grilled Sausages with, 154

preparing, for kebabs, 19

Red, and Zucchini, Grilled with Lemon-Basil Vinaigrette, 301, *301*

Onion(s) *(cont.)*

Red, Herbs, and Parmesan, Bruschetta with, 95

skewering, for grilling, 111, 150

Skirt Steak Fajitas, 174, *175*

Smoky Grilled Potato Salad, 294, *295*

and Vinegar Potato Hobo Packs, Grilled, 117

Wisconsin Brats and Beer, 152, *153*

Orange(s)

Avocado, and Pepita Salad, Grilled Tequila Chicken with, *218,* 219

-Chipotle Glaze, 68–69

Citrus-and-Spice Grilled Chicken, *236,* 236–37

Citrus-Cilantro Wet Spice Rub, 255

Cuban-Style Grill-Roasted Pork, 376–77

-Ginger Pork Tenderloin Steaks, Grilled Spicy, 207

-Ginger Sauce, Grilled Salmon Steaks with, 275

Jícama, and Pepita Relish, 45

Lime, and Cilantro Vinaigrette, 415–16

Mojo Sauce, 377

Salsa with Cuban Flavors, 375

-Sesame Glazed Salmon, 81

Sinaloa-Style Grill-Roasted Chickens, 392

Sour, Glaze, 123

storing, 23

-Tarragon Chicken Breasts, Grilled, 61

-Thyme Butter, Grilled Asparagus with, 101

zesting, 259

Oregano

Greek-Style Grilled Stuffed Chicken Breasts, 224

and Lemon, Grilled Potatoes with, 114

Overnight Mexican Crema, 267

Oysters

Clams, or Mussels, Grilled, 282–83

with Mignonette Sauce, 283

with Spicy Lemon Butter, 283

with Tangy Soy-Citrus Sauce, 283

grilled, serving, 282

P

Panade, adding to ground meat, 7

Paprika

Cajun Spice Rub, 66–67, 416

Dry Rub, 313

Dry Rub for Barbecue, 383

smoked, about, 292

Smoked, and Roasted Red Pepper Butter, 31

Spice Rub, 311, 411

Parmesan

Bruschetta with Sautéed Sweet Peppers, 96–98

Grilled Caesar Salad, 286, *287*

Grilled Chicken Caesar Salad, 288–89

Grilled Pesto Chicken, *388*, 389

Grilled Tomato and Cheese Pizzas, 284–85

Italian All-in-One Grilled Burgers, 131

Porcini and Artichoke Stuffing, 371

Red Onions, and Herbs, Bruschetta with, 95

taste tests on, 287

Parsley

curly- versus flat-leaf, 213

Greek-Style Grilled Stuffed Chicken Breasts, 224

Grilled Argentine Steaks with Chimichurri
Sauce, *164*, 164–65

Grilled Flank Steak with Garlic-Herb Sauce, 38, *39*

Grilled Rosemary Pork Loin, *204*, 204–5

Grilled Sweet Potatoes and Chimichurri Sauce, *296*, 297

Grilled Swordfish Steaks with Salsa Verde, *88*, 89

Lemon, and Garlic Butter, *30*, 31

-Lemon Chicken Breasts, Grilled, 60–61, *61*

Spice Marinade, Warm, with Ginger, 19

Peach(es)

-Glazed Grilled Chicken, 230, *231*

grilling, 123

-Habanero Chutney, 406–7

Sauce, Barbecued Pulled Chicken with, 387

Peanut butter

Peanut Sauce, 191, *191*

Satay Glaze, 211

Peanut(s)

Peri Peri Grilled Chicken, 240–41, *241*

Sauce, 191, *191*

Pears

grilling, 123

Korean Grilled Short Ribs (Kalbi), 338, *339*

Pecans

Charred Fingerling Potato Salad, 293

Pecorino Romano cheese

Mexican-Style Grilled Corn, *298*, 299

Pepita

Orange, and Avocado Salad, Grilled Tequila
Chicken with, *218*, 219

Orange, and Jícama Relish, 45

Pepper Jack cheese

Monterey Chicken, *222*, 222–23

taste tests on, 223

Pepper(s)

Bell, and Eggplant, Grilled, with Mint-Cumin
Dressing, 300

Pepper(s) *(cont.)*

bell, stemming, seeding, and slicing, 21

Charred Fingerling Potato Salad, 293

Chicken Souvlaki, 226–27, *227*

Grilled Beef Kebabs with Lemon-Rosemary
Marinade, 14–15, *15*

Grilled Beef Kebabs with North African Marinade, 15

Grilled Beef Kebabs with Red Curry Marinade, 15

Grilled Fish Tacos, 264–65

Grilled Lamb Kebabs, *18*, 18–19

Grilled Ratatouille, 120–21, *121*

Grilled Spanish-Style Potato Hobo Packs, 117

Grilled Stuffed Trout, 420–21, *421*

Grilled Vegetable and Bread Salad, 302, *303*

Grilled Vegetable Kebabs, 290, *290*

Grilled Vegetable Salad, 118

Grill-Roasted, 112, *112*

Grill-Roasted, with Rosemary, 112

Mediterranean-Style Portobello Burgers, 150–51, *151*

and Onions, Grilled Sausages with, 154

Red, Paste, Near East, Grilled Lamb Shoulder Chops with, 57

Roasted Red, and Smoked Paprika Butter, 31

Skirt Steak Fajitas, 174, *175*

Southwestern Stuffed Pork Chops, 196

Sweet, Sautéed, Bruschetta with, 96–98

Tunisian-Style Grilled Vegetables (Mechouia), 304

see also Chile(s)

Perfect Grilled Cheeseburgers, 4

Perfect Grilled Hamburgers, 4, *5*

Perfect Grilled Hamburgers with Cognac, Mustard, and Chives, 4

**Perfect Grilled Hamburgers with Garlic, Chipotles,
and Scallions, 4**

Peri Peri Grilled Chicken, 240–41, *241*

Pesto Chicken, Grilled, *388*, 389

Pickled Ginger Relish, 407

Pico de Gallo, 223

Pineapple

and Cucumber Salsa with Mint, 279

Grilled Caribbean Shrimp Skewers, 269

Grilled Fish Tacos, 264–65

grilling, 123

Huli Huli Chicken, 250–51

preparing, for salsa, 278

Salsa, Grilled Red Curry Mahi-Mahi with, 84, *85*

shopping for, 84

Tacos al Pastor, 366–67, *367*

Pine Nuts

Grilled Beef Kofte, 213

Grilled Lamb Kofte, 212–13, *213*

and Spinach, Grilled Stuffed Flank Steak with, 347

Pizzas, Grilled Tomato and Cheese, 284–85
Plantains
about, 113
Grilled, 113
Plastic wrap, ratings of, 201
Plums, grilling, 123
Polish sausages, about, 155
Porcini and Artichoke Stuffing, 371
Pork
Barbecued Pulled, *382*, 382–83
butt, cutting into steaks, 365
Chops
Ancho-Rubbed Grilled, *194*, 194–95
blade, about, 47
bone-in, flavor of, 200
Boneless, Grilled, 44–45
buying, 47
center cut, about, 47
Double-Thick, Smoked, 200–201
Grilled Honey-Glazed, *50*, 50–51
Grilled Stuffed, 196, *197*
Grill-Smoked, *198*, 198–99
rib, about, 47
Sausage-Stuffed, 196
sirloin, about, 47
Southwestern Stuffed, 196
Thick-Cut Bone-In, Grilled, 48, *49*
Thin-Cut, Grilled, 46
Thin-Cut, Grilled Caribbean, 46
Thin-Cut, Grilled Mediterranean, 46
Thin-Cut, Grilled Spicy Thai, 46
Cuban-Style Grill-Roasted, 376–77
Cutlets, Grilled Citrus-Marinated, *368*, 369
favorite cuts, for grill-roasting, 183
Kalua, *378*, 379
Kebabs, Grilled, with Barbecue Glaze, 192
Kebabs, Grilled, with Hoisin and Five-Spice, 192
Kebabs, Grilled, with Sweet Sriracha Glaze, 192, *193*
Lexington Pulled, *384*, 384–85
Loin
Grilled, with Apple-Cherry Filling with Caraway, 373
Grilled, with Apple-Cranberry Filling, *372*, 372–73
Grilled Rosemary, *204*, 204–5
Smoked, *202*, 202–3
Meatloaf Burgers, 132, *133*
Rib Roast, Bone-In, Grill-Roasted, *374*, 375
rib roast, carving, 375
Ribs
Atomic, *324*, 324–25
baby back, about, 310

Pork, Ribs *(cont.)*
Baby Back, Barbecued, 310–11, *311*
Chicago-Style Barbecued, *328*, 329
Cola-Barbecued, 316–17
country-style, about, 16
Country-Style, Sweet and Tangy Grilled, *314*, 314–15
Honey-Mustard Barbecued, 322–23
Kansas City Sticky, 326–27
Memphis-Style Wet, for a Crowd, 332–33
South Dakota Corncob-Smoked, 334, *335*
roasts, cuts of, 377
Shoulder, Tennessee Barbecued, *380*, 380–81
Skewers, Grilled, with Grilled Tomato Relish, *16*, 17
South Carolina Pulled, 385
Spareribs
Barbecued, 312
Chinese-Style Barbecued, 320–21
Memphis, 330–31, *331*
removing membrane from, 313
St. Louis, about, 331
Steaks, St. Louis Barbecued, *364*, 364–65
Tacos al Pastor, 366–67, *367*
Tenderloin
butterflying and pounding, 55
Chinese-Style Glazed, 54, *55*
Grilled, Coffee-and-Fennel Crusted, 208
Grilled, Everything Bagel–Crusted, 208
Grilled, Spice-Crusted, 208, *209*
Grilled Stuffed, 370–71, *371*
Roast, Grilled Glazed, *210*, 210–11
Steaks, Grilled Garlic-Lime, 206–7, *207*
Steaks, Grilled Lemon-Thyme, 207
Steaks, Grilled Spicy Orange-Ginger, 207
see also Bacon; Ham; Sausage(s)
Potato(es)
Charred Fingerling, Salad, 293
Grilled, with Garlic and Rosemary, 114, *115*
Grilled, with Oregano and Lemon, 114
Hobo Packs, Grilled, *116*, 116–17
Spanish-Style, 117
Spicy Home Fry, 117
Vinegar and Onion, 117
Maryland-Style Grilled Shrimp and Corn, *280*, 281
New England Clambake, *422*, 423
salad, food safety and, 295
Smoky Grilled, Salad, 294, *295*
Sweet, Grilled, and Chimichurri Sauce, *296*, 297
Poultry
duck breasts, shopping for, 406
Grilled Duck Breasts, 406

Poultry *(cont.)*
Grilled Duck Breasts with Tapenade, 407
Grill-Roasted Chinese-Style Duck, 408–9, *409*
Grill-Roasted Cornish Game Hens, 394–95
Pekin duck, about, 409
see also Chicken; Turkey
Propane tanks
checking level of, 52
propane indicators, ratings of, 139
remembering to turn off, 302
Prosciutto
and Fontina, Grilled Stuffed Chicken Breasts
with, *390*, 390–91
Grilled Stuffed Flank Steak, 346–47
Provolone cheese
Grilled Stuffed Flank Steak, 346–47

Q

Queso fresco cheese
about, 298
Mexican-Style Grilled Corn, *298*, 299
Quick Mexican Crema, 267

R

Radicchio
grilling, 120
and Napa Cabbage, Grilled, Topping, 129
Raita, Grilled Indian-Spiced Chicken with, *244*, 245
Ranch All-in-One Grilled Burgers, 131
Ratatouille, Grilled, 120–21, *121*
Red Chile Salsa, 343
Red Snapper
about, 87
Grilled Blackened, 278
or Striped Bass, Grilled Whole, *414*, 415
Relish
Fresh Tomato-Basil, 416
Grilled Tomato, Grilled Pork Skewers with, *16, 17*
Onion, Olive, and Caper, 45
Orange, Jícama, and Pepita, 45
Pickled Ginger, 407
serving, in muffin tin cups, 133
Tomato, Fennel, and Almond, 45
Remote thermometers, ratings of, 353

Rémoulade, 279
Rib racks
ratings of, 315
using V-rack as, 314
Roasted Red Pepper and Smoked Paprika Butter, 31
Rosemary
and Garlic, Grilled Portobellos with, 114, *115*
and Garlic, Inexpensive Grill-Roasted Beef with, 180, *181*
and Garlic, Spicy Grilled Butternut Squash with, *102,* 103
-Garlic Marinade, Grilled Butterflied Leg of Lamb with, 217
-Garlic Marinade, Grilled Lamb Shoulder Chops with, 57
Grilled Rack of Lamb, *214*, 214–15
Grill-Roasted Peppers with, 112
-Lemon Marinade, Grilled Beef Kebabs with, 14–15, *15*
Pork Loin, Grilled, *204,* 204–5
Rubs. *See* **Spice Rubs**
Rum
Drunken Steak, 166–67
-Molasses Glaze, 123
Simplified Caramel Sauce, 122, *122*

S

Safety practices
avoiding cross-contamination, 8, 18
avoiding flare-ups, 8, 33
consuming lobster tomalley, 425
consuming pink turkey meat, 399
keeping grill clean, 8
keeping potato salad safe, 295
location of grill, 8
Salads
Charred Carrot, 291
Charred Fingerling Potato, 293
Grilled Caesar, 286, *287*
Grilled Chicken Caesar, 288–89
Grilled Thai Beef, 170–71
Grilled Vegetable, 118
Grilled Vegetable and Bread, 302, *303*
Orange, Avocado, and Pepita, Grilled Tequila
Chicken with, *218,* 219
potato, keeping safe, 295
Smoky Grilled Potato, 294, *295*
Spinach, with Grilled Beef, Mushrooms,
and Miso-Ginger Dressing, *172,* 173
Salami and Mozzarella, Grilled Stuffed Chicken
Breasts with, 391

Salmon

about, 87

Apple Glazed, Spicy, 81

Barbecued Side of, 412–13, *413*

boning and skinning, 143

Burgers, 142–43

Grill-Smoked, 276, *277*

hot-smoked, serving, 412

Orange-Sesame Glazed, 81

Steaks

    Grilled, with Lemon-Caper Sauce, 274–75

    Grilled, with Lime-Cilantro Sauce, 275

    Grilled, with Orange-Ginger Sauce, 275

    prepping, 275

Sweet and Saucy Lime-Jalapeño Glazed, *80*, 81

wild versus farmed, 83

Wood-Grilled, *82*, 82–83

    Barbecued, 83

    Chinese-Style, 83

    Lemon-Thyme, 83

Salsa

Grilled Tomato, Sweet and Smoky, 179

Orange, with Cuban Flavors, 375

Pico de Gallo, 223

Pineapple, Grilled Red Curry Mahi-Mahi with, 84, *85*

Pineapple and Cucumber, with Mint, 279

Red Chile, 343

Santa Maria, 189

Verde, Grilled Chicken Tacos with, 220, *221*

Verde, Grilled Swordfish Steaks with, *88*, 89

Salt

preserving crunch from, 165

storing basting brush in, 68

Sandwiches

Baltimore Pit Beef, *186*, 186–87

Chicken Souvlaki, 226–27, *227*

Tennessee Barbecued Pork Shoulder, *380*, 380–81

Santa Maria Salsa, 189

Satay, Grilled Beef, 190–91, *191*

Satay Glaze, 211

Sauces

Burger, Apricot-Mustard, 141

Burger, Chile-Lime, 141

Burger, Malt Vinegar–Molasses, 141

Caramel, Simplified, 122, *122*

Chimichurri, Grilled Argentine Steaks with, *164*, 164–65

Chimichurri, Grilled Sweet Potatoes and, *296*, 297

Chipotle Chile Mayonnaise, 419

Sauces *(cont.)*

Chipotle-Lime, Creamy, 143

Garlic-Herb, Grilled Flank Steak with, 38, *39*

Gravy for Simple Grill-Roasted Turkey, 403

Horseradish Cream, with Chives, 413

Lemon-Caper, Grilled Salmon Steaks with, 274–75

Lemon-Garlic, Spicy, Grilled Shrimp with, 90–91

Lemon-Herb, Creamy, 143

Lime-Cilantro, Grilled Salmon Steaks with, 275

Mignonette, Grilled Clams, Mussels, or Oysters with, 283

Mint, and Zucchini, Grilled Lamb Loin or Rib

    Chops with, 59

Mojo, 377

Mustard, Mid-South Carolina, 383

Mustard-Dill, 413

Orange-Ginger, Grilled Salmon Steaks with, 275

Overnight Mexican Crema, 267

Peach, Barbecued Pulled Chicken with, 387

Peanut, 191, *191*

Quick Mexican Crema, 267

Rémoulade, 279

"Smoked Salmon Platter," 276

Soy-Citrus, Tangy, Grilled Clams, Mussels,

    or Oysters with, 283

Spicy Sweet and Sour Dipping, Thai-Style Grilled

    Chicken with, 246–47

Steak, 135

Sun-Dried Tomato and Caper Mayonnaise, 419

Tartar, 419

Tiger, 186–87

Tzatziki, 226

Wasabi Mayonnaise, 145

Yogurt, Grilled Eggplant with, 108, *109*

Yogurt-Garlic, 212–13

see also Salsa

Sauces, Barbecue

Basic, 67

Basic Pantry, 203

bottled, taste tests on, 71

bottled high-end, taste tests on, 358

Chinese-Style, 203

Eastern North Carolina, 383

Five-Alarm, 203

Honey-Mustard, 323

Honey-Scallion, 203

Kansas City, 70–71

Kentucky Smoked, 313

Lexington, 385

Sauces, Barbecue *(cont.)*

Louisiana Sweet, 313

Spicy Rio Grande, 313

Sweet and Tangy, Grill-Roasted Chicken with, 255

Tangy, 313

Vinaigrette, 93

Western South Carolina, 383

Sausage(s)

Argentine chorizo, about, 163

bratwurst, about, 155

chorizo, styles of, 163

Colombian chorizo, about, 163

fresh, for grilling, 155

Grilled, with Fennel, 154

Grilled, with Onions, 154

Grilled, with Peppers and Onions, 154

Grilled Beef and Chorizo Skewers, 162, *163*

Grilled Spanish-Style Potato Hobo Packs, 117

Grilled Stuffed Chicken Breasts with Salami
    and Mozzarella, 391

Mexican chorizo, about, 163

New England Clambake, *422,* 423

Polish, about, 155

Spanish chorizo, about, 163

-Stuffed Pork Chops, 196

sweet or hot Italian, about, 155

Texas Smoked, *156,* 157

Wisconsin Brats and Beer, 152, *153*

Sausages, chicken, about, 155

Scallion(s)

Grilled, Topping, 129

grilling, 120

-Hoisin Marinated Skirt Steak, Grilled, 42, *43*

-Honey Barbecue Sauce, 203

Smoked Beef Tenderloin, 350–51

Scallops

color coding, 271

Grilled, 92–93

Grilled Bacon-Wrapped, 270, *271*

preparing, 270

Seafood. *See* Fish; Shellfish

Serving platters

double-duty, tip for, 245

keeping warm, 157

Sesame

-Miso Glaze, 63

-Orange Glazed Salmon, 81

Shallot and Tarragon, Inexpensive Grill-Roasted
    Beef with, 180

Shellfish

clams, serving, 282

Grilled Bacon-Wrapped Scallops, 270, *271*

Grilled Clams, Mussels, or Oysters, 282–83

    with Mignonette Sauce, 283

    with Spicy Lemon Butter, 283

    with Tangy Soy-Citrus Sauce, 283

Grilled Lobsters, 424

Grilled Lobsters with Chili Butter, 424

Grilled Lobsters with Herbed Garlic Butter, 425

Grilled Scallops, 92–93

lobsters, buying, 423

lobsters, preparing for grilling, 425

lobster tomalley, consuming, 425

mussels, debearding, 283

mussels, serving, 282

New England Clambake, *422,* 423

oysters, serving, 282

scallops, color coding, 271

scallops, preparing, 270

see also Shrimp

Shrimp

Burgers, Grilled Southern, 146, *147*

and Corn, Maryland-Style Grilled, *280,* 281

frozen, buying, 269

Grilled, Tacos with Jícama Slaw, *266,* 267

Grilled, with Fresh Tomatoes, Feta, and Olives, 91

Grilled, with Spicy Lemon-Garlic Sauce, 90–91

sizes and counts, 269

Skewers, Grilled Caribbean, 269

Skewers, Grilled Jalapeño and Lime, *268,* 268–69

Skewers, Grilled Red Chile and Ginger, 269

threading onto skewers, 267

why they turn pink, 90

Simple Grill-Roasted Turkey, 402–3

Simple Refried Beans, 343

Simplified Caramel Sauce, 122, *122*

Sinaloa-Style Grill-Roasted Chickens, 392

Skewers

Grilled Beef and Chorizo, 162, *163*

Grilled Beef Kofte, 213

Grilled Lamb Kofte, 212–13, *213*

Grilled Pork, with Grilled Tomato Relish, *16, 17*

Grilled Shrimp, Caribbean, 269

Grilled Shrimp, Jalapeño and Lime, *268,* 268–69

Grilled Shrimp, Red Chile and Ginger, 269

Grilled Swordfish, with Basil Oil, *22,* 23

ratings of, 20

Skewers *(cont.)*
    sharpening chopsticks for, 17
    threading onions on, 111, 150
    threading shrimp on, 267
Skirt Steak Fajitas, 174, *175*
Smoked Beef Tenderloin, 350–51
Smoked Chicken, 252, *253*
Smoked Double-Thick Pork Chops, 200–201
Smoked Grill-Roasted Beef Tenderloin, 184
Smoked Paprika
    about, 292
    and Roasted Red Pepper Butter, 31
Smoked Pork Loin, *202,* 202–3
Smoked Roast Beef, 362, *363*
"Smoked Salmon Platter" Sauce, 276
Smoked Turkey Breast, 399
Smoker bags, ratings of, 331
Smokers, ratings of, 359
Smoky Chipotle Chile con Carne, 344–45
Smoky Grilled Potato Salad, 294, *295*
Snapper
    about, 87
    Red, Grilled Blackened, 278
    Red, or Striped Bass, Grilled Whole, *414,* 415
South Carolina, Mid-, Mustard Sauce, 383
South Carolina, Western, Barbecue Sauce, 383
South Carolina Pulled Pork, 385
South Dakota Corncob-Smoked Ribs, 334, *335*
Southern Shrimp Burgers, Grilled, 146, *147*
Southwestern Marinade, 37
Southwestern Marinade, Grilled Chicken Kebabs with, 21
Southwestern Stuffed Pork Chops, 196
Souvlaki, Chicken, 226–27, *227*
Soy
    -Citrus Sauce, Tangy, Grilled Clams, Mussels,
        or Oysters with, 283
    Garlic, and Ginger Marinade, 37
    -Ginger Glaze, 69
    -Ginger Glazed Tofu, Grilled, 78, *79*
    -Ginger Vinaigrette, Grilled Tuna Steaks with, 273
    -Honey Marinade, Grilled Butterflied Leg
        of Lamb with, 217
    sauce, taste tests on, 166
Spatulas, ratings of, 88
Spice-Crusted Grilled Pork Tenderloin, 208, *209*
Spice-Rubbed Grill-Roasted Turkey, 404–5, *405*
Spice Rubs
    for baby back ribs, 311
    Basic Barbecue, 416

Spice Rubs *(cont.)*
    for beer can chicken, 411
    Cajun, 66–67, 416
    Dry, Fragrant, 254
    Dry Rub, 313
    Dry Rub for Barbecue, 383
    Jamaican, 67
    New Mexican Chile, 158–59
    Tex-Mex, 67
    Wet, Citrus-Cilantro, 255
Spices
    storing, 416
    whole, buying and grinding, 416
    see also specific spices
Spicy Apple Glazed Salmon, 81
Spicy Garlic Oil, 285
**Spicy Grilled Butternut Squash with Garlic
    and Rosemary,** *102,* 103
Spicy Hoisin Glaze, 63
Spicy Molasses Glaze, 263
Spicy Old Bay Butter, 107
Spicy Rio Grande Sweet Barbecue Sauce, 313
Spinach
    Grilled Stuffed Pork Tenderloin, 370–71, *371*
    Grilled Stuffed Trout, 420–21, *421*
    and Pine Nuts, Grilled Stuffed Flank Steak with, 347
    Salad with Grilled Beef, Mushrooms, and Miso-Ginger
        Dressing, *172,* 173
Squash
    butternut, cutting up, 103
    Butternut, Grilled, *102,* 103
    Butternut, Spicy Grilled, with Garlic and
        Rosemary, *102,* 103
    Grilled Beef Kebabs with Lemon-Rosemary
        Marinade, 14–15, *15*
    Grilled Beef Kebabs with North African Marinade, 15
    Grilled Beef Kebabs with Red Curry Marinade, 15
    Grilled Lamb Loin or Rib Chops with Zucchini
        and Mint Sauce, 59
    Grilled Ratatouille, 120–21, *121*
    Grilled Vegetable and Bread Salad, 302, *303*
    Grilled Vegetable Kebabs, 290, *290*
    Grilled Vegetable Salad, 118
    Grilled Zucchini and Red Onion with Lemon-Basil
        Vinaigrette, 301, *301*
    Tunisian-Style Grilled Vegetables (Mechouia), 304
Squeeze bottle tops, saving, 131
Sriracha Glaze, Sweet, Grilled Pork Kebabs with, 192, *193*

Steak(s)

best, for grilling, 25

Boneless, Grilled, 24, *25*

bottom round, slicing, 189

California Barbecued Tri-Tip, 188, *189*

Carne Asada, *342*, 342–43

checking for doneness, 31

Chuck, Grilled, *32*, 33

cowboy-cut rib-eyes, about, 160

Cowboy-Cut Rib-Eyes, Grilled, 160, *161*

crosshatching, 179

Drunken, 166–67

Drunken, Margarita, 167

filet mignon, about, 25

filets, misshapen, dealing with, 31

Filets Mignons, Grilled, 30, *30*

Flank

  cooking, 170

  Grilled, with Garlic-Herb Sauce, 38, *39*

  Grilled Stuffed, 346–47

  Grilled Stuffed, with Spinach and Pine Nuts, 347

  Grilled Stuffed, with Sun-Dried Tomatoes

    and Capers, 347

  slicing, 38

flavoring with garlic, 32

grass-fed versus grain-fed, 161

Grilled, with New Mexican Chile Rub, 158–59

Grilled Argentine, with Chimichurri Sauce, *164*, 164–65

Grilled Beef and Chorizo Skewers, 162, *163*

Grilled Beef Satay, 190–91, *191*

Grilled Beef Teriyaki, *40*, 40–41

Grilled Free-Form Beef Wellington with Balsamic

  Reduction, *168*, 169

Grilled London Broil, 178–79

Grilled Thai Beef Salad, 170–71

poking, during cooking, 43

Porterhouse, about, 25, 29

Porterhouse, Grilled, *28*, 29

Porterhouse, slicing, 28

rib-eye, about, 25

sirloin tips, cutting, 41

Skirt

  cooking to 130 degrees, 343

  Fajitas, 174, *175*

  Grilled Black Pepper–Honey Marinated, 42

  Grilled Hoisin-Scallion Marinated, 42, *43*

  Grilled Marinated, 42

  and Poblano, Grilled, Tacos, 176–77

  shopping for, 175

Steak(s) *(cont.)*

Spinach Salad with Grilled Beef, Mushrooms,

  and Miso-Ginger Dressing, *172*, 173

strip, about, 25

T-Bone, about, 25, 29

T-Bone, Grilled, *28*, 29

T-Bone, slicing, 28

Tender, Juicy Grilled Burgers, 128

tips, buying most flavorful cut, 37

Tips, Grilled, *36*, 36–37

tri-tip, about, 188

turning chuck-eye roasts into, 32

Tuscan, Grilled, with Garlic Essence, 29

Ultimate Charcoal-Grilled, *348*, 349

Steak Sauce, 135

Steak sauce, taste tests on, 39

Sticky liquids, measuring, tip for, 51

St. Louis Barbecued Pork Steaks, *364*, 364–65

Striped Bass or Red Snapper, Grilled Whole, *414*, 415

Stuffings, for pork tenderloin

  Olive and Sun-Dried Tomato, 370

  Porcini and Artichoke, 371

Sun-Dried Tomato and Caper Mayonnaise, 419

Sweet and Saucy Lime-Jalapeño Glazed Salmon, *80*, 81

Sweet and Smoky Grilled Tomato Salsa, 179

Sweet and Spicy Hoisin Glaze, 211

Sweet and Tangy Barbecued Chicken, *234*, 234–35

Sweet and Tangy Grilled Country-Style Pork

  Ribs, *314*, 314–15

Sweet Curry Marinade with Buttermilk, 19

Sweet Potatoes, Grilled, and Chimichurri Sauce, *296*, 297

Swordfish

  about, 87

  Grilled Fish Tacos, 264–65

  Skewers, Grilled, with Basil Oil, *22*, 23

  Steaks, Grilled, with Salsa Verde, *88*, 89

T

Tacos

  al Pastor, 366–67, *367*

  Grilled Chicken, with Salsa Verde, 220, *221*

  Grilled Fish, 264–65

  Grilled Shrimp, with Jícama Slaw, *266*, 267

  Grilled Skirt Steak and Poblano, 176–77

Tamarind-Hoisin Glaze, 341

Tandoori Chicken Wings, Grilled, 76

Tandoori Marinade, Grilled Butterflied Leg

  of Lamb with, 217

Tangy Barbecue Sauce, 313

Tapenade, Grilled Duck Breasts with, 407

Tarragon

Grilled Marinated Portobello Mushrooms with, 110

-Orange Chicken Breasts, Grilled, 61

and Shallot, Inexpensive Grill-Roasted Beef with, 180

Tartar Sauce, 419

Tender, Juicy Grilled Burgers, 128

Tennessee Barbecued Pork Shoulder, *380*, 380–81

Tequila

Chicken, Grilled, with Orange, Avocado, and Pepita Salad, *218*, 219

Margarita Drunken Steak, 167

Teriyaki, Grilled Beef, *40*, 40–41

Texas Barbecued Beef Ribs, 336–37

Texas Smoked Sausages, *156*, 157

Tex-Mex All-in-One Grilled Burgers, 131

Tex-Mex Spice Rub, 67

Thai Grilled Beef Salad, 170–71

Thai-Style Grilled Chicken with Spicy Sweet and Sour Dipping Sauce, 246–47

Thai Thin-Cut Pork Chops, Grilled Spicy, 46

Thermometers

instant-read, description of, 64

instant-read, how to use, 183

instant-read, ratings of, 60

remote, ratings of, 353

Thyme

-Lemon Pork Tenderloin Steaks, Grilled, 207

-Lemon Wood-Grilled Salmon, 83

-Orange Butter, Grilled Asparagus with, 101

Tiger Sauce, 186–87

Tofu

Grilled Asian Barbecue Glazed, 78

Grilled Soy-Ginger Glazed, 78, *79*

Tomalley, lobster, consuming, 425

Tomatillos

about, 221

Grilled Chicken Tacos with Salsa Verde, 220, *221*

Tomato(es)

and Basil, Bruschetta with, 94, *97*

-Basil Relish, Fresh, 416

and Cheese Pizzas, Grilled, 284–85

coring and dicing, 95

Fennel, and Almond Relish, 45

Fresh, Feta, and Olives, Grilled Shrimp with, 91

Grilled, Relish, Grilled Pork Skewers with, *16*, 17

Tomato(es) *(cont.)*

Grilled, Salsa, Sweet and Smoky, 179

Mediterranean-Style Portobello Burgers, 150–51, *151*

paste, storing, 135

Pico de Gallo, 223

Santa Maria Salsa, 189

Sun-Dried

and Caper Mayonnaise, 419

and Capers, Grilled Stuffed Flank Steak with, 347

and Olives, Grill-Roasted Boneless Turkey Breast with, *397*, 398

and Olive Stuffing, 370

Tacos al Pastor, 366–67, *367*

Tunisian-Style Grilled Vegetables (Mechouia), 304

Tongs

description of, 64

opening bottle tops with, 152

ratings of, 107

Tool belt, for grilling equipment, 13

Tortillas

corn, taste tests on, 176

Grilled Chicken Tacos with Salsa Verde, 220, *221*

Grilled Fish Tacos, 264–65

Grilled Shrimp Tacos with Jícama Slaw, *266*, 267

Grilled Skirt Steak and Poblano Tacos, 176–77

Skirt Steak Fajitas, 174, *175*

Tacos al Pastor, 366–67, *367*

Trout

about, 87

Grilled Stuffed, 420–21, *421*

Tuna

about, 87

Burgers, *144*, 144–45

Steaks, Grilled, with Charmoula Vinaigrette, 273

Steaks, Grilled, with Soy-Ginger Vinaigrette, 273

Steaks, Grilled, with Vinaigrette, *272*, 272–73

Tunisian-Style Grilled Vegetables (Mechouia), 304

Turkey

Boneless Breast, Grill-Roasted, 396–98

Boneless Breast, Grill-Roasted, with Herb Butter, 398

Boneless Breast, Grill-Roasted, with Olives and Sun-Dried Tomatoes, *397*, 398

breast, removing bones from, 396

Breast, Smoked, 399

Burgers, Easy, *10*, 10–11

Burgers, Juicy Grilled, *140* 140–41

Grill-Roasted, Classic, *400*, 400–401

Turkey *(cont.)*

Grill-Roasted, Simple, 402–3

grill-roasting, 183

heritage, taste tests on, 401

pink meat, food safety and, 399

Spice-Rubbed Grill-Roasted, 404–5, *405*

Tuscan Steaks, Grilled, with Garlic Essence, 29

Twine

tying a butcher's knot with, 398

tying a surgeon's knot with, 347

types of, 203

Tzatziki Sauce, 226

U

Ultimate Charcoal-Grilled Steaks, *348,* **349**

Ultimate Veggie Burger, *148,* **148–49**

V

Vegetable(s)

and Bread, Grilled, Salad, 302, *303*

Grilled, Salad, 118

grilling, tips for, 119

Kebabs, Grilled, 290, *290*

Tunisian-Style Grilled (Mechouia), 304

see also specific vegetables

Veggie Burger, Ultimate, *148,* **148–49**

Vinaigrettes

Barbecue Sauce, 93

Basil, 93

Charmoula, Grilled Tuna Steaks with, 273

Chile-Lime, 93

Lemon-Basil, Grilled Zucchini and Red

Onion with, 301, *301*

Orange, Lime, and Cilantro, 415–16

Soy-Ginger, Grilled Tuna Steaks with, 273

Vinegar, red wine, taste tests on, 273

V-rack, as rib rack substitute, 314

W

Warm Spice Parsley Marinade with Ginger, 19

Wasabi Mayonnaise, 145

Water pans, grilling with, 235

Welder's brush, cleaning grate with, 147

Western South Carolina Barbecue Sauce, 383

Wine

-and-Herb Marinated Chicken, Grilled, 260, *261*

white, choosing, for cooking, 261

Wisconsin Brats and Beer, 152, *153*

Wood, for smoking

draining chips outdoors, 345

taste tests, 387

Wood-Grilled Salmon, *82,* **82–83**

Y

Yogurt

-Curry Glaze, 69

-Garlic Sauce, 212–13

Grilled Butterflied Leg of Lamb with Tandoori

Marinade, 217

Grilled Indian-Spiced Chicken with Raita, *244,* 245

Sauce, Grilled Eggplant with, 108, *109*

Tzatziki Sauce, 226

whole-milk, taste tests on, 245

Z

Zucchini

Grilled Beef Kebabs with Lemon-Rosemary

Marinade, 14–15, *15*

Grilled Beef Kebabs with North African Marinade, 15

Grilled Beef Kebabs with Red Curry Marinade, 15

Grilled Ratatouille, 120–21, *121*

Grilled Vegetable and Bread Salad, 302, *303*

Grilled Vegetable Kebabs, 290, *290*

Grilled Vegetable Salad, 118

and Mint Sauce, Grilled Lamb Loin or Rib

Chops with, 59

and Red Onion, Grilled with Lemon-Basil

Vinaigrette, 301, *301*

Tunisian-Style Grilled Vegetables (Mechouia), 304